Database Management Using dBASE IV and SQL

Robert Grauer

Maryann Barber

University of Miami

Mitchell McGRAW-HILL
New York St. Louis San Francisco Auckland Bogotá Caracas Hamburg
Lisbon London Madrid Mexico Milan Montreal New Delhi Paris
San Juan São Paulo Singapore Sydney Tokyo Toronto Watsonville

Mitchell **McGRAW-HILL**
Watsonville, CA 95076

Database Management Using dBASE IV and SQL

Disclaimer: This book and the accompanying magnetic disks are designed to help you improve your computer use. However, the author and publisher assume no responsibility whatsoever for the uses made of this material or for decisions based on its use, and make no warranties, either expressed or implied, regarding the contents of this book or any accompanying magnetic disks, its merchantability, or its fitness for any particular purpose.

Neither the publisher nor anyone else who has been involved in the creation, production, or delivery of this product shall be liable for any direct, incidental, or consequential damages, such as, but not limited to, loss of anticipated profits or benefits resulting from its use or from any breach of any warranty. Some states do not allow the exclusion or limitation of direct, incidental, or consequential damages, so the above disclaimer may not apply to you. No dealer, company, or person is authorized to alter this disclaimer. Any representation to the contrary will not bind the publisher or author.

1 2 3 4 5 6 7 8 9 0 SEM SEM 9 0 9 8 7 6 5 4 3 2

P/N 024154-6

ORDER INFORMATION
ISBN 0-07-911218-8 (text with 5¼″ data disk)
0-07-911219-6 (text with 3½″ data disk)
0-07-832710-5 (text with 5¼″ data disk and dBASE IV software)
0-07-832719-9 (text with 3½″ data disk and dBASE IV software)

The editor was Erika Berg.
The editorial assistant was Denise Nickeson.
The project manager was Greg Hubit
The cover designer was Gary Head.
The cover photo is © COMSTOCK INC./COMSTOCK INC
The text designer was John Edeen.
The printer and binder was Semline.
Library of Congress Card Catalog No. 91-062260

Contents in Brief

Contents in Detail

An alphabetical listing of the major dBASE commands as covered in the text, with the material on each command divided into four sections: syntax, discussion, tips, and related topics. The Programmer's Notebook provides a convenient reference for particular programming questions, but is not intended as a replacement for the Ashton-Tate/Borland Technical Manuals. The table on the following page lists the commands covered in the Programmer's Notebook.

Commands and Functions in the Programmer's Notebook

?/??
???
*/NOTE
&
&&
@...CLEAR
@...FILL
@...SAY...GET
@...TO
ACTIVATE MENU
ACTIVATE POPUP
ACTIVATE SCREEN
ACTIVATE WINDOW
APPEND
APPEND FROM
ASSIST
AVERAGE
BAR()
BOF()
BROWSE
CALCULATE
CANCEL
CDOW()
CHR()
CLEAR
CLOSE
CMONTH()
COMPILE
CONFIG.DB
CONTINUE
COPY
COPY INDEXES
COUNT
CREATE
CREATE APPLICATION
CREATE LABEL
CREATE QUERY
CREATE REPORT
CREATE SCREEN
CREATE VIEW
CREATE VIEW FROM ENVIRONMENT
CTOD()
DATE()
DAY()
DEACTIVATE MENU
DEACTIVATE POPUP
DEACTIVATE WINDOW
DEBUG
DEFINE BAR
DEFINE MENU
DEFINE PAD
DEFINE POPUP
DEFINE WINDOW
DELETE
DELETE TAG
DELETED()
DIR
DISPLAY
DISPLAY HISTORY
DISPLAY MEMORY
DISPLAY STATUS
DISPLAY STRUCTURE
DO
DO CASE
DO WHILE
DTOC()
DTOS()
EDIT
EJECT
EOF()
FIND
FOUND()
GO
HELP
IF
IIF()
INDEX ON
INSERT
ISCOLOR()
JOIN
LABEL FORM
LEN()
LINENO()
LIST
LIST HISTORY
LIST MEMORY
LIST STATUS
LIST STRUCTURE
LOCATE
LOWER()
LTRIM()
MAX()
MIN()
MODIFY COMMAND
MODIFY LABEL
MODIFY QUERY
MODIFY REPORT
MODIFY SCREEN
MODIFY STRUCTURE
MODIFY VIEW
MONTH()
MOVE WINDOW
ON ERROR/ESCAPE/KEY
ON PAD
ON SELECTION PAD
ON SELECTION POPUP
PACK
PARAMETERS
PRINTSTATUS()
PRIVATE
PROCEDURE
PROMPT()
PUBLIC
QUIT
READ
RECALL
RECNO()
REINDEX
RELEASE
REPLACE
REPORT FORM
RESTORE
RESTORE WINDOW
RESUME
RETURN
RTRIM()
RUN
SAVE
SAVE WINDOW
SCAN
SEEK
SELECT
SET
SET ALTERNATE
SET AUTOSAVE
SET BELL
SET BORDER
SET CATALOG
SET CENTURY
SET CLOCK
SET COLOR
SET CONFIRM
SET CONSOLE
SET DATE
SET DEBUG
SET DEFAULT
SET DELETED
SET DELIMITERS
SET DEVELOPMENT
SET DEVICE
SET DISPLAY
SET ECHO
SET ESCAPE
SET EXACT
SET FIELDS
SET FILTER
SET FORMAT
SET FUNCTION
SET HEADING
SET HELP
SET HISTORY
SET INDEX
SET INTENSITY
SET MEMOWIDTH
SET NEAR
SET ORDER
SET PATH
SET PRINTER
SET PROCEDURE
SET RELATION
SET SAFETY
SET SCOREBOARD
SET SKIP
SET SPACE
SET SQL
SET STATUS
SET STEP
SET TALK
SET TRAP
SET TYPEAHEAD
SET UNIQUE
SET VIEW
SET WINDOW
SHOW MENU
SHOW POPUP
SKIP
SORT
SPACE()
STORE
STR()
SUBSTR()
SUM
SUSPEND
TIME()
TRANSFORM()
TRIM()
UPPER()
USE
VAL()
WAIT
YEAR()
ZAP

Preface to the Instructor

Database Management Using dBASE IV and SQL began as a revision of our existing text on data management. We had planned simply on a second edition but soon realized that the changes we had in mind would be too extensive. Hence the new title, and the new book—one written exclusively for dBASE IV, which includes material on relational databases as well as a detailed introduction to SQL.

Database Management Using dBASE IV and SQL teaches you how to program in dBASE IV, but it is much more than a book on dBASE IV programming. It is intended for a first course in data management, relational databases, and SQL; but is also the perfect text for course(s) in dBASE IV. Our book is suitable for the first-time user; it begins at the dot prompt and continues with the dBASE IV control center. It is also appropriate for the experienced dBASE user, as it contains detailed information on over 200 dBASE IV commands and functions, with supplementary chapters on structured programming and design.

Database Management Using dBASE IV and SQL is built on a unique combination of business case studies, Student Data Disk, hands-on exercises, and Programmer's Notebook. Equally important, this book has been written for the classroom; it contains many elements associated with good teaching and sound pedagogy. Every chapter begins with a statement of objectives and ends with a list of key words and concepts. It encourages hands-on participation and provides an abundance of exercises. Solutions to all of the exercises in the text are contained in the accompanying Instructor's Manual.

Distinguishing Features

- **Business Case Studies**—describe problems in database management with which students can readily identify. The case solutions present theoretical concepts of database design, as well as information about the dBASE IV commands needed in the eventual solution.
- **Student Data Disk**—contains dBASE IV implementations of the various case studies, saves the tedium of data entry, and enables the reader to explore dBASE IV in ways that otherwise would not be possible.
- **Hands-on Exercises**—require the reader's participation at the computer. The exercises encompass all major elements in dBASE IV, including commands from the dot prompt, selecting options from the control center, command level programming, and SQL.
- **Programmer's Notebook**—contains detailed information on over 200 commands and functions in dBASE IV. This valuable reference tool is designed for both the novice and the experienced dBASE IV user.
- **Structured Methodology**—Two chapters provide information on structured programming and design, pseudocode, hierarchy charts, and top-down implementation.
- **Student Edition of dBASE IV**—This version of the commercial program limits the number of records in a DBF file or SQL table to 120, changes the dot prompt to include (DEMO), but otherwise enables students to fully utilize dBASE IV.

Instructor's Manual

Written by the authors, this comprehensive manual includes solutions to all exercises in the text. There is also a detailed lecture outline for each chapter, combined with teaching strategies and a series of "emergency lectures" in the form of pop quizzes.

Acknowledgments

The authors gratefully acknowledge the contribution of Erika Berg, sponsoring editor at Mitchell/McGraw Hill, without whom this book would not have been written. We are indebted to Greg Hubit, Betty Drury, and Jane Somers, who coordinated the production. We also thank our reviewers who, through their comments and constructive criticism, made this a far better book:

Daniel Dawson, Heald Business College
Raymond Frost, University of Miami
Dave Galligher, Datalogic
Scott Haynes, Ashton-Tate
Sebastian Kiteka, Vincennes University
Constance Knapp, Pace University
Sue Krimm, Pierce College
Robert Norton, San Diego Mesa College

Robert Grauer
Maryann Barber

PART

I

Introduction

CHAPTER

1 Introduction

OUTLINE

OBJECTIVES

After reading this chapter you will be able to:

1. Discuss the importance of subdirectories in DOS; list the DOS commands associated with subdirectories and describe the purpose of each.
2. Differentiate between installation and loading; install and load the student version of dBASE IV.
3. Install the data disk that accompanies this text; describe the tree structure of the data disk and how to change from one directory to another.
4. Distinguish between the different versions of dBASE.
5. Load dBASE and arrive at the dot prompt; provide the dBASE command to change the default drive.
6. Differentiate between report generation and data entry; describe the primary data entry operations.
7. List several types of data validation that may be done during the course of data entry; describe the effects of entering improper data into a system.

Overview

This book is about data base management; in particular, it is about data base systems as they are developed in dBASE IV. Our overall objective is to acquaint you with the potential of these systems via a case study approach, and to enable you to design and implement these systems in dBASE. We follow a learn-by-doing approach that leads you through a series of ***hands-on exercises*** requiring your participation at the computer.

The hands-on exercises make extensive use of a ***data disk,*** which we provide with the text. The data disk contains over 200 files and is divided into ***subdirectories*** for more efficient storage organization. It is absolutely critical, therefore, that you understand the organization of the data disk, so we include a brief review of subdirectories and their associated DOS commands.

We also think it important that you appreciate what dBASE can ultimately do, so we present a fully functional system in conjunction with the data disk. The second half of the chapter describes a case study for the Soleil America Corporation, then follows with a hands-on exercise to demonstrate the completed system. We take you through the steps of ***adding, editing,*** and ***deleting*** records in existing files, then to the ***report generation*** process to present information based on the data you entered. We show you the importance of ***data validation*** and the utility of ***on-line help.*** Our emphasis at this time is on the nontechnical (or less technical) individual who knows what an information system is supposed to do, but who is not concerned with programming per se.

The Origins of dBASE

There never was a dBASE I, nor was there a person named Ashton. The product was originally called ***Vulcan*** (after the home planet of *Star Trek*'s Mr. Spock, a character known for his total recall). It was initially a commercial failure (no more than fifty copies were sold), and did not even recoup its advertising budget. At least one prominent company chose not to market the product, and its author, ***Wayne Ratliff,*** seriously considered selling all rights to the program for $3,000.

Today it is the flagship product of a $250 million company. The ***dBASE*** series has been translated into more than twenty languages, including French, German, Italian, Spanish, Portuguese, Danish, Dutch, Swedish, and Norwegian. The program is available in more than fifty countries on six continents, has sold in excess of three million copies, and continues to dominate the market.

George Tate and Hal Lashlee are the individuals most responsible for transforming Vulcan into dBASE II, and its successors, dBASE III, dBASE III Plus, and dBASE IV. In 1980 the two founded the Discount Software Group, which offered a toll-free number, low prices, prompt delivery, and after-sale support. Within a short time the fledgling company was selling $100,000 worth of software a month, a phenomenal sum at the time (IBM would not announce the PC for another year and a half). They soon acquired exclusive rights to Vulcan in return for a generous royalty.

A new company was formed to market the product, with the intention that Ratliff would continue to improve the program. The name was changed to dBASE II, a catchy name that implied an improvement over dBASE I, which, in fact, never existed. ***Ashton-Tate*** was chosen as the name of the new company because it had a better ring than either Tate & Lashlee or Lashlee & Tate.

dBASE III was announced in 1984, followed by dBASE III Plus in 1986, and dBASE IV in 1988. Unfortunately for Ashton-Tate, dBASE IV was replete with problems and was initially rejected by industry. It took the company nearly two years to release the widely anticipated upgrade, ***dBASE IV, Version 1.1,*** but this time they did it right. The new release is stable and reliable, and continues to gain increased acceptance. This text is written for dBASE IV (Version 1.1 or 1.2), but henceforth we will simply use dBASE for ease of discussion.

About DOS

Very little is assumed in the way of previous knowledge of ***DOS*** (the disk operating system), yet it is essential you understand subdirectories in order to effectively use the data disk that accompanies this text. We had thought about placing this material in an appendix, but found that it is more effective if it appears at the very beginning of the text. Accordingly, please read and/or review the following sections *before* proceeding to the hands-on exercises.

Subdirectories

Subdirectories divide a disk into separate areas, and thus provide a means for efficient file organization; thus, just as a book is divided into chapters, a disk is divided into subdirectories. You can, for example, establish one subdirectory for a word processing program (e.g., WordPerfect) and a different subdirectory to hold the documents it creates. You can even create different subdirectories for each type of document you use, such as one subdirectory for business letters, a different subdirectory for school assignments, and a still different subdirectory for personal correspondence.

You can establish other directories (***directory*** and ***subdirectory*** are used interchangeably) for other programs; e.g., one subdirectory for Lotus, and a different subdirectory for dBASE IV. And you can create still other subdirectories to hold the various spreadsheets and/or data management applications created through Lotus and dBASE, respectively.

Figure 1.1 depicts a series of subdirectories as they might appear on a *hypothetical* disk. The arrangement in the figure is described as a ***tree structure,*** because the various entries branch downward from the ***root directory*** at the top of the figure. The root directory in our example contains four subdirectories—**DBASEIV**, **WP**, **LOTUS**, and **DOS**—three of which have subdirectories that branch from them. The **DBASEIV** subdirectory contains two subdirectories of its own, **SOCCER** and **LOANS**. The **LOTUS** subdirectory also contains two subdirectories, and one of these, **SCHOOL**, contains yet additional subdirectories.

Multiple subdirectories can have the same name; for example, **SCHOOL** and **HOME** exist in two places in Figure 1.1. DOS does not get confused, however, because the ***path specification*** is unique for each directory; i.e., the first **SCHOOL** belongs to **WP**, which in turn belongs to the root directory, whereas the second **SCHOOL** belongs to **LOTUS**, which in turn belongs to the root.

Another way to view Figure 1.1 is to regard the root directory as the parent, and the **DBASEIV**, **WP**, **LOTUS**, and **DOS** subdirectories as its children. The **DBASEIV** directory in turn is viewed as the parent of the **SOCCER** and **LOANS** subdirectories. The family tree can go down as many generations as desired, with each directory containing a combination of files and/or other subdirectories.

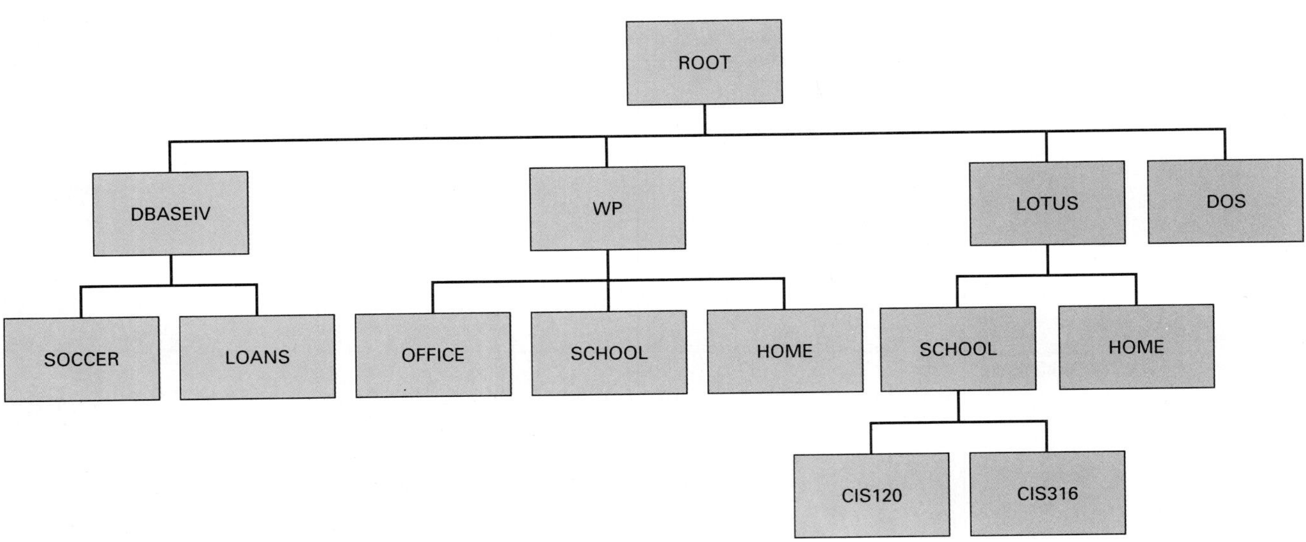

FIGURE 1.1
Tree Structure

At any given time you are logged into a specific (current) directory, which is treated *independently* of all other directories; i.e., any given command affects only (the files in) the current directory. In other words, **COPY *.*** or **ERASE *.*** pertain just to the files in the current directory, and not to all of the files on the disk. In similar fashion, execution of a **DIR** command displays only the names of the files and/or subdirectories in the current directory.

Figure 1.2a shows the output of a **DIR** command as it would appear when issued from the root directory of Figure 1.1. As you can see, the root directory contains three files and four subdirectories, and corresponds to the tree structure of Figure 1.1. Note, however, that the subdirectories **SOCCER**, **LOANS**, and so on, are not listed in the root directory, as these are children of other subdirectories.

Figure 1.2b shows the output of the **DIR** command as it would appear from the **DBASEIV** subdirectory. The **DBASEIV** directory contains seven program files as well as the names of two subdirectories (each one holding a different dBASE application). There are also two additional entries, a single and a double period, which appear in the directory listing of every subdirectory below the level of the root directory. The single period is a reference to the physical location of the subdirectory on the disk, while the double period is a reference to the physical location of its parent.

Finally, Figure 1.2c shows the output of the **DIR** command when issued from the **LOANS** subdirectory. This time there are five files but no subdirectories.

Commands for Subdirectories

DOS provides several commands that are used specifically with subdirectories. In particular, there are six such commands with which you should become familiar. These are:

MD to make (create) a subdirectory
CD to change to an existing subdirectory
RD to remove a subdirectory
TREE to display the tree structure of a disk
PATH to allow programs to be executed from other subdirectories
PROMPT to change the DOS prompt to include the current directory

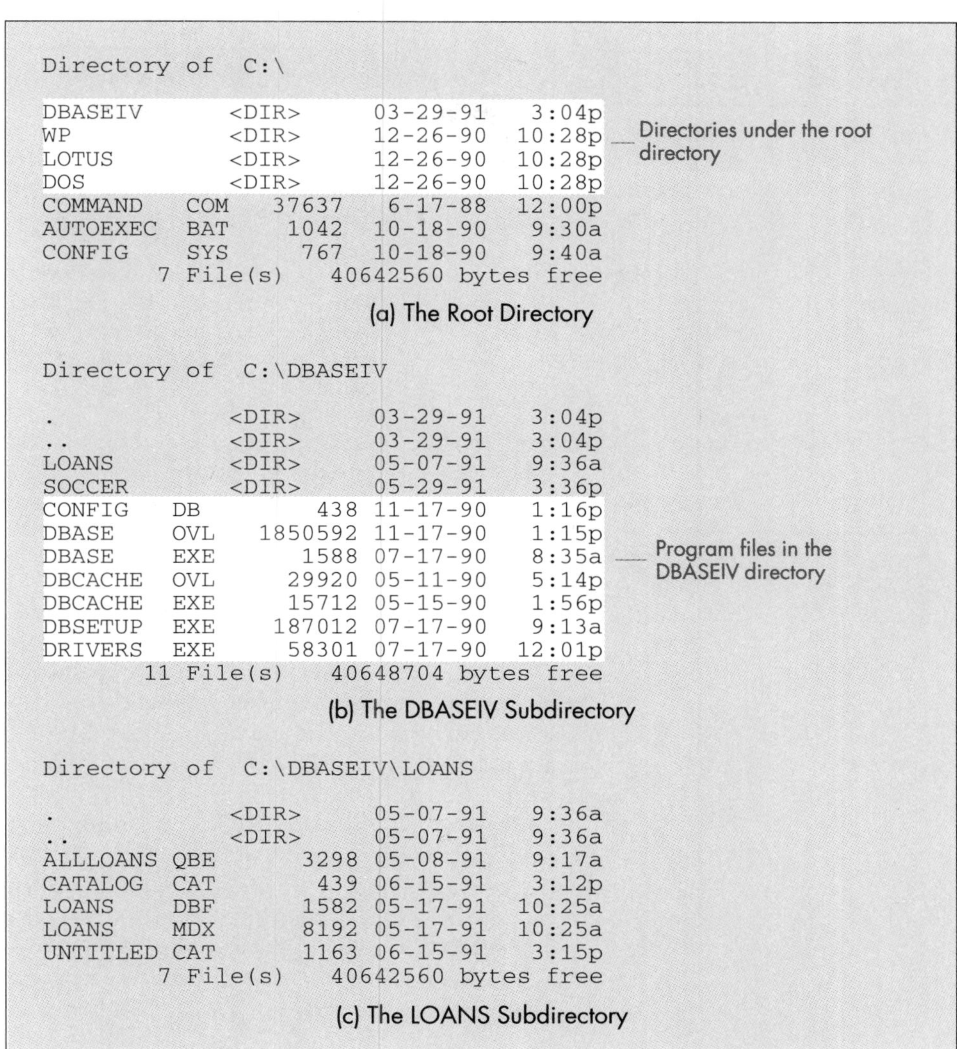

FIGURE 1.2
The DIR Command with Subdirectories

We provide a *brief* explanation of these commands, and summarize the discussion in Table 1.1. We then show you how these commands are used in conjunction with the ***data disk*** provided with the text, and finally direct you to a hands-on exercise.

The **M**ake **D**irectory (**MD**) command creates a new directory, but can create only one directory at a time. Thus, two distinct **MD** commands are needed to create the **SOCCER** directory of Figure 1.1; one to create the **DBASEIV** subdirectory, and a second to create the **SOCCER** subdirectory, which exists under the **DBASEIV** directory.

The ***backslash*** (\) separates one directory name from another, and thus indicates the path DOS is to take to reach a given subdirectory. A backslash immediately after the command name implies that the path begins with the root directory, with each successive backslash indicating a further downward path in the tree.

The **C**hange **D**irectory (**CD**) command changes the current directory; e.g., the commands **CD \DBASEIV** and **CD \DBASEIV\SOCCER** move to the **DBASEIV** and **SOCCER** subdirectories, respectively, regardless of where you were when the commands were executed. Alternatively, you could change to the **DBASEIV** directory by

TABLE 1.1 **DOS Commands for Subdirectories**

Command	Examples	Explanation
MD	MD \DBASEIV	Creates a **DBASEIV** directory under the root
	MD \DBASEIV\SOCCER	Creates a **SOCCER** subdirectory under the **DBASEIV** subdirectory
CD	CD \DBASEIV	Changes to the **DBASEIV** subdirectory
	CD \DBASEIV\SOCCER	Changes to the **SOCCER** subdirectory under the **DBASEIV** subdirectory
RD	RD \DBASEIV\SOCCER	Removes the **SOCCER** subdirectory, provided it is empty
TREE	TREE A:	Displays the tree structure of the disk in drive A
	TREE A:/F	Displays the tree structure and a list of files in each subdirectory
PATH	PATH C:\DBASEIV	Enables programs in the **dBASEIV** directory to be run from anywhere on the disk
	PATH	Displays the current path
	PATH C:\DBASEIV;C:\DOS	Enables programs in *both* the **DBASEIV** and **DOS** directories to be run from any directory
PROMPT	PROMPT pg	Changes the DOS prompt to display the drive and current directory.

omitting the initial backslash, provided you are in the root directory when the command is executed. In other words, the commands **CD \DBASEIV** and **CD DBASEIV** *are equivalent when issued from the root directory* because the absence of the initial backslash changes to a subdirectory under the current directory; realize, however, that **CD DBASEIV** if issued from any directory other than the root directory, would not work.

The **R**emove **D**irectory (**RD**) command removes a subdirectory. Under no circumstances, however, can it remove the root directory, nor should you be in the subdirectory you intend to remove. In addition, the subdirectory to be removed must be empty, i.e., all its files previously erased and all subdirectories (if any) removed.

The **TREE** command displays all subdirectories (and optionally the files within each directory). Note, too, that **TREE** is an *external* DOS command, which in turn requires access to the program **TREE.COM** found in the DOS subdirectory. In other words, to execute the **TREE** command successfully from a subdirectory other than **DOS**, you need to issue a **PATH** command to indicate where the **TREE.COM** program is found, e.g., **PATH C:\DOS.**

The **PATH** command enables execution of a program (or batch file) from a directory other than the current directory. Multiple paths can be specified in a single command by separating directories with semicolons, e.g., **PATH C:\DBASEIV;C:\DOS**. A **PATH** command remains in effect until the next **PATH** command is issued, or until the computer is turned off or rebooted. An existing path specification is canceled by issuing the command with just a semicolon (**PATH;**), and specification of the command by itself (that is, **PATH** with no parameters) displays the current path.

The normal ***DOS prompt*** (**A>** or **C>**) implies that DOS is waiting for a command, and, in addition, indicates the letter of the ***default drive,*** A or C, respectively. You can, however, use the command **PROMPT pg** to include the current directory in the DOS prompt, e.g., **C:\DBASEIV>** or **C:\DBASEIV\SOCCER>**. The additional information takes some getting used to, but the constant reminder of where you are (which directory you are in) saves mistakes in the long run.

DOS also provides the ability to establish an **AUTOEXEC.BAT** file, which, if it is present in the root directory of the default drive, executes automatically whenever the system is booted. In other words, you can store the commands you would like to execute at the start of every session—e.g., a **PATH** and **PROMPT** command—in the **AUTOEXEC.BAT** file and have them execute whenever you start the computer.

Getting Started

We come shortly to the first of many hands-on exercises that appear throughout the text. The exercise assumes the availability of dBASE IV, either the commercial version or the student version, which is (optionally) packaged with this text. The exercise also requires you to understand the DOS commands that were just discussed, and to distinguish between installing a program versus loading it.

Installation is the process by which a program, such as dBASE IV, is copied from floppy disks to a hard drive. During installation, you are asked questions about your system, such as what type of monitor and printer you have, so that the installation program can customize the program for your configuration. ***Loading,*** on the other hand, brings an installed program from disk into memory, from where it is executed. dBASE (or for that matter any other program) is *installed* once and only once, whereas it is *loaded* every time you use it.

The Student Version of dBASE IV

The ***student version of dBASE IV*** contains all essential features in the commercial version including the SQL implementation. There are, of course, some limitations, the most significant being a restriction on the number of records that can be stored in a **DBF** file or SQL table. The specific limitations of the student version are as follows:

1. A limit of 120 records in a **DBF** file or SQL table.
2. Only two printer drivers are supported: a generic driver that works with most printers and an ASCII driver.
3. The dot prompt is preceded by the word **DEMO** enclosed in parentheses.
4. The footer, **dBASE IV SAMPLER REPORT—FOR EVALUATION PURPOSES ONLY** appears at the bottom of all printed reports.
5. Applications created by the Application Generator are limited to five menus.
6. The Template Language for the Applications Generator, **DBSETUP**, Runtime, and Step IVWard (a utility to convert code from other applications into dBASE) are not supported.

The exercise instructs you to install the student version of dBASE IV on your computer if the commercial version has not been previously installed. It also explains how to modify the **PATH** command in the **AUTOEXEC.BAT** file to reference the dBASE IV subdirectory.

The Data Disk

The ***data disk(s)*** contains data files and partial solutions to the various case studies that appear throughout the text. (Since a 3½-inch disk holds approximately twice as much data as its 5¼-inch counterpart, you will find two 5¼-inch data disks, but only one 3½-inch data disk.) Whether or not you install the data disk(s) on your hard drive depends on whether or not you are sharing a computer with other people. If you have your own machine—that is, you are not sharing the computer, you should install the data disk(s) as described in the exercise.

HANDS-ON EXERCISE 1

Preliminaries

Objective

Install the student version of dBASE IV if the commercial version is not available; then modify the **PATH** command in the **AUTOEXEC.BAT** file to include the dBASE IV directory. Load dBASE IV and change to the dot prompt. Display the tree structure of the data disk and (optionally) install it.

STEP 1 **Verify the installation of dBASE IV**

Boot the system, then type **CD C:** to change to the root directory of drive C. Type **DIR** to view the contents of the root directory, which may or may not have a dBASE IV subdirectory, depending on whether or not dBASE IV has been previously installed.

STEP 2 **Install the student version of dBASE IV**

Do this step only if dBASE IV has not been previously installed on your computer. Insert the first dBASE disk into drive A, type **A:**, and press **return**. You are ready to install the student version of dBASE IV, but the precise command depends on your particular configuration. Type:

INSTALL C: C ——— *if you are installing dBASE to the C drive and you have a* color *monitor*

INSTALL C: M ——— *if you are installing dBASE to the C drive and you have a* monochrome *monitor*

The installation creates a new subdirectory, **C:\DBSAMPLE**, then copies the dBASE program files from the floppy disk to the newly created subdirectory. Follow the instructions displayed on the screen to complete the installation, which ends with the message, *Installation completed.*[1]

STEP 3 **Change and/or modify the DOS path**

The **PATH** command in the **AUTOEXEC.BAT** file should indicate the directory containing the dBASE program (e.g., **C:\DBASEIV** or **C:\DBSAMPLE** for the commercial and student versions, respectively). Type **PATH** to see the current path.

If the commercial version was previously installed on your computer, the existing **PATH** command may already reference the **dBASE IV** subdirectory, in which case no modifications are necessary. If, however, you installed the student version in step 2, then you *must* modify the existing **PATH** command to reflect the **DBSAMPLE** subdirectory. (Note, too, that a single **PATH** command may contain multiple directories, separated from one another by semicolons.) Use an ASCII editor to modify the **AUTOEXEC.BAT** file so that it contains the appropriate entry:

C:\DBASEIV ——— *if you are using the commercial version of dBASE IV*

C:\DBSAMPLE ——— *if you are using the student version of dBASE IV*

Press **Ctrl**, **Alt**, and then **Del** to reboot the computer, so that the modified **AUTOEXEC.BAT** file takes effect.

---

[1] Installation occasionally ends with the error message, *Out of environment space.* The problem is corrected by adding the statement, **SHELL=C:\DOS\COMMAND.COM C:\DOS\ /E:512 /p** as the first command in the **CONFIG.SYS** file. Be sure to reboot the computer after making the change, so that the new **CONFIG.SYS** file takes effect.

STEP 4 **Load dBASE**

Type **dBASE** to load dBASE. The Ashton-Tate Logo will appear briefly on your monitor, followed by the license agreement for dBASE IV. (Should you see the message, *Bad command or file name,* it means that dBASE has not been installed, or, more likely that the current DOS path does not include the dBASE directory. Either way, return to step 1 and proceed as indicated.)

Press the **return** key as instructed in the license agreement, and you should see the dBASE IV Control Center of Figure 1.3. (It is immaterial whether your control center is empty, as is the one in Figure 1.3, or whether it contains multiple entries in the various panels.)

STEP 5 **The dot prompt**

Press the **Esc** key to exit the dBASE Control Center; dBASE will display a confirming message, *Are you sure you want to abandon operation?* Type **y** (yes) to produce the screen of Figure 1.4. (The control center is introduced briefly in Chapter 2 and covered completely in Chapter 8; nothing further is said about the control center in this chapter.)

You are now at the ***dot prompt,*** the point at which all future hands-on exercises begin. The period (dot prompt) that appears at the lower left portion of the screen, just above the ***status line,*** is dBASE's way of telling you it is waiting for a command.

STEP 6 **Exit dBASE**

Type **QUIT** at the dot prompt to exit dBASE and return to the C> prompt. Steps 7 and 8 describe the additional and *optional* installation of the data disk.

STEP 7 **Install the data disk (optional)**

Do this step only if you have your own computer and are not sharing it with other students. Place the data disk (use data disk one if you have 5¼ inch disks) that came with this text in drive A, type **A:**, and press return. Type **DIR** to view the contents of the root directory, which contains the file INSTALL.BAT.

Type **INSTALL**, followed by the letter of the drive to which the data files are to be installed, e.g., **INSTALL C**. Do *not* type a colon after the drive letter. You will see additional messages as files are copied from the data disk to your hard drive. The

FIGURE 1.3
The Control Center

```
Catalog  Tools  Exit                                              3:02:34 pm
                         dBASE IV CONTROL CENTER

                         CATALOG: C:\UNTITLED.CAT

   Data      Queries     Forms      Reports      Labels     Applications
 <create>   <create>    <create>   <create>     <create>     <create>

File:        New file
Description: Press ENTER on <create> to create a new file

Help:F1  Use:◄┘  Data:F2  Design:Shift-F2  Quick Report:Shift-F9  Menus:F10
```

FIGURE 1.4
The Dot Prompt and Status Line

installation process ends with the message, *Installation complete,* at which point you will be returned to the A> prompt.

STEP 8 **Verify the installation of the data disk**

The installation process creates a `DATADISK` subdirectory on your hard drive, which in turn contains several subdirectories corresponding to various chapters in this book. Type the DOS command, **`CD C:\DATADISK`**, to change to the `DATADISK` directory, then type **`DIR`** to see the various subdirectories. One of the subdirectories, named `SOLEIL`, is the focus of the case study discussed later in this chapter. You can also experiment with various `CD` (and `DIR`) commands to change to various subdirectories; e.g., `CD \DATADISK\SOLEIL` followed by `DIR` to view the files in this subdirectory.

There's Always a Reason

We expect that you completed the hands-on exercise with little difficulty. There will be times, however, when not everything will go as smoothly as in this exercise, so we relate a favorite anecdote.[2] As you read our tale, remember that a computer does exactly what you tell it to do, which is not necessarily what you want it to do. It is a source of wonderful satisfaction when everything works, but also the cause of nearly unbelievable frustration when results are not what you expect.

Our story concerns a manager who purchased a PC and began to use it enthusiastically. Unfortunately, the feeling did not rub off on his assistant, who was apprehensive of computers in general, but who finally agreed to try the new technology.

As is frequently the case, the assistant's experience with the computer was as frustrating as the manager's was rewarding. Every time the assistant tried using the computer, an error message appeared; yet when the manager tried the same proce-

[2] "Mystery of the Month," *PC World Magazine,* April 1983.

dure, it worked fine. Finally the manager and assistant went through a systematic comparison of everything they did: turning the machine on and off, handling disks, using the keyboard, and so on. They could find no difference in their procedures and could not account for the repeated disk errors that plagued the assistant but left the manager alone.

Just as they were about to give up the manager noticed that his assistant was wearing a charm bracelet. He looked closely, and found that one of the charms was a tiny magnet containing just enough force to interfere with reading the disk. The assistant stored the bracelet in a drawer, and the machine has been fine ever since.

The point of our story is that there is always a logical reason for everything a computer does or does not do, although discovering that reason may be less than obvious. You are about to embark on a wonderful journey toward the productive use of a computer, with a virtually unlimited number of potential applications. Be patient, be inquisitive, and enjoy.

CASE PREVIEW

We come now to the main portion of the chapter, presenting a completely functional system developed in dBASE. The essence of the case study is in the specification of the system requirements from the viewpoint of the ***end-user.*** As you read further in the case, try to determine the information desired by the user, as well as the data required by the system in order to provide that information. Try to visualize how data will be entered into the system and how the corresponding reports will be generated. Above all, note the requirement for ease of use by a nontechnical individual.

CASE STUDY
Soleil America, Inc.

Stefan Soleil thought himself a very lucky young man. He was about to enter into a $10 million agreement with a well-known New York investment banking firm, whereby the firm would acquire a 75% interest in his shoe company, leaving him with the remaining 25%. They had also agreed to give him a three-year employment contract to manage the company, providing him with a salary of $500,000 in the first year and increasing by $500,000 each year to a salary of $1.5 million in the third and final year (with the stipulation, of course, that all agreed-upon sales and operating income targets were met).

It was not all luck, however, as years of hard work and sound business practices did much to bring about the good fortune. Stefan had always surrounded himself with bright and trusted employees, had paid them well, and was now reaping the rewards of being an effective manager and supervisor. In the old days he had known precisely how much every employee was earning, the date they were hired, and the date of their last salary review. This personal touch endeared him to his workers, but growth of the company in recent years had made it all but impossible to continue in this way. Accordingly, part of his plan for the transition included a computerized personnel information system through which he (and a soon-to-be-hired personnel manager) could track employee performance, promotions, and raises.

Of special importance in the new system are a series of reports, among them: 1) a listing of employees with outstanding performance evaluations, 2) a listing of employees who have not received a raise within the last year, and 3) a listing of employees earning below the expected salary for their job classification. (Each job within the company is assigned a responsibility or grade level, for which a standard formula is used to compute the expected salary. Each employee's salary is computed as a percentage of the expected salary, which provides a measure of how an individual is paid compared to others with a similar job classification.)

Six months ago Stefan hired a consultant to develop a customized, easy to use, menu-driven system according to his specifications. A prototype system was now in place for evaluation, after which the consultant would make final changes. Stefan hoped that the system would be simple enough to be used with relatively little training, yet sophisticated enough to provide the necessary information. He hoped that the final system would allow his personnel policies and philosophies to be kept in operation, even if he left the company at the end of his contract term.

Your job is to view the prototype system developed by the consultant and make a recommendation to Stefan Soleil.

CASE SOLUTION

The very last paragraph of the case presentation refers to a prototype system, which is used in the subsequent hands-on exercise. Indeed, the most essential portion of the chapter is the forthcoming hands-on exercise, which enables you better to appreciate an actual dBASE application. The system is fully functional and typical of systems you will use and/or develop.

The Soleil Personnel System is menu-driven and requires little in the way of user documentation. Although the subsequent hands-on exercise will take you through the system, it is useful to preview some of the screens at this time. It is helpful also to realize that the Soleil system, like many others, is divided into three major components, ***file maintenance, report generation,*** and ***utilities.*** This is apparent by examination of the main menu shown in Figure 1.5.

The menu in Figure 1.5 requires that the user select an option by entering 1, 2, 3, or 4 (the system will not accept any other response). Each of the first three options brings up a subsidiary menu, whereas the fourth will exit from the system, and return you to the operating system.

The relationship of the main menu in Figure 1.5 to its three subsidiary menus is shown in Figure 1.6. Figure 1.6a repeats the main menu from Figure 1.5, whereas Figures 1.6b, c, and d contain the file maintenance, report generation, and utility program menus, respectively. The file maintenance menu in Figure 1.6b provides for the typical operations of ***adding*** a new record, ***editing*** (changing) an existing record, or ***deleting*** an existing record.

The report generation menu of Figure 1.6c reflects the available options to produce the information desired by Stefan Soleil in the case description. It is important to emphasize, however, that the information (output) provided by the system is only as good as the data (input) on which it is based. No system, no matter how sophisticated, can produce valid output from invalid input, a principle aptly stated by the acronym ***GIGO*** (**G**arbage **I**n, **G**arbage **O**ut).

The utilities menu of Figure 1.6d offers five utilities (the meaning of which will become apparent as you read further in the text). The ***backup*** option, however, is critical, and you are reminded to keep *duplicate* copies of important files in *different* places, e.g., at home and in the office.

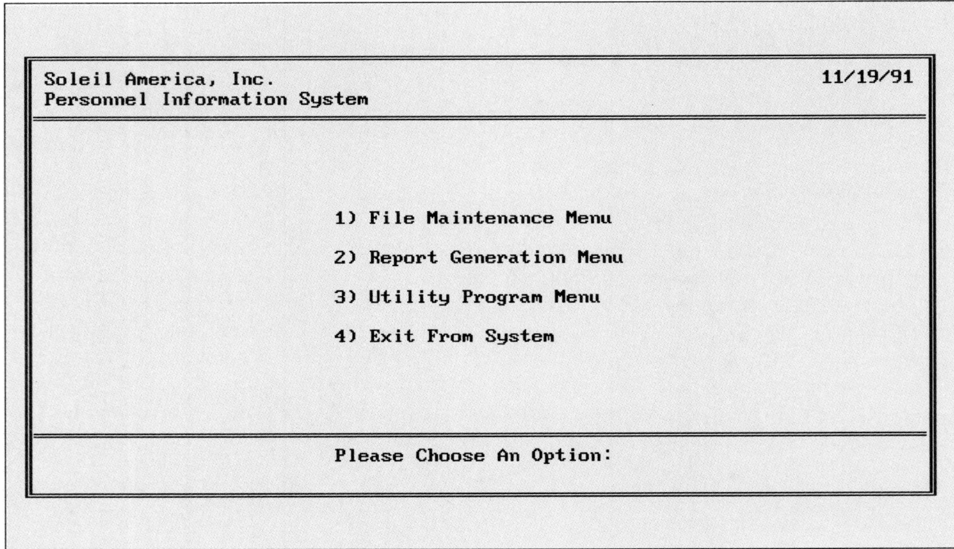

FIGURE 1.5
Main Menu of the Soleil Employee System

FIGURE 1.6
Main and Subordinate Menus

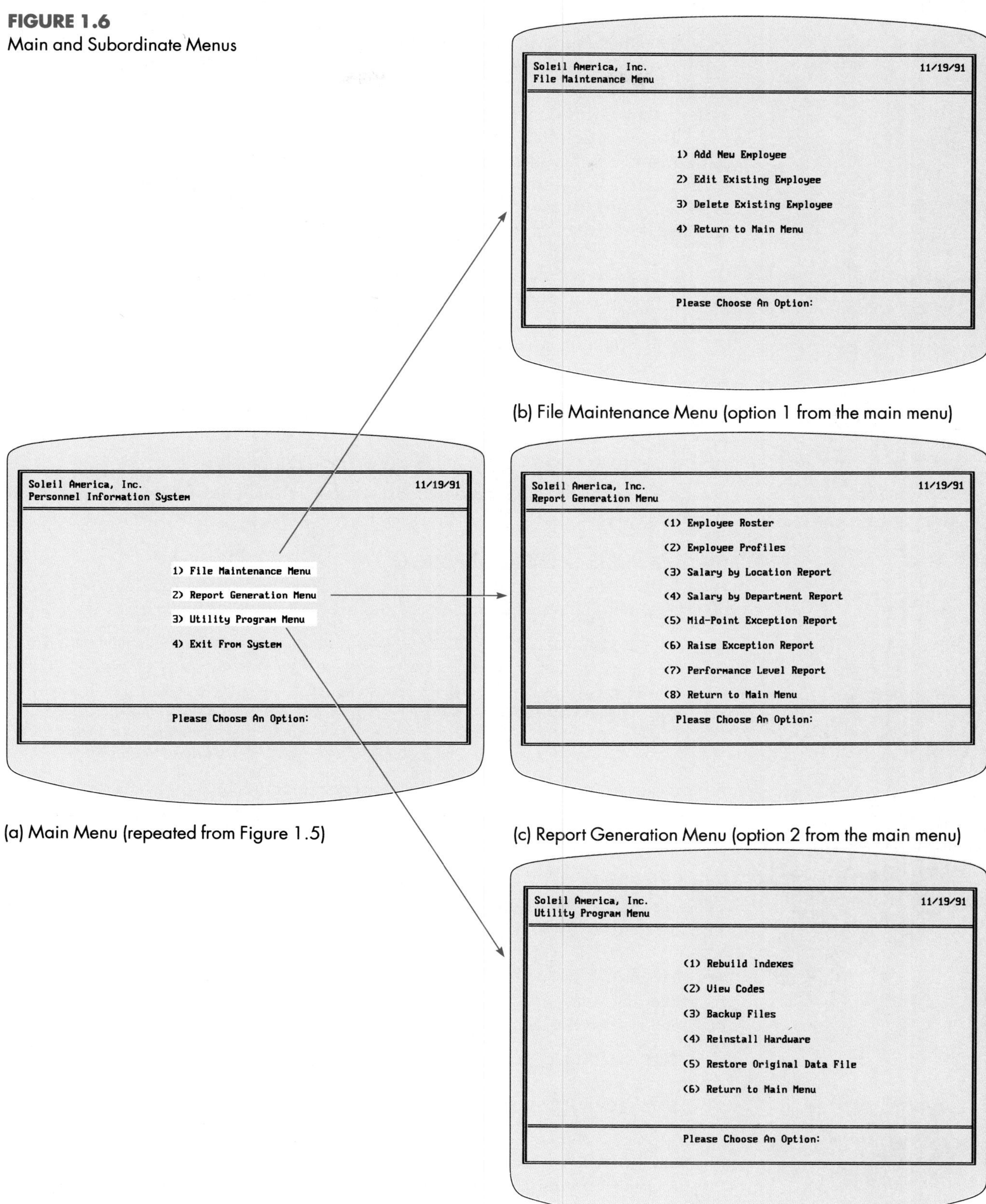

(a) Main Menu (repeated from Figure 1.5)

(b) File Maintenance Menu (option 1 from the main menu)

(c) Report Generation Menu (option 2 from the main menu)

(d) Utility Menu (option 3 from the main menu)

You should now have an overall appreciation for the goals of the Soleil System as well as an inkling as to its implementation. Remember that our objective at this time is for you to gain an appreciation for the power inherent within dBASE, as typified by a real application. Thus, it is not necessary now for you to be concerned with *how* the system works, only about *what* it does.

The exercise you are about to do is the very essence of the chapter. We urge you to experiment fully with the system, especially its file maintenance and report generation capabilities. Add, modify, and delete employee data, then generate several reports (before and after the various transactions). Visualize yourself as Stefan Soleil and decide whether the prototype is adequately developed for you to accept (and pay for) the system.

HANDS-ON EXERCISE 2

The Soleil Employee System

Objective

Load the Soleil Employee System and explore its capabilities from the viewpoint of an end user. Verify that the system does what it is intended to do and note any shortcomings.

STEP 1 **Change to the Soleil subdirectory**

Boot the system, ending at the DOS prompt. Type one of the following two commands, depending on whether you are sharing the hard drive with others:

CD C:\DATADISK\SOLEIL —— *if you installed the data disk on the hard drive and are not sharing your computer, or*

CD A:\DATADISK\SOLEIL —— *if you did not install the data disk, i.e., if you are sharing drive C with other students. (Use data disk one if you have 5¼ inch disks.)*

As you can see, the commands are identical except for the drive on which the **SOLEIL** directory is located. In other words, you will use drive C if you have the computer to yourself, or use drive A if you are sharing it with others.

STEP 2 **Load dBASE**

Type **dBASE** to load dBASE as you did in step 4 of the previous exercise. Press the **Esc** key to leave the control center and end at the dot prompt.

STEP 3 **Set the dBASE default drive**

As in the first step of this exercise, the command you enter depends on whether or not you installed the data disk to drive C. Type:

SET DEFAULT TO C ——— *if you installed the data disk, or*

SET DEFAULT TO A ——— *if you did not install the data disk, i.e., if you are sharing drive C with other students*

The **SET DEFAULT** command indicates where dBASE is to look for its data files, and thus depends on your configuration. Note, however, that all subsequent commands in this exercise are identical for either configuration.

STEP 4 **Load the Soleil system**

Type **DO SOLMAIN** to enter the Soleil system. You will be prompted for information about your configuration, i.e., whether you have a color monitor and what type of microprocessor you are using. These questions appear only the first time you run Soleil; they do not appear again, unless you specifically request reinstallation from the utility menu (see step 11).

STEP 5 **The opening screen and main menu**

The opening screen of Figure 1.7 appears automatically after you answer the configuration questions in step 4. The screen exhibits color (if applicable) as well as boldface. If you are using a monochrome monitor, the text in the middle portion of Figure 1.7 should be bold; if it isn't, adjust the contrast knob of your monitor.

Press **return** as instructed in Figure 1.7 to go to the main menu (Figure 1.5), which was discussed in the case solution.

STEP 6 **The file maintenance menu**

Type **1** to select the file maintenance menu, which enables you to execute any of the normal file maintenance operations; i.e., you can *add* a new record, or *edit* or *delete* an existing record. Type **1** to add a record; the system will prompt you for the social security number of the employee to be added; type **666-66-6666** (the hyphens are entered automatically). The system then checks to see that an employee with this social security number has not been entered previously, after which the screen of Figure 1.8a will appear. Add the employee as follows:

```
              Last Name:  Coulter
               Initials:  MA
 Social Security Number:  666-66-6666
             Birth Date:  06/22/45
              Education:  Bachelor's degree
              Hire Date:  November 14, 1991
               Location:  Italy
                  Title:  Sales representative
             Title Date:  November 14, 1991
                 Salary:  25,000
            Salary Date:  November 14, 1991
           Salary Grade:  5
```

Enter data for MA Coulter, one field at a time, into the screen of Figure 1.8a. The system is set up so that if an entry completely fills a field, as with the hire date, the cursor moves automatically to the next field. If, however, a field is not filled, as with a short last name, you must press **return** to go to the next field.

The input data for MA Coulter spells out the entries for education, location, and title, whereas the screen of Figure 1.8a requires that you enter the corresponding codes. To determine the correct codes, use the on-line help facility by pressing the appropriate function key indicated at the bottom of the figure. Press **F3**, for example, to display the location codes as shown in Figure 1.8b.

Complete the addition for MA Coulter, being careful to enter the data exactly as indicated. As you enter data, you may (deliberately or otherwise) encounter various validity checks; e.g., the system will not accept a nonnumeric character in a date field. Nor are you permitted to enter a dollar sign or comma in the salary field, as these characters are inserted for you. (The comma will at first appear to be in the wrong

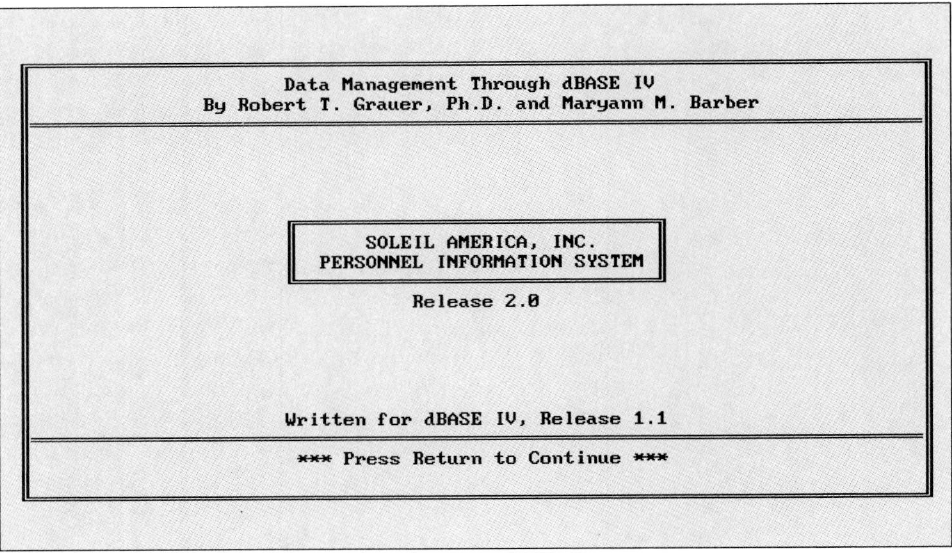

FIGURE 1.7
Opening Screen for Soleil System

place; e.g., 25,000 appears as 250,00; the entry corrects itself when you press the **return** key.) After completing the last field, you will see the following message at the bottom of the screen:

```
Enter A to Add another record, E to Edit above
    information, or S to Save and Quit
```

Type **S** to save the record and return to the file maintenance menu.

STEP 7 **Edit an existing record**

Type **2** to select the second option in the file maintenance menu, and edit data on an existing employee. The following message will appear on the screen with a place for the employee's name at the bottom:

```
Please enter name of Employee to edit below
    or press return twice to quit ...

Last Name:              Initials:
```

Enter the last name of the employee for editing, e.g., **Arnold**, and press **return**, then type the employee's initials, e.g., **JS**. Note that if you fill the initials field, as in this example, the system continues automatically; if, however, you enter only one initial, you must press the **return** key to continue. In actuality, you do not have to enter the initials, or even the complete last name; e.g., you can enter *Arn* in lieu of *Arnold,* in which case the system will retrieve the first employee whose last name begins with *Arn*. Realize, however, that if you enter only a partial last name, you must press the **return** key twice for the system to continue.

The system searches for the record to be edited and (if it is found) displays the record as shown in Figure 1.9; type **E** to edit the record as indicated on the screen. [Alternative choices are **P** to display the previous record (in alphabetical sequence), **N** for the next record, and **Q** to quit the editing operation altogether.]

Use the **up** and **down arrow** keys to move about the screen, and edit any field that requires a correction. For sake of illustration, change the hire date to **5/31/80.** In

FIGURE 1.8
Adding an Employee Record

```
Soleil America, Inc.                                          11/19/91
Personnel File Add Module

                Last Name:                        Initials:

        Social Security Number: 666-66-6666    Birthdate:   /  /


     Education Code:        Hire Date:    /  /           Location Code:

                Title Code:            Title Date:    /  /

     Salary:              Salary Date:    /  /            Salary Grade:
                                                            (1 - 9)

                 Please enter information at the cursor
     F2 - Education Codes     F3 - Location Codes     F4 - Title Codes
```

(a) Empty Template (only social security has been entered)

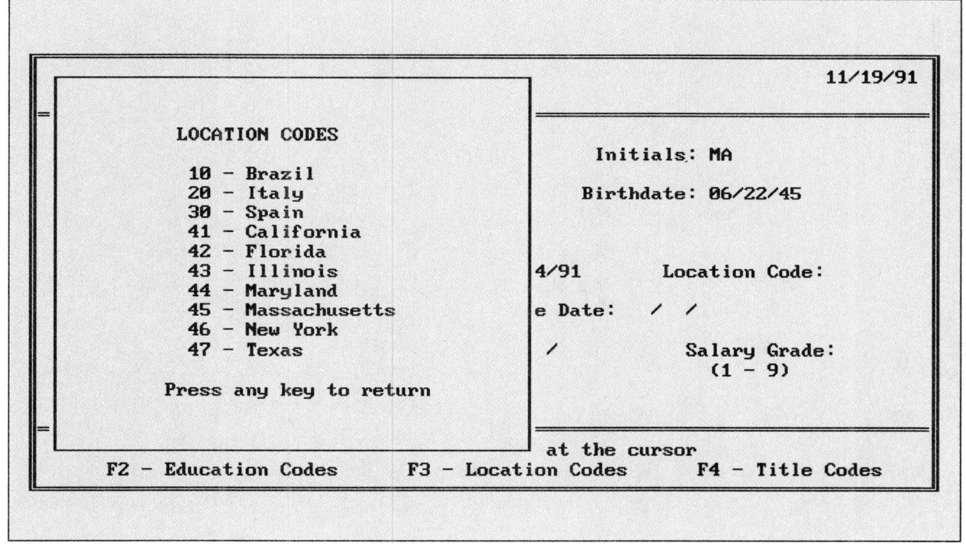

```
                                                              11/19/91

          LOCATION CODES
                                           Initials: MA
           10 - Brazil
           20 - Italy                     Birthdate: 06/22/45
           30 - Spain
           41 - California
           42 - Florida
           43 - Illinois                4/91      Location Code:
           44 - Maryland
           45 - Massachusetts           e Date:   /  /
           46 - New York
           47 - Texas                   /         Salary Grade:
                                                    (1 - 9)
          Press any key to return

                                          at the cursor
     F2 - Education Codes     F3 - Location Codes     F4 - Title Codes
```

(b) Help Screen (for location)

addition, change the title from *Sales Representative* (currently shown as title code 400) to *Production Coordinator.* (You can use on-line help, i.e., press **F4** to display the title codes.) When you reach the very last field on the screen, press **return** to produce the following message:

```
Enter E to Edit above information, S to Save and edit
    another record, or Q to save and Quit
```

Type **Q** to return to the file maintenance menu.

FIGURE 1.9
Editing an Employee Record

```
Soleil America, Inc.                                          11/19/91
Personnel File Edit Module

              Last Name: Arnold                  Initials: JS

         Social Security Number: 171-77-1777    Birthdate: 03/04/45

        Performance Rating: 1    Title Code: 302    Title Date: 02/12/87

       Education Code: 4     Hire Date: 06/25/81      Location Code: 42

                              Salary History
         Salary                Salary Date                 Salary Grade

         $ 78,000               02/17/88                        6
         $ 70,000               02/12/87                        6
         $ 67,000               01/10/86                        6

              Press E to Edit this record, N to see Next record,
                  P to see Previous record, or Q to Quit:
```

STEP 8 **Delete an existing employee**

Type **3** from the file maintenance menu to delete a record, which will produce the following message:

```
Please enter name of Employee to delete below
     or press return twice to quit

Last Name:              Initials:
```

Type **Stutz** as the employee slated for deletion and press **return** twice (the retrieval function works identically as in the previous transactions). The record for Stutz appears on the screen as shown in Figure 1.10. Type **D** to delete the record and note the presence of the confirming message, *Are you sure? (Y/N),* on the bottom of the screen. Answer appropriately and Stutz will be deleted.

STEP 9 **Report generation**

Although the emphasis of this exercise has been on the various file maintenance functions, it (file maintenance) is only a means to an end. The ultimate goal of this or any other system is to provide information to the decision maker. Exit from the file maintenance menu (Figure 1.6b) and return to the main menu (Figure 1.6a), then select the report generation menu shown in Figure 1.6c. Type **1** to select the employee roster, type **1** to list employees in alphabetical order, then relax as Figure 1.11 is produced on the monitor. Observe, too, that the report reflects the addition of MA Coulter, who was added in step 6, but does not mention Stutz, who was deleted in step 8.

STEP 10 **Experiment**

You should now have an understanding of both the file maintenance and reporting functions, yet you have only begun to scratch the surface. Accordingly, we suggest that you enter several additional transactions to further appreciate the capabilities inherent in this (and other) systems. Add, modify, and delete employee records; take advantage of the on-line help facility, and the ability to page through the employee file with the N and P options. Generate additional reports based on the data you enter.

Explore the data validation capabilities built into the system. See what happens if you select a menu option that doesn't exist, attempt to add a duplicate record, or try to edit a record that is not in the system.

FIGURE 1.10
Deleting an Employee Record

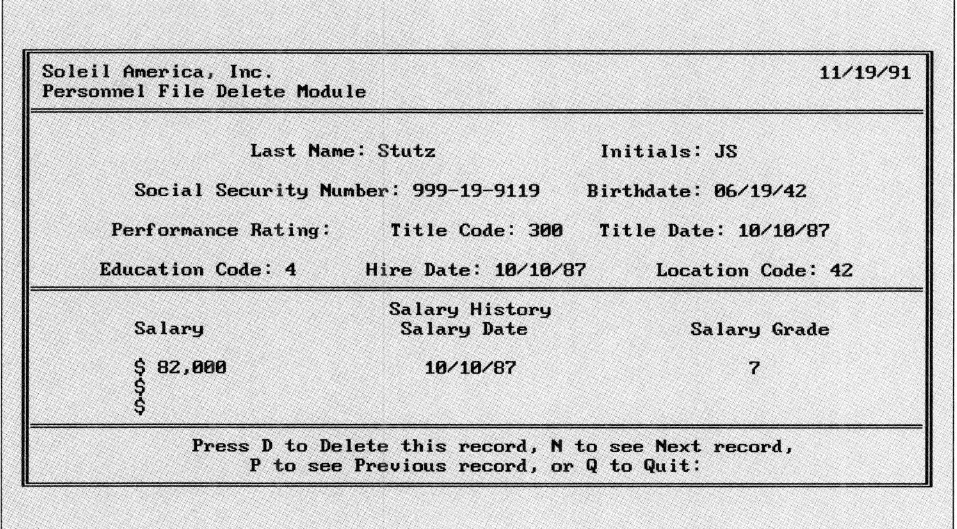

STEP 11 **The utilities menu**

Return to the main menu shown earlier and type **3** to select the utilities menu of Figure 1.6d. One option, restoring the data files, assumes particular significance at this time because completion of the exercise has changed the original Soleil data; i.e., you have added a record for Coulter, changed an existing record for Arnold, and deleted the record for Stutz. You may, however, restore the file to its original status, which enables you to repeat all (or part) of this exercise and obtain results identical to those previously. Type **5**, as indicated in the utility menu, to restore the file.

FIGURE 1.11
Employee Roster (report 1)

```
Page No.      1
11/19/91

                Soleil America, Inc.
            Employee Roster by Last Name

     Arnold, JS                             171-77-1777
     Baker, MJ                              333-33-3333
     Borow, LR                              111-11-1111
     Burke, HB                              313-13-1313
     Butler, LB                             188-18-8111
     Butler, WJ                             999-99-9999
     Center, BP                             454-54-5454
     Coulter, MA                            666-66-6666
     Hernandez, VL                          777-77-7777
     Jones, ME                              300-00-0000
     Kinzer, JL                             242-22-4444
     Marion, FM                             888-88-8888
     Mellon, SA                             999-22-9229
     Milgrom, ME                            121-21-2121
     Moldof, K                              222-22-2222
     Scholl, GT                             999-55-9665
     Smith, KL                              101-01-0101
     Smith, RT                              555-55-5555
     Sugrue, PK                             666-77-8668
```

As to the other options, we cannot overemphasize the need for backup and urge that it be done on a daily basis with real systems. The ability to view and/or alter codes comes into play during file maintenance, and the meaning of rebuilding indexes will become clear after reading Chapter 3. You may also reconfigure (reinstall) the system at any time, as done earlier in step 4.

STEP 12 **Exit the system**

Type **6** to exit the utility menu and return to the main menu. Type **4** to exit the Soleil system, which returns you to the DOS prompt.

Summary

Installation is the process of customizing a program to a particular hardware configuration; it is done once, and only once, when the program is first copied to the hard disk. ***Loading*** occurs when a program is read from disk into memory and is necessary every time the program is used.

The ***data disk*** that accompanies this text is divided into ***subdirectories*** corresponding to the chapters in the text. The availability of the data disk saves you the tedium of data entry and allows you to explore dBASE in a way that would otherwise not be possible.

The DOS **CD** command changes from one directory to another; the DOS **PATH** command makes it possible to load dBASEIV from any directory.

The **Esc** key exits the dBASE IV ***control center*** and ends at the dot prompt. The **QUIT** command exits dBASE and returns to DOS.

The dBASE product line is developed and marketed by ***Ashton-Tate Corporation; dBASE IV*** is the most current version of the dBASE line.

The Soleil Employee System was shown to be completely menu-driven with on-line help capabilities. The associated hands-on exercises took you through its ***file maintenance, report generation,*** and ***utility*** menus, which typify real-world applications.

Key Words and Concepts

Adding records	DOS prompt	**QUIT**
Ashton-Tate	Dot prompt	**RD** command
AUTOEXEC.BAT	Editing records	Report generation
Backup	End-user	Root directory
CD command	**Esc** key	**SET DEFAULT TO A**
CONFIG.SYS	File maintenance	**SET DEFAULT TO C**
Control center	GIGO	Status line
Data disk	Installing dBASE	Subdirectory
Data validation	Loading dBASE	**TREE** command
dBASE IV, Version 1.1	**MD** command	Tree structure
Default drive	On-line help	Utility programs
Deleting records	**PATH** command	Vulcan
DOS	**PROMPT pg**	Wayne Ratliff

True/False

1. The dBASE series is a product of IBM.
2. An end-user requires detailed knowledge of dBASE programming.
3. The dBASE series will run only on a PC manufactured by IBM.
4. The Soleil Employee System is contained on the dBASE program disk.
5. Additions, modifications, and deletions are the typical file maintenance functions.
6. The dot prompt refers to the "greater than" sign associated with PC DOS.
7. dBASE must be installed every time the Soleil system is executed.
8. A well-designed system will produce valid output from invalid input.
9. A well-designed system will reject the attempted addition of a record already present.
10. A given **PATH** command may specify more than one subdirectory.
11. The **DIR** command lists every file contained on a disk.
12. The DOS prompt can be changed to include the current directory of the default drive.
13. The data disk must be copied to drive C.

Exercises

1. Describe the procedure to:
   (a) Install the data disk
   (b) Install the student version of dBASE IV
   (c) Load dBASE
   (d) Load the Soleil system
   (e) Reconfigure the Soleil system
   (f) Restore the Soleil files to their original status
   (g) Backup the Soleil data files

2. Distinguish between:
   (a) The student and commercial versions of dBASE IV
   (b) The DOS prompt and the dBASE prompt
   (c) The DOS **TREE** command and the DOS **PATH** command
   (d) File maintenance and report generation
   (e) Drive A and drive C
   (f) Loading and installing dBASE

3. Process the following transactions for the Soleil Employee System:
   (a) Add a new employee with the following data:

```
             Last Name:  Small
              Initials:  MJ
Social Security Number:  787-88-7878
            Birth Date:  1/22/50
             Education:  Bachelor's degree
             Hire Date:  12/12/91
              Location:  Florida
                 Title:  Director of Purchasing
            Title Date:  12/12/91
                Salary:  36,000
           Salary Date:  12/12/91
          Salary Grade:  6
```

(b) Edit data for existing employee(s)—retrieve the following two employee records, changing the data as indicated:
   (i) Kinzer, JL—change education from "Other Graduate Degree" to "Master's Degree." (Use the on-line help facility as appropriate.)
   (ii) Smith, RT—change birth date from 10/10/47 to 11/10/47.

(c) Delete PK Sugrue (social security number 666-77-8668) from the system.

4. A well-designed system incorporates data validation procedures within the file maintenance function in an attempt to improve the quality of data entered into the system. These procedures typically take the form of error messages that prevent the user from entering transactions that are obviously incorrect. With respect to the Soleil system, what message (if any) will appear if you attempt to:
(a) Add an employee whose record is already in the system
(b) Delete an employee whose record is not in the system
(c) Exit the system without backing it up
(d) Enter alphabetic data in a numeric field, e.g., salary
(e) Enter an invalid option on a menu
(f) Enter a bad date, e.g., 13/25/92
(g) Enter a code not contained in the system, e.g., a location code of 84
Are there error messages you would like to see included in the system, which are not presently there?

5. The end-user is the individual ultimately responsible for providing the system specifications to a programmer or external consultant, who then implements the system. The end-user is also the person who ultimately accepts, and pays for, the completed system. With this in mind, are you ready to accept the Soleil system as it presently exists, or are there changes you would like incorporated?

CHAPTER

2 The Dot Prompt

OUTLINE

OBJECTIVES

After reading this chapter you will be able to:

1. Define the terms: field, record, file, file structure.
2. Create and/or modify a dBASE file structure; use the CREATE, MODIFY STRUCTURE, and DISPLAY STRUCTURE commands.
3. Add, modify, or delete records; use the APPEND, EDIT, BROWSE, DELETE, RECALL, and PACK commands.
4. List some or all records in a file through variations in the DISPLAY command.
5. Obtain summary information by the SUM, COUNT, and AVERAGE commands.
6. Explain the dBASE notation and record pointer.
7. Define the command buffer; explain the shortcut afforded through the up and down arrow keys when entering commands at the dot prompt.
8. Explain how to use the dBASE on-line help facility; describe the purpose of the Programmer's Notebook.
9. Describe the control center in dBASE IV and how its panels relate to the organization of this book.

Overview

dBASE IV bears little resemblance to the program that appeared over a decade ago. The ***dot prompt,*** however, has remained unchanged; it was the original user interface in dBASE II, and it has carried over to the present day. *We believe, therefore, that learning commands from the dot prompt continues as the best introduction to dBASE.* This approach not only provides continuity across the various releases; it also forces you to think for yourself, as opposed to simply selecting commands from a series of menus.

This chapter begins, therefore, with individual commands executed *interactively* from the dot prompt, as opposed to series of commands executed *collectively* as a program (as was done in Chapter 1). We show you how to create a file (**CREATE**), to enter, modify, and/or delete data in that file (**APPEND**, **EDIT**, **BROWSE**, **DELETE**, **RECALL**, and **PACK**), and to retrieve data from that file (**DISPLAY**, **SUM**, **COUNT**, and **AVERAGE**). You are then directed to a hands-on exercise in which you use these commands and gain an intuitive understanding of how they work.

After the exercise, we launch a more formal study of dBASE through discussion of the ***record pointer*** and ***dBASE notation,*** then review the exercise from this perspective. We show you that there is little need for memorization, provided you understand the command syntax as it is used in the ***on-line help*** facility. We present the ***Programmer's Notebook,*** a valuable reference at the end of this book. The chapter ends with an introduction to the dBASE IV ***control center.***

Vocabulary of Data Management

Imagine a situation in which you maintain employee data in manila folders (one folder per employee), with the entire set of folders kept in a filing cabinet. Every individual has the specifics of his or her employment (e.g., social security number, name, salary, and job title) written in one of these folders, with the data stored in the same format in every folder.

The system just described illustrates the basics of data management terminology. The data in a manila folder is called a ***record,*** with the full set of records (folders in the file cabinet) called a ***file.*** Each fact about an individual, e.g., his or her social security number, is termed a ***field.*** The order of fields within a record, the amount of space allocated to each field, and the type of data (character or numeric) in each field is constant from record to record, and is known as the ***file structure.***

The terminology is illustrated by Figure 2.1 (an abbreviated version of the file used in Chapter 1). Our illustrative file has six records, with each record containing five fields. The arrangement of fields within each record is identical (social security number, followed by name, followed by location, and so on), as is the allocated space for each field.

The various fields in Figure 2.1 are of different data types. Name, for example, is a ***character field,*** whereas salary is a ***numeric field.*** A character field may contain anything—i.e., letters, numbers, or special characters such as the apostrophe in O'Malley. A numeric field is more limited, as it can contain only numbers, a plus or minus sign, and a decimal point. A numeric field may be used in a calculation, whereas a character field, even one that contains only numbers, cannot. Thus, even though the social security number meets the criteria for a numeric field (it contains only numbers), it is more *efficiently* stored as a character field because it (the social security number) is never used in a calculation. Zip code and telephone number are other examples of so-called numeric fields that are better defined as character fields.

	Social Security Number (Field)	Name (Field)	Location (Field)	Salary (Field)	Title (Field)
Record 1 →	111111111	Borow	Florida	18000	Warehouse staff
Record 2 →	222222222	O'Malley	Brazil	24000	Sales rep
Record 3 →	333333333	Baker	Florida	14800	Sales support staff
Record 4 →	444444444	Benjamin	Florida	18800	Warehouse staff
Record 5 →	555555555	Smith	Brazil	14300	Clerical
Record 6 →	666666666	Jones	Texas	23500	Sales rep

FIGURE 2.1
Data Management Terminology

Merely putting data into the filing cabinet is easy; retrieving it in a meaningful form is quite another matter. In the course of normal business operations you will need information about some or all of your employees. You may, for example, want the folders of only those employees who are located in Florida, or only those employees who are warehouse staff, and so on. You may need to know the total of all salaries in the company, or the total salaries for just the warehouse staff.

You will also need to maintain your folders to reflect ongoing changes in the company. New employees will be added, necessitating the creation of new folders, whereas others may leave the company and their folders should be removed. Still others will require that their folders be updated as conditions change; e.g., employees may receive a raise, transfer to a new location, or change names.

dBASE, as well as all other data management systems, must make provision for all of these operations. There must be a way for you to define the file structure, and for the addition, modification, and deletion of records in an existing file. There must also be additional provisions to retrieve data once it has been entered. As we shall see, each of these operations is accomplished by a specific dBASE command, the most basic of which are explained in the next section.

Elementary dBASE Commands

Our approach to teaching dBASE is to get you on the computer as quickly as possible. Accordingly, rather than cover every detail of every command, we present an overview of the most basic commands, describe their general purpose, then turn you loose with a hands-on exercise. Programming in dBASE (or any other language) is best learned by doing, and the sooner you are on the computer, the better.

Table 2.1 lists the dBASE commands that will be covered. The initial task in any application is the creation of a file structure to specify the order of fields within a record, as well as the length and type of data in each field. Once the file structure has been created, you can display the structure to see if it is correct and, if not, modify it accordingly.

The commands for data entry allow you to add (**APPEND**) records to an existing file. You can make changes to existing records (one record at a time) through the **EDIT** command, or to several records at a time with the **BROWSE** command. You can

TABLE 2.1 **Elementary dBASE Commands**

Commands affecting the file structure:
CREATE, **DISPLAY STRUCTURE**, **MODIFY STRUCTURE**

Commands for file maintenance:
APPEND, **EDIT**, **BROWSE**, **DELETE**, **RECALL**, **PACK**

Commands for data retrieval:
DISPLAY, **SUM**, **AVERAGE**, **COUNT**

Miscellaneous commands:
HELP, **GOTO**, **USE**, **CLOSE DATABASES**, **SET DEFAULT**, **QUIT**

also remove existing records from a file, but you will need two commands to complete this task.

The **DELETE** command marks records for subsequent removal, but does not physically delete the records; i.e., dBASE gives you a chance to change your mind and **RECALL** the records slated for deletion. It is the **PACK** command that permanently (i.e., physically) removes the records marked for deletion.

The **DISPLAY** command shows some or all of the data for one or more records in the file; i.e., you can display one record, every record, or only those records that meet a specified criterion (e.g., employees in California). The **SUM**, **COUNT**, and **AVERAGE** commands are used for elementary arithmetic operations. **SUM** will total the value of a numeric field(s) for some or all of the records in the file; e.g., it can calculate the sum of every salary, or just the salaries for the warehouse staff. **COUNT**, on the other hand, will tally the number of records in the file or the number of records that meet a given criterion. In similar fashion the **AVERAGE** command can be made to apply to every record, or only to a subset.

The **SET DEFAULT** command establishes the ***default drive*** (i.e., the drive dBASE searches for existing files, and the drive to which dBASE writes any new files that are created). The **USE** command opens an *existing* dBASE file for processing, while **CLOSE DATABASES** closes (puts away) any files currently in use. The **GOTO** command moves from one record to another. The **QUIT** command exits dBASE and returns to DOS. The **HELP** command provides a source of on-line information about individual commands.

The hands-on exercise that follows illustrates how the ***file maintenance*** and ***data retrieval*** functions are implemented in dBASE. We think you will understand how the commands work from the way in which they are used, but we do include additional explanation after the exercise. In other words, we think it easiest to first gain an intuitive understanding through experimentation, prior to a more rigorous explanation.

HANDS-ON EXERCISE 1

Elementary dBASE Commands

Objective

Create a dBASE file structure corresponding to Figure 2.1; add, modify, and delete records in the file; and display individual records and/or summary information from the file.

STEP 1 **Change to the appropriate subdirectory**

Boot the system, ending at the DOS prompt. Type one of the following two commands, depending on whether you are sharing the hard drive with others:

CD C:\DATADISK\INTRO —— *if you installed the data disk on the hard drive and are not sharing your computer, or*

CD A:\DATADISK\INTRO —— *if you did not install the data disk, i.e., if you are sharing drive C with other students. (Use data disk one if you have 5¼-inch disks.)*

The commands are identical except for the drive on which the **INTRO** directory is located. In other words, you will use drive C if you have the computer to yourself, or use drive A if you are sharing it with others.

STEP 2 **Load dBASE**

Type **dBASE** to load dBASE, then press the **Esc** key to leave the control center and arrive at the dot prompt. The next command again depends on whether or not you installed the data disk to drive C, i.e., type:

SET DEFAULT TO C ——— *if you installed the data disk, or*

SET DEFAULT TO A ——— *if you did not install the data disk, i.e., if you are sharing drive C with other students.*

The **SET DEFAULT** command tells dBASE where to look for its files and, as indicated, depends on your configuration. All subsequent commands, however, are identical regardless of the location of your files.

STEP 3 **Define the file structure**

Type **CREATE EMPLOYEE** to establish the file structure **EMPLOYEE.DBF**. The file name is optional; i.e., you could choose a file name other than **EMPLOYEE**, providing it (the file name) is one to eight characters in length, in accordance with the rules of DOS. The **DBF** extension, however, is assigned automatically by dBASE.

dBASE then displays the screen of Figure 2.2, which asks for information about the file structure you wish to create. Type the name of the first field, **SOCSEC**, and press the **return** key to move to the next column. Type **C** to specify a character field (recall that the social security number is defined as a character rather than a numeric field, because it is not used in arithmetic operations), type **9** and press the **enter** key for the field width, and **N** to indicate that an index is not requested. (Indexes are discussed in detail in Chapter 3.) Enter the information shown for all remaining fields.

When information for the last field (**TITLE** in our example) has been entered, press the **enter** key to signify the end of the file structure. dBASE will ask you to press **return** a second time, to confirm that you are finished, then asks if you want to input data at this time. Respond **N** (no), and you will be returned to the dot prompt.

STEP 4 **Verify the file structure**

Type **DISPLAY STRUCTURE**, as shown in Figure 2.3, to review the file structure just created. You will see all fields in the file structure, the type and width of each field, and the order in which the fields appear within a record. You will also see the number of records in the file (none to this point), and the date of the last file update, in this case the date on which the file structure was created.

Verify that the file structure is exactly as you intend it to be. (Do not be concerned that the total number of positions in the record, 57 in our example, is one

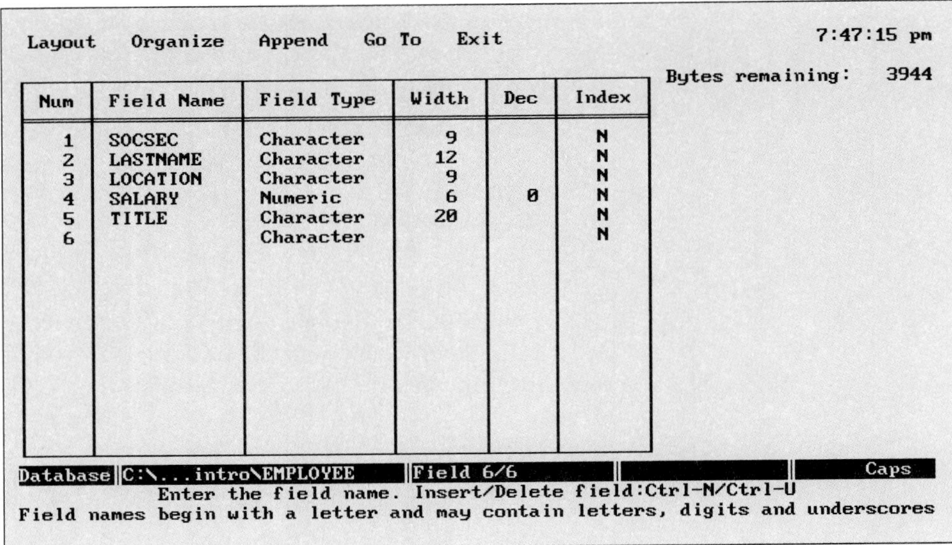

FIGURE 2.2
Defining a File Structure

more than the sum of the individual field lengths, as dBASE uses this extra position for its internal file management.) If you discover an error, e.g., an extra or omitted field, an incorrect data type, or wrong field size, you can change the file structure through the **MODIFY STRUCTURE** command as described in the Programmer's Notebook.

STEP 5 **Adding records**

Type **APPEND** (at the dot prompt) to begin entering data, bringing the ***input template*** of Figure 2.4 into view. (APPEND is an example of a full-screen command in that it first clears the screen of any previous output.) The input template in Figure 2.4 displays the field names and field widths of the file structure. Enter data *exactly* as it appears in Figure 2.1, beginning with the first field for the first record. dBASE commands are case sensitive, and thus you need to pay attention to capitalization; e.g., type **Florida**, not FLORIDA or florida.

Press the **return** key after completing the data for one field in order to move to the next field. The only exception is if the data completely fills the field width, as happens for the social security number, in which case dBASE automatically takes you to the next field *without* your pressing the **return** key. In other words, completion of the social security number automatically positions you in the first position of the last name field, because the data completely fills the space allocated for social security

FIGURE 2.3
The DISPLAY STRUCTURE Command

EMPLOYEE.DBF file is in INTRO subdirectory

```
. DISPLAY STRUCTURE
Structure for database: C:\DATADISK\INTRO\EMPLOYEE.DBF
Number of data records:          0
Date of last update     : 02/17/91
Field  Field Name  Type        Width    Dec    Index
    1  SOCSEC      Character       9                N
    2  LASTNAME    Character      12                N
    3  LOCATION    Character       9                N
    4  SALARY      Numeric         6                N
    5  TITLE       Character      20                N
** Total **                       57
```

FIGURE 2.4
Input Template for Data Entry

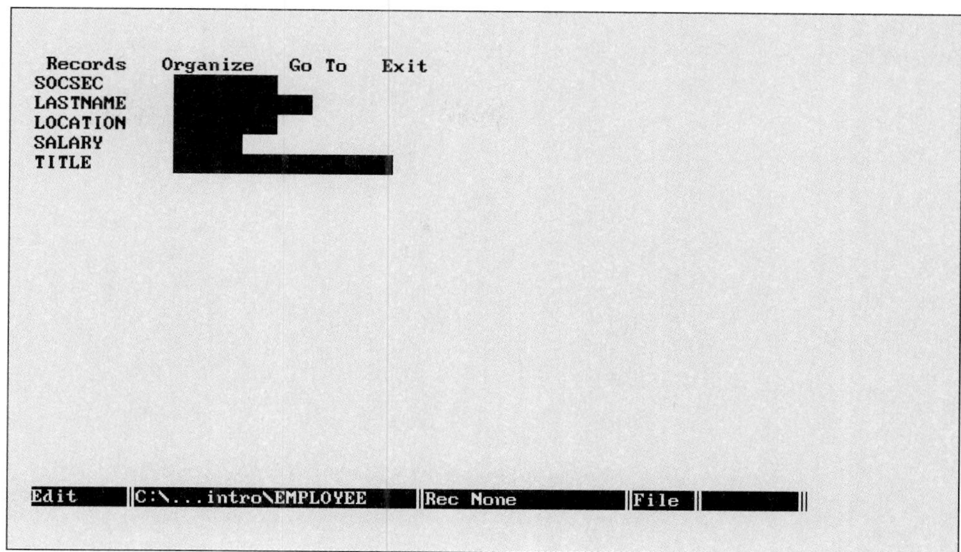

number. You may, however, have to press the **return** key after entering a last name, in order to move to the location field.

When you have entered data for the last field in record 1, press the **enter** key to move on to record 2. After completing the field entries for O'Malley, press the **enter** key to bring up a blank input screen for the third record, and enter data for this record as well. Enter data for the remaining records in Figure 2.1, then press **Ctrl+End** to terminate data entry. You must, however, press **Ctrl+End** while still in record 6, otherwise a blank record will be appended to the file. (In the event record 7 does appear, press the **enter** or **Esc** key while the cursor is positioned in the first field.)

STEP 6 **Modify data in existing records**

There are two ways in which erroneous data can be corrected. You can *edit* an individual record, or you can *browse* the entire file. All that is required in either mode is to retype the field(s) in error, rather than retyping the entire record.

The specific record affected by the EDIT command depends on the position of the record pointer at the time the command is issued, a concept discussed at the end of the exercise. For the time being, however, enter the following from the dot prompt and observe what happens:

```
. 3

. EDIT
```

Typing a 3 at the dot prompt positions the record pointer at record number three (Baker), so that the subsequent EDIT command brings up that record for modification. In similar fashion, typing a **1** prior to a second EDIT command would bring you to record number one (Borow).

Screens for both the EDIT and BROWSE commands are shown in Figures 2.5a and 2.5b, respectively. EDIT, like APPEND, is a full-screen command in which one record at a time is placed on the screen for modification. The EDIT command displays a template with the current value of each field, enabling you to change (edit) any or all fields in much the same way data was entered initially. The PgUp and PgDn keys will display the previous and following records, and allow you to continue editing.

FIGURE 2.5
Data Modification

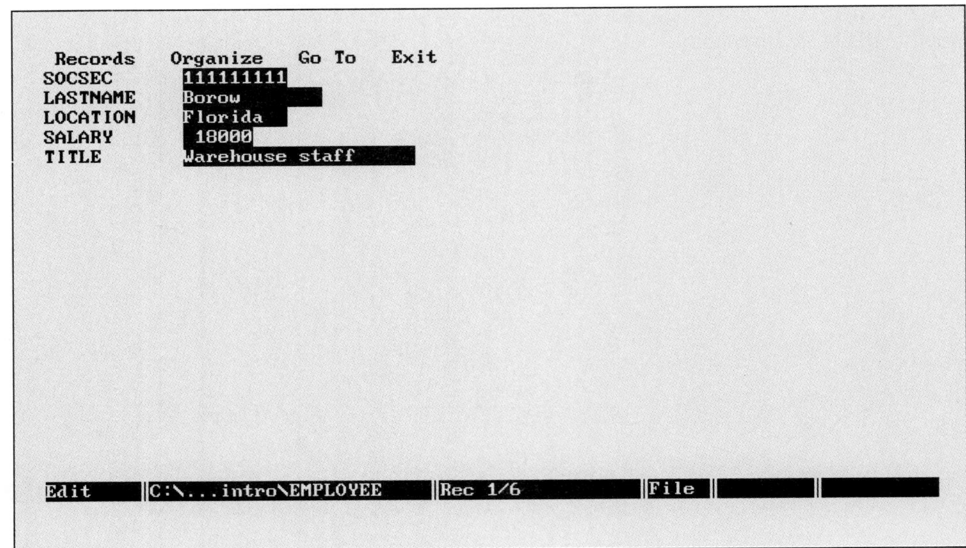

(a) The EDIT Command

Records Organize Fields Go To Exit

SOCSEC	LASTNAME	LOCATION	SALARY	TITLE
111111111	Borow	Florida	18000	Warehouse staff
222222222	O'Malley	Brazil	24000	Sales rep
333333333	Baker	Florida	14800	Sales support staff
444444444	Benjamin	Florida	18800	Warehouse staff
555555555	Smith	Brazil	14300	Clerical
666666666	Jones	Texas	23500	Sales rep

Browse C:\...intro\EMPLOYEE Rec 1/6 File

(b) The BROWSE Command

The **BROWSE** command in Figure 2.5b displays several records simultaneously, as opposed to the **EDIT** command, which views only a single record.

Press **Ctrl+End** to return to the dot prompt.

STEP 7 **Delete a record**

Two commands, **DELETE** and **PACK**, are needed to remove a record from a file. The **DELETE** command marks a record for deletion, but does not remove the record from the file (i.e., the record is logically, but not physically, deleted). In other words, dBASE enables you to change your mind and restore a record through the **RECALL** command. Execution of the **PACK** command, however, permanently (i.e., physically) removes the records marked for deletion.

Figure 2.6 illustrates all three commands. The two **DELETE** commands mark records 3 and 6 for deletion, a fact confirmed by the **DISPLAY ALL** command in Figure 2.6a, which shows asterisks next to these record numbers. Record 3 is recalled in Figure 2.6b, so that the **PACK** command of Figure 2.6c deletes only record 6. The **DISPLAY ALL** command confirms that record 6 has been deleted, but that record 3 is still in the file.

Follow the command sequence in the figure, after which your file should contain five records (Borow, O'Malley, Baker, Benjamin, and Smith).

STEP 8 **Displaying individual record(s)**

The **DISPLAY** command can show a single record, every record, or only those records meeting a specified condition. **DISPLAY**, with no additional parameters as in Figure 2.7a, shows only the record at the current position of the record pointer. **DISPLAY ALL**, however, shows every record in the file, as illustrated in Figure 2.7b.

FIGURE 2.6
The DELETE, RECALL, and PACK Commands

```
. 3                    ---- Record pointer is moved to record 3

EMPLOYEE: Record No       3

. DELETE               ---- Record 3 is logically deleted
      1 record deleted

. 6
EMPLOYEE: Record No       6

. DELETE               ---- Record 6 is logically deleted
      1 record deleted

. DISPLAY ALL
Record#  SOCSEC    LASTNAME     LOCATION  SALARY TITLE
      1  111111111 Borow        Florida    18000 Warehouse staff
      2  222222222 O'Malley     Brazil     24000 Sales rep
      3 *333333333 Baker        Florida    14800 Sales support staff
      4  444444444 Benjamin     Florida    18800 Warehouse staff
      5  555555555 Smith        Brazil     14300 Clerical
      6 *666666666 Jones        Texas      23500 Sales rep
        └ Asterisk indicates record 6 is marked for deletion
```

(a) The DELETE Command

```
. 3
EMPLOYEE: Record No       3

. RECALL               ---- Record 3 is recalled
       1 record recalled
```

(b) The RECALL Command

```
. PACK                 ---- PACK command physically deletes marked records
      5 records copied

. DISPLAY ALL
Record#  SOCSEC    LASTNAME     LOCATION  SALARY TITLE
      1  111111111 Borow        Florida    18000 Warehouse staff
      2  222222222 O'Malley     Brazil     24000 Sales rep
      3  333333333 Baker        Florida    14800 Sales support staff
      4  444444444 Benjamin     Florida    18800 Warehouse staff
      5  555555555 Smith        Brazil     14300 Clerical
```

(c) The PACK Command

```
. 2                                    Record pointer is moved to record 2
EMPLOYEE: Record No         2

. DISPLAY                              Only one record is displayed

Record#  SOCSEC     LASTNAME     LOCATION  SALARY TITLE
      2  222222222  O'Malley     Brazil     24000 Sales rep
```

(a) Displaying a Single Record

```
. DISPLAY ALL                          All records are displayed

Record#  SOCSEC     LASTNAME     LOCATION  SALARY TITLE
      1  111111111  Borow        Florida    18000 Warehouse staff
      2  222222222  O'Malley     Brazil     24000 Sales rep
      3  333333333  Baker        Florida    14800 Sales support staff
      4  444444444  Benjamin     Florida    18800 Warehouse staff
      5  555555555  Smith        Brazil     14300 Clerical
```

(b) Displaying All Records

```
. DISPLAY FOR LOCATION = "Florida"      Character field enclosed in quotes
Record#  SOCSEC     LASTNAME     LOCATION  SALARY TITLE
      1  111111111  Borow        Florida    18000 Warehouse staff
      3  333333333  Baker        Florida    14800 Sales support staff
      4  444444444  Benjamin     Florida    18800 Warehouse staff
```

(c) Displaying Selected Records (character field)

```
. DISPLAY FOR SALARY < 15000            Numeric field does not use quotes

Record#  SOCSEC     LASTNAME     LOCATION  SALARY TITLE
      3  333333333  Baker        Florida    14800 Sales support staff
      5  555555555  Smith        Brazil     14300 Clerical
```

(d) Displaying Selected Records (numeric field)

FIGURE 2.7
The DISPLAY Command

Inclusion of the **FOR** parameter limits the displayed records to those that meet the designated condition. Hence, you can display only the employees located in Florida (Figure 2.7c) or the employees whose salary is less than $15,000 (Figure 2.7d). Note, too, the use of quotes in the condition of Figure 2.7c, and that quotes are *not* used with the numeric field in Figure 2.7d.

STEP 9 **Obtaining summary information**

The **SUM**, **AVERAGE**, and **COUNT** commands are used to obtain summary information about the file as a whole, or about those records meeting a specified condition. The commands are illustrated in Figure 2.8.

STEP 10 **The command buffer (the up and down arrow keys)**

The last 20 commands executed from the dot prompt are stored automatically in a ***command buffer.*** You can retrieve any of these commands (and thus avoid the associated retyping) by pressing the **up arrow** key the appropriate number of times; i.e., pressing the **up arrow** key at the dot prompt retrieves the previous command, pressing it again retrieves the second previous command, and so on. The **down arrow** key works in reverse and displays the next command in the buffer (after a previous command has been retrieved).

Press the **up arrow** key once and the last command from step 9 will appear at the dot prompt; press the **up arrow** key a second time and the previous (i.e., the

FIGURE 2.8
The SUM, AVERAGE, and COUNT Commands

```
. SUM SALARY
      5 records summed
   SALARY
    89900

. AVERAGE SALARY
      5 records averaged
   SALARY
    17980

. AVERAGE SALARY FOR TITLE = "Warehouse staff"
      2 records averaged
   SALARY
    18400

. COUNT FOR TITLE = "Warehouse staff"
      2 records
```

second-to-last) command will appear. Experiment with the **up** and **down arrow** keys until you are comfortable with their function. You can *reexecute* any retrieved command simply by pressing the **enter** key, or you can use the **Ins** and/or **Del** keys to *edit* a retrieved command, then press the **enter** key to execute the modified command.

STEP 11 **The CLOSE DATABASES and USE commands**

Type **CLOSE DATABASES** to close (put away) the **EMPLOYEE.DBF** file you have been using. The command is important because it causes dBASE to write the **EMPLOYEE.DBF** file (currently in memory) to disk. In other words, dBASE does not necessarily write changes as they are made, but stores them temporarily in memory for more efficient execution; it is the **CLOSE DATABASES** command that causes the file to be written to disk. Note, too, that although this exercise began with a **CREATE EMPLOYEE** command, all subsequent exercises that refer to this file will begin with a **USE** command because it (the **EMPLOYEE.DBF** file) exists by virtue of this exercise.

STEP 12 **The QUIT command**

Type **QUIT** to exit dBASE and return to DOS.

The Basics of dBASE

The exercise just completed provides an intuitive appreciation for many commands as they are given from the dot prompt, but in no way suffices as an adequate introduction to dBASE. We expect that the exercises have, in fact, raised at least as many questions as they have answered, especially with respect to how specific commands work. Nevertheless, we hope that the exercise has piqued your curiosity, and thus motivated an interest in the information about to follow.

We are now ready to begin a detailed study of dBASE, starting with the presentation of two very basic and important concepts, the ***record pointer*** and ***dBASE***

notation. As we shall see, these concepts apply to all commands, and provide a firm foundation for a more formal study of the language.

The Record Pointer

The records within a **DBF** file are numbered consecutively, beginning with 1; i.e., the first record is record number 1, the second record is record number 2, and so on. dBASE keeps track of its position within a file by maintaining a record pointer whose location in a file is continually updated as commands are executed. Even when dBASE is processing an entire file (e.g., during execution of a **DISPLAY ALL** command), it still looks at one record at a time, as it continually changes the location of the record pointer.

The importance of the record pointer becomes apparent as we review individual commands from the hands-on exercise. The **EDIT**, **DELETE**, **RECALL**, and **DISPLAY** commands, for example, affect only a single record, but which record? Will the same record always be selected with any of these commands? The answer is that dBASE chooses whichever record is indicated by the current position of the record pointer.

You can move the record pointer with the **GO** command, e.g., **GO 3**, **GOTO 3**, or simply **3**, to move the record pointer to record number 3. Type **DISPLAY** at this point and record 3 is shown on the monitor. **GO TOP** and **GO BOTTOM** move the record pointer to the first and last records, respectively.

Other commands also affect the position of the record pointer. The **USE** command opens (i.e., uses) an existing **DBF** file and positions the record pointer to the first record. **DISPLAY ALL** and **PACK** place the record pointer at the end of the file beyond the last record.

Suffice it to say that since dBASE always knows where it is within a **DBF** file, it is also important for you to know this information. Accordingly, you should always be thinking of the record pointer as you execute individual commands.

The dBASE Notation

dBASE employs a precise notation to describe all of the variations permitted within a given command. Consider, for example, the **DISPLAY** command as it would appear (in abbreviated form) in the dBASE reference manual:

```
DISPLAY [<expression list>] [OFF] [<scope>] [FOR
    <condition>] [TO PRINTER/TO FILE <file name>]
```

The notation uses four distinct elements: upper-case letters, lower-case letters with angled brackets, square brackets, and a slash. ***Upper-case letters*** denote a dBASE term (e.g., **DISPLAY**, **FOR**, and **TO**), which must be spelled exactly as it appears within the command. ***Lower-case letters*** (enclosed within angled brackets) indicate user-supplied information; e.g., field names as they are defined within a file structure. ***Square brackets*** imply an optional parameter; i.e., a clause that may or may not be included, depending on the user's objectives. A ***slash*** indicates a choice between two entries.

Figure 2.9 shows several variations in the **DISPLAY** command, which illustrate the inclusion (omission) of the different parameters. Realize, however, that since every parameter in the command syntax is enclosed in square brackets, every parameter is optional; i.e., the only required portion of the **DISPLAY** command is the command itself. Omitting all parameters, as in Figure 2.9a, results in the assumption of default values for all parameters, which in the case of the **DISPLAY** command lists all fields for the current record.

```
. USE EMPLOYEE
. DISPLAY
Record#  SOCSEC     LASTNAME       LOCATION  SALARY TITLE
      1  111111111 Borow           Florida     18000 Warehouse staff
```

(a) With No Parameters

```
. DISPLAY SOCSEC,LASTNAME
Record#  SOCSEC     LASTNAME
      1  111111111 Borow
```

(b) Expression List

```
. DISPLAY SOCSEC,LASTNAME OFF
 SOCSEC    LASTNAME
 111111111 Borow
```

(c) OFF Parameter

```
. DISPLAY ALL
Record#  SOCSEC     LASTNAME       LOCATION  SALARY TITLE
      1  111111111 Borow           Florida     18000 Warehouse staff
      2  222222222 O'Malley        Brazil      24000 Sales rep
      3  333333333 Baker           Florida     14800 Sales support staff
      4  444444444 Benjamin        Florida     18800 Warehouse staff
      5  555555555 Smith           Brazil      14300 Clerical
```

(d) Scope Parameter

```
. DISPLAY ALL FOR TITLE='Warehouse staff'
Record#  SOCSEC     LASTNAME       LOCATION  SALARY TITLE
      1  111111111 Borow           Florida     18000 Warehouse staff
      4  444444444 Benjamin        Florida     18800 Warehouse staff
```

(e) FOR Condition (character field)

```
. DISPLAY LASTNAME,TITLE OFF ALL FOR TITLE='Warehouse staff' TO PRINTER
 LASTNAME     TITLE
 Borow        Warehouse staff
 Benjamin     Warehouse staff
```

(f) Multiple Parameters

FIGURE 2.9
The dBASE Notation (variations in the DISPLAY command)

Inclusion of an ***expression list*** causes only the specified fields to be displayed, as in Figure 2.9b, whereas omitting the expression list (as in the first example) implies that every field is to be shown. Specification of the **OFF** parameter (Figure 2.9c) displays the record *without* the associated record number.

The ***scope*** parameter designates the records in the file that are to be affected by the command. A scope of **ALL** means the command is to be applied to every record, a scope of **NEXT 2** applies to only two records (beginning with the current record), whereas a scope of **REST** applies to the remaining records (again from the current position of the record pointer). The default scope for the **DISPLAY** command is the current record, which explains why only one record was shown in the first three examples. Specification of **ALL**, as in Figure 2.9d, displays all records.

The **FOR** parameter further limits which records are to appear (e.g., only those records whose title is 'Warehouse staff'). The **FOR** condition works in conjunction with the scope parameter as all records within the scope are considered, but only those meeting the condition are displayed as in Figure 2.9e.

A ***slash*** implies a choice between two elements and appears once within the **DISPLAY** command; i.e., between **TO PRINTER** and **TO FILE**. Inclusion of the optional entry implies a subsequent choice between directing output to the printer versus a file on disk. Figure 2.9f shows how multiple parameters can be included in a single dBASE command.

More about the Basic Commands

Recall that the hands-on exercise was preceded by a table of basic commands, accompanied by a cursory explanation of the individual commands. Table 2.2 is an expanded version of that earlier table, with the formal dBASE syntax included for each command. Were we to say nothing further about the commands in the table, you would (from your knowledge of the dBASE notation) already have a fair understanding of how these commands work.

Consider, for example, the **SUM**, **AVERAGE**, and **COUNT** commands, and how their syntax is similar to the **DISPLAY** command just explained. Only the command names themselves (**SUM**, **AVERAGE**, and **COUNT**) are required in their respective commands; i.e., all other entries are enclosed in square brackets and consequently are optional. Hence **SUM**, with no scope and no expression list, will total the value of each numerical field over all records within the **DBF** file (the default scope is **ALL**). Inclusion of an expression list (e.g., **SUM SALARY**), causes only the field(s) mentioned to be totaled, just as its inclusion in a **DISPLAY** statement causes only those fields to be displayed. The **AVERAGE** and **COUNT** commands function in similar fashion.

Return once more to the hands-on exercise, reviewing the various commands with respect to the syntax presented in Table 2.2. Try to determine why we selected (or omitted) individual parameters as we sought to introduce the basic dBASE commands. Repeat the exercise with additional command variations you would like to try.

TABLE 2.2 **Syntax of Elementary Commands**

Commands affecting the file structure:

```
CREATE <filename>
MODIFY STRUCTURE
DISPLAY STRUCTURE [TO PRINTER/TO FILE <filename>]
```

Commands for file maintenance:

```
APPEND
BROWSE [FIELDS <field list>]
EDIT [<record number>]
DELETE [<scope>] [FOR <condition>]
RECALL [<scope>] [FOR <condition>]
PACK
```

Commands for data retrieval:

```
DISPLAY [<expression list>] [OFF] [<scope>] [FOR <condition>]
     [TO PRINTER/TO FILE <filename>]
SUM [<expression list>] [<scope>] [FOR <condition>]
AVERAGE [<scope>] [<expression list>] [FOR <condition>]
COUNT [<scope>] [FOR <condition>]
```

Miscellaneous commands:

```
HELP <dBASE IV key word>
GO/GOTO [BOTTOM/TOP] [<record number>]
USE <filename>
CLOSE DATABASES
SET DEFAULT TO <drive:>
QUIT
```

Getting Help

As you work with dBASE, questions will inevitably arise about the syntax and/or capabilities of individual commands that go beyond the material in Table 2.2. Accordingly, we describe two additional sources of information, the **HELP** command and the Programmer's Notebook.

The HELP Command

The **HELP** command is perhaps the most important command in dBASE, as it provides access to the dBASE on-line help facility. You must, by now, be slightly overwhelmed with all of the commands we have covered, and the inherent variation within a command. Our intent, however, is not to have you memorize all of the variations within all of the commands, but to gain an overall understanding of the way in which commands are issued, and, equally important, to know how to obtain additional information when you need it. That is the purpose of the on-line help facility as illustrated in Figure 2.10.

Type **HELP** at the dot prompt to enter on-line help, and produce the screen of Figure 2.10a. Use the up and down arrows to highlight the first choice, then press return to produce the alphabetic list of commands shown in Figure 2.10b. Highlight **DISPLAY** and press return once more to produce Figure 2.10c. A shortcut to obtaining help on a particular command is to type **HELP**, followed by the name of the command, such as **HELP DISPLAY**, after which Figure 2.10c would appear immediately.

Figure 2.10c contains the syntax of the **DISPLAY** command, which we just discussed. Realize, however, that this screen, coupled with your knowledge of the dBASE notation, gives you immediate and total information about the **DISPLAY** command. *There is no need to memorize anything, provided you understand the dBASE notation*. All the information about every dBASE command is at your fingertips. It's that easy!

FIGURE 2.10
The dBASE Help Facility
(1 of 2)

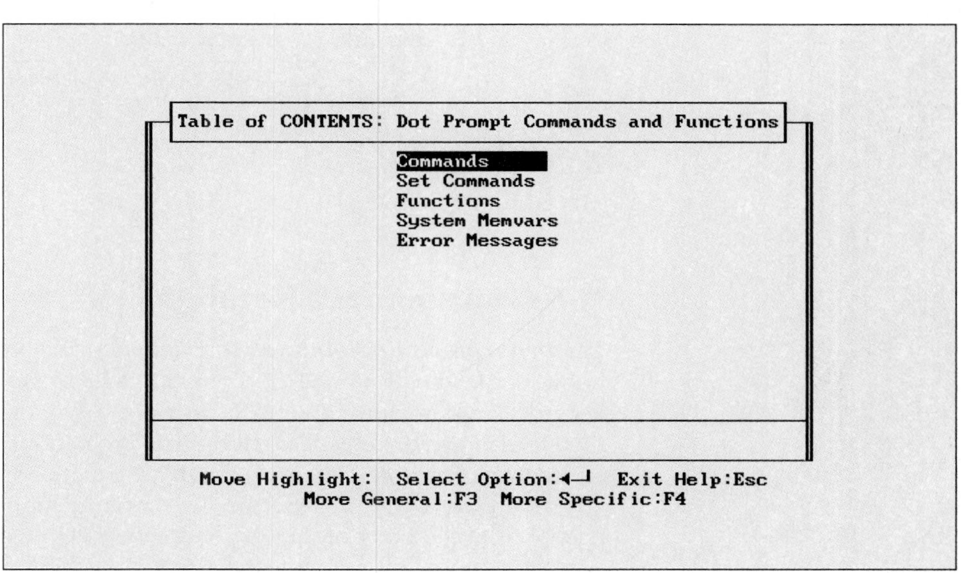

(a) Opening HELP Menu

FIGURE 2.10
The dBASE Help Facility (continued)

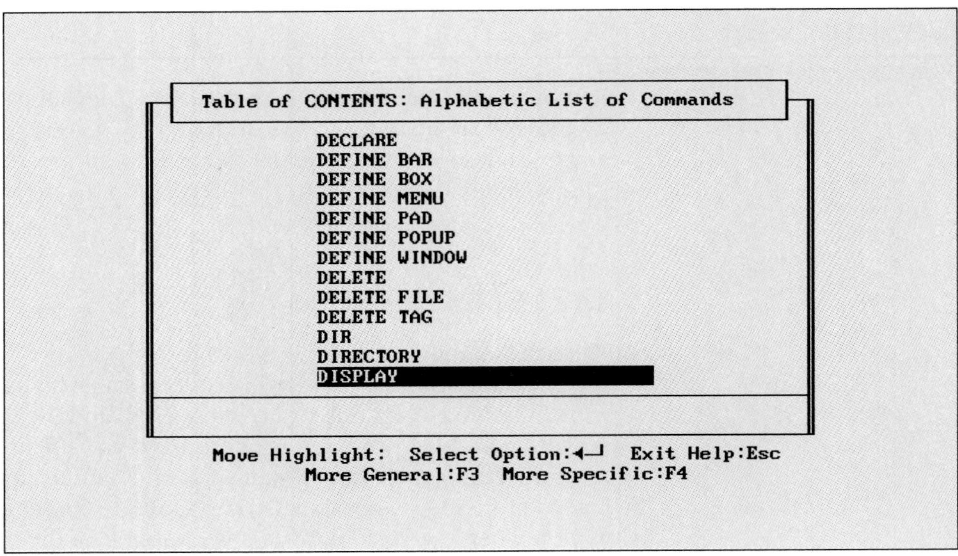

(b) Alphabetic List of Commands

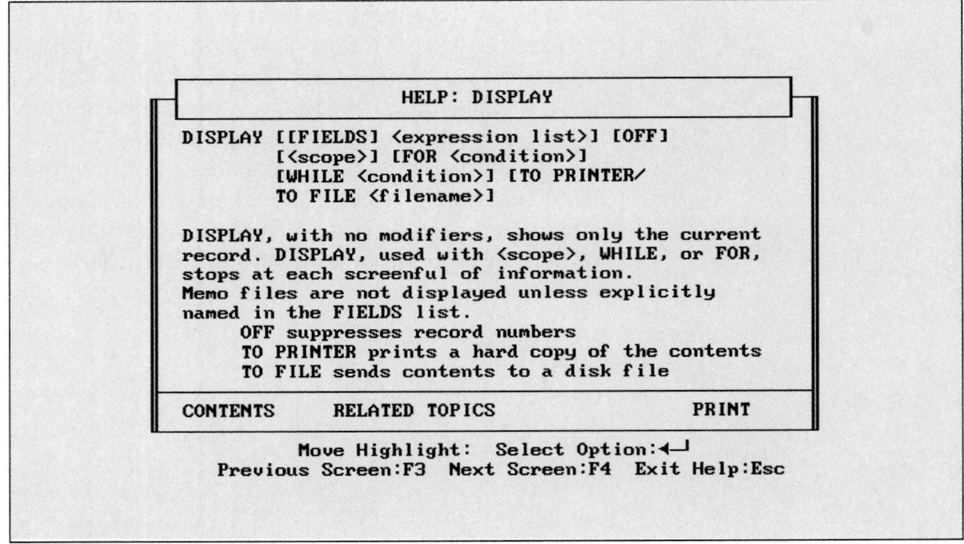

(c) The DISPLAY Command

The Programmer's Notebook

The ***Programmer's Notebook*** is an independent reference section at the end of the book. Unlike the dBASE **HELP** command, which displays its information on the monitor, the Programmer's Notebook provides a written copy of its suggestions and is therefore more convenient for study. The Programmer's Notebook also provides substantially more information than the **HELP** command.

We expect you will use the Notebook to supplement what you learn in class and/or from the body of the text. It is especially helpful in answering specific questions about individual commands. Commands from the text are listed in alphabetical order, with the material on each command divided into four sections: syntax, discussion, tips, and related topics.

A Look Ahead

As indicated in the chapter opening, the dot prompt has remained unchanged and thus serves as the ideal introduction to dBASE. Nevertheless, dBASE IV represents a major overhaul of Ashton-Tate's flagship product, with significantly more capability than its predecessors. One of the most visible changes is the introduction of an entirely new user interface, the dBASE IV ***control center,*** illustrated in Figure 2.11.

Figure 2.11 may seem familiar because it appeared each time dBASE was loaded in the hands-on exercises. We told you, however, to press the **Esc** key to exit the control center and arrive at the dot prompt, because it (the dot prompt) is our preferred means of introducing you to dBASE. It is appropriate now, however, to introduce the control center as it provides a preview of the next several chapters.

The control center is divided into six panels (columns), each of which implies a major capability within dBASE, which in turn is covered in its own chapter. Consider:

- **Data** The data panel provides access to existing **DBF** files through pull-down menus, with options parallel to the **APPEND**, **EDIT**, **DELETE**, **RECALL**, and **PACK** commands covered in this chapter. The data panel is discussed in Chapter 8.
- **Queries** Queries provide a restricted view of a **DBF** file that considers only a subset of records in the file and/or a subset of fields for selected records. Queries are developed in Chapter 6.
- **Forms** Forms provide a more visually appealing means for data entry than the unformatted screens in this chapter; forms are created through the screen generator as described in Chapter 7.
- **Reports** Reports enable more sophisticated output than what is possible through individual commands (**DISPLAY**, **SUM**, **AVERAGE**, and **COUNT**) at the dot prompt. Reports are covered in Chapter 4.
- **Labels** Labels enable the creation of mailing labels for form letters and other applications. Labels are developed in Chapter 5.
- **Applications** Applications link entries in the other panels together through a customized menu generated by dBASE for the user. Applications are developed in Chapter 8 after all of the other capabilities have been discussed.

FIGURE 2.11
The dBASE IV Control Center

```
Catalog   Tools   Exit                                        9:49:13 pm
                          dBASE IV CONTROL CENTER

                  CATALOG: C:\DATADISK\INTRO\UNTITLED.CAT

   Data       Queries      Forms       Reports      Labels    Applications
 <create>    <create>    <create>     <create>     <create>     <create>

File:         New file
Description:  Press ENTER on <create> to create a new file

 Help:F1  Use:◄┘  Data:F2  Design:Shift-F2  Quick Report:Shift-F9  Menus:F10
```

This discussion is intended as only the briefest of introductions to the control center; as indicated, we will return to the control center in Chapter 8 after all of the individual capabilities have been developed.

Summary

A ***file*** is a set of records. A ***record*** contains one or more ***fields*** that describe a logical entity. The ***file structure*** describes the order of fields within a record, and the length and data type of each field.

The **CREATE** command defines a file structure, the **DISPLAY STRUCTURE** command shows an existing file structure, and the **MODIFY STRUCTURE** command enables the structure to be changed.

The **APPEND** command adds records to a file, whereas the **EDIT** and **BROWSE** commands modify existing records. The **DELETE** command *logically* deletes a record, which can still be restored by the **RECALL** command; the **PACK** command *physically* deletes records marked for deletion.

The **SUM**, **AVERAGE**, and **COUNT** commands provide summary data about the records in a file. The **DISPLAY** command shows an individual record, all records in a file, or only the records meeting a specified criterion.

The ***record pointer*** indicates the current record and is implicitly affected by all dBASE commands. You can move to the first or last record in a file with the **GO TOP** or **GO BOTTOM** command, respectively; you can also move to a specific record with the command **GO <record number>**.

The ***dBASE notation*** explains all of the variations allowed within a given command. The notation consists of four distinct elements: upper-case letters, lower-case letters with angled brackets, square brackets, and a slash.

The ***command buffer*** provides access to the last 20 commands executed from the dot prompt. Access to the command buffer is provided by the up and down arrow keys.

The **HELP** command provides on-line access to all dBASE commands. The ***Programmer's Notebook*** provides more detailed information in written form.

The ***dot prompt*** is the original user interface and is unchanged from the earliest release. dBASE IV also offers a new interface known as the ***control center.***

Key Words and Concepts

ALL
APPEND
AVERAGE
BROWSE
Character field
CLOSE DATABASES
Command buffer
Control center
COUNT
CREATE
Ctrl+End
Data retrieval
dBASE notation
DBF extension
Default drive
DELETE
DISPLAY
DISPLAY STRUCTURE
Dot prompt
EDIT
Expression list
Field
File
File maintenance
File structure
FOR condition
GO BOTTOM
GOTO
GO TOP
HELP
Input template
MODIFY STRUCTURE
NEXT
Numeric field
OFF
On-line help
PACK
Programmer's Notebook
QUIT
RECALL
Record
Record pointer

`REST`	`SUM`	`USE`
Scope	`TO FILE`	
`SET DEFAULT TO`	`TO PRINTER`	

True/False

1. The default scope of the **DISPLAY** command is all records.
2. A file structure cannot be changed after it has been created and saved.
3. The **DELETE** command physically deletes a record.
4. The **EDIT** command displays multiple records simultaneously on the screen.
5. A file contains one or more records.
6. A record contains one or more fields.
7. The Programmer's Notebook is part of the Ashton-Tate dBASE reference manual.
8. The prompt characters for DOS and dBASE are the same.
9. The **ADD** command adds records to a file.
10. Every record in a file has the same number of fields.
11. Output of the **DISPLAY** command can be directed to the printer.
12. Records listed by the **DISPLAY** command must be shown with their record numbers.
13. Specific information on the **DISPLAY** command can be obtained with the command, **HELP DISPLAY**.
14. The **PACK** command physically deletes all records marked for deletion.
15. The **SUM** and **COUNT** commands are equivalent.
16. The **SUM** command must include values from every record in the file in computing a total.
17. The **USE** command positions the record pointer to the first record within a file.
18. Most dBASE commands operate independently of the record pointer.
19. Pressing the down arrow key will retrieve the last command issued from the dot prompt.

Exercises

1. Supply the dBASE command(s) to:
   (a) Correct individual records
   (b) Display multiple records on the screen at one time while simultaneously allowing you to correct any of the displayed records
   (c) Create (modify) a file structure
   (d) Add records to the end of an existing data file
   (e) Mark a record for subsequent deletion
   (f) Physically delete records marked for deletion
   (g) Save changes and exit from the edit or browse modes
   (h) Position the record pointer at record one
   (i) Obtain additional information on the **EDIT** command

2. Distinguish between:
   (a) **HELP** and **HELP DISPLAY**
   (b) **DELETE** and **PACK**
   (c) Editing and browsing
   (d) **DISPLAY** and **DISPLAY ALL**
   (e) A field and a file

(f) Upper- and lower-case letters within the dBASE syntax
(g) The DOS prompt and the dBASE prompt
(h) The **SUM** and **COUNT** commands
(i) Character fields and numeric fields
(j) **GO TOP** and **GO BOTTOM**
(k) Pressing the up and down arrow keys at the dot prompt

3. Indicate the number of records that will be returned for each of the following **COUNT** commands with respect to the file associated with Figure 2.5. Some of the commands are invalid, however, in which case you are to indicate how the commands should be corrected.
(a) `COUNT`
(b) `COUNT FOR SALARY = 18000`
(c) `COUNT FOR SALARY = '18000'`
(d) `COUNT FOR TITLE = 'Warehouse staff'`
(e) `COUNT FOR LOCATION = Brazil`
(f) `COUNT FOR LOCATION = 'BRAZIL'`
(g) `COUNT FOR LOCATION = 'Brazil' AND TITLE = 'Warehouse staff'`
(h) `COUNT FOR LOCATION = 'Brazil' .OR. TITLE = 'Warehouse staff'`

4. Perhaps the best source of information about dBASE is dBASE itself; i.e., *to find out the effect of a particular command or parameter, execute the command from the dot prompt and draw your own conclusions.* With this in mind, execute the following sets of commands, pausing at the end of each set to answer the associated questions.

Set 1

```
.DISPLAY OFF
.DISPLAY SOCSEC,LASTNAME
.DISPLAY ALL LASTNAME,SOCSEC
.DISPLAY
.DISPLAY STRUCTURE TO PRINTER
```

(a) What is the effect of including the field names of only two of the five fields? Does the order of the field names in the command make any difference?
(b) What is the effect of the **TO PRINTER** parameter? the **OFF** parameter?
(c) What is the difference between **DISPLAY**, **DISPLAY ALL**, and **DISPLAY STRUCTURE**?
(d) What happens to the record pointer after a **DISPLAY ALL** command has been executed?
(e) What is the default scope of the **DISPLAY** command? What is the effect of **ALL**?

Set 2

```
.3
.EDIT
.GO TOP
.EDIT
.BROWSE
```

(f) Which record is edited as a result of the first **EDIT** command? the second **EDIT** command? Why were different records edited?
(g) What is the difference between the **EDIT** and **BROWSE** commands? How many records are on the screen (at one time) as a result of the two commands?

Set 3

```
.GO 2
.DELETE
.DISPLAY ALL
.PACK
.DISPLAY ALL
```

(h) How many records are displayed by the first **DISPLAY ALL** command? by the second **DISPLAY** command?

(i) Which record is missing? How was it deleted?

Set 4

```
.SUM
.SUM ALL
.COUNT FOR TITLE = 'Warehouse staff'
.AVERAGE SALARY
.AVERAGE SALARY FOR TITLE = 'Warehouse staff'
```

(j) What is the difference between **SUM** and **SUM ALL**? What is the default scope of the **SUM** command?

(k) What is the difference between **AVERAGE SALARY** and **AVERAGE SALARY FOR TITLE = 'Warehouse staff'**?

5. Use dBASE to establish a file structure consistent with the data in Figure 2.12. Enter data into the file and verify that the data has been entered correctly. Use whatever commands are necessary to produce the following information. Note, however, that some of the requests are not possible, in which case you should indicate why the information cannot be provided.

(a) The names, salaries, and titles of all employees earning less than $30,000
(b) The number of all employees earning less than $30,000
(c) The total salary of all employees
(d) The average salary of all employees
(e) The average salary of all managers
(f) The names and hire dates of all employees with at least eight years of service
(g) The names and birth dates of all employees who are 30 or older
(h) The names and salaries of all account reps

FIGURE 2.12
Data for Problem 5

SOCSEC	NAME	TITLE	SALARY	HIREDATE	LOCATION
100000000	Davis	Account Rep	34000	01/02/89	Boston
200000000	Friedel	Manager	48000	02/17/87	Miami
300000000	Kendrick	Account Rep	26500	02/16/89	Miami
333333333	McGrath	Account Rep	37000	04/25/89	Chicago
400000000	Cordell	Account Rep	27200	04/02/90	Boston
444444444	Facella	Account Rep	24750	01/15/90	Los Angeles
500000000	Pattishall	Account Rep	38500	11/11/87	Miami
555555555	Ferraro	Account Rep	26400	02/02/88	Miami
600000000	Tillberg	Manager	35500	10/29/85	Boston
666666666	Grauer	Account Rep	37500	03/16/88	Miami
700000000	Fitzgerald	Manager	53000	04/19/86	Chicago
777777777	Ticich	Account Rep	27000	03/16/91	Boston
800000000	Martineau	Manager	48000	02/28/86	Los Angeles
888888888	Seaman	Account Rep	29000	01/03/89	Los Angeles
900000000	Beyer	Account Rep	32900	01/19/85	Chicago
999999999	Hirschberg	Account Rep	28500	06/19/87	Miami

FIGURE 2.13
Data for Problem 6

NAME	OLDSALARY	BIRTHDATE
Davis	32000	07/12/69
Friedel	45000	09/26/57
Kendrick	24500	12/06/68
McGrath	32000	05/25/59
Cordell	26200	06/12/70
Facella	23000	07/15/71
Pattishall	35000	02/24/62
Ferraro	24400	03/30/68
Tillberg	34000	12/25/65
Grauer	32500	03/31/62
Fitzgerald	50000	06/10/66
Martineau	47000	09/18/61
Ticich	23500	11/24/45
Seaman	26000	11/23/67
Beyer	29900	11/29/65
Hirschberg	26000	10/09/67

(i) The names, titles, and salaries of all employees in Miami and Chicago
(j) The names and salary increases (in dollars) for all employees

6. Figure 2.13 contains the additional data needed to complete exercise 5. Modify the file structure just created, add the indicated data to the appropriate records, then supply the answers to complete parts (g) and (j) from exercise 5.

7. The potential applications of dBASE are limited only by your imagination. You could, for example, use dBASE to monitor a record collection and provide reports such as the following:
(a) All music by a particular artist
(b) All music on a particular medium, e.g. cassette or compact disk
(c) All music on a particular label
(d) All music in a particular style, e.g. country, rock, or classical
(e) All music released in a given year

Design a file structure capable of accomplishing these objectives. What other reports might you want to include?

CHAPTER

3

Indexing

OUTLINE

OBJECTIVES

After reading this chapter you will be able to:

1. Describe the concept of indexing and how indexes are created in dBASE; discuss how it is possible to list records in multiple sequences.
2. Distinguish between files with extensions of MDX and DBF; describe how to view the DOS directory from within dBASE.
3. Differentiate between a master and an open index; describe how the distinction is made in dBASE.
4. Distinguish between the `INDEX ON` and `SET ORDER TO TAG` commands; describe the purpose of the `DISPLAY STATUS` command.
5. Define and build a concatenated index.
6. Describe how to list records in ascending as well as descending sequence; also how to index on a calculated field.

Overview

All of the examples in Chapter 2 listed records in social security order; i.e., in the sequence in which the records were entered into the **DBF** file. There will be many times, however, when data is more meaningful if it is presented in a different sequence, e.g., alphabetically or in order of increasing (decreasing) salary. ***Indexing*** makes this possible.

We begin with a conceptual discussion of indexing, then introduce the commands (**INDEX ON** and **SET ORDER TO TAG**) needed for implementation. We distinguish between a ***master index*** and an ***open index,*** and describe how indexes are updated automatically during maintenance operations on a **DBF** file. We cover the finer points of indexing, including the use of ***concatenated*** and/or ***calculated*** keys, and processing records in ***ascending*** as well as ***descending sequence.*** The chapter includes two hands-on exercises, both of which are essential if you are truly to understand the all-important concept of indexing.

You should also know that dBASE IV introduced a new type of index, the ***multiple index (MDX) file,*** which offers several advantages over the ***NDX files*** used in dBASE III Plus and all earlier releases. The multiple index is discussed here exclusively; you are, however, referred to the Programmer's Notebook for information on the earlier type of index.

The Concept of Indexing

Figure 3.1a depicts an employee file, consisting of five records, which we created in the previous chapter. The records appear in ***physical sequence,*** i.e., in the order in which they were entered into the **EMPLOYEE.DBF** file in Chapter 2. It is entirely possible, however, that we might wish to access the records in a different ***logical sequence,*** e.g., alphabetically or in order of increasing salary.

Assume, for example, that the five employee records are to be retrieved in alphabetical order. A person looking at the file of Figure 3.1a would know to list the records in the sequence Baker, Benjamin, Borow, O'Malley, and Smith. In other words, rather than retrieving records in the physical order in which they are stored (i.e., record 1, 2, 3, 4, and 5), we present them in the logical sequence of record 3 (Baker), then record 4 (Brown), then records 1, 2, and 5 (Borow, O'Malley, and Smith). The file that specifies the logical sequence in which records are processed is known as an ***index;*** the field on which the index is based is termed a ***key.***

Figures 3.1b, c, and d contain an alphabetical, salary, and social security index, respectively, all of which are associated with the data file of Figure 3.1a. Each index specifies a different logical sequence in which records in the **DBF** file may be processed. Records are listed alphabetically in accordance with the last name index of Figure 3.1b, in increasing order of salary in conjunction with the salary index of Figure 3.1c, and by social security number in accordance with the index of Figure 3.1d. (The last example is trivial at this time because the logical sequence of the social security index matches the physical order in which records appear in the **DBF** file; that would no longer be true if additional records were added to the **DBF** file.)

As can be seen from the figure, an index contains only the key on which the index is based, together with the corresponding record number in the **DBF** file. In other words, the index provides no data per se, only the sequence in which records are retrieved from the associated **DBF** file. Thus, to retrieve records alphabetically according to the index in Figure 3.1b, dBASE would first retrieve record 3 (Baker),

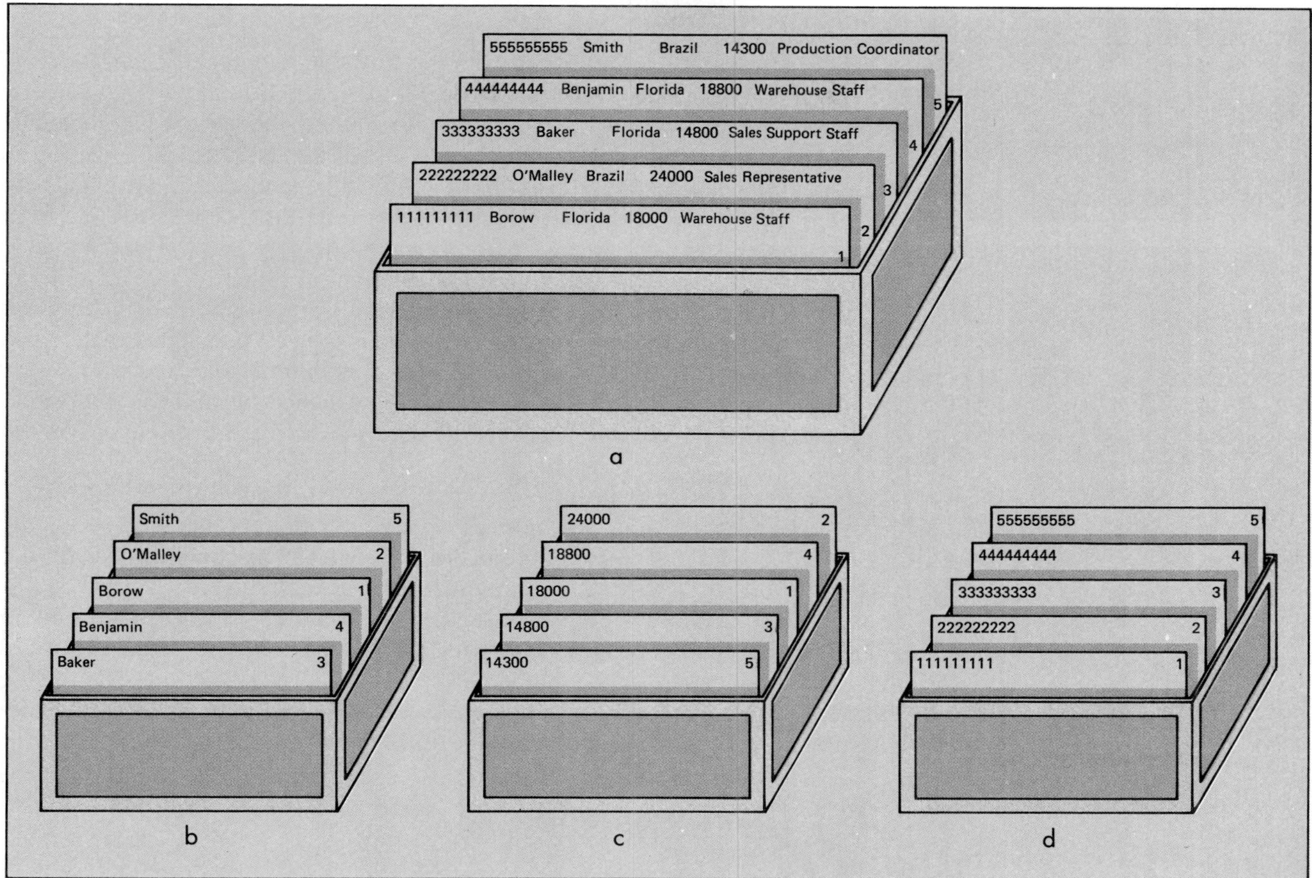

FIGURE 3.1
A File and Its Indexes

then record 4 (Benjamin), then records 1, 2, and 5 (Borow, O'Malley, and Smith, respectively).

You can draw an analogy between the index of a book and a dBASE index. Both are arranged according to a key phrase or field, and both indicate where the corresponding information may be found, by providing the page number in the book or record number in the file. In addition, just as the index of a book is kept in a separate section, an index in dBASE is stored as a separate (index) file.

Implementation in dBASE IV

Two types of indexes are available in dBASE IV. An **NDX *(single index) file*** stores exactly one index and was the only type available in dBASE III Plus. Since dBASE III Plus is *upward compatible* with dBASE IV, you can use **NDX** files in dBASE IV in exactly the same way they were used in dBASE III Plus. The second type of index is the **MDX *(multiple index) file,*** which is new to dBASE IV, and which can hold up to 47 indexes in the same file. The multiple index file simplifies the way in which indexes are created and maintained, and hence, we suggest you use this type of index exclusively; all subsequent discussion in the text refers to the **MDX** index.

Creating an Index

The easiest way to create an index is within the **CREATE** command, when you first define the file structure. This assumes, of course, that you know the field (or fields) within the file structure that will be used as the key(s) for the index(es). Alternatively, after the file has been created, you can use the **MODIFY STRUCTURE** command to designate specific fields as index keys. Both commands produce screens similar to that of Figure 3.2, which displays the file structure of the **EMPLOYEE.DBF** file from Chapter 2.

As you already know, the definition (modification) of a file structure includes all field names in a file with the associated field type, width, and (for numeric fields only) the number of decimal places. All of these items are displayed as column headings in Figure 3.2. Note, too, the presence of an additional column to indicate whether an index should be created; i.e., all that is necessary to establish an index is to position the cursor in the index column of the appropriate row (field), and toggle the option to **Y**es.

Three indexes are established in conjunction with Figure 3.2, for **SOCSEC, LASTNAME**, and **SALARY**. All three indexes are stored within the multiple index file, **EMPLOYEE.MDX**, which is created automatically by dBASE in conjunction with the **CREATE (MODIFY STRUCTURE)** command for **EMPLOYEE.DBF**.

The indexes within a multiple index file are identified by ***tags,*** with the tag name equal to the field name (key) on which the index is based. Thus, the social security index is identified by the tag name **SOCSEC**, the last name index by the tag **LASTNAME**, and the salary index by the tag **SALARY**. The importance of the tag name becomes apparent as we consider the **SET ORDER** command.

The SET ORDER Command

As we have just seen, multiple indexes can be easily created for a single **DBF** file. At any given time, however, there can be only one ***master index***—the index that determines the logical sequence in which the records are accessed. The master index may be changed as often as necessary, with records in the **DBF** file processed according

FIGURE 3.2
Creation of Indexes

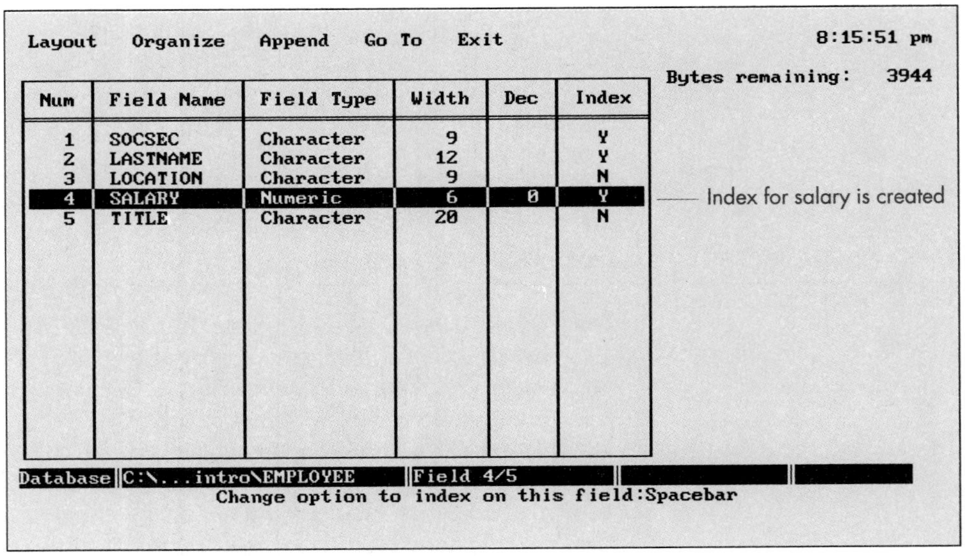

Layout Organize Append Go To Exit 8:15:51 pm

Bytes remaining: 3944

Num	Field Name	Field Type	Width	Dec	Index
1	SOCSEC	Character	9		Y
2	LASTNAME	Character	12		Y
3	LOCATION	Character	9		N
4	SALARY	Numeric	6	0	Y
5	TITLE	Character	20		N

Index for salary is created

Database C:\...intro\EMPLOYEE Field 4/5

Change option to index on this field:Spacebar

to the current master index, e.g., by last name, *or* by salary, *or* by social security number.

The **SET ORDER** command selects the master index through reference to its tag name. Consider:

Syntax

```
SET ORDER TO [TAG <tag name>]
```

Examples

```
SET ORDER TO TAG LASTNAME
SET ORDER TO TAG SALARY
SET ORDER TO TAG SOCSEC
SET ORDER TO
```

The SET ORDER command designates a previously created index as the master index. For example, SET ORDER TO TAG LASTNAME, in Figure 3.3a, selects last name as the master index, causing all subsequent commands to process records in alphabetical order. The SET ORDER commands of Figures 3.3b and 3.3c designate different master indexes, which in turn process the records in different sequences.

The tag name, however, is *optional* in the SET ORDER statement, and omission of the tag name, as in Figure 3.3d, restores the file to its ***natural order;*** i.e, the physical sequence in which the records were entered into the DBF file.

Updating Indexes

The contents of a DBF file change continually with time; new records will be added, existing records will be modified, while still other records will be deleted. Suffice it to say that the indexes associated with a file must change in parallel with the file itself. Consider now Figure 3.4, which continues our earlier example of a single DBF file with three indexes (last name, salary, and social security number). A sixth record (Brown) has been appended at the end of Figure 3.4a, which in turn produced changes in the indexes of Figures 3.4b, 3.4c, and 3.4d.

As can be seen from Figure 3.4a, Brown is *physically* the sixth (last) record in the DBF file, whereas his name is *logically* the fourth record when the file is processed alphabetically. In other words, the index in Figure 3.4b has been adjusted to reflect the addition of the new record and maintain the correct alphabetical sequence (Baker, Benjamin, Borow, *Brown,* O'Malley, and Smith). In similar fashion, the indexes in Figures 3.4c and 3.4d have also been updated to maintain the salary and social security sequences, respectively. You should be able to trace through any of the indexes in Figure 3.4 and retrieve all six records in alphabetical, salary, or social security order.

The biggest advantage to the MDX file of dBASE IV is that it is opened automatically (by dBASE) in conjunction with the DBF file, and thus all of its indexes are updated whenever changes are made in the DBF file. [This is in contrast to the NDX files of dBASE III Plus, which had to be opened explicitly by the user, a requirement that was often overlooked. The unfortunate result was that NDX files often became incompatible (out-of-date) with their associated DBF file, which in turn produced all kinds of errors.]

Implicit in this discussion is the critical difference between a ***master index*** and an ***open index.*** All indexes within a multiple index file are always open, and hence will be updated with any changes to the DBF file. At any given time, however, there can be only one master index, i.e., the index that determines the sequence in which records are processed as described earlier in Figure 3.3.

Hands-on Exercise 1 implements these concepts in dBASE. It is a short exercise, but it effectively demonstrates the capabilities inherent in indexing.

```
. SET ORDER TO TAG LASTNAME ———————— Records are listed by last name

Master index: LASTNAME
. DISPLAY ALL
Record#  SOCSEC     LASTNAME     LOCATION  SALARY TITLE
      3  333333333 Baker         Florida    14800 Sales support staff
      4  444444444 Benjamin      Florida    18800 Warehouse staff
      1  111111111 Borow         Florida    18000 Warehouse staff
      2  222222222 O'Malley      Brazil     24000 Sales rep
      5  555555555 Smith         Brazil     14300 Clerical
```

(a) Last Name Index

```
. SET ORDER TO TAG SALARY ———————— Records are listed by salary

Master index: SALARY
. DISPLAY ALL
Record#  SOCSEC     LASTNAME     LOCATION  SALARY TITLE
      5  555555555 Smith         Brazil     14300 Clerical
      3  333333333 Baker         Florida    14800 Sales support staff
      1  111111111 Borow         Florida    18000 Warehouse staff
      4  444444444 Benjamin      Florida    18800 Warehouse staff
      2  222222222 O'Malley      Brazil     24000 Sales rep
```

(b) Salary Index

```
. SET ORDER TO TAG SOCSEC ———————— Records are listed by social security number

Master index: SOCSEC
. DISPLAY ALL
Record#  SOCSEC     LASTNAME     LOCATION  SALARY TITLE
      1  111111111 Borow         Florida    18000 Warehouse staff
      2  222222222 O'Malley      Brazil     24000 Sales rep
      3  333333333 Baker         Florida    14800 Sales support staff
      4  444444444 Benjamin      Florida    18800 Warehouse staff
      5  555555555 Smith         Brazil     14300 Clerical
```

(c) Social Security Index

```
. SET ORDER TO ———————— No tag is specified

Database is in natural order
. DISPLAY ALL
Record#  SOCSEC     LASTNAME     LOCATION  SALARY TITLE
      1  111111111 Borow         Florida    18000 Warehouse staff
      2  222222222 O'Malley      Brazil     24000 Sales rep
      3  333333333 Baker         Florida    14800 Sales support staff
      4  444444444 Benjamin      Florida    18800 Warehouse staff
      5  555555555 Smith         Brazil     14300 Clerical
```

(d) Natural Order

FIGURE 3.3
The SET ORDER Command

HANDS-ON EXERCISE 1

Indexing

Objective

Show how a DBF file may be accessed in different logical sequences through indexing; demonstrate that indexes within an MDX file are updated automatically in conjunction with changes to the associated DBF file.

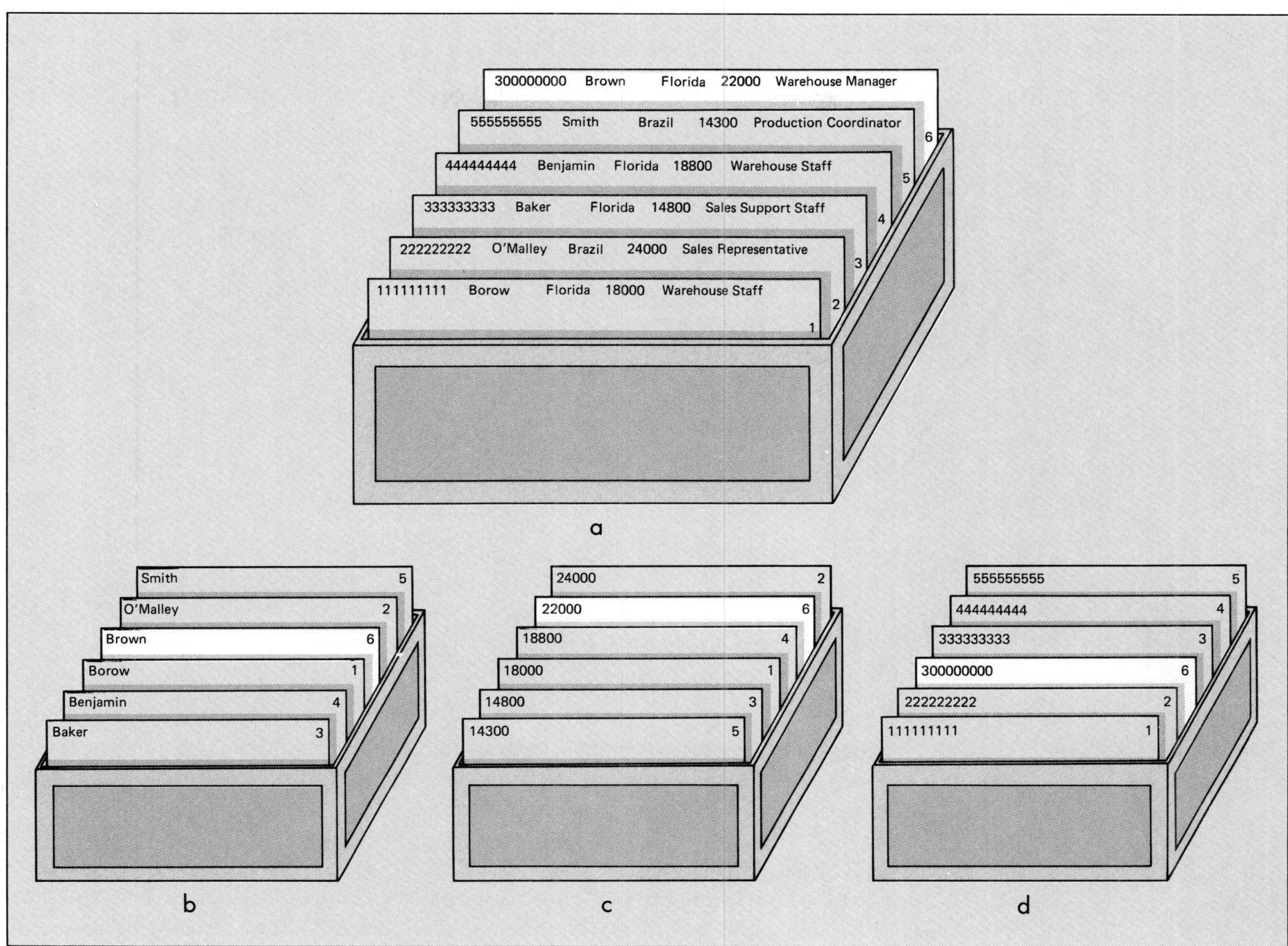

FIGURE 3.4
Adding Records to an Indexed File

STEP 1 **Load dBASE**

Repeat steps 1 and 2 from the hands-on exercise in Chapter 2 to log into the **INTRO** directory and load dBASE. You should end at the dot prompt with the default drive set to drive A or drive C (depending on whether you installed the data disk).

STEP 2 **Retrieve the EMPLOYEE.DBF file**

Type **USE EMPLOYEE** to retrieve the **EMPLOYEE.DBF** file created in Chapter 2, then type **DISPLAY STRUCTURE** to show the file structure of Figure 3.5a. As you can see, the indexes have *not* yet been created so the **DISPLAY ALL** command of Figure 3.5b lists the records in physical sequence.

STEP 3 **Create the indexes**

Type **MODIFY STRUCTURE** to produce the screen of Figure 3.2. Use the **Tab** key to move from column to column within the file structure until you come to the column labeled Index. Press the space bar to toggle the index option from (N to Y) to create indexes for SOCSEC, LASTNAME, and SALARY.

```
. USE EMPLOYEE ———————————— Retrieves EMPLOYEE.DBF file from Chapter 2

. DISPLAY STRUCTURE
Structure for database: C:\DATADISK\INTRO\EMPLOYEE.DBF
Number of data records:       5
Date of last update    : 02/17/91
Field  Field Name  Type       Width    Dec    Index
    1  SOCSEC      Character      9              N  —— Indexes have not yet been created
    2  LASTNAME    Character     12              N
    3  LOCATION    Character      9              N
    4  SALARY      Numeric        6              N
    5  TITLE       Character     20              N
** Total **                      57
```

(a) The File Structure

```
. DISPLAY ALL ———————————— Records are listed in physical sequence

Record#  SOCSEC     LASTNAME     LOCATION  SALARY TITLE
      1  111111111  Borow        Florida    18000 Warehouse staff
      2  222222222  O'Malley     Brazil     24000 Sales rep
      3  333333333  Baker        Florida    14800 Sales support staff
      4  444444444  Benjamin     Florida    18800 Warehouse staff
      5  555555555  Smith        Brazil     14300 Clerical
```

(b) Employee Records

FIGURE 3.5
The EMPLOYEE.DBF File

Press **Ctrl+End** when you have toggled all three indexes to Y. You will see three messages flash across the screen as dBASE creates the requested indexes, after which you will be returned to the dot prompt.

STEP 4 **View the file directory**

Type **RUN DIR** to view the DOS directory from within dBASE. (The dBASE RUN command provides access to DOS and executes whatever DOS command follows; e.g., RUN DIR will execute the DOS DIR command.) The output produced by the **DIR** command shows both an **EMPLOYEE.DBF** file and an **EMPLOYEE.MDX** file, the latter corresponding to the multiple index file just created. dBASE assigns the extension **MDX** to the multiple index file, and uses the same file name (**EMPLOYEE**, in the example) as in the associated **DBF** file.

STEP 5 **Choose a master index**

Type the command, **SET ORDER TO TAG LASTNAME**, then type **DISPLAY ALL** to list records by last name. Enter the **SET** and **DISPLAY** commands shown in Figure 3.3 to view the file in other sequences; i.e., type **SET ORDER TO TAG SALARY** to display records in salary sequence, and **SET ORDER TO TAG SOCSEC** to view the records by social security number.

Finally, enter the command, **SET ORDER TO**, without a tag, as shown in Figure 3.3d, to display the records in natural order, i.e., in the physical sequence in which they were entered.

STEP 6 **Add a record**

All indexes within an **MDX** file are automatically updated in conjunction with changes to the associated **DBF** file. To show that this is true, type **APPEND** at the dot prompt, then add the record shown in Figure 3.6. Press **Ctrl+End** after completing the title to save the record and return to the dot prompt.

FIGURE 3.6
Adding a Record

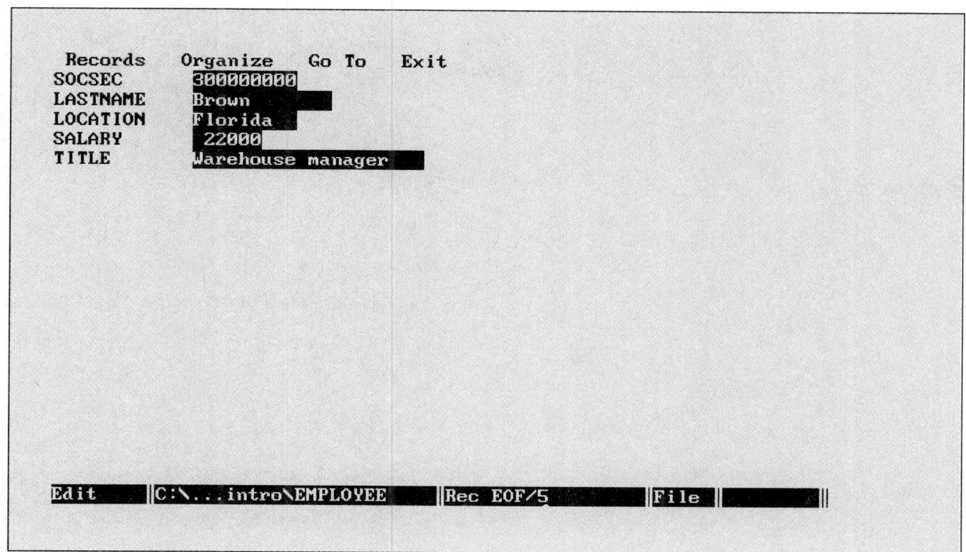

STEP 7 **Verify that the indexes have been updated**
Enter the various **SET ORDER** and **DISPLAY** commands of Figure 3.7 to show that the existing indexes have been updated to accommodate the addition of Brown's record. In other words, even though Brown is physically the last record in the file, it appears in its proper logical sequence according to the different master indexes in Figures 3.7a, 3.7b, and 3.7c.

STEP 8 **Exit dBASE**
Type **QUIT** to exit dBASE.

Finer Points of Indexing

Each of the indexes we have been using processed records in ascending (the default) sequence according to the value of a single field within the file structure (e.g., last name, social security number, and salary). An index can also be based on a combination of fields, and/or can access records in descending rather than ascending sequence. These concepts are illustrated in Figure 3.8.

Figure 3.8b contains an index based on a ***concatenated*** key, which combines the location and last name fields to list employees by location, and alphabetically within each location. The index in Figure 3.8c is based on the ***calculated*** values of percent salary increase, a field not found in the file structure, but which is calculated from other fields (salary and old salary) that are. (The **DBF** file in Figure 3.8a has been expanded to include an old salary field in order that the percent increase may be computed.) Finally, Figure 3.8d sequences employees in ***descending*** (rather than ascending) order of salary. All of these indexes are produced by the **INDEX ON** command.

```
. SET ORDER TO TAG LASTNAME
Master index: LASTNAME
. DISPLAY ALL
Record#  SOCSEC     LASTNAME     LOCATION  SALARY TITLE
      3  333333333  Baker        Florida    14800 Sales support staff
      4  444444444  Benjamin     Florida    18800 Warehouse staff
      1  111111111  Borow        Florida    18000 Warehouse staff
      6  300000000  Brown        Florida    22000 Warehouse manager
      2  222222222  O'Malley     Brazil     24000 Sales rep
      5  555555555  Smith        Brazil     14300 Clerical
```

(a) Last Name Index

```
. SET ORDER TO TAG SALARY
Master index: SALARY
. DISPLAY ALL
Record#  SOCSEC     LASTNAME     LOCATION  SALARY TITLE
      5  555555555  Smith        Brazil     14300 Clerical
      3  333333333  Baker        Florida    14800 Sales support staff
      1  111111111  Borow        Florida    18000 Warehouse staff
      4  444444444  Benjamin     Florida    18800 Warehouse staff
      6  300000000  Brown        Florida    22000 Warehouse manager
      2  222222222  O'Malley     Brazil     24000 Sales rep
```

(b) Salary Index

```
. SET ORDER TO TAG SOCSEC
Master index: SOCSEC
. DISPLAY ALL
Record#  SOCSEC     LASTNAME     LOCATION  SALARY TITLE
      1  111111111  Borow        Florida    18000 Warehouse staff
      2  222222222  O'Malley     Brazil     24000 Sales rep
      6  300000000  Brown        Florida    22000 Warehouse manager
      3  333333333  Baker        Florida    14800 Sales support staff
      4  444444444  Benjamin     Florida    18800 Warehouse staff
      5  555555555  Smith        Brazil     14300 Clerical
```

(c) Social Security Index

```
. SET ORDER TO
Database is in natural order
. DISPLAY ALL
Record#  SOCSEC     LASTNAME     LOCATION  SALARY TITLE
      1  111111111  Borow        Florida    18000 Warehouse staff
      2  222222222  O'Malley     Brazil     24000 Sales rep
      3  333333333  Baker        Florida    14800 Sales support staff
      4  444444444  Benjamin     Florida    18800 Warehouse staff
      5  555555555  Smith        Brazil     14300 Clerical
      6  300000000  Brown        Florida    22000 Warehouse manager
```

(d) Natural Order

FIGURE 3.7
The SET ORDER Command with Added Record

The INDEX ON Command

The **INDEX ON** command creates an index from a key expression, which until now has consisted of a single field within the file structure. Indeed, we have not needed the **INDEX ON** command at all, since all previous indexes were based on a single field within the file structure, and thus were created through the **CREATE** and/or **MODIFY STRUCTURE** commands. The **INDEX ON** command, however, makes it possible to create more complex indexes of the type illustrated in Figure 3.8. Consider:

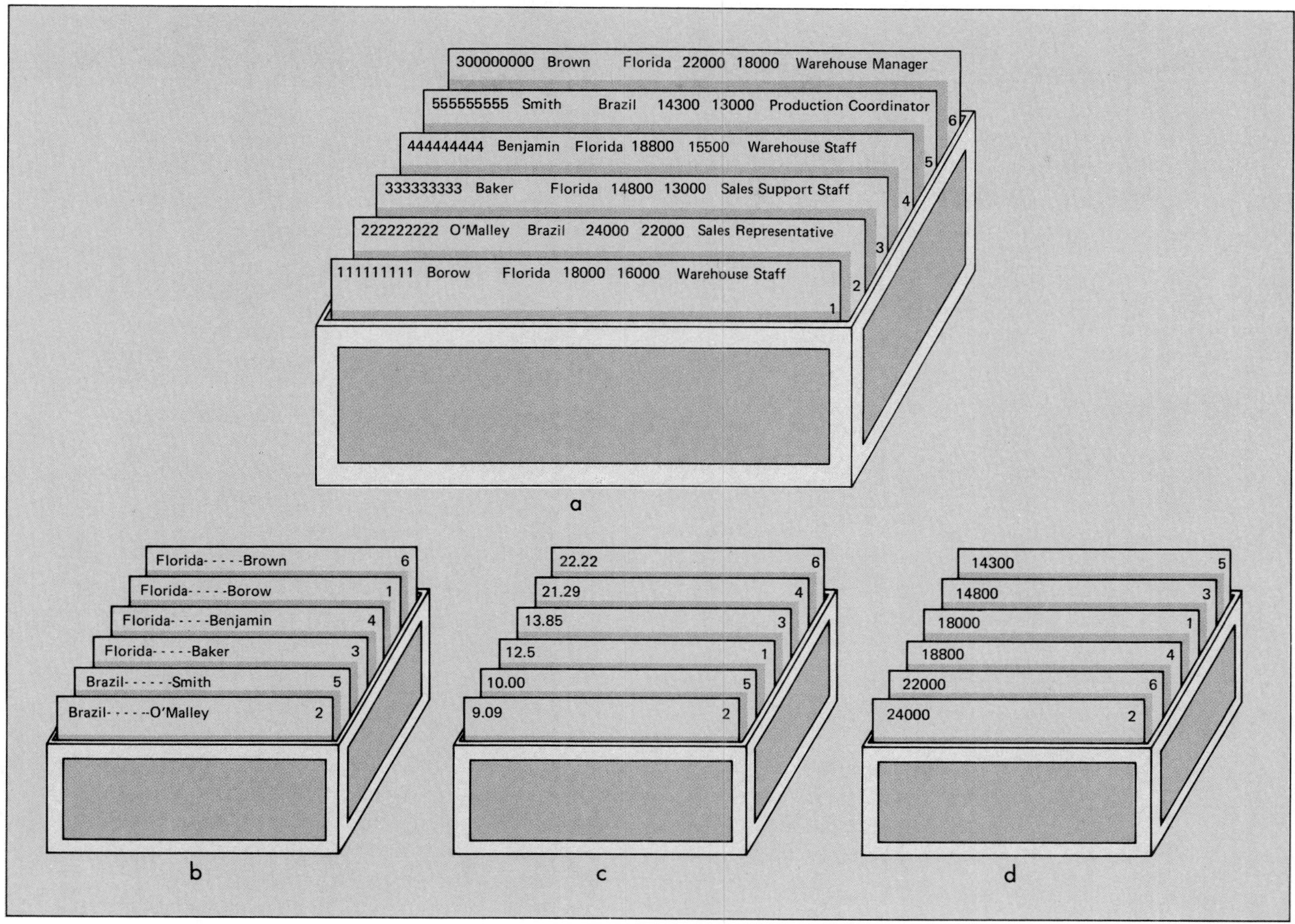

FIGURE 3.8
Finer Points of Indexing

Syntax

```
INDEX ON <key expression> TAG <tag name> [DESCENDING]
```

Examples

```
INDEX ON LOCATION + LASTNAME TAG LOCATION
INDEX ON SALARY TAG DESCSALARY DESCENDING
INDEX ON (SALARY-OLDSALARY)/OLDSALARY*100 TAG INCREASE
```

The ***key expression*** in the command syntax specifies the key on which the index is based, and can consist of a single field or a *combination* of fields within the file structure. The tag specifies the tag name within the associated multiple index file. The index created by the **INDEX ON** command is immediately made the current master index, so that all subsequent commands access the file according to the newly created index. The master index can be changed with a subsequent **SET ORDER** command or through execution of another **INDEX ON** command.

Indexing on a Concatenated Key

The key expression in the **INDEX ON** command of Figure 3.9a contains two fields, **LOCATION** *and* **LASTNAME**. **LOCATION** is listed first, and is considered the more

Concatenated key is based on two fields

```
. INDEX ON LOCATION+LASTNAME TAG LOCATION
  100% indexed            6 Records indexed
. DISPLAY ALL
Record#  SOCSEC     LASTNAME      LOCATION  SALARY OLDSALARY TITLE
      2  222222222  O'Malley      Brazil     24000     22000 Sales rep
      5  555555555  Smith         Brazil     14300     13000 Clerical
      3  333333333  Baker         Florida    14800     13000 Sales support staff
      4  444444444  Benjamin      Florida    18800     15500 Warehouse staff
      1  111111111  Borow         Florida    18000     16000 Warehouse staff
      6  300000000  Brown         Florida    22000     18000 Warehouse manager
```

(a) Concatenated Key

DESCENDING included in INDEX command

```
. INDEX ON SALARY TAG DESCSALARY DESCENDING
  100% indexed            6 Records indexed
. DISPLAY ALL
Record#  SOCSEC     LASTNAME      LOCATION  SALARY OLDSALARY TITLE
      2  222222222  O'Malley      Brazil     24000     22000 Sales rep
      6  300000000  Brown         Florida    22000     18000 Warehouse manager
      4  444444444  Benjamin      Florida    18800     15500 Warehouse staff
      1  111111111  Borow         Florida    18000     16000 Warehouse staff
      3  333333333  Baker         Florida    14800     13000 Sales support staff
      5  555555555  Smith         Brazil     14300     13000 Clerical
```

(b) Descending Index

FIGURE 3.9
Finer Points of Indexing

important or primary field, whereas **LASTNAME** is the less important or secondary field. The resulting index sequences employees according to location and alphabetically within location; i.e., all Brazil employees appear together in alphabetical order, followed by all Florida employees, who are also in alphabetical order. The combination of two or more fields in this fashion is known as a concatenated key.

A concatenated key may consist of any number of fields, but the combined key cannot exceed 220 characters. A second restriction is that each of the fields within the concatenated key must be a character field. (Date and/or numeric fields may be included in a concatenated key, provided they are first converted to an equivalent character field as described in the Programmer's Notebook.)

Indexing in Descending Sequence

The syntax of the **INDEX ON** command ends with the word **DESCENDING** enclosed in brackets, indicating an *optional* entry to produce a descending index. The option is illustrated in Figure 3.9b, which lists records in descending (high to low) sequence of salary. The key expression is a single field, **SALARY**, which is the same field used to produce the earlier ascending index on salary; the tag name, however, is different to differentiate it (the tag) from the earlier tag, which sequenced records in ascending sequence. In other words, the multiple index file, **EMPLOYEE.MDX**, now contains the tags, **SALARY** and **DESCSALARY**, either of which can be made the master index by the appropriate **SET ORDER** command.

Indexing on a Calculated Numeric Field

An index may be based on a ***calculated numeric key,*** i.e., a key expression not contained in the DBF file per se, but which is computed from one or more fields in the file structure. Assume, for example, that the **EMPLOYEE.DBF** file has been

Key expression is a calculated field

```
. INDEX ON (SALARY-OLDSALARY)/OLDSALARY*100  TAG INCREASE
  100% indexed            6 Records indexed
```

(a) INDEX ON Command

```
. DISPLAY ALL

Record#  SOCSEC     LASTNAME      LOCATION   SALARY OLDSALARY TITLE
      2  222222222  O'Malley      Brazil      24000     22000 Sales rep
      5  555555555  Smith         Brazil      14300     13000 Clerical
      1  111111111  Borow         Florida     18000     16000 Warehouse staff
      3  333333333  Baker         Florida     14800     13000 Sales support staff
      4  444444444  Benjamin      Florida     18800     15500 Warehouse staff
      6  300000000  Brown         Florida     22000     18000 Warehouse manager
```

(b) DISPLAY Command without Field List

Calculated field is included in field list

```
. DISPLAY ALL LASTNAME,SALARY,OLDSALARY,(SALARY-OLDSALARY)/OLDSALARY*100

Record#  LASTNAME      SALARY OLDSALARY SALARY-OLDSALARY)/OLDSALARY*100
      2  O'Malley       24000     22000                            9.09
      5  Smith          14300     13000                           10.00
      1  Borow          18000     16000                           12.50
      3  Baker          14800     13000                           13.85
      4  Benjamin       18800     15500                           21.29
      6  Brown          22000     18000                           22.22
```

(c) DISPLAY Command with Field List

FIGURE 3.10
Indexing on a Calculated Field

expanded to include an **OLDSALARY** field (as shown in Figure 3.8a), and that records are to be processed in order of percent salary increase. (Percent salary increase is computed by taking the difference between the present and old salaries, dividing by the old salary, and multiplying the result by 100.) The **INDEX ON** command to create this index is shown in Figure 3.10a.

Figure 3.10b lists records in order of percent salary increase but does *not* display the value of the increase, because the key expression is stored within the index rather than the **DBF** file. In other words, a **DISPLAY** statement (without an expression list) displays only fields explicitly defined in the file structure. The latter include **SALARY** and **OLDSALARY**, but not the calculated value of percent salary increase.

A **DISPLAY** statement with a field list, including the calculation, is needed to show the percent salary increase as illustrated in Figure 3.10c.

HANDS-ON EXERCISE 2

Finer Points of Indexing

Objective

Demonstrate finer points of indexing by creating indexes based on a concatenated key, a descending sequence, and a calculated field.

STEP 1 Modify the file structure

Load dBASE as you did in the previous exercise, being sure you are logged into the appropriate drive and directory. Type **USE EMPLOYEE** to open the existing

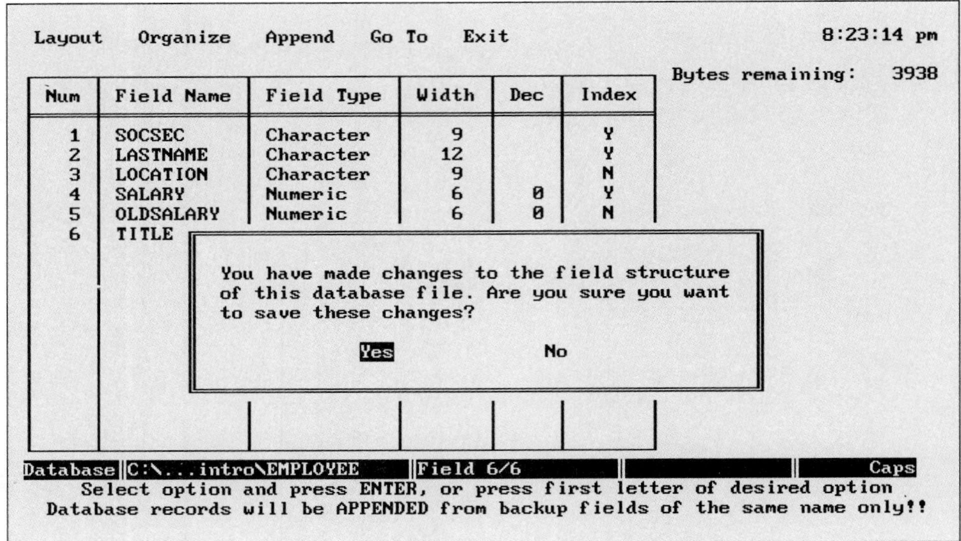

FIGURE 3.11
The MODIFY STRUCTURE Command

`EMPLOYEE.DBF` file, then type the command, **`MODIFY STRUCTURE`**, so that the `OLDSALARY` field can be added to the file structure.

Position the cursor on the line containing the `TITLE` field, then press **`Ctrl + N`** to add the new field. Enter the field name, type, length, and decimal places (`OLDSALARY`, Numeric, 6, and 0, respectively), then press **`Ctrl + End`** to save these changes in the file structure. You will be asked to confirm the changes as shown in Figure 3.11, after which the message *`6 records added`* will appear, indicating that the six existing records have been modified to accommodate the new field.

STEP 2 **Add the new salary data**

Type **`BROWSE`** to enter the browse mode and add the `OLDSALARY` values to the existing records. Enter the data as shown in Figure 3.12. Press **`Ctrl + End`** to save the modifications.

STEP 3 **Create a concatenated index**

Type **`INDEX ON LOCATION + LASTNAME TAG LOCATION`** to create the concatenated index of Figure 3.9a. Type **`DISPLAY ALL`** after the index has been created to display the file by city and alphabetically within city.

STEP 4 **Create a descending index**

Type **`INDEX ON SALARY TAG DESCSALARY DESCENDING`** to create the descending index of Figure 3.9b. Type **`DISPLAY ALL`** after the index has been created to display the file in descending salary sequence.

STEP 5 **Create an index based on a calculated key**

Type **`INDEX ON (SALARY-OLDSALARY)/OLDSALARY*100 TAG INCREASE`** to create the index of Figure 3.10a. Type **`DISPLAY ALL`** to list records in sequence by percent salary increase, but note that the increase itself is not displayed, because the increase is not a field within the `DBF` file structure. Accordingly, you need to enter a `DISPLAY` statement with a field list including the calculation to display the actual increase.

FIGURE 3.12
Adding a Field (BROWSE command)

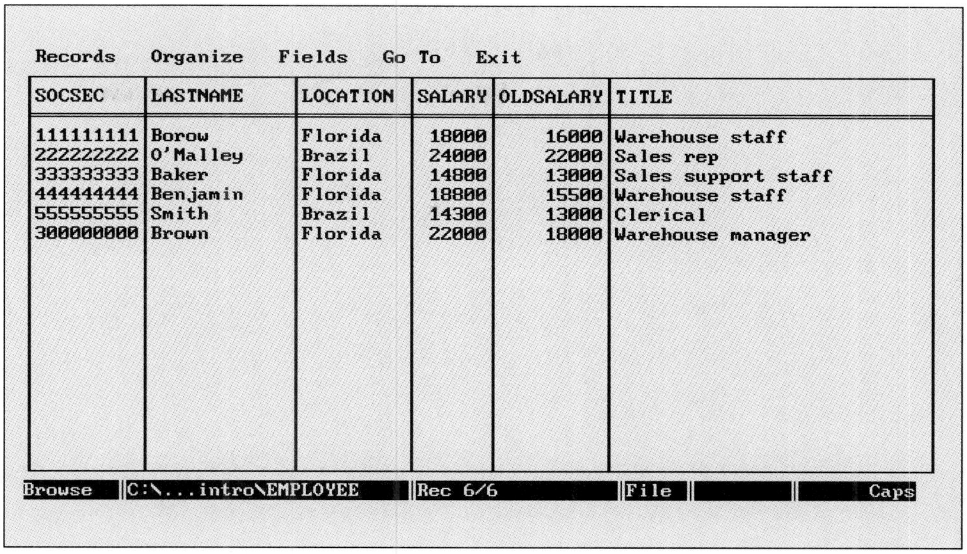

```
Records   Organize   Fields   Go To   Exit

SOCSEC    |LASTNAME  |LOCATION |SALARY|OLDSALARY|TITLE
111111111 |Borow     |Florida  | 18000|    16000|Warehouse staff
222222222 |O'Malley  |Brazil   | 24000|    22000|Sales rep
333333333 |Baker     |Florida  | 14800|    13000|Sales support staff
444444444 |Benjamin  |Florida  | 18800|    15500|Warehouse staff
555555555 |Smith     |Brazil   | 14300|    13000|Clerical
300000000 |Brown     |Florida  | 22000|    18000|Warehouse manager

Browse ||C:\...intro\EMPLOYEE ||Rec 6/6 ||File || || Caps
```

STEP 6 **Exit dBASE**
Type **QUIT** to exit dBASE.

Additional Commands

We introduce three additional commands before leaving the subject of indexing. These commands do not add any capability per se, but facilitate the use of indexes, and hence are worth knowing.

DISPLAY STATUS Command

As you might expect, it is quite easy to forget the indexes that have been created, the keys on which the indexes are based, or simply to lose track of the current master index. The **DISPLAY STATUS** command recaps all of this information and is shown in Figure 3.13a.

The SET ORDER command in Figure 3.13a establishes **SALARY** as the master index, a fact reflected by the subsequent DISPLAY STATUS command. The command also displays all indexes in the **MDX** file and the key expressions on which those indexes are based. You can see, for example, the various indexes developed in the chapter, which include a concatenated key, a calculated key, and a descending index.

USE with ORDER Command

The **USE with ORDER** command accomplishes the identical function as separate USE and SET ORDER commands. Consider:

Syntax
```
USE filename [ORDER <.mdx tag> ]
```

Example 1
```
USE EMPLOYEE ORDER LOCATION
```

Example 2
```
USE EMPLOYEE
SET ORDER TO TAG LOCATION
```

```
. SET ORDER TO TAG SALARY
Master index: SALARY

. DISPLAY STATUS ———————————— The DISPLAY STATUS command

Currently Selected Database:
Select area: 1   Database in Use: C:\DATADISK\INTRO\EMPLOYEE.DBF
Production   MDX file:  C:\DATADISK\INTRO\EMPLOYEE.MDX
             Index TAG:      SOCSEC  Key: SOCSEC
             Index TAG:      LASTNAME  Key: LASTNAME
      Master Index TAG:      SALARY  Key: SALARY
        |    Index TAG:      INCREASE  Key: (SALARY-OLDSALARY)/OLDSALARY*100
        |    Index TAG:      LOCATION  Key: LOCATION+LASTNAME
        |    Index TAG:      DESCSALARY  Key: SALARY (Descending)
        |
        └— Master index is indicated
```

(a) After SET Command

```
                          ┌—— Use command designates LOCATION as master index
. USE EMPLOYEE ORDER LOCATION
Master index: LOCATION

. DISPLAY STATUS
Currently Selected Database:
Select area: 1   Database in Use: C:\DATADISK\INTRO\EMPLOYEE.DBF
Production   MDX file:  C:\DATADISK\INTRO\EMPLOYEE.MDX
             Index TAG:      SOCSEC  Key: SOCSEC
             Index TAG:      LASTNAME  Key: LASTNAME
             Index TAG:      SALARY  Key: SALARY
             Index TAG:      INCREASE  Key: (SALARY-OLDSALARY)/OLDSALARY*100
      Master Index TAG:      LOCATION  Key: LOCATION+LASTNAME
             Index TAG:      DESCSALARY  Key: SALARY (Descending)
```

(b) After USE Command

```
. SET ORDER TO
Database is in natural order

. DELETE TAG SOCSEC ———————————— SOCSEC tag is removed from MDX file

. DISPLAY STATUS
Currently Selected Database:
Select area: 1   Database in Use: C:\DATADISK\INTRO\EMPLOYEE.DBF
Production   MDX file:  C:\DATADISK\INTRO\EMPLOYEE.MDX
             Index TAG:      LASTNAME  Key: LASTNAME
             Index TAG:      SALARY  Key: SALARY
             Index TAG:      INCREASE  Key: (SALARY-OLDSALARY)/OLDSALARY*100
             Index TAG:      LOCATION  Key: LOCATION+LASTNAME
             Index TAG:      DESCSALARY  Key: SALARY (Descending)
```

(c) After USE Command

FIGURE 3.13
DISPLAY STATUS Command (partial output)

The two examples are equivalent. Example 1 combines the **USE** and **SET** commands into a single statement, whereas example 2 uses a separate **SET ORDER** command to designate the master index. Figure 3.13b follows the **USE** command of example 1 with a **DISPLAY STATUS** command, confirming that **LOCATION** has indeed been established as the master index.

DELETE TAG Command

A multiple index file holds up to 47 indexes (tags), which is more than adequate for virtually any application. Realize, however, that each of these indexes has to be continually maintained to reflect changes in the associated `DBF` file, and thus each index adds significantly to the overhead of the system. The **`DELETE TAG`** command removes an existing index and is illustrated in Figure 3.13c. The subsequent **`DISPLAY STATUS`** command indicates five (rather than six) tags in the multiple index file, and confirms the deletion of the **`SOCSEC`** tag.

Error Messages

We hope that you have followed our presentation without difficulty. Experience tells us, however, that you will make certain mistakes, either as you follow our exercises or experiment further on your own. Accordingly, consider Figure 3.14, which illustrates two common error messages associated with indexing.

Figure 3.14a *repeats* an earlier **`INDEX ON`** command to create a concatenated index with the tag name **`LOCATION`**. The dBASE message indicates that this tag already exists; i.e., you executed the command previously, and hence dBASE is asking whether you want to overwrite (replace) the existing index. Press return when the *overwrite* option is highlighted to replace the index; alternatively, you can cancel the command and return to the dot prompt.

The error in Figure 3.14b—***data type mismatch***—occurs because we are attempting to concatenate two fields with *different* field types; i.e., **`LOCATION`** and **`SALARY`** were defined as character and numeric fields, respectively, and cannot be combined as written. You can, however, use the **`STR( )`** function to convert **`SALARY`** to a character field, as described in the Programmer's Notebook.

FIGURE 3.14
Error Messages Associated with Indexing

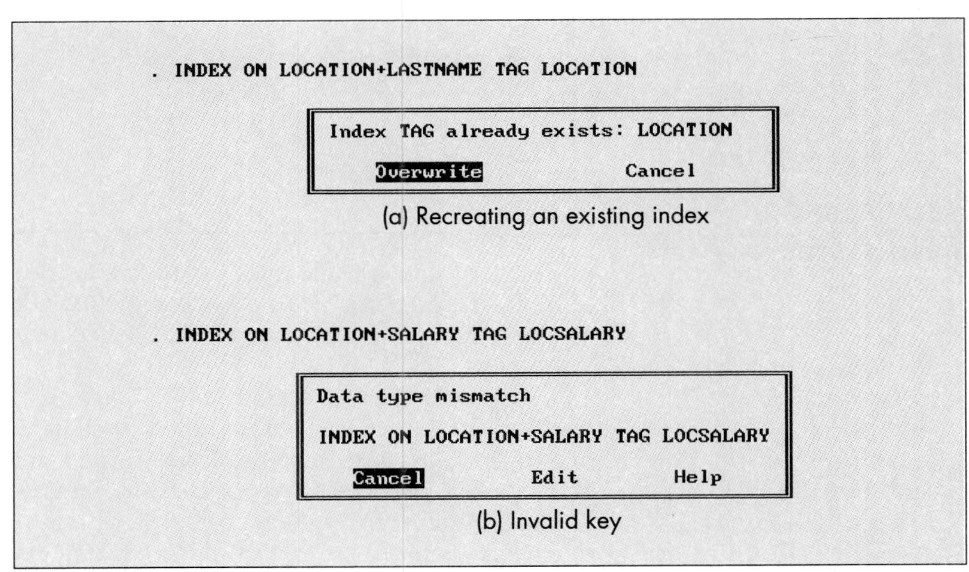

(a) Recreating an existing index

(b) Invalid key

Summary

The records in a DBF file are stored in ***physical (natural) sequence*** according to the sequence in which they were entered; a file, however, may be accessed in a different ***logical sequence*** through ***indexing.***

dBASE IV supports two types of indexes, a ***multiple index* (MDX)** file unique to dBASE IV and a ***single index* (NDX)** file that was supported in dBASE III Plus and all earlier releases. The chapter focused exclusively on the MDX file of dBASE IV.

The easiest way to create an index is in conjunction with the definition or modification of the file structure, i.e., with the **CREATE** or **MODIFY STRUCTURE** command. More complex indexes, e.g., those based on a ***concatenated*** or ***calculated*** key, or those in a ***descending*** sequence, can be created only through the **INDEX ON** command.

The multiple index file is created and/or opened automatically in conjunction with the associated DBF file; thus, all indexes within the MDX file are updated automatically to reflect changes to the DBF file.

At any instant there can be many ***open indexes*** but only one ***master index,*** the latter being determined by the last **SET ORDER** or **INDEX ON** command that was executed.

The **USE with INDEX** command opens the DBF file and designates a master index. The **DISPLAY STATUS** command displays all indexes within the MDX file, the keys on which they are based, and the current master index.

Key Words and Concepts

Ascending sequence
Calculated field
Concatenated index
CREATE
Data type mismatch
Descending sequence
DELETE TAG
DESCENDING
DISPLAY STATUS
Index
INDEX ON
Key
Key expression
Logical sequence
Master index
MDX file
Multiple index file
MODIFY STRUCTURE
Natural order
NDX file
Open index
Overwrite index
Physical sequence
RUN command
SET ORDER TO
Single index file
Tag
USE with ORDER

True/False

1. dBASE IV supports both NDX and MDX index files.
2. dBASE III PLUS supports both NDX and MDX index files.
3. The dBASE IV multiple index file is opened automatically in conjunction with its DBF file.
4. A single MDX file may contain up to 47 tags (indexes).
5. It is possible for a given file to have several indexes (tags) associated with it.
6. The DOS directory cannot be accessed from within dBASE.
7. The same field can be used to create an index in ascending sequence, and another in descending sequence.
8. An index must be created just prior to being used.
9. The **SET ORDER** command changes the master index.
10. An index may be created from several fields within a file structure.

11. The multiple (MDX) index file was available in dBASE III Plus.
12. The SET ORDER command may be specified *without* a tag.
13. The INDEX ON command is the only way to create an index.

Exercises

1. Supply the dBASE commands to:
   (a) Open a DBF file together with its existing index(es)
   (b) View the file directory from within dBASE
   (c) Create an index for an existing DBF file
   (d) Change the master index for a DBF file
   (e) Create a descending index
   (f) Create a concatenated index

2. Distinguish between:
   (a) The two uses of SALARY in the command, INDEX ON SALARY TAG SALARY
   (b) An open index and a master index
   (c) A key and a tag
   (d) An NDX file and an MDX file
   (e) The command USE EMPLOYEE ORDER SALARY
   versus USE EMPLOYEE
   SET ORDER TO TAG SALARY
   (f) The command INDEX ON SALARY TAG SALARY DESCENDING
   versus SET ORDER TO TAG SALARY
   (g) The command SET ORDER TO TAG SOCSEC
   versus SET ORDER TO
   (h) The command INDEX ON LASTNAME TAG LASTNAME
   versus INDEX ON LASTNAME+FIRSTNAME TAG LASTNAME
   (i) The command INDEX ON LOCATION+LASTNAME TAG EMPLOYEES
   versus INDEX ON LASTNAME+LOCATION TAG EMPLOYEES
   (j) The command INDEX ON SALARY TAG DESCSALARY DESCENDING
   versus INDEX ON -SALARY TAG DESCSALARY

3. Begin with the EMPLOYEE.DBF file (of Figure 3.12) and do the following:
   (a) Add a new record for Rudolph (with social security number 400000000, located in Chicago, with salaries of 24,000 and 21,000, and a job title of Sales representative)
   (b) Delete the existing record for Benjamin
   (c) Be sure that all existing indexes (last name, social security, salary, location, descending salary, and salary increase) are properly updated; list the file in each of these sequences after the addition and deletion have been accomplished

4. Create a file structure to hold the data in Figure 3.15, then enter the data into the file structure. Create whatever indexes are necessary, then enter the required commands to produce the following lists of students. List all fields in the file structure in every report. The students' grade point averages (quality points earned/credits taken) are to appear as well.
   (a) A master list of all students in alphabetical order
   (b) A list of those students on the Dean's List (grade point average of 3.00 or higher) in decreasing order of grade point average
   (c) An alphabetical list of students on academic probation (grade point average less than 2.00)
   (d) A master list of all students by major, and alphabetically within major

FIGURE 3.15
Data for Problem 4

Student Name	Major	Quality Points Earned	Credits Taken
Alan Moldof	Business	60	20
Joel Stutz	Business	180	50
Marion Milgrom	Education	140	38
Jessica Grauer	Business	96	28
Adam Moldof	Education	160	84
John Smith	Business	180	75
Eleanor Rudolph	Education	140	75
Benjy Grauer	Business	96	50
Toni Essman	Business	120	38
Karen Levine	Business	180	85
Michael Essman	Education	140	66
Jessica Blatt	Business	60	28

5. Figure 3.16 contains data for thirty-one (arbitrarily chosen) countries. Create the appropriate **DBF** file, then prepare the following reports based on the data:

(a) Display the five largest countries (in terms of area) in descending order of area; display only the country's name and area

(b) Display the five smallest countries (in terms of area) in ascending order of area; display only the country's name and area

(c) Display the eight largest countries (in terms of population) in descending order of population; display only the country's name and population

FIGURE 3.16
Data for Problem 5

Country	Year Admitted to the UN	Population (est 1990)	Area (sq miles)
Algeria	1962	25,714,000	918,497
Argentina	1945	32,291,000	1,065,189
Australia	1945	16,646,000	2,966,200
Bangladesh	1974	117,976,000	55,598
Belgium	1945	9,895,000	11,799
Brazil	1945	153,771,000	3,286,470
Canada	1945	26,527,000	3,851,790
China	1945	1,130,065,000	3,705,390
Congo	1960	2,306,000	132,046
Egypt	1945	54,139,000	385,201
Finland	1955	4,977,000	130,119
France	1945	56,184,000	220,688
Germany	1973	77,553,000	137,674
Ghana	1957	15,310,000	92,098
Greece	1945	10,066,000	51,146
Hungary	1955	10,546,000	35,919
India	1945	850,067,000	1,266,595
Israel	1949	4,371,000	7,847
Japan	1945	123,778,000	145,846
Kenya	1963	25,393,000	224,960
Mexico	1945	88,335,000	761,604
Portugal	1955	10,526,000	36,390
Spain	1955	39,623,000	194,896
Sweden	1946	8,407,000	173,731
Switzerland	1945	6,628,000	15,941
Togo	1960	3,566,000	21,622
USSR	1945	290,939,000	8,649,496
United Kingdom	1945	57,121,000	94,226
United States	1945	250,372,000	3,615,123
Vietnam	1977	68,488,000	128,401
Zaire	1960	35,330,000	905,563

Quarterback	Yds Gained	TD Passes	Interceptions	Rating
Aikman, Dallas	2754	11	10	86.7
Brister, Pittsburgh	1350	9	9	72.9
DeBerg, Kansas City	2965	17	14	79.3
Elway, Denver	3253	13	12	75.4
Esiason, Cincinnati	2883	13	16	72.5
Everett, Los Angeles	3438	11	20	68.9
Friesz, San Diego	2896	12	15	67.1
Gannon, Minnesota	2166	12	6	81.5
George, Indianapolis	2910	10	12	73.8
Harbaugh, Chicago	3121	15	16	73.7
Hostetler, New York	2032	5	4	84.1
Kelly, Buffalo	3844	33	17	97.6
Kosar, Cleveland	3487	18	9	87.8
Kramer, Detroit	1635	11	8	71.8
Krieg, Seattle	2080	11	12	82.5
Majkowski, Green Bay	1362	3	8	59.3
Marino, Miami	3970	25	13	85.8
McMahon, Philadelphia	2239	12	11	80.3
Millen, New England	3073	9	18	72.5
Miller, Atlanta	3103	26	18	80.6
Moon, Houston	4690	23	21	81.7
O'Brien, New York	3300	10	11	76.6
Rypien, Washington	3564	28	11	97.9
Schroeder, Los Angeles	2562	15	16	71.6
Testeverde, Tampa Bay	1994	8	15	59.0
Tupa, Phoenix	2053	6	13	62.0
Walsh, New Orleans	1638	11	6	79.5
Young, San Francisco	2517	17	8	101.8

FIGURE 3.17
Data for Problem 6

(d) Display the eight smallest countries (in terms of population) in ascending order of population; display only the country's name and population
(e) Display the ten countries with the highest population density (population/area) in descending order of population density; display the country's name, population, area, and population density
(f) Display the ten countries with the lowest density (population/area) in ascending order of population density; display the country's name, population, area, and population density

6. Figure 3.17 contains data for NFL quarterbacks at the end of the 1991 season. Create the appropriate **DBF** file, then prepare the following reports:
(a) A list of all quarterbacks in ascending order of quarterback rating; print all fields for each quarterback
(b) A list of the ten quarterbacks with the highest number of touchdowns in descending order; print only the quarterback's name and number of touchdowns
(c) A list of the ten quarterbacks with the highest number of interceptions in descending order; print only the quarterback's name and number of interceptions
(d) A list of the ten quarterbacks with the largest difference between touchdowns and interceptions; print the quarterback's name, number of touchdowns, number of interceptions, and computed difference (touchdowns minus interceptions)
(e) A list of all quarterbacks who threw for at least 3,000 yards in ascending order of yardage

What modifications are needed to list the quarterbacks alphabetically within conference (i.e., National and American)? What is the required **INDEX** command?

7. Research the Fortune 500 (or a similar list) to obtain the gross revenue and net income, for the present and previous year, for the twenty largest corporations. Use dBASE to create a file containing this data, then prepare the following reports:

(a) An alphabetical list of all twenty companies, showing every field for every company

(b) A list of the ten companies with the highest revenue in the current year, in ascending order of revenue; list the company name and revenue for the current year

(c) A list of all companies with a net income of at least $1 billion, in descending order of income; list the company name and net income for the current year

(d) A list of those companies with an increase in net income over the previous year of at least ten percent, in ascending order of the percentage increase; list the company name, net income for both years, and rate of increase in net income

PART

II

The Control Center

CHAPTER

4 The Report Generator

OUTLINE

OBJECTIVES

After reading this chapter you will be able to:

1. Distinguish between data and information; describe how one is converted into the other.
2. Use the dBASE report generator to create and/or modify report forms; describe the use of pull-down menus within the report generator and the significance of the quick-layout option.
3. Describe the relationship between the **DBF**, **MDX**, and **FRM** files in conjunction with the report generator.
4. Access the dBASE **HELP** facility to display the syntax of the **REPORT FORM** command; describe the purpose of all optional parameters.
5. Define the dBASE record pointer; discuss how the **SET ORDER** and **REPORT FORM** commands alter its position within a **DBF** file.
6. Define a report band; list the different types of report bands and describe when and where they are generated.

Overview

The chapter uses a new example with which we are all familiar, the United States of America. We present a table containing statistical data for the fifty states, then show several reports that present the data in more useful fashion. We stress the importance of viewing computer-generated output with a critical eye, for all too often we are guilty of accepting printed reports at face value, without regard for underlying validity.

The dBASE specific material focuses on the ***report generator,*** and how to create and modify ***report forms.*** We do not, however, cover every option of every command, nor do we think it necessary to do so. We view the report generator as a means to an end, that of producing useful information, rather than as an end unto itself.

Nevertheless, the chapter contains three hands-on exercises, each of which is essential if you are to use this very powerful facility effectively. The first exercise has you manipulate existing report forms to examine variations in the **REPORT FORM** command, and the critical relationship between report forms, indexes, and the associated DBF file. The second exercise introduces the ***quick-layout*** menu to create a report form with a minimum of effort, then modifies the report through various ***pull-down menus.*** The final exercise stresses the importance of ***report bands*** within the development process.

Data versus Information

Figure 4.1 lists the United States in alphabetical order, and includes the year a state entered the union, its estimated population in 1988, its area in square miles, and the geographic region of the country in which it is located. Figure 4.2 contains four reports that were derived from this data, and lists the original thirteen states, the ten smallest states according to area, the ten largest states according to population, and the five states with the highest population density.

The two figures effectively illustrate the difference between ***data*** and ***information.*** Data refers to a fact or facts about a person, place, or thing, and in our example (Figure 4.1) includes items such as the state name, year admitted, population, and region. Information, on the other hand, is data that has been rearranged into a form perceived as useful by the recipient, e.g., the five states with the highest population density (population/area). Put another way, data is the raw material, whereas information is the finished product. Information can be used to make decisions, raw data cannot.

The distinction between data and information is often difficult to discern. In general, however, data is seen as something less than information, although what one person perceives as data may be viewed as information by another. The alphabetical listing of all fifty states, with the associated facts on every state, may be viewed as information by one person, and as raw data by someone else.

Data is converted to information through ***calculation*** (e.g., computation of population density), ***selection*** (listing only a subset of the file), and ***sequencing*** (presenting records in a different order). As you view the reports of Figure 4.2, try to determine which operations were needed for their creation.

The dBASE Report Generator

The reports in Figures 4.1 and 4.2 were produced with the dBASE ***report generator,*** a powerful menu-driven facility that we shall describe in depth. Each report is based

United States Statistical Data

State Name	Admitted to Union	Population (est 1988)	Area (sq miles)	Region
Alabama	1819	4,102,000	51,609	South Central
Alaska	1959	524,000	589,757	Pacific
Arizona	1912	3,489,000	113,909	Mountain
Arkansas	1836	2,395,000	53,104	South Central
California	1850	28,314,000	158,693	Pacific
Colorado	1876	3,301,000	104,247	Mountain
Connecticut	1788	3,233,000	5,009	New England
Delaware	1787	660,000	2,057	Middle Atlantic
Florida	1845	12,335,000	58,560	South Atlantic
Georgia	1788	6,342,105	58,876	South Atlantic
Hawaii	1959	1,098,000	6,450	Pacific
Idaho	1890	1,003,000	83,557	Mountain
Illinois	1818	11,614,000	56,400	North Central
Indiana	1816	5,556,000	36,291	North Central
Iowa	1846	2,834,000	56,290	North Central
Kansas	1861	2,495,000	82,264	North Central
Kentucky	1792	3,727,000	40,395	South Central
Louisiana	1812	4,408,000	48,523	South Central
Maine	1820	1,205,000	33,215	New England
Maryland	1788	4,622,000	10,577	Middle Atlantic
Massachusetts	1788	5,889,000	8,257	New England
Michigan	1837	9,240,000	58,216	North Central
Minnesota	1858	4,307,000	84,068	North Central
Mississippi	1817	2,620,000	47,716	South Central
Missouri	1821	5,141,000	69,686	North Central
Montana	1889	805,000	147,138	Mountain
Nebraska	1867	1,602,000	77,227	North Central
Nevada	1864	1,054,000	110,540	Mountain
New Hampshire	1788	1,085,000	9,304	New England
New Jersey	1787	7,721,000	7,836	Middle Atlantic
New Mexico	1912	1,507,000	121,666	Mountain
New York	1788	17,909,000	49,576	Middle Atlantic
North Carolina	1789	6,489,000	52,586	South Atlantic
North Dakota	1889	667,000	70,665	North Central
Ohio	1803	10,855,000	41,222	North Central
Oklahoma	1907	3,242,000	69,919	South Central
Oregon	1859	2,767,000	96,981	Pacific
Pennsylvania	1787	12,001,000	45,333	Middle Atlantic
Rhode Island	1790	993,000	1,214	New England
South Carolina	1788	3,470,000	31,055	South Atlantic
South Dakota	1889	713,000	77,047	North Central
Tennessee	1796	4,895,000	42,244	South Central
Texas	1845	16,841,000	267,338	South Central
Utah	1896	1,690,000	84,916	Mountain
Vermont	1791	557,000	9,609	New England
Virginia	1788	6,015,000	40,817	South Atlantic
Washington	1889	4,648,000	68,192	Pacific
West Virginia	1863	1,876,000	24,181	South Atlantic
Wisconsin	1848	4,855,000	56,154	North Central
Wyoming	1890	479,000	97,914	Mountain
Totals		245,190,105	3,618,400	

FIGURE 4.1
United States Statistical Data

on its own ***report form,*** and was created with a different index (the states are listed in different sequences in each report). Different indexes are *not* a requirement, however, as the states could have been listed in the same sequence in all four reports. The reports are more meaningful, however, when the states are listed in a sequence tailored to the specific report form; hence we (optionally) use a different index with each report.

FIGURE 4.2
Data versus Information

State Name	Admitted to Union
Delaware	1787
New Jersey	1787
Pennsylvania	1787
Connecticut	1788
Georgia	1788
Maryland	1788
Massachusetts	1788
New Hampshire	1788
New York	1788
South Carolina	1788
Virginia	1788
North Carolina	1789
Rhode Island	1790

(a) The Thirteen Original States

State Name	Area (sq miles)
Rhode Island	1,214
Delaware	2,057
Connecticut	5,009
Hawaii	6,450
New Jersey	7,836
Massachusetts	8,257
New Hampshire	9,304
Vermont	9,609
Maryland	10,577
West Virginia	24,181

(b) The Ten Smallest States

State Name	Population (est 1988)
California	28,314,000
New York	17,909,000
Texas	16,841,000
Florida	12,335,000
Pennsylvania	12,001,000
Illinois	11,614,000
Ohio	10,855,000
Michigan	9,240,000
New Jersey	7,721,000
North Carolina	6,489,000

(c) The Ten Most Populous States

State Name	Population (est 1988)	Area (sq miles)	Density (pop'n/area)
New Jersey	7,721,000	7,836	985.32
Rhode Island	993,000	1,214	817.96
Massachusetts	5,889,000	8,257	713.21
Connecticut	3,233,000	5,009	645.44
Maryland	4,622,000	10,577	436.99

(d) The Five Most Densely Populated States

A report form can be thought of as an empty report (or template), containing a report's title, formatting characteristics (margins and spacing), column headings, and so on. It does not, however, contain any data. The report generator creates the report form, which is later merged with the **USSTATES.DBF** file (sequenced by the desired index) to produce the finished report. The process is shown in Figure 4.3, which depicts the relationship between a **DBF** file, its various indexes, and associated report forms.

The four reports use the same **DBF** file, but different report forms; i.e., one report form contains the state name and year of admission, a second report form the state name and area, and so on. Four different report forms are required because the report designs are different, and each report form is created individually through the report generator. Four different indexes were also used in order to list states in different sequences.

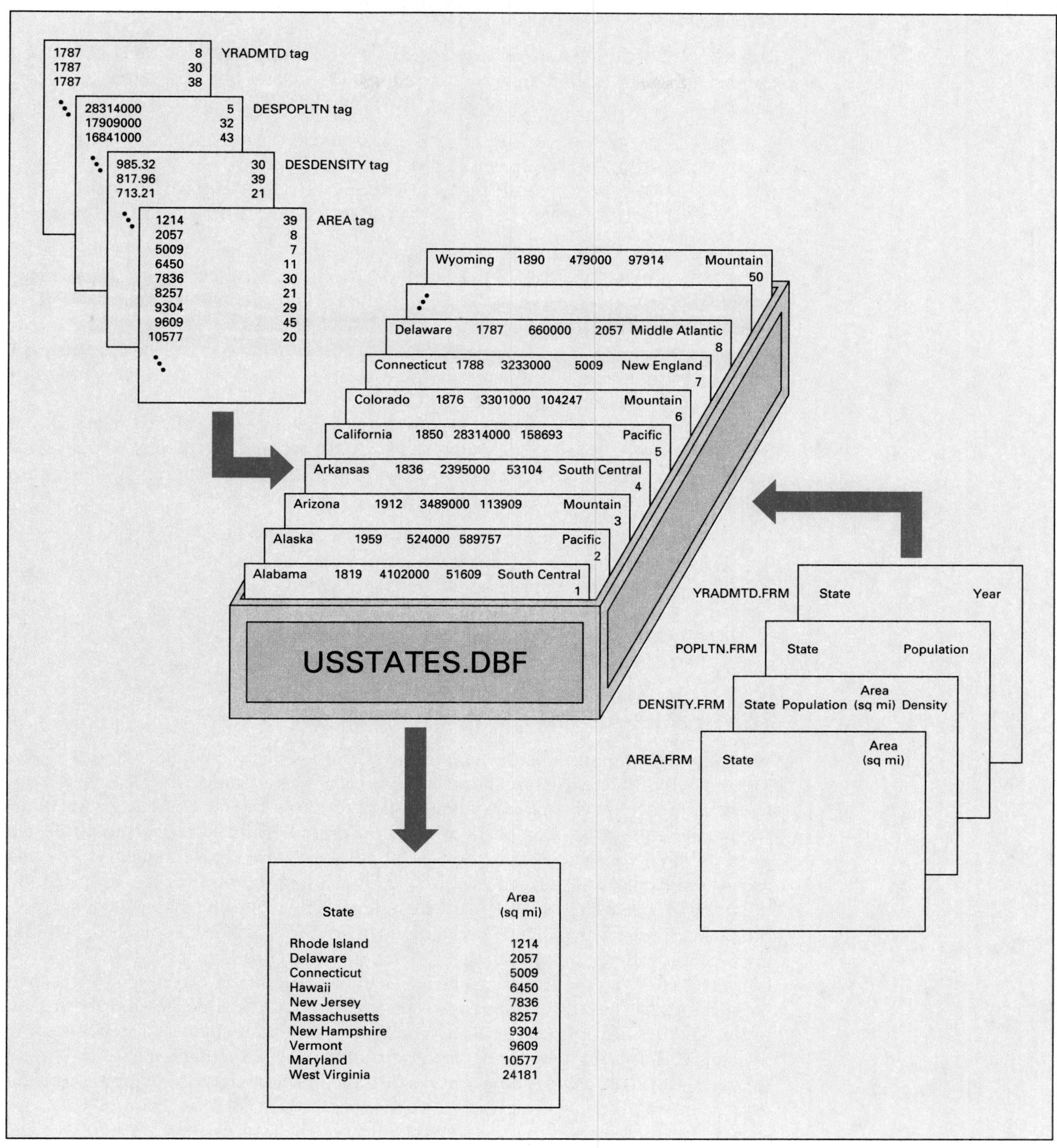

FIGURE 4.3
Understanding Report Forms
(file relationships)

The REPORT FORM Command

The **REPORT FORM** command displays data from an open **DBF** file, in sequence by the master index, beginning at the current position of the record pointer, in accordance with the designated report form. The syntax of the command is as follows:

```
REPORT FORM <report form file name> [PLAIN]
    [HEADING <expression>]
    [NOEJECT] [SUMMARY] [<scope>] [FOR <condition>]
    [WHILE <condition>] [TO PRINTER/TO FILE <file name>]
```

Variations in the **REPORT FORM** command are explained within the context of the dBASE notation that was introduced in Chapter 2. Recall that upper-case letters denote a dBASE reserved word, which must be spelled exactly as shown; lower-case letters indicate a user-supplied value. Square brackets imply an optional entry, and as you can see, every entry (except for the command and report form file name) is enclosed in square brackets, and therefore optional. A slash within an entry indicates a choice, e.g., **TO PRINTER** *or* **TO FILE**.

The scope, **FOR**, and **WHILE** parameters function identically to other dBASE commands. (The default scope of the **REPORT FORM** command is **ALL**, so that omission of the scope parameter lists all records in the **DBF** file.) The other clauses are unique to the **REPORT FORM** command and are explained below:

PLAIN	Suppresses headers and footers except on first page
HEADING	Prints text at the top of each page
NOEJECT	Suppresses an initial form feed
SUMMARY	Prints only subtotals and totals
TO PRINTER	Sends the report to the printer
TO FILE	Writes the report to a disk file

The Importance of the Record Pointer

We cannot overemphasize the importance of indexing in conjunction with report forms. Each of the reports in Figure 4.2 listed a different number of records in a different sequence, making it absolutely critical to know the current master index, as well as the current position of the ***record pointer.*** Recall that records in a **DBF** file are numbered consecutively as they are physically entered into the file; i.e., the first record is record 1, the second record is record 2, and so on. Realize, too, that the records in the **USSTATES.DBF** file were entered alphabetically; thus, Alabama is record 1, Alaska is record 2, and Wyoming is record 50. All dBASE commands work in conjunction with the record pointer and underlying record numbers.

The effect of the record pointer is seen by comparing the results of the two identical **REPORT FORM** commands in Figure 4.4a. **AREA** is designated the master index, and the first **REPORT FORM** command lists the four smallest states according to area; i.e., *it lists the first four records beginning with the current record.* The second (identical) **REPORT FORM** command also lists the first four records beginning with the current record, but since the record pointer was *not* reset, four different states are shown. In all likelihood the user intended to see the four smallest states; he or she was successful with the first **REPORT FORM** command but not with the second, because the record pointer was not set properly.

The results are even more peculiar in Figure 4.4b. The **SET ORDER** command changes the master index, presumably with the intent of listing the first 13 states admitted to the union. Note, however, the unexpected results. The **SET ORDER** command did *not* reset the record pointer from the example in Figure 4.4a, and thus the selected states begin at New Hampshire, rather than at the top of the **YRADMTD** index.

FIGURE 4.4
Resetting the Record Pointer

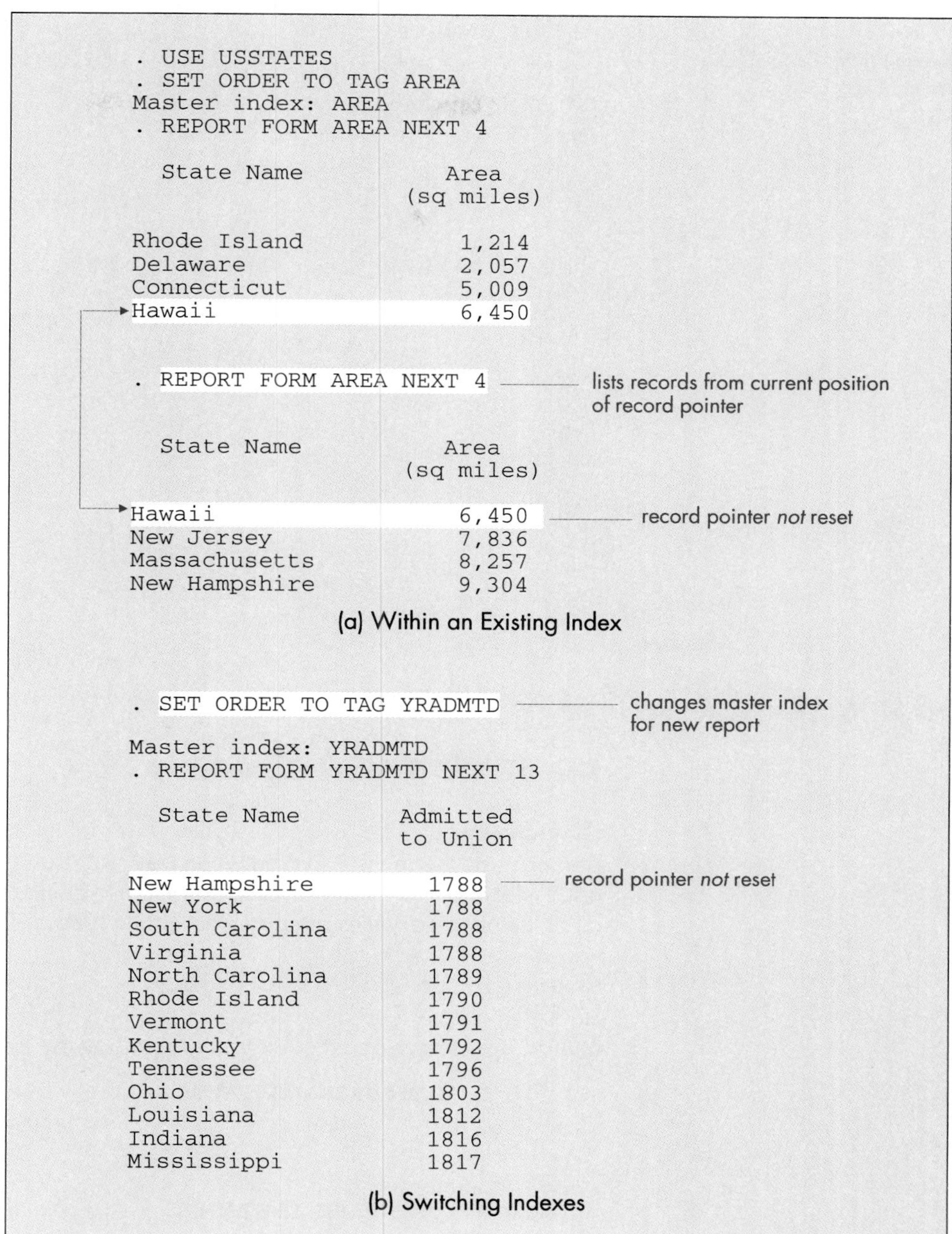
```
. USE USSTATES
. SET ORDER TO TAG AREA
Master index: AREA
. REPORT FORM AREA NEXT 4

  State Name               Area
                        (sq miles)

Rhode Island              1,214
Delaware                  2,057
Connecticut               5,009
Hawaii                    6,450

. REPORT FORM AREA NEXT 4

  State Name               Area
                        (sq miles)

Hawaii                    6,450
New Jersey                7,836
Massachusetts             8,257
New Hampshire             9,304
```


(a) Within an Existing Index

```
. SET ORDER TO TAG YRADMTD
Master index: YRADMTD
. REPORT FORM YRADMTD NEXT 13

  State Name            Admitted
                        to Union

New Hampshire              1788
New York                   1788
South Carolina             1788
Virginia                   1788
North Carolina             1789
Rhode Island               1790
Vermont                    1791
Kentucky                   1792
Tennessee                  1796
Ohio                       1803
Louisiana                  1812
Indiana                    1816
Mississippi                1817
```


(b) Switching Indexes

The **GO TOP** command is the only proper way to set the record pointer, as shown in Figure 4.4c on page 78. The master index is unchanged from the previous example, but since the record pointer was properly set, we get the original 13 states.

We come now to the first of three hands-on exercises, which recreates the various reports of Figure 4.2. The exercise uses report forms that exist on the data disk to stress the relationship between a **DBF** file, its various indexes, the report forms, and the generated reports. Rest assured, however, that you will have ample opportunity to create report forms for yourself in subsequent exercises. The ensuing exercise also explores various options in the **REPORT FORM** command.

FIGURE 4.4
Resetting the Record Pointer (continued)

```
. GO TOP ———————————————— GO TOP command resets record pointer

USSTATES: Record No        8
. REPORT FORM YRADMTD NEXT 13

   State Name          Admitted
                       to Union

Delaware                  1787
New Jersey                1787
Pennsylvania              1787
Connecticut               1788
Georgia                   1788
Maryland                  1788
Massachusetts             1788
New Hampshire             1788
New York                  1788
South Carolina            1788
Virginia                  1788
North Carolina            1789
Rhode Island              1790
```

(c) GO TOP Command

HANDS-ON EXERCISE 1

The dBASE Report Generator

Objective
Demonstrate the relationship between DBF, MDX, and FRM files. The intent of this exercise is not to burden you with data entry, but to demonstrate the report generator; thus, all of the necessary files already exist on the data disk.

STEP 1 **Change to the USSTATES directory**
Boot the system, ending at the DOS prompt. Type one of the following two commands, depending on whether you are sharing the hard drive with others:

CD C:\DATADISK\USSTATES —— *if you installed the data disk on the hard drive and are not sharing your computer, or*

CD A:\DATADISK\USSTATES —— *if you did not install the data disk, i.e., if you are sharing drive C with other students. (Use data disk one if you have 5¼-inch disks.)*

Type **DIR** to view the directory of Figure 4.5; you will see **USSTATES.DBF** file, its index, **USSTATES.MDX**, and the four **FRM** files required for the reports in Figure 4.2.

STEP 2 **Open the USSTATES.DBF file**
Type **dBASE** to load dBASE, then set the default drive as you have in previous exercises. Type **USE USSTATES** to open the data file, then enter the **DISPLAY STRUCTURE** command as shown in Figure 4.6a. The reports that will be produced in this exercise list the states in different sequences, which requires the existence of corresponding indexes. You can verify that the indexes already exist through the **DISPLAY STATUS** command shown in Figure 4.6b.

FIGURE 4.5
The USSTATES Directory

```
USSTATES DBF       2794 03-13-91   10:04a

USSTATES MDX      18432 03-13-91   10:04a

AREA      FRM       985 03-13-91    9:26a
DENSITY   FRM      1402 03-13-91    9:21a
POPLTN    FRM      1004 03-13-91    9:21a
YRADMTD   FRM       985 03-13-91    9:27a
```

MDX file contains multiple indexes

Report forms for Figure 4.2

STEP 3 **Reproduce the reports of Figure 4.2**

Each of the reports in Figure 4.2 is based on the same **USSTATES.DBF** file, but uses a different report form and a different index. Enter the commands below to reproduce the four reports, observing how each set uses a different index and references a different report form. (The **REPORT FORM** commands contain a **NOEJECT** clause to eliminate the blank page that would otherwise appear at the beginning of each report.)

```
.SET ORDER TO TAG YRADMTD
.GO TOP
.REPORT FORM YRADMTD NEXT 13 NOEJECT TO PRINTER

.SET ORDER TO TAG AREA
.GO TOP
.REPORT FORM AREA NEXT 10 NOEJECT TO PRINTER
```

FIGURE 4.6
The USSTATES.DBF File

```
. USE USSTATES
. DISPLAY STRUCTURE
Structure for database: C:\DATADISK\USSTATES\USSTATES.DBF
Number of data records:       50
Date of last update   : 03/13/91
Field  Field Name  Type       Width    Dec    Index
    1  STATE       Character     14               N
    2  YRADMTD     Numeric        4               Y
    3  POPLTN      Numeric       10               Y
    4  AREA        Numeric        8               Y
    5  REGION      Character     15               N
** Total **                      52
```

(a) File Structure

```
. DISPLAY STATUS
. Select area: 1    Database in Use: C:\DATADISK\USSTATES\USSTATES.DBF
Production     MDX file:   C:\DATADISK\USSTATES\USSTATES.MDX
           Index TAG:     DENSITY  Key: popltn/area
           Index TAG:     AREA  Key: area
           Index TAG:     POPLTN  Key: popltn
           Index TAG:     YRADMTD  Key: yradmtd
           Index TAG:     REGION  Key: region+state
           Index TAG:     DESPOPLTN  Key: popltn (Descending)
           Index TAG:     DESDENSITY  Key: popltn/area (Descending)
```

(b) Existing Indexes (partial output)

```
.SET ORDER TO TAG DESPOPLTN
.GO TOP
.REPORT FORM POPLTN NEXT 10 NOEJECT TO PRINTER

.SET ORDER TO TAG DESDENSITY
.GO TOP
.REPORT FORM DENSITY NEXT 5 NOEJECT TO PRINTER
```

STEP 4 **The HELP command**

Type **HELP REPORT** to display the syntax of the REPORT FORM command shown earlier in the chapter. Press **Esc** to exit the help mode. Experiment with some or all of the options. (Type **EJECT** to force a form feed after you produce the report.)

STEP 5 **The HEADING parameter**

The HEADING parameter is one of the most useful options in the REPORT FORM command as it enables you to assign different headings to the same report form. Type the following commands to see the flexibility provided by this parameter:

```
.SET ORDER TO TAG AREA
.GO TOP
.REPORT FORM AREA NEXT 10 HEADING 'The 10 Smallest States'
.GO TOP
.REPORT FORM AREA NEXT 5 HEADING 'The 5 Smallest States'
```

Practice makes perfect, so experiment away, creating additional reports of your own design. Do not leave this exercise until you truly understand the relationship between the DBF file, MDX file, and multiple FRM files.

Use and Abuse of the Computer

The reports we have been discussing are simple and straightforward, and easily produced without error. Unfortunately, that statement is a bit too optimistic because we all make careless errors, and/or are too accepting of reports produced by others. Consider, for example, Figure 4.7, which contains two erroneous attempts at producing the report listing the original thirteen states. It is important to say that these examples are *not* contrived, but are reproduced from student assignments. The errors seem obvious now, but nevertheless went undetected by students who submitted the reports for a grade.

Figure 4.7a lists the first thirteen records in the **USSTATES.DBF** file, rather than the first thirteen states admitted. The report was produced by using the DBF file *without* opening the associated YRADMTD index.

The error in Figure 4.7b is more subtle and was caused by failing to reset the record pointer. Remember our earlier discussion, which illustrated how the REPORT FORM command alters the position of the record pointer, and how this action must be recognized or else the wrong states appear. Consider:

```
.USE USSTATES
.SET ORDER TO TAG YRADMTD
.REPORT FORM YRADMTD NEXT 13
```

FIGURE 4.7
Use and Abuse of the Computer

Original 13 States		Original 13 States	
State Name	Admitted to Union	State Name	Admitted to Union
Alabama	1819	Rhode Island	1790
Alaska	1959	Vermont	1791
Arizona	1912	Kentucky	1792
Arkansas	1836	Tennessee	1796
California	1850	Ohio	1803
Colorado	1876	Louisiana	1812
Connecticut	1788	Indiana	1816
Delaware	1787	Mississippi	1817
Florida	1845	Illinois	1818
Georgia	1788	Alabama	1819
Hawaii	1959	Maine	1820
Idaho	1890	Missouri	1821
Illinois	1818	Arkansas	1836
(a) Wrong index		(b) Record Pointer in Wrong Position	

Given that the report form, data file, and associated index are correct, these statements will correctly produce the report in question. However, after the **`REPORT FORM YRADMTD NEXT 13`** command has been executed, the record pointer remains on the 13th record in the year admitted sequence (Rhode Island). Thus, if one were to repeat the statement, **`REPORT FORM YRADMTD NEXT 13`**, without resetting the record pointer (i.e., without specifying **`GO TOP`**), states 13 through 25 would appear on the subsequent report. In all probability, the student who submitted Figure 4.7b was dissatisfied with a heading in the report form and/or the paper alignment, made the proper adjustment, then reran the report without resetting the record pointer.

Our point is simply that *most individuals are not critical enough when viewing computer output*. Beginning students and/or first-time computer users, especially, are often so happy when they produce output that they automatically assume it to be correct. Nothing could be further from the truth. Now that our point is made, we trust you will have little difficulty in evaluating the reports in problems 3 and 4 at the end of the chapter.

Report Bands

We come now to a discussion of how report forms are created, which leads shortly to a second hands-on exercise. As you shall see, the report generator has a ***quick-layout*** option to produce a report form with a minimum of effort, as well as ***pull-down menus*** to create more polished report forms. The difference is seen by comparing the reports in Figures 4.8a and 4.8b. Consider:

1. The column headings in Figure 4.8a appear in upper-case letters and correspond to the field names within the **`USSTATES.DBF`** file; the column headings in Figure 4.8b are more descriptive.
2. The numeric fields are unedited in Figure 4.8a and edited in Figure 4.8b.
3. The total line in Figure 4.8a contains a nonsensical total on the year admitted field, which is removed in Figure 4.8b; the latter also contains a label to identify the line.

Both reports, however, are produced through description of various ***report bands*** as entered through the report generator. A report band consists of one or more lines

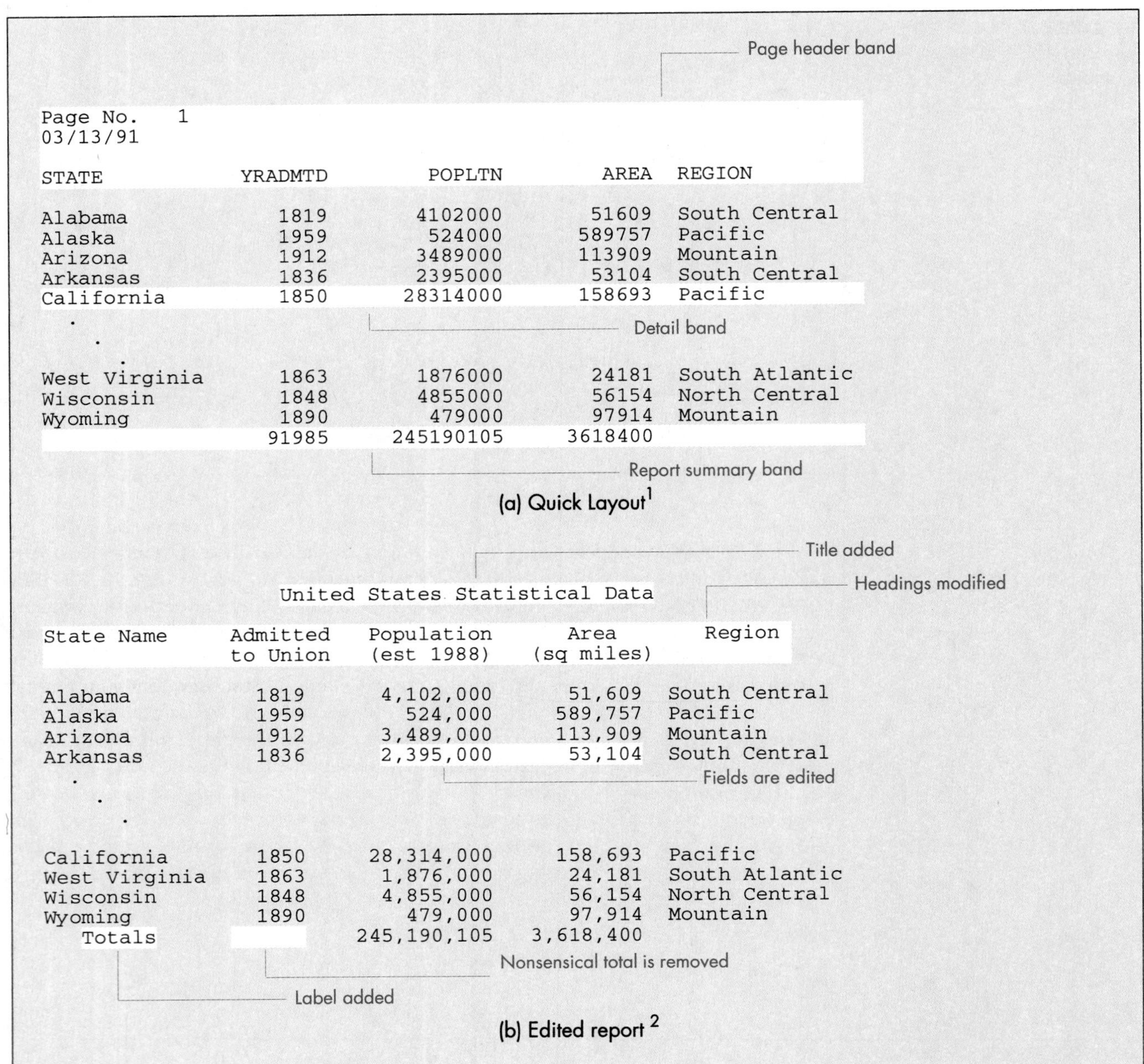

Page No. 1
03/13/91

STATE	YRADMTD	POPLTN	AREA	REGION
Alabama	1819	4102000	51609	South Central
Alaska	1959	524000	589757	Pacific
Arizona	1912	3489000	113909	Mountain
Arkansas	1836	2395000	53104	South Central
California	1850	28314000	158693	Pacific
.				
.				
.				
West Virginia	1863	1876000	24181	South Atlantic
Wisconsin	1848	4855000	56154	North Central
Wyoming	1890	479000	97914	Mountain
	91985	245190105	3618400	

(a) Quick Layout[1]

United States Statistical Data

State Name	Admitted to Union	Population (est 1988)	Area (sq miles)	Region
Alabama	1819	4,102,000	51,609	South Central
Alaska	1959	524,000	589,757	Pacific
Arizona	1912	3,489,000	113,909	Mountain
Arkansas	1836	2,395,000	53,104	South Central
.				
.				
.				
California	1850	28,314,000	158,693	Pacific
West Virginia	1863	1,876,000	24,181	South Atlantic
Wisconsin	1848	4,855,000	56,154	North Central
Wyoming	1890	479,000	97,914	Mountain
Totals		245,190,105	3,618,400	

(b) Edited report[2]

FIGURE 4.8
Introduction to Report Forms

that appear at designated places within a report. There are seven different types of report bands:

Page header band:	One or more lines that appear at the top of every page
Page footer band:	One or more lines that appear at the bottom of every page
Report intro band:	One or more lines that appear at the beginning of a report (after the page header for the first page)

[1] The report of Figure 4.8a is created through the quick layout menu as shown in Figure 4.9 and described in steps 1 through 4 of Hands-on Exercise 2.

[2] The report of Figure 4.8b is created through pull-down menus as shown in Figure 4.10 and described in steps 5 through 10 of Hands-on Exercise 2.

Report summary band:	One or more lines that appear at the end of a report (before the page footer for the last page)
Group intro band:	One or more lines that appear before the first record in a group (groups are discussed in conjunction with the third hands-on exercise and do not appear in Figure 4.8)
Group summary band:	One or more lines that appear after the last record in a group
Detail band:	One or more lines that appear in conjunction with every selected record in the associated **DBF** file

In essence, a report form is created by describing the appearance of various report bands to the report generator. Report bands (except for the detail band) are defined in pairs; e.g., there is a page header band and a page footer band. However, there is no requirement for both bands to appear in the same report; e.g., Figure 4.8a contains a page header band but not a page footer band. Moreover, a given report need not contain all seven types of report bands.

The report form for Figure 4.8a was created through the quick-layout option, whereas the one in Figure 4.8b required considerably more effort. Our intent is to make you productive as quickly as possible, and so the following exercise begins with the quick-layout option; we then show you how to improve the appearance of the report through options in the various pull-down menus.

The report forms are created through the dBASE report generator, a menu-driven process that is illustrated in the ensuing exercise. The report generator is initiated by the **CREATE REPORT** command, and results in a permanent (**FRM**) file, which can be used repeatedly.[1] The report form can, if necessary, be subsequently modified through the **MODIFY REPORT** command. (We expect that you will be able to use the report generator with just the explanation provided in the exercise, but direct you to the Programmer's Notebook for additional information.)

HANDS-ON EXERCISE 2

Creating Report Forms

Objective

Create a simple report form through the quick-layout command; create more sophisticated reports through various pull-down menus.

STEP 1 **Reset the record pointer**

We assume you are still at the dot prompt with the **USSTATES.DBF** file open. You must, however, change the master index to natural order so that states will be listed alphabetically; accordingly, type the commands, **SET ORDER TO** *and* **GO TOP**.

STEP 2 **Enter the report generator**

Type **CREATE REPORT** to initiate the report generator, then enter **USDATA** (or any other suitable name) as the name of the report. You will see the opening screen of the report generator in Figure 4.9a; it is confusing at first, but do not be concerned, because the report generator is nowhere nearly as complicated as it looks.

---

[1] The **REPORT FORM** command creates two additional files, with extensions of **FRG** and **FRO** for each report form; i.e., **AREA.FRM** produces the files **AREA.FRG** and **AREA.FRO**. The purpose of these additional files is explained in Chapter 8 and beyond the scope of the present discussion.

FIGURE 4.9
Creating a Report Form through Quick Layout

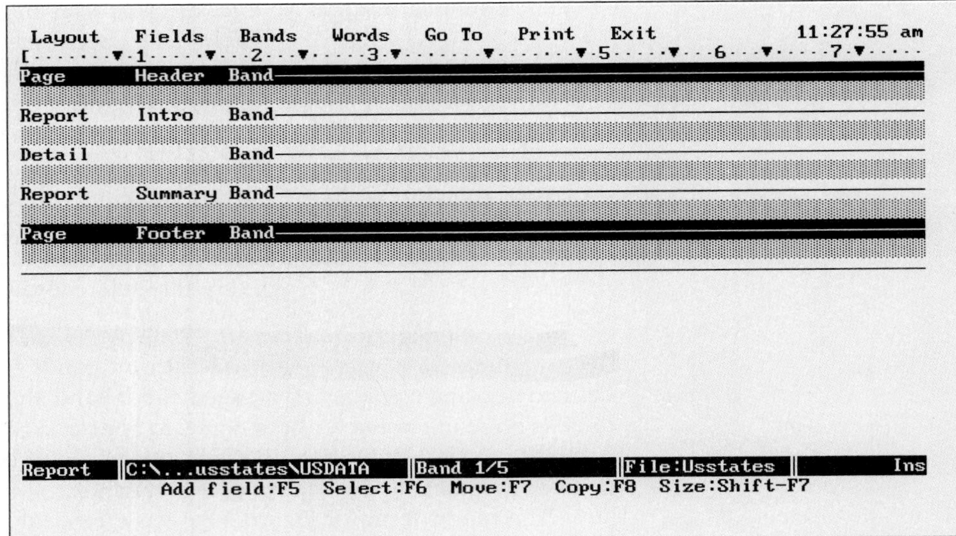

(a) Opening Screen

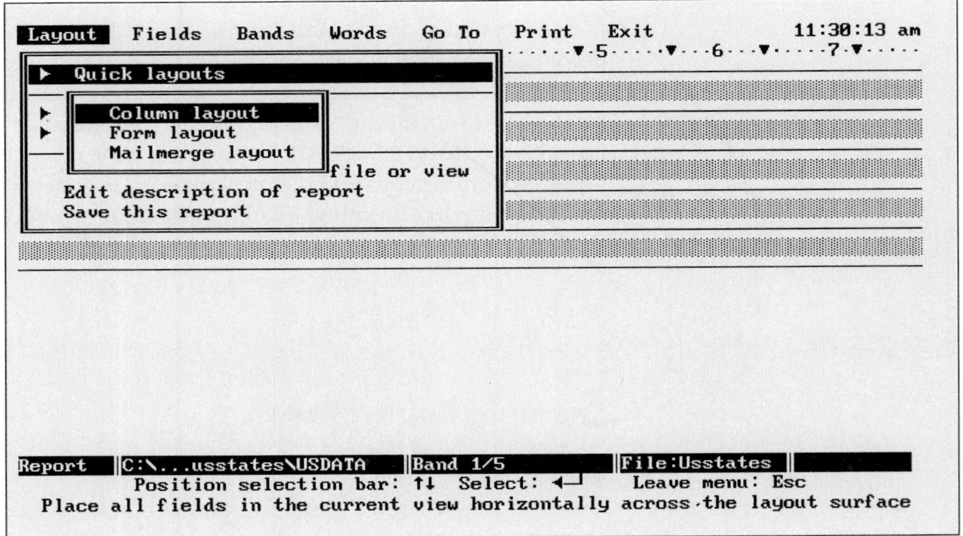

(b) Layout Menu

As we have already indicated, all reports are divided into report bands. Look again at Figure 4.9a, observing that five different bands are shown. Move the **up** and **down arrow** keys and see how the different bands are highlighted as the cursor position changes. That's all you need to know, because report forms are constructed simply by moving to the appropriate band and entering the desired information in the correct location.

STEP 3 **Pull-down menus**

Press the **Alt** key, and while holding the **Alt** key down, press the letter **L** to pull down the layout menu. (We subsequently use the notation **Alt+L** to indicate that the two keys must be pressed together.)

Use the **up** and **down arrow** keys to highlight *Quick layouts,* then press the **enter** key to produce the menu in Figure 4.9b. Highlight *Column layout* and press

FIGURE 4.9
Creating a Report Form through Quick Layout (continued)

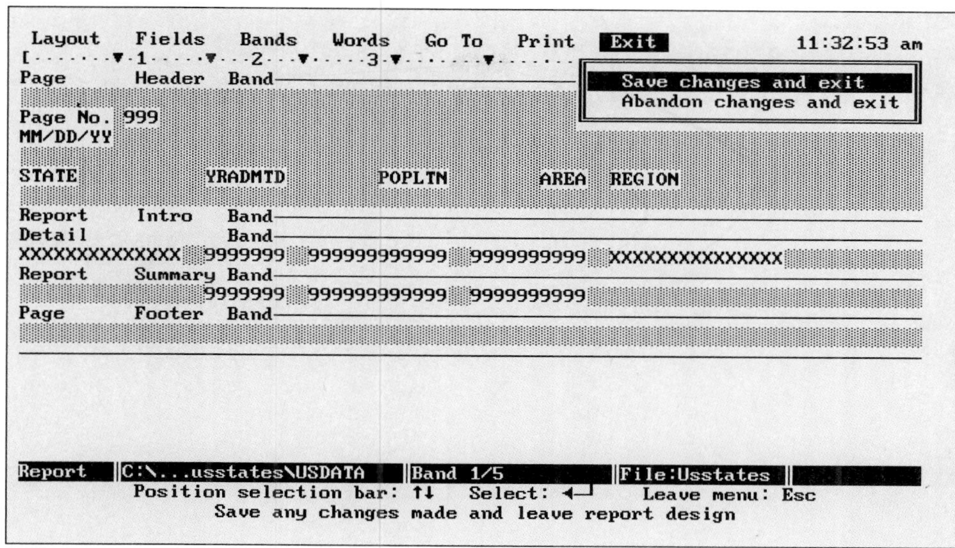

(c) Default Format and Exit Menu

return to produce Figure 4.9c. The design process is finished! i.e., you have created your first report form.

STEP 4 **The Exit menu**

Press **Alt+E** to pull down the exit menu. Highlight *Save changes and exit* and press **return** to exit to the dot prompt. Type **REPORT FORM USDATA TO PRINTER** to recreate the report of Figure 4.8a. Easy, wasn't it?

STEP 5 **Modify the report form**

The report in Figure 4.8a is improved significantly through changes shown in Figure 4.8b, and the remainder of this exercise is aimed at achieving that result. Type **MODIFY REPORT USDATA** to retrieve the USDATA report form just created, and begin the modification process.

Position the cursor within the page header band and add the heading line **United States Statistical Data**. Add the remaining lines in similar fashion, using the revised column titles shown in Figure 4.8b, and the insertion or replacement mode as appropriate. Stay in the page header band and move the cursor to any existing line you wish to remove, e.g., the line containing the page number or date. Press **Alt+W** to pull down the words menu of Figure 4.10a, highlight the *Remove line* option, then press **return** to remove the line. Delete the other lines from the original heading in similar fashion.

STEP 6 **Save the report and continue editing**

You are well advised to save changes continually as they are made successfully during the modification process; accordingly, press **Alt+L** to pull down the layout menu, highlight the *Save this report* option, and press **return**.

STEP 7 **Change the field templates**

The next several changes alter the appearance of fields within the detail band. Move the cursor to the POPLTN field in the detail band, then press **Alt+F** to pull down the

FIGURE 4.10
Modifying a Report Form

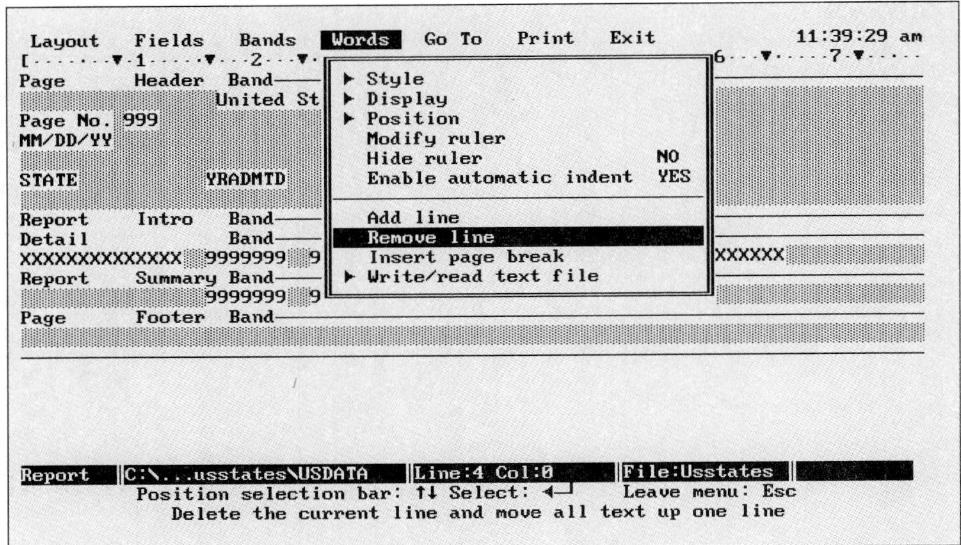

(a) The Words Menu

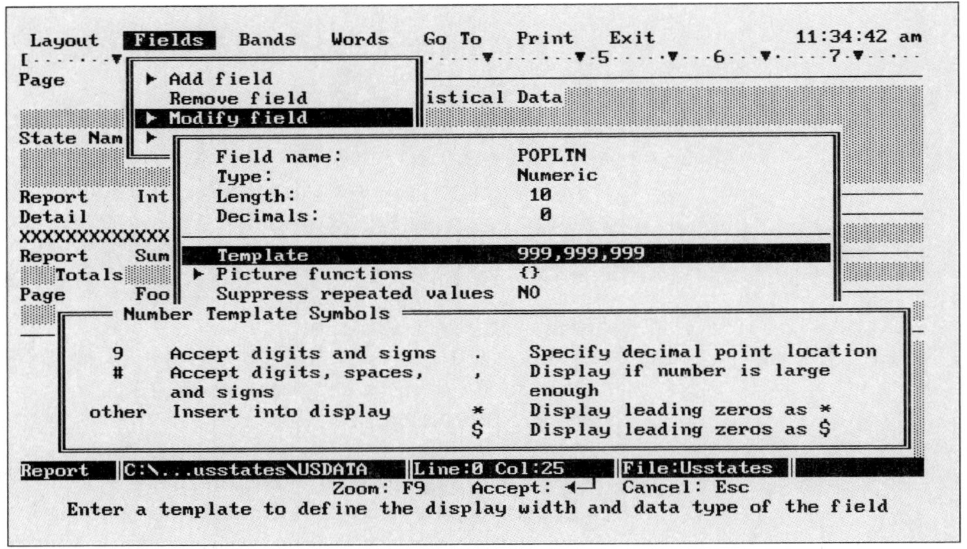

(b) Editing a Template

fields menu. Highlight the *Modify field* option and press **return**, then highlight the *Template* option and press **return** once more. Change the template to include commas as shown in Figure 4.10b, then press **return** when you are finished. Press **Ctrl+End** to accept the changes. Modify the templates of other fields (including those in the report summary band) that require similar editing. Press **Alt+L** to pull down the layout menu to save the report form.

STEP 8 **Deleting a field**

Move the cursor to the **YRADMTD** total in the report summary band, then press the **Del** key to remove this total from the report. Press **Alt+L** to pull down the layout menu to save the report form.

FIGURE 4.10
Modifying a Report Form (continued)

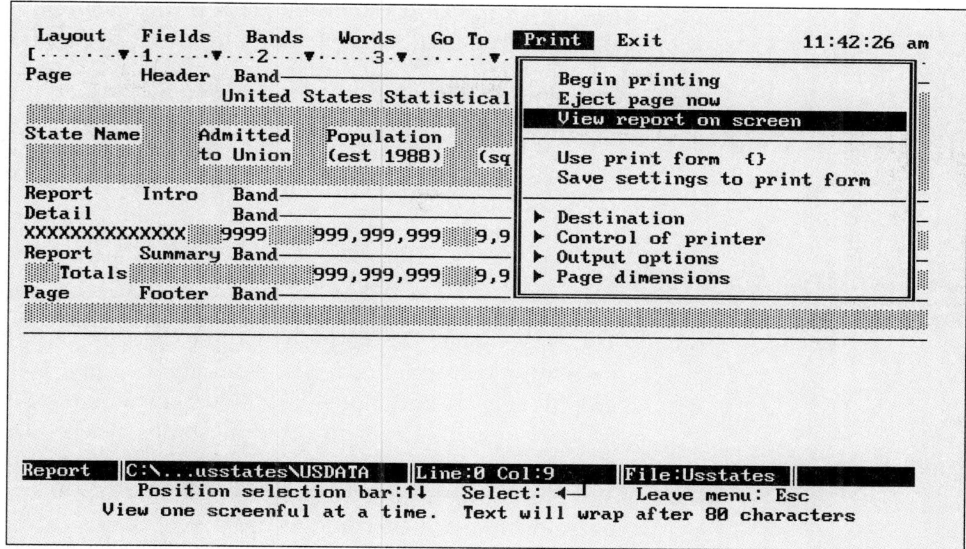

(c) The Print Menu

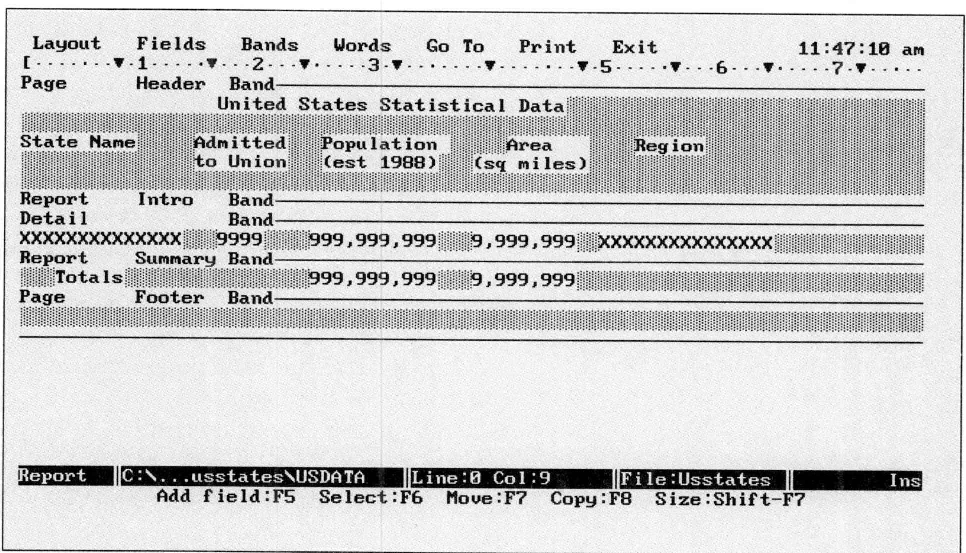

(d) The Finished Report Form

STEP 9 **View the report**

Press **Alt+P** to pull down the print menu, highlight *View report on screen,* and press **return**. The report should match the one in Figure 4.8b, in which case you can select the *Begin printing* option to print from within the report generator. More than likely, however, you will have to make additional corrections according to the steps just described. When you are finished making corrections, and are satisfied with the finished report, press **Alt+E** to pull down the exit menu, highlight *Save changes and exit,* and press **return**.

STEP 10 **Printing from the dot prompt**

You can print a report from the dot prompt in lieu of printing from the print menu; e.g., type **REPORT FORM USDATA TO PRINTER** to print the finished report. Remember, too, you can use the same report form with different indexes; e.g., you can list states by year of admission, rather than alphabetically, with these commands:

```
.SET ORDER TO TAG YRADMTD
.REPORT FORM USDATA TO PRINTER
```

Obtaining Subtotals

The United States is often divided into sections according to history, geography, or for simple convenience for studying the country. Figure 4.11 lists the states by geographic region, and alphabetically within region, with summary statistics computed for each region. The figure also illustrates a new capability of the report generator, namely, to group records and produce subtotals or averages.

As we have already indicated, reports are created through the report generator by specifying the contents of the report bands that appear at various places in the report. It helps, therefore, to view Figure 4.11 in terms of the report bands it contains, and further how these bands differ from those that appeared in the report of Figure 4.8b. Accordingly, note the following characteristics of Figure 4.11:

1. States are listed by region, and alphabetically within region; they were listed in strict alphabetical order in Figure 4.8b.
2. A modified page header band includes a page number and the date of execution; the column headings have been changed to reflect the density field of the detail band.
3. A new ***group intro band*** appears *before* the first state in each region; the band contains a double line, followed by the name of the region.
4. A modified detail band includes a new field, density, obtained by dividing population by area, which calculates the number of people per square mile. Note, too, that the region field has been deleted from the detail band.
5. A new ***group summary band*** appears *after* the last state in each region; the band contains the total population and area for the region, and the average density for the region.
6. A modified report summary band includes the *average* density for the entire country.

The final hands-on exercise uses the **USDATA** report form as the basis for the report of Figure 4.11. At the same time, the **USDATA** report form is useful in its own right and should be kept permanently. The exercise begins, therefore, by copying **USDATA.FRM** to a second file (**REGION.FRM**), which is modified in the exercise.

HANDS-ON EXERCISE 3

Report Bands

Objective

Change the appearance of a report by modifying the various bands within an existing report form; introduce subtotals into a report.

STEP 1 **Copy the existing USDATA report form**

The DOS **COPY** command is the normal way of copying a file; however, since you are already in dBASE, it is easier to use the dBASE **RUN** command that provides access to

Page header band

Group intro band

Detail band

Group summary band

```
Page   1                                                Date: 03/14/91

              United States Statistical Data by Region

State Name      Admitted   Population      Area        Density
                to Union   (est 1988)   (sq miles)  (people/sq mi)

===================================================================
Middle Atlantic
  Delaware         1787       660,000       2,057       320.86
  Maryland         1788     4,622,000      10,577       436.99
  New Jersey       1787     7,721,000       7,836       985.32
  New York         1788    17,909,000      49,576       361.24
  Pennsylvania     1787    12,001,000      45,333       264.73
   Totals/Averages         42,913,000     115,379       473.83

===================================================================
Mountain
  Arizona          1912     3,489,000     113,909        30.63
  Colorado         1876     3,301,000     104,247        31.67
  Idaho            1890     1,003,000      83,557        12.00
  Montana          1889       805,000     147,138         5.47
  Nevada           1864     1,054,000     110,540         9.54
  New Mexico       1912     1,507,000     121,666        12.39
  Utah             1896     1,690,000      84,916        19.90
  Wyoming          1890       479,000      97,914         4.89
   Totals/Averages         13,328,000     863,887        15.81

===================================================================
New England
  Connecticut      1788     3,233,000       5,009       645.44
  Maine            1820     1,205,000      33,215        36.28
  Massachusetts    1788     5,889,000       8,257       713.21
  New Hampshire    1788     1,085,000       9,304       116.62
  Rhode Island     1790       993,000       1,214       817.96
  Vermont          1791       557,000       9,609        57.97
   Totals/Averages         12,962,000      66,608       397.91

===================================================================
North Central
  Illinois         1818    11,614,000      56,400       205.92
  Indiana          1816     5,556,000      36,291       153.10
  Iowa             1846     2,834,000      56,290        50.35
  Kansas           1861     2,495,000      82,264        30.33
  Michigan         1837     9,240,000      58,216       158.72
  Minnesota        1858     4,307,000      84,068        51.23
  Missouri         1821     5,141,000      69,686        73.77
  Nebraska         1867     1,602,000      77,227        20.74
  North Dakota     1889       667,000      70,665         9.44
  Ohio             1803    10,855,000      41,222       263.33
  South Dakota     1889       713,000      77,047         9.25
  Wisconsin        1848     4,855,000      56,154        86.46
   Totals/Averages         59,879,000     765,530        92.72
```

FIGURE 4.11
Modified Report (statistics by region)

DOS and enables you to execute any DOS command. Be sure you are at the dot prompt, then type the command **`RUN COPY USDATA.FRM REGION.FRM`** to duplicate the existing `USDATA.FRM` file.

STEP 2 **Establish the master index**

The report of Figure 4.11 groups states by region, and alphabetically within region. Although we are not yet ready to produce the report (we haven't even begun to mod-

```
Page    2                                           Date: 03/14/91

            United States Statistical Data by Region

State Name      Admitted     Population       Area        Density
                to Union     (est 1988)    (sq miles)  (people/sq mi)

==================================================================
Pacific
  Alaska             1959        524,000      589,757         0.89
  California         1850     28,314,000      158,693       178.42
  Hawaii             1959      1,098,000        6,450       170.23
  Oregon             1859      2,767,000       96,981        28.53
  Washington         1889      4,648,000       68,192        68.16
   Totals/Averages            37,351,000      920,073        89.25

==================================================================
South Atlantic
  Florida            1845     12,335,000       58,560       210.64
  Georgia            1788      6,342,105       58,876       107.72
  North Carolina     1789      6,489,000       52,586       123.40
  South Carolina     1788      3,470,000       31,055       111.74
  Virginia           1788      6,015,000       40,817       147.37
  West Virginia      1863      1,876,000       24,181        77.58
   Totals/Averages            36,527,105      266,075       129.74

==================================================================
South Central
  Alabama            1819      4,102,000       51,609        79.48
  Arkansas           1836      2,395,000       53,104        45.10
  Kentucky           1792      3,727,000       40,395        92.26
  Louisiana          1812      4,408,000       48,523        90.84
  Mississippi        1817      2,620,000       47,716        54.91
  Oklahoma           1907      3,242,000       69,919        46.37
  Tennessee          1796      4,895,000       42,244       115.87
  Texas              1845     16,841,000      267,338        63.00
   Totals/Averages            42,230,000      620,848        73.48

   Totals/Averages           245,190,105    3,618,400       156.16
```


FIGURE 4.11
Modified Report (statistics by region) (continued)

ify the report form), we suggest you select the index now, so that you don't forget to do it later. Type **SET ORDER TO TAG REGION** to select the appropriate master index.

Type **MODIFY REPORT REGION** to enter the report generator and create the necessary report form.

STEP 3 **Modify the page header band**

Place the cursor within the page header band at the extreme left of the first line and type the word **Page**, followed by a space. Press **Alt+F** to pull down the fields menu, select *Add a field,* highlight the predefined *pageno* field as shown in Figure 4.12a, press **return**, and finally press **Ctrl+End** to accept this field.

Move the cursor to the extreme right of this line, type **Date:** followed by a space, pull down the fields menu once again, and add the predefined *date* field. Modify the title on the next line to include the words **by Region** at the end of the line. Move to the line containing the column headings, add an appropriate heading for the density field, and remove the heading for the region field. Pull down the layout menu (**Alt+L**) to save your work to this point.

FIGURE 4.12
Creating a Report Form/II

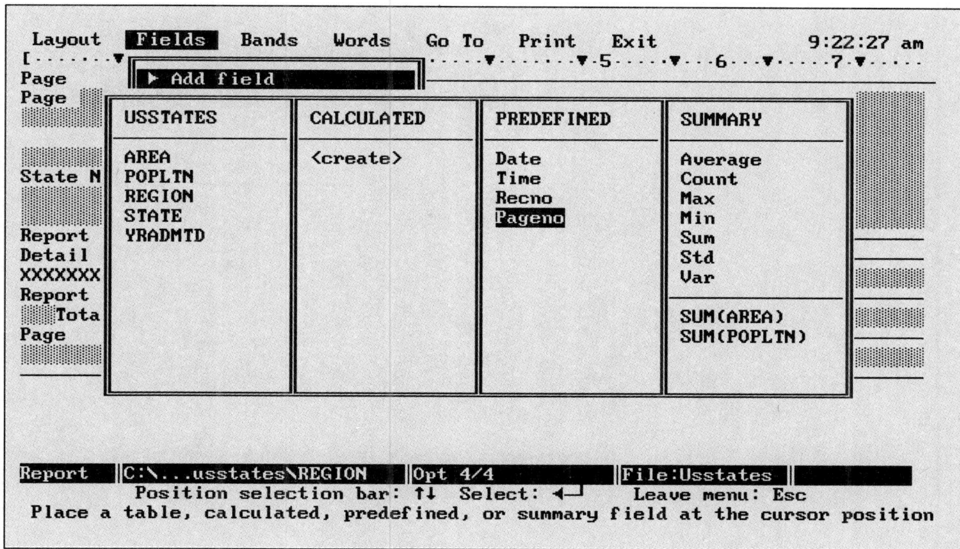

(a) Adding a Predefined Field (in page header band)

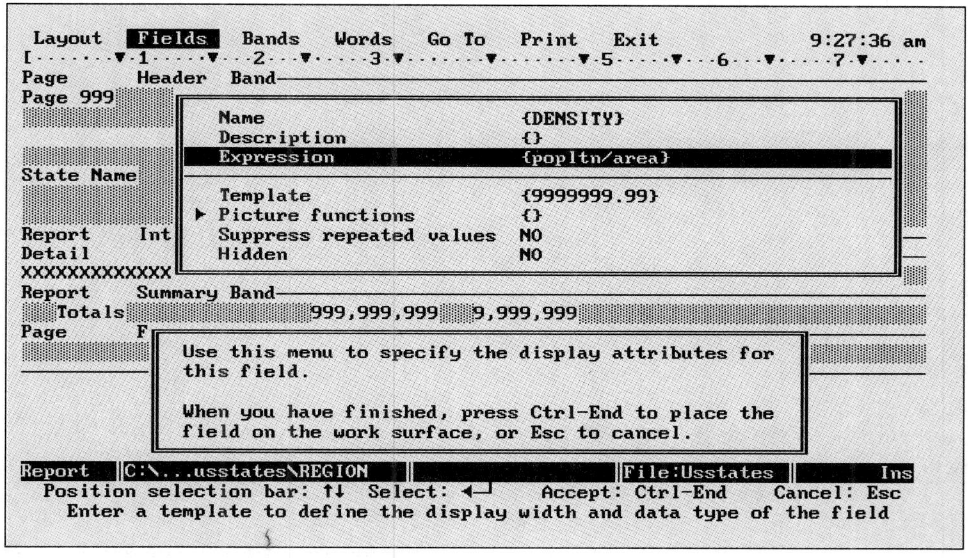

(b) Adding a Calculated Field (in detail band)

STEP 4 **Modify the detail band**

Move to the detail band, then position the cursor on the region field (which appears as a series of X's) within the detail band. Press the **Del** key to delete this field from the existing report.

Press **Alt+F** to pull down the fields menu, select *Add a field,* highlight *<create>,* and press **return** to add the density field as shown in Figure 4.12b. Use the **up** and **down arrow** keys to highlight *Name* and press **return**, then type **DENSITY** as the field name. Use the cursor keys once again to highlight *Expression,* press **return**, then type **POPLTN/AREA** as the expression used to compute density. Press **Ctrl+End** to exit this operation.

FIGURE 4.12
Creating a Report Form/II (continued)

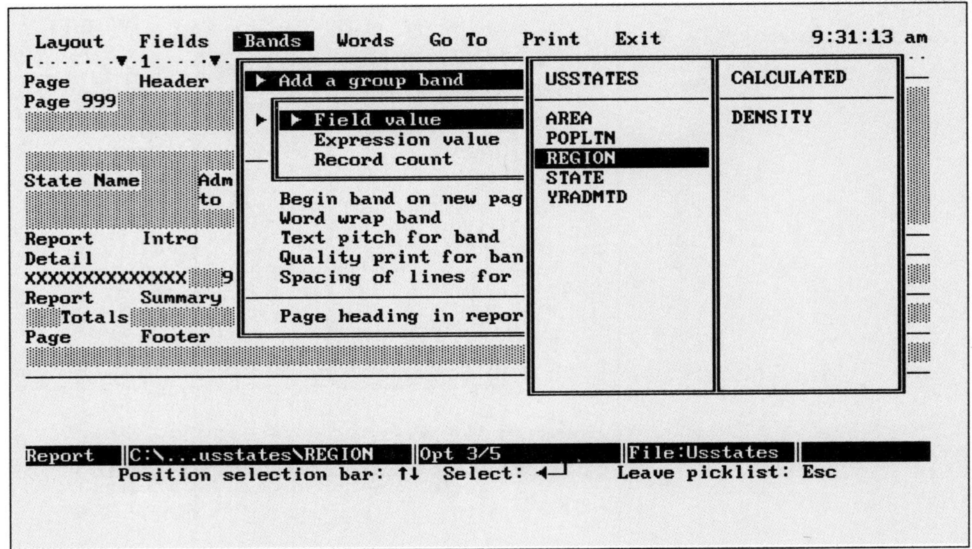

(c) Adding a Group

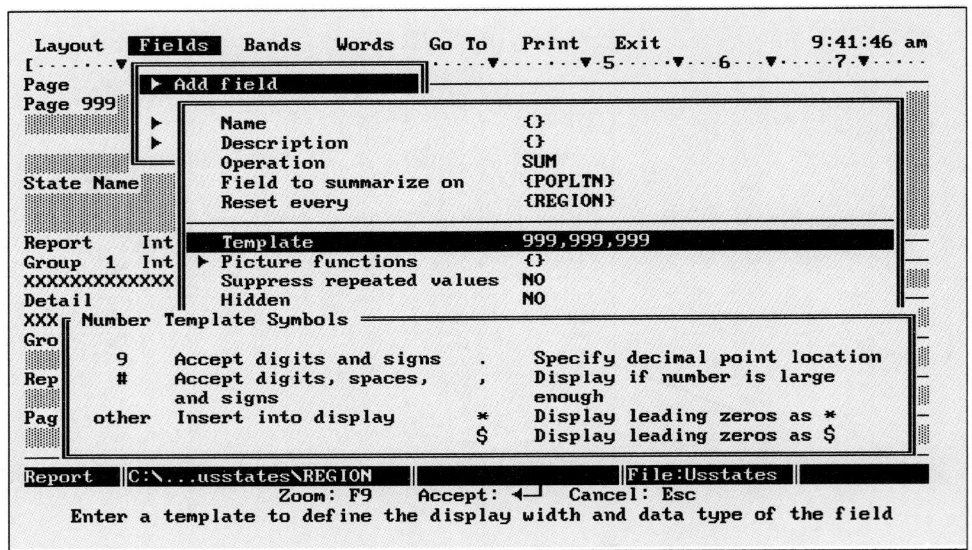

(d) Adding a Field (group summary band)

STEP 5 **Add a Group**

Move the cursor to the report intro band, press **`Alt+B`** to pull down the bands menu of Figure 4.12c, highlight *Add a group band,* and press **`return`**. Highlight *Field value* and press **`return`**, then highlight `REGION` and press **`return`** once more.

STEP 6 **Define the group intro band**

Place the cursor at the extreme left of the first line of the group intro band. Press **`Alt+F`** to pull down the fields menu, select *Add a field,* highlight the `REGION` field and press **`return`**, and then press **`Ctrl+End`** to accept the new field. Check your progress by viewing the report on the screen from the print menu (press **`Alt+P`** to pull down the print menu, then select the view option).

FIGURE 4.12
Creating a Report Form/II (continued)

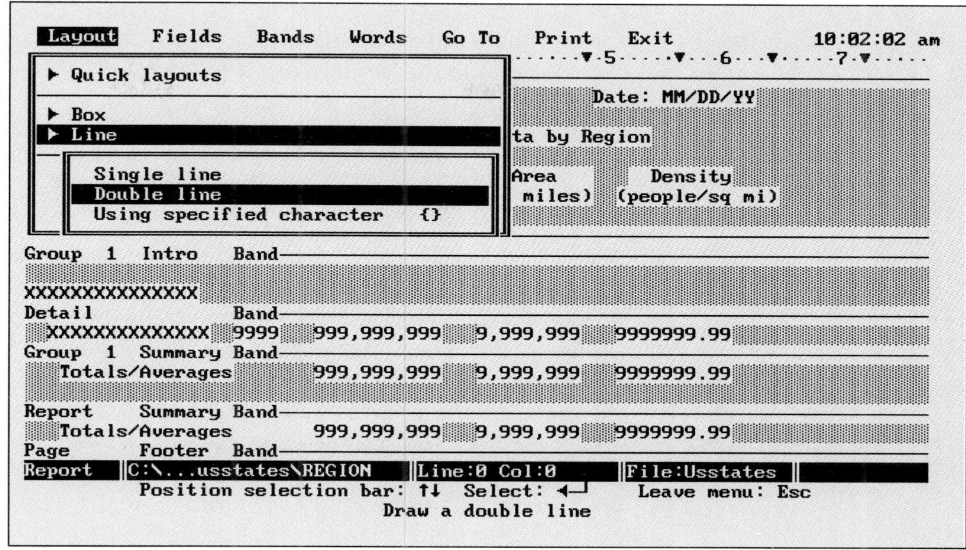

(e) Creating a Double Line

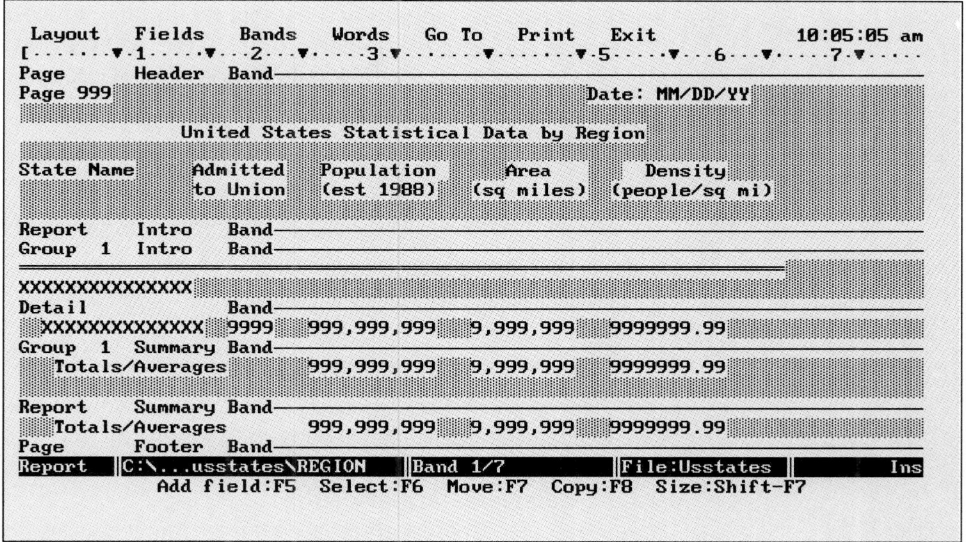

(f) Completed Report Form

States should be listed by region and alphabetically within region (if this is not the case, complete steps 7 and 8, then return to step two to select the appropriate index). Pull down the layout menu (**Alt+L**) to save your work to this point.

STEP 7 **Define the group summary band**

Move to the group summary band under the existing population column. Press **Alt+F** to pull down the fields menu and select *Add a field.* Move the cursor to the **SUMMARY** column, select *Sum* as the operation, then (at the next menu) select **POPLTN** as the *field to summarize on* (see Figure 4.12d). Highlight *Template,* modify the template as indicated in the figure, and press **Ctrl+End** to accept the changes. Note, too, how the summation is automatically reset on **REGION**; i.e., dBASE computes the total population for all states in a given region, then sets the total back to zero when the region changes.

Remain in the group summary band and add a similar summation field under area. Then perform a parallel series of operations for the density field except select **AVERAGE** rather than **SUM** as the indicated operation. View and/or save the report as you see fit.

STEP 8 **Add a line to the group intro band**
Return to the group intro band, placing the cursor at the extreme left of the line. Press **return** to add a blank line to this band, move the cursor to the blank line, then press **Alt+L** to pull down the layout menu. Highlight the *Line* option and press **return** to bring up the menu of Figure 4.12e. Highlight the *Double line* option and press **return** once more. Move the cursor to the beginning of the blank line and press **return**, use the arrow keys to draw the line, and press **return** when you reach the end of the line. The completed report form should match Figure 4.12f.

Save your work, then view the finished report through the print menu. Ideally, your report will match Figure 4.11, but more than likely it will not be an exact duplicate of our report. Compare your completed report form to Figure 4.12f and make any necessary changes.

STEP 9 **Produce hard copy of the finished report**
Press **Alt+E** to pull down the exit menu, highlight *Save changes and exit,* and press **return** to exit to the dot prompt. Type **REPORT FORM REGION TO PRINTER** to obtain hard copy of the finished report. Congratulations on a job well done!

STEP 10 **Exit dBASE**
Type **QUIT** to exit dBASE.

Summary

The ***information*** produced by a system is only as good as the quality of the ***data*** on which it is based. Data is converted to information through calculation, selection, and sequencing. Reports produced by a computer should be examined critically rather than accepted on blind faith.

The dBASE ***report generator*** creates a ***report form*** through the **CREATE** and/or **MODIFY REPORT** commands. The ***quick-layout*** menu is the fastest way to produce a report form, but more polished reports can be developed through ***pull-down menus*** within the report generator. Individual menus are accessed by pressing the **Alt** key and the first letter of the menu; e.g., **Alt+L** activates the layout menu.

The **REPORT FORM** command presents data from a **DBF** file in sequence according to the master index, and in the format described in the designated report form (**FRM**) file. Multiple report forms, each of which can be used with multiple indexes, can be associated with a single **DBF** file.

The **NEXT** clause in the **REPORT FORM** command limits the records that appear in the designated report to a specific number; the **FOR** clause includes an indeterminate number of records that meet a given criterion.

The **TO PRINTER** clause in the **REPORT FORM** command directs output to the printer; it is often followed by an **EJECT** command, which issues a form feed to the printer. The **HEADING** parameter enables the same report form to create multiple reports with different titles.

A report form contains one or more ***report bands,*** each of which appears at a designated time in the report generation processes. Seven different types of bands are possible (***page header*** and ***page footer, report intro*** and ***report summary, group intro*** and ***group summary,*** and ***detail***).

Key Words and Concepts

`Alt` key	Information	Report form
Bands menu	Layout menu	`REPORT FORM`
`CREATE REPORT`	`MODIFY REPORT`	Report generator
Data	`NOEJECT`	Record pointer
Detail band	Page footer band	Report intro band
Exit menu	Page header band	Report summary band
Fields menu	`PLAIN`	`SET ORDER TO`
`GO TOP`	Print menu	`SUMMARY`
Group intro band	Pull-down menus	`TO PRINTER`
Group summary band	Quick-layout	`TO FILE`
`HEADING`	Report band	Words menu

True/False

1. Data and information are synonymous.
2. The `SET ORDER` command always positions the record pointer to the top of the file.
3. Multiple report forms can be associated with a single `DBF` file.
4. A report form cannot be modified after it has been created.
5. A sophisticated data management system will produce correct reports from invalid data.
6. The output of the `REPORT FORM` command can be directed to the monitor, printer, or a file.
7. The order in which records appear in a given report is most likely immaterial.
8. The `REPORT FORM` command must include every record in the associated `DBF` file.
9. The `REPORT FORM` command cannot be used in conjunction with an index file.
10. The syntax of the `REPORT FORM` command contains several optional parameters.
11. If a given report contains a page intro band, then it must contain a page footer band.
12. Every report must contain every type of report band.
13. The total(s) displayed in a group summary band are normally reset only at the end of the report.

Exercises

1. Distinguish between:
   (a) A group intro band and a group summary band
   (b) The files `AREA.FRM`, `POPLTN.FRM`, and `DENSITY.FRM`
   (c) The save option in the layout menu versus the save option in the exit menu
   (d) The commands, `CREATE REPORT` and `MODIFY REPORT`
   (e) The commands, `HELP` and `HELP REPORT`

FIGURE 4.13
Reports for Problem 2

State Name	Population (est 1988)	Area (sq miles)	Density (pop'n/area)
New Jersey	7,721,000	7,836	985.32
Rhode Island	993,000	1,214	817.96
Massachusetts	5,889,000	8,257	713.21
Connecticut	3,233,000	5,009	645.44
Maryland	4,622,000	10,577	436.99
New York	17,909,000	49,576	361.24
Delaware	660,000	2,057	320.86
Pennsylvania	12,001,000	45,333	264.73
Ohio	10,855,000	41,222	263.33
Texas	16,841,000	67,338	250.10

(a) First Erroneous Report

State Name	Population (est 1988)	Area (sq miles)	Density (pop'n/area)
Alaska	524,000	589,757	0.89
Wyoming	479,000	97,914	4.89
Montana	805,000	147,138	5.47
South Dakota	713,000	77,047	9.25
North Dakota	667,000	70,665	9.44
Nevada	1,054,000	110,540	9.54
Idaho	1,003,000	83,557	12.00
New Mexico	1,507,000	121,666	12.39
Utah	1,690,000	84,916	19.90
Nebraska	1,602,000	77,227	20.74

(b) Second Erroneous Report

State Name	Population (est 1988)	Area (sq miles)	Density (pop'n/area)
New Jersey	7,721,000	7,836	985.32
Rhode Island	993,000	1,214	817.96
Massachusetts	5,889,000	8,257	713.21
Connecticut	3,233,000	5,009	645.44
Maryland	4,622,000	10,577	436.99
New York	17,909,000	49,576	361.24
Delaware	660,000	2,057	320.86
Pennsylvania	12,001,000	45,333	264.73
Ohio	10,855,000	41,222	263.33
Florida	12,335,000	58,560	210.64
Totals	76,218,000	229,641	5019.72

(c) Third Erroneous Report

2. Figure 4.13 contains three erroneous attempts at a report listing the ten states with highest population density. Identify the error in each report and the likely cause of the mistake.

3. Identify the error in each series of commands that prevents the report from successfully listing the ten smallest states. (Assume that each command is entered on a single line.)

   (a)
   ```
   USE USSTATES
   REPORT FORM AREA HEADING 'The 10 Smallest States'
   ```
   (b)
   ```
   USE USSTATES ORDER AREA
   REPORT FORM AREA NEXT 10 SUMMARY HEADING 'The 10
   Smallest States'
   ```

FIGURE 4.14
Reports for Problem 4

```
State Name     Admitted  Population     Area         Density
               to Union  (est 1988)  (sq miles) (people/sq mi)
=============================================================
Middle Atlantic
  Delaware        1787      660,000       2,057        320.86
  Maryland        1788    4,622,000      10,577        436.99
  New Jersey      1787    7,721,000       7,836        985.32
  New York        1788   17,909,000      49,576        361.24
  Pennsylvania    1787   12,001,000      45,333        264.73
   Totals/Averages       42,913,000     115,379        473.83
=============================================================
Mountain
  Arizona         1912    3,489,000     113,909         30.63
  Colorado        1876    3,301,000     104,247         31.67
  Idaho           1890    1,003,000      83,557         12.00
  Montana         1889      805,000     147,138          5.47
  Nevada          1864    1,054,000     110,540          9.54
  New Mexico      1912    1,507,000     121,666         12.39
  Utah            1896    1,690,000      84,916         19.90
  Wyoming         1890      479,000      97,914          4.89
   Totals/Averages       56,241,000     979,266        191.97
  .
   .
    .
```

(a) First Erroneous Report

```
State Name     Admitted  Population     Area         Density
               to Union  (est 1988)  (sq miles) (people/sq mi)
=============================================================
South Central
  Alabama         1819    4,102,000      51,609         79.48
   Totals/Averages        4,102,000      51,609         79.48
=============================================================
Pacific
  Alaska          1959      524,000     589,757          0.89
   Totals/Averages          524,000     589,757          0.89
=============================================================
Mountain
  Arizona         1912    3,489,000     113,909         30.63
   Totals/Averages          3,489,000     113,909         30.63
  .
   .
    .
```

(b) Second Erroneous Report

(c) **USE USSTATES ORDER AREA**
REPORT FORM AREA NEXT 10 NOEJECT HEADING 'The 10 Largest States'

(d) **USE USSTATES ORDER AREA**
REPORT FORM AREA NEXT 10 HEADING The 10 Smallest States

(e) **USE USSTATES ORDER AREA**
REPORT FORM AREA FOR AREA < 40000 HEADING '10 Smallest States'

4. Figure 4.14 contains two erroneous attempts to produce statistical data by region. Identify the error in each report.

5. Use the existing report forms on the data disk (**AREA.FRM**, **YRADMTD.FRM**, **POPLTN.FRM**, and **DENSITY.FRM**) in conjunction with the **USSTATES.DBF** and **USSTATES.MDX** files to produce the reports listed below. Use the **HEADING**

FIGURE 4.15
Screens for Problem 8

```
 Soc Security Number   Last Name       Salary       Title

Location:  Boston
     400-00-0000       Cordell        $27,200    Account Rep
     100-00-0000       Davis          $34,000    Account Rep
     777-77-7777       Ticich         $27,000    Account Rep
     600-00-0000       Tillberg       $35,500    Manager
                                      -------
       Location total               $ 123,700
.
  .
   .
Location:  Miami
     555-55-5555       Ferraro        $26,400    Account Rep
     200-00-0000       Friedel        $48,000    Manager
     666-66-6666       Grauer         $37,500    Account Rep
     999-99-9999       Hirschberg     $28,500    Account Rep
     300-00-0000       Kendrick       $26,500    Account Rep
     500-00-0000       Pattishall     $38,500    Account Rep
                                      -------
       Location total               $ 205,400

        Company total             $   553,750
```

(a) Report

```
 Layout   Fields   Bands   Words   Go To   Print   Exit            4:13:33 pm
[·······▼·1·····▼···2···▼·····3·▼·······▼·······▼·5·····▼···6···▼·····7·▼·····
Page        Header  Band
     Soc Security Number       Last Name         Salary          Title

Report      Intro   Band
Group  1    Intro   Band
Location:  XXXXXXXXX
Detail              Band
       999-99-9999          XXXXXXXXXXXX      $99,999    XXXXXXXXXXXXXXXXXXXX
Group  1    Summary Band

            Location total               $ 999,999

Report      Summary Band
            Company total               $    999,999
Page        Footer  Band
```

(b) Report Form (dBASE screen)

parameter of the **REPORT FORM** command to change the title of each report. Create any additional indexes as necessary.

(a) A list of states with area greater than 100,000 square miles in descending order of area
(b) An alphabetical list of states with population density less than 50 people per square mile
(c) An alphabetical list of states admitted to the union in the 20th century
(d) The last 10 states admitted to the union with the most recent state listed first

(e) A list of states with population greater than 10,000,000 in descending order of population

6. Which pull-down menu contains the command to do each of the following?
(a) View the report without printing it
(b) Save the report form and continue editing
(c) Save the report form and exit from the report generator
(d) Remove a line from the report
(e) Add a group to the report
(f) Create a report by using the quick-layout option
(g) Add a single line, double line, or box to the report
(h) Change the template of an existing field

7. Use the data on thirty-one arbitrarily chosen countries that was presented in Figure 3.16 to prepare the following reports:
(a) A list of the ten largest countries in terms of area in decreasing order of area; do not total the area for these countries
(b) A list of the ten largest countries in terms of population in decreasing order of population; compute the total population for the listed countries
(c) A list of the five countries with the highest population density in decreasing order of density
(d) A list of the five countries with the lowest population density in ascending order of density

8. (a) Identify the various report bands present in Figure 4.15; use the finished report in Figure 4.15a and/or the final report form in Figure 4.15b to indicate the precise contents of each report band.
(b) Create the **EMPLOYEE.FRM** file corresponding to Figure 4.15, then use it with the **EMPLOYEE.DBF** file (in Figure 2.12 in Chapter 2) to produce the finished report of Figure 4.15a.

CHAPTER

5 Mail Merge and Label Forms

OUTLINE

OBJECTIVES

After reading this chapter you will be able to:

1. Discuss elementary considerations of file design.
2. Differentiate between character, numeric, date, and logical fields as they are used within a file structure.
3. Create a set of mailing labels through the **CREATE (MODIFY) LABEL** and **LABEL FORM** commands.
4. Define mail merge; create a set of form letters through the **CREATE (MODIFY) REPORT** and **REPORT FORM** commands.
5. Describe several similarities associated with the procedure for creating mailing labels and form letters.

Overview

The creation of ***mailing labels*** is one of the easiest and most useful capabilities in dBASE IV, as you can create labels of almost any dimension and/or use them in unusual ways, e.g., as badges for a meeting or entries in a Rolodex. The material is presented within the context of a new case study, the Dade County Metro Zoo, which focuses on this powerful facility.

Mailing labels are created through the **CREATE (MODIFY) LABEL** and **LABEL FORM** commands, which parallel the commands for report forms introduced in the previous chapter. As you shall see, there are many similarities and overlapping menus between report forms and mailing labels, and thus coverage of one topic implicitly reviews the other. Indeed, we return to the report generator to cover its ***mail merge*** facility, which enables you to prepare the associated ***form letters*** for which the mailing labels are intended.

Although the emphasis of the chapter is on the concept of a mail merge operation, the case solution raises several issues about the ***file design.*** We discuss which fields should (and should not) be included, as well as considerations of ***field type*** and ***field size.*** We begin with the case presentation.

CASE PREVIEW

The case you are about to read is centered on the development of a fund-raising system for the Dade County Metro Zoo. Karen Jackson, the recently appointed Director of Special Programs, is given the task of building a mailing list, soliciting donations, and monitoring contributions as they are received. Solution of the case requires the preparation of form letters to solicit donations, the generation of mailing labels to use in conjunction with the form letters, and an analysis of contributions as they come in. You will see that Ms. Jackson is interested in knowing the average contribution, the number of people contributing, and so on.

As you read the case, try to determine precisely what information is required from the system, and what data inputs are necessary to generate that information. Since our solution begins with the design of the file structure, we suggest that you develop your own file structure prior to viewing ours. Think carefully about which fields to include, and what the ***field size*** and ***data type*** should be for each field included in the file structure.

CASE STUDY
The Dade County Metro Zoo[1]

Karen Jackson was feeling very good about her new position as Director of Special Programs for the Dade County Metro Zoo, one of the most popular and exciting attractions in South Florida. Already she had wonderful plans for week-long summer camps for elementary and junior high students, picnic dinners under the stars, special seminars, and so on. She realized, however, that those functions would have to wait until there were sufficient funds to finance them. The opening of the most recent exhibits had met a cost overrun, and there was little money left for new programs.

Karen settled quickly into one of her primary functions, the grim reality of fund raising, and was determined to make

[1] Although the case study is based on the Dade County Metro Zoo in Dade County, Florida, it is in fact a simplification of programs that actually exist. Ms. Jackson and Mr. Marder are products of the authors' imagination.

her first project a very successful one. She knew she needed a clever basis for the appeal and was stuck for two days, until the idea of an "Adopt an Animal" campaign popped into her mind during her daily five-mile run through the zoo's nature trail. She would solicit contributions on three levels: $25 for a reptile, $50 for a bird, and $100 for a mammal. Adopting "parents" would receive a personalized adoption certificate, a picture of their animal, and educational information about the zoo. Karen also thought of using the guest book, maintained at the zoo entrance, as the source for a mailing list. She hoped that those persons who had already visited the zoo would be as excited as she about the zoo's potential.

Feeling good about her proposal, she approached Mr. Marder, the Zoo Director. He gave her an enthusiastic approval, but cautioned her about the need to maintain accurate records. Luckily, Karen had been exposed to application software as an undergraduate business major, and to dBASE IV in particular. The Zoo provided access to an IBM PC, and she knew that it, along with dBASE IV, would be an invaluable tool in organizing and producing the information she needed to follow the progress of the fund-raising campaign.

Karen had already determined that her first task would be to generate a series of form letters and associated mailing labels to use in conjunction with her appeal. She recognized the need to update her records to reflect contributions as they were received, and to prepare reports reflecting the source and amount of the donations. She also wanted the system to be capable of future mailings, and hence wanted to record the date on which a donation was received. Karen took out a yellow legal pad, and in organized fashion, began to list the reports she wanted:

1. A set of personalized letters to potential donors soliciting donations and a set of mailing labels to accompany these letters.
2. A set of personalized thank-you notes to individuals who contributed to the campaign and a set of mailing labels to accompany the thank-you notes; a list of people who contributed but who had not yet been sent thank-you notes.
3. A master list (in alphabetical order) of people who contributed to the campaign. Also summary information on the total amount of money raised, the number of people who contributed, and the amount of the average contribution.

CASE SOLUTION

We begin our solution with a detailed discussion of the file structure, the first consideration of which is to reconcile the available input with the desired output. *You must be absolutely certain that the data entered into a system is sufficient to provide all necessary information,* else the system is almost guaranteed to fail.

Unfortunately, the design of the file structure is often taken for granted, and consequently is done quickly and poorly. We have seen too many instances of clients requesting additional reports only to be told that extensive (and expensive) programming changes would be necessary, or worse, that the system contained insufficient data to enable the modification they requested. Accordingly, *we cannot overemphasize the need for careful design of the file structure.*

Designing the File Structure

Figure 5.1 contains our suggested file structure, which may or may not correspond to what you envisioned as you read the case. Indeed, whether or not our solutions are the same is not really important, as there are many satisfactory answers. What is essential, however, is that the structure that is chosen contain all necessary data so that the required reports can be generated.

Suffice it to say that there are many acceptable solutions, and that there is no single right or wrong answer. Nevertheless, *the design of a file structure is the most important step in the development of a system,* and consequently we will discuss it at length. Figure 5.1 may seem obvious upon presentation, but it does reflect the results of many decisions, all of which affect the eventual success of a system. These decisions encompass:

1. The fields to be included
2. The size of each field

FIGURE 5.1
Suggested File Structure

```
Structure for database: C:\DATADISK\ZOO\ZOO.DBF [1]
Number of data records:        16
Date of last update    : 04/01/91
Field  Field Name   Type         Width       Dec      Index
    1  LASTNAME     Character       16                    N
    2  FIRSTNAME    Character       12                    N
    3  PREFIX       Character        3                    N
    4  STREET       Character       24                    N
    5  CITY         Character       18                    N
    6  STATE        Character        2                    N
    7  ZIPCODE      Character        5                    N
    8  DONATION     Numeric          3                    N
    9  DONOR_DATE   Date             8                    N
   10  ADOPT        Character        1                    N
   11  THANK_YOU    Logical          1                    N
```

3. The data type of each field
4. The order of the fields within a record

Consider, for example, how these questions affect the most "obvious" of fields, a person's name. No one is likely to contest that a name field is necessary, and further that the system should include an individual's first and last name, as well as a prefix (e.g., Mr. or Ms.) for that name. It is less obvious what the size of the name field should be, and that the name should be divided into three separate fields as was done in Figure 5.1.

What would be wrong, for example, if name were treated as a single field (31 positions in all), consisting of the prefix, first name, and last name in that order? Consider the consequences of a single field (instead of the three in the figure), in light of the following names:

Dr. Joel Stutz
Mr. Philip Glassman
Ms. Helen Rumsch

Whether you realize it or not, the names are listed in alphabetical order (according to the design criteria of a single field), and therein lies the problem. In other words, when dBASE indexes records by name, it does so beginning with the *leftmost position* (i.e., the prefix), and hence the rather unusable sequence. It should be apparent, therefore, that last name requires its own field if the system is to list records alphabetically by last name.

Given the necessity of separating the last name, is anything further to be gained by treating the prefix as yet another field, as opposed to its being part of the first name? The answer is yes, in that the case description alludes to the need for both solicitation letters and thank-you notes. Perhaps we will use salutations in the form of "Dear Joel" or even the more formal "Dr. Stutz," both of which require that the prefix be separate from the first name. This may or may not happen, but it costs nothing at this point to opt for the separate fields.

Consider also what other decisions were made with respect to including (omitting) fields within the file structure of Figure 5.1. We use two lines for the address on our letters and labels (consisting of street on line one, and city, state, and zip code on line two) instead of three (omitting a line for company name). The shorter address

---

[1] The **ZOO.DBF** file has been created for you and exists on the data disk for use in subsequent Hands-on Exercises.

requires less storage and also simplifies programming for both report forms and mailing labels. It does, however, preclude the use of a business affiliation. Two lines were chosen in this instance only after examining the potential data and finding that residential addresses appeared exclusively.

Regardless of whether you go with two- or three-line addresses, zip code must be stored as a separate field, in order to be able to index on this field, and thereby take advantage of bulk mail (which requires presorting by zip code). The *length* of the zip code should not, however, be automatically set to five positions in every application, as some systems may require the newer zip + 4 designation. Five positions was deemed suitable in our system, given the preponderance of residential addresses.

The size of the first and last name fields is more arbitrary. Sixteen positions were specified for the last name, but 15 or 17 would have sufficed equally well. Does that mean that lengths of 12 or 24 positions are also acceptable? Probably not. Our experience has been that 12 is generally too small, and 24 too large; i.e., the allotted space should be large enough to contain the names in the file, but not so large as to continually waste space when shorter names are present. Accordingly, we have settled on a length of 16 positions and use that in virtually all of our systems.

Even with the specification of ***field type,*** things are not always as they seem. Zip code is designated as a ***character field*** rather than a ***numeric field,*** because arithmetic is never performed on zip code; i.e., the numeric data type is reserved for fields that are used in calculations, rather than for any field composed of digits. In similar fashion, a social security number (when called for) should also be specified as a character field.

The case description suggested that future (or repeated) mailings might be necessary, and hence a ***date field*** is included in the file structure. Knowing when a donation was received will ensure that individuals who do contribute will not be solicited too often (e.g., more than once a year).

The adoption field illustrates the use of a one-position ***code*** to designate the type of animal (`R`, `B`, and `M` for reptile, bird, and mammal, respectively), as opposed to spelling out the animal name. Use of coded, rather than expanded, values results in considerable savings of disk space, and also results in more efficient (and less error-prone) processing.

The final field in the file structure is an example of a ***logical field,*** i.e., a field with two possible values, true or false (which may be entered as `T`, `F`, `t`, `f`, `Y`, `N`, `y`, or `n`). The purpose of the field in our example is to indicate whether or not a thank-you note has been sent. Although a one-position character field would appear to satisfy this requirement equally well, dBASE processes logical fields more efficiently, and hence its use at this time.

The result of these deliberations has produced the file structure shown in Figure 5.1. As can be inferred from the discussion, there are no hard and fast rules for designing a file structure. The decisions that are made as to the fields needed, their sizes and types, reflect the needs of the present (and future) system, and are often subjective in nature. As you proceed through the text, you will be exposed to many different applications that help you develop the experience necessary to design your own systems.

The Mail-Merge Operation

A ***mail merge*** combines a ***form letter*** with a file of names and addresses to produce a series of personalized letters such as those shown in Figure 5.2. In essence, the process creates the "same" letter many times by merging the form letter with the data file, changing only the personalized information from letter to letter. The letters are

FIGURE 5.2
Form Letters

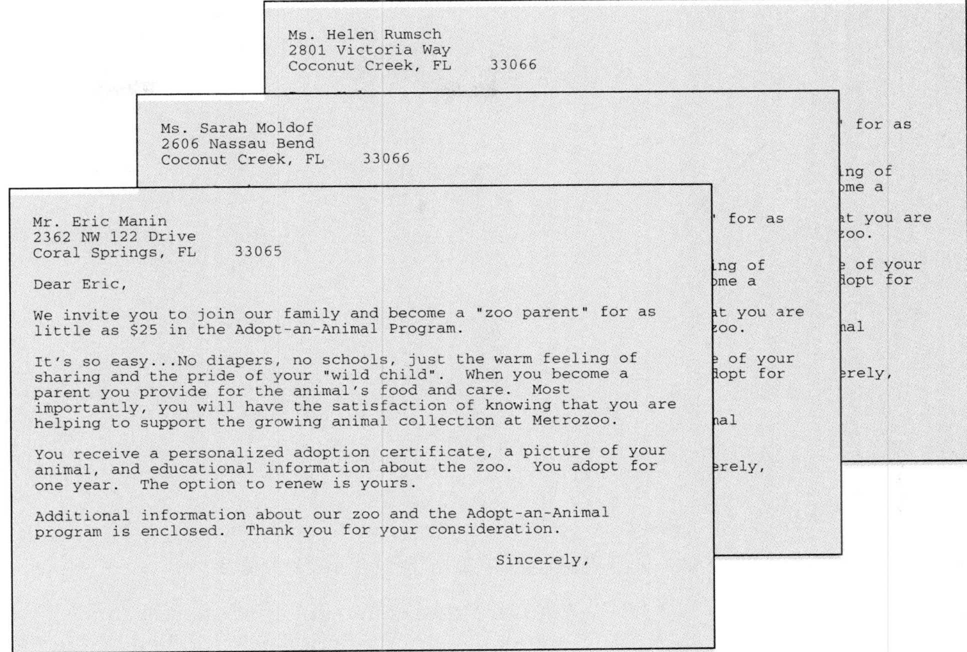

Ms. Helen Rumsch
2801 Victoria Way
Coconut Creek, FL 33066

Ms. Sarah Moldof
2606 Nassau Bend
Coconut Creek, FL 33066

Mr. Eric Manin
2362 NW 122 Drive
Coral Springs, FL 33065

Dear Eric,

We invite you to join our family and become a "zoo parent" for as little as $25 in the Adopt-an-Animal Program.

It's so easy...No diapers, no schools, just the warm feeling of sharing and the pride of your "wild child". When you become a parent you provide for the animal's food and care. Most importantly, you will have the satisfaction of knowing that you are helping to support the growing animal collection at Metrozoo.

You receive a personalized adoption certificate, a picture of your animal, and educational information about the zoo. You adopt for one year. The option to renew is yours.

Additional information about our zoo and the Adopt-an-Animal program is enclosed. Thank you for your consideration.

Sincerely,

produced one at a time, with each letter containing a different name and address, and beginning on a new page, until the records have been exhausted.

We implement the mail merge of Figure 5.2 later in the chapter, but for the present we move directly to the creation of the ***mailing labels*** required to address the envelopes containing the letters. dBASE is truly at its best in this regard, for its mailing label facility is both fast and easy to use.

Mailing Labels

Figure 5.3 contains a set of ***two-up mailing labels*** (the labels are printed in two columns) for use with the form letters of Figure 5.2. The labels were produced in zip code sequence to take advantage of bulk mail (and alphabetically within zip code) and match the sequence in which the form letters were produced.

The generation of mailing labels is accomplished in much the same way as reports were created in the previous chapter. A ***label form*** (analogous to a report form) contains the characteristics of the mailing labels (e.g., the number of lines per label, the number of labels across a page, and the fields within a label) but no actual data. The labels are produced by merging the **DBF** file (sequenced according to the master index) with the designated label form. The process is shown in Figure 5.4.

The label form itself is created via a menu driven process that functions in similar fashion to the report generator. The procedure is initiated by the **CREATE LABEL** command, and results in the creation of a permanent label form (with extension **LBL**[2]). The label form can, if necessary, be subsequently modified through the **MODIFY LABEL** command.

[2] The **LABEL FORM** command creates two additional files, with extensions of **LBG** and **LBO**, for each label form; i.e., **ZOO.LBL** produces the files **ZOO.LBG** and **ZOO.LBO**. The purpose of these additional files is explained in Chapter 8 and goes beyond the scope of the present discussion.

FIGURE 5.3
Two-up Mailing Labels

```
Mr. Eric Manin                       Ms. Sarah Moldof
2362 NW 122 Drive                    2606 Nassau Bend
Coral Springs, FL    33065           Coconut Creek, FL    33066


Ms. Helen Rumsch                     Mr. Chris Anderson
2801 Victoria Way                    8137 NW 2nd Court
Coconut Creek, FL    33066           Coral Springs, FL    33071

   .
      .
         .

Ms. Tobi Cohen                       Mr. Jack Hill
7110 High Sierra Circle              Century Village
West Palm Beach, FL    33411         Deerfield Beach, FL    33441
```

The LABEL FORM Command

The **LABEL FORM** command prints mailing labels by merging the existing label form with a **DBF** file, just as reports were printed by the **REPORT FORM** command in conjunction with a report form. Consider:

```
LABEL FORM <label form file name> [<scope>]
    [FOR <condition>] [WHILE <condition>] [SAMPLE]
    [TO PRINTER/TO FILE <file name>]
```

Variations in the **LABEL FORM** command are explained within the context of the dBASE notation; all entries, except for the command and label form file name, are enclosed in brackets and therefore optional. All parameters (except for the **SAMPLE** clause) function identically as in the **REPORT FORM** command and are not discussed further. The **SAMPLE** parameter is unique to the **LABEL FORM** command and prints test labels to check the printer for alignment.

The label generator is illustrated in the ensuing exercise. The process is initiated by the **CREATE LABEL** command, which creates an **LBL** file containing the label form. The **LABEL FORM** command produces the actual labels, using data from the associated **DBF** file. The command can be used with different indexes to present the labels in different sequences, and/or include a **FOR** and/or a **WHILE** clause to limit the records for which labels are produced.

The TRIM Function

The mailing labels in Figure 5.3 are unremarkable in that they appear exactly as we would like them to. There are, for example, no extra spaces between the first and last name, nor between the city and state. We make these observations only to make you aware of the ***TRIM function*** that is built automatically into the label form. (See the Programmer's Notebook for additional discussion.)

The importance of the **TRIM** function is easily realized when you remember that every field in a file structure is defined as a ***fixed-length field,*** requiring a constant amount of space in the input file. **FIRSTNAME**, for example, is a 12-position field, so that a first name of **Chris**, followed by a last name of **Anderson**, would normally appear as **Chris   Anderson**, rather than **Chris Anderson**. The **TRIM** function, however, is built into the label form and thus eliminates the ***trailing blanks*** after the first name, placing **Anderson** one space after the **s** in **Chris**.

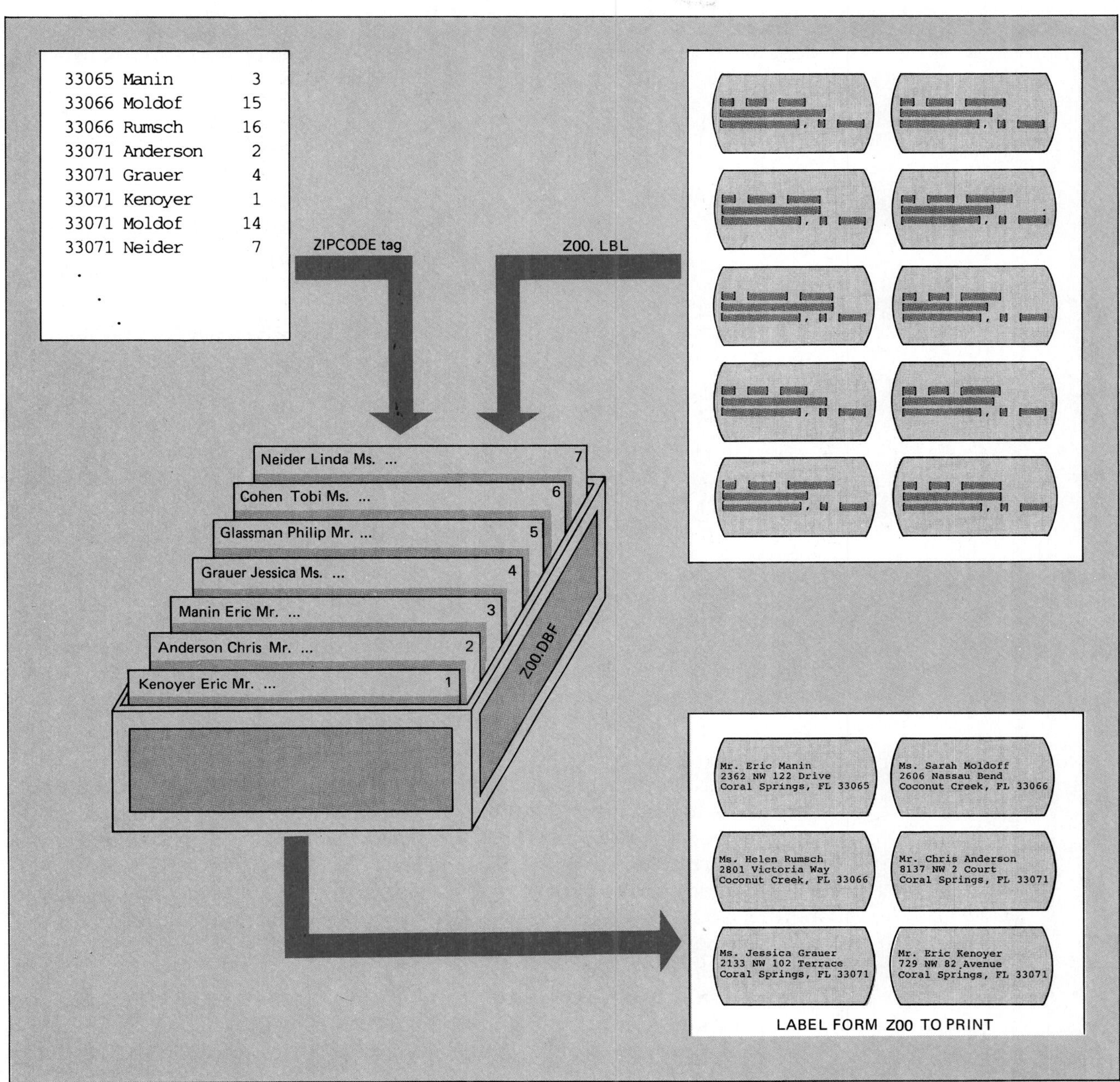

FIGURE 5.4
Understanding Mailing Labels (file relationships)

HANDS-ON EXERCISE 1

Mailing Labels

Objective

Create mailing labels; demonstrate the relationship between the `DBF`, `MDX`, and `LBL` files.

STEP 1 **Change to the ZOO directory**
Boot the system, ending at the DOS prompt. Type one of the following two commands, depending on whether you are sharing the hard drive with others:

CD C:\DATADISK\ZOO —— *if you installed the data disk on the hard drive and are not sharing your computer, or*

CD A:\DATADISK\ZOO —— *if you did not install the data disk, i.e., if you are sharing drive C with other students. (Use data disk two if you have 5¼-inch disks.)*

STEP 2 **Open the ZOO.DBF file**
Type **dBASE** to load dBASE, then set the default drive as you have in previous exercises. Type **USE ZOO** at the dot prompt to open the existing **ZOO.DBF** file shown in Figure 5.1.

STEP 3 **Enter the mailing label facility**
Type **CREATE LABEL** to initiate the label generator, then enter **ZOO** (or any other suitable name) as the name of the label form. You will see the work surface of Figure 5.5a (which is inherently less confusing than the opening screen of the report generator).

STEP 4 **The dimensions menu**
Press **Alt+D** to pull down the dimensions menu. Use the **up** and **down arrow** keys to highlight *predefined size,* then press **return** to produce the menu of Figure 5.5b. Highlight the second choice from this menu (15⁄16 × 3½ by 2) and press **return**.

STEP 5 **Create line one**
The first line of the mailing label is to contain three fields; **PREFIX**, **FIRSTNAME**, and **LASTNAME**, in that order. Check that the cursor is positioned in the first column of line one, then press **Alt+F** to pull down the fields menu. Highlight *Add field,* and press **return** to produce the screen in Figure 5.5c. Use the arrow keys to highlight **PREFIX**, then press **return** to produce the screen in Figure 5.5d; this confirms that **PREFIX** has been selected, that it is a three-position character field, and that its template will appear as **XXX** (a three-position character field). Press **Ctrl+End** to accept this field in the label form.

Press the **space bar** to leave a space between **PREFIX** and **FIRSTNAME**, the field you will select next. Press **Alt+F** to pull down the fields menu a second time, select *Add field,* select **FIRSTNAME**, and proceed as before to add the first name. Press the **space bar** once again, pull down the fields menu a third time, then add the **LASTNAME** field to complete the first line of the mailing label.

STEP 6 **Complete the label form**
Press the **return** key to move to the second line of the label form and add the **STREET** field. Move to the third line and add **CITY**, type a comma and a space after **CITY**, then add **STATE** and **ZIPCODE** in that order. The completed label appears in Figure 5.5e.

STEP 7 **Save the label form**
Press **Alt+L** to pull down the layout menu, highlight *Save this label,* and press **return**. You will see a second window with the cursor positioned after the name of the label form (**ZOO.LBL**); press **return** to save the file and return to the work surface.

FIGURE 5.5
Creating a Mailing Label

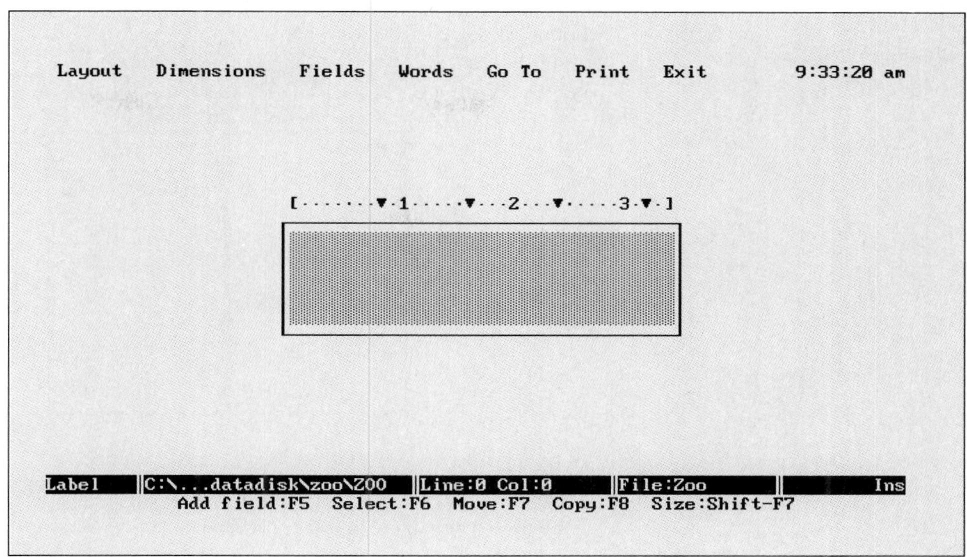

(a) The Work Surface

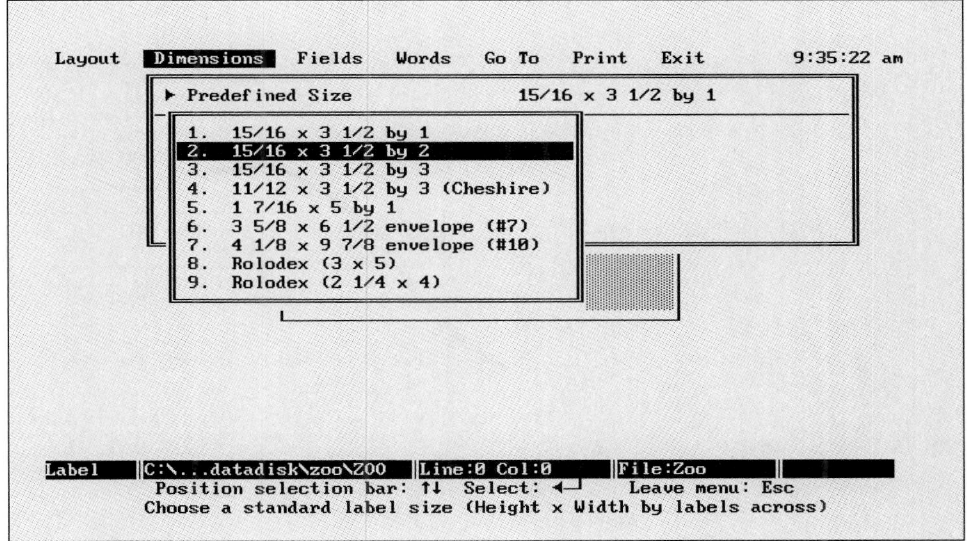

(b) Dimensions Menu

STEP 8 **View the mailing labels**

Press **Alt+P** to pull down the print menu of Figure 5.5f, highlight *View label on screen,* and press **return**. The appearance of the mailing labels should match those in Figure 5.3, although the labels will appear in a *different* sequence. If necessary, you can change the appearance of the labels through the fields (and/or words) menu. When you are satisfied with the appearance of the label form, press **Alt+E** to pull down the exit menu, select *Save changes and exit,* and return to the dot prompt.

STEP 9 **Print the mailing labels**

Type **SET ORDER TO TAG ZIPCODE** to change the master index, then type the command, **LABEL FORM ZOO TO PRINTER**, to print the labels in zip code order.

FIGURE 5.5
Creating a Mailing Label (continued)

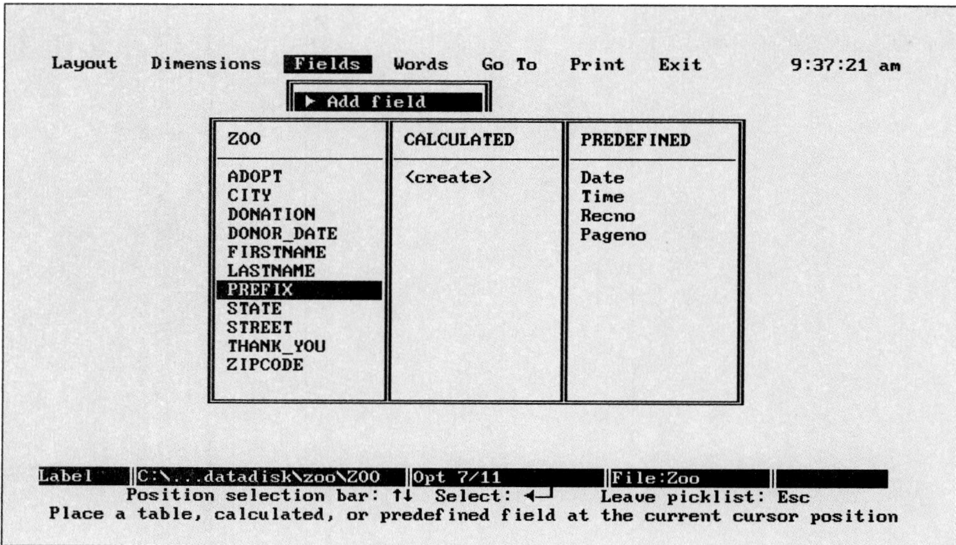

(c) Adding a Field

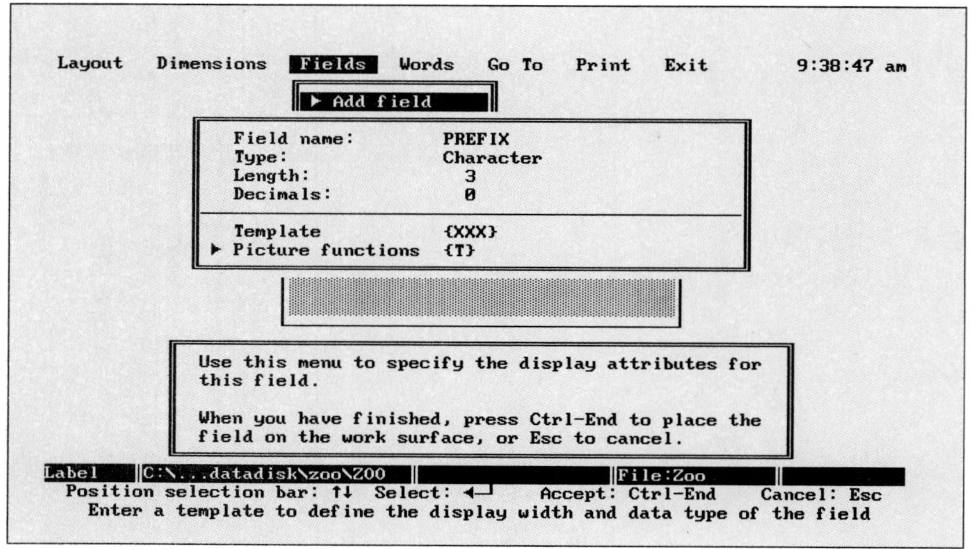

(d) Field Template

Creating the Form Letters

The preparation of mailing labels is only one step in the case solution, which also requires a set of personalized letters to go with the mailing labels. It remains to create the form letter and then to merge it with the file of names and addresses to produce the set of personalized letters.

Historically, a mail merge was done through a word processor because the word processor was the only means of creating a form letter. dBASE IV, however, incorporates the basic capabilities of a word processor (word wrap, changing margins and tabs, search-and-replace, and so on) into its report generator, making it possible to create the form letter *without* resorting to an external word processor.

FIGURE 5.5
Creating a Mailing Label (continued)

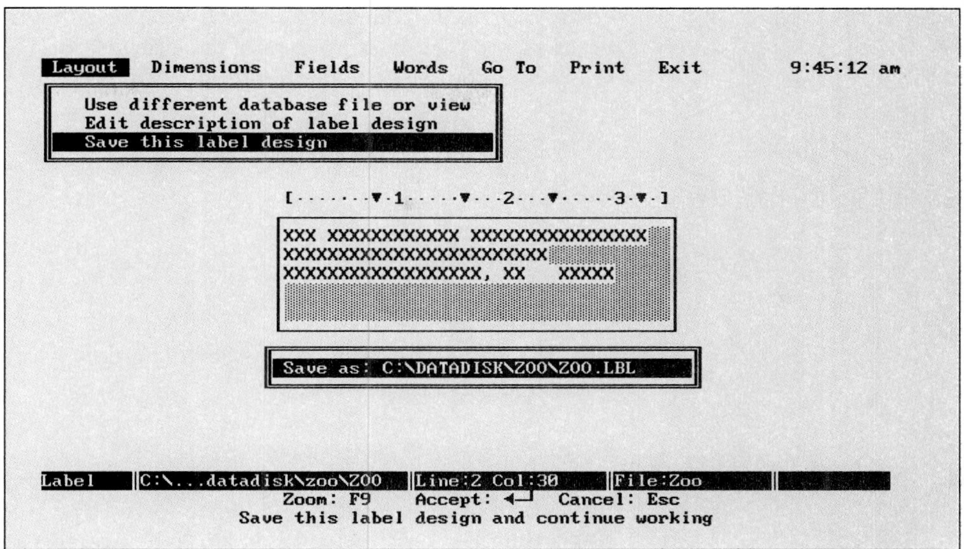

(e) Saving the Label

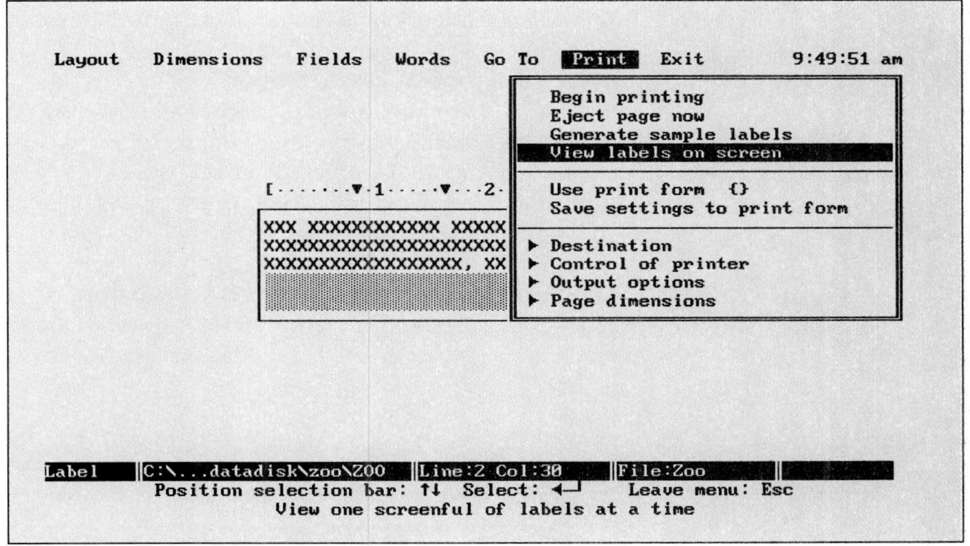

(f) Print Menu

The procedure to produce the personalized letters is conceptually the same as the process to produce the mailing labels. It begins with the creation of a form letter through the report generator, which is initiated by the **CREATE REPORT** command; in similar fashion, a label form is created through the mailing label facility and is initiated with the **CREATE LABEL** command. The individual letters are produced with the **REPORT FORM** command, just as the mailing labels are produced by the **LABEL FORM** command.

The ensuing exercise shows you how to create the set of personalized letters through the report generator. Many of the steps in the exercise will seem familiar, almost as if you have already done them, because the report generator contains many of the same menus as the label facility. You will find, for example, that both the mailing label and form letter contain a three-line address, and that the fields for this address are added through a fields menu present in both facilities. In similar fashion, you will find a print menu to print the labels or form letters, and an exit menu to save your work and return to the dot prompt.

HANDS-ON EXERCISE 2

Mail Merge

Objective
Use the mail-merge facility of dBASE IV to create a form letter; refer to Figure 5.2 as a guide in producing the letters.

STEP 1 **Enter the report generator**
The **ZOO.DBF** file should still be open from the previous exercise, but if not, type **USE ZOO** to open the **ZOO.DBF** file, followed by the command, **SET ORDER TO TAG ZIPCODE** to access the records in zip code sequence (to match the sequence in which the mailing labels were generated).

Type **CREATE REPORT** to initiate the report generator, then enter **LETTER** (or any other suitable name) as the name of the report that will contain the form letter. You will see the opening screen of the report generator as shown in Figure 5.6a.

STEP 2 **Select the mail-merge layout**
Press **Alt+L** to pull down the layout menu as shown in Figure 5.6b. Highlight *Quick layouts* and press **return**, then select *Mailmerge layout*. Press **return** once more, to produce the mail-merge layout of Figure 5.6c. Note the appearance of the work surface in Figure 5.6c, which has an expanded detail band to hold the form letter you are about to create.

STEP 3 **Create the letter heading and salutation**
The address in the form letter consists of three lines that match the contents of the mailing labels just created; i.e., the first line of the address contains three fields—

FIGURE 5.6
Creating a Form Letter

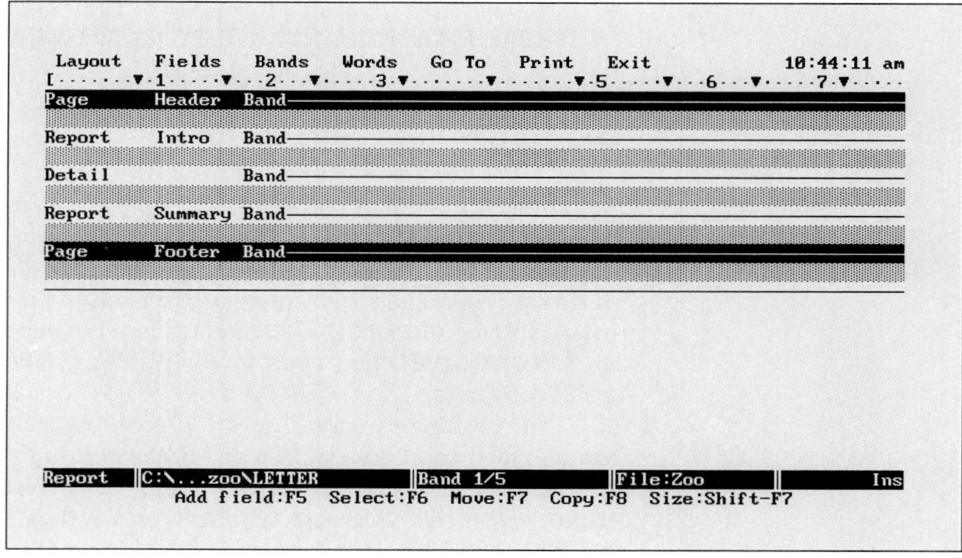

(a) Opening Screen

FIGURE 5.6
Creating a Form Letter (continued)

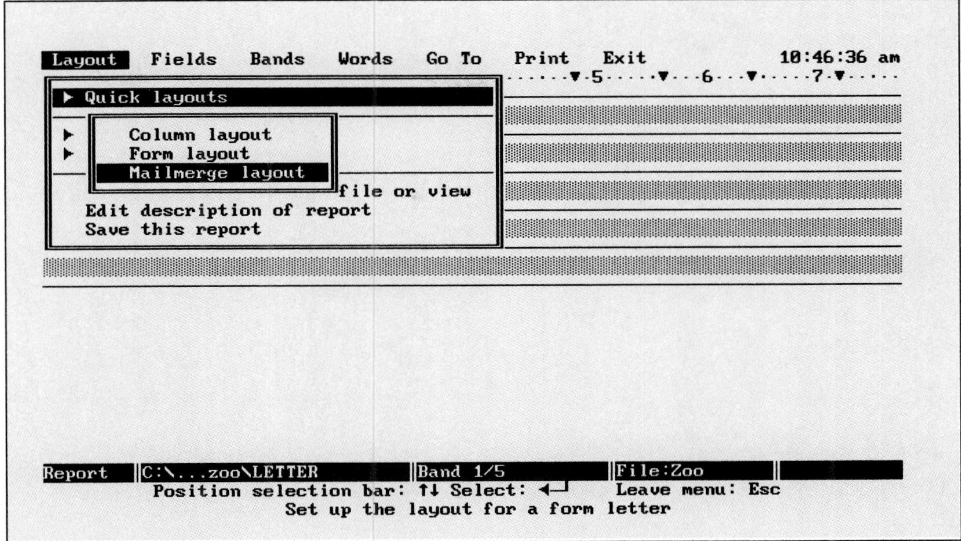

(b) Layout Menu

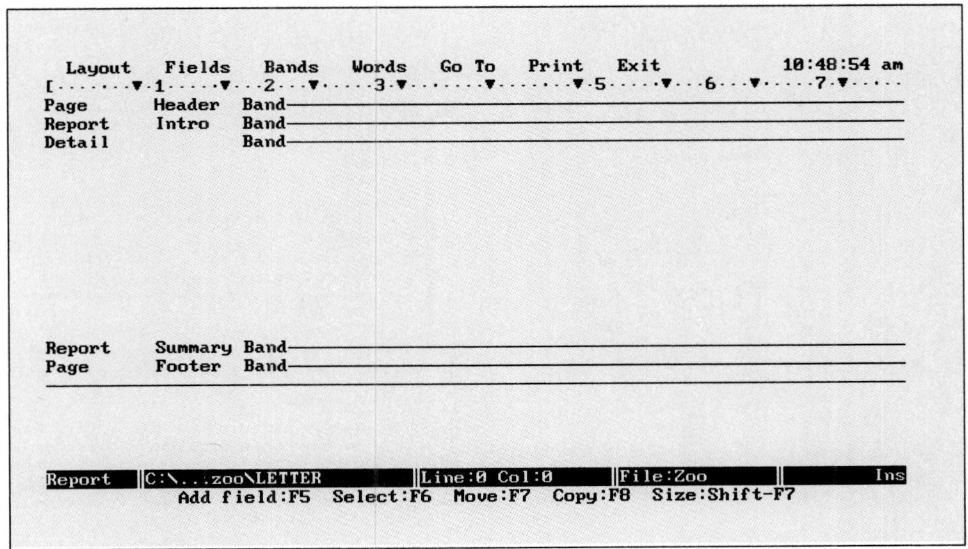

(c) Mail-merge Layout

PREFIX, **FIRSTNAME**, and **LASTNAME**—in that order. Check that the cursor is positioned in line 0, column 0 (as shown in the status line of Figure 5.6c), then press **Alt+F** to pull down the fields menu. Highlight *Add field,* and press **return** to produce the screen in Figure 5.6d. Use the arrow keys to highlight **PREFIX**, then press **return** to produce the screen in Figure 5.6e; this confirms that **PREFIX** has been selected, that it is a three-position character field, and that its template will appear as **XXX** (a three-position character field). Press **Ctrl+End** to accept this field in the report form. Press the **right arrow** key to move to the end of the field.

Press the **space bar** to leave a space between **PREFIX** and **FIRSTNAME**, press **Alt+F** to pull down the fields menu, select *Add field,* select **FIRSTNAME**, and press **Ctrl+End** to accept the field. Press the **right arrow** key to move to the end of the field, press the **space bar** to leave a space between the first and last name,

FIGURE 5.6
Creating a Form Letter (continued)

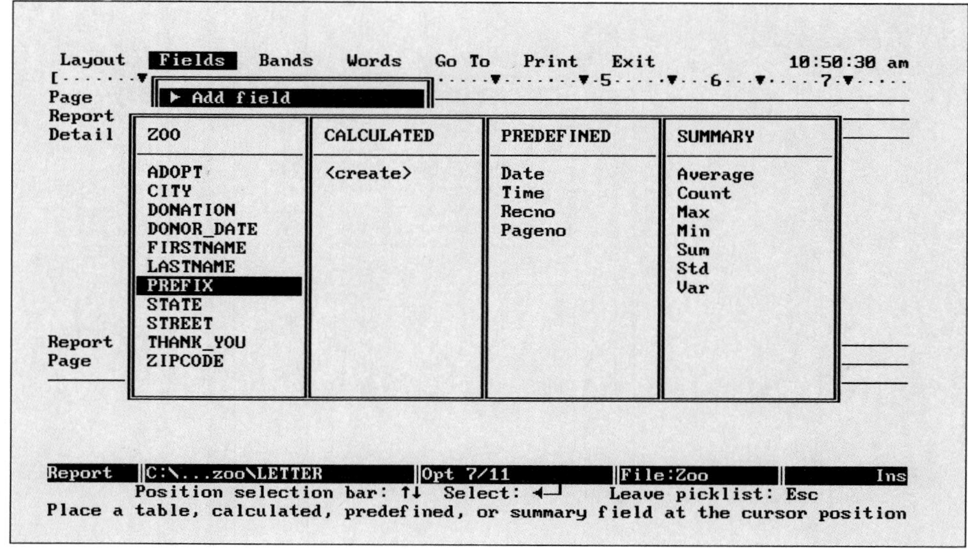

(d) Adding a Field

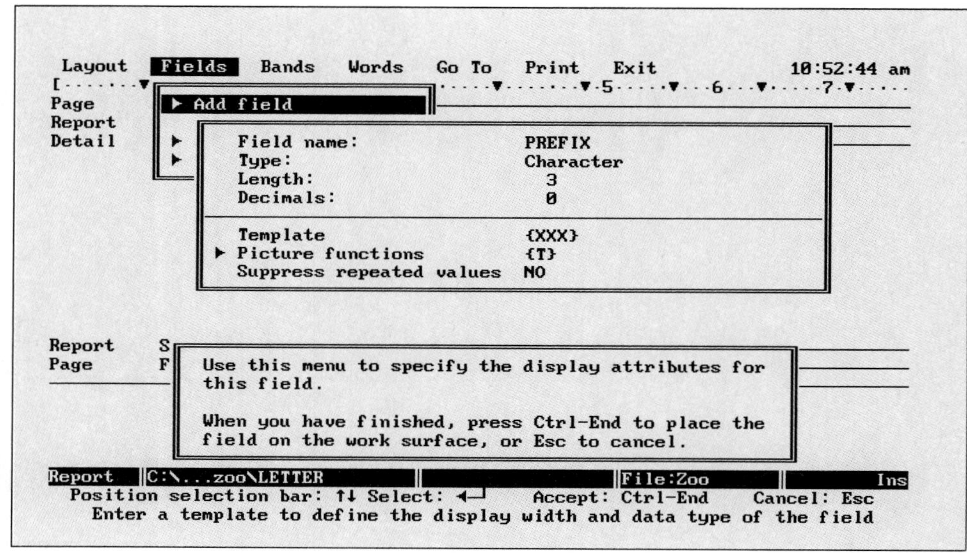

(e) Adding a Field (continued)

pull down the fields menu a third time, then add the **LASTNAME** field to complete the first line of the address. Press the **return** key to move to the second line of the address and add **STREET**, then press **return** to move to the third line and add **CITY**, a comma after **CITY**, **STATE**, and **ZIPCODE** in that order. You have completed the address and have to add the salutation. Press **return** twice more, type **Dear**, leave a space, then add the **FIRSTNAME** field, followed by a comma. Press the **return** key twice more to move to the first line of the letter.

STEP 4 **Change the right margin**

Press **Alt+W** to pull down the words menu, highlight *Modify ruler* as shown in Figure 5.6f, and press **return**. You should now be positioned at the very top of the screen in the ruler line. Press the **right arrow** key to move to column 66, and press the **]**

FIGURE 5.6
Creating a Form Letter (continued)

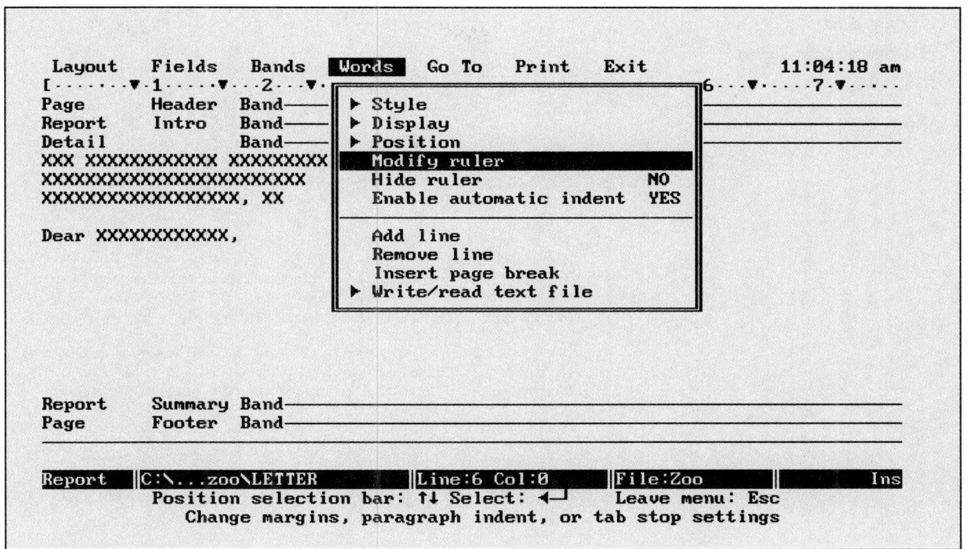

(f) Words Menu

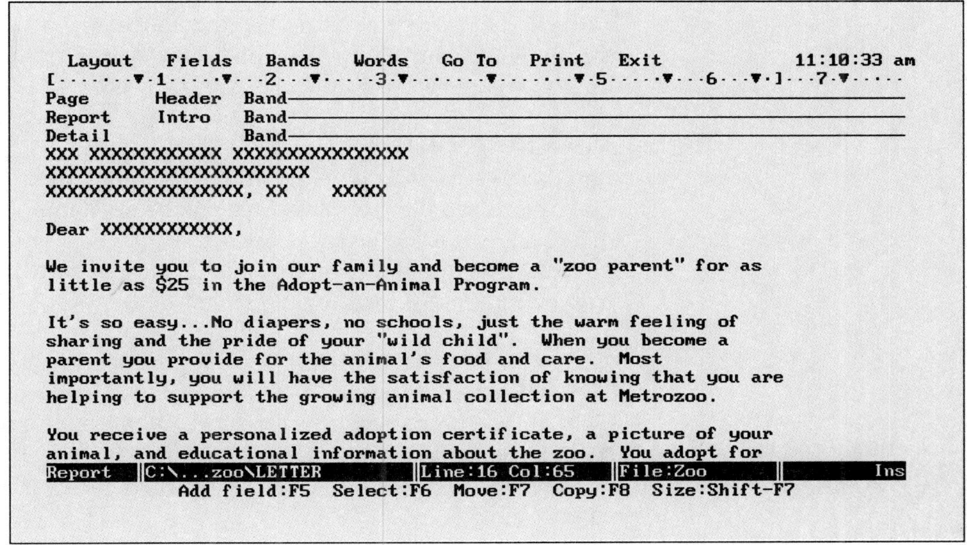

(g) Word Wrap

(right bracket) key to set the right margin. Press the **down arrow** key to leave the ruler line and return to the detail band, where you will enter the letter.

STEP 5 **Save the letter**

So far, so good, and thus you want to save what you have done. Press **Alt+L** to pull down the layout menu, highlight *Save this report,* and press **return**. You will see a second window with the cursor positioned after the name of the report form (**LETTER.FRM**); press **return** to save the file and return to the work surface.

STEP 6 **Type the letter**

Type the letter as it appears in Figures 5.6g and 5.6h. Enter text just as you would with any word processor, pressing the **return** key *only* at the end of a paragraph, and *not*

FIGURE 5.6
Creating a Form Letter (continued)

```
Mr. Eric Manin
2362 NW 122 Drive
Coral Springs, FL    33065

Dear Eric,

We invite you to join our family and become a "zoo parent" for as
little as $25 in the Adopt-an-Animal Program.

It's so easy...No diapers, no schools, just the warm feeling of
sharing and the pride of your "wild child".  When you become a
parent you provide for the animal's food and care.  Most
importantly, you will have the satisfaction of knowing that you are
helping to support the growing animal collection at Metrozoo.

You receive a personalized adoption certificate, a picture of your
animal, and educational information about the zoo.  You adopt for
one year.  The option to renew is yours.

Additional information about our zoo and the Adopt-an-Animal
program is enclosed.  Thank you for your consideration.

                                                    Sincerely,

                Cancel viewing: ESC,  Continue viewing: SPACEBAR
```

(h) Viewing the Completed Letter

at the end of every line; text will automatically wrap from one to the next. Note, too, that the top of the letter will scroll off the screen as you near the end. Press **Alt+L** to pull down the layout menu and save your work.

STEP 7 **View the form letters**

Press **Alt+P** to pull down the print menu, highlight *View report on screen,* and press **return** to see the completed letter for Eric Manin as shown in Figure 5.6h. Check that you are satisfied with the finished letter, and if not, make corrections as necessary. Press **Alt+E** to pull down the exit menu when you are finished, select *Save changes and exit,* and return to the dot prompt.

STEP 8 **Print the first two letters**

Type **GO TOP** to move to the first record in zip code sequence. Check that the printer is on, then type **REPORT FORM LETTER NEXT 2 TO PRINTER NOEJECT** to print the first two letters.

Summary

The ***design*** of a file structure is the most important step in the development of a system. You must be absolutely certain that the data entered as input is sufficient to provide all information desired as output.

Mailing labels are created in a process analogous to that for report forms as described in Chapter 4. The **CREATE** and/or **MODIFY LABEL** command creates a label form, just as **CREATE** and/or **MODIFY REPORT** created a report form.

The **LABEL FORM** command generates the set of mailing labels just as the **REPORT FORM** command produced the finished report. Mailing labels can be generated in different sequences in conjunction with different indexes.

The report generator contains a ***mail-merge*** option to create form letters. The **CREATE REPORT** command creates the empty form letter, which is subsequently merged with a DBF file through the **REPORT FORM** command.

Key Words and Concepts

Character field
`CREATE LABEL`
`CREATE REPORT`
Data type
Date field
Dimensions menu
Exit menu
Field size
Field type
Fields menu
File design
Fixed-length field
Form letter
Label form
`LABEL FORM`
Layout menu
Logical field
Mail merge
Mailing label
`MODIFY LABEL`
`MODIFY REPORT`
Numeric field
Print menu
`REPORT FORM`
`SAMPLE`
Trailing blanks
`TRIM` function
Two-up mailing labels
Words menu

True/False

1. A logical field always has a field length of 1.
2. Last name, first name, and middle initial should generally be defined as separate fields, as opposed to being grouped together.
3. The zip code is usually defined as a separate field, as opposed to including it in a larger address field.
4. A zip code contains only numbers, and hence should be defined as a numeric field.
5. A two-line address will suffice in all applications.
6. A label form is created through the `LABEL FORM` command.
7. Creation of a form letter requires the use of an external word processor; i.e., it *cannot* be done in dBASE IV.
8. Form letters are typically created through the `CREATE LABEL` command.
9. Report forms and mailing labels share several common menus.
10. The dBASE label facility can produce entries for a Rolodex in addition to a variety of label sizes.
11. A given `LBL` file can produce labels in only one sequence, e.g., alphabetically or by zip code, but not both.
12. The `TRIM` function is built automatically into a label form.

Exercises

1. Distinguish between:
   (a) A mailing label and a form letter
   (b) A one-position character field and a logical field
   (c) Field length and field type
   (d) The file extensions, `LBL` and `FRM`
   (e) The commands, `CREATE REPORT` and `MODIFY REPORT`
   (f) The commands, `CREATE LABEL` and `LABEL FORM`
2. As indicated in the chapter, careful attention must be given to designing the file structure, or else the resulting system will not perform as desired. Consider the following:
   (a) An individual's age may be calculated from his or her birth date, which in turn can be stored as a field within a record. An alternate technique would be to store age directly in the record and thereby avoid the calculation. Which field—age or birth date—would you use? Why?

(b) Social security number is typically chosen as a record key in lieu of a person's name. What attribute does the social security number possess that often makes it the superior choice?

3. How many *unique* codes can be developed from a four-position numeric (numbers only) code? From a four-position alphabetic (letters only) code? From a four-position alphanumeric (letters and numbers) code?

4. Given the existence of the **ZOO.DBF** and **ZOO.LBL** files as presented in the chapter, for which records, and in which sequence, will mailing labels be produced, given the commands below?
(a) **LABEL FORM ZOO**
(b) **SET ORDER TO TAG ZIPCODE**
LABEL FORM ZOO
(c) **SET ORDER TO TAG LASTNAME**
LABEL FORM ZOO
(d) **LABEL FORM ZOO FOR ADOPT = 'M'**
(e) **LABEL FORM ZOO FOR THANK_YOU**
(f) **LABEL FORM ZOO FOR ZIPCODE = '33065'**

5. Which facility—the report generator, mailing labels, or both—is associated with the following menus?
(a) Fields menu
(b) Dimensions menu
(c) Print menu
(d) Words menu
(e) Bands menu
(f) Exit menu

6. The following *erroneous* set of commands is intended to create a form letter for thank-you notes and associated mailing labels. Only people who have contributed but have not yet been thanked are to receive a thank-you note.

```
.USE ZOO
.CREATE REPORT THANKS
   .
     .
       Menu selections to create form letter
   .
     .
.SET ORDER TO TAG ZIPCODE
.REPORT FORM THANKS

.CREATE LABEL THANKS
   .
     .
       Menu selections to create mailing labels
     .
      .

.SET ORDER TO
.LABEL FORM THANKS FOR DONATION > 0
```

Identify the various errors in the command sequence. In so doing, it will be helpful to determine the following:
(a) For which records, and in what sequence, are the thank-you notes created?

(b) For which records, and in what sequence, are the mailing labels created?
(c) How is it possible for the `CREATE REPORT` and `CREATE LABEL` commands to both reference the same name (`THANKS`)?

7. Use the report generator to create a form letter for thank-you notes addressed to only those people who sent in a donation. Your solution should meet the following requirements:
(a) The thank-you notes are to be produced in alphabetical order.
(b) Individual thank-you notes are to contain the current date (i.e., the date you send the note), the date the contribution was received, and the amount of the contribution.
(c) Create a set of mailing labels for use with the thank-you notes; realize, however, that you should print labels only for those individuals who actually contributed, and the labels are to be printed in alphabetical order.

CHAPTER

6 Queries and Conditions

OUTLINE

OBJECTIVES

After reading this chapter you will be able to:

1. Describe the relational and logical operators that may be present in a dBASE condition.
2. Explain the error message, *Data type mismatch,* and why a date conversion function may be required within a condition.
3. Use the **FIND** and **LOCATE** commands to move to individual records within a **DBF** file; describe the differences between these commands.
4. Explain why a **DISPLAY** or **EDIT** command is often used in conjunction with a **FIND** and **LOCATE** command.
5. Use the **SET FILTER TO** command to establish a filter condition; explain how the existence of a filter condition affects a **DBF** file.
6. Differentiate between the **SET FIELDS** and **SET FILTER** commands; explain how to negate the effects of both of these commands.
7. Create a dBASE query file.

Overview

The use of a ***condition*** is fundamental to almost every dBASE command because it defines the records on which a command is to operate. Although many conditions are simple in appearance and have been used throughout the text, other conditions grow quite complex and require additional explanation. The chapter begins, therefore, with a formal discussion of dBASE conditions and covers the use of both ***relational*** and ***logical operators.***

The chapter includes a discussion of the **FIND** and **LOCATE** commands to identify a record that meets a specified condition, and the associated use of the **SKIP** and **CONTINUE** commands. We present the **SET FILTER** command to limit the ***view*** of a file to a group of records that meet a specified condition and the **SET FIELDS** command to display a limited set of fields.

The final topic is the development of a ***query,*** a specialized dBASE file that permanently stores a filter condition and associated information. We take you through the process of building a ***query file*** in detail, showing how it parallels the development of report forms and mailing labels from earlier chapters. All of this is done within the context of a new example, to again remind you of the diversity of data management applications for which dBASE is suitable.

A New Example

Figure 6.1 displays the file structure for a **LOANS.DBF** file as it might exist in a banking environment. The **DBF** file is included on the data disk and is the basis for all examples in this chapter. The meaning of the various fields should be apparent from the field names and a lay person's knowledge of banking. We include personal data about the individual (first and last name, address, and telephone number) as well as specific data for the loan (the amount, interest rate, term, type of loan, and date on which the loan was granted).

The choice of field type is consistent with the earlier discussion in Chapter 5. The designation of a character field is obvious for the **FIRSTNAME**, **LASTNAME**, **STREET**, **CITY**, and **STATE**; character is also specified for the **LOAN_NUM**, **ZIPCODE**,

FIGURE 6.1
The LOANS.DBF File

```
Structure for database: C:\DATADISK\LOANS\LOANS.DBF
Number of data records:       10
Date of last update    : 05/08/91
Field  Field Name  Type         Width    Dec
    1  LOAN_NUM    Character        4
    2  AMOUNT      Numeric          7
    3  INTEREST    Numeric          5      3
    4  TERM        Numeric          2
    5  LOAN_DATE   Date             8
    6  TYPE        Character        1
    7  COSIGNER    Logical          1
    8  FIRSTNAME   Character       10
    9  LASTNAME    Character       12
   10  STREET      Character       24
   11  CITY        Character       18
   12  STATE       Character        2
   13  ZIPCODE     Character        5
   14  TELEPHONE   Character       10
```

and **TELEPHONE** (even though these fields contain only numbers) because they are not used in calculations. The **AMOUNT**, **INTEREST**, and **TERM** are numeric, as these fields are used in the calculation of the monthly payment. The **TYPE** of loan is a character field and contains one of four codes, depending on the nature of the loan (**M**ortgage, **A**utomobile, **P**ersonal, or **B**oat.) The **LOAN_DATE** is an obvious date field, whereas **COSIGNER** is designated a logical field because it is either true or false; i.e., there either is or is not a cosigner (a second individual responsible for repayment should the first person default).

Conditions

A ***condition*** has one of two values, true or false; i.e., a condition evaluates the relationship between two quantities and returns a value of true or false, depending on whether or not the relationship is satisfied. The most frequent way of using a condition in dBASE is through the **FOR** clause, an optional parameter in many commands. Consider, for example, the following **DISPLAY** statements, each of which is written in conjunction with the **LOANS.DBF** file of Figure 6.1:

```
DISPLAY ALL FOR AMOUNT > 5000
DISPLAY ALL FOR TYPE = "P"
```

The first statement lists every record where the amount borrowed is greater than $5,000, whereas the second statement lists every record with a personal loan. Both statements examine every record in the file, one record at a time, to determine whether the indicated condition is true, and if so, the record is displayed. The record is passed over when the condition is false.

The condition in the first statement is **AMOUNT > 5000** and it (the condition) is either true or false; i.e., the value of the **AMOUNT** field in the current record is either greater than $5,000 or it isn't. In similar fashion, the condition in the second statement is also true or false; i.e., the value of the **TYPE** field in the current record is either an upper-case **P** or it isn't.

Relational Operators

In simplest form, a condition consists of two quantities separated by a ***relational operator,*** with the set of relational operators summarized in Table 6.1. The condition must, however, compare like quantities to one another, e.g., a numeric field to a numeric value or a character field to a character string; failure to do so produces the dBASE error message, **Data type mismatch**, which indicates that the quantities on either side of the relational operator are of different data types.

TABLE 6.1 **Relational Operators**

Operation	Operator
Less than	<
Greater than	>
Equal to	=
Not equal to	< > or #
Less than or equal to	< =
Greater than or equal to	> =

Consider once again the conditions in the two **DISPLAY** statements, remembering that the type of loan is defined as a character field, and thus must be compared to a character string enclosed in quotation marks (or apostrophes). The amount of the loan, however, is a numeric field and thus is compared to a numeric quantity consisting of numbers, an optional sign and/or a decimal point, and is written without quotation marks (or apostrophes).

Table 6.2 contains additional examples of valid and invalid conditions for all four data types: character, numeric, logical, and date. Conditions for character and numeric fields, e.g., **LASTNAME** and **INTEREST**, are straightforward, whereas those for logical and date fields are more subtle. **COSIGNER**, for example, was defined as a logical field and appears without a relational operator, because the variable name itself implies a true condition. Thus, the statement **DISPLAY ALL COSIGNER** will list all records where the value of the **COSIGNER** field is true (**T**, **t**, **Y**, or **y**) whereas **DISPLAY .NOT. COSIGNER** lists those records where the value of the logical variable is false (**F**, **f**, **N**, or **n**).

The use of a date field requires ***curly braces*** around the literal date, so that both sides of the relational operator contain similar, i.e., date, values. Failure to use the braces will produce the message, **Data type mismatch**, as previously indicated.

Logical Operators

The logical operators, **.AND.**, **.OR.**, and **.NOT.** (set off by periods), are used to combine two (or more) ***simple conditions*** into a ***compound condition*** as shown in Figure 6.2. Figure 6.2a lists all loans of less than $100,000, whereas Figure 6.2b lists all mortgage loans. (The **LIST** command is similar to the **DISPLAY** command except that it has a default scope of **ALL**, whereas **DISPLAY** has a default scope of the current record. Accordingly, **LIST** is often easier to use and appears throughout the chapter. Additional differences between the two commands are found in the Programmer's Notebook.)

The individual conditions are combined in Figures 6.2c and 6.2d. The **.AND.** operator of Figure 6.2d requires *both* individual conditions to be true in order for the compound condition to be true; i.e., the amount of the loan has to be less than $100,000 *and* the loan must be a mortgage. The logical **.OR.** needs only *one* of the

TABLE 6.2 **Conditions**

Example	Comments
LASTNAME= 'Anderson'	Valid.
LASTNAME= "ANDERSON"	Valid syntactically, but match will not be found since all capital letters were used in the search string.
LASTNAME= Anderson	Invalid; character field requires either quotation marks or apostrophes.
INTEREST> .10	Valid.
INTEREST> 10%	Invalid; numeric fields may not contain a comma, dollar sign, or percent sign.
COSIGNER	Valid as **COSIGNER** is a logical field; condition will return all records where the value of the logical field is true (**T, t, Y,** or **y**).
COSIGNER= 'F'	Invalid; relational operators are not used with logical fields.
.NOT. COSIGNER	Valid; condition will return all records where the value of the logical field is false (**F, f, N,** or **n**).
LOAN_DATE> 01/01/90	Invalid; a date field cannot be compared to a numeric field.
LOAN_DATE> '01/01/90'	Invalid; a date field cannot be compared to a character field.
LOAN_DATE> {01/01/90}	Valid; Braces are used to convert a character date to an equivalent date value.

FIGURE 6.2
Compound Conditions

```
. LIST LASTNAME,AMOUNT,TYPE FOR AMOUNT < 100000 OFF
LASTNAME       AMOUNT TYPE
Milgrom         95000 M
Flynn            9500 A
Simpson         65000 B
Lee             15500 A
Anderson         8500 A
Mills           88500 M
Flynn           10000 P
```

(a) Condition 1 (AMOUNT < 100000)

```
. LIST LASTNAME,AMOUNT,TYPE FOR TYPE = "M" OFF
LASTNAME       AMOUNT TYPE
Milgrom         95000 M
Taylor         500000 M
Mills           88500 M
Moldof         250000 M
Milgrom        178500 M
```

(b) Condition 2 (TYPE = "M")

```
. LIST LASTNAME,AMOUNT,TYPE FOR AMOUNT <100000 .OR. TYPE = "M"
LASTNAME       AMOUNT TYPE
Milgrom         95000 M
Flynn            9500 A
Simpson         65000 B
Taylor         500000 M
Lee             15500 A
Anderson         8500 A
Mills           88500 M
Moldof         250000 M
Flynn           10000 P
Milgrom        178500 M
```

(c) OR Operation

```
. LIST LASTNAME,AMOUNT,TYPE FOR AMOUNT < 100000 .AND. TYPE = "M" OFF
LASTNAME       AMOUNT TYPE LOAN_DATE
Milgrom         95000 M    11/24/89
Mills           88500 M    05/13/91
```

(d) AND Operation

two simple conditions to be true; i.e., the amount is less than $100,000 *or* the loan is a mortgage.

Precedence of Operations

More than one logical operation can be included in a compound condition, which makes the result of the condition (whether it is true or false) dependent on the *sequence* in which the logical operations are evaluated. Accordingly, dBASE provides a ***precedence of operations*** so that the condition is evaluated without ambiguity. **.NOT.** is evaluated first, followed by **.AND.**, and then **.OR.**. Consider, for example, how the evaluation of **.AND.** *before* **.OR.** affects the outcome of the following condition:

```
                                       ┌AND is evaluated first
.                                      │
  TERM = 15 .OR. AMOUNT > 100000 .AND. INTEREST < .12
```

The **.AND.** condition (**AMOUNT > 100000 .AND. INTEREST < .12**) is evaluated first, after which its outcome (true or false) is evaluated in conjunction with the **.OR.** condition (**TERM = 15**). The *compound* condition will be considered true if the amount of the loan is greater than $100,000 *and* the interest rate is less than 12 percent, or failing this, the compound condition will still be considered true if the term of the loan is 15 years.

Parentheses can be used at any time to *clarify* the sequence of operations; e.g., you could rewrite the preceding condition with parentheses to clarify (for a human reader; dBASE needs no such help) the sequence of operations. Since any expression within parentheses is evaluated first, the meaning of the following condition is unchanged from the example without the parentheses; i.e., **.AND.** is still evaluated before **.OR.**.

```
                 Parentheses clarify sequence of operations
TERM = 15 .OR. (AMOUNT > 100000 .AND. INTEREST < .12)
```

Parentheses can also be used to *alter* the sequence of operations (if necessary) and thus change the interpretation of the condition. Any operation that appears within a set of parentheses is evaluated first; thus, in the example below, the compound condition in parentheses is true if either the term is 15 years or the amount is greater than $100,000, but in any event the interest must be less than 12 percent for the entire condition to be considered true.

```
              Parentheses alter the sequence of operations
(TERM = 15 .OR. AMOUNT > 100000) .AND. INTEREST < .12
```

Identifying Individual Records

Virtually all of the material so far has dealt with a subset of records, e.g., the records that satisfy the specified condition in a **FOR** clause. It is also necessary to isolate *individual* records that satisfy a condition, a task accomplished with either the **FIND** or **LOCATE** command. The terms are synonymous in English, but function very differently in dBASE. Each command is discussed in detail.

The LOCATE Command

The **LOCATE** command searches the **DBF** file for the first record that satisfies a specified **FOR** condition. A successful search displays the record number of the first record meeting the condition, whereas an error message (**End of LOCATE scope**) is displayed if a match is not found. Consider:

Syntax `LOCATE FOR condition`

Example `LOCATE FOR LASTNAME = "Milgrom"`

The **LOCATE** command is illustrated in Figure 6.3. The last names for all ten records in the **LOANS.DBF** file are listed in Figure 6.3a, and these values are used to illustrate variations in the command as shown in the remainder of the figure.

A successful **LOCATE** command positions the record pointer at the first record satisfying the condition; it does *not,* however, display the record; consequently, a **LOCATE** command is almost invariably followed by a **DISPLAY** (or **EDIT**) command as shown in Figure 6.3b. At the risk of repetition, the **LOCATE** command positions the

FIGURE 6.3
The LOCATE Command

```
. USE LOANS
. LIST LASTNAME
Record#  LASTNAME
      1  Milgrom
      2  Flynn
      3  Simpson
      4  Taylor
      5  Lee
      6  Anderson
      7  Mills
      8  Moldof
      9  Flynn
     10  Milgrom
```

(a) The LOANS.DBF File

```
. LOCATE FOR LASTNAME = "Milgrom"
Record =         1        ---- Only the record number is displayed
. DISPLAY LASTNAME
Record#  LASTNAME
      1  Milgrom
. LOCATE FOR LASTNAME = "Milgrom"
Record =         1        ---- LOCATE command always returns the
                               same record
```

(b) Repetition of Same Command

```
. LOCATE FOR LASTNAME = "Milgrom"
Record =         1
. CONTINUE                ---- CONTINUE command alters starting position
Record =        10
. CONTINUE
End of LOCATE scope       ---- The last Milgrom has been found
```

(c) The CONTINUE Command

```
. LOCATE FOR LASTNAME = "MILGROM"   ---- There is no record for a lastname
End of LOCATE scope                      MILGROM
```

(d) Case Sensitive

```
. LOCATE FOR LASTNAME = "Mi"   ---- Partial lastname is entered
Record =         1
. CONTINUE
Record =         7             ---- Mills rather than Milgrom is returned
. CONTINUE
Record =        10
. CONTINUE
End of LOCATE scope
```

(e) Partial Last Name

record pointer at the *first* record satisfying the designated condition, and so repetition of the same **LOCATE** command always retrieves the same record.

The **CONTINUE** command begins its search from the current record and positions the record pointer on the next record that matches the condition specified in the previous **LOCATE** command. A **LOCATE** command is used in Figure 6.3c to find the first record with a last name of Milgrom, whereupon successive **CONTINUE** commands step through the remainder of the file until the last Milgrom has been identified.

As with all conditions involving character fields, the condition in the **LOCATE** command is ***case sensitive,*** as seen in Figure 6.3d, where a search for MILGROM is unsuccessful. The condition can also specify a partial last name, as shown in Figure 6.3e, where we search for records with a last name beginning with "Mi". The **LOCATE** command returns the same Milgrom as before, but the initial **CONTINUE** command returns Mills rather than Milgrom.

The FIND Command

The **FIND** command is the fastest way to locate individual records in a DBF file, but its use requires that the file be opened with an index. The FIND command searches the key field of the master index for the first record matching the specified ***search-string;*** a successful search positions the record pointer at the associated record, whereas a *Find not successful* message is displayed if a match cannot be found. Consider:

Syntax

```
FIND search-string
```

Examples

```
SET ORDER TO TAG LASTNAME
FIND Milgrom
```

The FIND command is illustrated in Figure 6.4. The last names for all 10 records in the **LOANS.DBF** file are listed in alphabetical sequence in Figure 6.4a, and these values are used to illustrate variations in the command as shown in the remainder of the figure. Note, too, that several similarities exist between the FIND and LOCATE commands, as can be seen by comparing Figures 6.3 and 6.4.

As indicated, a successful FIND command positions the record pointer at the first record containing an index key matching the search-string; it does *not,* however, display the record, and so FIND, like LOCATE, is typically followed by a DISPLAY command as shown in Figure 6.4b. At the risk of repetition, the FIND command positions the record pointer at the *first* record matching the search-string, i.e., at the first Milgrom according to the active index, which means that repetition of the same FIND command always retrieves the same record.

The **SKIP** command moves the record pointer to the next record according to the active index. Successive SKIP commands are used, therefore, to find other records that match the search string as shown in Figure 6.4c. SKIP is different from CONTINUE, however, in that SKIP moves directly to the next record *regardless* of whether it matches the condition, whereas CONTINUE implies a search for the next matching record. Thus, while a CONTINUE command will eventually display the message End of LOCATE scope when all Milgroms have been identified, no such message is associated with a SKIP command. The FIND command in Figure 6.4c moves the record pointer to the first Milgrom, the first SKIP command moves to the second Milgrom, but the next SKIP moves to record 7 (Mills) without explicit indication that the last Milgrom has been found.

The search-string in the FIND command is case sensitive as shown in Figure 6.4d. The FIND command can also search for a partial last name as shown in Figure 6.4e.

FIND versus LOCATE

The main difference between the two commands is that LOCATE searches the file *sequentially,* whereas FIND goes *directly* to the desired record by using the associated index. Thus, a FIND command is *faster* than the corresponding LOCATE command, although the difference between the commands, FIND Milgrom and

FIGURE 6.4
The FIND Command

```
. USE LOANS
. SET ORDER TO TAG LASTNAME ———— Index is required for FIND command
Master index: LASTNAME
. LIST LASTNAME
Record#   LASTNAME
      6   Anderson
      2   Flynn
      9   Flynn
      5   Lee
      1   Milgrom
     10   Milgrom
      7   Mills
      8   Moldof
      3   Simpson
      4   Taylor
```

(a) The LOANS.DBF FILE (in sequence by last name)

```
. FIND Milgrom
. DISPLAY LASTNAME
Record#   LASTNAME
      1   Milgrom
. FIND Milgrom ———— FIND command always returns the same record
. DISPLAY LASTNAME
Record#   LASTNAME
      1   Milgrom
```

(b) Repetition of Same Command

```
. FIND Milgrom
. DISPLAY LASTNAME
Record#   LASTNAME
      1   Milgrom
. SKIP
LOANS: Record No       10 ——— SKIP command returns next record (Milgrom)
. SKIP
LOANS: Record No        7 ——— SKIP command returns next record in sequence (Mills)
```

(c) The SKIP Command

```
. FIND MILGROM
Find not successful
```

(d) Case sensitive

```
. FIND Mi ———— Partial lastname is entered
. DISPLAY LASTNAME
Record#   LASTNAME
      1   Milgrom
```

(e) Partial Key

LOCATE FOR lastname = 'Milgrom', will not be apparent in the existing **LOANS.DBF** file because it is so small (only ten records). Note, too, that quotation marks (or apostrophes) are required for the character string in the **LOCATE** statement, but are not used in the search-string associated with the **FIND** command.

The **LOCATE** command does, however, offer three advantages of its own. First, the lack of an index allows you to search on any field, not just those for which an index exists. Second, the condition in the **LOCATE** command may specify an inequality; e.g., **LOCATE FOR AMOUNT > 100000**, whereas no comparable search is possible with the **FIND** operation. And finally, the **LOCATE** command will accommodate a compound condition—e.g., **LASTNAME = "Milgrom" .AND. TYPE = "M"**—something you cannot do in a **FIND** command.

The subtleties associated with finding or not finding records underscore the importance of proper data entry; i.e., inadvertently entering upper-case letters where lower-case letters were intended, misspelling a name, including extra blanks where they don't belong, and so on will invariably cause problems in the operation of the system.

FOR versus WHILE Condition

Most dBASE commands allow a **FOR** condition and/or a **WHILE** condition—a subtle, but significant, difference. The **FOR** and **WHILE** conditions in the **LIST** commands in Figures 6.5a and 6.5b produce identical output as both figures display the loan information for all records with a last name of Milgrom. The difference, therefore, is not in the output per se, but in how that output was produced.

Execution of the **LIST FOR** command in Figure 6.5a causes dBASE to search *every* record in the associated file, whereas the **LIST WHILE** command ceases processing as soon as the condition is no longer met. Note, however, that the **LIST WHILE** command must be preceded by a **SET ORDER** command to list records alphabetically, and by a **FIND** command to position the record pointer to the first record satisfying the designated condition.

The increased efficiency of the **WHILE** condition is seen from Figure 6.5c, which begins processing at the first Milgrom and continues as long as the indicated condition is true, i.e, until a last name other than Milgrom is found. The **WHILE** condition ceases execution after only three records (the two Milgroms and Mills), whereas the **FOR**

FIGURE 6.5
FOR versus WHILE Condition

```
. USE LOANS
. LIST LASTNAME,AMOUNT,TERM,INTEREST FOR LASTNAME = "Milgrom"
Record#  LASTNAME        AMOUNT TERM INTEREST
      1  Milgrom          95000   30    0.110
     10  Milgrom         178500   30    0.095
```

(a) FOR Condition

```
. SET ORDER TO TAG LASTNAME
Master index: LASTNAME
. FIND Milgrom
. LIST LASTNAME,AMOUNT,TERM,INTEREST WHILE LASTNAME =
"Milgrom"
Record#  LASTNAME        AMOUNT TERM INTEREST
      1  Milgrom          95000   30    0.110
     10  Milgrom         178500   30    0.095
```

FIND command prior to WHILE condition

(b) WHILE Condition

FIND command moves to first record with a last name of Milgrom

```
. LIST LASTNAME,AMOUNT,TERM,INTEREST
Record#  LASTNAME        AMOUNT TERM INTEREST
     6  Anderson          8500    3    0.130
     2  Flynn             9500    4    0.125
     9  Flynn            10000    3    0.140
     5  Lee              15500    3    0.135
     1  Milgrom          95000   30    0.110
    10  Milgrom         178500   30    0.095
     7  Mills            88500   15    0.095
     8  Moldof          250000   15    0.097
     3  Simpson          65000   10    0.095
     4  Taylor          500000   15    0.115
```

(c) Efficiency Considerations

condition has to consider all 10. The difference in execution speed can be dramatic with large files.

A Restricted View

Until now we have had an unrestricted ***view*** of any **DBF** file in use; i.e., every command provided implicit access to every field in every record. There are times, however, when it is useful to limit the view in effect, i.e., to see only certain records and/or certain fields within those records. This is accomplished through combination of the **SET FIELDS** and **SET FILTER** commands.

The SET FIELDS Command

The **LIST** and/or **DISPLAY** commands normally show every field in each record they display. While this is not a problem in records with a limited (in size) file structure, it is inconvenient in larger structures in that the fields from one record wrap around the screen, making the output difficult to read.

The **SET FIELDS** command acts as a filter to limit the fields accessible in subsequent commands. Consider:

Syntax

```
SET FIELDS TO [<field-1>...<field-n>]
```

Examples

```
SET FIELDS TO LASTNAME,AMOUNT
SET FIELDS TO
```

The **SET FIELDS** command in Figure 6.6a includes two fields, **LASTNAME** and **AMOUNT**, causing the subsequent **LIST** command to display the values of only these two fields. The remaining fields have not disappeared from the file structure but are simply hidden from view.

The effect of the **SET FIELDS** command is *cumulative*; i.e., the fields in each subsequent command are added to the field list established by any previous command(s). In other words, three additional fields, **TYPE, LOAN_DATE**, and **COSIGNER**, are added to the field list of Figure 6.6a by the **SET FIELDS** command of Figure 6.6b, and hence the **LIST** command in Figure 6.6b displays five fields rather than three.

The **SET FIELDS** command can be issued *without* any fields at all, as was done in Figure 6.6c. This action will cancel the existing field list, causing any subsequent **LIST** (or **DISPLAY**) command to again show all of the fields in the original file structure.

The SET FILTER Command

The **SET FILTER** command restricts the view of a **DBF** file to those records meeting a designated filter condition. After the command has been executed—i.e., once a filter condition is in effect—it is as though the file in use consists of only those records that satisfy the condition; the other records have *not* been deleted, but are treated as though they weren't there. Consider:

Syntax

```
SET FILTER TO [<condition>]
```

Examples

```
SET FILTER TO AMOUNT > 200000
SET FILTER TO
```

FIGURE 6.6
The SET FIELDS Command

```
. USE LOANS
. SET FIELDS TO LASTNAME,AMOUNT
. LIST OFF
LASTNAME      AMOUNT
Milgrom        95000
Flynn           9500
Simpson        65000
Taylor        500000
Lee            15500
Anderson        8500
Mills          88500
Moldof        250000
Flynn          10000
Milgrom       178500
```

(a) Initial Command

Fields are added to existing field list

```
. SET FIELDS TO TYPE,LOAN_DATE,COSIGNER
. LIST OFF
LASTNAME      AMOUNT TYPE LOAN_DATE COSIGNER
Milgrom        95000 M    11/24/89   .F.
Flynn           9500 A    11/11/90   .T.
Simpson        65000 B    05/05/91   .F.
Taylor        500000 M    10/18/88   .F.
Lee            15500 A    05/15/91   .T.
Anderson        8500 A    02/02/91   .T.
Mills          88500 M    05/13/91   .T.
Moldof        250000 M    05/10/91   .F.
Flynn          10000 P    06/30/91   .T.
Milgrom       178500 M    06/30/91   .F.
```

(b) Adding to the Field List

Original field list is restored

```
. SET FIELDS TO
. LIST OFF
LOAN_NUM  AMOUNT . . . LASTNAME . . .    TELEPHONE
1000       95000 . . . Milgrom  . . .    3059749876
1005        9500 . . . Flynn    . . .    3057778888
1010       65000 . . . Simpson  . . .    3057520998
8000      500000 . . . Taylor   . . .    4077772222
2400       15500 . . . Lee      . . .    3057531752
3050        8500 . . . Anderson . . .    3053445000
4000       88500 . . . Mills    . . .    3055554444
4100      250000 . . . Moldof   . . .    3053448765
4269       10000 . . . Flynn    . . .    3057778888
5000      178500 . . . Milgrom  . . .    3059992222
```

(c) Restoring the Field List

The **SET FILTER** command in Figure 6.7a limits the view of the **LOANS.DBF** file to those records with an amount greater than $200,000. Hence, the subsequent **LIST** command displays only two records (i.e., the records meeting the filter condition), although the **LOANS.DBF** file still contains the original ten records. Note, too, that the **LIST** command displays only five fields for each of the listed records, which assumes that the **SET FIELDS** commands of Figures 6.6a and 6.6b are still in effect.

The execution of a **SET FILTER** command *replaces* the condition in effect from any previous command. Thus, the **SET FILTER** command in Figure 6.7b limits our view to records with an automobile loan (regardless of the amount), the command in

FIGURE 6.7
The SET FILTER Command (assumes the SET FIELDS commands of Figures 6.6a and 6.6b are in effect)

```
. SET FILTER TO AMOUNT>  200000
. LIST OFF
 LASTNAME       AMOUNT TYPE LOAN_DATE COSIGNER
 Taylor         500000 M     10/18/88  .F.
 Moldof         250000 M     05/10/91  .F.
```

(a) Numeric Field

```
. SET FILTER TO TYPE = "A"
. LIST OFF
 LASTNAME       AMOUNT TYPE LOAN_DATE COSIGNER
 Flynn            9500 A     11/11/90  .T.
 Lee             15500 A     05/15/91  .T.
 Anderson         8500 A     02/02/91  .T.
```

(b) Character Field

```
. SET FILTER TO COSIGNER
. LIST OFF
 LASTNAME       AMOUNT TYPE LOAN_DATE COSIGNER
 Flynn            9500 A     11/11/90  .T.
 Lee             15500 A     05/15/91  .T.
 Anderson         8500 A     02/02/91  .T.
 Mills           88500 M     05/13/91  .T.
 Flynn           10000 P     06/30/91  .T.
```

(c) Logical Field

```
. SET FILTER TO LOAN_DATE > {06/01/91}
. LIST OFF
 LASTNAME       AMOUNT TYPE LOAN_DATE COSIGNER
 Flynn           10000 P     06/30/91  .T.
 Milgrom        178500 M     06/30/91  .F.
```

(d) Date Field

```
. SET FILTER TO
. LIST OFF
 LASTNAME       AMOUNT TYPE LOAN_DATE COSIGNER
 Milgrom         95000 M     11/24/89  .F.
 Flynn            9500 A     11/11/90  .T.
 Simpson         65000 B     05/05/91  .F.
 Taylor         500000 M     10/18/88  .F.
 Lee             15500 A     05/15/91  .T.
 Anderson         8500 A     02/02/91  .T.
 Mills           88500 M     05/13/91  .T.
 Moldof         250000 M     05/10/91  .F.
 Flynn           10000 P     06/30/91  .T.
 Milgrom        178500 M     06/30/91  .F.
```

(e) Restoring the Filter Condition

Figure 6.7c limits the view to loans with a cosigner, while the command in Figure 6.7d restricts it to loans made after June 1, 1991. Note, too, how the format of the condition in each of the four figures depends on the field type, and how a different syntax is used for numeric, character, logical, and date fields as described previously in conjunction with Table 6.2.

The **SET FILTER** command in Figure 6.7e *omits* a condition, which in turn restores the view to all records in the associated file; consequently, the subsequent **LIST** command displays the ten records in the **LOANS.DBF** file.

HANDS-ON EXERCISE 1

Finding (Locating) Individual Records

Objective

Demonstrate the `FIND`, `LOCATE`, `SKIP`, and `CONTINUE` commands to identify individual records; change the current view through the `SET FIELDS` and `SET FILTER` commands.

STEP 1 **Change to the LOANS directory**

Boot the system, ending at the DOS prompt. Type one of the following two commands, depending on whether you are sharing the hard drive with others:

`CD C:\DATADISK\LOANS` ——	*if you installed the data disk on the hard drive and are not sharing your computer, or*
`CD A:\DATADISK\LOANS` ——	*if you did not install the data disk, i.e., if you are sharing drive C with other students. (Use data disk two if you have 5¼-inch disks.)*

STEP 2 **Open the LOANS.DBF file**

Type **dBASE** to load dBASE, then set the default drive as you have in previous exercises. Type **USE LOANS** at the dot prompt to use the existing `LOANS.DBF` file, then type **LIST LASTNAME** to list the last name and record numbers of the ten existing records as shown in Figure 6.3a.

STEP 3 **The LOCATE and CONTINUE commands**

Enter the command, **LOCATE FOR LASTNAME = "Flynn"**, to find the *first* Flynn in the `LOANS.DBF` file; the search is successful with dBASE indicating a match in record number 2. Reenter the *identical* `LOCATE` command (by pressing the **up arrow** key) and dBASE will again return record 2, because the same `LOCATE` command always returns the same record. Type **CONTINUE** (rather than `LOCATE`) to begin the search after record 2, and this time the match occurs at record number 9. Type **CONTINUE** a *second* time (to begin the search after record 9), whereupon dBASE returns the message *End of LOCATE scope,* indicating that there are no more individuals with this last name.

STEP 4 **The FIND command**

Enter the command, **SET ORDER TO TAG LASTNAME,** then type **FIND FLYNN** in *upper-case*; dBASE returns the message *Find not successful* because the `FIND` command is case sensitive. Type the command, **FIND Flynn**, which results in a successful search but a mere dot prompt as dBASE provides no explicit indication of a successful `FIND` command. Type **DISPLAY LASTNAME** to verify that you are positioned at record number 2 and that the last name is indeed Flynn.

Press the **up arrow** key twice and then press **return** to repeat the successful **FIND Flynn** command. Press the **up arrow** key as necessary to retrieve the **DISPLAY** command, then press **return**, and you will see that you are still at record number 2, because `FIND`, like `LOCATE`, always returns the same record. Type **SKIP**, followed by **DISPLAY LASTNAME**, and you will see the second Flynn (record 9); type **SKIP** and **DISPLAY LASTNAME**, and you will see Lee (record 5); note, however, that the `SKIP` command did not indicate that there were no more matching records.

STEP 5 **The SET FIELDS command**

Enter the following `LIST` and `SET FIELDS` commands or use the **up** and **down arrow** keys as appropriate:

```
.LIST
.SET FIELDS TO LASTNAME,AMOUNT,TERM,TYPE
.LIST
```

The first `LIST` command shows every field for every record and presents a rather confusing screen. The second `LIST` command produces a better screen with fewer fields because of the field list established by the `SET FIELDS` command.

STEP 6 **The SET FILTER command**

Enter the following `SET FILTER` and `LIST` commands or use the **up** and **down arrow** keys as appropriate:

```
.SET FILTER TO TYPE = "M" .AND. TERM = 15
.LIST
```

The `SET FILTER` command reduces our view of the database to those records with a mortgage loan *and* a term of 15 years. Thus the subsequent `LIST` command displays only three records and only four fields for each record (`LASTNAME`, `AMOUNT`, `TERM`, and `TYPE`) because the `SET FIELDS` command of the previous step is still in effect. Note, too, that the three records are listed in alphabetical order because the `SET ORDER TO TAG LASTNAME` command is still in effect from step 4.

STEP 7 **Cancel existing settings**

Type the commands, **SET ORDER TO**, **SET FIELDS TO**, and **SET FILTER TO**, each with no additional parameters, to cancel the effects of earlier commands issued in steps 4, 5, and 6, respectively. Type **LIST** to verify that the existing settings have been canceled; i.e., you will see all fields for all records in natural (record number) order.

STEP 8 **The SET VIEW command**

Type the command, **SET VIEW TO MORTGAGE** to utilize an existing query file, `MORTGAGE.QBE`, which exists on the data disk. (The concept of a query file is discussed immediately following the exercise.) Type **LIST** and you will again see the three records from step 7, with four fields for each record, and with the records listed in alphabetical order.

Query Files

The `LIST` commands in steps 6 and 8 of the just completed hands-on exercise display identical information, namely, a list of the 15-year mortgage loans in alphabetical sequence according to the borrower's last name. The outputs are the same, but they are produced through very different command sequences as shown in Figure 6.8.

Figure 6.8a shows the `SET` commands used in steps 4, 5, and 6 of the hands-on exercise to designate a sequence (`SET ORDER`), establish a field list (`SET FIELDS`), and implement a filter condition (`SET FILTER`). Figure 6.8b, on the other hand, contains a single command, `SET VIEW TO MORTGAGE`, that produces the identical result. We conclude, therefore, that the **SET VIEW** command represents a shorter way to achieve the effect of several other commands. As we shall see, the `SET VIEW` com-

FIGURE 6.8
The SET VIEW Command

```
. USE LOANS
. SET ORDER TO TAG LASTNAME
. SET FIELDS TO LASTNAME,AMOUNT,TERM,TYPE
. SET FILTER TO TYPE = "M" .AND. TERM = 15
. LIST
Record#  LASTNAME        AMOUNT TERM TYPE
      7  Mills            88500   15 M
      8  Moldof          250000   15 M
      4  Taylor          500000   15 M
```

(a) Commands from the Dot Prompt

```
. SET VIEW TO MORTGAGE
. LIST
Record#  LASTNAME        AMOUNT TERM TYPE
      7  Mills            88500   15 M
      8  Moldof          250000   15 M
      4  Taylor          500000   15 M
```

(b) Query File

mand activates a query file, in this case **MORTGAGE.QBE**, which contains the equivalent of the individual commands shown in Figure 6.8a.

A query file is created in much the same way as report forms and mailing labels. You are presented with a work surface and set of pull-down menus, and you use the **CREATE QUERY** and **MODIFY QUERY** commands just as you used their counterparts for report forms and mailing labels.

Query by Example

Figure 6.9 displays the query design work surface for the **MORTGAGE.QBE** file. The figure resembles the work surfaces for report forms and mailing labels in that it contains a ***menu bar*** at the top and a ***navigation line*** at the bottom. The essence of the query work surface, however, is in two new elements—a ***file skeleton*** and a ***view skeleton.***

The file skeleton is a graphic representation of a file structure, containing the name of the file (**LOANS.DBF**) and all of the fields in that file (although not all of the fields are visible at once). The view skeleton indicates which fields from the file skeleton will appear in the completed query and corresponds to the execution of a **SET FIELDS** command. Observe, therefore, that three of the fields in the file skeleton (**TERM**, **TYPE**, and **LASTNAME**), are preceded by a down arrow, indicating that they appear in the view skeleton. The other fields (**LOAN_DATE**, **COSIGNER**, **FIRSTNAME**, and **STREET**) appear without the down arrow, which implies that they are not in the view.

The file skeleton uses a **QBE** (***Query by Example***) interface to implement the conditions for selecting a record as well as the sequence in which the selected records are to appear; i.e., the file skeleton enables you to achieve the equivalent of a **SET FILTER** and/or a **SET ORDER** command. The **Asc1** entry under the **LASTNAME** field indicates that records are to appear in *asc*ending sequence by last name and that this is the primary (only) field on which sorting is to take place. In similar fashion the entries under the **TERM** and **TYPE** fields impose the equivalent of the filter condition **TERM = 15 .AND. TYPE = "M"**.

FIGURE 6.9
Query Design Work Surface

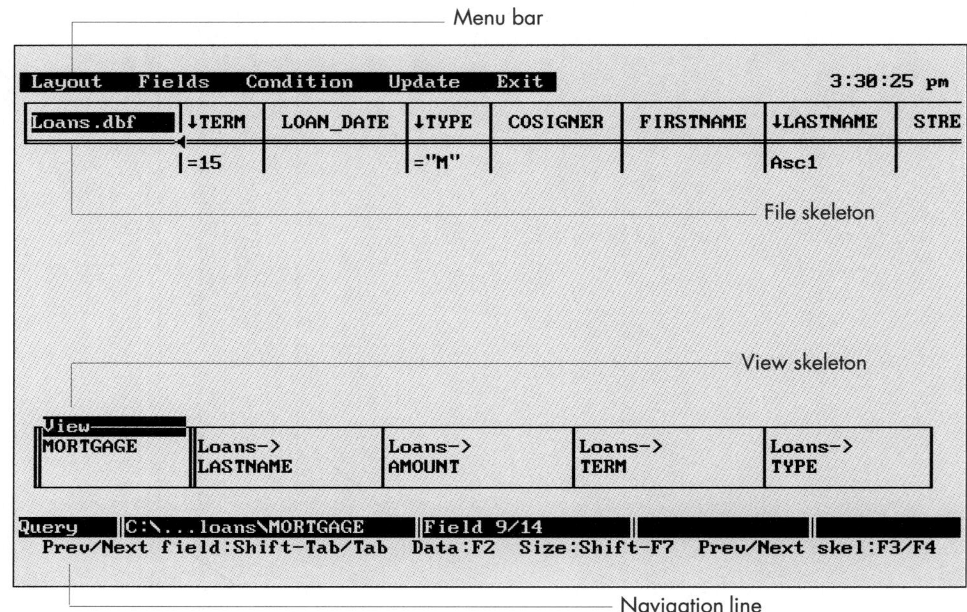

Figure 6.10 further illustrates the **QBE** approach with respect to implementation of the **.OR.** and **.AND.** operations. Figure 6.10a implements the **.OR.** operation in which each simple condition appears on a *separate* line in the work surface. Figure 6.10b, on the other hand, implements the **.AND.** operation in which all of the simple conditions appear on the *same* line.

Note, too, that our illustration uses four different field types with a different syntax required for each. Thus, **TERM** was defined as a numeric field, and its condition appears without quotation marks; **LOANDATE** is defined as a date field and requires curly braces to select records after June 30, 1990; **TYPE** is a character field and needs quotation marks for its condition, whereas **COSIGNER** is a logical field requiring a true-or-false operator.

FIGURE 6.10
Query by Example

Loans.dbf	AMOUNT	INTEREST	TERM	LOAN_DATE	TYPE	COSIGNER
			=30			
				>{06/30/90}		
					="A"	
						.T.

(a) .OR. Function

Loans.dbf	AMOUNT	INTEREST	TERM	LOAN_DATE	TYPE	COSIGNER
			=30	>{06/30/90}	="A"	.T.

(b) .AND. Function

The Calculated Fields Skeleton

The query design work surface can also contain a third component, the ***calculated fields skeleton,*** which was not shown in Figure 6.9. As its name implies, the calculated field skeleton is used to define a calculated field, i.e., a field that is not in the file structure, but whose value is determined from other fields that are. A good example of a calculated field is the monthly payment of a loan, a field whose value is calculated from three other fields: the amount borrowed (i.e., principal), the interest rate per period, and the number of periods.

The computation of the monthly payment is facilitated through the **PAYMENT *function,*** one of several functions included within dBASE to perform a specified calculation. The PAYMENT function determines the periodic loan payment for a loan and has the following format:

Syntax

```
PAYMENT(Principal, Interest per period, Number of periods)
```

Examples

```
PAYMENT(100000,.10/12,15*12)
PAYMENT(AMOUNT,INTEREST/12,TERM*12)
```

The first example computes the *monthly* payment for a $100,000 loan at 10 percent annual interest, payable over 15 years. Observe, therefore, how the annual interest is divided by 12 within the payment function, and further how the 15-year term is multiplied by 12. The second example computes the monthly payment, based on the field names AMOUNT, INTEREST, and TERM, rather than on specific values.

We are ready now for our second hands-on exercise, in which you develop your own query file to compute the monthly payment of all mortgage loans.

HANDS-ON EXERCISE 2

Query by Example

Objective

Create a query to list the loan number and monthly payment for all mortgage loans in sequence by loan number.

STEP 1 **The CREATE QUERY command**

Type **USE LOANS** to reopen the LOANS.DBF file as well as negate the effects of any existing SET FILTER or SET FIELDS commands. Then type **CREATE QUERY YOURTURN** (where YOURTURN is the name of the query you will create) to display the query design work surface of Figure 6.11a; you will see the file skeleton for LOANS.DBF at the top of the screen and the view skeleton for the YOURTURN query (view) at the bottom.

STEP 2 **Explore the work surface**

Press the **F3/F4** function key to toggle back and forth between the file skeleton and the view skeleton. Stop in either place and use the **Tab** key to move from one field to the *next* field or the **Shift+Tab** keys to move to the *previous* field.

STEP 3 **Changing the view skeleton**

The F5 key adds or removes a field(s) from the view skeleton; i.e., pressing the F5 key when a field is not in the view skeleton will add the field, while pressing the key when the field is in the view skeleton removes it. Note, however, that every field in

FIGURE 6.11
Creating a Query File

```
Layout   Fields   Condition   Update   Exit                        10:30:47 am
Loans.dbf | ↓LOAN_NUM | ↓AMOUNT | ↓INTEREST | ↓TERM | ↓LOAN_DATE | ↓TYPE | ↓COSIGNE

View
YOURTURN | Loans->   | Loans-> | Loans->  | Loans->
         | LOAN_NUM  | AMOUNT  | INTEREST | TERM

Query  C:\...loans\YOURTURN  File 1/1                               CapsIns
 Next field:Tab  Add/Remove all fields:F5  Zoom:F9  Prev/Next skeleton:F3/F4
```

(a) Opening Screen

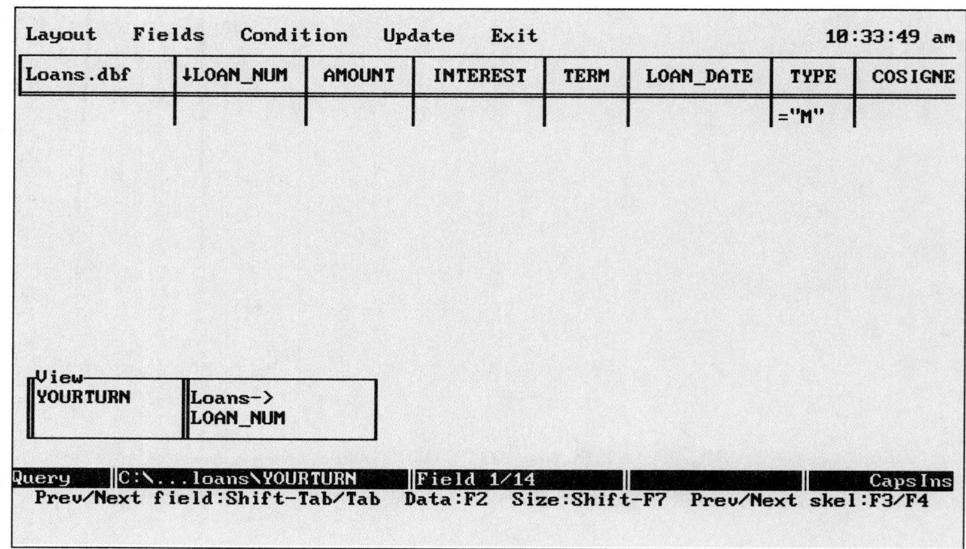

(b) Setting a Filter

the file skeleton is initially present in the view skeleton, whereas the finished view will contain only the **LOAN_NUM** field from the file skeleton. Accordingly, we need to delete several fields from the view skeleton.

Use the **F3/F4** key to move to the file skeleton, then use the **Tab/Shift+Tab** key to move to the **LOANS.DBF** column in the file skeleton. Press the **F5** key to remove *all* fields currently in the view skeleton (you can replace the fields by pressing the **F5** key a second time). Stay in the file skeleton and tab to the **LOAN_NUM** field, then press **F5** to add this field to the view skeleton as shown in Figure 6.11b.

FIGURE 6.11
Creating a Query File (continued)

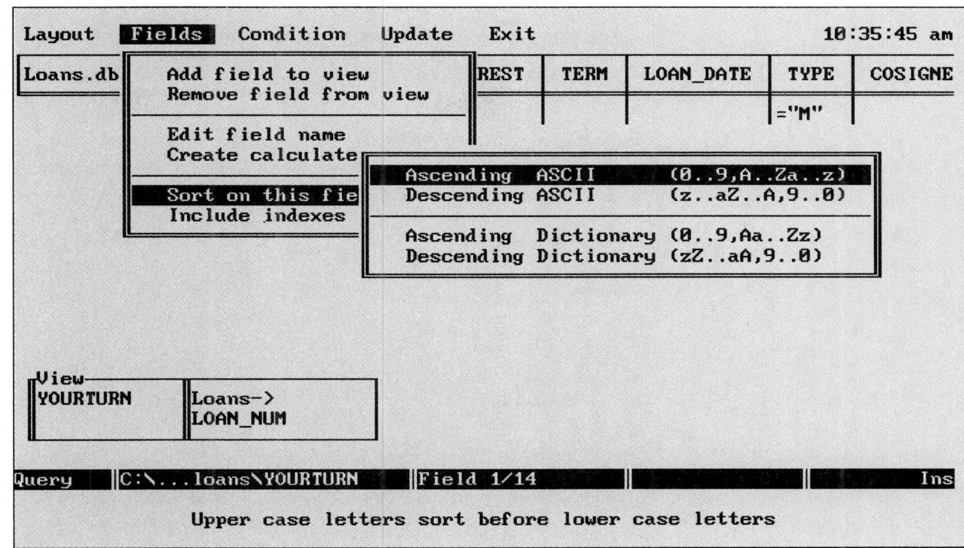

(c) Selecting a Sequence

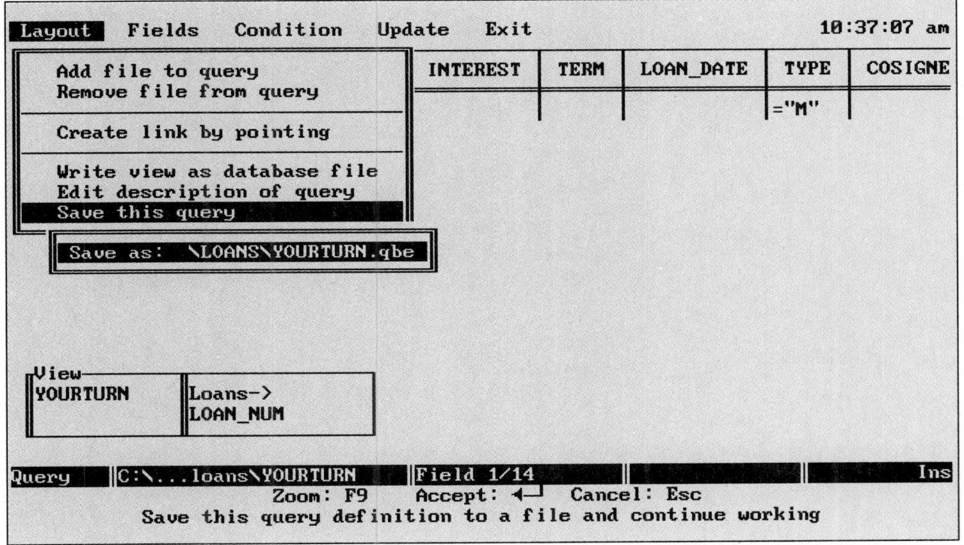

(d) Saving the Query

STEP 4 **Enter the filter condition**

Tab to the **TYPE** field in the file skeleton, then enter the filter condition for mortgages by typing **="M"** and pressing **return**. Your screen should match Figure 6.11b exactly.

STEP 5 **Selecting a sequence**

Press **Shift+Tab** to move backward to the **LOAN_NUM** field, then press **Alt+F** to pull down the fields menu. Highlight *Sort on this field* and press **return**, then highlight *Ascending ASCII* as shown in Figure 6.11c and press **return** once more. You

FIGURE 6.11
Creating a Query File (continued)

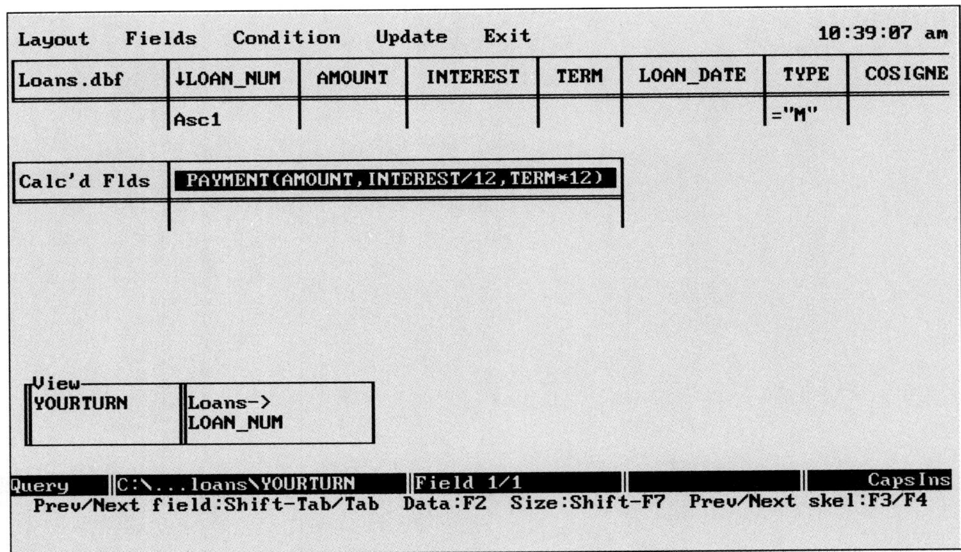

(e) Defining a Calculated Field

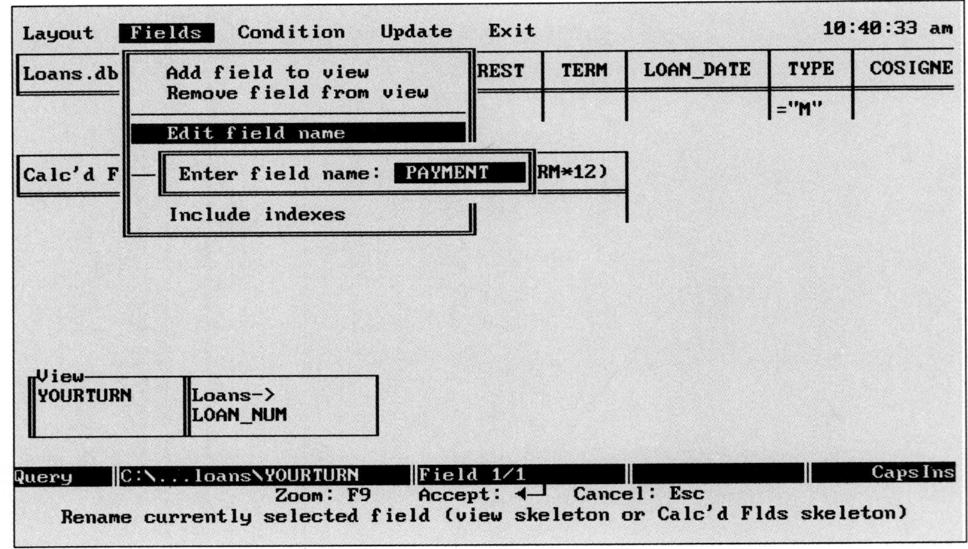

(f) Naming the Calculated Field

will see **Asc1** under the **LOAN_NUM** field, indicating an ascending sort in ASCII sequence; the number one indicates that this is the primary (in this case only) field on which the sort is to be based.

STEP 6 **Save the query**

We cannot overemphasize the need to repeatedly save your work; accordingly, press **Alt+L** to pull down the layout menu, highlight *Save this query,* and press **return**, then press **return** a second time to save it as **YOURTURN.QBE** as shown in Figure 6.11d. (dBASE automatically appends the **QBE** extension, whereas **YOURTURN** was

FIGURE 6.11
Creating a Query File (continued)

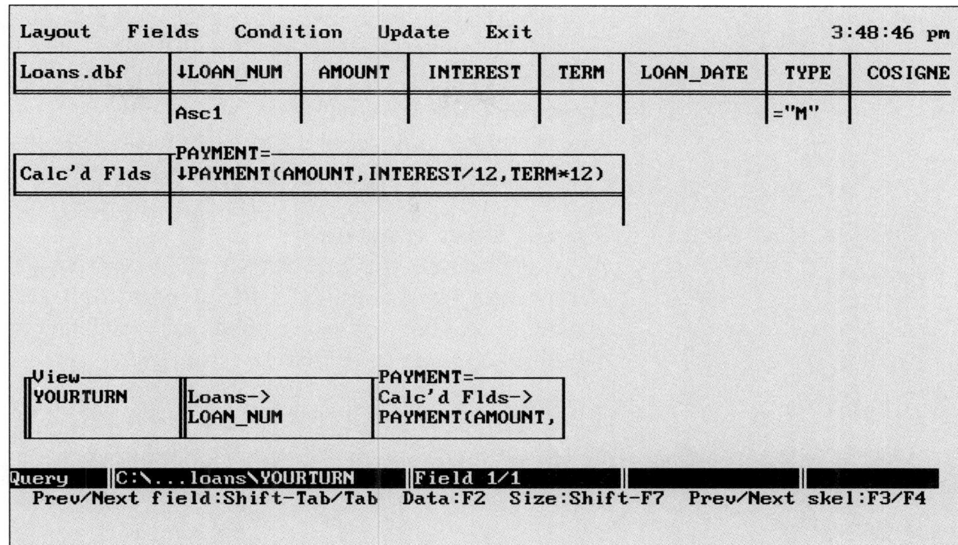

(g) The Completed Query

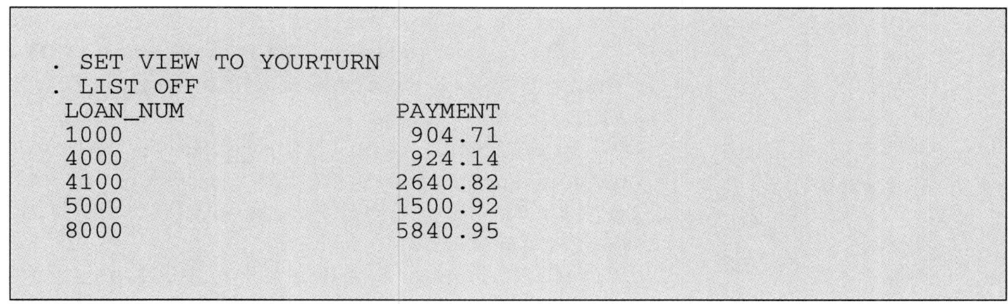

```
. SET VIEW TO YOURTURN
. LIST OFF
 LOAN_NUM                    PAYMENT
 1000                         904.71
 4000                         924.14
 4100                        2640.82
 5000                        1500.92
 8000                        5840.95
```

(h) SET VIEW Command

taken as the name of the query in accordance with the initial **CREATE QUERY** command from step 1.)

STEP 7 **Add a calculated field**

Press **Alt+F** to again pull down the fields menu, highlight *Create calculated field,* and press **return** to produce the calculated fields skeleton shown in Figure 6.11e. Enter the payment function as **PAYMENT(AMOUNT,INTEREST/12,TERM*12)**, and press **return**.

STEP 8 **Name the calculated field**

Press **Alt+F** a final time, select *Edit field name,* and press **return**. Type **PAYMENT** as the name of the calculated field as shown in Figure 6.11f. Press **return** to complete the operation.

STEP 9 **Add the PAYMENT field to the view skeleton**

Use the **F3/F4** key to once again move about the work surface, but notice how this time you move between three skeletons: the file skeleton at the top of the screen, the calculated fields skeleton in the middle, and the view skeleton at the bottom. Stop in the calculated fields skeleton and press the **F5** key to add this field to the view skeleton, producing the completed query of Figure 6.11g.

STEP 10 **Save the completed query**
Press **Alt+E** to pull down the exit menu, save the completed query, and return to the dot prompt.

STEP 11 **The SET VIEW command**
Type **SET VIEW TO YOURTURN**, then type **LIST OFF** to list all records in the LOANS.DBF file according to the query **YOURTURN**. You should see five records in ascending sequence of loan number as shown in Figure 6.11h, with the monthly payment printed for each record.

Summary

A ***condition*** evaluates the relationship between two quantities and returns a value of true or false, depending on whether or not the relationship is satisfied. The two quantities on either side of the condition must be of the same data type.

The logical operators, **.AND.**, **.OR.**, and **.NOT.** combine two (or more) simple conditions into a ***compound condition;*** .NOT. is evaluated first, followed by .AND., and then .OR.

The **FIND** command is the fastest way to locate individual records in a DBF file, but its use requires that the file have been previously opened with an index. The **LOCATE** command searches sequentially through the file. Both commands are case sensitive.

Most commands enable a choice between a **FOR** and a **WHILE** condition; the commands can be used to produce equivalent output, but the WHILE condition executes more efficiently.

The **SET FIELDS** and/or **SET FILTER** commands limit our view of the **DBF** file. The equivalent of both commands can be stored in a dBASE ***query file.***

The query design work surface consists of a ***file skeleton, view skeleton,*** and optional ***calculated fields skeleton.*** The query is developed through a **QBE** (Query By Example) interface unique to dBASE IV.

The dBASE **PAYMENT** function computes a periodic payment, based on three arguments: the principal, interest rate per period, and number of periods.

Key Words and Concepts

.AND.
Ascl
Calculated fields skeleton
Case sensitive
Compound condition
Condition
CONTINUE
CREATE QUERY
Curly braces
Data type mismatch
Fields menu
File skeleton
F3/F4 function key
F5 function key
FIND
FOR condition
Layout menu
LOCATE
Logical operators
Menu bar
MODIFY QUERY
Navigation line
.NOT.
.OR.
PAYMENT function
Precedence of operations
Query file
Query by example
Relational operators
Search-string

SET FIELDS	Simple condition	View
SET FILTER	SKIP	View skeleton
SET VIEW	Tab key	
Shift+Tab key	WHILE condition	

True/False

1. The **LOCATE** command requires an index.
2. The **FIND** command requires an index.
3. The **FIND** command can be expected to execute quicker than the corresponding **LOCATE** command.
4. **SET FILTER** may not be used in conjunction with **SET FIELDS**.
5. A given condition may not include more than one **.AND.**, **.OR.**, or **.NOT.** operation.
6. Both the **FIND** and **LOCATE** commands merely move the record pointer, but do not display the associated record.
7. A date field may not appear in a dBASE condition.
8. The **SET FILTER** command physically deletes from the database all records that do not meet the filter condition.
9. The **REMOVE FILTER** command negates the effect of a pre-existing filter condition.
10. A query file permanently stores a filter condition.
11. The **SET FIELDS** command can be used with either the **DISPLAY** or **LIST** command.
12. The **PAYMENT** function has three arguments.

Exercises

1. Distinguish between:
   (a) A simple condition and a compound condition
   (b) A **SET FIELDS** command and a **SET FILTER** command
   (c) A **LOCATE** command and a **FIND** command
   (d) A **LOCATE** command and a **CONTINUE** command
   (e) A **FOR** condition and a **WHILE** condition
   (f) The file skeleton and the view skeleton
   (g) Pressing **Tab** or **Shift+Tab** within the query design surface
   (h) Pressing the **F3** and the **F4** keys within the query design surface

2. Use the file structure in Figure 6.1 to write an appropriate **LIST** command to display all loans meeting the specified conditions:
   (a) All loans less than $100,000
   (b) Mortgage loans less than $100,000
   (c) All loans with an interest rate of less than 10% *or* a term greater than 5 years
   (d) All mortgage loans with an interest rate less than 10% *and* a term of 15 years
   (e) All loans with a monthly payment greater than $1,000
   (f) Any loan that is not a mortgage
   (g) All loans made after January 1, 1991

3. Indicate the effect that each of the following commands will have on the **LOANS.DBF** file as it appears in Figure 6.5c, i.e., with **LASTNAME** as the master

index. Be sure to include the approximate text of any dBASE messages produced as a result of the command.

(a) **FIND FLYNN**
(b) **LOCATE FOR LASTNAME = 'FLYNN'**
(c) **FIND Flynn**
(d) **LOCATE FOR LASTNAME = 'Flynn'**
(e) **CONTINUE** (issued immediately after part d)
(f) **CONTINUE** (issued immediately after part e)
(g) **LOCATE FOR LASTNAME = 'Flynn**
(h) **LOCATE FOR LASTNAME = Flynn**

4. Figure 6.12 contains a completed query upon which the following questions are based.
   (a) What is the name of the view?
   (b) What is the filter condition; i.e., which records will appear in this view?
   (c) Which fields appear in the view?
   (d) What is the significance of the down arrow that appears next to the **LASTNAME** field in the file skeleton?
   (e) What effect does pressing the F5 function key have when you are positioned in the **LASTNAME** field of the *file* skeleton?
   (f) In which sequence will the records appear?
   (g) Why does **PAYMENT** appear twice in the calculated fields skeleton?

5. Develop a query, **AUTOLOAN.QBE**, corresponding to the commands shown in Figure 6.13.

6. Each of the following conditions (developed in accordance with the file structure in Figure 6.1) has a problem of one type or another. Some of the conditions are invalid syntactically, whereas others are syntactically valid, but produce results different from what the user intended. Indicate the difficulty in each.
   (a) **TYPE = "m"**
   (b) **TYPE = M**
   (c) **TYPE = "M" AND AMOUNT > 100000**
   (d) **TYPE = "M" .OR. AMOUNT > 100,000**

FIGURE 6.12
Query for Problem 4

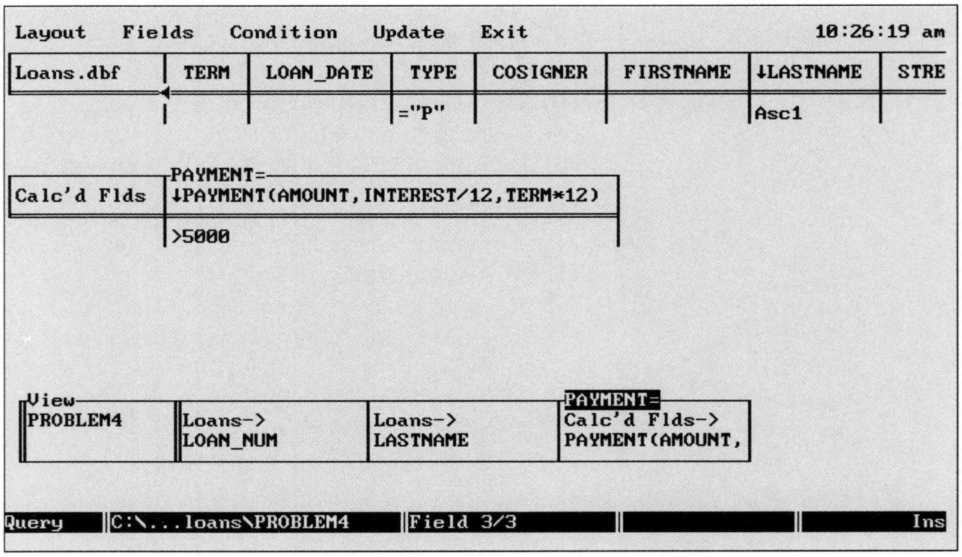

```
Layout   Fields   Condition   Update   Exit                              10:26:19 am
Loans.dbf | TERM | LOAN_DATE | TYPE  | COSIGNER | FIRSTNAME | ↓LASTNAME | STRE
          |      |           | ="P"  |          |           | Asc1      |

              PAYMENT=
Calc'd Flds | ↓PAYMENT(AMOUNT,INTEREST/12,TERM*12)
            | >5000

View                                                    PAYMENT=
PROBLEM4     | Loans->     | Loans->     | Calc'd Flds->
             | LOAN_NUM    | LASTNAME    | PAYMENT(AMOUNT,

Query    |C:\...loans\PROBLEM4    |Field 3/3    |    |    Ins
```

FIGURE 6.13
Commands for Problem 5

```
. USE LOANS
. SET ORDER TO TAG LASTNAME
. SET FIELDS TO LOAN_NUM,LASTNAME,AMOUNT,LOAN_DATE,TYPE
. SET FILTER TO TYPE = "A" .AND. LOAN_DATE > {03/01/91}
. LIST OFF
```

(e) **TYPE <> "M" .OR. TYPE <> "P"**
(f) **LOAN_DATE > 11/24/91**
(g) **COSIGNER = "F"**
(h) **NOT COSIGNER**

7. Which command, **FIND** or **LOCATE**,
   (a) Is the fastest way to find an individual record?
   (b) Is associated with an index?
   (c) Uses quotation marks around the value of a character field?
   (d) Searches the **DBF** file sequentially?
   (e) Always returns the same record?
   (f) Is associated with a **CONTINUE** command?
   (g) Is associated with a **SKIP** command?
   (h) Can search the **DBF** file for a portion of an individual's last name, e.g., Sm rather than Smith?
   (i) Can search on an inequality, e.g., an amount greater than $100,000?
   (j) Can find a record based on two conditions, e.g., a mortgage loan for Milgrom?

8. Which command, **SET FIELDS** or **SET FILTER**,
   (a) Includes a condition?
   (b) Is cumulative, i.e., the effects of a subsequent command are added to a previous command(s)?
   (c) Is analogous to the view skeleton in the query design work surface?
   (d) Corresponds to implementation of query by example in the file skeleton?
   (e) May be issued without any additional parameters?
   (f) Limits the records returned by a subsequent **LIST** or **DISPLAY** command?

CHAPTER

7 The Screen Generator

OUTLINE

OBJECTIVES

After reading this chapter you will be able to:

1. Discuss several considerations in the design of a file structure.
2. Use the dBASE screen generator to create customized screens for data entry and file maintenance.
3. List at least three types of data validation; describe how these checks may be implemented within the context of the dBASE screen generator.
4. Describe in general terms the functions of various statements in the format file produced by the screen generator.
5. Differentiate between the **APPEND** and **SET FORMAT** commands with respect to adding records to a file.

Overview

dBASE includes several special capabilities to facilitate system development, among them report forms (Chapter 4), mailing labels (Chapter 5), and queries (Chapter 6). In this chapter we present the ***screen generator,*** a powerful feature that enables you to design formatted screens to facilitate data entry. Implicit within this discussion is the concept of ***data validation,*** and how various error-checking procedures can be incorporated into the screen generation process.

These subjects are presented within the context of an entirely new case study because one of the major objectives of our book is to expose you to a wide variety of potential dBASE applications. The introduction of a new case is done with this in mind, and it affords you the opportunity to review earlier material on the design of a file structure. We suggest, therefore, that you reread the portions of earlier chapters that dealt with file design, study the present case, and then develop your own file structure prior to viewing our solution.

CASE PREVIEW

The case you are about to read deals with a stock broker interested in attracting additional clients. As you read the discussion, visualize what data is necessary for the broker to accomplish his goals, and what form that data should take within the file structure. Recall, also, the many decisions that are reflected within a file structure, namely:

1. The fields required
2. The size of each field
3. The data type of each field
4. The order of the fields within the record

As you wrestle with your own solution, realize that the major decision in designing any system is, in essence, which fields to include in the file structure. Some of the fields will be obvious, e.g., name and address, which are common to virtually every application. Others will be less obvious, for example, a prospect's telephone number (which was omitted by many of our students when we initially assigned this case as a homework assignment).

Information on precisely which fields to include requires a true understanding of the physical system, which is gained only from discussions with the personnel involved. Since our broker is unavailable, you may want to contact someone else to determine what he or she would want in the way of a system similar to the one we describe. Incorporate your findings into a file structure, then compare your solution to ours.

We continue now with the case description.

CASE STUDY
Michael Essman, Stock Broker

As the 747 taxied to the end of the runway, Michael Essman turned to his wife, smiled, then settled back into his seat for the long ride home. The two weeks in Australia had been fabulous, and the fact that his brokerage house had picked up the tab for the truly deluxe accommodations made it even better. Indeed he was one of only 180 brokers, out of the firm's 11,000, to have achieved sufficient sales production to merit the trip. The realization that he had accomplished this in less than five years made it all the more gratifying.

Last year's success was in the past, however, and as the plane took off, Mike's thoughts turned to increasing his sales level in the coming year. He was motivated now more by ego than by money, although the money certainly helped, especially as his income had grown from almost nothing to well into six figures. Moreover, the client assets he had under management virtually guaranteed a very comfortable income as long as he maintained his existing accounts. Yes, he had what he wanted materially, but he still craved recognition within the industry as being among the very best. His problem was that of any salesman, namely, how to increase sales production.

Mike knew he was lucky to have entered the business during the early 1980s, yet he also knew it was more than luck. He thought of the approximately 10,000 cold calls he had made over the last year (40 calls a day, 5 days a week, 50 weeks a year), and of the 9,500 rejections those calls had produced. Still, they had yielded some 500 new accounts, which is how he got to Australia in the first place. He thought fondly of his first manager, Norm MacGregor, who effectively reduced selling to a "numbers game," whereby if the number of contacts was sufficiently large, the accounts would follow. Norm's advice to him was simply that "selling is like shaving; do it every day or you're a bum." Mike knew that he couldn't rest on last year's laurels, no matter how great a year it had been.

The problem was that there were only so many hours in a day, and that it simply wasn't possible to increase the amount of time on the phone. He had gotten to the point where he could tell within the first minute of a conversation whether the contact was worth pursuing, and it took him only another two minutes to determine the prospect's investment objective (growth or income), the investment vehicle (stocks and/or bonds), whether he or she was interested in a retirement account, and finally the amount of money available to invest. He realized for the first time that the system he maintained on 3 by 5 index cards was not efficient for following up those contacts who had expressed an interest for additional information. Clearly, he needed a better way to manage repeat phone calls and/or follow-up mailings, especially when a prospect said, "Call me in two weeks," or "Send me the next annual report." Perhaps a computer might help, but how?

The major brokerage he worked for provided adequate computer support for existing clients, but did nothing in the way of data management for prospective clients. Then it hit him: his goal for the coming year would be to use the PC sitting on his desk to solicit new accounts.

CASE SOLUTION

The solution to this (or any other) case begins with the design of the file structure, the importance of which we cannot overemphasize. A logical starting place is to ask yourself the information expected from the system, and then determine the data needed to produce that information; in other words, determine the input needed to produce the required output. Mike Essman, for example, wants the system to tell him:

1. The investment needs of a specific prospect; i.e., whether the person seeks growth or income, whether he or she is interested in stocks, bonds, and/or a retirement account.
2. The date a specific prospect was last contacted, as well as the date for follow-up; also the means of follow-up, i.e., a letter, telephone call, or both.
3. The addresses of all prospects who appear interested, regardless of the amount of money they have to invest.
4. The telephone numbers of all prospects with at least $50,000 to invest, regardless of how interested they seem.

The list goes on and on, but you can begin to appreciate the type of information the system is to produce, and also the data required to produce that information. You can then develop a file structure consistent with the information requirements.

Our solution is shown in Figure 7.1, which may or may not correspond to what you envisioned as you read the case. Indeed, whether or not our solutions are the same is not really important, as there are many satisfactory answers. What is essential, however, is that the structure that is chosen contain all necessary data so that the system can perform as intended.

The need to include the prospect's name, address, and telephone number is apparent from the case preview and discussion. The prospect's name is separated into three fields (last name, first name, and prefix) so that we can index on last name and/

FIGURE 7.1
Suggested File Structure

Field	Field Name	Type	Width
1	LASTNAME	Character	16
2	FIRSTNAME	Character	12
3	PREFIX	Character	3
4	STREET	Character	24
5	CITY	Character	18
6	STATE	Character	2
7	ZIPCODE	Character	5
8	TELEPHONE	Character	10
9	AMOUNT	Numeric	7
10	INTEREST	Character	1
11	LASTCALL	Date	8
12	NEXTCALL	Date	8
13	CALL_MAIL	Character	1
14	STOCKS	Character	1
15	BONDS	Character	1
16	RETIREMENT	Character	1
17	OBJECTIVE	Character	1

or address the person informally by first name. The address is similarly divided so that we can sort on zip code.

The decision on field type (character, numeric, logical, or date) is trivial for most fields. Note, however, that zip code and telephone were designated as character (rather than numeric) even though they contain only numbers, because arithmetic is not performed on these fields.

The length of the telephone field also merits discussion. Given the necessity for including the area code, you might be inclined to specify a field size of fourteen positions rather than ten—i.e., a phone number of the form (305) 284-6105, as opposed to 3052846105, which is more difficult to read. Note, however, that only ten positions are required for the phone number itself, with the additional characters (the left and right parentheses, space, and hyphen) needed only for printed reports or data entry screens. As you will see, it is possible to save space in the file structure by designating the smaller length, with a subsequent conversion to the more readable form accomplished through dBASE commands at the appropriate time.

The file structure must also be broad enough to include all data necessary to fulfill the system's objectives, regardless of whether those objectives are stated implicitly or explicitly. It is logical, for example, to assume that the persons contacted will express different degrees of interest (e.g., high, moderate, or low), and provision must be made to capture this important field. Two date fields are included, perhaps to do a special mailing to all people contacted within the last month, to drop all contacts over a year old, to know whom to contact next week, and so on. Realize, too, that Mike is more interested in clients with large amounts of money to invest (it takes no more time to buy 1000 shares of stock than 100), and so this field should be included as well.

The investment objective is stored as a one-position code containing either a `G` or an `I`, for growth or income, respectively, as opposed to spelling out the data. In addition to saving space, the use of codes facilitates data entry, reduces the chance for error, and simplifies data validation. Three additional fields for stocks, bonds, and retirement are also included, and contain either a Y or an N to indicate whether the prospect is interested in the specific item. We had thought about designating these fields as logical fields; i.e., fields with only two possible values, but opted for the more flexible character field for future expansion. In other words, the broker may eventually want to characterize the degree of interest (e.g., very strong, strong, moderate, none), as opposed to a simple yes/no answer.

The result of these deliberations has produced the file structure shown in Figure 7.1. As can be inferred from the discussion, there are no hard and fast rules for designing a file structure. The decisions that are made as to the fields needed, their sizes and types, reflect the needs of the present (and future) system, and are often subjective in nature.

Data Entry

The **APPEND** command was introduced in Chapter 2 as the means of adding records to a file. The **APPEND** command positions the record pointer at the end of the existing **DBF** file, whereupon the new record is added using the input template shown in Figure 7.2a. Adding records in this fashion may not pose problems for the knowledgeable dBASE user, but it can be intimidating for the less sophisticated end-user; e.g., a prospect's telephone number is entered without parentheses or a hyphen. More importantly, the user is given no guidance in terms of what to enter in other fields, the meaning of which may not be readily apparent; what, for example, is the expected response in the **OBJECTIVE** or **INTEREST** fields?

A better approach is through the formatted screen of Figure 7.2b, in which the fields slated for data entry are spaced attractively on the monitor with appropriate formatting; e.g., the parentheses and hyphen within the phone number. The fields themselves are also labeled more completely; e.g., "Degree of Interest" appears in lieu of **INTEREST**. In addition, a series of ***prompting messages*** (not shown in the *completed* screen of Figure 7.2b) will appear prior to each field being entered. These messages tell the user the response that is expected; i.e., a **G** or **I** (**G**rowth or **I**ncome) in the **OBJECTIVE** field; an **H**, **M**, or **L** (**H**igh, **M**edium, or **L**ow) in the **INTEREST** field; and so on.

Data Validation

Data validation is the all-important process of checking a user's input to prevent erroneous data from being accepted as valid. This procedure is absolutely critical because the objective of any system is to provide information, yet the quality of that information can be only as good as the data on which it is based. No system, no matter how sophisticated, can compensate for inaccurate or incomplete data, a principle aptly stated by the acronym **GIGO** (**G**arbage **I**n, **G**arbage **O**ut).

Figure 7.3a depicts the entry of an erroneous record for Joel Stutz as it would appear at the dot prompt. The record contains an inordinate number of mistakes, each of which was made deliberately, simply to illustrate just how porous dBASE is with respect to data validation. By contrast, Figure 7.3b contains the validated record that was entered through a formatted screen.

Consider now the various types of data validation procedures that are built into this (and other) system(s). Our sytem includes a ***numeric check*** in the telephone number and zip code fields and an ***alphabetic check*** in the state field. A numeric check ensures that only numbers will be accepted into the designated field, whereas an alphabetic check allows only the letters A through Z. Note, too, that an alphabetic field may also employ ***case conversion,*** whereby a user's response is automatically converted to upper (lower) case as with the state abbreviation, e.g., FL.

A ***range*** (or limit) ***check*** ensures that a given entry is within prescribed limits; e.g., the amount to invest must be at least $10,000. A ***code check*** for a valid code confirms that a proper entry has been made in the designated field—e.g., that the degree of interest is **H**, **M**, or **L** (high, medium, or low), or that the investment objective is **G** or **I** (growth or investment). A ***completeness check*** verifies that all necessary fields have been filled; you would not, for example, want to accept a prospect's rec-

FIGURE 7.2
Appending Records

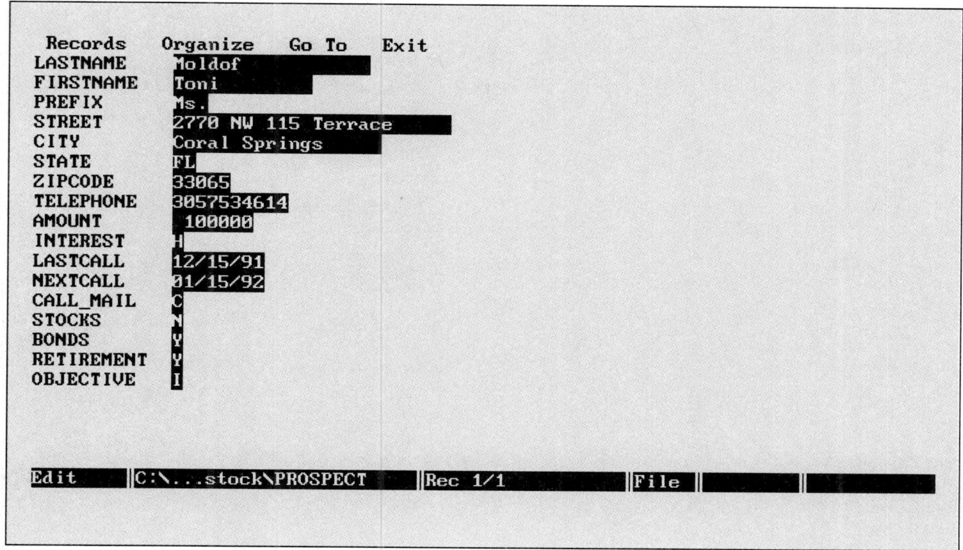

(a) Data Entry via Standard Screen

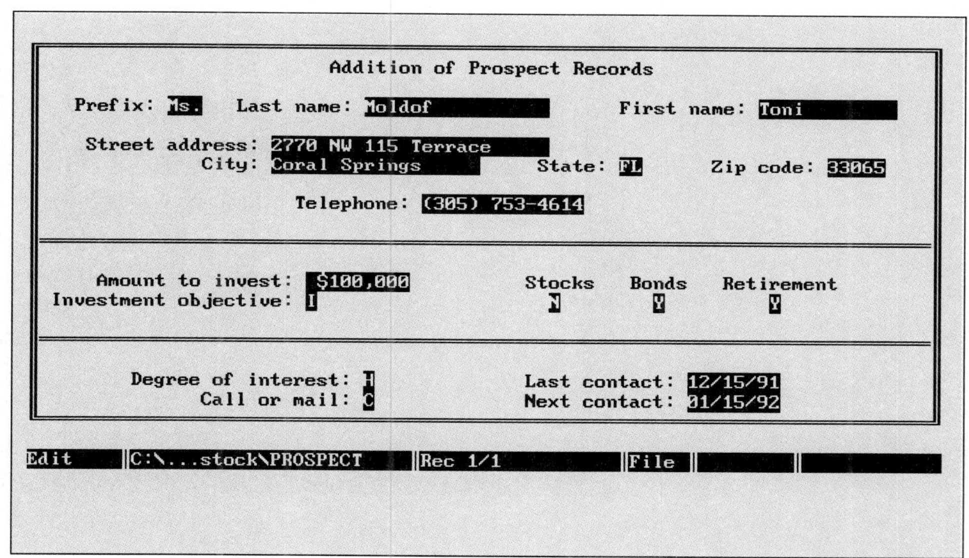

(b) Data Entry via Formatted Screen

ord without a name, address, and telephone number. A ***date check*** ensures a valid date; e.g., a month between one and twelve, inclusive. A date check can also be expanded to validate dates within the context of a particular system—e.g., a minimum of two weeks before a follow-up call (as the broker does not want to annoy his prospects by calling too often).

All of these procedures are built directly into the formatted screen of Figure 7.3b and are illustrated in the ensuing hands-on exercise. There is, however, one type of data validation that is not included, the procedure to prevent a ***duplicate addition,*** i.e., adding a record which is already in the file. This is a critically important check, but one that can be implemented only through programming; it is discussed completely in Chapter 11.

FIGURE 7.3
Data Validation

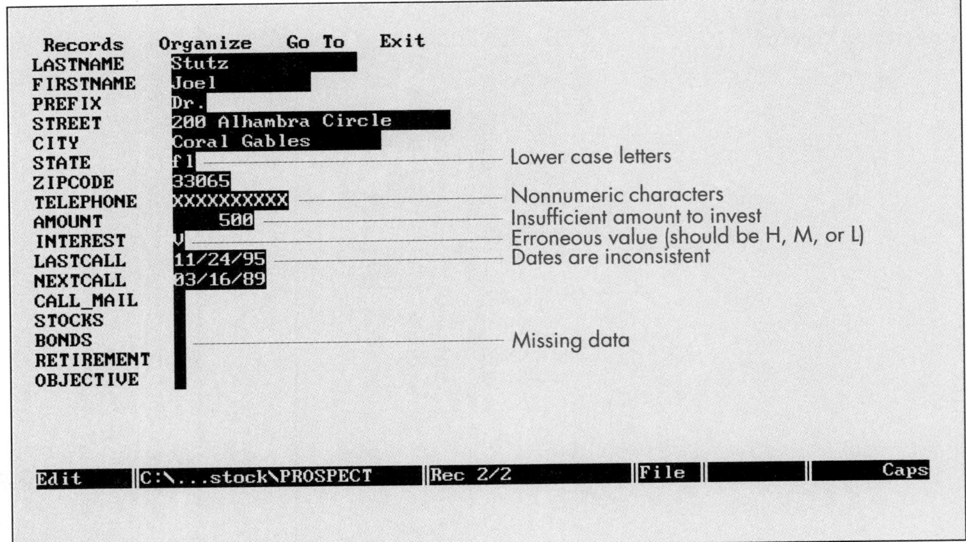

(a) Erroneous Record

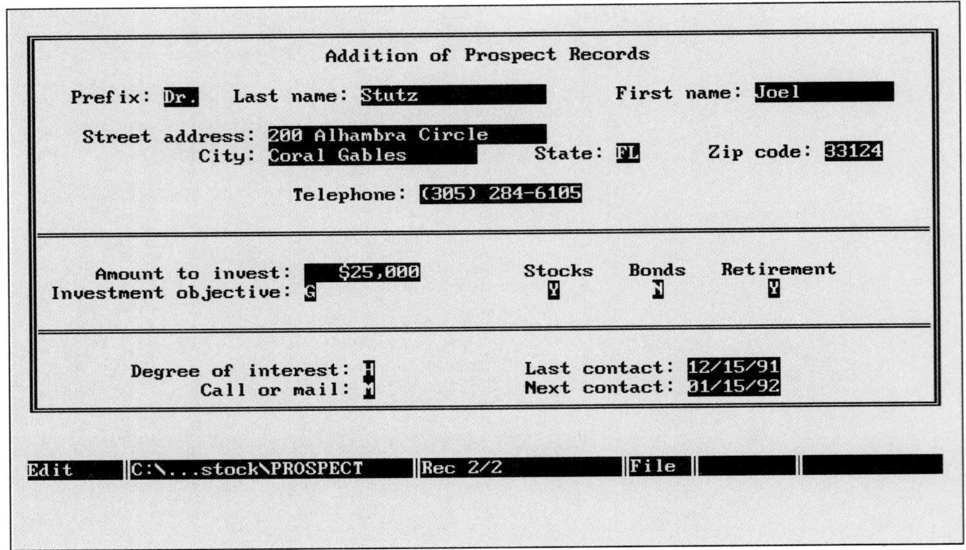

(b) Validated Record

The SET FORMAT Command

As indicated in the chapter opening, dBASE provides a ***screen generator*** (covered in the second half of the chapter) to create the formatted screens we have been discussing. For the present, however, we use an *existing* screen to demonstrate the ease of data entry and associated data validation. The **SET FORMAT** command opens the existing ***format* (FMT) *file*** containing the formatted screen, and activates it in conjunction with a subsequent **APPEND** or **EDIT** command. Figure 7.4 illustrates the command as it is used in the ensuing hands-on exercise.

Figure 7.4a contains two commands, **USE** and **APPEND**, to add records to an existing **PROSPECT.DBF** file, which has been created for you on the data disk. These

FIGURE 7.4
The APPEND and SET FORMAT Commands

```
. USE PROSPECT
. APPEND
```

Records will be added according to the unformatted screen of Figure 7.2a
Press Ctrl+End to terminate data entry

(a) APPEND Command

```
. USE PROSPECT
. SET FORMAT TO PROSPECT
. APPEND
```

Assumes the existence of PROSPECT.FMT

Records will be added according to the formatted screen of Figure 7.2b
Press Ctrl+End to terminate data entry

(b) SET FORMAT Command

```
. USE PROSPECT
. SET FORMAT TO
. APPEND
```

Omission of a file name returns to unformatted screen

Records are once again added according to the unformatted screen of Figure 7.2a
Press Ctrl+End to terminate data entry

(c) Omitted File Name

commands were previously covered in Chapter 2, and they append records using the unformatted screen of Figure 7.2a.

Figure 7.4b contains an additional command, **SET FORMAT TO PROSPECT**, which assumes the existence of a **PROSPECT.FMT** file that was previously created using the screen generator. The **SET FORMAT** command is issued *before* the **APPEND** command, which then adds records using the formatted screen of Figure 7.2b.

You can return to an unformatted screen by issuing a **SET FORMAT** command without specifying a file name as shown in Figure 7.4c. You are ready for our first hands-on exercise, which illustrates the use of an existing format file.

HANDS-ON EXERCISE 1

Data Validation

Objective
Append records with and without a formatted screen; demonstrate various data validation procedures as implemented in the screen generator.

STEP 1 **Change to the STOCK directory**
Boot the system, ending at the DOS prompt, then enter one of the following two commands, depending on whether or not you are sharing the hard drive:

CD C:\DATADISK\STOCK — *if you installed the data disk on the hard drive and are not sharing your computer, or*

CD A:\DATADISK\STOCK — *if you did not install the data disk, i.e., if you are sharing drive C with other students. (Use data disk two if you have 5¼-inch disks.)*

STEP 2 **Open the PROSPECT.DBF file**

Load dBASE and exit to the dot prompt. Set the default drive as in previous exercises, then type **USE PROSPECT** to open the existing PROSPECT.DBF file. Type **DISPLAY STRUCTURE** to display the structure shown in Figure 7.1, observing that although we have created the file structure, no records have as yet been entered.

STEP 3 **Append records to the file**

Type **APPEND** to bring up the data entry screen shown in Figure 7.2a, then enter data for Toni Moldof exactly as it appears in the figure. Remember that dBASE takes you automatically from one field to the next, whenever the first field is filled, but that you must press the **return** key when this is not so. Thus, you must press **return** to move from LASTNAME to FIRSTNAME, and again from FIRSTNAME to PREFIX, but not from PREFIX to STREET.

Complete the record for Toni Moldof, then enter data for another record or two, making as many mistakes as possible in the process. You will see that dBASE does have limited data validation built in; you cannot, for example, enter alphabetic data into a numeric field, nor can you enter an invalid date such as December 32nd. There are, however, far too many mistakes that will get through, as described earlier in conjunction with Figure 7.3a.

Press **Alt+E** to pull down the exit menu and return to the dot prompt.

STEP 4 **The SET FORMAT command**

Type **SET FORMAT TO PROSPECT** to use the existing PROSPECT.FMT file, which has been created for you, then type **APPEND** to bring up a formatted screen similar to Figure 7.3b. Enter the name, address, and telephone fields for Joel Stutz as shown in Figure 7.3b. Type the state in *lower-case;* i.e., type **fl**, and see how it is automatically converted to its upper-case equivalent. Note, too, that the form will not let you enter anything other than numbers in the zip code and telephone fields.

STEP 5 **Data validation**

Type **500** as the amount to invest and press **return**; you will hear a beep at the same time an error message is displayed at the bottom of the screen, indicating a minimum investment of $10,000. Press the **space bar** as indicated, enter a corrected amount, then press **return** to move to the next field, investment objective.

STEP 6 **Prompting messages**

The cursor should now be positioned in the investment-objective field, with a corresponding message, *Enter investment objective (Growth or Income),* displayed at the bottom of the screen. Prompting messages such as this are especially important as they guide the user in entering the data that is expected. Type anything other than a **g** or an **i**, which in turn produces a beep and an error message. Make the correct entry (in either upper or lower case) and move to the next field.

STEP 7 **Toggling between valid responses**

You are now in the stocks field, which in turn displays a different prompting message at the bottom of the screen. This time you do not even have to enter a response, but can press the **space bar** to toggle between Y and N, according to the prospect's interest in stocks. A similar response is required for the bonds and retirement fields.

STEP 8 **Validation of dates**

Move to the field containing the date the prospect was last contacted and attempt to enter an invalid date such as February 31st; you can't, as dBASE automatically checks that the days and months are consistent with one another. Note, too, that we have built additional checks into this field; e.g., you cannot enter a future date as the date the prospect was last contacted. Moreover, the date for the next contact must be at least two weeks later than the date of the last contact.

Complete the record for Joel Stutz, then enter one or two additional records of your own. Press **Alt+E** to pull down the exit menu and return to the dot prompt when you are finished.

The Screen Generator

The exercise you have just completed made use of an *existing* format file to demonstrate the ease of data entry and associated data validation. We come now to a discussion of how that file was created, which leads to a second hands-on exercise on the screen generator.

We have commented several times on the consistency between one dBASE facility and another; e.g., the parallels that exist between report forms and mailing labels. Formatted screens are no exception and are created through a similar series of commands and menu options. The **CREATE SCREEN** command invokes the screen generator, just as CREATE REPORT and CREATE LABEL initiated their respective facilities. In similar fashion, **MODIFY SCREEN** alters an existing screen, and parallels the commands for report forms and mailing labels.

The screen generator also makes use of a ***work surface*** and ***pull-down menus*** that are common to the other facilities. Figure 7.5a shows the empty work surface produced by execution of the CREATE SCREEN command, whereas Figure 7.5b shows the completed screen. The latter is created through options contained in the various pull-down menus in Figure 7.5; the menu names should look familiar because they also appear with the work surfaces for report forms and mailing labels.

The screen generator creates a format file with an ***FMT extension***, which actually is a dBASE program consisting of statements to display the formatted screen.[1] Figure 7.6 contains the **PROSPECT.FMT** file used in the first exercise, a file that was *produced by the screen generator* as a consequence of the menu options selected from the work surface. In other words, you move around the work surface and select options to describe what the finished screen should look like, then trust in the screen generator to create the program to produce that screen.

It isn't necessary, therefore, for you to know the details of every statement in a format file because dBASE creates the file for you. We believe, however, that a quick description of the various entries will help you in the ensuing hands-on exercise, and so we list the purpose of several commands in the format file. Consider:

- **@...SAY** statements to display literal information in the indicated position; e.g., @ 6,59 SAY "Zip code:" displays the literal **Zip code:** in row 6, column 59.
- **@...GET** statements to display an input template in the indicated position; e.g., 6,69 GET Zipcode, displays the template for **Zipcode** in row 6, column 69.

[1] Two other file types, with extensions of **SCR** and **FMO**, are associated with the screen generator, but are beyond the scope of the present discussion. These additional files are explained in Chapter 8.

FIGURE 7.5
The Work Surface

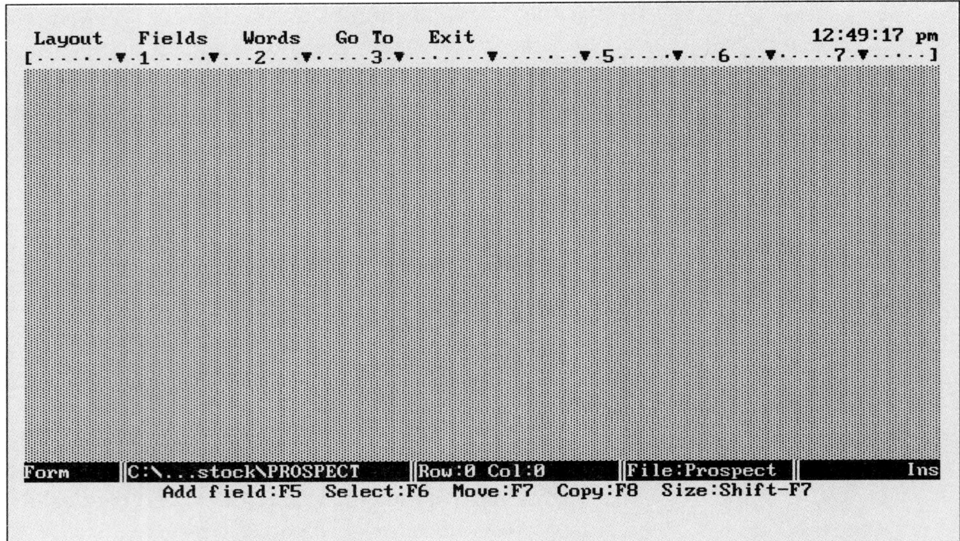

(a) Empty Work Surface

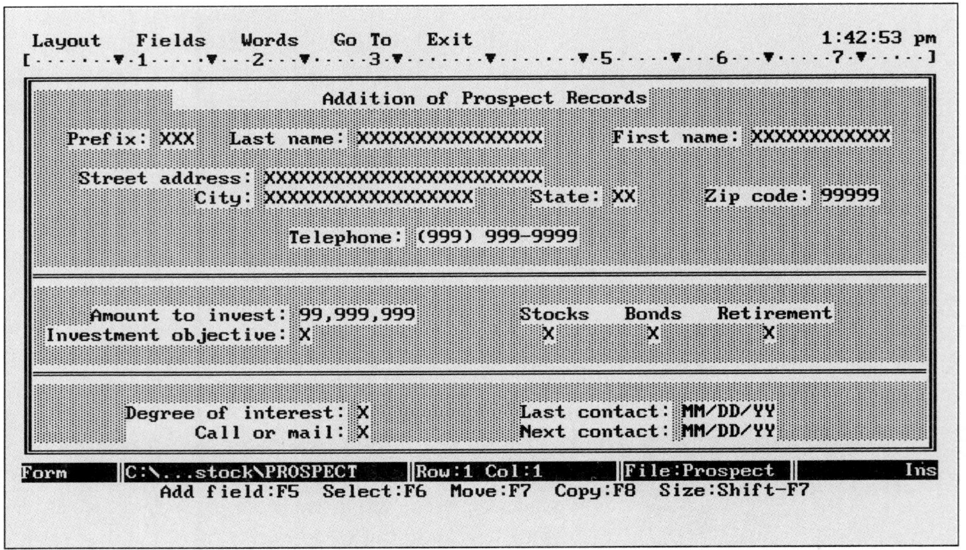

(b) Completed Screen

- **`PICTURE` clauses** to indicate the length and type of data that is accepted; e.g., `PICTURE "XXX"` (associated with the `Prefix` field) indicates a three-position character field, whereas `PICTURE "99999"` (associated with the `Zipcode` field) indicates a five-position numeric field. You can also have different data types within the same entry; e.g., `PICTURE "AA999"` represents a five-position field in which the first two positions are alphabetic (i.e., the letters A through Z) and the last three are numeric.
- **Functions,** denoted by an `@` sign, that appear within a `PICTURE` clause and further qualify the incoming data. The exclamation function, `@!`, enables case conversion; e.g., `@"A!X"` appears within the `PICTURE` clause for `State` and converts the user's entry to its upper-case equivalent. The multiple choice

```
@ 0,0 TO 19,79 DOUBLE
@ 1,26 SAY "Addition of Prospect Records"
@ 3,4 SAY "Prefix:"
@ 3,12 GET Prefix PICTURE "XXX"
@ 3,18 SAY "Last name:"
@ 3,29 GET Lastname PICTURE "XXXXXXXXXXXXXXXX"
@ 3,51 SAY "First name:"
@ 3,63 GET Firstname PICTURE "XXXXXXXXXXXX"
@ 5,5 SAY "Street address:"
@ 5,21 GET Street PICTURE "XXXXXXXXXXXXXXXXXXXXXXXXX"
@ 6,15 SAY "City:"
@ 6,21 GET City PICTURE "XXXXXXXXXXXXXXXXXX"
@ 6,44 SAY "State:"
@ 6,51 GET State PICTURE "@A! XX"
@ 6,59 SAY "Zip code:"
@ 6,69 GET Zipcode PICTURE "99999"
@ 8,23 SAY "Telephone:"
@ 8,34 GET Telephone PICTURE "@R (999) 999-9999"
@ 10,1 SAY "══════════════════════════════════════════════════════════════"
@ 12,6 SAY "Amount to invest:"
@ 12,24 GET Amount PICTURE "@$ 99,999,999" ;
   VALID amount=>10000 ;
   ERROR "A minimum of $10,000 is required" ;
   MESSAGE "Enter the amount available to invest"
@ 12,43 SAY "Stocks   Bonds   Retirement"
@ 13,2 SAY "Investment objective:"
@ 13,24 GET Objective PICTURE "@A! X" ;
   VALID objective='G'.or.objective='I' ;
   ERROR "Enter G or I only!" ;
   MESSAGE "Enter investment objective (Growth or Income)"
@ 13,45 GET Stocks PICTURE "@M Y,N" ;
   MESSAGE "Press space to toggle between Y and N"
@ 13,54 GET Bonds PICTURE "@M Y,N" ;
   MESSAGE "Press space to toggle between Y and N"
@ 13,64 GET Retirement PICTURE "@M Y,N" ;
   MESSAGE "Press space to toggle between Y and N"
@ 15,1 SAY "══════════════════════════════════════════════════════════════"
@ 17,9 SAY "Degree of interest:"
@ 17,29 GET Interest PICTURE "@A! X" ;
   VALID interest='H'.OR.interest='M'.OR.interest='L' ;
   ERROR "Enter H, M, or L" ;
   MESSAGE "Enter degree of interest (High, Medium, or Low)"
@ 17,43 SAY "Last contact:"
@ 17,57 GET Lastcall ;
   VALID date()-lastcall=>0 ;
   ERROR "You cannot enter a day in the future!" ;
   MESSAGE "Enter date of last contact"
@ 18,15 SAY "Call or mail:"
@ 18,29 GET Call_mail PICTURE "@A! X" ;
   VALID call_mail='C'.OR.call_mail='M'.OR.call_mail='B' ;
   ERROR "Enter C, M, or B!" ;
   MESSAGE "Enter means of contact (Call, Mail, or Both)"
@ 18,43 SAY "Next contact:"
@ 18,57 GET Nextcall ;
   VALID nextcall-lastcall=>14 ;
   ERROR "You must allow at least two weeks between sales calls" ;
   MESSAGE "Enter planned date for follow-up"
```

FIGURE 7.6
Partial Contents of Generated PROSPECT.FMT File

function, **@M**, provides choices to the user; e.g., **"@M Y,N"** appears within the **PICTURE** clauses for **Stocks**, **Bonds**, and **Retirement** and lets the user toggle between a value of **Y** and **N**. The insertion function, **@R**, displays additional characters not stored in the file structure; e.g., **"@R (999) 999-9999"** in the **PICTURE** clause for **Telephone** causes the parentheses, blank, and hyphen to appear on the screen but not in the file structure.

- **MESSAGE clauses** to display a prompting message prior to data entry, e.g., `MESSAGE "Enter the amount available to invest"` for the `Amount` field.
- **VALID clauses** to indicate the conditions under which an entry will be accepted as valid, e.g., `VALID amount => 10000` to indicate the minimum amount to invest.
- **ERROR clauses** to display an error message should the user attempt an invalid entry, e.g., `ERROR "A minimum of $10,000 is required".`

The hands-on exercise that follows next takes you through the pull-down menus in the screen generator to produce the completed screen of Figure 7.5b. As you do the exercise, remember that the completed screen in Figure 7.5b corresponds exactly to the format file of Figure 7.6; it is useful, therefore, to reconcile the two figures; e.g., show how the **@...GET** and **@...SAY** statements correspond to the positions of the various fields as they appear on the screen. Note, too, the various clauses that appear within the format file and recall their effect on data entry from the previous exercise.

HANDS-ON EXERCISE 2

The Screen Generator

Objective
Use the dBASE screen generator to create the customized screen of Figure 7.2b, using the format file of Figure 7.5b as a guide.

STEP 1 **The CREATE SCREEN command**
Return to the dot prompt, then type **CREATE SCREEN YOURTURN** to begin creating the form called **YOURTURN.FMT. YOURTURN** was chosen as the name of the form to differentiate it from the **PROSPECT.FMT** form, which already exists and which was used in the first exercise. In other words, the objective of this exercise is for you to create your own form, **YOURTURN.FMT**, which functions identically to ours.

You should see the empty work surface of Figure 7.5a displayed on your monitor.

STEP 2 **Enter literal data**
Use the arrow keys to move around the work surface, and as you do, enter all of the literal information shown in Figure 7.7a. Refer to the various **@...SAY** statements in the format file of Figure 7.6 to determine the exact location of a literal; e.g., *Addition of Prospect Records* begins in row 1, column 26 of the work surface. Note, too, that the position of the cursor is always displayed in the middle of the status bar; e.g., Row 18, Column 56, in Figure 7.7a.

STEP 3 **Save the form**
As always, you should save your work repeatedly during the development process; accordingly, press **Alt+L** to pull down the layout menu, highlight *Save this form,* and press **return**. You will see a second window with the cursor positioned after the form name, **YOURTURN.SCR**, in this example. Press **return** to save the form and continue working.

STEP 4 **Add a field**
Move the cursor to row 3, column 12 (which should be one space to the right of the literal **Prefix:**), then press **Alt+F** to pull down the fields menu. Use the **up** and

FIGURE 7.7
The Forms Generator

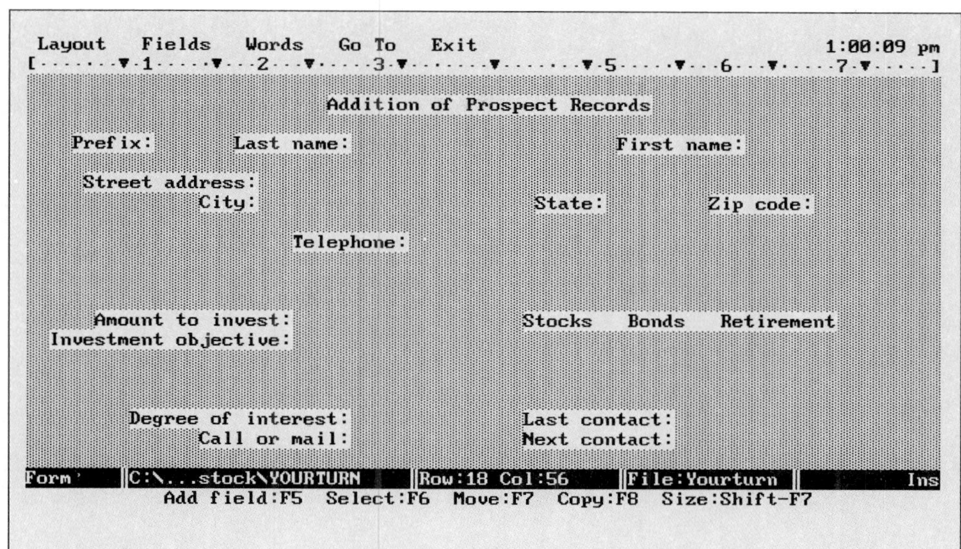

(a) Entering Literal Information

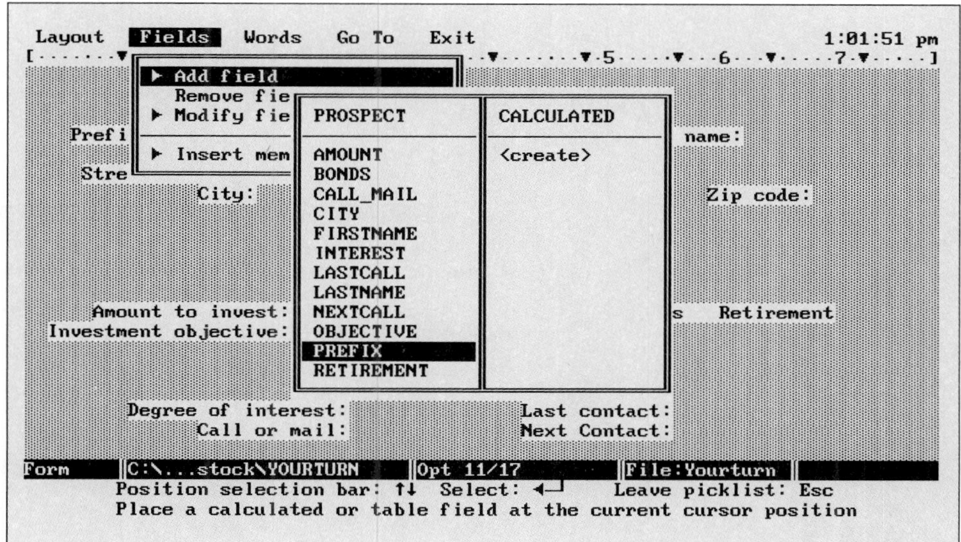

(b) Adding a Field

down arrow keys to highlight *Add field* as shown in Figure 7.7b, press **return**, highlight PREFIX, press **return** a second time, and finally press **Ctrl+End** to accept the field and indicated template. You will be returned to the work surface, where you should see three X's (beginning in row 3, column 12) to indicate that a three-position character field (PREFIX) will be obtained at this point. The three X's correspond to the width (three), and type (character), of the PREFIX field as described in the file structure for PROSPECT.DBF.

In similar fashion, add the LASTNAME, FIRSTNAME, STREET, and CITY fields to the work surface. Once again, you will want to refer to the format file of Figure 7.6 to determine the exact location of the individual fields. This time, however, you will need to look at the @...GET (rather than the @...**SAY**) statements, because you are telling dBASE where the input templates for specific fields will be displayed; e.g., the template for FIRSTNAME will begin in row 3, column 63.

FIGURE 7.7
The Forms Generator (continued)

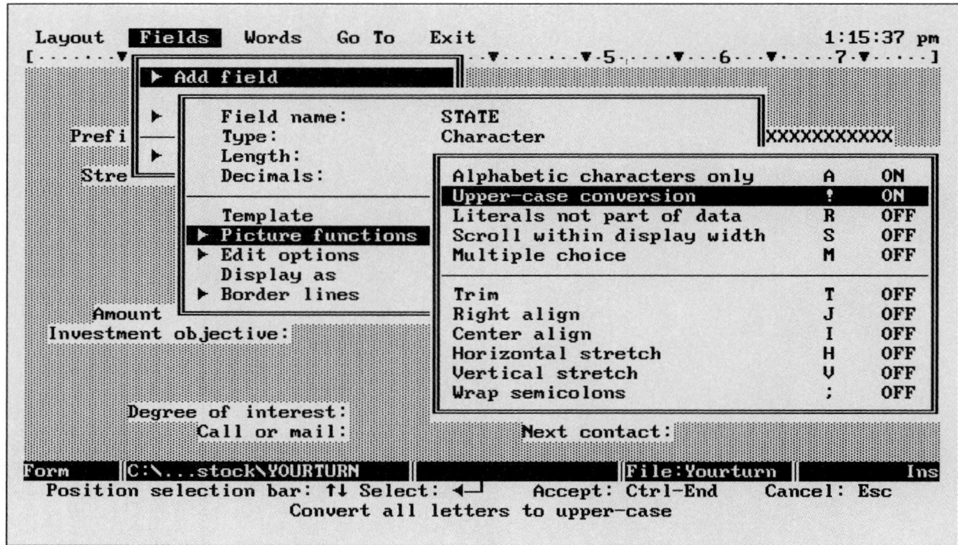

(c) Picture Functions (STATE field)

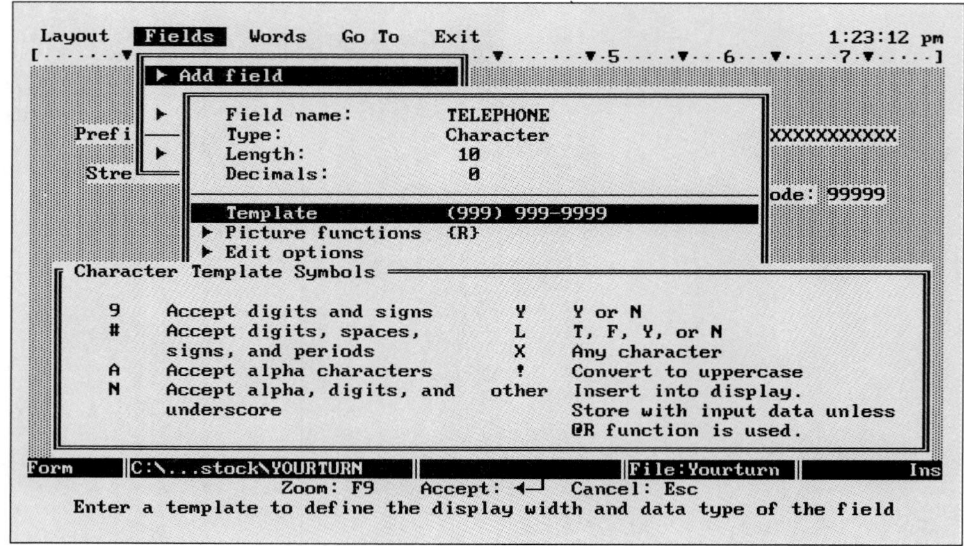

(d) Template (TELEPHONE field)

STEP 5 **Picture functions**

Move the cursor to row 6, column 51, press **`Alt+F`** to pull down the fields menu, and add the **`STATE`** field; do *not,* however, press **`Ctrl+End`** as yet, because we will introduce data validation through inclusion of a ***picture function.***

Use the **`down arrow`** key to highlight *Picture functions,* then press **`return`** to bring up the screen of Figure 7.7c. Highlight *Alphabetic characters only* and press the **`space bar`** to toggle the option on, then highlight *Upper-case conversion* and toggle that option on as well. You have just enabled data validation to the extent that only alphabetic characters (i.e., the letters A through Z) will be accepted in the **`STATE`** field, and further, any letters that are entered will be automatically converted to their upper-case equivalents. Press **`Ctrl+End`** twice to accept these entries.

FIGURE 7.7
The Forms Generator (continued)

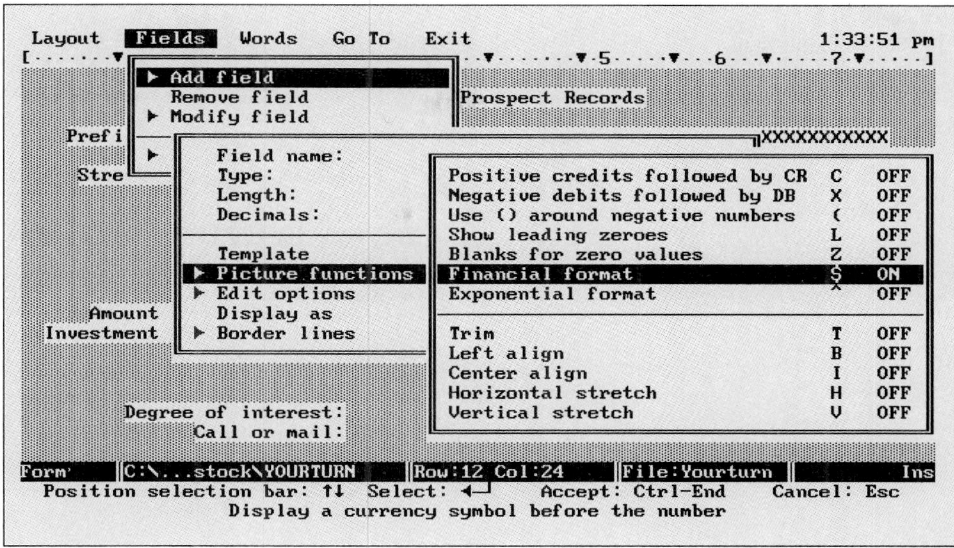

(e) Picture Functions (AMOUNT field)

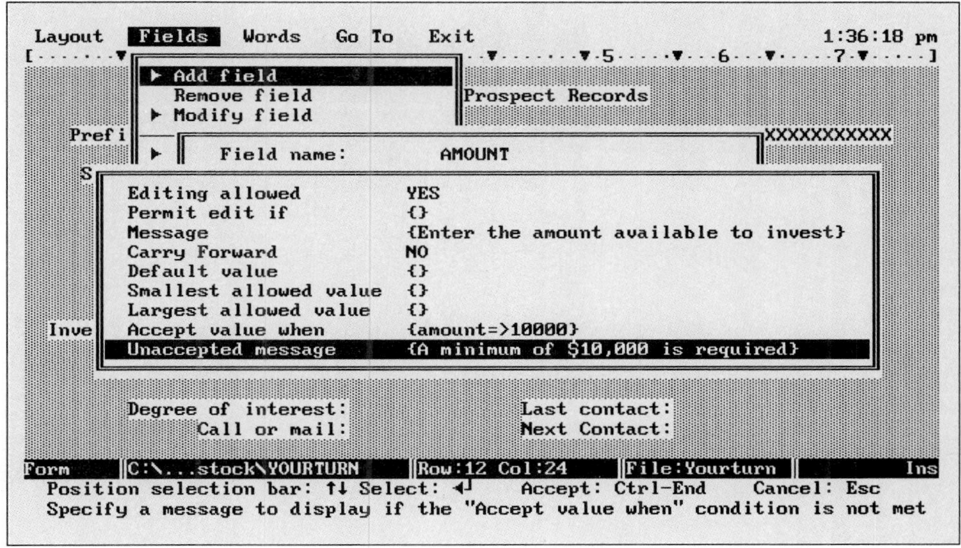

(f) Data Validation (AMOUNT field)

Move the cursor to row 6, column 69, press **Alt+F** to pull down the fields menu, then add the `ZIPCODE` field with a ***picture template*** of 99999.

STEP 6 **Insertion characters**

As you already know, the telephone number displayed on the monitor includes left and right parentheses around the area code, a space between the area code and phone number, and a hyphen within the phone number itself, for a total of 14 characters, whereas only 10 are specified in the file structure itself. The additional ***insertion characters*** are made possible through the insertion function.

Move the cursor to row 8, column 34 and add the `TELEPHONE` field, then highlight *Picture functions* and press **return**. Select the third option, *Literals not part of*

FIGURE 7.7
The Forms Generator (continued)

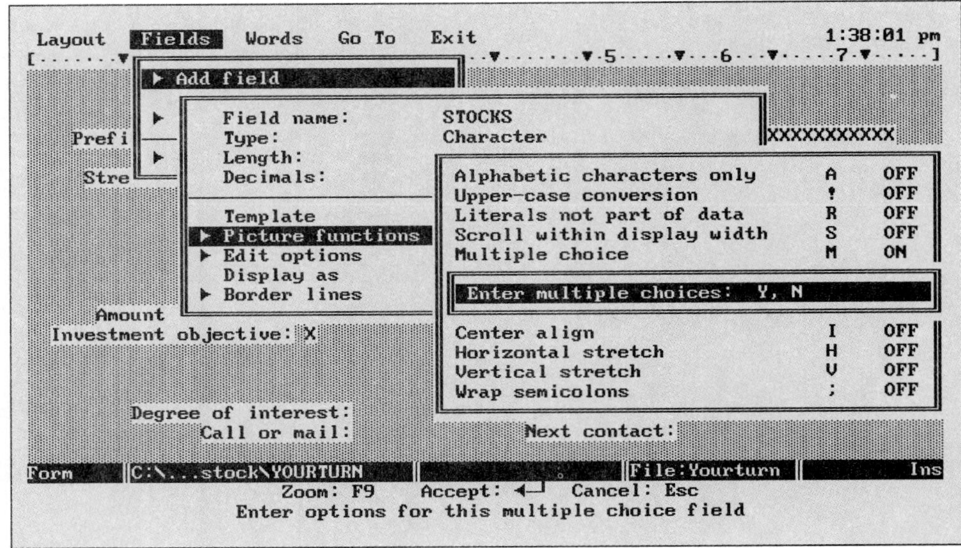

(g) Multiple Choice (STOCK field)

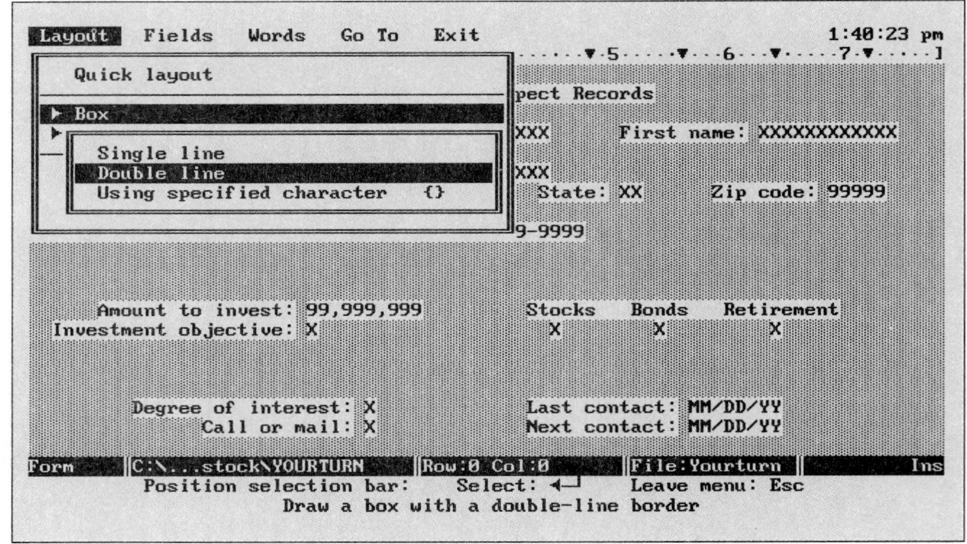

(h) Adding a Box

data, toggle it on with the **space bar**, and press **Ctrl+End** to accept the entry. Use the **up arrow** key to highlight *Template* as shown in Figure 7.7d (note that the picture function is displayed as **{R}** to indicate that the insertion option is on) and press **return**. Replace the existing template (consisting of X's) with **(999) 999-9999**, press **return** to complete the field, and press **Ctrl+End** to accept it.

STEP 7 **Financial format**

Move the cursor to row 12, column 24 and add the AMOUNT field. Select *Picture functions,* toggle *Financial format* on as shown in Figure 7.7e, and press **Ctrl+End** to accept this field. Highlight *Template,* press **return**, insert commas as appropriate, and press **return**. Leave the cursor positioned where it is, to introduce a range check and prompting message into the AMOUNT field as described in step 8.

STEP 8 **Edit options**

Highlight *Edit options* and press **return** to display the screen of Figure 7.7f. Use the **down arrow** key to highlight *Message,* press **return**, then enter the prompting message for the AMOUNT field, e.g., **Enter the amount available to invest**. Press **return** when the message is complete.

Use the **down arrow** key to highlight *Accept value when,* press **return**, and enter the appropriate condition, e.g., **AMOUNT=>10000**. Press **return** when finished. Now highlight *Unaccepted message,* press **return**, and enter the error message, e.g., **A minimum of $10,000 is required.** Press **return** once more.

Press **Ctrl+End** twice to accept the two messages and associated error condition. Pull down the layout menu and save your work to this point.

STEP 9 **Multiple choice entries**

Multiple choice entries provide the ultimate in data entry, as they enable the user to simply toggle between all acceptable entries. Move the cursor to row 13, column 45, pull down the fields menu, and add the **STOCKS** field. Highlight *Picture functions* and press **return**, then highlight *Multiple choice* and press **return** a second time to produce Figure 7.7g. Type the acceptable entries for this field, separated by a comma; i.e., type **Y,N**, press **enter**, and then press **Ctrl+End**.

Choose *Edit options* and create a prompting message for this field—e.g., **Press space to toggle between Y and N**—then press **Ctrl+End** three times to accept the multiple choice entries and associated messages.

STEP 10 **Add the remaining fields**

Add the remaining fields for OBJECTIVE, BONDS, RETIREMENT, INTEREST, CALL_MAIL, LASTCALL, and NEXTCALL using Figure 7.6 as a guide. Note, too, that the last two fields are date fields, and you can use date arithmetic for validation. The valid value for LASTCALL is entered as **date()-lastcall=>0**, which implies that the system date has to be greater than or equal to the date of the last call. In similar fashion, the valid value for NEXTCALL is entered as **nextcall-lastcall=>14** to ensure that the next call occurs at least 14 days after the last call.

STEP 11 **Boxes and lines**

Press **Alt+L** to pull down the layout menu, highlight *Box,* and press **return** to produce the screen of Figure 7.7h. Highlight *Double line* and press **return**; you are in position to draw a box as indicated by the message, *Position upper left with cursor keys, complete with enter.*

Move the cursor to row 0, column 0, (the upper left corner on the screen) and press **return** to fix the starting position of the box. Use the cursor keys to move to the bottom right of the screen; i.e., to row 19, column 79, and press **return** to complete the box. You can add the double lines in rows 10 and 15 by selecting *Line* rather than *Box* from the layout menu.

STEP 12 **Test your work**

Press **Alt+E** to pull down the exit menu, highlight *Save changes and exit,* then press **return** to exit to the dot prompt. Type **SET FORMAT TO YOURTURN**, followed by **APPEND**, at which point you should see the formatted screen for data entry. Add one or more records to the PROSPECT.DBF file, using the format file (YOURTURN.FMT) just created. Hopefully, your screen and underlying data validation will duplicate ours; if not, type **MODIFY SCREEN YOURTURN** and make changes as necessary.

Step 13 **Disable the bell**

You can disable the beep, which normally sounds when a field is filled during data entry, by typing **SET BELL OFF** at the dot prompt. Note, however, that if the bell is suppressed, and you attempt to enter invalid data, the system simply refuses to accept the invalid entry.

STEP 14 **Return to DOS**

Type **QUIT** at the dot prompt to exit dBASE and return to DOS. Congratulations on a job well done.

Summary

The design of any system begins by specifying the information expected, and then determining the data needed to produce that information; in other words, determine the input needed to produce the required output.

The ***screen generator*** is a powerful facility that creates formatted screens for data input. There is a remarkable consistency from one dBASE feature to another, e.g., in the process to create report forms and label forms. ***Formatted screens*** are no exception and are created through a similar series of menus and options.

Data validation is especially important because the information provided by a system is dependent entirely on the quality of the data on which it is based. No system, no matter how sophisticated, can compensate for inaccurate or incomplete data.

A ***numeric check,*** an ***alphabetic check,*** a ***range check,*** a ***completeness check,*** and checking for a ***valid code*** are among the data validation procedures that can be implemented through the screen generator. A check for a ***duplicate addition*** requires programming.

The **SET FORMAT** command opens an existing format (**FMT**) file that was previously created by the screen generator; a subsequent **APPEND** command will add records to the associated **DBF** file according to the formatted screen.

Key Words and Concepts

@ !
@ M
@ R
@...GET
@...SAY
Alphabetic check
Case conversion
Code check
Completeness check
CREATE SCREEN
Data validation
Date check
Duplicate addition
ERROR clause
Exit menu
Fields menu
FMT extension
Format file
GIGO
Insertion characters
Layout menu
MESSAGE clause
MODIFY SCREEN
Numeric check
Picture function
Picture template
Prompting messages
Pull-down menus
Range check
SET BELL
SET FORMAT
Screen generator
VALID clause
Work surface

True/False

1. A sophisticated system will produce valid output from invalid input.
2. It is preferable to store an individual's age rather than his or her birth date, since the latter requires a calculation to determine age.

3. Zip code should be stored as a character field rather than as a numeric field.
4. A fully edited telephone number requires a field width of 14 positions in the file structure.
5. The **SET FORMAT TO** command negates the need for an **APPEND** command.
6. Execution of a **SET FORMAT** command, without specification of a format file, returns to an unformatted screen.
7. dBASE will not accept numeric values in a character field.
8. dBASE will not accept alphabetic values in a numeric field.
9. dBASE will automatically convert lower-case letters entered in a character field to upper case.
10. A given field cannot have both a picture function and a picture template.
11. A picture clause can include data of different types; e.g., **PICTURE "99AAA"**.
12. dBASE will never append a new record to a file unless a value has been entered for every field within that record.
13. dBASE will never append a new record to a file if an existing record has the same first and last name as the record to be added.
14. When designing a file structure, a person's first and last name should be designated as a single field for efficiency.
15. The **@...SAY** statement indicates the position of literal information on a formatted screen.
16. The **@...GET** statement indicates the position where the user will enter the value of an input field.

Exercises

1. Distinguish between
   (a) A numeric check and an alphabetic check
   (b) An alphabetic check and case conversion
   (c) A picture clause of **999** versus one of **XXX**
   (d) A picture clause of **AAA** versus one of **AA**
   (e) A prompting message and an error message
   (f) The **@...GET** and **@...SAY** statements
   (g) An **APPEND** command preceded by a **SET FORMAT TO** command, as opposed to an **APPEND** command given in isolation
   (h) Appending data with and without **SET BELL OFF** in effect
   (i) The commands, **USE PROSPECT** and **SET FORMAT TO PROSPECT**

2. Explain how it is possible for a ten-position field such as telephone (as defined in the file structure of Figure 7.1) to require 14 positions in a data entry screen (e.g., Figure 7.2b). What is gained by this technique? Why is a similar approach *not* followed for a date field (i.e., the date on which the prospect was last contacted requires eight positions in both the file structure and data entry screen).

3. Describe what is meant by each one of the following data validation checks. In each case indicate whether the procedure can be accomplished within the screen generator or whether it requires additional programming.
   (a) Completeness check
   (b) Range (limit) check
   (c) Date check
   (d) Checking for a duplicate addition
   (e) Checking for a valid code
   (f) Alphabetic check
   (g) Numeric check

FIGURE 7.8
World Series Data

Year	Winning Team	Losing Team	Winning League	Number of Games
1991	Minnesota	Atlanta	AL	7
1990	Cincinnati	Oakland	NL	4
1989	Oakland	San Francisco	AL	4
1988	Los Angeles	Oakland	NL	5
1987	Minnesota	St. Louis	AL	7
1986	New York	Boston	NL	7
1985	Kansas City	St. Louis	AL	7
1984	Detroit	San Diego	AL	5
1983	Baltimore	Philadelphia	AL	5
1982	St. Louis	Milwaukee	NL	7
1981	Los Angeles	New York	NL	6

4. Figure 7.8 contains data from the World Series for the years 1981 through 1991. Each year lists the winning and losing team, the winning league (American or National), and the number of games in the series. (The World Series uses a best-of-seven format; i.e., the first team to win four games is the winner.) Design the appropriate file structure, then develop a suitable format file to facilitate data entry.

(a) For which field(s) does it make sense to implement a numeric range check? What should the range(s) be?

(b) Which field is suitable for multiple-choice input? What should the choices be?

CHAPTER

8 The Control Center

OUTLINE

OBJECTIVES

After reading this chapter you will be able to:

1. Name the six panels in the control center; describe how the **CREATE** and **MODIFY** commands associated with each panel are executed from the control center.
2. State the command to enter the control center from the dot prompt; indicate how to exit the control center and return to the dot prompt.
3. Describe two different techniques to access a pull-down menu; name the pull-down menus available from the browse/edit screen.
4. Differentiate between the data (**F2**) and design (**Shift+F2**) function keys as they are executed from the control center.
5. Use the application generator to create a quick application consisting of a sign-on banner, input screen, report form, and label form.
6. Differentiate between a DOS directory and dBASE catalog; list several file types present in a DOS directory but not in a dBASE catalog.

Overview

The ***control center*** is one of the most visible changes in dBASE IV. It is an entirely new user interface intended to simplify the execution of commands that would otherwise be issued at the dot prompt. The control center will seem familiar because it appeared each time dBASE was loaded in the hands-on exercises, although we told you to press the **Esc** key to arrive at the dot prompt, because the dot prompt is our preferred means of introducing you to dBASE. Now, however, it is appropriate to discuss the control center as its panels (queries, report forms, mailing labels, and so on) provide an effective review of earlier material. The control center also provides access to the ***application generator,*** a facility that links entries in the various panels to one another through a user-defined menu.

The control center manages its files through ***catalogs,*** which contain the name, location, and description of every file in every panel. The discussion of the control center, therefore, is also an opportunity to review the many ***file types*** that exist in dBASE IV and that you have encountered in the preceding chapters.

The Control Center

The ***control center*** is a graphic display that provides simplified access to commands that would otherwise be executed from the dot prompt. Consider, for example, the control center of Figure 8.1, which is divided into six panels. The panel names—Data, Queries, Forms (screens), Reports, Labels, and Applications—should seem familiar, because they correspond to capabilities which (except for Applications) were covered in earlier chapters.

The essence of the control center is the use of the cursor keys to select files and operate on those files. If, for example, you highlight **STUDENTS** in the data panel of Figure 8.1 and then press the enter key, you accomplish the identical result as exe-

FIGURE 8.1
The Control Center

```
Catalog   Tools   Exit                                              3:10:38 pm
                          dBASE IV CONTROL CENTER

                 CATALOG: C:\DATADISK\STUDENTS\UNTITLED.CAT

    Data       Queries       Forms       Reports       Labels     Applications

 <create>     <create>     <create>     <create>     <create>     <create>

 STUDENTS     BSNSFEM      INPUT        ACADEMIC     ROLODEX      SIMPLE
              FLORIDA                   ADDRESS      TWOCOLMN
              GPA_30                    CONTACT
              SENIORS                   MAJOR

File:         STUDENTS.DBF
Description:  STUDENTS.DBF stores data on currently enrolled students

 Help:F1  Use:◄┘  Data:F2  Design:Shift-F2  Quick Report:Shift-F9  Menus:F10
```

Menu bar
Catalog name
File description
Navigation line

cuting the command **USE STUDENTS** from the dot prompt. In similar fashion, choosing **<create>** in the reports column corresponds to executing the command **CREATE REPORT**, while selecting the **TWOCOLMN** entry in the labels panel is equivalent to executing the command **LABEL FORM TWOCOLMN** at the dot prompt.

We expect you will already have an intuitive appreciation for the various panels included in the control center; nevertheless, it is worthwhile to review how the entries in these panels were created. Note, too, that all of the files in Figure 8.1 are contained on the data disk, and further, that this specific control center is the focus of a subsequent hands-on exercise.

The ***data panel*** lists the existing **DBF** files. The **<create>** option is equivalent to typing **CREATE** at the dot prompt, after which you will be required to define the file structure. Once this is done, the data in a file is entered through ***pull-down menus*** that include the equivalent of the **APPEND**, **EDIT**, **BROWSE**, **DELETE**, **RECALL**, and **PACK** commands. Other menu options allow you to create or change the master index, so that the data panel, with its ***menu system,*** embraces all of the commands that were covered in Chapters 2 and 3.

The ***queries panel*** lists the views that were created through the techniques of Chapter 6. The **<create>** option is equivalent to the **CREATE QUERY** command, whereas highlighting an existing entry, e.g. **SENIORS**, corresponds to the command, **SET VIEW TO SENIORS**.

The ***forms panel*** lists the forms (formatted screens) that were created through the screen generator of Chapter 7. The **<create>** option is equivalent to the **CREATE SCREEN** command, whereas highlighting an existing entry, e.g. **INPUT**, corresponds to the command, **SET FORMAT TO INPUT**.

The ***reports panel*** lists the report forms that were created through the report generator in Chapter 4. The **<create>** option is equivalent to the **CREATE REPORT** command, whereas highlighting an existing entry, e.g. **MAJOR**, corresponds to the command, **REPORT FORM MAJOR**.

The ***labels panel*** lists existing label forms that were created through the procedure described in Chapter 5. The **<create>** option is equivalent to the **CREATE LABEL** command, whereas highlighting an existing entry, e.g. **ROLODEX**, corresponds to the command, **LABEL FORM ROLODEX**.

The ***applications panel*** lists dBASE applications (programs) that were created by the application generator and links entries in the other panels to one another through customized menus. The **<create>** option is equivalent to the **CREATE APPLICATION** command, whereas highlighting an existing entry will run (execute) that application. The ***application generator*** is covered in detail in the second half of the chapter.

All six panels provide the ability to modify an existing file, i.e., the equivalent of the individual commands to **MODIFY STRUCTURE**, **MODIFY QUERY**, **MODIFY SCREEN**, **MODIFY REPORT**, **MODIFY LABEL**, and **MODIFY APPLICATION**. Still the control center does *not* offer any additional capability over the dot prompt, because every action taken at the control center can also be accomplished at the dot prompt.

The control center is actually more limited than the dot prompt, because it does not account for the many optional parameters available with individual commands. There is, for example, no equivalent to the **FOR** parameter in the **REPORT** and/or **LABEL FORM** commands; i.e., the labels produced by highlighting **TWOCOLMN** in the labels panel include *every* record in the associated **DBF** file, as opposed to the command, **LABEL FORM TWOCOLMN FOR ZIPCODE = '33071'**, which prints labels selectively. Nevertheless, the control center is popular because of its ease of use. Moreover, you can overcome some of its limitations through creative use of the other panels, e.g., the use of queries as a substitute for the **FOR** parameter.

The Navigation Line

The ***navigation line*** is displayed at the bottom of the control center and indicates the means of moving from one screen to the next. Six choices are offered at the bottom of Figure 8.1, each of which is described in detail.

The **F1** ***(help) key*** enters the *context-sensitive* help facility, which was first described in Chapter 2. Figure 8.2, for example, shows how a user may go from one topic to another within the help facility, with each new screen superimposed on its predecessor. Observe, too, how the displayed information leads eventually to help for specific commands, once again reminding us that the control center is simply an alternate way to execute dBASE commands. Note also the **PRINT** option at the bottom of the help screen that enables you to produce your own hard copy of the reference material.

The ↵ ***(enter) key*** opens the highlighted file, but its exact effect depends on the panel from where it is issued. The enter key is equivalent to a simple **USE** command when pressed from the data panel as in Figure 8.1, where it is equivalent to the command, **USE STUDENTS**. The result is different, however, if you press the key from other panels; e.g., pressing enter when **MAJOR** is highlighted in the reports panel is equivalent to the command, **REPORT FORM MAJOR**. The precise effect of the enter key is shown in Table 8.1.

The **F2** ***(data) key*** switches to the browse or edit screen, depending on which of these commands was issued last. The **F2** key also functions as a toggle switch when you are already in the browse or edit screen; i.e., pressing the key when you are in the browse mode toggles to the edit mode, and vice versa.

The **Shift+F2** ***(design) key*** is the equivalent of a **MODIFY** command, with the exact effect dependent on the panel from where it is pressed. (See Table 8.1.) The **Shift+F2** combination enables you to modify the entry currently highlighted; i.e., pressing **Shift+F2** from the data panel is equivalent to a **MODIFY STRUCTURE** command issued at the dot prompt, whereas pressing **Shift+F2** from the reports or labels panel corresponds to **MODIFY REPORT** or **MODIFY LABEL**, respectively.

The **Shift+F9** ***(quick report) key*** produces an unformatted (quick) report through the report generator and is not discussed further in this chapter. (Return to Chapter 4 for details on the report generator.)

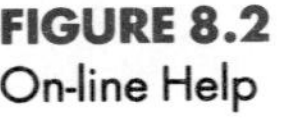
FIGURE 8.2
On-line Help

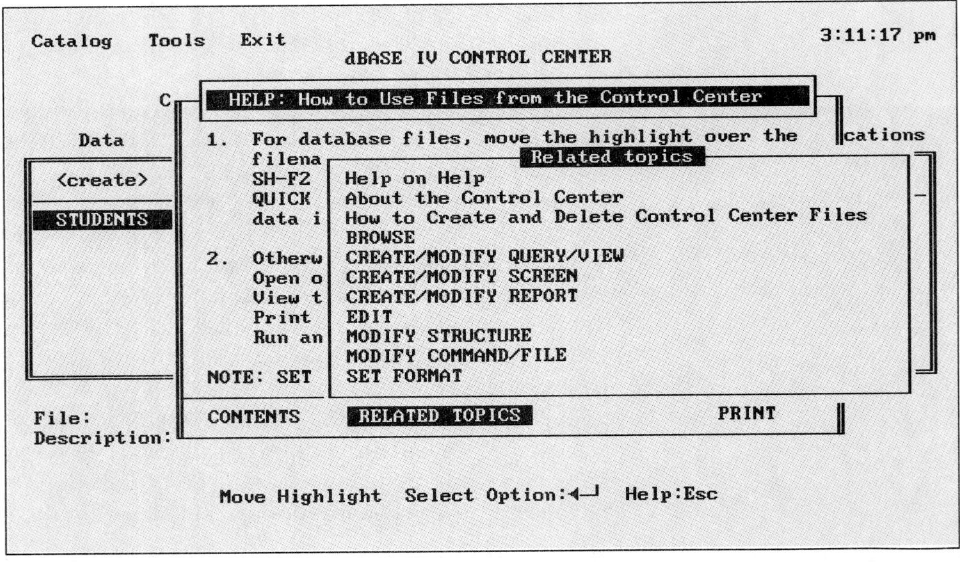

TABLE 8.1 **Control Center Actions and Equivalent Commands**

Panel	↵ (Enter)	Shift+F2 (Design)	F2 (Data)
Data	Uses (closes) the **DBF** file (**USE** or **CLOSE**)	Modify the file structure (**MODIFY STRUCTURE**)	Browse/edit the **DBF** file
Queries	Uses (or closes) the highlighted view (**SET VIEW TO**)	Modify the query definition (**MODIFY VIEW**)	Browse/edit the **DBF** file
Forms	Edits/appends to the open **DBF** file using this form (**SET FORMAT TO**)	Modify the form design (**MODIFY SCREEN**)	Browse/edit the **DBF** file
Report Forms	Prints the report form (**REPORT FORM**)	Modify the report design (**MODIFY REPORT**)	Browse/edit the **DBF** file
Label Forms	Prints the mailing label (**LABEL FORM**)	Modify the label design (**MODIFY LABEL**)	Browse/edit the **DBF** file
Applications	Run the application	Modify the application (**MODIFY APPLICATION**)	Not applicable

The **F10** ***(menus) key*** pulls down one of three menus—catalog, tools, or exit—from the menu bar at the top of the screen. The catalog and tools menus are discussed at the end of the chapter when we review all of the various file types contained within the control panel. The exit menu provides a choice between returning to the dot prompt and returning to the DOS prompt.

We come now to the first of two hands-on exercises illustrating the control center.

HANDS-ON EXERCISE 1

The Control Center

Objective

Introduce the dBASE IV control center and access its menu system and on-line help.

STEP 1 **Change to the STUDENTS directory**

Boot the system, ending at the DOS prompt. Type one of the following two commands, depending on whether you are sharing the hard drive with others:

CD C:\DATADISK\STUDENTS —— *if you installed the data disk on the hard drive and are not sharing your computer*

CD A:\DATADISK\STUDENTS —— *if you did not install the data disk, i.e., if you are sharing drive C with others. (Use data disk two if you have 5¼-inch disks.)*

STEP 2 **The control center**

Type **dBASE** at the DOS prompt to load dBASE as you have done throughout the text. This time, however, we want you to remain in the control center; i.e., do *not* press the **Esc** key to exit to the dot prompt. If you are already at the dot prompt, or for some reason the control center did not appear, type **ASSIST** to restore the control center shown in Figure 8.1.

FIGURE 8.3
Opening a File

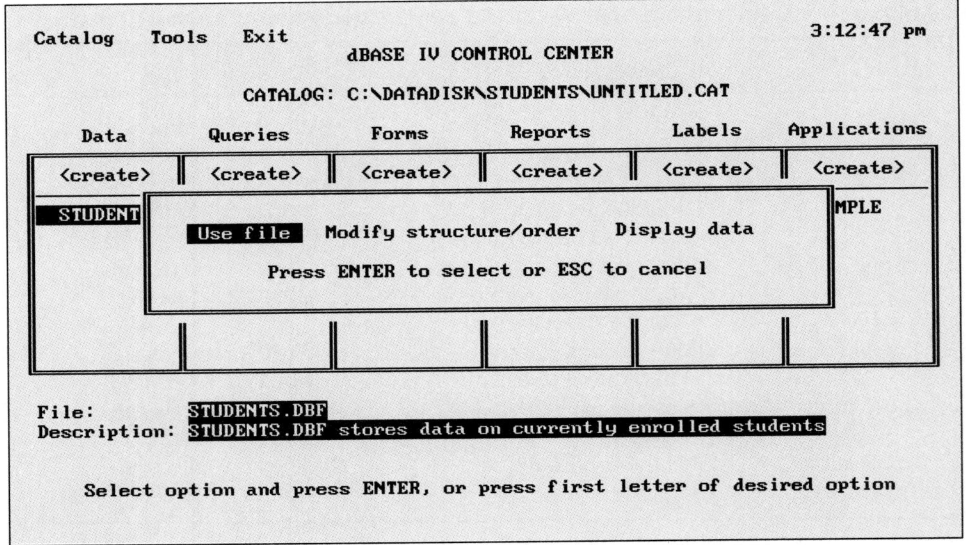

(a) Closed File (STUDENTS is below the line)

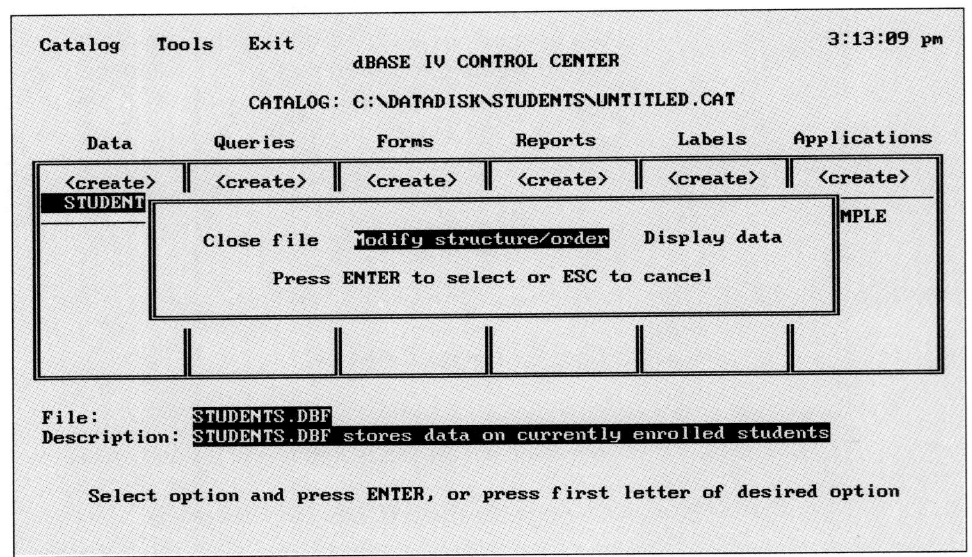

(b) Open File (STUDENTS is above the line)

STEP 3 **Open the STUDENTS.DBF file**

Use the **left** and **right arrow** keys to move to the data panel, then use the **up** and **down** keys to highlight **STUDENTS**, and press **return**. You should see Figure 8.3a on your monitor. Note that you are offered three choices, and realize, too, that each choice corresponds to a different command issued from the dot prompt. Highlight the first choice, *Use file,* and press **enter**; this action opens the **STUDENTS.DBF** file and returns you to the control center.

There is, however, a subtle change in the appearance of the control center as **STUDENTS** appears *above* the line in the data panel, whereas it was *below* the line in Figure 8.3a. The new position indicates that the **STUDENTS.DBF** file is now open; i.e., the file is in use as a consequence of the previous action.

Be sure that **STUDENTS** is still highlighted, then press **return**; this will bring up Figure 8.3b, which exhibits a subtle change in the available choices: *Close file,* as opposed to *Use file,* which appeared in Figure 8.3a. The difference is completely consistent with what has taken place; i.e., **STUDENTS.DBF** is now open and so you are given the option to close the file, whereas previously the file was not in use and so you could open it.

STEP 4 **The MODIFY STRUCTURE and BROWSE commands**

Highlight *Modify structure/order* (in Figure 8.3b) and press **return**; your screen will resemble Figure 8.4a, but will have the ***organize menu*** superimposed on the figure.

FIGURE 8.4
Access to the Dot Prompt

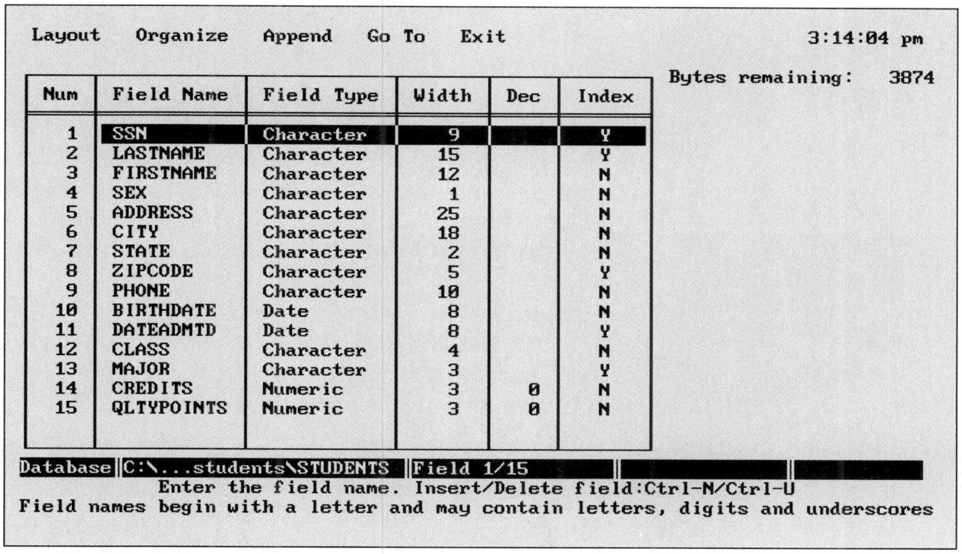

Layout Organize Append Go To Exit 3:14:04 pm

Bytes remaining: 3874

Num	Field Name	Field Type	Width	Dec	Index
1	SSN	Character	9		Y
2	LASTNAME	Character	15		Y
3	FIRSTNAME	Character	12		N
4	SEX	Character	1		N
5	ADDRESS	Character	25		N
6	CITY	Character	18		N
7	STATE	Character	2		N
8	ZIPCODE	Character	5		Y
9	PHONE	Character	10		N
10	BIRTHDATE	Date	8		N
11	DATEADMTD	Date	8		Y
12	CLASS	Character	4		N
13	MAJOR	Character	3		Y
14	CREDITS	Numeric	3	0	N
15	QLTYPOINTS	Numeric	3	0	N

Database C:\...students\STUDENTS Field 1/15
Enter the field name. Insert/Delete field:Ctrl-N/Ctrl-U
Field names begin with a letter and may contain letters, digits and underscores

(a) MODIFY STRUCTURE Command

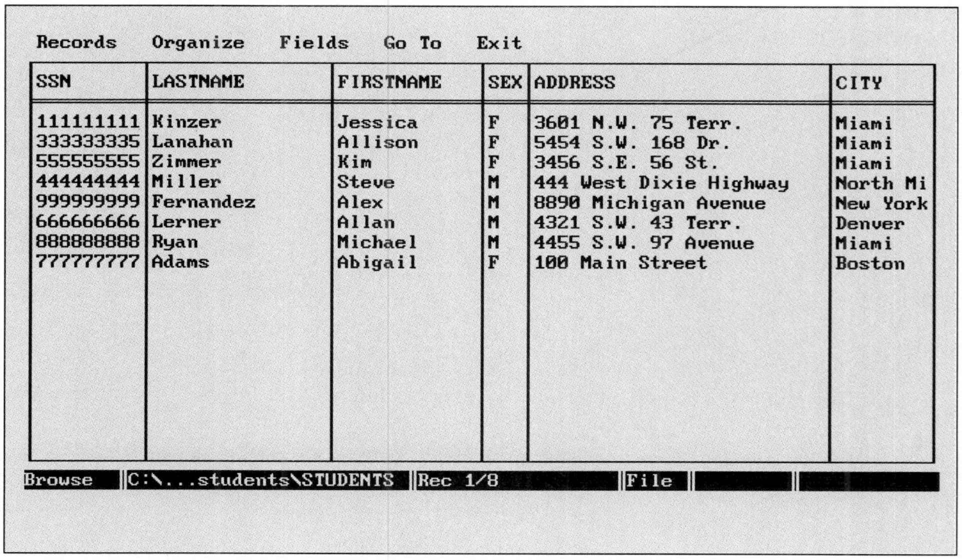

Records Organize Fields Go To Exit

SSN	LASTNAME	FIRSTNAME	SEX	ADDRESS	CITY
111111111	Kinzer	Jessica	F	3601 N.W. 75 Terr.	Miami
333333335	Lanahan	Allison	F	5454 S.W. 168 Dr.	Miami
555555555	Zimmer	Kim	F	3456 S.E. 56 St.	Miami
444444444	Miller	Steve	M	444 West Dixie Highway	North Mi
999999999	Fernandez	Alex	M	8890 Michigan Avenue	New York
666666666	Lerner	Allan	M	4321 S.W. 43 Terr.	Denver
888888888	Ryan	Michael	M	4455 S.W. 97 Avenue	Miami
777777777	Adams	Abigail	F	100 Main Street	Boston

Browse C:\...students\STUDENTS Rec 1/8 File

(b) BROWSE Command

Press the **Esc** key to make the menu disappear, then press **Alt+E** to pull down the exit menu and return to the control center.

Highlight **STUDENTS** in the data panel and press **return**, then select *Display data* to produce Figure 8.4b. Can you see that the actions just taken at the control center are equivalent to issuing the **MODIFY STRUCTURE** and **BROWSE** commands from the dot prompt?

STEP 5 **On-line help**

Press **Alt+E** to pull down the exit menu and return to the control center, but this time concentrate on the function keys displayed on the navigation line at the bottom of the screen. Press the **F1** function key to enter the help facility, then let your imagination roam as you explore whatever command is of interest. Note, too, the availability of the **PRINT** option to obtain hard copy on your current topic. When you are finished with the ***on-line help,*** press the **Esc** key to return to the control center.

STEP 6 **Shortcuts**

Be sure that **STUDENTS** is highlighted in the data panel, then press **Shift+F2** (as shown on the navigation line) to return to the **MODIFY STRUCTURE** screen of Figure 8.4a. Pull down the exit menu to return to the control center, then press the **F2** function key to produce the **BROWSE** screen of Figure 8.4b. Can you see that the **Shift+F2** (design) and **F2** (data) key combinations are shortcuts to executing the **MODIFY STRUCTURE** and **BROWSE** commands?

STEP 7 **Pull down the records menu**

The menu bar in Figure 8.4b has five choices—Records, Organize, Fields, Go To, and Exit—each of which offers multiple options as shown in Figure 8.5. You can access any of the five menus in one of two ways:

1. Press the **F10** function key, then use the **left** and **right arrow** keys to arrive at the desired menu.
2. Press the **Alt** key plus the first letter in the menu name, e.g., **Alt+R** to go directly to the Records menu.

FIGURE 8.5
BROWSE/EDIT Pull-Down Menus

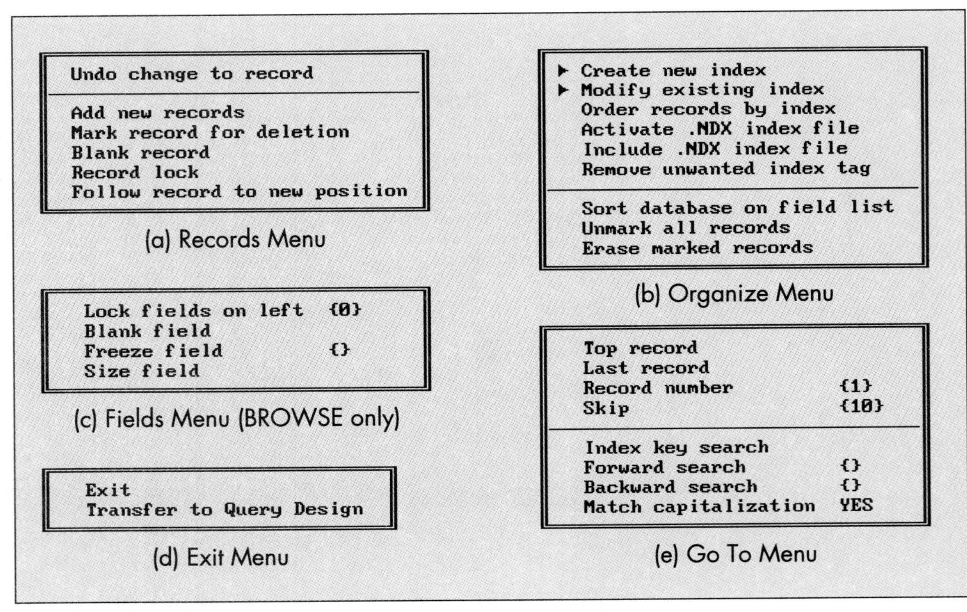

Pull down the records menu, then use the **up** and **down arrow** keys to move from option to option within the menu. You will find, however, that not all options are available in that the cursor stops on only those options shown in bold; an explanation for the highlighted option always appears at the bottom of the screen. You should also realize how the various menu options correspond directly to commands that were introduced earlier from the dot prompt; *Add new records,* for example, corresponds to the APPEND command.

STEP 8 **Explore the other menus**

Pull down the organize and exit menus, using either the **F10** function key or the appropriate Alt key combinations, **Alt+O** and **Alt+E**, respectively. Explore these menus as well, being sure to notice the explanations at the bottom of the screen. Once again you should recognize how the various menu options correspond directly to commands issued at the dot prompt; e.g., *Unmark all records* and *Erase marked records,* both of which are in the organize menu, correspond to the RECALL and PACK commands, respectively. Press **Alt+E** to pull down the exit menu, highlight *Exit,* and press **enter** to return to the control center.

STEP 9 **The forms panel**

Use the **left** and **right arrow** keys to move to the forms panel, highlight INPUT, then press the **F2** (data) key. Press **Alt+R** to pull down the records menu, highlight *Add new records,* and press **return**. You should see the data entry screen of Figure 8.6, which uses the formatted screen of the INPUT form. Add a record or not as you see fit, then press **Alt+E** to return to the control center.

STEP 10 **The labels panel**

Use the **left** and **right arrow** keys to move to the forms panel, highlight ROLODEX, and press **return**. Select *Print label* as shown in Figure 8.7a, then choose *View labels on screen* from the menu in Figure 8.7b to view the labels, after which you will be returned to the control center.

FIGURE 8.6
The Forms Panel

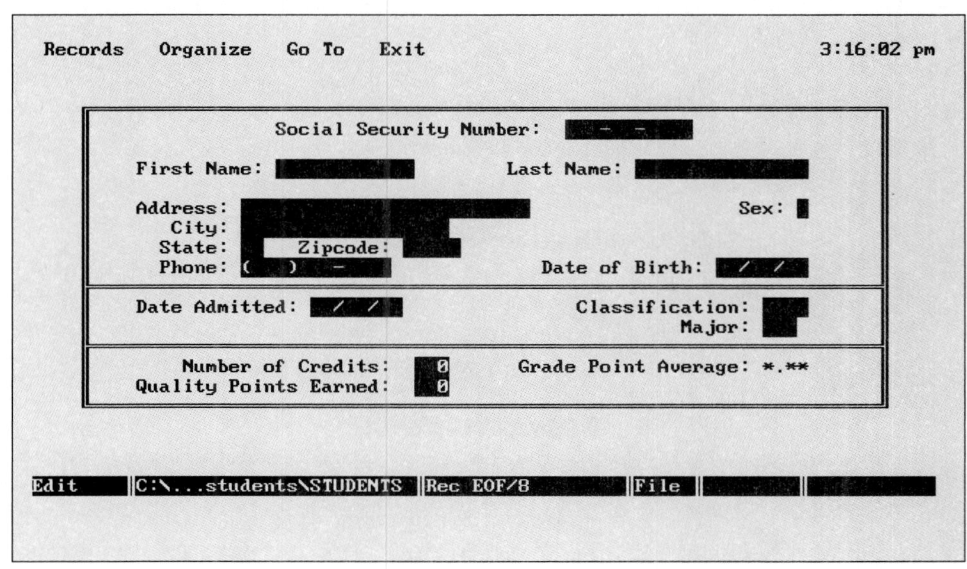

FIGURE 8.7
The Labels Panel

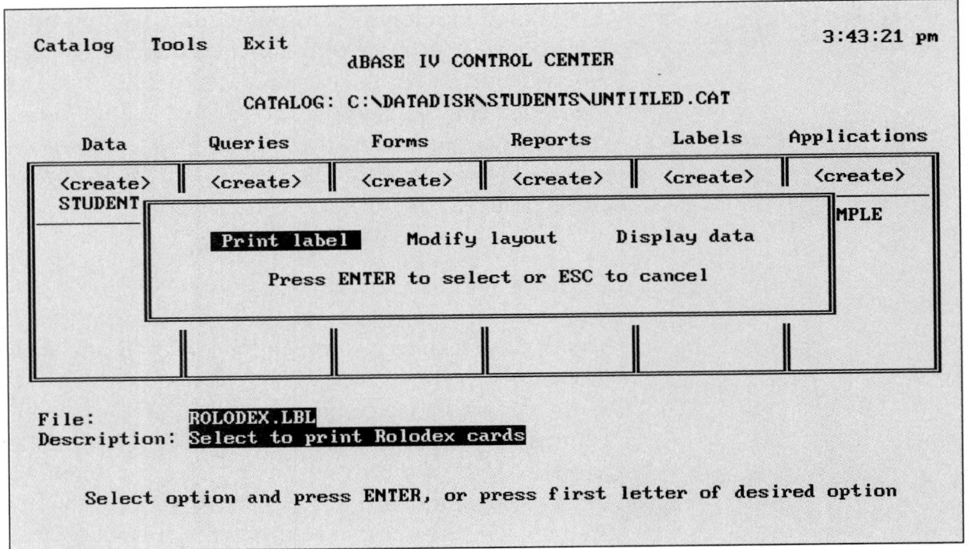

(a) First Prompt

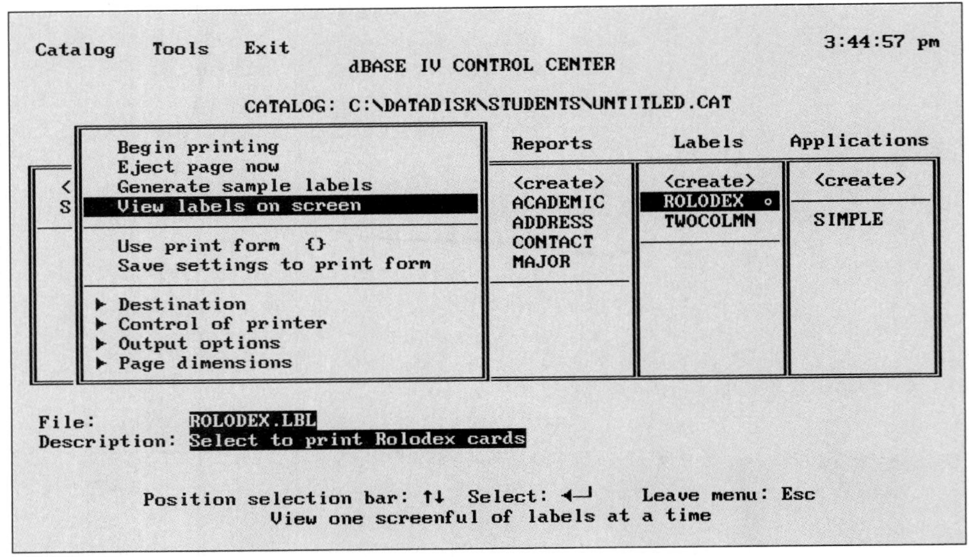

(b) Second Prompt

STEP 11 **The queries panel**

Use the **left** and **right arrow** keys to move to the queries panel, highlight `GPA_30`, press **return**, highlight *Use view,* and press **return** once more. All subsequent commands will be processed with this view, which limits records to those students whose grade point average is 3.00, or higher.

STEP 12 **The reports panel**

Use the **left** and **right arrow** keys to move to the reports panel, highlight `ACADEMIC`, and press **return**. Highlight *Print report* and press **return**, then choose *Current view* as shown in Figure 8.8a. Highlight *View report on screen* from the next menu and press **return**; you should see Figure 8.8b, which contains six

FIGURE 8.8
The Reports Panel (with active view)

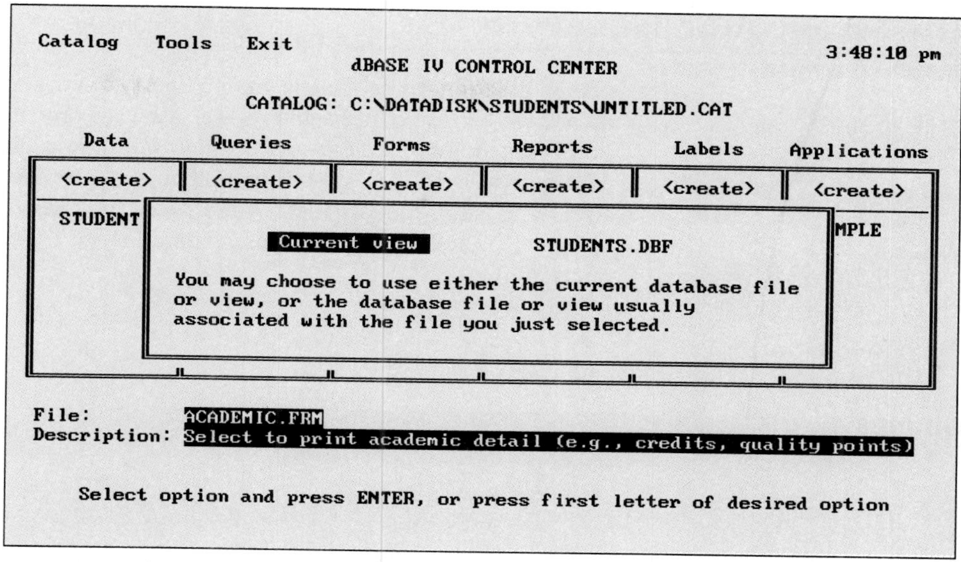

(a) Selecting the View

STUDENT ACADEMIC INFORMATION

Social Security Number	Last Name	First Name	Number of Credits	Quality Points	GPA
111-11-1111	Kinzer	Jessica	75	256.00	3.41
333-33-3335	Lanahan	Allison	33	120.00	3.64
999-99-9999	Fernandez	Alex	110	345.00	3.14
666-66-6666	Lerner	Allan	15	60.00	4.00
888-88-8888	Ryan	Michael	105	320.00	3.05
777-77-7777	Adams	Abigail	45	140.00	3.11

Cancel viewing: ESC, Continue viewing: SPACEBAR

(b) Printed Report

students, each with a grade point average of 3.00 or higher, in accordance with the view you selected in step 11.

STEP 13 **Close the student file**

Move to the data panel, highlight **STUDENTS**, and press **return**, then select *Close file,* and press **return** once more. Press **Alt+E** to pull down the exit menu from the control center, highlight *Exit to dot prompt,* and press **return**.

The Application Generator

dBASE functions at two levels, interactively or at the command (program) level. Commands are executed interactively—i.e., one at a time from the dot prompt as was done in the preceding chapters—or through the equivalent key strokes from the control center as we have just described. Either way, the user continually retypes the same command sequence(s), each time with the possibility of error. An alternative approach is to store the set of commands in a ***program*** and then execute the program.

FIGURE 8.9
The Application Generator

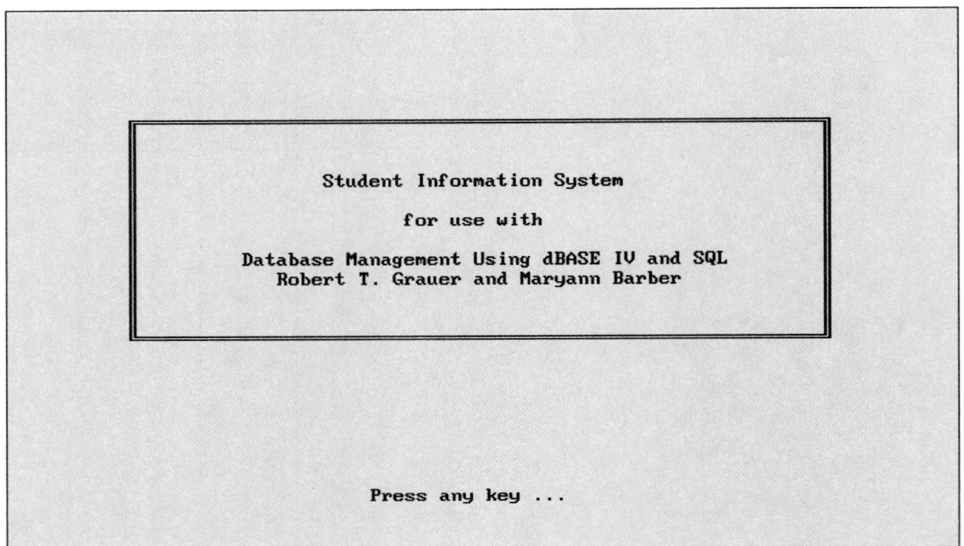

(a) Sign-on Banner

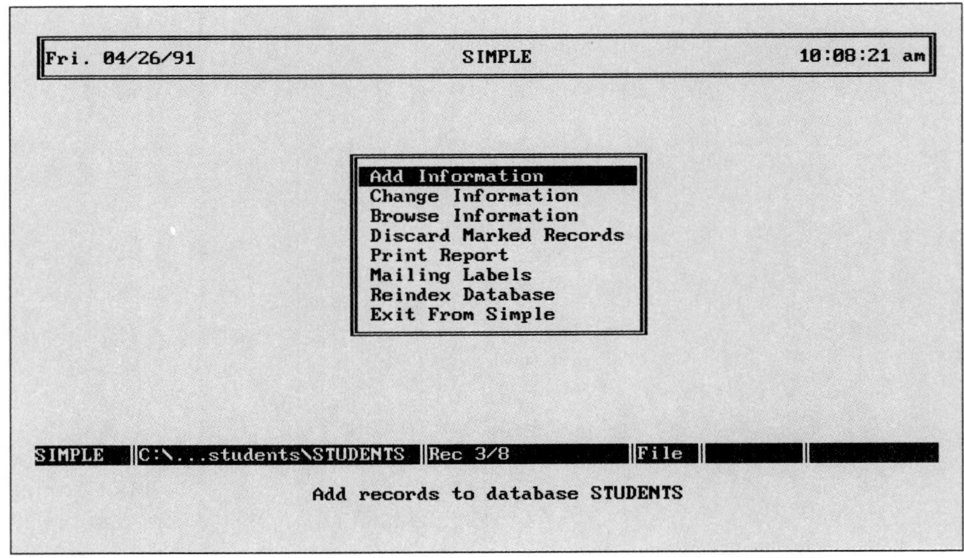

(b) Pop-up Menu

Programming, however, is not easy and is beyond the interest or ability of many individuals who nevertheless need access to the data management facilities in dBASE. The solution is to let dBASE create the program for you, through its ***application generator,*** a menu-driven facility accessed through the control center. To appreciate the potential of this powerful tool, consider again the control center of Figure 8.1.

The applications panel contains a single entry, **SIMPLE**, which as you shall see, links entries in the other five panels to one another. To run this application, you move to the applications panel in the control center, highlight **SIMPLE**, select *Run Application,* and press **enter**. You then see the ***sign-on banner*** of Figure 8.9a, a more personal and appealing greeting than either the dot prompt or control center.

Figure 8.9b displays a customized ***pop-up menu*** for this application, offering a choice of file maintenance operations and/or the ability to print a report or set of mailing labels. The user selects an option from this menu in the same fashion as from any other dBASE menu, i.e., by highlighting the option and pressing **return** or simply by typing the first letter of the option itself.

Impressive as the application may be, it is aptly named for it was indeed simple to create, and was developed by selecting appropriate entries from the control center. Consider now Figure 8.10, and how its highlighted entries correspond to various files in the control center. The name of the database file in Figure 8.10 is **STUDENTS** and corresponds to the **DBF** file in the data panel of Figure 8.1. In similar fashion, the screen format file is entered as **INPUT**, and matches the entry in the forms panel of the control center.

The report format file (**ACADEMIC**) and label format file (**TWOCOLMN**) also correspond to entries in their respective panels. Note, however, that while the control center contains multiple entries in both the reports and labels panels, there is room for only one each in Figure 8.10. That is because **SIMPLE** was designed as a ***quick application,*** i.e., an application requiring a minimum of effort to create but limited in its capacity. More powerful applications can be created, however, but are beyond the scope of our discussion.

The ensuing hands-on exercise introduces you to the existing **SIMPLE** application, then takes you through the steps necessary to create an application of your own.

FIGURE 8.10
Application Definition

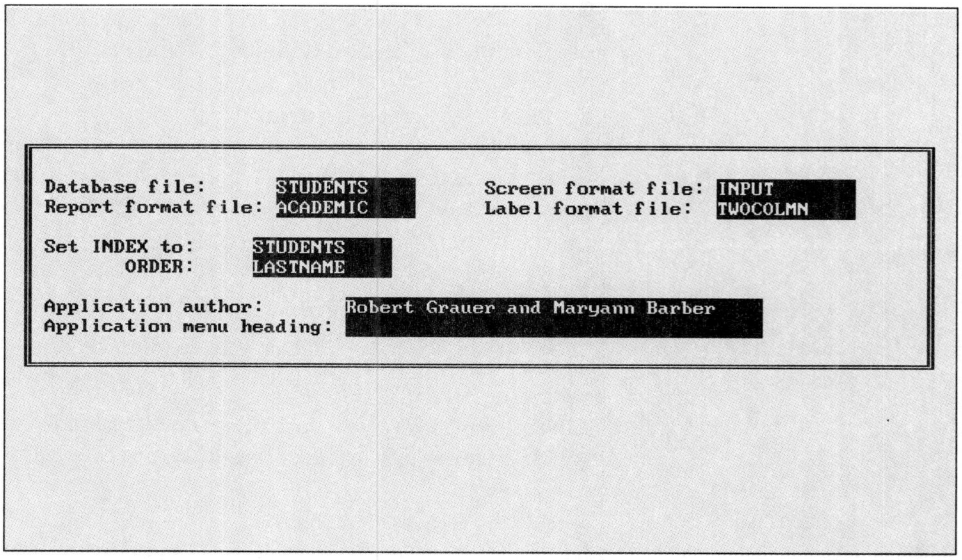

```
Database file:        STUDENTS          Screen format file: INPUT
Report format file:   ACADEMIC          Label format file:  TWOCOLMN

Set INDEX to:       STUDENTS
      ORDER:        LASTNAME

Application author:         Robert Grauer and Maryann Barber
Application menu heading:
```

HANDS-ON EXERCISE 2

The Application Generator

Objective
Execute an existing application produced through the application generator; create a second application.

STEP 1 **Using an existing application**
Type **ASSIST** at the dot prompt to enter the control center, move to the applications panel, highlight SIMPLE, and press **return**. Select *Run application,* press **return**, then answer *Yes,* indicating you want to run the application called SIMPLE. You will see the sign-on banner shown in Figure 8.9a (press any key as instructed), after which the pop-up menu of Figure 8.9b will appear.

Select any of the menu choices through highlighting with the **up** and **down arrow** keys, or by typing the first letter of the option. The first four choices—*Add, Change, Browse,* and *Discard Marked Records*—are the normal file maintenance operations and correspond to the APPEND, EDIT, BROWSE, and PACK commands. All append and edit operations will be done through the formatted screen shown in Figure 8.6. The *Print Report* option will run the report form ACADEMIC, while *Mailing Labels* will run the label form TWOCOLMN.

Experiment as you see fit, then exit the SIMPLE application and return to the control center.

STEP 2 **Create a new application**
Move to the applications panel, highlight <create>, and press **enter** at which point you will be asked whether you want to create a dBASE program or use the application generator. Select *Application Generator* and press **return**, then complete the application definition as shown in Figure 8.11a.

We chose SECOND as the name of the application with the indicated description. We choose a pop-up menu (type **P** for pop-up or press the **space bar** to toggle between the different menu types. In actuality, the type of menu is immaterial because we are creating a quick application, which can use only a pop-up menu. The menu name is also immaterial and could be omitted entirely). The database/view and index are both STUDENTS and correspond to the names of the DBF and MDX files, respectively; ZIPCODE is the tag within the index file. Press **Ctrl+End** when you complete the application definition as indicated at the bottom of the screen.

STEP 3 **Create the sign-on banner**
The initial sign-on banner will appear on your monitor. You will want, however, to replace the text in the default message (This is an APPLICATION OBJECT...) with a message of your own as shown in Figure 8.11b. Use the arrow keys to position yourself within the box and press the Ins key to toggle between insertion and replacement modes as necessary. You can also press **Ctrl+Y** to delete an entire line of text. Enter the text of your sign-on banner.

STEP 4 **Display the sign-on banner**
Press **Alt+A** to pull down the application menu as shown in Figure 8.11c. Highlight *Display sign-on banner* and press **return**, highlight *Yes* and press **return** once more. Remain in the application menu and proceed to step 5.

STEP 5 **Generate the application**
Highlight *Generate quick application* and press **return** to produce the screen of Figure 8.11d, where you choose the options to be included in the application. Note,

FIGURE 8.11
Creating an Application

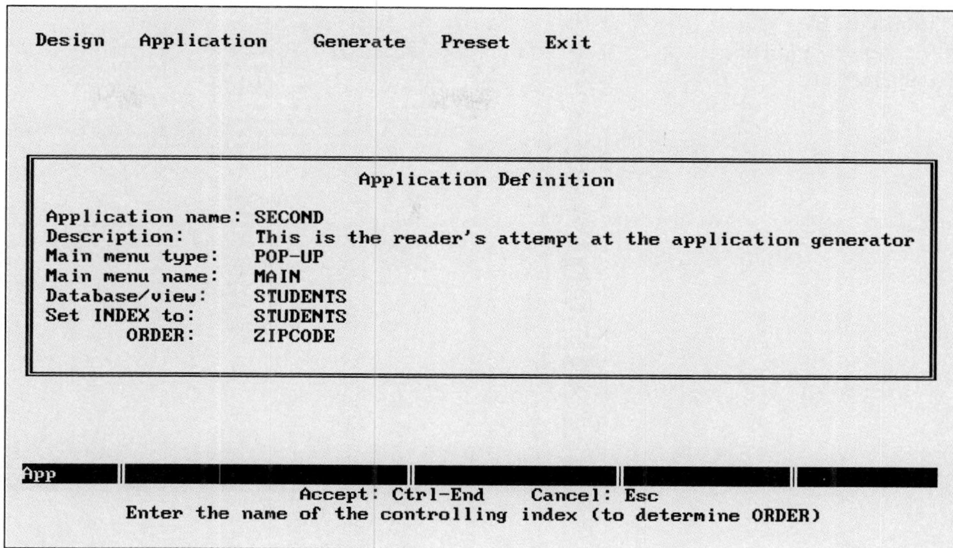

(a) Opening Screen

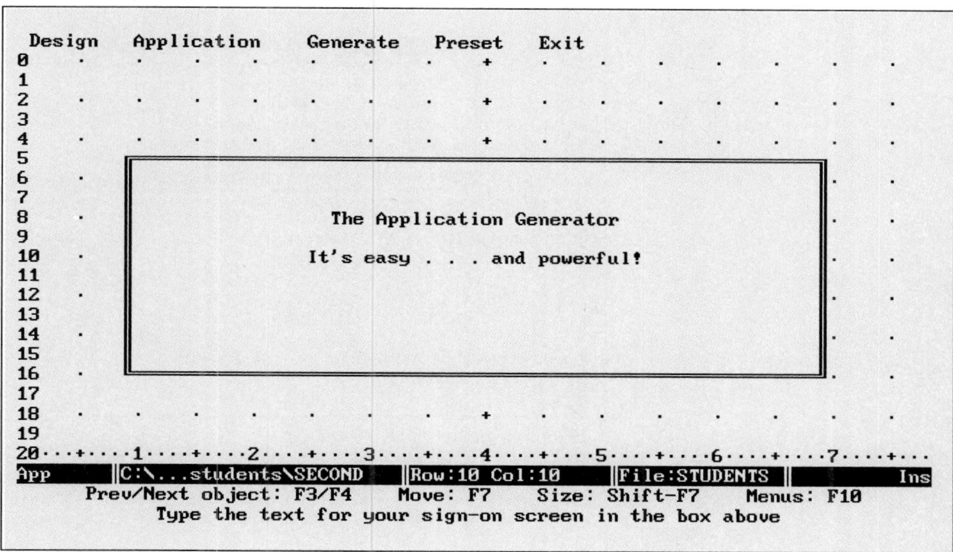

(b) Creating a Sign-on Banner

however, that some options have already been entered according to the application definition you supplied in step 2; i.e., **STUDENTS** is the name of the database and index files, and **ZIPCODE** appears as the order.

You are free, however, to select the remaining entries (from files that exist in the control panel). Type **INPUT** as the name of the format file, **CONTACT** as the name of the report form, and **ROLODEX** as the name of the label form. Press **Ctrl+End** when you have completed the screen, then select *Yes* to generate the application. Press any key as instructed after the generation is complete.

STEP 6 **Save the application**

Press **Alt+E** (or use the **right arrow** key) to pull down the exit menu, highlight *Save all changes and exit,* and press **enter** to complete the operation. You are back

FIGURE 8.11
Creating an Application (continued)

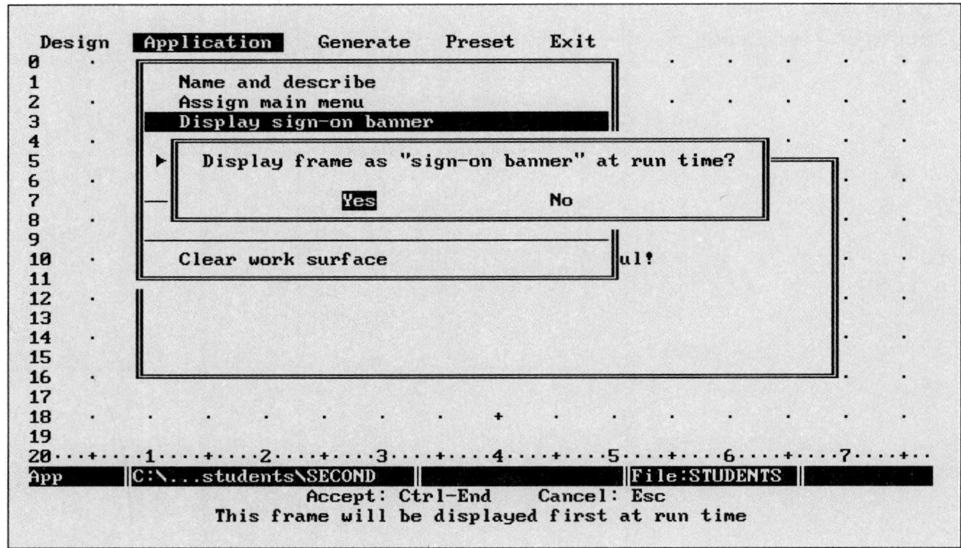

(c) Displaying the Sign-on Banner

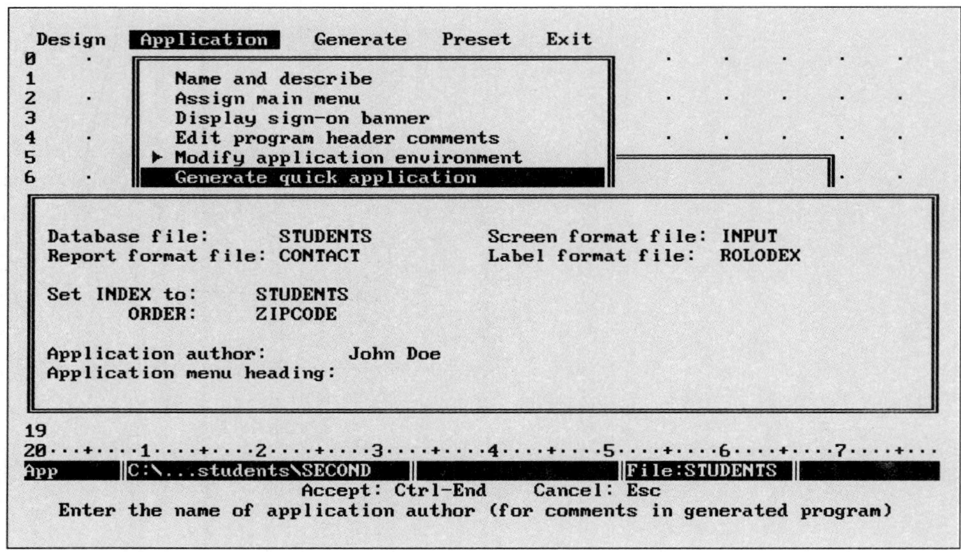

(d) Generating the Application

at the control center, which now contains a new entry in the applications panel corresponding to the application you just created.

STEP 7 **Run the new application**

Use the arrow keys to highlight the **SECOND** entry in the applications panel of Figure 8.11e, and press **return**. Highlight *Run application* and press **enter**, then answer *Yes* to the confirming prompt to run the application.

You should see your sign-on banner, and after pressing any key as indicated, you will see the pop-up menu in Figure 8.11f. Experiment with the various options in your application, then exit from the application to return to the control center.

FIGURE 8.11
Creating an Application (continued)

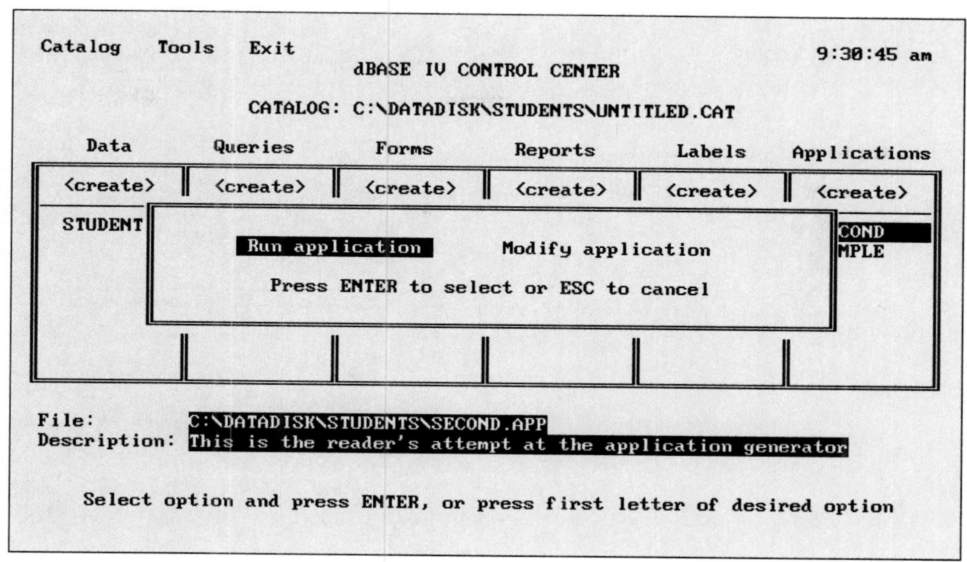

(e) Running the Application

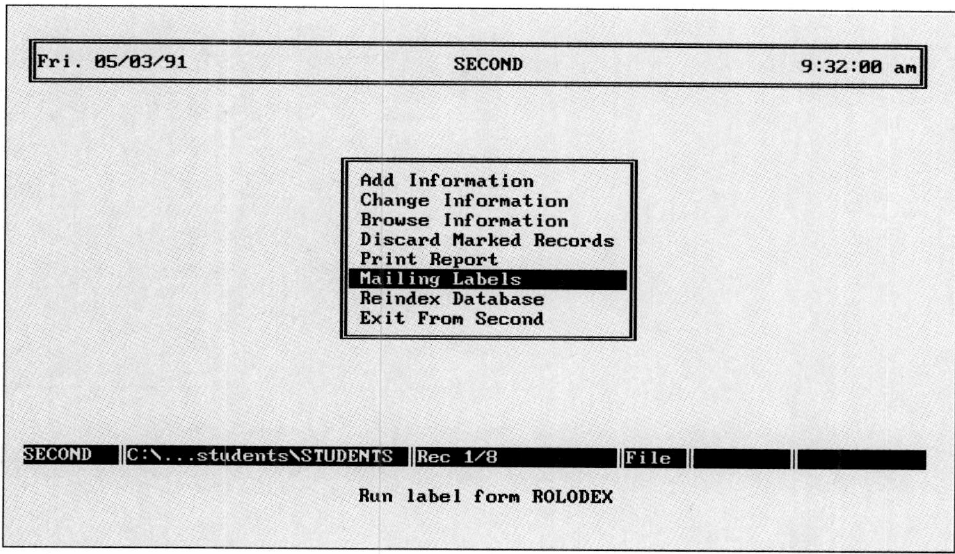

(f) User's Pop-up Menu

STEP 8 **The catalog menu (file descriptions)**

Move from file to file within the control center, and as you do, observe the following:

1. The name of the highlighted file appears at the lower left of the control center.
2. A description of the file appears immediately under its name.

You can change the description of the highlighted file by pressing **Alt+C** to pull down the catalog menu, selecting *Change description of highlighted file,* and then entering the new description as shown in Figure 8.11g.

FIGURE 8.11
Creating an Application (continued)

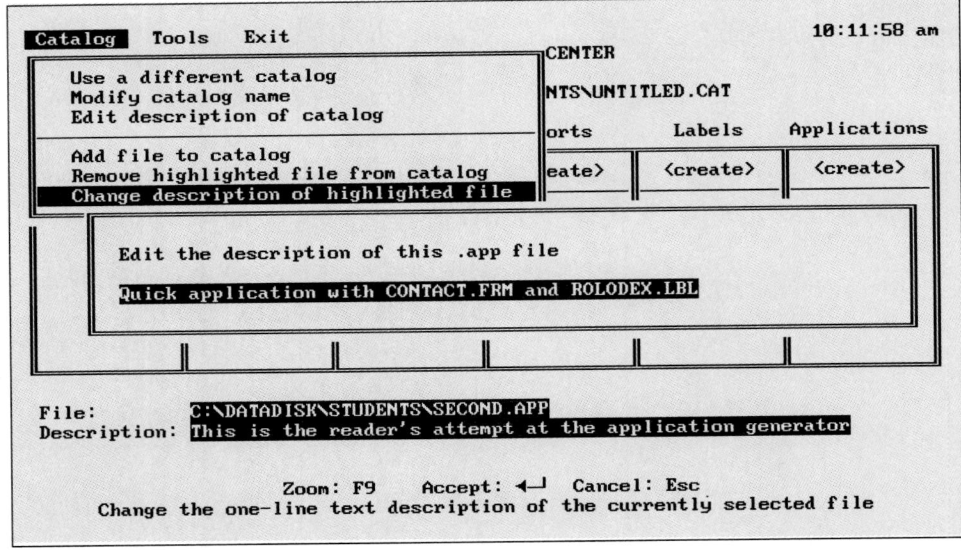

(g) The Catalog Menu

DOS Files Sort Mark Operations Exit 10:18:32 am

C:\DATADISK\STUDENTS

Name/Extension		Size	Date & Time		Attrs	Space Used
SECOND	APP	1,083	May 3,1991	9:01a	♦♦♦♦	2,048
SECOND	DBO	16,208	May 9,1991	8:50a	a♦♦♦	16,384
SECOND	PRG	19,126	May 3,1991	9:01a	♦♦♦♦	20,480
SENIORS	QBE	3,847	Apr 12,1991	10:25a	♦♦♦♦	4,096
SIMPLE	APP	1,138	Apr 26,1991	10:05a	♦♦♦♦	2,048
SIMPLE	DBO	16,800	May 9,1991	8:48a	a♦♦♦	18,432
SIMPLE	PRG	19,633	Apr 26,1991	10:05a	♦♦♦♦	20,480
STUDENTS	DBF	1,530	May 3,1991	8:52a	♦♦♦♦	2,048
STUDENTS	MDX	12,288	May 1,1991	2:10p	♦♦♦♦	14,336
TWOCOLMN	LBL	1,363	Apr 12,1991	8:14a	♦♦♦♦	2,048
UNTITLED	CAT	3,335	May 9,1991	9:46a	a♦♦♦	4,096
Total ◄marked►		0	(0 files)			0
Total ◄displayed►		148,461	(27 files)			172,032

Files:*.* Sorted by: Name

DOS util C:\...datadisk\STUDENTS

Position selection bar ↑↓ Mark file:◄┘ Directories:F9

(h) The Tools Menu

STEP 9 **The tools menu**

Press **Alt+T** to pull down the tools menu, select *DOS utilities,* and press **return**; you will see an alphabetic listing of the files in the current DOS directory, similar to Figure 8.11h. Press the **down arrow** key several times to scroll through the file list until you see either **SECOND** or **SIMPLE**, which correspond to the applications we have been using. Each file name appears three times, with three different extensions: **APP**, **DBO**, and **PRG**; the significance of this is explained after the exercise. Press **Alt+E** to exit this screen and return to the control center.

STEP 10 **Exit dBASE**

Press **Alt+E** to pull down the exit menu in the control center. Highlight *Quit to DOS* and press **return** to exit dBASE and return to DOS.

dBASE IV File Types

The multitude of dBASE IV ***file types,*** each with a different function, can be overwhelming. The **SECOND** application, for example, is associated with three files, each with a different extension (**APP**, **PRG**, and **DBO**) as shown in Figure 8.11h. In similar fashion report forms are associated with the file types **FRM**, **FRG**, and **FRO**, while labels use yet a different set—**LBL**, **LBG**, and **LBO**. Still other extensions are used with forms and query files as shown in Table 8.2, which summarizes dBASE file types of interest from the control panel.

The reason for the different file types is best understood by considering one set in detail, e.g., applications, remembering that the application generator assigns us the simpler task of describing *what* an application is to do, rather than the more complex task of developing the logic to produce that application. In other words, we define the application according to the process described in the hands-on exercise, then store that information in a file with extension **APP**, e.g., **SECOND.APP**.

After the application has been defined—i.e., after we have created the sign-on banner and specified the report and label forms the application is to include—we tell dBASE to generate the application, which converts the specifications in the **SECOND.APP** file to a program file, **SECOND.PRG**. The latter consists of programming statements (which are understandable to us and which can in fact be modified through a program editor). The last step is to run the application, which causes dBASE to translate the source program in the **PRG** file to an ***object program,*** **SECOND.DBO**, consisting of machine language statements understandable to the computer.

A similar process occurs for both report forms and label forms. We use the **CREATE REPORT** command to initiate the report generator and store the description in a report form, e.g., **ACADEMIC.FRM**. We then produce a finished report through the **REPORT FORM** command, which creates a program file, **ACADEMIC.FRG**, and finally an object program, **ACADEMIC.FRO**, consisting of machine language statements. In similar fashion, the **CREATE LABEL** command produces a label form (with

TABLE 8.2 **dBASE IV File Extensions**[1]

File Type	Design	Program	Object
Data File[2]	DBF		
Query	QBE		QBO
Form (Screen)	SCR	FMT	FMO
Report Form	FRM	FRG	FRO
Label Form	LBL	LBG	LBO
Application	APP	PRG	DBO

[1] Certain file types, (e.g., **FRG** and **FRO**) are created only through commands from the dot prompt (e.g., **REPORT FORM**) and will *not* be created from the control center.

[2] Execution of a **MODIFY STRUCTURE** command produces backup files with extension of **DBK** and **MBK** for the **DBF** and **MDX** files, respectively.

extension **LBL**), which in turn produces a program file (extension **LBG**), and finally an object program (extension **LBO**). Parallel files are created for queries and formatted screens.

Figure 8.12 shows the files in *our* directory at the end of the hands-on exercises. There is, however, one significant difference between executing the **REPORT FORM** and **LABEL FORM** commands from the dot prompt, versus highlighting the existing forms from the control panel, in that the latter does *not* save the program and object files. In other words, the multiple extensions for the report and label forms (**FRG**, **FRO**, **LBG**, and **LBO**) shown in Figure 8.12 are there because we executed the commands from the dot prompt, and these files would not appear if you operated exclusively from the control center. As indicated, your directory will most likely differ from ours according to the commands you executed during the hands-on exercises.

Catalogs

One unstated advantage of the control center is that it provides a more organized display of files than the DOS directory, as can be seen by comparing the control center in Figure 8.1 with the directory of Figure 8.12. The control center shows at a glance how many files are in each panel, whereas the directory makes it difficult to locate individual files within the myriad of file types.

The display of files in the control center is determined by the dBASE ***catalog*** currently in effect. The control center in Figure 8.1, for example, is associated with the catalog **UNTITLED.CAT**, which is the name of the default catalog whenever dBASE is loaded. You can, however, use the catalog menu of Figure 8.11h to change the name of this catalog and/or use a different catalog (if one exists).

FIGURE 8.12
File Directory

```
C:\DATADISK\STUDENTS> DIR
.             <DIR       04-26-91    9:58a
..            <DIR       04-26-91    9:58a
ACADEMIC FRG       4683 05-09-91    9:44a
ACADEMIC FRM       1759 04-12-91    9:59p
ACADEMIC FRO       4696 05-09-91    9:45a
ADDRESS  FRM       1890 04-12-91   10:01p
BSNSFEM  QBE       3964 04-12-91   10:27p
CATALOG  CAT        439 05-09-91    9:54a
CONTACT  FRM       1385 04-12-91   10:03p
FLORIDA  QBE       3576 04-12-91   10:26p
GPA_30   QBE       3929 05-01-91    1:59p
INPUT    FMO       4096 05-09-91    9:40a
INPUT    FMT       3989 04-26-91   12:05p
INPUT    SCR       4388 04-26-91   12:05p
MAJOR    FRM       1568 04-12-91    9:54p
ROLODEX  LBG       4450 05-09-91    9:45a
ROLODEX  LBL       1854 04-12-91    8:21p
ROLODEX  LBO       5444 05-09-91    9:45a
SECOND   APP       1083 05-03-91    9:01a
SECOND   DBO      16208 05-09-91    8:50a
SECOND   PRG      19126 05-03-91    9:01a
SENIORS  QBE       3847 04-12-91   10:25p
SIMPLE   APP       1138 04-26-91   10:05a
SIMPLE   DBO      16800 05-09-91    8:48a
SIMPLE   PRG      19633 04-26-91   10:05a
STUDENTS DBF       1530 05-03-91    8:52a
STUDENTS MDX      12288 05-01-91    2:10p
TWOCOLMN LBL       1363 04-12-91    8:14p
UNTITLED CAT       3335 05-09-91    9:54a
```

DIR command (entered at DOS prompt)

Three file types for report form; FRM and FRO are created at dot prompt

Three file types for application

Catalog file for control center

A catalog is simply a list of files, containing some (usually not all) files in the DOS directory in which it is located. The catalog, **UNTITLED.CAT** in our example, is itself a file as can be seen from the directory of Figure 8.12. How, you may ask, are catalogs created in the first place, and further how are files added to (deleted from) an existing catalog? The answers are very simple.

dBASE creates a default catalog for you, **UNTITLED.CAT**, and uses that catalog unless you specify otherwise. *All files created from the control panel are automatically added to the active catalog, whereas files created at the dot prompt are not.* Thus, if you were to select **<create>** in the labels panel for a new label form called **EXAMPLE**, the file **EXAMPLE.LBL** would be added to the catalog and **EXAMPLE** would appear in the labels panel. Creating the identical label form from the dot prompt (**CREATE LABEL EXAMPLE**) would *not* add the label form to the catalog, and thus **EXAMPLE** would not appear in the control center even though **EXAMPLE.LBL** would still appear in the DOS directory.

The pull-down catalog menu allows you to add files to, or remove files from, an existing catalog; e.g., *Add file to catalog* will add files created at the dot prompt (and thus not in the catalog), while *Remove highlighted file from catalog* erases a file from the catalog. Note, however, that removing a file from the catalog does not erase it from the DOS directory.

Summary

The ***control center*** provides simplified (but limited) access to commands executed at the dot prompt. The control center contains six panels—***Data, Queries, Forms, Reports, Labels,*** and ***Applications***—each of which displays the indicated file type.

The **ASSIST** command exits the dot prompt and enters the control center; pressing the **Esc** key exits the control center and returns to the dot prompt.

Pull-down menus are accessed by pressing the **F10** function key, then using the left and right arrows to arrive at the menu of choice. Alternatively, you can press the **Alt** key plus the first letter of the menu; e.g. **ALT+C** pulls down the catalog menu from the control center.

The ***menu system*** consists of the control center plus the screens you can reach from the control center. Four pull-down menus—records, organize, fields, and go to—encompass the operations for file maintenance and are accessed from the browse/edit screen.

The ***application generator*** creates a dBASE program that enables the user to select one or more options from appropriate menus. A ***quick application*** may include a formatted screen for file maintenance, a report form, and a label form.

As many as three different ***file types*** can be associated with each entry in the control center. The applications panel, for example, is associated with file types **APP**, **DBO**, and **PRG**.

Key Words and Concepts

Alt key
Application
Application generator
Application menu
Applications panel
ASSIST
Catalog
Catalog menu
Control center
CREATE APPLICATION
Ctrl+Y
Data panel
Esc key
F1 (help) key
F2 (data) key
F10 (menus) key
File maintenance
File type

Forms panel
Go to menu
Labels panel
Menu system
MODIFY APPLICATION
Navigation line
Object program
On-line help
Organize menu
Pop-up menu
Program
Pull-down menus
Queries panel
Quick application
Records menu
Reports panel
Shift+F2 (design) key
Shift+F9 (quick report)
Sign-on banner
Tools menu
UNTITLED.CAT

True/False

1. The **ASSIST** command enters the control center from the dot prompt.
2. The exit menu in the control center will exit to either the dot prompt or the DOS prompt.
3. The control center provides complete access to all dBASE commands as issued from the dot prompt.
4. Catalog, tools, and exit are among the panels present in the control center.
5. All options in the **LABEL FORM** command can be reached through the labels panel in the control center.
6. The precise effect of the **F2** function key in the control center depends on the panel in which it is pressed.
7. The **F2** function key will toggle between the browse and edit screens.
8. Pressing the **F10** function key and/or pressing **Ctrl+R** will pull down the records menu from the browse/edit screen.
9. All files in a dBASE catalog appear in the corresponding DOS directory.
10. All files in a DOS directory are listed in the associated dBASE catalog.
11. Selecting **<create>** from the reports panel will automatically create three files, with extensions of **FRM**, **FRG**, and **FRO**.
12. On-line help is *not* available from the control center.
13. The tools menu is used to change the description of a file in the control center.

Exercises

1. Which menu—records, organize, or go to—provides the equivalent of the following dBASE commands entered at the dot prompt?
   (a) **APPEND**
   (b) **DELETE**
   (c) **RECALL**
   (d) **FIND**
   (e) **PACK**
   (f) **SET ORDER TO**
   (g) **GO TOP**

2. Indicate the dBASE command or control center operation that will create the following files in conjunction with the control center displayed in Figure 8.1.
   (a) **ACADEMIC.FRG**
   (b) **ACADEMIC.FRO**
   (c) **TWOCOLMN.LBG**
   (d) **TWOCOLMN.LBO**
   (e) **SIMPLE.DBO**
   (f) **SECOND.APP**
   (g) **INPUT.FMO**

FIGURE 8.13
Screen for Problem 3

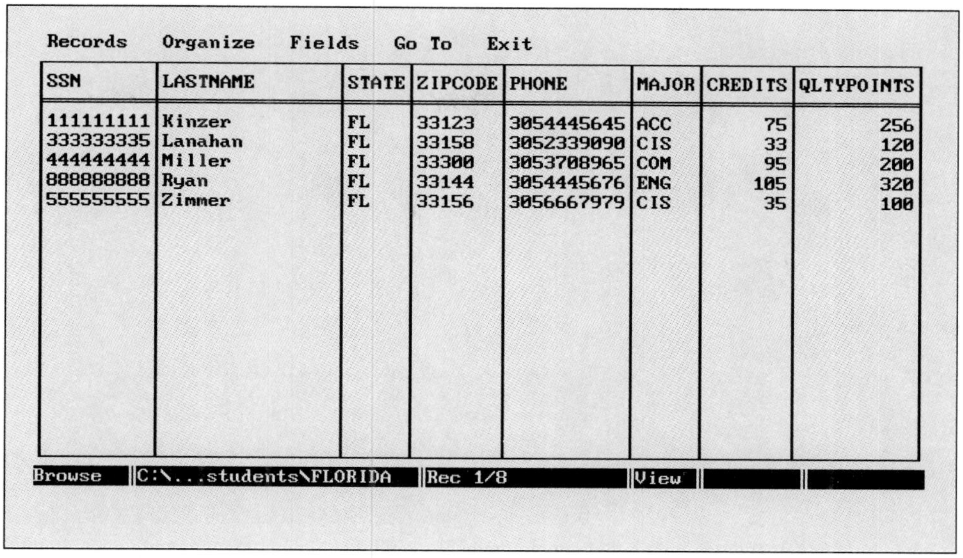

Records Organize Fields Go To Exit

SSN	LASTNAME	STATE	ZIPCODE	PHONE	MAJOR	CREDITS	QLTYPOINTS
111111111	Kinzer	FL	33123	3054445645	ACC	75	256
333333335	Lanahan	FL	33158	3052339090	CIS	33	120
444444444	Miller	FL	33300	3053708965	COM	95	200
888888888	Ryan	FL	33144	3054445676	ENG	105	320
555555555	Zimmer	FL	33156	3056667979	CIS	35	100

Browse | C:\...students\FLORIDA | Rec 1/8 | View

3. Figure 8.13 was produced from the identical **STUDENTS.DBF** file as Figure 8.3, but contains only a subset of the records in the original figure. In addition, Figure 8.13 displays different fields for the records that are shown, and further lists its records in different sequence. All three changes were brought about by various menu options and/or selections from the control center of Figure 8.1.
   (a) What criterion was used to select the records in Figure 8.13? What action, taken at the control center of Figure 8.1, implemented this selection?
   (b) In which order are the records displayed in Figure 8.13? Which menu, and which option in that menu, produced the new sequence?
   (c) The **FIRSTNAME**, **ADDRESS**, and **CITY** fields are not displayed in Figure 8.13 even though those fields follow immediately after the **LASTNAME** field in the file structure of Figure 8.3b. Which menu, and which option in that menu, caused these fields to be omitted from the display in Figure 8.13?

4. Which of the following commands can be executed through suitable action at the control panel of Figure 8.1 and/or through subsequent pull-down menus?
   (a) `MODIFY LABEL ROLODEX`
   (b) `REPORT FORM MAJOR HEADING 'CIS Majors'`
   (c) `LABEL FORM TWOCOLMN FOR ZIPCODE='33123'`
   (d) `SET FORMAT TO INPUT`
   (e) `MODIFY SCREEN INPUT`
   (f) `SET VIEW TO SENIORS`
   (g) `CREATE LABEL`
   (h) `CREATE`
   (i) `MODIFY STUDENTS`
   (j) `USE STUDENTS`
   (k) `CREATE APPLICATION`
   (l) `MODIFY APPLICATION`
   (m) `QUIT`

5. Figure 8.14 displays two screens associated with attempts to create a **THIRD** application from the control panel of Figure 8.1.
   (a) Why did the error in Figure 8.14a occur?
   (b) Figure 8.14b appeared immediately after pressing any key as instructed. What

FIGURE 8.14
Errors in the Application Generator

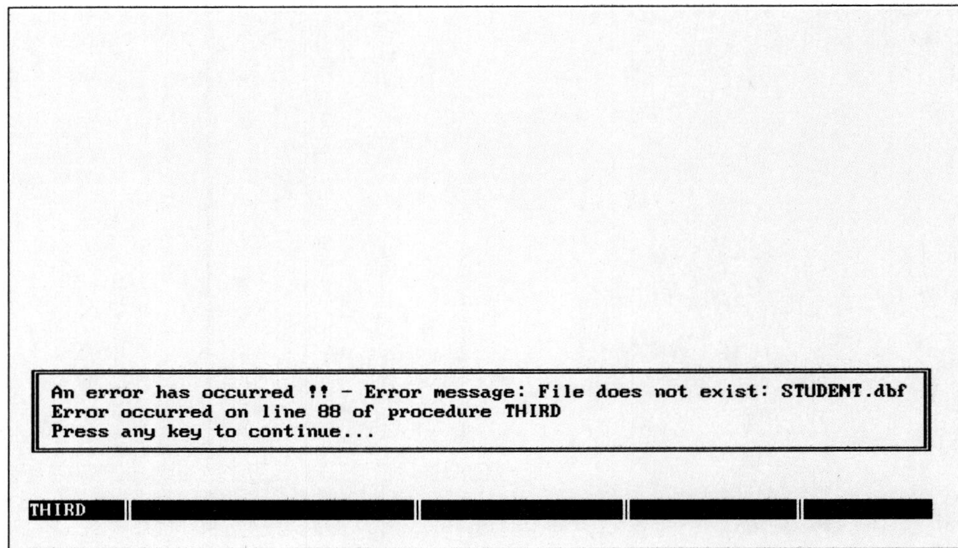

(a) First Error

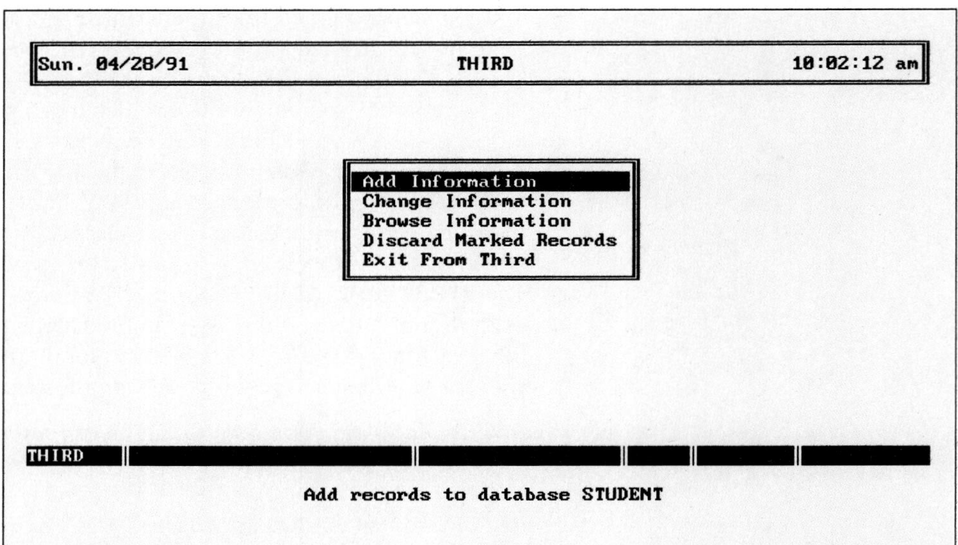

(b) Second Error

is your best guess as to why this menu contains only five choices, as opposed to eight choices present in the other applications developed in the chapter?

(c) The status bar at the bottom of parts (a) and (b) is empty except for the name of the application (**THIRD**). Why?

PART

Command-Level Programming

CHAPTER

9

Introduction to Programming

OUTLINE

OBJECTIVES

After reading this chapter you will be able to:

1. Describe the requirements of a menu-driven program.
2. Define structured programming; explain what is meant by the one entry point/one exit point philosophy.
3. Define pseudocode; list two conventions to follow in writing pseudocode.
4. List the dBASE statements used to implement the basic building blocks of structured programming.
5. Distinguish between the dBASE interactive and command modes.
6. Discuss why coding standards are necessary in dBASE; suggest at least three standards to follow in writing dBASE programs.
7. Define debugging and describe how this is accomplished in dBASE; distinguish between errors in compilation and errors in execution.
8. Discuss the need for proper documentation of programs; describe several elements used in program documentation.

Overview

Although we were pleased with the reports produced in previous chapters, and said nothing to the contrary, the methodology is really quite primitive. The requirement for entering commands one at a time from the dot prompt (or through the control center) is severely limited, and results in having to continually retype command sequences. This is, to say the least, an inefficient and error-prone procedure.

This chapter introduces *programming* and develops a ***menu-driven program*** capable of producing a variety of reports based on the United States example from Chapter 4. We develop the logic necessary to write the program and, in so doing, discuss both ***structured programming*** and ***pseudocode.*** We introduce a variety of new dBASE statements and discuss how they are used in the menu-driven program. Our goal, however, is not to present every nuance of every statement (the details are in the Programmer's Notebook), but rather to present an overview of why programming is necessary and what it can accomplish.

The most important part of the chapter is the hands-on exercises, which incorporate all of this material. More than likely, you will make mistakes along the way, and so we introduce you to ***debugging,*** with emphasis on the difference between errors in ***compilation*** versus errors in ***execution.***

A Menu-Driven Program

Let us return to the four reports on the United States, which were created originally in Chapter 4, reviewing how the reports were produced in the hands-on exercises. In particular, recall how we continually entered commands from the dot prompt, in order to produce the various reports. Wouldn't it be simpler if we could simply call up a program that asked us in English which report(s) we wanted?

Figure 9.1 demonstrates exactly that capability. The screens in Figures 9.1a, b, and c request information from the user on the type of report desired (area, population, year of admission, or density), the sequence in which states are to be listed (ascending or descending), and the number of states to be included. The program collects all three responses and then produces the resulting report, as shown in Figure 9.1d. Imagine how much easier this ***user-friendly*** program is to use than entering the individual commands from the dot prompt or control center.

Implicit in these screens is a ***data validation*** capability, in that the program will reject invalid responses. In other words, the program is expecting a response of A, B, C, or D to indicate the type of report desired, and it must be smart enough to reject any invalid response (i.e., a response other than A, B, C, or D). In similar fashion, the program should validate the desired sequence (either A or D for ***ascending*** or ***descending,*** respectively) as well as the number of states to include in the report (a number from 1 to 50, inclusive). Once all three valid responses have been obtained, the report can be generated.

It is also important to recognize the ***flexibility*** inherent in the input screens of Figures 9.1a, b, and c. We could just as easily have asked for a report listing the states in ascending order of admission to the union, descending order of population, and so on. We see, therefore, that the menu driven system is not only easy to use, but flexible as well, in terms of its ability to generate a large number of reports.

Figure 9.1 effectively establishes the requirements of the menu-driven program that will be developed in this chapter; the program is to be:

1. Able to produce four types of reports (area, population, year of admission, or density), listing a variable number of states for each report in either ascending or descending sequence.

FIGURE 9.1
Output of Interactive dBASE Program

```
UNITED STATES REPORT MENU

A) AREA REPORT
B) 1990 POPULATION REPORT
C) DATE OF ADMISSION REPORT
D) POPULATION DENSITY REPORT

WHICH REPORT DO YOU WISH TO SEE: A
```

(a) First Prompting Message
(A has been entered)

```
ASCENDING OR DESCENDING SEQUENCE?

ENTER A OR D: A
```

(b) Second Prompting Message
(A has been entered)

```
HOW MANY STATES DO YOU WANT LISTED?

ENTER NUMBER: 10
```

(c) Third Prompting Message
(10 has been entered)

```
AREA REPORT

Rhode Island          1214
Delaware              2057
Connecticut           5009
Hawaii                6450
New Jersey            7836
Massachusetts         8257
New Hampshire         9304
Vermont               9609
Maryland             10577
West Virginia        24181
```

(d) Output Produced by the Program

2. Capable of validating the user's inputs for the type of report, sorting sequence, and number of states.
3. Easy to use and not require any knowledge of programming languages or data management systems.

The entire chapter is aimed at developing a menu-driven program with these capabilities. As you shall see, much of the discussion will not be concerned with dBASE per se, but with the underlying logic of the program. That, in turn, leads us to a discussion of programming methodology, a discipline known as ***structured programming.***

Structured Programming

Much time and effort has been devoted to finding the best way to write programs. The outcome of that research has given rise to a discipline known as structured programming, which applies to any language, be it dBASE, BASIC, COBOL, etc. The discipline seeks to produce programs that are logically correct and that can be easily read and maintained by someone other than the original author.

The theory that we are about to discuss may seem somewhat abstract, without any immediate application. It is, however, the basis on which good programming is based, and its relevance will become apparent as the menu-driven program is developed. Accordingly, you may want to read this section now, then reread it later as you code the program in dBASE.

The logic in a structured program can be viewed as a set of basic building blocks, put together in various combinations to solve a problem. Only three types of building blocks are necessary: ***sequence, selection*** (a decision), and ***iteration*** (a loop). The fact that these structures are sufficient to express any desired logic was first postulated in a now-classic paper by Bohm and Jacopini.[1]

The elementary building blocks of structured programming are shown in Figure 9.2. Each building block is expressed as a ***flowchart,*** or pictorial representation of programming logic. Flowcharts use special symbols to communicate information. A rectangle indicates a processing statement, a diamond indicates a decision, and a small circle connects portions of the flowchart. Each of the building blocks in the figure has one key feature in common, namely, *one entry point* and *one exit point.*

The sequence block of Figure 9.2a implies that program statements are executed sequentially, i.e., in the order in which they appear. The two blocks, A and B, could denote anything from single statements to complete programs.

The selection block of Figure 9.2b shows a choice between two actions. A condition is tested, and if the condition is true, block A is executed; if it is false, block B is executed. The condition is the single entry point to the structure, and both paths meet in a single exit point.

Iteration (or looping) in Figure 9.2c calls for the repeated execution of one or more statements. A condition is tested and, if it is true, block A is executed. If, however, the condition is false, control passes to the next sequential statement after the iteration structure. Again, there is exactly one entry point and one exit point from the structure.

Figure 9.2d contains a fourth type of building block, known as the ***case structure,*** which expresses a multibranch situation. Although case is really a special instance of selection, it is convenient to extend the definition of structured programming to include this fourth type of building block. The case construct evaluates a condition and branches to one of several paths, depending on the value of the condition. As with the other fundamental building blocks, there is one entry point and one exit point.

Sufficiency of the Basic Structures

The theory of structured programming says simply that an appropriate combination of the elementary building blocks may be derived to solve any problem in logic. This is possible because an entire structure (sequence, selection, iteration, or case) may be *substituted* anywhere block A or B appears. Figure 9.3 contains a combination of the basic structures to illustrate this point.

Figure 9.3 is essentially a selection structure. However, instead of specifying a single statement for the true and false branches (as was done in Figure 9.2b), an iteration structure is substituted for block A and a sequence structure for block B. Both the iteration and sequence structures meet at a single point, which in turn becomes the exit point for the initial selection structure.

---

[1] Bohm and Jacopini, "Flow Diagrams, Turing Machines and Languages with Only Two Formation Rules," *Communications of the ACM,* May 1966.

FIGURE 9.2
The Building Blocks of Structured Programming

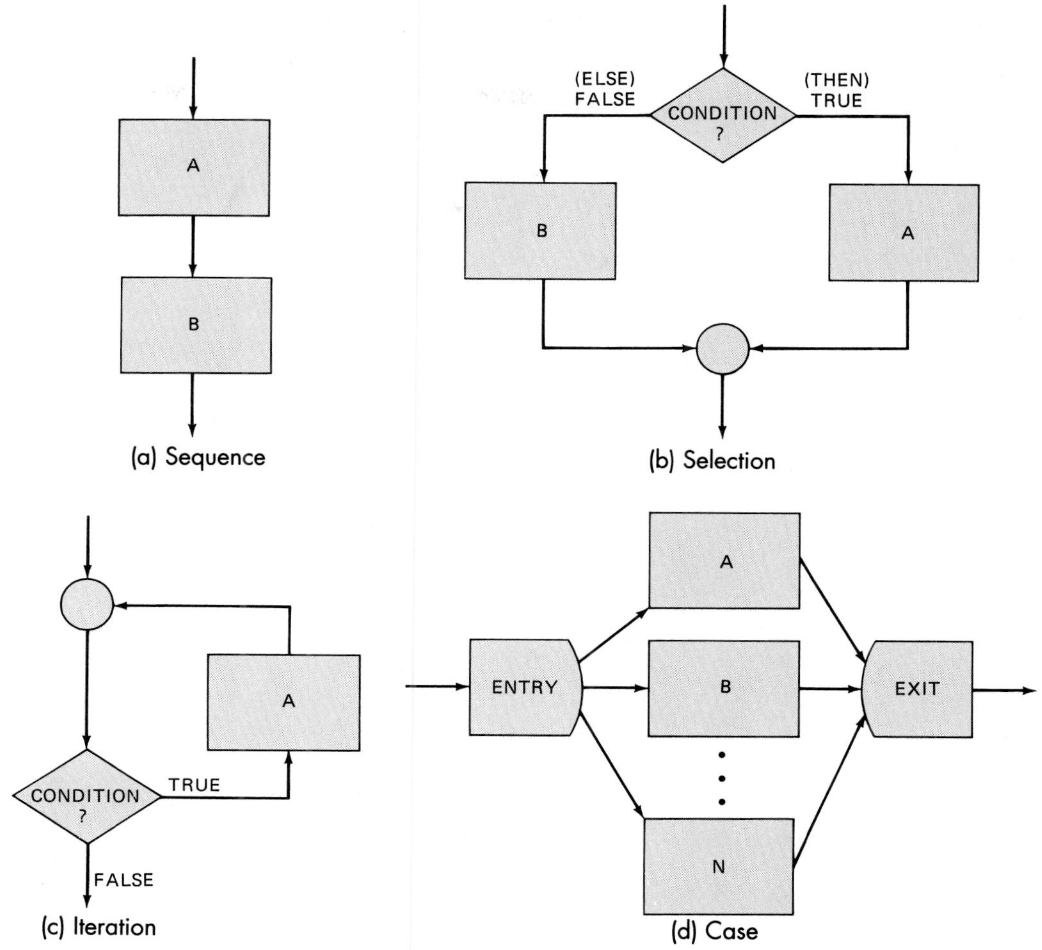

FIGURE 9.3
Sufficiency of the Basic Structures

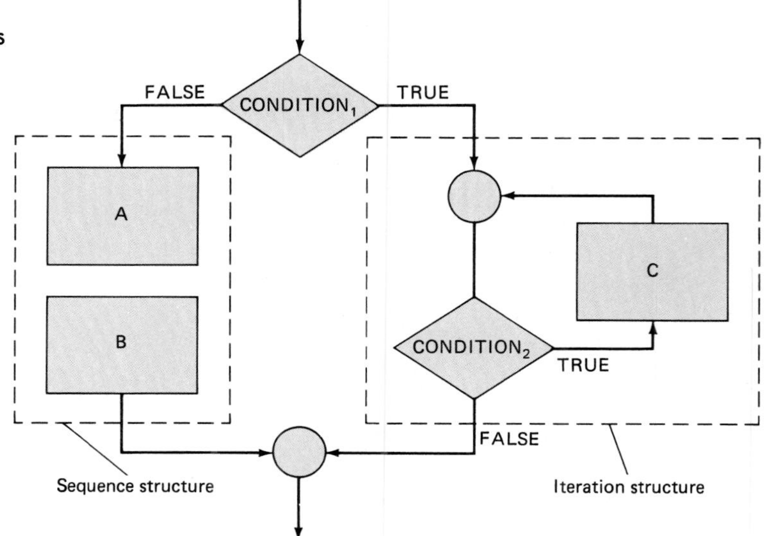

Pseudocode

Pseudocode, or neat notes to oneself, is a commonly accepted technique for expressing program logic. Pseudocode uses English-like statements similar to computer instructions and has a very distinct block structure, which is extremely conducive to structured programming. An example of pseudocode, corresponding to the flowcharts of Figure 9.2, is shown in Figure 9.4.

Pseudocode is *not* bound by formal syntactical rules as is a programming language. Nor is it bound by rules of indentation, which is done strictly at your discretion. We suggest, however, the use of certain conventions to make pseudocode easier to read. We use indentation, in conjunction with vertical lines, to indicate the extent of the various building blocks. We use the key words **IF**, **DO WHILE**, and **DO CASE** for selection, iteration, and case, respectively, and end each block with **ENDIF**, **ENDDO**, and **ENDCASE** as indicated. The only real limitation is a restriction to the elementary building blocks (sequence, selection, iteration, and case), which causes the pseudocode to flow easily from the top down.

Good pseudocode should be sufficiently precise to serve as a real aid in writing a program, while informal enough to be intelligible to nonprogrammers. The very nature of the technique prohibits the establishment of precise rules as that would imply a formalism that pseudocode does not possess. Nevertheless, we suggest you take a second look at Figure 9.4 and try to adhere to our suggestions for indentation and the use of vertical lines to indicate the extent of a block.

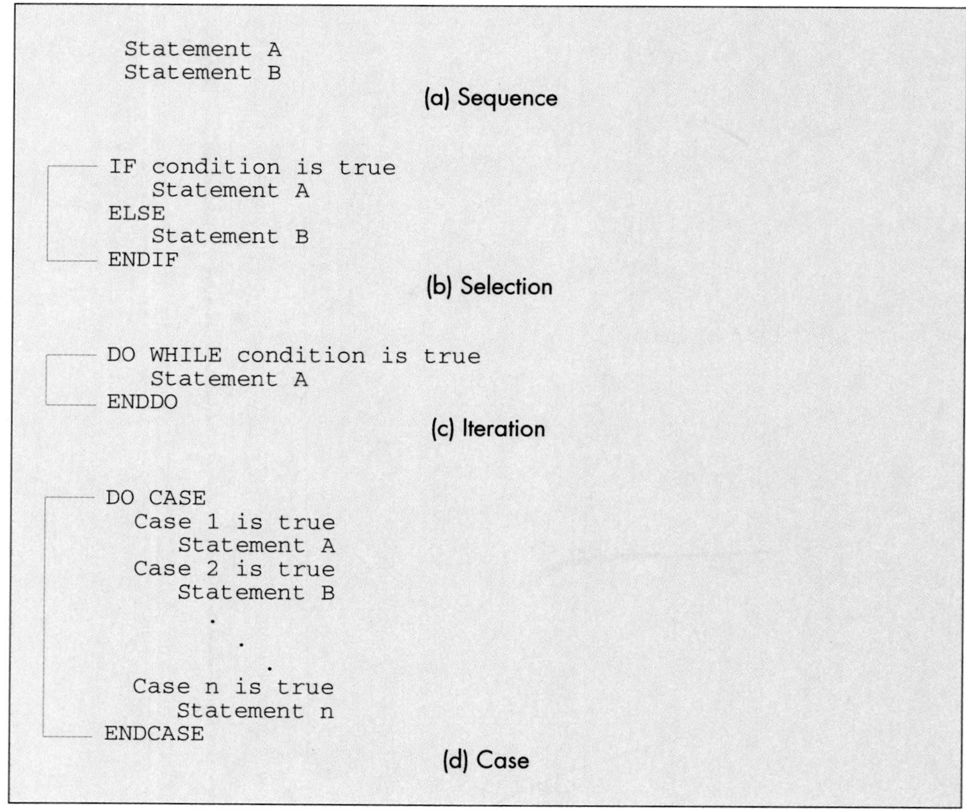

FIGURE 9.4
Structured Programming in Pseudocode

Developing the Menu-Driven Program

Thus far we have stated that the basic building blocks of structured programming are sufficient to develop the logic to solve any problem, and have chosen pseudocode as the preferred method for expressing that logic. Now we are ready to apply these concepts to the problem at hand.

Review the requirements of the menu-driven program, which we postulated earlier, and realize that the eventual program will consist of two major sections, ***user input*** and ***report generation.*** The user-input portion will accept and validate responses from the user, after which the report generation segment will create a report based on the inputs provided. Thus, in very general terms, the program will execute statements in sequence to:

1. Obtain the report type (area, population, date of admission, or density).
2. Obtain the report sequence (ascending or descending).
3. Obtain the number of states to include in the report.
4. Generate the report.

There is a great deal of detail implied in the user-input portion of the program. The user is asked to input a response, e.g., the type of report. The program then checks the validity of that response, and if invalid, asks the user to once again enter the type of report desired. The new response must also be validated, and the process should continue until a valid answer has been obtained. Similar sets of statements must then be executed to obtain the other responses, i.e., the report sequence and the number of states to include in the report. Can you begin to see how the basic building blocks will be used to describe a procedure for obtaining a valid response?

The logic for the user-input portion of the menu-driven program is expressed in the pseudocode in Figure 9.5. The figure contains three parallel sets of instructions for each of the three responses—report type (area, population, year of admission or density), report sequence (ascending or descending), and number of states (1 to 50).

Consider the logic to obtain the report type, i.e., Figure 9.5a. A loop is established in which the user is continually asked for a response, until a valid response is obtained. The execution of that loop is controlled by a ***switch,*** i.e., a variable that can assume one of two values (yes or no). The switch is initially set to 'no' (i.e., a valid response has not yet been obtained), and the loop is entered. The user supplies a response. If the response is valid, the switch is set to 'yes' and the loop is terminated. If, on the other hand, an invalid response is supplied, an error message is displayed but the switch remains set to 'no,' which in turn causes the loop to be repeated. The user is again asked for a response, the response is checked, and so on. The process continues an indeterminate number of times, until a valid response is obtained. Figures 9.5b and 9.5c contain similar logic to obtain the remaining responses from the user.

Figure 9.6 depicts the logic to create a particular report, once the three valid user inputs have been received. The report-generation process begins by opening the file and then establishing a case structure to evaluate the report type. Based on this value, an appropriate heading is written and the proper index is selected. (Implicit in this logic is the assumption that four distinct indexes—on area, population, year of admission, and density—have been previously created.)

Next we determine whether the states in the report are to be listed in ascending or descending sequence. States will be listed in ascending sequence by starting at the beginning of the appropriate index and moving forward; they will be listed in descending sequence by starting at the end of the index and moving backward.

FIGURE 9.5
Pseudocode for Data Entry

```
Set valid-report-switch to 'no'
DO WHILE valid-report-switch = 'no'
   Get user's response
   IF user's response is valid
      Set valid-report-switch to 'yes'
   ELSE
     Tell user to input a valid report type
   ENDIF
ENDDO
```

(a) Obtaining the Report Type

```
Set valid-sequence-switch to 'no'
DO WHILE valid-sequence-switch = 'no'
   Get user's response
   IF user's response is valid
     Set valid-sequence-switch to 'yes'
    ELSE
      Tell user to input a valid report sequence
   ENDIF
ENDDO
```

(b) Obtaining the Report Sequence

```
Set valid-number-switch to 'no'
DO WHILE valid-number-switch = 'no'
   Get user's response
   IF user's response is valid
      Set valid-number-switch to 'yes'
   ELSE
      Tell user to input a valid number of states
   ENDIF
ENDDO
```

(c) Obtaining the Number of States

(Implicit in this logic is the assumption that the indexes were created in ascending order; e.g., the area index begins with Rhode Island and continues to Alaska. Thus, if the user requested that states be listed in descending order (the largest state first), we would go to the end of the index, i.e., Alaska, and move backward to Texas, California, and so on).

The **DO WHILE** loop at the end of Figure 9.6 writes the requested number of detail lines (one for each state in the report). The loop is controlled by a ***counter,*** which is initialized to zero outside the loop and incremented by one within the loop. Note that when the proper number of lines have been written, the value of the counter will be equal to the desired number of states, which terminates the loop and ends the program.

The case construct within the loop writes the appropriate detail line, depending on the report type. (Detail lines for the various reports contain different fields; e.g., the area report contains the state name and area, whereas the population report has the name and population.) Observe, also, the **IF** statement within the loop, which determines whether the record pointer is moved to the next or previous record, based on the sequence requested.

The logic for the menu-driven program is complete as depicted in the pseudocode of Figures 9.5 and 9.6. These figures do not contain dBASE statements per se, and must therefore be converted in order that the program run on the computer. This in turn leads to a discussion of dBASE programming.

FIGURE 9.6
Pseudocode for Report-Generation Portion

```
Clear screen
Open USSTATES file

DO CASE
   CASE 1: Write report heading for Area report
           Set tag to area index
   CASE 2: Write report heading for Population report
           Set tag to population index
   CASE 3: Write report heading for Admission report
           Set tag to admission index
   CASE 4: Write report heading for Density report
           Set tag to density index
ENDCASE


IF report sequence is ascending
   Start with first state in index (and move forward)
ELSE
   Start with last state in index (and move backward)
ENDIF


Set counter to zero
DO WHILE counter < number of states requested
   DO CASE
      CASE 1: Write detail line for Area report
      CASE 2: Write detail line for Population report
      CASE 3: Write detail line for Admission report
      CASE 4: Write detail line for Density report
   ENDCASE

   IF report sequence is ascending
      Go to next state
   ELSE
      Go to previous state
   ENDIF

   Increment counter by 1
ENDDO
```

Implementation in dBASE

There are essentially two ways to teach programming. The first is to spend an inordinate amount of time explaining all of the nuances associated with the necessary dBASE statements and then, and only then, write a program. The second is to plunge right in with only an intuitive understanding, and leave the details for later. We are firm advocates of the latter approach, believing strongly that quick exposure to programming helps remove the mystical aura that too often surrounds the subject.

Let us review, for a moment, what has been accomplished so far. We began the chapter with the requirements of a generalized menu-driven program, developed the required logic via the building blocks of structured programming, and expressed that logic in pseudocode. It remains, however, to convert that logic to dBASE code, which in turn requires the introduction of several new dBASE statements.

However, in keeping with our philosophy of a quick entry into programming, we present only the bare essentials of the necessary dBASE statements, and refer you to the Programmer's Notebook for additional information. We suggest also that you skip back and forth between the discussion and the completed program of Figure 9.7.

The presentation of the required dBASE statements is divided into three groups as described below:

1. Statements related to structured programming (**IF...ENDIF**, DO WHILE ...**ENDDO**, and DO CASE...ENDCASE)
2. Statements pertaining to input/output (@...**SAY** @...**GET**, **READ**, and **?**)
3. Memory variables
4. Statements affecting the record pointer (GO **TOP**, GO **BOTTOM**, **SKIP +1**, and **SKIP -1**)

Statements for Structured Programming

The extended definition of structured programming indicates that a structured program is one consisting entirely of four types of building blocks: sequence, selection, iteration, and case. It follows therefore that the implementation of structured programming in dBASE must accommodate these building blocks. Implementation of the sequence structure is trivial in that dBASE statements appear in a program in the order in which they are to be executed. Selection is implemented by the dBASE IF statement, iteration by the dBASE DO WHILE statement, and case by the dBASE DO CASE statement. As we shall see, the dBASE syntax of these statements closely resembles the pseudocode shown in Figure 9.4. (You may want to look ahead to Figure 9.7 to find an example of each statement.)

The **IF** statement determines whether a condition is true or false, and if the condition is true, executes the indicated series of commands; it may also include an optional **ELSE** clause with an alternative set of statements that are executed when the condition is false. An IF statement *must* terminate with **ENDIF**.

The **DO WHILE** statement repeatedly tests a condition, executing a set of commands as long as the stated condition is true. A DO WHILE statement *must* end with **ENDDO**.

Finally, **DO CASE** evaluates a condition with multiple outcomes, enabling the execution of one of several possible paths (cases), including one alternative or error-checking condition. A DO CASE statement must end with an **ENDCASE.**

Input/Output Statements

All programs make provision to receive input and generate output. Figure 9.1, for example, displayed various messages asking the user for information on which to base a report, accepted his or her responses, and subsequently displayed the resulting report.

The **@...SAY** command displays text on the screen, e.g., a request for user input, while the **@...GET** command (in conjunction with a **READ** command) obtains and stores that response. Both statements contain row and column coordinates to indicate the location of the text or input template. The screen display is divided into 25 rows (numbered from 0 to 24) and 80 columns (numbered from 0 to 79). The upper left corner has the coordinates (0,0).

The relationship between the various @...SAY and @...GET statements in the program also merits attention. Consider, for example, the statement @ 13,23 SAY 'WHICH REPORT DO YOU WISH TO SEE:', which displays the indicated text, starting in row 13, column 23. The prompting message ends in column 55 of the same row and the associated @ 13,56 GET mselect PICTURE 'A' displays the input template for the user response in row 13, column 56.

Recall, too, that a **PICTURE** clause indicates the type and length of the memory variable expected in the user response. A PICTURE of **A** indicates an alphabetic response of one character (**AA** would imply a two-character response). In similar fashion, a picture clause of **99** implies a two-digit numeric response (and is used in connection with the number of states).

The **?** command prints the lines in the eventual report. The command may print a literal by enclosing the text to be printed in apostrophes—e.g., **? 'Area report'**—or it may display the contents of a field within a **DBF** file—e.g., **? state,area** to print the value of the **state** and **area** fields for the current record in the open **DBF** file.

Memory Variables

A ***memory variable*** is a temporary storage location used by a program to hold data that is not part of a **DBF** file. Several such variables are present in the program of Figure 9.7; e.g., **mselect**, **mseq**, and **mnum**, which store the user responses for the type of report, sequence, and number of states, respectively. The values of these memory variables are obtained through the various **@...GET** commands at the beginning of the program. Note, too, that a memory variable must be defined in a **STORE** statement before it can be used elsewhere in the program.

Statements Affecting the Record Pointer

Consider again the requirements of the menu-driven program, which lists selected states in one of eight possible ways, i.e., in ascending or descending order by area, population, date of admission, and population density. Recall also that the program assumes the existence of a single **DBF** file (**USSTATES.DBF**), together with a master index (**USSTATES.MDX**) containing four indexes (area, population, year of admission, and population density). The **USE** statement, in conjunction with the appropriate **SET ORDER TO TAG** statement, opens the **DBF** file and designates the active index; e.g., **SET ORDER TO TAG AREA** indicates that states will be processed in order of area.

The **GO** or **GOTO** statement positions the record pointer to a specific record number; e.g., **GOTO 3** moves to record three in the file. **GO TOP** and **GO BOTTOM** position the pointer at the first and last records, respectively, *according to the active index*—e.g., to Rhode Island and Alaska, respectively, if area is the active index.

SKIP (or **SKIP +1**) moves the record pointer one record forward in the file, according to the order of the active index. In similar fashion, **SKIP −1** moves one record backward, also according to the order of the active index. Thus the statements

```
USE usstates
SET ORDER TO TAG area
GO TOP
DISPLAY
SKIP +1
DISPLAY
```

will display first Rhode Island and then Delaware, whereas the statements

```
USE usstates
SET ORDER TO TAG area
GO BOTTOM
DISPLAY
SKIP -1
DISPLAY
```

will display Alaska and California.

The Completed Program

The completed menu-driven program is shown in Figure 9.7. (The vertical lines in the figure are only to highlight the overall program logic and are not part of the program per se.) Your objective at this time should be to gain a conceptual understanding of

```
CLEAR
SET BELL OFF
SET TALK OFF
@ 4,23 SAY '    UNITED STATES REPORT MENU'
@ 6,23 SAY 'A) AREA REPORT'
@ 7,23 SAY 'B) 1990 POPULATION REPORT'
@ 8,23 SAY 'C) DATE OF ADMISSION REPORT'
@ 9,23 SAY 'D) POPULATION DENSITY REPORT'
@ 13,23 SAY 'WHICH REPORT DO YOU WISH TO SEE: '
STORE 'no ' to mrepmenu
DO WHILE mrepmenu = 'no '
   STORE ' ' TO mselect
   @13,56 GET mselect PICTURE 'A'
   READ
   @18,20 SAY SPACE(50)
   STORE UPPER(mselect) to mselect
   IF mselect < 'A' .OR. mselect > 'D'
      @18,20 SAY 'Please choose one of the options listed!'
   ELSE
      STORE 'yes' TO mrepmenu
   ENDIF
ENDDO
CLEAR
@ 9,23 SAY 'ASCENDING OR DESCENDING SEQUENCE?'
@ 11,23 SAY '        ENTER A OR D:'
STORE 'no ' to morder
DO WHILE morder = 'no '
   STORE ' ' TO mseq
   @11,47 GET mseq PICTURE 'A'
   READ
   @18,20 SAY SPACE(50)
   STORE UPPER(mseq) to mseq
   IF mseq = 'A' .OR. mseq = 'D'
      STORE 'yes' TO morder
   ELSE
      @18,27 SAY 'Please enter A or D only!'
   ENDIF
ENDDO
CLEAR
@ 9,23 SAY 'HOW MANY STATES DO YOU WANT LISTED?'
@ 11,23 SAY '         ENTER NUMBER: '
STORE 'no ' to mnumber
DO WHILE mnumber = 'no '
   STORE 0 TO mnum
   @11,47 GET mnum PICTURE '99'
   READ
   @18,23 SAY SPACE(50)
   IF mnum < 1 .OR. mnum > 50
      @18,23 SAY 'Please enter a number from 1 to 50 only!'
   ELSE
      STORE 'yes' TO mnumber
   ENDIF
ENDDO
```

(a) User Input portion of the Menu Driven Program

FIGURE 9.7
Menu-driven Program in dBASE

the program, as opposed to becoming bogged down with the details of dBASE. We do expect you, however, to be able to follow the overall flow, noting especially how the building blocks of structured programming are incorporated.

As with the pseudocode, the program is divided into two segments, user input and report generation. Figure 9.7a contains the user-input portion, which obtains the user's responses; Figure 9.7b depicts the report generation segment, which creates the desired report (based on the user-supplied inputs).

The first three statements—**CLEAR**, **SET BELL OFF**, and **SET TALK OFF**—clear the screen, suppress the bell at the end of a user response, and prevent dBASE messages from echoing on the screen during program execution. The effect of the latter two statements is best illustrated by coding and executing the program, with and without the statements, in the subsequent hands-on exercise.

The next several statements obtain the user's response for the type of report desired, by first prompting the user for an appropriate response. Remember, too, the requirement for data validation in which the program rejects an invalid response—

FIGURE 9.7
Menu-driven Program in dBASE (continued)

```
CLEAR
USE usstates
DO CASE
   CASE mselect = 'A'
      STORE '      AREA REPORT' to mheading
      SET ORDER TO TAG area
   CASE mselect = 'B'
      STORE '1990 POPULATION REPORT' to mheading
      SET ORDER TO TAG popltn
   CASE mselect = 'C'
      STORE 'DATE OF ADMISSION REPORT' to mheading
      SET ORDER TO TAG yradmtd
   CASE mselect = 'D'
      STORE 'POPULATION DENSITY REPORT' to mheading
      SET ORDER TO TAG density
ENDCASE
? '                 ',mheading
? ' '
IF mseq ='A'
   GO TOP
ELSE
   GO BOTTOM
ENDIF
STORE 0 TO mcounter
DO WHILE mcounter < mnum
   DO CASE
      CASE mselect = 'A'
         ? '         ',state,'            ',area
      CASE mselect = 'B'
         ? '         ',state,'            ',popltn
      CASE mselect = 'C'
         ? '         ',state,'            ',yradmtd
      CASE mselect = 'D'
         ? '         ',state,'            ',popltn/area
   ENDCASE
   STORE mcounter + 1 TO mcounter
   IF mseq = 'A'
      SKIP
   ELSE
      SKIP-1
   ENDIF
ENDDO
CLOSE DATABASES
RETURN
```

(b) Report Generation Portion of the Menu-driven Program

e.g., a report type other than A, B, C, or D—until a proper response is received. The latter task is accomplished in a data validation loop controlled by the memory variable, **mrepmenu**.

The value of **mrepmenu** is defined and initialized to *no* via a **STORE** statement, after which the program obtains the value of another memory variable, **mselect** which stores the report type. The **UPPER** function is used within the **STORE** statement to convert the value of **mselect** (i.e., the user-supplied report type) to its upper-case equivalent prior to validating the response. If the report type is other than A, B, C, or D (i.e., if the value of **mselect** is less than A or greater than D), the report type is invalid and the message, *Please choose one of the options listed,* appears. If, however, the report type is valid, the switch controlling the loop (i.e., **mrepmenu**) is set to *yes,* which terminates the loop.

A similar procedure is followed to obtain the report sequence and number of states. The data validation loop is controlled by the memory variable **msequence**, and the sequence itself (ascending or descending) is stored in **mseq**. In similar fashion, **mnumber** controls the final data validation routine, with the user-supplied parameter stored in **mnum**.

The user-input portion of the program ends with valid responses having been supplied for the memory variables: **mselect** (the type of report), **mseq** (ascending or descending sequence), and **mnum** (the number of states). The report generation program of Figure 9.7b then creates the desired report, based on the values of these parameters.

Report generation begins by clearing the screen and opening the data file. Next a **DO CASE** statement is entered, which stores (but does not write) the appropriate report heading in a memory variable, based on the value of **mselect**, indicating the desired report. (The heading is displayed only after leaving the case statement, and a blank line is displayed after the heading.) Observe also that the case statement is used to open the appropriate index, which enables the chosen report to appear in its proper sequence; e.g., the area report lists states by area, whereas the population report lists them by population.

The record pointer is positioned at the beginning (**TOP**) or end (**BOTTOM**) of the master index by the **IF** statement. We are now able to print the detail lines in the report by moving the record pointer forward, beginning at the top (if ascending sequence was selected), or backward, from the bottom (for descending sequence).

Recall that the memory variable **mnum** contains the number of states that are to appear in the completed report. We can generate a report with the proper number of lines by establishing a loop to print a detail line, and then executing that loop *mnum* times. This is accomplished with the aid of a counter (**mcounter**), which is initialized to zero *outside* the loop and incremented by one *inside* the loop, as explained in the pseudocode of Figure 9.6.

The loop itself contains a case statement to write the proper detail line. The loop also contains a statement to move the record pointer forward to the next record (**SKIP**), or backward to the previous record (**SKIP -1**), according to the sequence selected. The program ends with statements to close all files (**CLOSE DATABASES**) and return to the dot prompt (**RETURN**).

Implementation on the Computer

The ensuing hands-on exercise tells you how to implement the completed program on the computer. The process may appear complicated initially, but it will soon become second nature; nevertheless, it is helpful to describe the various steps in the exercise before you sit down at the computer.

The first requirement is to convert the hand-written program to a form suitable for input to the computer; this can be done using the dBASE editor, **MODIFY COMMAND**, and results in a file containing the dBASE statements of Figure 9.7. After the program is created, two additional operations, ***compilation*** and ***execution,*** take place. Compilation is the process that translates a dBASE ***source program*** into machine language so that the machine language program can be subsequently run on the computer; execution occurs when the generated machine language or ***object program*** gains control, requests the user's inputs, and produces the desired reports.

Errors can occur during compilation and/or execution. dBASE, like all other programming languages, has a rigid syntax that must be followed precisely so that the compiler is able to translate dBASE into machine language. In other words, failure to enter dBASE statements according to the rules of the language produces compilation errors, as the compiler is unable to interpret the erroneous statements.

After compilation comes execution, and therein lie the strength and weakness of the computer. *The computer does precisely what it is instructed to do, not necessarily what you want it to do.* Hence, if you wrote syntactically correct statements for a logically incorrect program, the program would compile cleanly, but would produce errors during execution, i.e., results that were different from what was intended. Mistakes of either type are known as ***bugs,*** and thus ***debugging*** is the process of detecting and correcting programming errors.

Perhaps we should warn you that you may become quite confused in your initial confrontation with dBASE error messages. You may even think that dBASE is a bit unreasonable in its demands for precision, and that it should be smart enough to know what you meant even if you made a mistake. Unfortunately, that is not the case. Just be patient, and try to remain calm and collected. Reflect a moment and the error often becomes quickly apparent. Remember, too, that experience is the best teacher, and that you will get better with practice. Good luck and on with the exercise.

HANDS-ON EXERCISE 1

Menu-Driven Programs

Objective

Use the dBASE editor, `MODIFY COMMAND`, to create the menu-driven program of Figure 9.7; compile, execute, and debug the program.

STEP 1 **Change to the USSTATES directory**

Type one of the following two commands, depending on whether you are sharing the hard drive with others:

`CD C:\DATADISK\USSTATES` —— *if you installed the data disk on the hard drive and are not sharing your computer, or*

`CD A:\DATADISK\USSTATES` —— *if you did not install the data disk, i.e., if you are sharing drive C with other students. (Use data disk two if you have 5¼-inch disks.)*

Type **dBASE** to load dBASE, then set the default drive as you have in previous exercises.

STEP 2 **Create the menu-driven program**

Type **MODIFY COMMAND MENU** (MENU is the name we have selected for the program file) to bring up the opening screen of the dBASE text editor shown in Figure 9.8. The

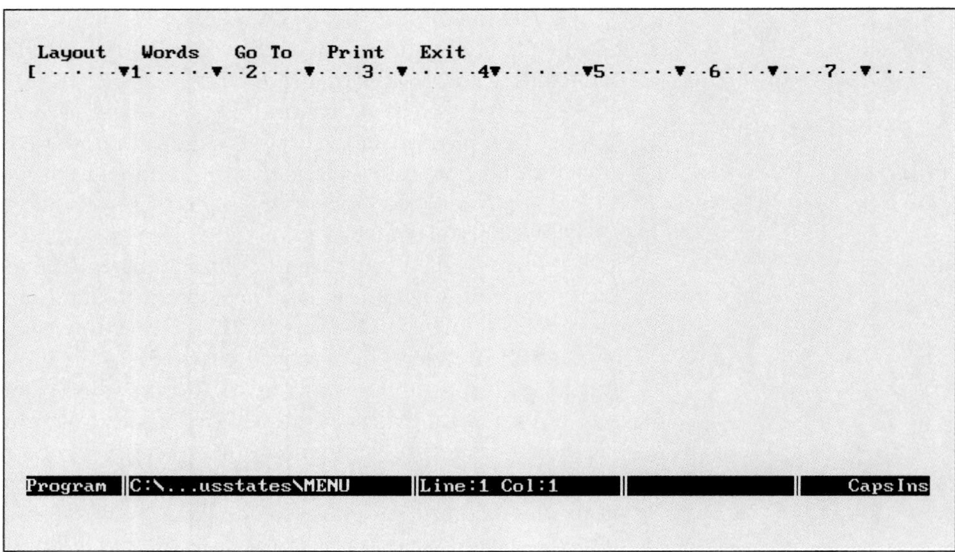

FIGURE 9.8
MODIFY COMMAND (opening screen)

dBASE editor has most of the capabilities you would expect in a full-featured word processor—search-and-replace, block move and copy, and so on—and these commands are described in the Programmer's Notebook. You will find it easier initially, however, to stick with the basics and alternate between the insertion and replacement modes as necessary.

Enter the menu-driven program exactly as it appears in Figure 9.7, being sure to press the **return** key at the end of every line. Remember, too, to save your program *periodically* as it is being entered; i.e., press **Alt+L** to pull down the layout menu, highlight *Save this program,* and press **return**. When you have finished entering the program, press **Alt+E** to pull down the exit menu, highlight *Save changes and exit,* and press the **enter** key to return to the dot prompt.

STEP 3 **Create the necessary index files**

Enter the commands below to create the necessary indexes. (You may have already created some or all of these indexes in Chapter 4, whereupon dBASE will ask whether to overwrite the index tag; answer yes.)

```
.USE USSTATES
.INDEX ON YRADMTD TAG YRADMTD
.INDEX ON AREA TAG AREA
.INDEX ON POPLTN TAG POPLTN
.INDEX ON POPLTN/AREA TAG DENSITY
```

Verify that the necessary files are present by typing **DIR *.*** at the dot prompt. Your directory should contain the **USSTATES.DBF** file, the multiple index file (**USSTATES.MDX**), and the program file (**MENU.PRG**) created in step 2. Remember the significance of the different extensions: **DBF** (data file), **MDX** (master index file), and **PRG** (program file).

STEP 4 **Compile the program**

Type **DO MENU** to compile (and execute) the **MENU.PRG** program. You will see a message indicating that compilation is taking place, and then if all goes well, the prompting messages of Figure 9.1, after which dBASE will generate the requested report. *It is more than likely, however, that you will have made one or more errors in*

FIGURE 9.9
Debugging in dBASE (compilation errors)

```
USE usstates
DO CASE
   CASE mselect = 'A'
      STORE '      AREA REPORT to mheading
      SET ORDER TO TAG area
   CASE mselect = 'B'
      .
        .
          .
ENDCASE
```

Ending apostrophe is missing

(a) Erroneous Source Statement

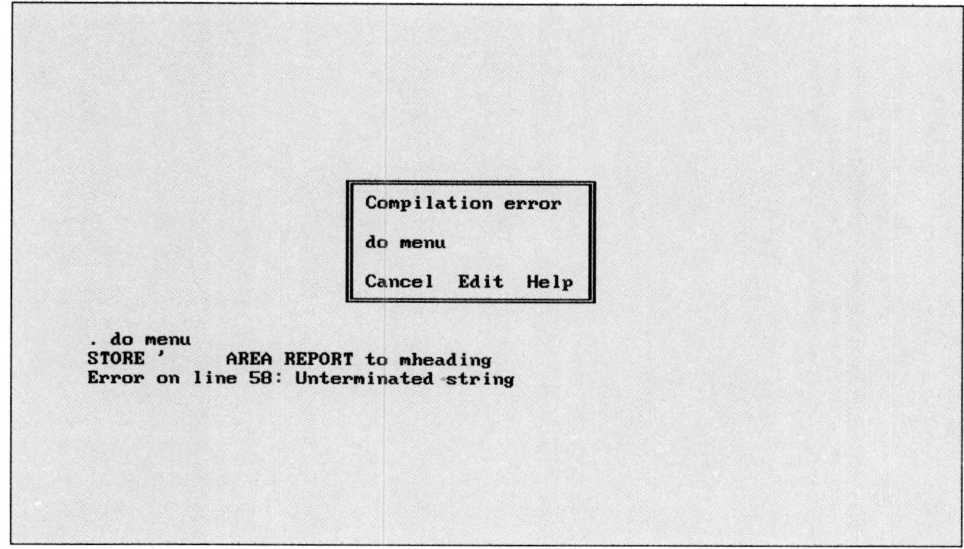

(b) dBASE Error Message

entering your program, which will require you to consider steps 5 and 6 on debugging.

STEP 5 **Debugging (errors in compilation)**

To illustrate what is likely to happen, consider Figure 9.9a, which contains a *modified but erroneous* portion of the original program from Figure 9.7. Figure 9.9b displays the messages produced by dBASE and consist of the statement itself, its line number within the program, and a description of the error. The indicated cause, *unterminated string,* is quite common and implies that a closing quotation mark was omitted at the end of a character string (i.e., a message) in our program.

Use the arrow keys to highlight the cancel option and press **return**, then type **MODIFY COMMAND MENU** (or MODI COMM MENU for short) to reenter the dBASE editor. Use the arrow keys to position the cursor at the proper place in the program (e.g., line 58) and make the necessary correction(s). Press **Alt+E** to pull down the exit menu, highlight *Save changes and exit,* and press **return**. You will once again be returned to the dot prompt, from where you reenter the command **DO MENU** and repeat the cycle, until all compilation errors are gone.

STEP 6 **Additional debugging (errors in execution)**

To illustrate the nature of execution errors, we present a *different* modification to the original program as shown in Figure 9.10. The altered statements are shown in Figure

FIGURE 9.10
Debugging in dBASE (execution errors)

```
DO CASE
  CASE mselect = 'A'
    STORE '      AREA REPORT' to mheading
    SET ORDER TO TAG areas
  CASE mselect = 'B'
    STORE '1990 POPULATION REPORT' to mheading
    SET ORDER TO TAG popltn
  CASE mselect = 'C'
    STORE 'DATE OF ADMISSION REPORT' to mhead
    SET ORDER TO TAG year
  CASE mselect = 'D'
    STORE 'POPULATION DENSITY REPORT' to mheading
    SET ORDER TO TAG density
ENDCASE
? '                  ',mhead
```

tag spelled incorrectly

variable-name spelled incorrectly

(a) Erroneous Source Statements

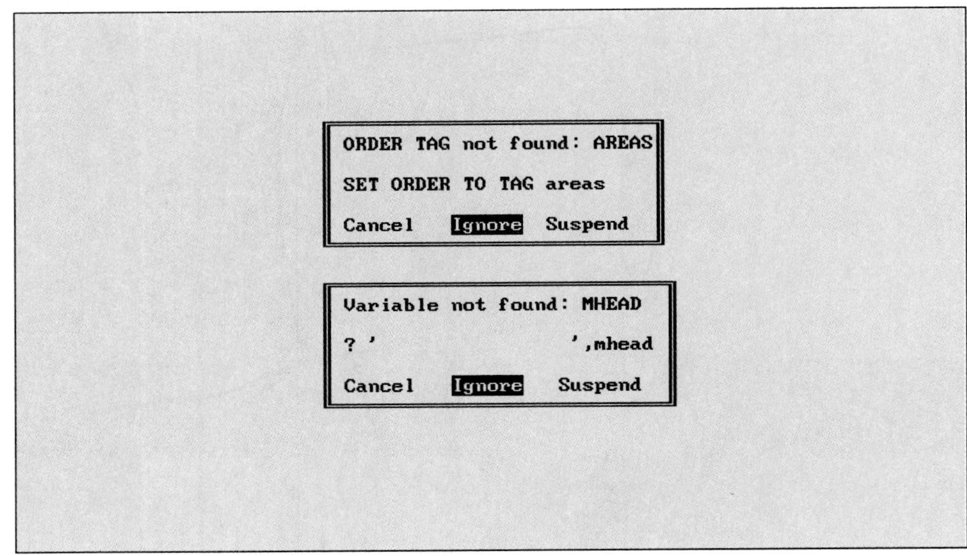

(b) dBASE Error Messages

```
Alabama          51609
Alaska          589757
Arizona         113909
Arkansas         53104
California      158693
Colorado        104247
Connecticut       5009
Delaware          2057
Florida          58560
Georgia          58876
```

(c) Erroneous Output

9.10a, the associated error messages in Figure 9.10b, and the resulting output in Figure 9.10c. The intended output (based on the user's responses) was to be the same as in Figure 9.1d, i.e., the ten states with the smallest area.

Each error is followed immediately by the message, *Cancel, Ignore, or Suspend,* which is dBASE's way of asking what action you wish to take as a result of the error. ***Cancel*** terminates execution immediately and returns you to the dot prompt, ***Ignore*** disregards the error and continues execution, whereas ***Suspend*** returns you to the dot prompt from where you can enter additional commands, after which execution may be resumed. Initially you should ignore the errors (as was done in the figure) in order to execute as much of the program as possible, but be sure to write down all mistakes for subsequent correction.

Note, too, the effects of ignoring the errors on the resulting output. The first error refers to the `SET ORDER` statement misspelling the requested index; i.e., `areas` rather than `area`. The error message indicates that dBASE cannot find the `areas` tag, and ignoring the error causes states to be listed alphabetically; i.e., as they were entered in the `DBF` file. The second message pertains to a print statement referencing `mhead` rather than `mheading`; dBASE is unable to find the misspelled entry, causing the report in Figure 9.10c to be printed without the `AREA REPORT` heading that appeared in the original output of Figure 9.1d.

Finally, when execution is completed, you must once again use the command `MODI COMM MENU` to reenter the dBASE editor and correct the program. Continue debugging until your program runs without error.

STEP 7 **Print the MENU program**

It is convenient to end the session with hard copy (printed output) of your completed program. Type **`MODI COMM MENU`** to enter the dBASE text editor and press **`Alt+P`** to pull down the print menu as shown in Figure 9.11. Highlight *Line number* and press **`return`** to toggle the option to *Yes*. Move the **`down arrow`** key to highlight *Destination* and press **`return`**, check that *Write to PRINTER* is highlighted and press **`Esc`** to exit, and finally highlight *Begin printing* and press **`return`**. Pull down the exit menu and return to the dot prompt. Congratulations on a job well done!

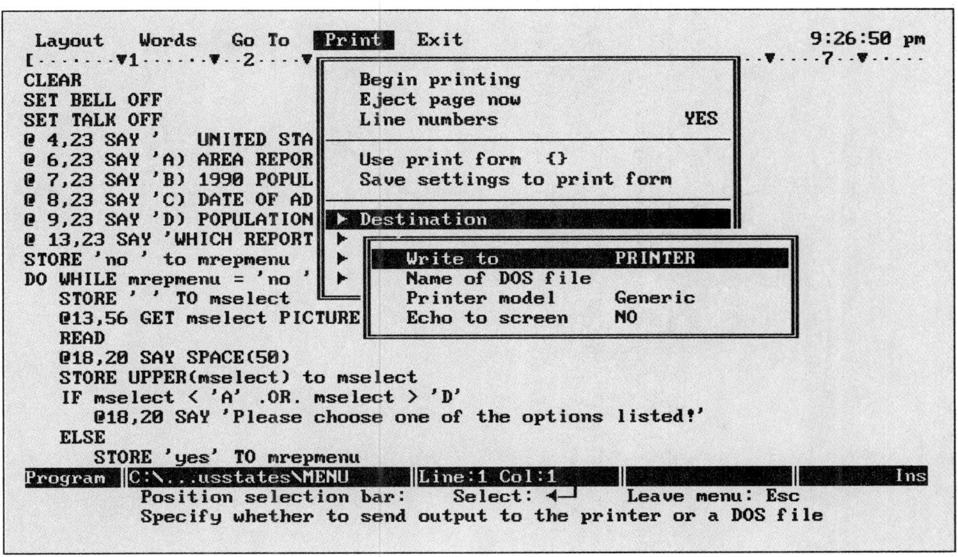

FIGURE 9.11
MODIFY COMMAND (print menu)

Errors in Execution

The errors depicted in steps 5 and 6 of the hands-on exercise were accompanied by dBASE error messages, a fortunate occurrence in that dBASE indicates that something is wrong. It is also possible, however, that a program will appear to execute successfully, i.e., it will execute without any error messages at all, yet still be incorrect.

Figure 9.12a contains still another example of modified code from the original menu-driven program. Unlike the examples in the hands-on exercise, these modifications compile and execute cleanly, yet the output of Figure 9.12b is hardly what was expected. (Once again we attempted to list the ten smallest states in terms of area.) Only five states are listed, and these are listed without their respective areas.

The problem is that dBASE does exactly what we tell it to do, which is not necessarily what we want it to do. As you can see, the erroneous print statement in Figure 9.12a omits the **area** field, so **area** is not printed. In addition, the variable **mcounter** is incremented by two, which produces five iterations rather than ten.

The DEBUG Command

The **DEBUG** command executes a dBASE program within the context of the full-screen debugger, a powerful tool that monitors the execution of a dBASE program, letting you see statements as they execute. You can, for example, execute one statement at a time or many statements at once, then pause after the designated statement(s) have executed to display the value of one or more variables in the program. You can also designate ***breakpoints,*** or specific statements where the program is to pause, then take whatever action you like when the breakpoint is reached.

FIGURE 9.12
Errors in Execution

```
DO WHILE mcounter < mnum
   DO CASE
      CASE mselect = 'A'
         ? '          ',state
      CASE mselect = 'B'
         ? '          ',state,'          ',popltn
      CASE mselect = 'C'
         ? '          ',state,'          ',yradmtd
      CASE mselect = 'D'
         ? '          ',state,'          ',popltn/area
   ENDCASE
   STORE mcounter + 2 TO mcounter
   IF mseq = 'A'
      SKIP
   ELSE
      SKIP-1
   ENDIF
ENDDO
```

area field is missing

increment is wrong

(a) Erroneous Source Statements

```
              AREA REPORT

          Rhode Island
          Connecticut
          New Jersey
          New Hampshire
          Maryland
```

(b) Erroneous Output

Figure 9.13a displays the initial debugging screen as it would appear in conjunction with the menu-driven program. The screen is divided into four windows: an ***edit window*** containing the menu program, a ***display window*** to show the value of variables at any point in the program, a ***breakpoint window*** indicating the places where the program is to pause, and a ***debug window*** where you enter commands. Note too, that the **CLEAR** statement (line 1) is highlighted in the edit window; the debug window indicates the current line is line 1; and the message, *stopped for step,* appears below the debug window. In other words, the debugger is about to execute line 1 in the menu program, but it is asking you for information on how to proceed.

The essence of the debugger is the debug window, which displays information about the program, e.g., the name of the open database file, the current record, and the statement about to be executed. The window also provides you with the ***action***

FIGURE 9.13
The DEBUG Command

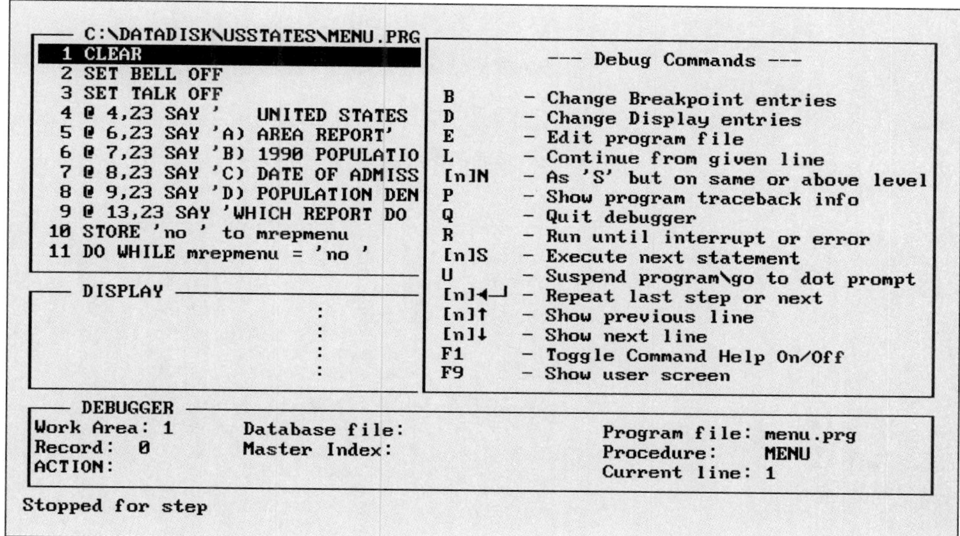

(a) Initial Debugging Screen

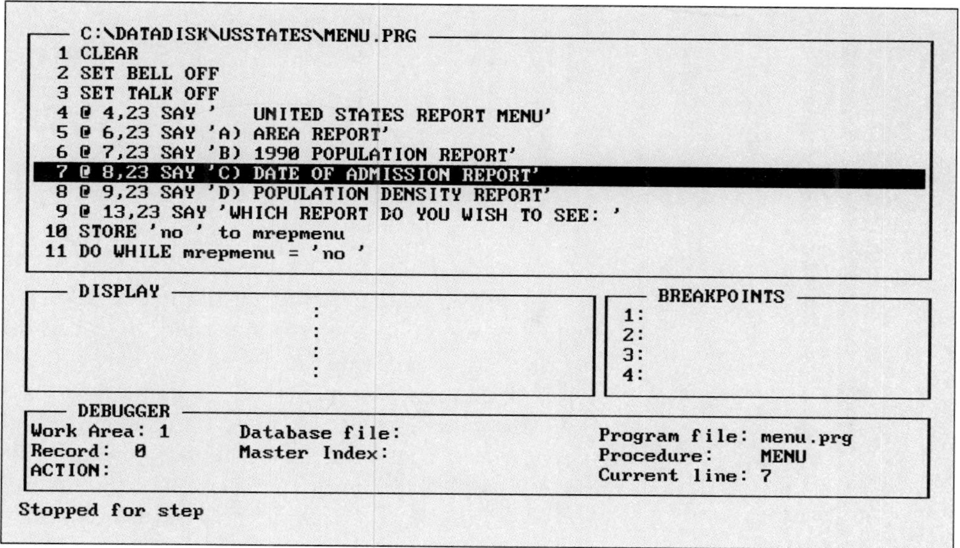

(b) Stepping Through the Program

FIGURE 9.13
The DEBUG Command (continued)

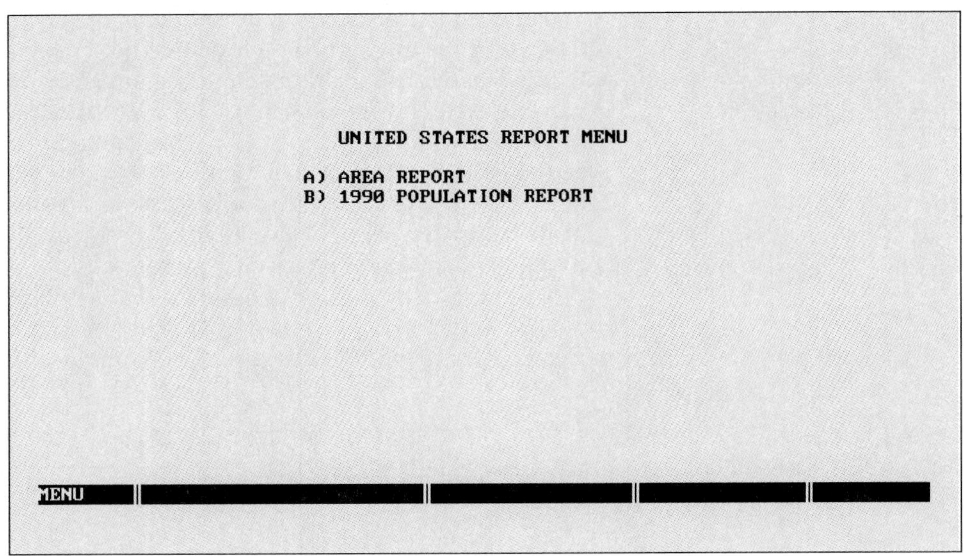

(c) Showing the User Screen (F9 Key)

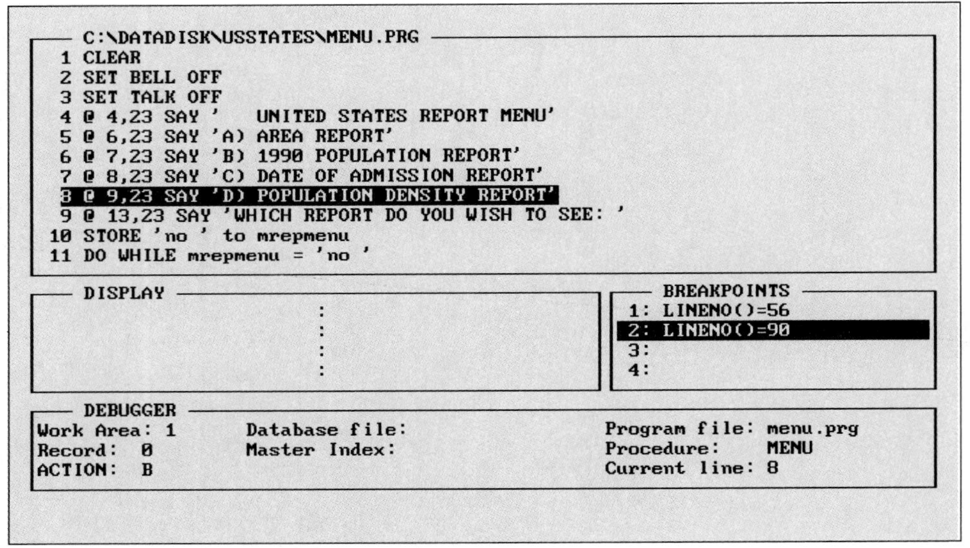

(d) Setting Breakpoints

line where you enter a debugging command; e.g., **B** to set a **b**reakpoint, **D** to **d**isplay a value, **S** to execute the next **s**tatement, **R** to **r**un the program until a breakpoint is encountered, or **Q** to **q**uit the debugger and return to the dot prompt.

The debugger is an excellent tool, not only for debugging, but also for learning about programming. Accordingly, the ensuing exercise returns to the *original and correctly written menu-driven program,* and uses the debugger to demonstrate the flow of control in that program. You will see, for example, how to enter a simple series of step and display commands, how to set breakpoints, and how to view the output of the program as it is being produced.

FIGURE 9.13
The DEBUG Command (continued)

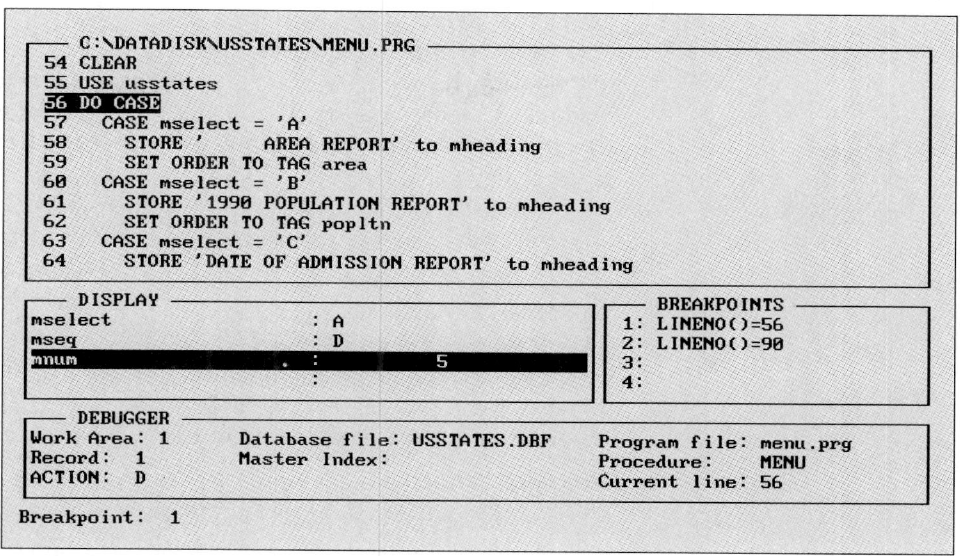

(e) The Display Command (first breakpoint)

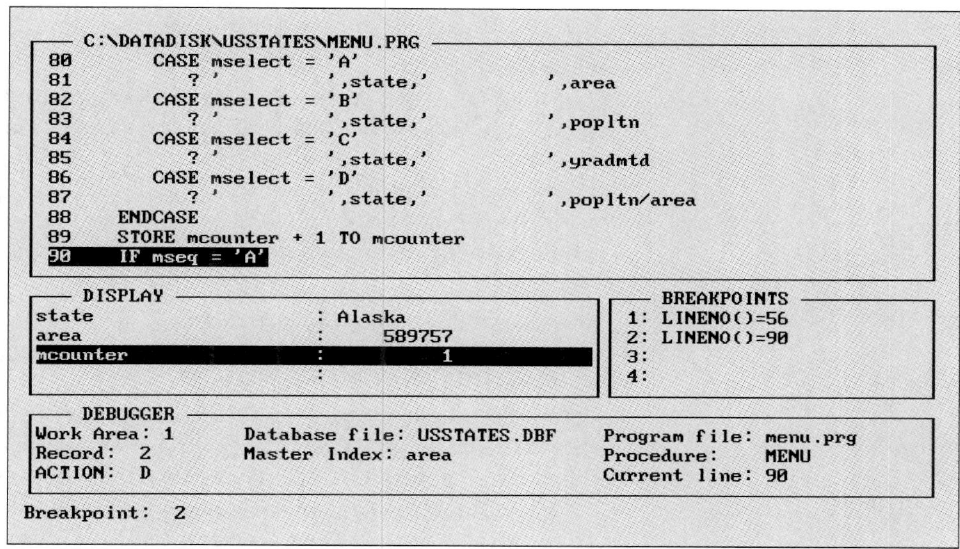

(f) The Display Command (second breakpoint)

HANDS-ON EXERCISE 2

The Debugger

Objective

Demonstrate the dBASE IV debugger with the *original and correctly written menu-driven program.* You will find it useful to refer to the printed copy of the menu program obtained in step 7 of the previous exercise, which lists the program with line numbers to help determine breakpoints.

STEP 1 **Enter the debugger**

Type **DEBUG MENU**, where MENU is the name of the program file to debug. You will see the initial debugging screen of Figure 9.13a, which (as explained earlier) is divided into four windows. The highlight is on line one of the program, the cursor is flashing on the action line, and the message, *Stopped for step,* appears at the bottom of the screen.

Press the **F1** help key to remove the window of debug commands from the monitor; press the **F1** key a second time to restore the commands to view.

STEP 2 **The step command**

Type **S** for step to execute the next statement, i.e., the CLEAR command of line one, which moves the highlight to line two. Type **S** five more times, causing the highlight to move five lines until it pauses at line seven in Figure 9.13b.

STEP 3 **The user screen**

Press the **F9** function key to display the user screen of Figure 9.13c, showing output of the program through line six; i.e., before line seven is executed. Press the **F9** key a second time to toggle back to the debugger, type **S** to execute the next statement, then press **F9** again to toggle to the user screen and see the additional line of output on the monitor.

STEP 4 **Set breakpoints**

Type **B** to set a breakpoint, moving you to the BREAKPOINTS window shown in Figure 9.13d. Type **LINENO()=56** and press **return**, then type **LINENO()=90** and press return once more. The first breakpoint, line 56, will occur after you have entered all three required inputs; the second breakpoint, line 90, will occur in the middle of the loop to display the desired report. Press **Ctrl+End** to exit the breakpoint window and return to the debug window.

STEP 5 **The run and display commands**

Type **R** to run the program until the first breakpoint is encountered, which occurs after the program has promped you for input—i.e, the type of report (type **A** for the area report), the sequence (type **D** for descending), and the number of states (type **5** to see the five largest states). The program then pauses at the first breakpoint, line 56, as shown in Figure 9.13e, where you are expected to enter a response.

Type **D** for display, which transfers you to the DISPLAY window. Then type **mselect** (and press **return**), **mseq** (and press **return**), and finally **mnum** (and press **return**), noting that in each instance the debugger returns the value of the indicated memory variable. The displayed output confirms that you did, in fact, request the area report, in descending sequence, for five states as **A**, **D**, and **5** are the values of **mselect**, **mseq**, and **mnum** respectively. Press **Ctrl+End** to leave the display window and return to the debug window.

STEP 6 **Continue execution**

Type **R** to continue running the program until the next breakpoint occurs prior to line 90. Then type **D** to transfer to the DISPLAY window, then enter **state**, **area**, and **mcounter** to obtain the values of these variables as shown in Figure 9.13f; note, too, that Alaska is the largest state and hence it is the first to appear in an area report that lists states in descending sequence. Press **Ctrl+End** to return to the debug window, then type **R** to run to the next breakpoint. Once again the program pauses at line 90 (within the loop to print the output), but this time you see Texas. Press **F9** to toggle to the user screen and view the area report as it is being developed. Continue execution as you see fit.

STEP 7 **The quit command**
Type **Q** to quit the debugger and return to the dot prompt.

Coding Standards

We expect that you were successful in the hands-on exercise, and that our intuitive explanation of the program makes more sense to you now than previously. We suggest that you return to the listing of Figure 9.7 and review the individual dBASE statements. In particular, we want to make you aware of several ***coding standards*** (i.e., conventions) that we follow in order to make our programs easier to read.

The conventions we are about to discuss are not required by dBASE, but are used to make programs easier to understand and maintain. Indeed, you will best appreciate the significance of this section if you are ever called on to read and/or modify someone else's program. Our suggestions are as follows:

- *Indent detail lines under `IF`, `DO WHILE`, and `DO CASE` statements:* Indentation, by a consistent amount (e.g., three columns), is a tremendous aid in showing the scope associated with these basic building blocks. Thus the statement

```
IF mchoice = 'A'
    GO TOP
ELSE
    GO BOTTOM
ENDIF
```

  is inherently easier to read than

```
IF mchoice = 'A'
GO TOP
ELSE
GO BOTTOM
ENDIF
```

  Similar examples can be constructed for the `DO WHILE` and `DO CASE` statements. We think that indentation is perhaps the most important convention to follow.
- *Use upper and lower case to differentiate between dBASE commands and programmer-supplied variables:* We follow the general convention of having upper-case letters denote dBASE reserved words, whereas lower-case letters imply programmer-chosen names. Thus, we code ***`USE usstates`***, as opposed to ***`USE USSTATES`***, both of which are acceptable to dBASE. Although the implementation of this guideline is perhaps a bit tedious, it is followed almost universally and hence is recommended strongly.
- *Use spaces before and after operational symbols:* We believe that the appearance of a program is improved significantly by proper spacing within a line. Thus, we prefer

```
CASE select = 'A'
STORE mcounter + 1 TO mcounter
```

as opposed to

```
CASE select='A'
STORE mcounter+1 TO mcounter
```

Program Documentation

In addition to following the coding standards just described, your program should be accompanied by written ***documentation*** to provide further description of its function. Unfortunately, documentation is something most programmers do poorly, if at all. Nevertheless, the individuals who do the poorest job of documentation are generally the ones who yell the loudest when maintaining someone else's programs. Documentation for the menu-driven program is shown in Figure 9.14. (Note that the pseudocode appeared earlier in Figures 9.5 and 9.6 and hence is not repeated even though it is part of the documentation.)

Proper documentation does require time and effort. Documentation per se is not fun, but it is part of the programming function. Hence it should be done, and done well. Although there is no common agreement on precisely what constitutes proper documentation, we suggest that the following elements be present:

- *Pseudocode:* Given that individuals naturally write notes to themselves prior to coding, the pseudocode is essentially done and should not pose a burden. This is perhaps the most essential piece of documentation.
- *Program narrative:* The narrative is a verbal description of the program's overall function and is helpful as a prelude to viewing the program.
- *File description(s):* You should include a listing of all **DBF** files with their record structure; you should also list all associated index files together with the fields on which they are indexed.
- *Data dictionary:* The data dictionary lists all memory variables in the program, together with a description of their intended purposes and possible values.

Summary

A ***program*** consists of a series of dBASE commands stored in a file and executed collectively. This chapter developed a ***menu-driven*** program with requirements for ***ease of use, flexibility,*** and ***data validation.***

The logic of any program can be developed with just the basic building blocks of ***structured programming,*** namely, ***sequence, selection,*** and ***iteration,*** each of which has ***one entry point*** and ***one exit point.*** The definition is frequently extended to include a fourth building block, ***case.*** Programming logic is commonly expressed in ***pseudocode.***

Compilation is the process of translating a ***source program*** into machine language; ***execution*** occurs when the generated machine language or ***object program*** gains control, accepts user input, and produces the associated output. dBASE source and object programs use the extensions **PRG** and **DBO,** respectively.

Debugging is the process of detecting and correcting programming errors. The **DEBUG** command executes a program and allows you to see its commands as they are executing.

Program Narrative: MENU.PRG

MENU.PRG is a menu-driven program capable of generating four distinct report types, based on user supplied input. The program is divided into two main modules: *user input,* in which user responses are requested on the screen, and *report generation,* in which the reports are created, based on the inputs furnished.

The user-input portion begins with the display of three successive menus to determine: 1) the type of report, 2) the sequence of records within the report, and 3) the number of states to appear within the report. Each user response is checked for validity; i.e., the program will continue to ask for user responses until valid choices are supplied.

The report-generation segment creates a heading and opens the data file and appropriate index, based on the report type selected by the user. The record pointer is positioned at the top or bottom of the file, depending on whether an ascending or descending report sequence was selected. A loop is then entered to print the proper number of detail lines according to a user-specified number. Each time the loop is executed, a report line is generated with the content of the detail line dependent on the report type. The record pointer is moved to either the next or previous record, depending on the user-specified sequence.

Data Base File: USSTATES.DBF

Structure:

1	STATE	Character	14	(Name of state)
2	YRADMTD	Numeric	4	(Year of admission to union)
3	POPLTN	Numeric	10	(Population in 1990)
4	AREA	Numeric	8	(Area in square miles)
5	REGION	Character	15	(Region of country)

Production Index: USSTATES.MDX

Memory Variables:

mrepmenu — keeps report-type menu on screen; assumes value of *yes* or *no*
mselect — user-supplied value to indicate report type; assumes value of *A, B, C,* or *D*
msequence — keeps sequence menu on screen; assumes value of *yes* or *no*
mseq — user-supplied value to indicate report sequence; assumes value of *A* or *D*
mnumber — keeps number-of-states menu on screen; assumes value of *yes* or *no*
mnum — user-supplied value to indicate number of states; assumes value of *1* to *50*
mheading — first line of report heading
mcounter — counter to control the number of states in the report; will eventually equal mnum, at which point report is finished

FIGURE 9.14
Program Documentation

Key Words and Concepts

?
@...GET
@...SAY
Action line
Ascending sequence
Breakpoint
Breakpoint window
Bug
Cancel
Case structure
CLEAR
Coding standards
Compilation
Counter
Data validation

DBO extension
DEBUG command
Debug window
Debugging
Descending sequence
Display window
DO CASE
DO WHILE
Documentation
Edit window
ELSE
ENDCASE
ENDDO
ENDIF
Execution
Flexibility
Flowchart
GO BOTTOM
GO TOP
IF
Ignore
Iteration structure
Memory variable
Menu-driven program
MODIFY COMMAND
Object program
PRG extension
Pseudocode
READ
Report generation
Selection structure
Sequence structure
SET TALK
SET BELL
SKIP +1
SKIP -1
Source program
STORE
Structured programming
Suspend
Switch
User-friendly
User input

True/False

1. A structured program is guaranteed not to contain logical errors.
2. Structured programming can be implemented in a variety of languages.
3. The logic of any program can be expressed as a combination of only three types of logic structures.
4. The one entry/one exit philosophy is essential to structured programming.
5. The case construct is one of the three basic logic structures.
6. SKIP and SKIP+1 are equivalent statements.
7. Pseudocode has precise syntactical rules.
8. Output of a dBASE program can be directed to either the monitor or the printer.
9. Indentation is not important when writing dBASE programs.
10. dBASE requires MENU.PRG as the name of a menu-driven program.
11. The dBASE IF statement requires an ELSE clause.
12. A person using a menu-driven system needs a detailed knowledge of database programming.
13. Pseudocode makes no provision for an unconditional branch.
14. If a program compiles cleanly, it must execute correctly.
15. Compilation is the process of translating a source program into an object program.
16. MENU.PRG and MENU.DBO contain the source and object versions of a program called MENU.

Exercises

1. The following problem pertains neither to dBASE nor to a common business application. It is a problem with which the reader is totally unfamiliar, and consequently a problem for which he or she has no preexisting bias toward a solution. Nevertheless the exercise serves to demonstrate the applicability of both structured programming and pseudocode to virtually any physical setting.

   A robot is sitting on a chair, facing a wall a short distance away. The objective is to (1) develop the necessary logic (restricted to the basic building blocks of structured programming) to have the robot walk to the wall and return to its initial position, and (2) to express that logic in pseudocode. The robot understands the following commands, which are to be used in your solution:

STAND
SIT
TURN (turns right ninety degrees)
STEP

In addition, the robot can raise its arms and sense the wall with its fingertips. (However, it cannot sense the chair on its return trip, since the chair is below arm level.) Accordingly, the robot must count the number of steps to the wall or chair using the following commands:

ADD (increments counter by 1)
SUBTRACT (decrements counter by 1)
ZERO COUNTER (sets counter to zero)
ARMS UP
ARMS DOWN

The wall is assumed to be an integer number of steps away. It is highly recommended that various student solutions should be presented in class. Select a volunteer to act as the robot, and see whether the submitted solutions actually accomplish the objective.

2. Use the following program fragment to answer parts a–f below. (**EOF** is a dBASE variable that will assume a true value when the end of file is reached; in other words, **EOF** is a switch used to control the loop in the program, enabling us to process every record in the file.)

```
USE employee
INDEX ON salary TAG salary
DO WHILE .NOT. EOF()
   ? name,salary
   SKIP +1
ENDDO
```

(a) What is the name of the **DBF** file in use?
(b) What is the name of the tag in use?
(c) What is the record key? In which order (ascending or descending) will the records be listed?
(d) What would happen if the **SKIP +1** statement were replaced by **SKIP -1**?
(e) What would happen if the **SKIP +1** statement were eliminated entirely?
(f) What changes would have to be made for records to list in the opposite order from part c? (Do not create any additional indexes.)

3. Assume that the **USSTATES.DBF** file has been modified to include an additional field containing the 1980 population of each state. Modify the program of Figure 9.7 to include a fifth permissible report type, namely, the percentage of population growth (from 1980 to 1990). Is this change(s) difficult to make? Can you see how well-written programs facilitate the task of program maintenance?

4. Several improvements can be made to the program in Figure 9.7 to enhance the user interface. Accordingly, supply the necessary modifications to:
(a) Produce a "beep" when the user inputs an erroneous response, e.g., a report type other than A, B, C, or D. (The dBASE statement **? CHR(7)** produces the desired beep.)
(b) Allow the user to direct output of the program to the printer. (The dBASE statement **SET PRINTER ON** directs all subsequent output to the printer.)

FIGURE 9.15
Contents of Memory Variables

```
MCOUNTER     priv  N           13
MHEADING     priv  C  "DATE OF ADMISSION REPORT"
MNUM         priv  N           13
MNUMBER      priv  C  "yes"
MSEQ         priv  C  "A"
MORDER       priv  C  "yes"
MSELECT      priv  C  "C"
MREPMENU     priv  C  "yes"
```

(c) Enhance the appearance of the menus in Figure 9.1; e.g., surround each set of messages with a box of asterisks. (This is accomplished via additional **@...SAY** statements to display the asterisks at designated points on the screen.)

5. It is often very useful to examine the contents of memory variables during program execution, which is accomplished simply by including the statement **DISPLAY MEMORY** at the point(s) within the program where you wish to see the memory variables. (The command may also be entered from the dot prompt if execution was suspended, the output produced by the **DISPLAY MEMORY** command studied, whereupon execution can be resumed.) Figure 9.15 was produced by placing the **DISPLAY MEMORY** statement two lines from the end of the program in Figure 9.7. (The entry **priv**, which follows each memory variable, indicates the variable is private and pertains only to the **MENU** program. The concept of private versus public variables will be explained further in Chapter 11.)

Use the information in Figure 9.15 to determine the report requested by the user (i.e., work backward and determine the user responses to the questions produced by the program).

FIGURE 9.16
Erroneous Program and Associated Output for Problem 7

```
@ 9,23 SAY 'HOW MANY STATES DO YOU WANT LISTED?'
@ 11,23 SAY '         ENTER NUMBER: '
STORE 'no ' to mnumber
DO WHILE mnumber = 'no '
   STORE 0 TO mnum
   @11,47 GET mnum PICTURE '99'
   READ
   @18,23 SAY SPACE(50)
   IF mnum < 1 .OR. mnum > 50
      @18,23 SAY 'Please enter a number from 1 to 50 only!'
   ELSE
      STORE 'yes' TO number
   ENDIF
ENDDO
```

(a) Modified Program Statements

```
HOW MANY STATES DO YOU WANT LISTED?

         ENTER NUMBER: 10
```

(b) Erroneous Output (Infinite Loop)

FIGURE 9.17
Erroneous Program and Associated Output for Problem 8

```
STORE 'no ' to mrepmenu
DO WHILE mrepmenu = 'no '
   STORE ' ' TO mselect
   @13,56 GET mselect PICTURE 'A'
   READ
   @18,20 SAY SPACE(50)
   STORE UPPER(mselect) to mselect
   IF mselect < 'a' .OR. mselect > 'd'
      @18,20 SAY 'Please choose one of the options listed!'
   ELSE
      STORE 'yes' TO mrepmenu
   ENDIF
ENDDO
```

(a) Modified Program Statements

```
           UNITED STATES REPORT MENU

              A) AREA REPORT
              B) 1990 POPULATION REPORT
              C) DATE OF ADMISSION REPORT
              D) POPULATION DENSITY REPORT

            WHICH REPORT DO YOU WISH TO SEE: C


        Please choose one of the options listed!
```

(b) Erroneous Output (Valid response is rejected)

6. Describe what will be printed as a result of the following statements. Assume in each instance that the file **USSTATES.DBF** is open, and that it contains these fields: **STATE**, **AREA**, and **POPLTN**. In each instance indicate precisely what will print, rather than what was probably intended. Note, too, that some of the statements are syntactically invalid and will produce dBASE error messages.
   (a) `? state`
   (b) `? density`
   (c) `? 'state'`
   (d) `? 'density'`
   (e) `? 'state`
   (f) `? state,area,popltn`
   (g) `? 'state,area,popltn'`
   (h) `? state,' ',area`
   (i) `? 'state   area'`

7. Figure 9.16a contains a portion of *modified* code from the original **MENU.PRG** program, producing the erroneous results shown in Figure 9.16b. The program accepts the user's response for the number of states, e.g., 10, as valid (i.e., it does not display an error message), but remains in a loop requesting the user to input the number of states. Identify the cause of the problem.

8. Figure 9.17a contains a *different* portion of modified code from the **MENU.PRG** program, producing the erroneous result shown in Figure 9.17b. This time, a correct user response of A, B, C, or D produces the indicated error message, causing

Quarterback	Yds Gained	TD Passes	Interceptions	Rating
Aikman, Dallas	2754	11	10	86.7
Brister, Pittsburgh	1350	9	9	72.9
DeBerg, Kansas City	2965	17	14	79.3
Elway, Denver	3253	13	12	75.4
Esiason, Cincinnati	2883	13	16	72.5
Everett, Los Angeles	3438	11	20	68.9
Friesz, San Diego	2896	12	15	67.1
Gannon, Minnesota	2166	12	6	81.5
George, Indianapolis	2910	10	12	73.8
Harbaugh, Chicago	3121	15	16	73.7
Hostetler, New York	2032	5	4	84.1
Kelly, Buffalo	3844	33	17	97.6
Kosar, Cleveland	3487	18	9	87.8
Kramer, Detroit	1635	11	8	71.8
Krieg, Seattle	2080	11	12	82.5
Majkowski, Green Bay	1362	3	8	59.3
Marino, Miami	3970	25	13	85.8
McMahon, Philadelphia	2239	12	11	80.3
Millen, New England	3073	9	18	72.5
Miller, Atlanta	3103	26	18	80.6
Moon, Houston	4690	23	21	81.7
O'Brien, New York	3300	10	11	76.6
Rypien, Washington	3564	28	11	97.9
Schroeder, Los Angeles	2562	15	16	71.6
Testeverde, Tampa Bay	1994	8	15	59.0
Tupa, Phoenix	2053	6	13	62.0
Walsh, New Orleans	1638	11	6	79.5
Young, San Francisco	2517	17	8	101.8

FIGURE 9.18
Data for Problem 9

the program to remain in a loop and prevent additional execution. Identify the source of the problem.

9. Figure 9.18 contains data for quarterbacks in the National Football League at the end of the 1991 season. Develop a menu-driven program that will enable the user to specify:
   (a) One of four report types: touchdown passes, interceptions, overall quarterback rating, or total passing yardage.
   (b) The number of quarterbacks to include in the report (from 1 to 28).
   (c) Whether the quarterbacks are to appear in ascending or descending sequence of the statistic requested.

CHAPTER

10 Design and Implementation

OUTLINE

OBJECTIVES

After reading this chapter you will be able to:

1. Show how various management concepts apply to both organizations and information systems.
2. Differentiate between structured programming and structured design; distinguish between the functional nature of a hierarchy chart and the procedural nature of pseudocode.
3. Describe how a hierarchy chart is developed; discuss three criteria used to evaluate a completed hierarchy chart.
4. State how a system may be tested before its programs are completed; describe what is meant by top-down testing.
5. Describe the dBASE statements used to implement the basic building blocks of structured programming.
6. Describe the dBASE statements used to pass control from one program to another within a system.

Overview

The United States example of the previous chapter introduced the command mode of dBASE, and demonstrated the flexibility inherent in a menu-driven program. However, powerful as that example might have been, it consisted of only a single program, whereas an ***information system*** contains multiple programs carefully related to one another. The Soleil America System introduced in Chapter 1, for example, contains some 40 programs and approximately 5,000 lines of code.

Rest assured that we will not take you through the detailed coding of all 40 programs. We do think it important, however, that you understand how the programs are related to one another, and how the overall system is developed and tested. This in turn leads to a discussion of ***structured design,*** a methodology that goes beyond the structured programming concepts of the previous chapter.

We begin with a review of the Soleil America System, then present a ***hierarchy chart*** that lists the major programs in that system. We develop the logic necessary to relate those programs to one another, express that logic in ***pseudocode,*** then test the system in a hands-on exercise. This in turn causes us to review many of the dBASE statements presented in Chapter 9. Thus, you will once again see the `IF`, `DO WHILE`, and `DO CASE` statements for ***structured programming,*** and the `READ`, `@...GET`, and `@...SAY` statements for input/output operations.

The most important portion of the chapter, however, deals with the relationship of the many programs in the system to one another, and how that system is implemented and tested. We discuss the use of ***stub programs*** (partially completed programs) to enable testing to begin before the system is fully completed. We also introduce the necessary dBASE statements to pass control from one program to another within a system.

CASE STUDY
Soleil America, Revisited

Return briefly to the case description and hands-on exercises associated with Soleil, as they were first presented in Chapter 1. Recall in particular the menu-driven nature of the system as typified by Figure 10.1.

The opening menu on the left side of the figure provides four choices: file maintenance, report generation, utilities, and leaving the system. More specific options are provided in the subordinate menus (shown in the middle of the figure), which are displayed in accordance with the respective choice from the opening menu. For example, a response of 1 to the opening menu brings up the file maintenance menu to add, edit, or delete an employee record. In similar fashion, a response of 2 returns the report-generation menu, which allows a choice of one of seven reports. The utilities menu allows for yet additional functions (backup, reinstalling the hardware, and so on).

The flow of the overall system is easily understood by viewing Figure 10.1 (and perhaps by repeating some or all of the hands-on exercise from Chapter 1). Entry into the system presents the user with the opening menu (shown in the leftmost portion of the figure), whereupon he or she is presented with one of three subordinate menus (shown in the middle), which in turn leads to additional screens (shown on the right) appropriate to the specific function selected.

Control of the system passes continually from menu to menu within Figure 10.1. It flows initially from left to right [e.g., from the opening menu, to the file maintenance menu (given a response of 1), to the screen to add a new record (given a second response of 1)]. After the addition is completed, control passes from right to left, i.e., back to the file maintenance menu, which in turn goes back to the opening menu, whereupon the process begins anew. It is also possible to stop at an intermediate menu and reverse direction, rather than going all the way back to the opening menu. Hence after completing the addition, another file maintenance function (adding, editing, or deleting) could be selected from the file maintenance menu in lieu of returning to the opening menu.

(Continued on p. 228)

FIGURE 10.1
Overall View of the Soleil America System

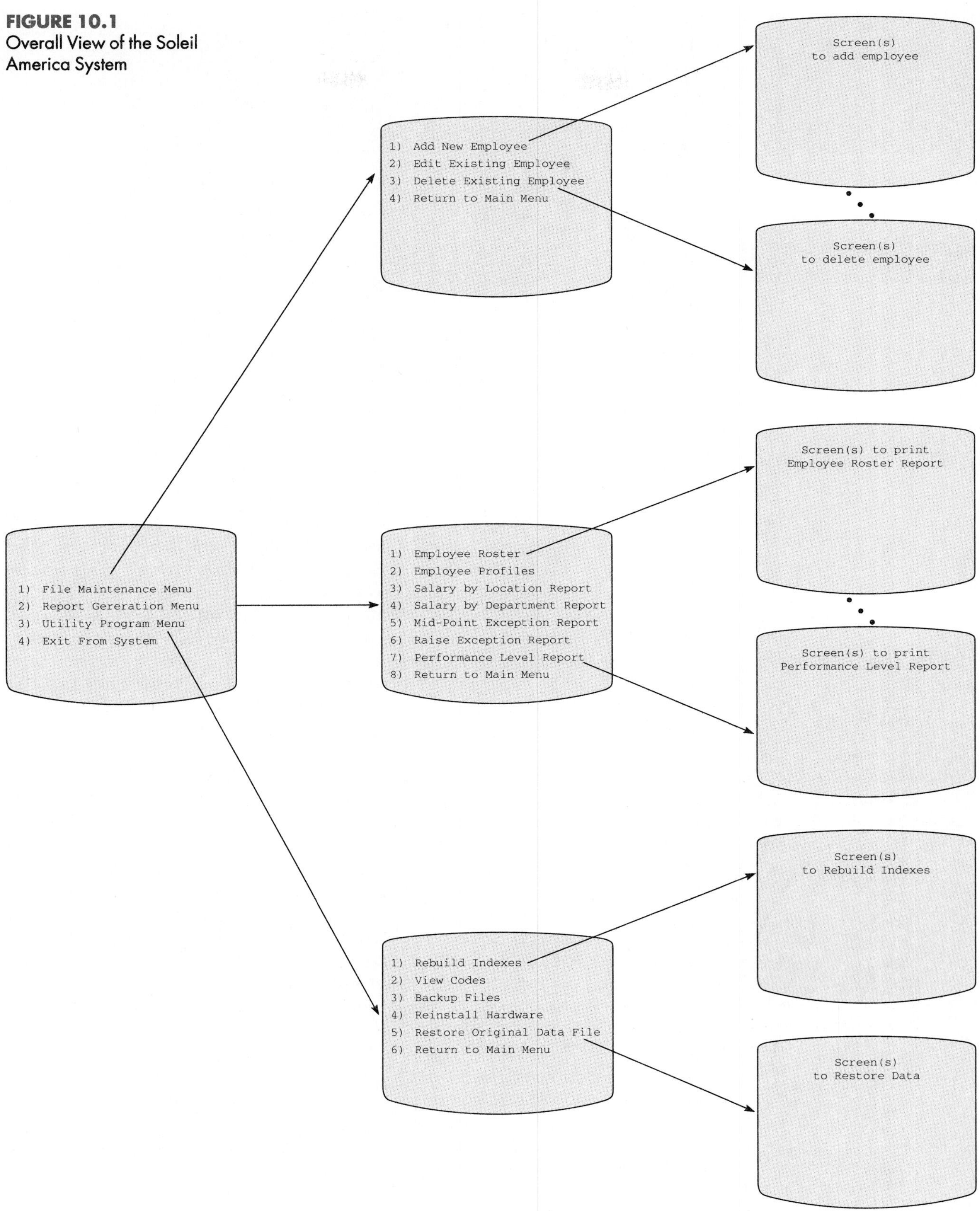

Although it is theoretically possible to develop a single program capable of all of the functions implied by Figure 10.1, that program would be extremely unwieldy. It is necessary, therefore, to develop a system of programs, which is indeed a major undertaking, and which goes beyond the capabilities of a single program. In other words, our concern is with the development of several programs and the *relationship* of these programs to one another. That, in turn, leads to a discussion of structured design, which forms the bulk of this chapter.

Structured Design

Structured design is a methodology that ensures individual programs fit properly together to form a system. It embodies a series of techniques that identify the tasks a system is to accomplish, then relates those tasks to one another in *hierarchical* fashion. In essence, this has already been accomplished for the Soleil system by the menu descriptions of Figure 10.1.

Use your imagination to turn Figure 10.1 on its side (rotate it 90 degrees to the right so that the main menu is on top of the page). Imagine, also, that each box in the figure no longer represents a computer screen, but a person in an organization together with his or her job description. Thus, the person at the top of the organization chart (the chief executive of the organization) is in charge of displaying the main menu. He or she has three subordinates who display the file maintenance, report, and utility menus, respectively. Each of these middle managers has several lower-level subordinates for the more elementary functions, e.g., adding a record, preparing the employee roster report, and backing up the data.

We have, in effect, turned Figure 10.1 into a ***hierarchy chart*** of the kind used in structured design, and have redrawn it as such in Figure 10.2. *The hierarchy chart is the primary tool of structured design* and is analogous to a company's organization chart. The blocks in a hierarchy chart represent programs in a system, just as blocks in an organization chart correspond to positions in a company. The levels within the hierarchy chart describe the relationships between the programs in a system, just as levels in an organization chart describe manager/subordinate relationships among positions. The program at the top of the hierarchy chart is the "boss" of the system, just as the person at the top of an organization chart runs the company. The programs on any level (except the first) are called from a program on the next higher level, and may in turn call programs on a still lower level in the hierarchy chart. In much the same way, people in an organization chart report to the individual on the level immediately above them, while other people on lower levels report to them.

With respect to the hierarchy chart of Figure 10.2, **DISPLAY-MAIN-MENU** will, at different times, call **DISPLAY-MAINTENANCE-MENU**, **DISPLAY-REPORT-MENU**, and **DISPLAY-UTILITY-MENU**. **DISPLAY-MAINTENANCE-MENU** will call either **ADD-EMPLOYEE-RECORD**, **EDIT-EMPLOYEE-RECORD**, or **DELETE-EMPLOYEE-RECORD**. In similar fashion, the other middle managers, **DISPLAY-REPORT-MENU** and **DISPLAY-UTILITY-MENU**, will call their lower-level subordinates. Eventually the lowest-level program completes its function, returns control to its middle manager, which in turn returns control to the overall boss of the system. The process continues indefinitely with control passing back and forth between programs, just as control was passed between the screens of Figure 10.1.

The hierarchy chart is by far the most important tool of structured design. It is useful both as a design aid *before* programs are written, and as a documentation aid to facilitate maintenance *after* the system is completed. In this chapter we concen-

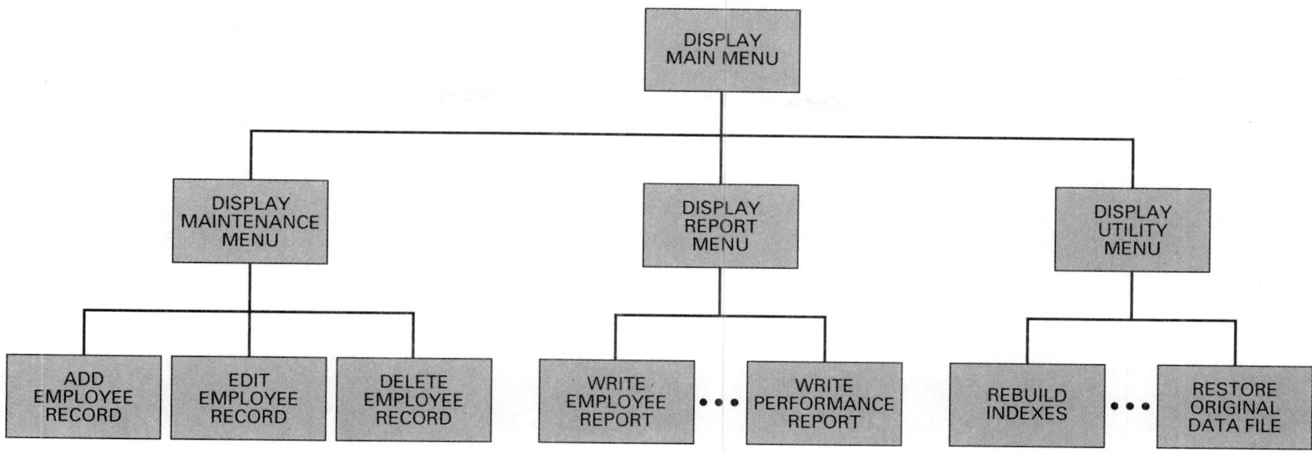

FIGURE 10.2
The Soleil America Hierarchy Chart

trate on its role in system development. We discuss how to create a hierarchy chart and how to evaluate hierarchy charts drawn by others.

Creating the Hierarchy Chart

A hierarchy chart is created in levels, beginning at the top of the chart and working down to the bottom. It helps, perhaps, to envision the entire system as consisting initially of a single, albeit complex, program at the top of the hierarchy chart. Given the impracticality of coding such a program, however, we choose instead to divide it into subordinate tasks, and place those subordinate tasks (each of which represents a potential program) on the next lower level of the hierarchy chart. We continue in this manner until the subordinate tasks can no longer be logically subdivided; i.e., we develop the hierarchy chart by repeatedly dividing a complex task into smaller and smaller pieces, until eventually the lowest-level programs can be coded without difficulty.

The earlier analogy between a system's hierarchy chart and a corporate organization chart is applicable to this discussion as well. Consider, for example, that when an individual is sufficiently motivated to create a new company, he or she proceeds from the *top* of the organization down. More than likely, the entrepreneur installs him- or herself as president, then hires vice-presidents for engineering, finance, marketing, and so on. Eventually, when the top of the organization is in place, assembly line workers, sales personnel, etc., are hired at the bottom of the organization to make and sell the product.

In much the same way the development of a system's hierarchy chart is begun by recognizing the major functions the system is to accomplish, and placing these directly under the main program (on level 1) in the hierarchy chart. Each of these primary tasks is divided into more elementary tasks, which are placed on lower levels (level 2 and beyond) of the hierarchy chart. The decision as to how many programs to include, and how they should be related to one another, is necessarily subjective. Sooner or later, however, one will reach a point where the lower-level functions cannot be further subdivided, whereupon the hierarchy chart is finished. The completed hierarchy chart can then be reviewed for effectiveness, just as one periodically reviews a company's organization chart.

Evaluating the Hierarchy Chart

As already indicated, the design of a hierarchy chart is somewhat subjective. Nevertheless, certain guidelines can be applied to this procedure and result in selecting one design over another. In particular, consider the following criteria:

1. Are the programs *functional*?
2. Is the hierarchy chart *complete*?
3. Is there proper *subordination*?

Each of these is discussed in turn with respect to the hierarchy chart of Figure 10.2.

Functionality

A ***functional program*** is defined as a program that does one, and only one, job, the nature of which is apparent from the program's name. Again, the analogy to a corporation is appropriate in that individuals who try to do too many different things are generally ineffective, as indicated in the cliche, "a jack of all trades, but a master of none." In similar fashion, a single program that performs many functions is also a cause for concern.

The function of a program should be clear from examination of its name alone. Note, for example, that the name of every program in Figure 10.2 consists of a verb, an adjective or two, and an object, e.g., `DISPLAY-MAINTENANCE-MENU` or `ADD-EMPLOYEE-RECORD`. Naming programs in this fashion is an ideal way for ensuring that a system consists entirely of functional programs; indeed, if a program cannot be named in this fashion, its function is probably not clearly defined and the hierarchy chart should be redone.

Another way of expressing the need for functional programs is to strive for ***program independence;*** i.e., the internal workings of one program should not affect the internal workings of another. Perhaps you have already been associated with a working system in which changes were requested. As often as not when a programmer or consultant attempts to modify one part of a system, some other, apparently unrelated, portion of the system no longer works properly. The problem may be due in part to various programs being unnecessarily dependent on one another.

What we are saying is that changes made to one program should not affect the results produced by another, because the programs are independent of one another. (In a practical sense programs have to be somewhat related, else they would not be parts of the same system; however, the amount of interdependence between programs should be minimized to the greatest extent possible.) With respect to Figure 10.2, for example, a change in the procedure for adding an employee record should not affect how employee records are deleted because the programs, `ADD-EMPLOYEE-RECORD` and `DELETE-EMPLOYEE-RECORD`, are each functional in their own right, and consequently independent of one another. The analogy to a corporate organization pertains here as well, as the actions of a marketing manager, for example, should not have any effect on how an accountant balances the books.

Completeness

The next criterion in the evaluation of a hierarchy chart is to verify its ***completeness,*** i.e., that the hierarchy chart provides for every function required by the system. You test for completeness in a hierarchy chart on a level by level basis, starting at the top, and working your way down.

With respect to Figure 10.2, for example, ask yourself whether the three functions on level one—`DISPLAY-MAINTENANCE-MENU`, `DISPLAY-REPORT-MENU`, and **DISPLAY-UTILITY-MENU**—do everything implied by the **DISPLAY-MAIN-MENU** program located on the level above. In other words, are these functions sufficient to carry out the requirements associated with displaying the main menu?

Next drop down to level two and repeat the process. Do the programs, **ADD-EMPLOYEE-RECORD**, **EDIT-EMPLOYEE-RECORD**, and **DELETE-EMPLOYEE-RECORD**, fulfill all of the requirements associated with **DISPLAY-MAINTENANCE-MENU**? Do the various **WRITE-REPORT** programs complete the objectives associated with **DISPLAY-REPORT-MENU**, and so on? Proceed in this manner until you are satisfied that the hierarchy chart contains all of the tasks required by the overall system.

Subordination

Proper ***subordination*** implies that every lower-level program reports to the appropriate higher-level program. In Figure 10.2, for example, it would be wrong to have **DISPLAY-REPORT-MENU** subordinate to **DISPLAY-MAINTENANCE-MENU** instead of **DISPLAY-MAIN-MENU**. It may seem obvious in this example, but mistakes are often made.

Proper subordination also implies that a given program should have only a single manager, although that program can (and does) have multiple subordinates. Thus, **DISPLAY-MAINTENANCE-MENU** is subordinate to a single manager (**DISPLAY-MAIN-MENU**), but has three subordinates (**ADD-EMPLOYEE-RECORD**, **EDIT-EMPLOYEE-RECORD**, and **DELETE-EMPLOYEE-RECORD**) reporting to it.

Finally, proper subordination has to do with ***span of control***, the number of subordinates reporting to a manager. Consider, for example, the organization chart in Figure 10.3a, which depicts the Hatfield family business. The president, A. Hatfield, has been complaining of falling profits since he brought his children, B. and C. Hatfield, into the company.

It doesn't take an extensive management background to realize that the Hatfield organization is top heavy. A. Hatfield does nothing other than manage B. Hatfield, who in turn controls C. Hatfield, whose role in life is to manage I. R. Milgrom. I. R. Milgrom, on the other hand, is overloaded in that 21 people report to him. The problems are related to span of control, i.e., the number of subordinates reporting directly to a manager. I. R. Milgrom has too many, whereas each member of the Hatfield family has too few.

A better structure is exhibited by the McCoy family in Figure 10.3b. Here the president manages three vice-presidents, who in turn each manage seven subordinates. Profits have continued to rise, even after the introduction of the McCoy offspring, and the company appears to be well run. This does not imply that every organization needs to have exactly three vice-presidents, nor must every vice-president have exactly seven subordinates. It does say, however, that there is a more effective span of control in the McCoy organization.

Similar criteria can be applied to a system's hierarchy chart. Systems with ineffective spans of control (too many or too few) can generally be said to be poorly designed, and are difficult to follow and/or maintain.

Structured Design versus Structured Programming

Structured design is a *functionally* oriented technique, whereas structured programming is *procedural* in nature. The difference is significant, and both methodologies are required in the development process. One begins by creating the hierarchy chart for a system by using the methodology of structured design, then links the programs

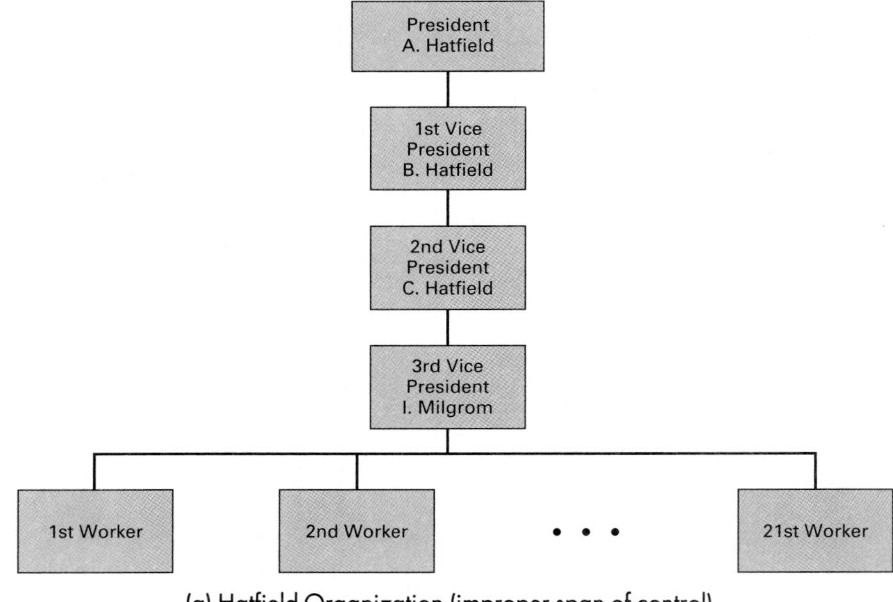

(a) Hatfield Organization (improper span of control)

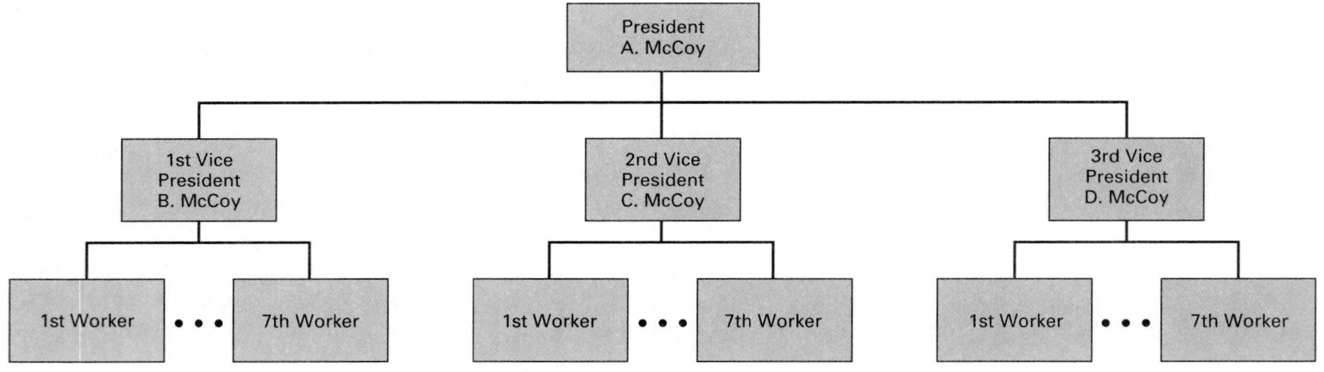

(b) McCoy Organization (proper span of control)

FIGURE 10.3
Span of Control within an Organization

together within the context of structured programming, presenting this logic in pseudocode.

To put it another way, the hierarchy chart indicates *what* functions are necessary, but not when (or how often) they are to be performed. It contains no decision-making logic, nor does it imply anything about the order or frequency in which various programs within a system are executed. Pseudocode, on the other hand, depicts the sequence in which the functions (programs) are executed, using only the basic blocks of sequence, selection, iteration, and case.

Examination of the hierarchy chart in Figure 10.2 indicates that the highest-level program in the system, **DISPLAY-MAIN-MENU**, will call three subordinate programs, **DISPLAY-MAINTENANCE-MENU**, **DISPLAY-REPORT-MENU**, and **DISPLAY-UTILITY-MENU**. It does not, however, specify how often these programs will be called, nor does it indicate the conditions for calling one subordinate in lieu of another. That in turn is specified within the logic of the **DISPLAY-MAIN-MENU** program, developed according to the building blocks of structured programming, expressed first in pseudocode, and eventually converted to a programming language.

The DISPLAY-MAIN-MENU Program

Review in your mind the operation of the Soleil system as evidenced by the hands-on exercises and other experimentation from Chapter 1. The system displayed an opening menu, which led to other menus for the file maintenance, reporting, and utility functions. You selected a subservient function, made the necessary user inputs, and were eventually returned to the opening menu, whereupon the process began again. The cycle repeated itself an indeterminate number of times, until you elected to exit the system entirely, but at no time were you allowed to input an invalid selection in response to any menu. The **DISPLAY-MAIN-MENU** program, located at the top of the hierarchy chart, demonstrates these capabilities.

Pseudocode for the **DISPLAY-MAIN-MENU** program is displayed in Figure 10.4. Recall from the discussion in Chapter 9 that pseudocode describes logic in terms of the basic building blocks of structured programming, i.e., sequence, selection, iteration, and case. Remember, too, that pseudocode only *resembles* a programming language and that it eventually must be translated to dBASE.

The pseudocode of Figure 10.4 contains an outer loop to continually display the opening menu, and an inner loop that requests input until a valid response is received. In other words, the outer loop redisplays the main menu after the system returns from a lower-level program, and thus enables the user to select another function. The inner loop guarantees that the user will always input a valid response.

The outer loop in Figure 10.4 is controlled by the variable *mainloop,* which is set to *true* initially, and remains at that setting until the user elects to exit from the system by entering a *4* in response to the opening menu. That, in turn, causes *mainloop* to be set to *false,* which terminates the outer loop and exits the system. The inner loop is controlled by the variable *menuloop,* which is set to *true* initially and remains set to *true* until a valid response (1, 2, 3, or 4) is entered. When this occurs, *menuloop* is set to *false* and the appropriate lower-level program is called. Remember, too, that while pseudocode contains the logic inherent in a program, it is not written in an actual programming language, and thus eventually it has to be translated into dBASE.

The completed program is shown in Figure 10.5. It contains little that is new in the way of specific dBASE statements other than the `DO` statements used to call the

FIGURE 10.4
Pseudocode for DISPLAY-MAIN-MENU

```
Set mainloop to true
DO WHILE mainloop is true
   Clear screen
   Display menu choices
   Set menuloop to true
   DO WHILE menuloop is true
      Get user's menu choice
      DO CASE
         CASE 1: Call file maintenance program
                 Set menuloop to false
         CASE 2: Call report program menu
                 Set menuloop to false
         CASE 3: Call utility program menu
                 Set menuloop to false
         CASE 4: Display backup information
                 Set menuloop to false
                 Set mainloop to false
      OTHERWISE: Display error message
      ENDCASE
   ENDDO
ENDDO
Exit system and return to DOS
```

```
***SOLMAIN.PRG
***This program maps the main menu
***
CLEAR
SET BELL OFF
SET TALK OFF
SET STATUS OFF
STORE 'T' TO mainloop
DO WHILE mainloop = 'T'
   CLEAR
   @ 2,70 SAY DATE() ———————— Displays system date
   @ 2,2 SAY 'Soleil America, Inc.'
   @ 3,2 SAY 'Personnel Information System'
   @ 4,2 SAY 'Release 2.0'
   @ 09,27 SAY '1) File Maintenance'
   @ 11,27 SAY '2) Report Menu'
   @ 13,27 SAY '3) Utility Programs'
   @ 15,27 SAY '4) Exit From System'
   @ 21,27 SAY 'Please Choose An Option: '
   STORE 'T' TO menuloop
   DO WHILE menuloop = 'T'
      STORE ' ' TO opt
      @ 21,52 GET opt PICTURE '9'
      READ
      DO CASE
         CASE opt='1'
            DO SOLFILE ———————— Call to lower level program
            STORE 'F' TO menuloop
         CASE opt='2'
            DO SOLREP ———————— Call to lower level program
            STORE 'F' TO menuloop
         CASE opt='3'
            DO SOLUTIL ———————— Call to lower level program
            STORE 'F' TO menuloop
         CASE opt='4'
            STORE 'F' TO menuloop
            STORE 'F' TO mainloop
      OTHERWISE
         ? CHR(7) ———————— Beeps for invalid response
         @ 23,17 SAY '*** Please Choose One of the Options Listed! ***'
      ENDCASE
   ENDDO
ENDDO
QUIT ———————— Exits dBASE and returns to DOS
```

FIGURE 10.5
Soleil Main Menu Program

lower-level programs; i.e., virtually all of the statements used in Figure 10.5 were introduced in the previous chapter in conjunction with the menu for the United States example. The program begins with three **SET** statements to:

1. Eliminate the bell on data input—**SET BELL OFF**.
2. Suppress the intermediate dBASE messages—**SET TALK OFF**.
3. Inhibit the display of the dBASE status line—**SET STATUS OFF**.

The outer and inner loops are controlled by the variables *mainloop* and *menuloop,* respectively, as was explained earlier. The beginning statements within the outer loop clear the screen, display the date and title information, then display the opening menu. The inner loop is executed as many times as necessary until a valid response is obtained. Note the use of the various **@...SAY** statements to display information on the screen, and the combination of the **@...GET** and **READ** statements to obtain user input via the keyboard.

The **DO CASE** statement within the inner loop directs control to the appropriate lower-level program according to the value of the variable *opt* (obtained via the **GET** statement). A simple `DO` statement of the form, `DO program-name`, transfers control to the lower-level program. For example, if the user responded 1 initially (i.e., he or she requested the file maintenance function from the main menu), control would pass from the main menu program in Figure 10.5 to the program `SOLFILE.PRG`. The latter, lower-level program would execute in its entirety, whereupon control would return to the main menu program at the statement below the `DO` statement that transferred control in the first place. (The continual transfer of control from one program to another is best appreciated after completing the first hands-on exercise later in the chapter.)

The `DO CASE` statement also prevents the system from accepting an invalid value (i.e., a number other than 1, 2, 3, or 4). Should this occur, the `? CHR(7)` statement causes the system to beep, the subsequent `@...SAY` statement displays an error message, and the inner loop is re-executed. The system once again prompts for a proper response, the user inputs his or her choice, and the process continues.

Eventually, the user will elect to leave the system by responding 4 to the opening menu, which in turn causes two things to happen. First, *menuloop* is set to *F* (as it is whenever a valid response is received), terminating the inner loop that requests a valid user response. Next, *mainloop* is set to *F*, terminating the outer loop and causing control in the program to pass to the `QUIT` statement, which exits dBASE and returns control to DOS.

We hope that you were able to follow our discussion, and that the listing in Figure 10.5 is perfectly clear. Do not be concerned, however, if you are unsure about the operation of one or more statements. Proceed to the next section on top-down implementation and its associated hands-on exercise. Remember, dBASE programming is best learned by doing, and completion of the hands-on exercise will go a long way in helping you understand Figure 10.5.

Top-Down Implementation

Completion of the Soleil system requires that we eventually write a program for every box in the hierarchy chart of Figure 10.2. Our intent, however, is not to spend an undue amount of time in programming per se, but rather to provide an appreciation for the system development process. Accordingly, we describe how the system would be implemented and tested, omitting the detailed program listings.

Realize, also, that while the process of formatting menus in an attractive fashion (with respect to row and column placement on the screen) is time consuming, it is not very difficult. Far more important is the logic to accept the user response, as that determines which screen will be displayed, and which programs within the system will be executed next. In other words, our initial concern should be that the system guarantee a valid response from the user, which in turn will transfer control to the appropriate lower-level program, rather than decide whether the message requesting that response appears in row 18 or row 20.

Unfortunately, many students make the mistake of developing the screen layouts first, leaving the more complex portions of the system for later. By contrast, the ***top-down*** philosophy of system implementation requires simply that the more important programs in a system (those at or near the top of the hierarchy chart) be developed first, with the details left for later. The concept is simple, even obvious, yet one which is ignored too often in practice. Again the analogy between a system's hierarchy chart and a corporate organization chart is appropriate. A new company begins with the president and not the janitor, so why not begin system development at the top as well? Moreover, the higher a person appears on an organization chart, the more responsible his or her position. In much the same way, programs appearing near the top of a hierarchy chart are generally more important than those near the bottom.

The top-down philosophy espouses simply that testing begin as soon as possible, *even before all of the programs in a system have been completed.* Although this may sound implausible, it is easily accomplished by supplying partially completed programs, known as ***stub programs,*** for the lower-level programs in the system.

Consider, for example, the **DISPLAY-MAIN-MENU** program of Figure 10.5. As can be seen, three additional programs (**SOLFILE**, **SOLREP**, and **SOLUTIL**) are necessary before testing can begin. What if, however, we initially developed very simple versions of these programs, as shown in Figure 10.6? We could then proceed to fully test the **DISPLAY-MAIN-MENU** program which, as indicated earlier, is the most important program in the entire system. The results of the early testing will indicate that the subordinate programs are called in proper sequence, and also provide a sense of how the completed system will operate.

The stub programs in Figure 10.6 are easy to code, trivial in nature, and consist of four types of statements:

1. A **CLEAR** statement to erase the screen.
2. An **@...SAY** statement to print a message indicating that the program has been called.
3. A **WAIT** statement requiring only that the user press any key to continue (signifying that he or she has read the message).
4. A **RETURN** statement to return control to the calling program, in this case the **DISPLAY-MAIN-MENU** program.

The availability of the stub programs enables us to test the **DISPLAY-MAIN-MENU** program and confirm that it is performing correctly. Recall that the function of the **DISPLAY-MAIN-MENU** program is to display an opening menu, request a user response, validate that response (i.e., check that it is 1, 2, 3, or 4), and then transfer control to an appropriate lower-level program corresponding to the user's response.

After the testing of the **DISPLAY-MAIN-MENU** program is completed, we will know that it interacts properly with its subordinate programs, and that it is also capa-

FIGURE 10.6
Level One Program Stubs

```
***SOLFILE.PRG
CLEAR
@10,10 SAY 'The file maintenance menu would be located here'
@11,10 SAY 'The user would add, edit, or delete employee records'
WAIT
RETURN
```

(a) File Maintenance Program Stub

```
***SOLREP.PRG
CLEAR
@10,10 SAY 'The report menu would be located here'
@11,10 SAY 'The user would choose one of several reports'
WAIT
RETURN
```

(b) Report Menu Program Stub

```
***SOLUTIL.PRG
CLEAR
@10,10 SAY 'The utility menu would be located here'
@11,10 SAY 'The user would choose a utility function'
WAIT
RETURN
```

(c) Utility Menu Program Stub

ble of rejecting invalid user responses. We will not know anything about whether the lower-level programs are working, only that they have been called correctly. Nevertheless, the accomplishment is significant as can be appreciated by completing the ensuing hands-on exercise.

HANDS-ON EXERCISE 1

Top-down Testing/1

Objective

Illustrate the concept of top-down testing with stub programs.

STEP 1 **Change to the SOLSTUB directory**

Boot the system, ending at the DOS prompt. Type one of the following two commands, depending on whether you are sharing the hard drive with others:

CD C:\DATADISK\SOLSTUB —— *if you installed the data disk on the hard drive and are not sharing your computer, or*

CD A:\DATADISK\SOLSTUB —— *if you did not install the data disk, i.e., if you are sharing drive C with other students. (Use data disk two if you have 5¼-inch disks.)*

Type **DIR** to verify the presence of the necessary program files in this directory. You should see a total of four files: SOLMAIN.PRG (containing the main menu program of Figure 10.5), as well as the three subordinate stub programs shown in Figure 10.6 (SOLFILE.PRG, SOLREP.PRG, and SOLUTIL.PRG). Observe that all four files have the ***PRG extension*** corresponding to the dBASE convention for program files.

STEP 2 **Load dBASE**

Type **dBASE** to load dBASE as you have been doing throughout the text. Set the dBASE default drive with the appropriate **SET DEFAULT** command in accordance with step 1.

STEP 3 **Test the system**

Enter the dBASE command, **DO SOLMAIN**, to invoke the main menu program, and bring up the menu shown in Figure 10.7. Observe how the menu displayed on the screen corresponds to the @...SAY statements present in the program of Figure 10.5.

Supply a value other than 1, 2, 3, or 4 to verify that the system rejects invalid entries. Enter responses of 1, 2, and 3 (in several different sequences and/or combinations) to invoke the appropriate lower-level programs, obtaining output as shown in Figures 10.8a, b, and c, respectively. Note that after each lower-level program is executed, control returns to the main menu. Eventually, supply a response of 4 to leave the Soleil system and return to DOS.

Additional Testing

Successful completion of the hands-on exercise demonstrates that the system successfully passes control from one program to another as well as rejects invalid user responses. Realize, however, that the exercise encompassed only 4 of the 19 required

FIGURE 10.7
The Main Menu as Displayed on the Monitor (output produced by the program of Figure 10.5)

```
Soleil America, Inc.                                    02/04/91
Personnel Information System
Release 2.0


                        1) File Maintenance

                        2) Report Menu

                        3) Utility Programs

                        4) Exit From System



                        Please Choose An Option:
```

```
          The file maintenance menu would be located here
          The user would add, edit, or delete employee records
Press any key to continue...
```

(a) Output of File Maintenance Stub Program
(output produced by the program of Figure 10.6a)

```
           The report menu would be located here
           The user would choose one of several reports
Press any key to continue...
```

(b) Output of Report Menu Stub Program
(output produced by the program of Figure 10.6b)

```
           The utility menu would be located here
           The user would choose a utility function
Press any key to continue...
```

(c) Output of Utility Menu Stub Program
(output produced by the program of Figure 10.6c)

FIGURE 10.8
Output of Stubs Program

programs (and that three of these existed as stubs). Clearly, additional work is required before the system is finally operational.

The next step is to expand each of the three stub programs to accept user input, while simultaneously developing additional stub programs for the next lower level of the hierarchy chart. The testing would then expand to encompass every program within the hierarchy chart, the successful completion of which would verify that all 19 programs interact properly with one another.

Consider, for example, Figure 10.9, which expands the stub program for file maintenance (shown earlier as Figure 10.6a). The logic is straightforward and closely parallels that of the **DISPLAY-MAIN-MENU** program, which was explained earlier. Note, further, the requirement for three additional stub programs (**SOLADD.PRG**, **SOLEDIT.PRG**, and **SOLDEL.PRG**) to fully test the file maintenance program.

```
***SOLFILE.PRG
***This program maps the file maintenance menu
***
STORE 'T' TO filemenu
DO WHILE filemenu = 'T'
   CLEAR
   @ 3,2 SAY 'File Maintenance Menu'
   @ 08,27 SAY '1) Add New Employee'
   @ 10,27 SAY '2) Edit Existing Employee'
   @ 12,27 SAY '3) Delete Existing Employee'
   @ 14,27 SAY '4) Exit to Main Menu'
   @ 21,27 SAY 'Please Choose An Option: '
   STORE 'T' TO menuloop
   DO WHILE menuloop = 'T'
      STORE ' ' TO fileopt
      @ 21,52 GET fileopt PICTURE '9'
      READ
      @ 22,2 SAY SPACE(77)
      DO CASE
         CASE fileopt='1'
           DO SOLADD ---------------------------- Stub program
           STORE 'F' TO menuloop
         CASE fileopt='2'
           DO SOLEDIT --------------------------- Stub program
           STORE 'F' TO menuloop
         CASE fileopt='3'
           DO SOLDEL ---------------------------- Stub program
           STORE 'F' TO menuloop
        CASE fileopt = '4'
           STORE 'F' TO filemenu
           STORE 'F' TO menuloop
      OTHERWISE
         ? CHR(7)
         @ 23,17 SAY '*** Please Choose One of the Options Listed! ***'
      ENDCASE
   ENDDO
ENDDO
RETURN ------------------------------------ Returns control to calling program
```

FIGURE 10.9
Expanded File Maintenance Program (requires additional stubs programs for testing)

In similar fashion, it will be necessary to expand the other stub programs of Figure 10.6 (for report generation and utilities), creating additional lower-level programs for each of these as well. A second round of testing would begin as indicated in the next hands-on exercise. Once again we have created all necessary stub programs for you, and have placed them in a different subdirectory.

HANDS-ON EXERCISE 2

Top-down Testing/2

Objective

Continue testing the stubs system by expanding the first-level programs, through additional stubs for the next lowest level.

STEP 1 **Log into the SOLSTUB2 subdirectory**

The steps in this exercise parallel those of the preceding exercise except that you are testing an expanded version of the system, which is located in a *different* subdirectory. Be sure you are at the DOS prompt, then type one of the following two commands, depending on whether you are sharing the hard drive with others:

```
SOLMAIN   PRG       1222 02-03-91   10:06a ——— Main menu program (unchanged)

SOLFILE   PRG       1059 02-03-91   11:42a ——— Expanded file maintenance program
SOLREP    PRG       1559 02-03-91   10:17a
SOLUTIL   PRG        923 02-03-91   10:26a

SOLADD    PRG        128 02-03-91    9:22a
SOLDEL    PRG         84 02-03-91   12:03p ——— File maintenance program stubs
SOLEDIT   PRG        128 02-03-91    9:22a

REPORT1   PRG         96 02-03-91   10:19a
REPORT2   PRG         98 02-03-91   10:16a
REPORT3   PRG         99 02-03-91   10:20a
REPORT4   PRG         99 02-03-91   10:21a
REPORT5   PRG         98 02-03-91   10:21a
REPORT6   PRG         94 02-03-91   10:22a
REPORT7   PRG         96 02-03-91   10:22a

SOLBUILD  PRG         99 03-01-91    8:33p
SOLCODES  PRG         79 02-03-91   10:27a
SOLBKUP   PRG         98 02-03-91   10:27a
REINSTAL  PRG        100 03-01-91    8:34p
SOLCOPY   PRG        100 03-01-91    8:34p
```

FIGURE 10.10
Completed System with Program Stubs (directory of C:\DATADISK\SOLSTUB2)

CD C:\DATADISK\SOLSTUB2 — *if you installed the data disk on the hard drive and are not sharing your computer, or*

CD A:\DATADISK\SOLSTUB2 — *if you did not install the data disk, i.e., if you are sharing drive C with other students. (Use data disk two if you have $5^1/_4$-inch disks.)*

Type **DIR** to verify that this directory contains the nineteen program files shown in Figure 10.10. The **SOLMAIN** program is unchanged from the previous exercise, but the **SOLFILE**, **SOLREP**, and **SOLUTIL** programs have been expanded from their earlier stub versions. This in turn required us to add additional stub programs (**SOLADD**, **SOLDEL**, and so on) so that we could fully test the expanded programs.

STEP 2 **Load dBASE**

Type **dBASE** to load dBASE as you have been doing throughout the text. Use the **SET DEFAULT** command to set the dBASE default drive to drive A or drive C, in accordance with your action in step 1.

STEP 3 **Test the file maintenance menu**

Type **DO SOLMAIN** to begin testing, but realize you are testing a *different* version of the system because you are in a different directory than in the previous exercise. Once again, you will see the main menu of the Soleil System (shown in Figure 10.7), which provides three options: file maintenance, report generation, and utilities.

Enter a **1** to invoke the file maintenance menu, which in turn allows you to select one of three file maintenance functions. Respond 1, 2, or 3 to add, edit, or delete an employee record, which in turn invokes a lower-level stub program. You might also try entering an invalid response to check the data validation capabilities built into the system. Output produced by testing the file maintenance program (and its associated stubs) is shown in Figure 10.11.

When you are satisfied that the file maintenance menu works, type **4** to return to the main menu of Figure 10.7.

```
  File Maintenance Menu

                          1) Add New Employee

                          2) Edit Existing Employee

                          3) Delete Existing Employee

                          4) Exit to Main Menu

                          Please Choose An Option:
```

(a) File Maintenance Menu (produced by Figure 10.9)

```
              Employee record is added
Press any key to continue...
```

(b) Output of Program Stub to Add Employee

```
              Employee record is edited
Press any key to continue...
```

(c) Output of Program Stub to Edit Employee

```
              Employee record is deleted
Press any key to continue...
```

(d) Output of Program Stub to Delete Employee

FIGURE 10.11
Testing the File Maintenance Menu

STEP 4 **Continue testing**

Enter a **2** from the main menu (Figure 10.7) to invoke the report generation menu. Experiment with various responses, both valid and invalid, eventually returning to the main Soleil Menu. Continue testing the utility menu and its associated stub programs. Eventually, when you are satisfied that the "complete" system works, exit and return to the DOS prompt.

Advantages of Top-down Implementation

The top-down approach to testing enables the highest (and most important) programs in a hierarchy chart to be tested earlier, and more often, than the lower-level (and often trivial) programs. It makes it possible to begin testing earlier in the development cycle with the consequence that any errors that do exist are found sooner and, consequently, are easier to correct. Of course, later versions of the system can still contain bugs, but these will be in lower-level programs, where correcting them is easier. The more difficult problems will already have been resolved in the initial tests.

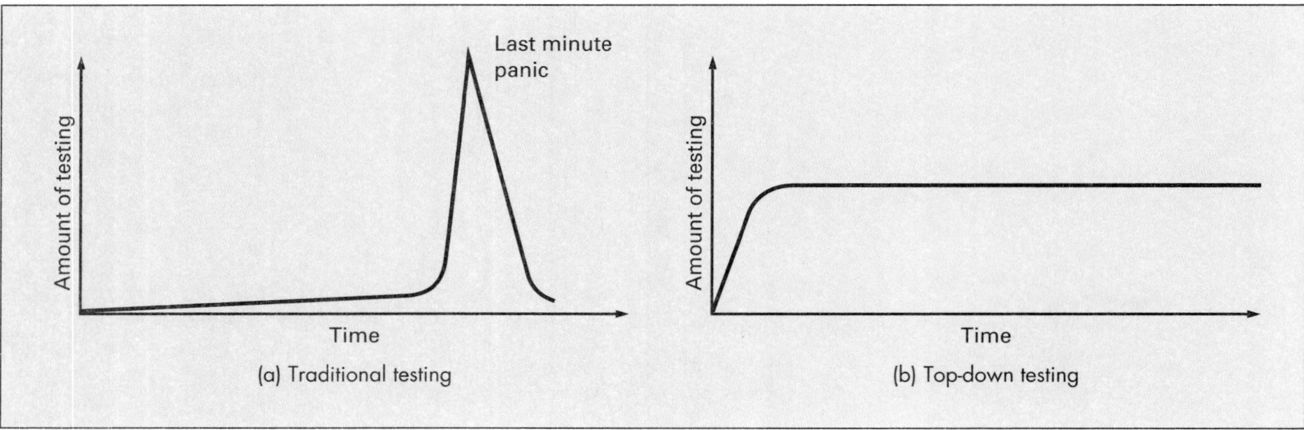

FIGURE 10.12
Top-down versus Traditional Testing

A second advantage of top-down testing is that testing and coding become parallel activities, which means that users (and project sponsors) continually see previews of the completed system. Thus, they are in an excellent position to correct any major flaws in the implementation of the system well before it is completed.

The differences between top-down and traditional testing are contrasted in Figure 10.12. Figure 10.12a depicts the traditional way of testing, in which no testing is done until the weekend before the system goes live (or your assignment is due). Last-minute panic sets in, with abundant overtime and chaos. By contrast, Figure 10.12b indicates a more uniform pattern of testing, which begins almost immediately and continues throughout the project's duration.

Summary

Structured design is a methodology that identifies the tasks a system is to accomplish, then relates those tasks to one another in a hierarchy chart. The boxes in a ***hierarchy chart*** correspond one to one with the programs in the system.

A hierarchy chart is evaluated for ***completeness, functionality,*** and ***span of control.*** A program in a hierarchy chart can be entered only from the program immediately above it, and must return control to that program when execution is complete.

The dBASE ***DO program*** statement transfers control to a lower-level program. The dBASE ***RETURN*** statement returns control back to the higher-level program.

Structured design is a ***functionally*** oriented technique indicating what has to be done, but not when or if in fact a task will be performed. Structured programming, on the other hand, is ***procedural*** in nature and contains decision-making logic depicting the sequence in which the program tasks will be executed.

Top-down testing begins early in the development process, even before a system is completely coded; top-down testing requires the use of ***stub programs.***

Key Words and Concepts

? CHR(7)	CLEAR	Functional program
@...GET	Completeness	Hierarchy chart
@...SAY	DO	Information system

PRG extension	**SET BELL OFF**	Structured programming
Program independence	**SET STATUS OFF**	Stub programs
Pseudocode	**SET TALK OFF**	Subordination
QUIT	Span of control	Top-down testing
RETURN	Structured design	**WAIT**

True/False

1. A system must be completely coded before any testing can begin.
2. A program in a hierarchy chart can be called from another program at its own level.
3. The highest-level programs in a hierarchy chart should be tested first.
4. Pseudocode and hierarchy charts depict the same thing.
5. In a given system, the same program cannot be both a called and a calling program.
6. No program in a hierarchy chart should have more than one subordinate program.
7. Every program within a system should eventually return control to the program that called it initially.
8. No program in a hierarchy chart should have more than one managing program.
9. When designing a hierarchy chart, one should strive to include programs that accomplish multiple functions for efficiency purposes.
10. An information system can be partially tested even if no data files are available.
11. Structured design is a procedurally oriented technique.
12. Structured programming is a functionally oriented technique.
13. A span of control of 1 or 2 is reasonable for most programs within a system.
14. A hierarchy chart is best developed from the bottom up.
15. System testing should be concentrated in the last twenty-five percent of the development phase.
16. The optimal number of programs in a system is equal to the number of programmers available.

Exercises

1. Distinguish between
   (a) A called and a calling program
   (b) A stub program and its completed version
   (c) Structured design and structured programming
   (d) A system's hierarchy chart and a company's organization chart
   (e) The **CLEAR** and **WAIT** statements
   (f) The **DO CASE** and **DO WHILE** statements
   (g) The **@...SAY** and **@...GET** statements
   (h) The **RETURN** and **QUIT** statements
   (i) A functionally oriented technique versus a procedurally oriented technique
2. Indicate precisely what the following dBASE statements do:
   (a) **QUIT**
   (b) **CLEAR**
   (c) **RETURN**
   (d) **@ 2,70 SAY DATE()**
   (e) **WAIT**

(f) `SET BELL OFF`
(g) `? CHR(7)`
(h) `SET TALK OFF`
(i) `SET STATUS OFF`

3. Develop pseudocode for either the file maintenance, report generation, or utility menu programs (**DISPLAY-MAINTENANCE-MENU**, **DISPLAY-REPORT-MENU**, or **DISPLAY-UTILITY-MENU**) shown in the hierarchy chart of Figure 10.2. Use Figure 10.4 as a guide.

4. With respect to the completed programs and associated lower-level stub programs for the second hands-on exercise, indicate precisely what messages will be produced if the user enters the following responses in sequence: 5, 1, 3, 4, and 4. Can you begin to appreciate the results of top-down testing?

5. This problem specifically avoids a business context, and was selected because you are unfamiliar with it and consequently have no preexisting bias toward a solution.

   Develop a hierarchy chart (which is the eventual basis for a programming solution) to allow a person to play a series of tic-tac-toe games interactively against a computer. The following programs are used in our solution: **PLAY-SERIES**, **PLAY-GAME**, **CLEAR-BOARD**, **GET-USER-MOVE**, **VALIDATE-USER-MOVE**, **CHECK-FOR-WINNER**, **UPDATE-BOARD**, **GET-COMPUTER-MOVE**, **DISPLAY-BOARD**, **DISPLAY-MESSAGE**. (The last program, **DISPLAY-MESSAGE**, may be called from several places.)

   Note that in developing the hierarchy chart you are concerned only with *what* the individual programs will do, not *how* they will do it (The logic for the latter is developed in pseudocode when the programs are actually written.)

6. Again we have chosen a nonbusiness problem to give you further practice with structured design. Develop a hierarchy chart for the game of blackjack (also known as "21"). Indicate sufficient programs in your solution to accommodate:
   (a) Doubling down—if the player's first two cards total 11, he or she may double the bet and receive one additional card.
   (b) Purchasing insurance—if the dealer's "up" card is an ace, the player may place an additional side bet. If the dealer has "blackjack," the player receives a payout of 2 to 1 on the side bet, but loses the initial bet. If the dealer does not have blackjack, the side bet is lost and play continues.
   (c) Splitting pairs—if the player has a pair, he or she may double the bet and play two hands.

   The rules of blackjack state that the dealer must draw with 16 or less, and stand with 17 or more. Your hierarchy chart should contain the necessary programs to keep a running total of the player's winnings (or losses).

CHAPTER

11 File Maintenance

OUTLINE

OBJECTIVES

After reading this chapter you will be able to:

1. List the three basic file maintenance operations.
2. Distinguish between file maintenance at the dot prompt versus file maintenance through a program; describe advantages and disadvantages of each approach.
3. Differentiate between a program and a procedure; explain what is meant by a dBASE procedure file.
4. Describe the general function of **SET** commands; list at least five such commands and the specific purpose of each.
5. Explain the role of memory variables in dBASE programming.

Overview

The subject of ***file maintenance*** has already been broached in several places, beginning with the Soleil system in Chapter 1. The initial example presented a completed, menu-driven system that allowed you to *add, edit,* or *delete* a record within the context of the Soleil system. Later chapters discussed file maintenance from the dot prompt, included presentation of the necessary commands (**APPEND**, **EDIT**, **BROWSE**, **DELETE**, and **PACK**), and covered the use of format files and the screen generator to facilitate these operations. That discussion, however, has for the most part taken place at the dot prompt, which has only limited capabilities for ***data validation.*** Accordingly, this chapter covers the subject in considerably more detail to produce the program(s) necessary to prevent the addition of duplicate and/or incomplete records.

The present chapter continues the development of the student system of Chapter 8 and follows the precepts of structured programming and design from Chapters 9 and 10, respectively. We introduce new dBASE commands as necessary for file maintenance: the **SEEK** statement for random retrieval, ***memory variables, public*** and ***private variables,*** and ***procedures.*** Our objective, however, is not to cover every option of every command, but rather to present an overview of why programming is necessary for file maintenance, and further, to offer insight into how programs are developed. Accordingly, you are once again referred to the Programmer's Notebook for additional information on any of the statements discussed in the chapter.

Limitations of the Dot Prompt

The all-important subject of data validation was introduced in Chapter 7 in conjunction with the screen generator. We saw that opening a format file prior to the subsequent addition of records via the **APPEND** command, automatically invoked various dBASE validation procedures. It was not possible, for example, to place alphabetic data into a numeric field, nor could invalid values be entered into a date field. We saw, too, that a range check could be imposed on numeric fields, and further that character fields could be checked for specific values.

Impressive as these capabilities are, they stop far short of what is necessary in a practical application. They do not, for example, preclude the addition of ***duplicate records,*** or the inclusion of records with ***incomplete data.*** Accordingly, to demonstrate the difference between what can and cannot be accomplished from the dot prompt, we begin with a hands-on exercise that contrasts a simple **APPEND** command, with and without a format file, to a customized program for adding records.

The exercise will demonstrate the limitations of adding records from the dot prompt, specifically how easy it is to add a duplicate record and/or a record missing critical data, or even a record that is altogether blank. We then attempt to enter the identical (erroneous) records through a data validation program, which checks each record as it is being entered, and rejects duplicate additions as well as records with missing fields and/or invalid data. The program also enables the addition of many records in a single session, by continually asking whether another record should be added or the program ended.

The actual data validation is done in two phases. The record to be added is first checked against existing records in the file to prevent duplication, after which the fields within the new record are checked for completeness and accuracy. To ensure that the record about to be added is not already in the file, the program searches the file to see if the record already exists, and if not, proceeds to add the record. If, on the other hand, the record is already in the file, that fact must be made known to the user in the form of an error message, and the addition rejected.

The main question is how to search the existing file to determine whether or not the record is present. Do we look for the entire record, or just a particular field(s) within the record, and if the latter, which field? Given the impracticality of checking for every field in every record, the search is normally restricted to a single field, known as a ***key,*** the value of which must be unique. Social security number is chosen over last name because social security number is a ***unique key;*** i.e., no two individuals can have the same social security number, whereas several individuals can have the same last name.

The program also precludes the addition of incomplete records as well as records with invalid codes. It must check, therefore, for the presence of a value in ***critical fields*** (e.g., first and last name), and further that the values of certain fields are within specified ranges (e.g., that sex is either **M** or **F**). It is not necessary, however, to check every field, especially if the field is not likely to be known initially. Note, too, that the determination of which fields are considered critical depends on the application. Phone number, for example, is not considered critical in this system, whereas it is absolutely crucial in the stock broker example of Chapter 7.

As you shall see in the exercise, data validation takes time, a price that the user is not always willing to pay, especially as he or she sits idly at the computer while the checking routines are executed. Nevertheless, we cannot overstate the case for data validation, because once errors are allowed into a system, they have a disturbing tendency to remain. We continue with the hands-on exercise.

HANDS-ON EXERCISE 1

Limitations of the Dot Prompt

Objective

Add (append) records from the dot prompt, with and without a format file, using the STUDENTS.DBF file from Chapter 8. Show the inability of this technique to reject duplicate additions and/or incomplete records.

STEP 1 **Change to the STUDENT2 directory**

Boot the system, ending at the DOS prompt. Type one of the following two commands, depending on whether you are sharing the hard drive with others:

CD C:\DATADISK\STUDENT2 — *if you installed the data disk on the hard drive and are not sharing your computer*

CD A:\DATADISK\STUDENT2 — *if you did not install the data disk, i.e., if you are sharing drive C with others. (Use data disk two if you have 5¼-inch disks.)*

STEP 2 **Open the STUDENTS.DBF file**

Type **dBASE** to load dBASE, then set the default drive as you have in previous exercises. Type **USE STUDENTS** at the dot prompt to open the existing STUDENTS.DBF file.

STEP 3 **Examine the existing file**

Type **BROWSE** at the dot prompt to display the eight records currently in the STUDENTS.DBF file as shown in Figure 11.1a. The entry in the status line, *Rec 1/8,* indicates that there are currently eight records in the file and the record pointer is currently on the first record.

FIGURE 11.1
Limitations of the Dot Prompt

Records Organize Fields Go To Exit

SSN	LASTNAME	FIRSTNAME	SEX	ADDRESS	CITY
111111111	Kinzer	Jessica	F	3601 N.W. 75 Terr.	Miami
333333335	Lanahan	Allison	F	5454 S.W. 168 Dr.	Miami
555555555	Zimmer	Kim	F	3456 S.E. 56 St.	Miami
444444444	Miller	Steve	M	444 West Dixie Highway	North M
999999999	Fernandez	Alex	M	8890 Michigan Avenue	New Yor
666666666	Lerner	Allan	M	4321 S.W. 43 Terr.	Denver
888888888	Ryan	Michael	M	4455 S.W. 97 Avenue	Miami
777777777	Adams	Abigail	F	100 Main Street	Boston

Browse C:\...student2\STUDENTS Rec 1/8 File

(a) File before Data Entry

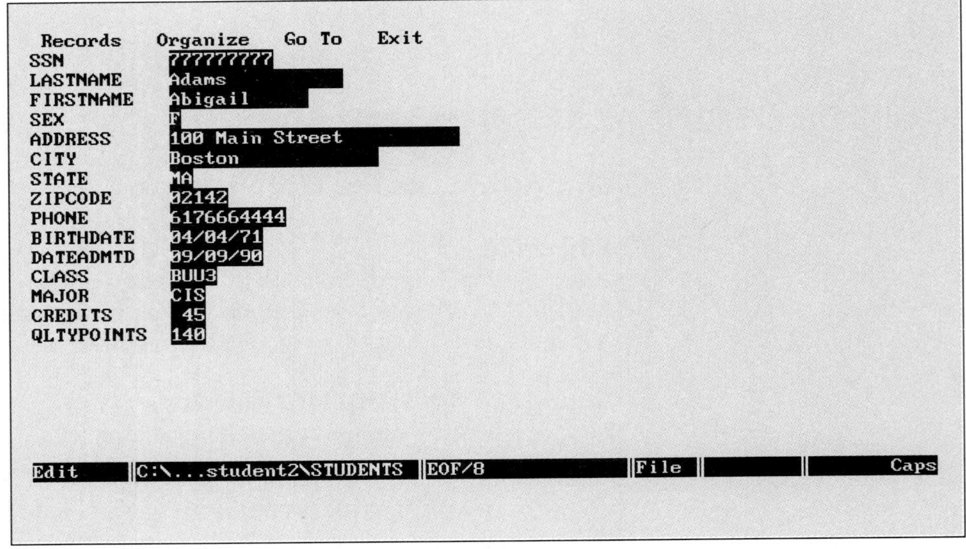

(b) Adding from the Dot Prompt (duplicate record)

STEP 4 **Add a duplicate record**

Press **Alt+E** to pull down the exit menu, highlight *Exit,* and press **enter** to return to the dot prompt. Type **APPEND** to bring up the template for a new record, then add a duplicate record for Abigail Adams as shown in Figure 11.1b.

STEP 5 **Add a blank record**

Press the **enter** key after completing the last field for Abigail's duplicate record, which should bring up the template for another new record; press **Ctrl+End** immediately to exit the append (edit) mode and return to the dot prompt. You have, whether you realize it or not, added a blank record to the file, which will be shown in step 7.

FIGURE 11.1
Limitations of the Dot Prompt (continued)

```
Records   Organize   Go To   Exit

              Social Security Number: 123-45-6789
   First Name:                       Last Name:
   Address: 1718 Vestal Drive                         Sex:
      City: Coral Springs
     State: FL   Zipcode: 33071
     Phone: (305)777-8888              Date of Birth: 03/16/74

   Date Admitted: 09/09/91             Classification: BUU1
                                                Major: UND

       Number of Credits:  60     Grade Point Average:
   Quality Points Earned: 210

Edit  C:\...student2\STUDENTS  EOF/10  File
```

(c) Adding with Format File (incomplete record)

Records Organize Fields Go To Exit

SSN	LASTNAME	FIRSTNAME	SEX	ADDRESS	CITY
111111111	Kinzer	Jessica	F	3601 N.W. 75 Terr.	Miami
333333335	Lanahan	Allison	F	5454 S.W. 168 Dr.	Miami
555555555	Zimmer	Kim	F	3456 S.E. 56 St.	Miami
444444444	Miller	Steve	M	444 West Dixie Highway	North M
999999999	Fernandez	Alex	M	8890 Michigan Avenue	New Yor
666666666	Lerner	Allan	M	4321 S.W. 43 Terr.	Denver
888888888	Ryan	Michael	M	4455 S.W. 97 Avenue	Miami
777777777	Adams	Abigail	F	100 Main Street	Boston
777777777	Adams	Abigail	F	100 Main Street	Boston
123456789				1718 Vestal Drive	Coral S

Browse C:\...students\STUDENTS Rec 1/11 File

(d) File after Data Entry

STEP 6 **Add an incomplete record**

Type **SET FORMAT TO INPUT** to use the existing format file, then type **APPEND** to add the incomplete record in Figure 11.1c (the student's first name, last name, and sex are missing). Note, too, that while the format file will not accept an invalid code for sex, it does let you omit the field entirely.

STEP 7 **Examine the updated file**

Press the **F2** function key to toggle to the browse mode, then press the **PgUp** key to move to the first record and display the screen of Figure 11.1d. As you can see, Adams appears twice, followed by a blank record, followed by an incomplete record for the last student. Note, too, the status line contains the entry *Rec 1/11* to indicate that the file now contains eleven records, and that the record pointer is currently on the first record. Press **Alt+E** to pull down the exit menu and return to the dot prompt.

STEP 8 **The ADDRECD program**
Type **DO ADDRECD** to execute the add record program, then attempt to reenter the erroneous records from steps 4, 5, and 6. The program begins with a prompt for the social security number of the new student; type **777-77-7777** (the hyphens are supplied by the program), and the program will reject your entry and indicate that Abigail Adams is already in the file. Try to enter a blank record, or a record with a missing first or last name, or missing sex, and you will be similarly rejected. Eventually you will be forced to enter at least a social security number, first and last name, and sex, after which you can type **Q** to exit the program and return to the dot prompt.

The ADDRECD Program

The hands-on exercise just completed has demonstrated the difference between adding records from the dot prompt versus the use of a custom program. It has also acquainted you with data validation capabilities contained within the addition program, and the sequence in which these functions are executed. Hence, while you may have originally viewed the process of adding records to a file as a single task, it is in reality made up of several subservient functions.

It is necessary, for example, to map the screen so that values for the input variables can be entered. It is also necessary to check for the presence of a duplicate record, for the existence of the critical fields, for the validity of the input data, and so on. Although a single program could have been written to encompass the entire addition process, the length of that program would make its development extremely difficult. Accordingly, the **ADDRECD** program is divided into functional modules based on the principles of structured design, with each subservient function developed as a separate program.

The Hierarchy Chart

The relationship of the individual programs to one another within the addition process is depicted by the hierarchy chart of Figure 11.2. The names of the subordinate programs are restricted to a maximum of eight characters, yet the function of each program should still be apparent. The **INITVAR** program initializes (and defines) the memory variables that are subsequently used by the other programs. The **GETINPUT** program obtains input values from the user for the various fields within a student record. The **DATACHK** program checks the critical fields for completeness and verifies

FIGURE 11.2
The Hierarchy Chart

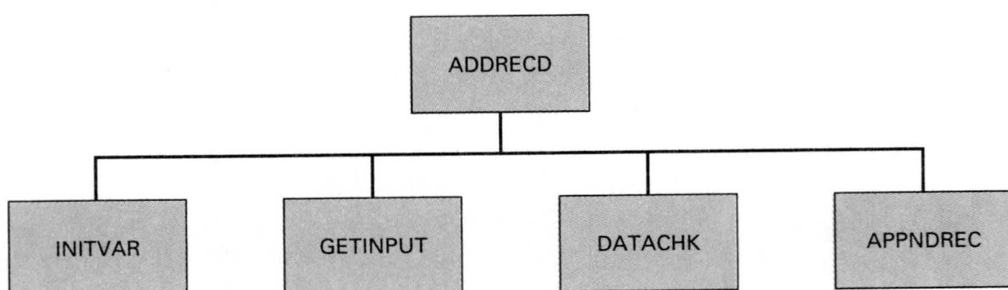

that the data is within specified limits. The **APPNDREC** program is the last one to be executed, and appends the newly created record to the **STUDENT.DBF** file, replacing fields in the **DBF** file with the corresponding values of their associated memory variables.

The necessity for the subordinate functions implies that a new record is not added immediately to a **DBF** file, but that it is stored temporarily in memory until the individual fields have been verified as correct. In other words, the values entered by the user are first placed into memory variables, checked for accuracy and completeness in the critical fields, and only when proven correct is the data moved to permanent variables, i.e., to the appropriate fields within a student record.

Recall, therefore, that the **ADDRECD** program in the hands-on exercise began by asking for the social security number of the record to be added. The program then checked that the record about to be added did not already exist, and only after an appropriate (i.e., nonduplicate) number was obtained, would the program display the screen for data entry. The critical fields in the new record were checked for completeness and validity, and the record was added only after the data was entered correctly; i.e., the program would continually prompt for a missing first or last name and/or an acceptable sex code. Each of these tasks is accomplished in a separate program in the hierarchy chart.

Explanation of the hierarchy chart of Figure 11.2 is now complete in the sense that we know the function of each of its programs. It remains, however, to link the programs to one another, and to indicate when (and how often) they are called. That in turn is the purpose of pseudocode, which implies sequence and decision-making logic, and which is developed in the next section.

Pseudocode

The **ADDRECD** program allowed several records to be added in a single session, and hence the pseudocode of Figure 11.3 is driven by an outer loop that enables records to be added continually until the user decides to quit. The loop is controlled by a switch, **add-more-records-switch**, which is set to *true* outside the loop, and reset to *false* when the user chooses to exit.

Within the loop itself there are many distinct operations, each of which has to occur in order to add a record. The user enters the social security number of the record to be added, and the program checks that the number is not already in the file. This logic is contained within an inner loop, controlled by **duplicate-switch**, that gives the user as many chances as necessary to enter a nonduplicate number.

Once a valid (i.e., nonduplicate) social security number is obtained, the program displays a screen requesting values for the remaining fields (last name, first name, and so on), checks for completeness of the critical fields and for proper entries in designated fields, and then adds the validated record. At this point the addition of the current record is finished, whereupon the program asks whether additional records are to be added or the program terminated. The logic to obtain this response is contained within yet another loop, controlled by **user-answer-switch**, that requires the user to make a valid response.

The dBASE Listing

The dBASE listing for the **ADDRECD** program is shown in Figure 11.4, and its associated documentation in Figure 11.5. The logic in the program parallels that of the pseudocode just developed, whereas its several **DO** statements provide for the transfer of control to subordinate programs within the hierarchy chart.

```
   Set add-more-records-switch to true
 ┌─DO WHILE add-more-records-switch is true
 │    Set duplicate-switch to true
 │  ┌─DO WHILE duplicate-switch is true
 │  │  ┌─DO WHILE social security number equals spaces
 │  │  │    Display message to enter social security number
 │  │  │    Get social security number of record to be entered
 │  │  └─ENDDO
 │  │  ┌─IF social security number is in file
 │  │  │    Display message indicating duplicate number
 │  │  │  ELSE
 │  │  │    Set duplicate-switch to false
 │  │  └─ENDIF
 │  └─ENDDO
 │
 │    Display screen requesting user to enter data
 │    Get user inputs for all fields
 │    Check critical user inputs for completeness
 │    Check critical user inputs for valid ranges
 │    Add validated record to file
 │
 │    Set user-answer-switch to true
 │  ┌─DO WHILE user-answer-switch is true
 │  │    Display message to add more records or exit program
 │  │  ┌─DO CASE
 │  │  │    CASE A: (Add more records)
 │  │  │       Set user-answer-switch to false
 │  │  │    CASE B: (Exit program)
 │  │  │       Set user-answer-switch to false
 │  │  │       Set add-more-records-switch to false
 │  │  │    OTHERWISE:
 │  │  │       Display message requesting valid response
 │  │  └─ENDCASE
 │  └─ENDDO
 └─ENDDO
   RETURN
```

FIGURE 11.3
Pseudocode for ADDRECD Program

The documentation in Figure 11.5 contains a program narrative to describe the overall function of the program, a listing of the called programs and procedures (a concept we explain shortly), a copy of the associated file structure, and a brief description of the memory variables contained in the program.

The **ADDRECD** program, and its associated subprograms, contain several dBASE programming statements that require additional explanation. These include various **SET** commands, ***procedures,*** the **STORE** command, the **SEEK** command, and ***public*** versus ***private variables.*** Each of these is explained below, with additional information provided in the Programmer's Notebook.

SET Commands

dBASE contains an almost inordinate number of **SET** statements that allow the programmer to control virtually every aspect of the dBASE environment. Thirty-nine **SET** commands are shown in Figure 11.6, with default values as indicated. The programmer, however, often changes the default values to conform to the requirements of a specific program, as is done in the first several statements of the **ADDRECD** program. This section provides a brief explanation of the affected parameters.

SET STATUS (default **ON**) turns the dBASE status line on or off. The status line is of little value, given the presence of custom menus within a program, and hence the parameter is set to off.

```
***ADDRECD.PRG
SET STATUS OFF
SET SAFETY OFF
SET BELL OFF
SET TALK OFF
SET SCOREBOARD OFF
SET PROCEDURE TO proclib
@ 0,0 TO 24,79 PANEL COLOR R
USE students ORDER ssn
STORE .T. TO addrecs
DO WHILE addrecs
   STORE .T. TO duplicate
   DO WHILE duplicate
      DO scrnclr
      STORE "         " TO mssn
      @ 3,20 TO 9,59 PANEL COLOR R
      @ 6,23 SAY "Social Security Number: "
      DO WHILE mssn = "         "
         @ 6,47 GET mssn PICTURE "@R 999-99-9999"
         STORE "Enter student's social security number" TO message
         DO printmsg WITH message
         READ
      ENDDO
      SEEK mssn
      IF FOUND()
         @ 7,40 TO 13,69 PANEL COLOR GR+
         STORE TRIM(firstname) + " " + lastname TO name
         @ 10,45 SAY name
         STORE "Student in file - Press any key to continue" TO message
         DO printmsg WITH message
         SET CONSOLE OFF
         WAIT
         SET CONSOLE ON
      ELSE
         STORE .F. to duplicate
      ENDIF
   ENDDO
   DO initvar
   DO getinput
   STORE "Checking data ... Please wait" TO message
   DO printmsg WITH message
   DO datachk
   STORE "Record Being Added" TO message
   DO printmsg WITH message
   DO appndrec
   DO msgclear
   @ 22,19 SAY "Enter A to add another record or Q to quit"
   STORE .T. TO needanswer
   DO WHILE needanswer
      STORE " " TO moreadd
      @ 22,63 GET moreadd PICTURE "!"
      READ
      DO msgclear
      DO CASE
         CASE moreadd = "A"
            STORE .F. TO needanswer
         CASE moreadd = "Q"
            STORE .F. TO needanswer
            STORE .F. TO addrecs
         OTHERWISE
            STORE "Please enter either A or Q" TO message
            DO printmsg WITH message
      ENDCASE
   ENDDO
ENDDO
USE
RETURN
```

FIGURE 11.4 The ADDRECD Program

Program Narrative: ADDRECD.PRG

The ADDRECD program adds records to the STUDENTS.DBF file until the user inputs a response to quit the system. Each addition is preceded by a prompt to the user to input the social security number for the record to be added. The existing file is then checked for the presence of that number, and if the record is not already in the file, the program displays an additional screen to collect the input data. Incoming records are checked for completeness, and only when a record passes all validity checks is it added to the system. The actual routines to display the input screen, validate the incoming data, and add the record to the DBF file, are performed within various called programs.

Called Programs:

INITVAR — Initializes all memory variables used to hold the input values for the various DBF fields (see Figure 11.10)
GETINPUT — Maps the screen in which the user inputs values for the various DBF fields; (see Figure 11.11)
DATACHK — Checks for the presence of data in critical fields (see Figure 11.12)
APPNDREC — Performs the actual addition to the DBF file via a series of REPLACE statements in which the values of the input memory variables are entered into the corresponding DBF fields (see Figure 11.13)

Procedures:

SCRNCLR — Clears out the inside of the box
MSGCLEAR — Clears out the message portion (line 23) of the box
PRINTMSG — Displays a message in line 23 of the screen; uses the current value of the message parameter from the ADDRECD program and centers message between margins

Data Base File: STUDENTS.DBF

Field	Field Name	Type	Width	Index	Field	Field Name	Type	Width	Index
1	SSN	Character	9	Y	9	PHONE	Character	10	N
2	LASTNAME	Character	15	Y	10	BIRTHDATE	Date	8	N
3	FIRSTNAME	Character	12	N	11	DATEADMTD	Date	8	Y
4	SEX	Character	1	N	12	CLASS	Character	4	N
5	ADDRESS	Character	25	N	13	MAJOR	Character	3	Y
6	CITY	Character	18	N	14	CREDITS	Numeric	3	N
7	STATE	Character	2	N	15	QLTYPOINTS	Numeric	3	N
8	ZIPCODE	Character	5	Y					

Memory Variables:

addrecs — switch that controls major loop of entire program; set to true initially, then set to false when user elects to quit system
duplicate — switch that prevents the addition of duplicate records; set to true prior to requesting social security number of new record; set to false when social security number is not found in the file
mssn — contains the actual social security number of the record to be added
message — contains any one of several messages, which is passed to the PRINTMSG procedure
needanswer — switch that controls the routine to obtain a user's response for adding addtional records or quitting the system
moreadd — contains the user's response to add more records or to quit system

FIGURE 11.5
Program Documentation

SET SAFETY (default ON) controls whether a confirmation message—e.g., *index file already exists, overwrite (yes or no)*—will be provided before certain files are overwritten. This information is useful from the dot prompt, but confusing to a user within the programming mode, and the parameter is turned off.

SET BELL (default ON) determines whether a beep is heard during certain operations, e.g., during data entry when the end of an input field is reached. Although

FIGURE 11.6
SET Statements

ALTERNATE	- OFF	ECHO	- OFF	NEAR	- OFF
AUTOSAVE	- OFF	ENCRYPTION	- ON	PAUSE	- OFF
BELL	- OFF	ESCAPE	- ON	PRINT	- OFF
CARRY	- OFF	EXACT	- OFF	SAFETY	- OFF
CATALOG	- OFF	EXCLUSIVE	- OFF	SCOREBOARD	- OFF
CENTURY	- OFF	FIELDS	- OFF	SPACE	- ON
CONFIRM	- OFF	FULLPATH	- OFF	SQL	- OFF
CONSOLE	- ON	HEADING	- ON	STATUS	- OFF
DEBUG	- OFF	HELP	- ON	STEP	- OFF
DELETED	- OFF	HISTORY	- ON	TALK	- OFF
DELIMITERS	- OFF	INSTRUCT	- ON	TITLE	- ON
DESIGN	- ON	INTENSITY	- ON	TRAP	- OFF
DEVELOP	- ON	LOCK	- ON	UNIQUE	- OFF

this warning may seem appropriate initially, one tires quickly of the noise and hence the parameter is turned off.

SET TALK (default ON) controls whether responses from dBASE commands are displayed on the screen. This information is useful at the dot prompt, but confusing to a user in the program mode, where it interferes with the screen design and other messages displayed by the program. The parameter is turned off.

SET SCOREBOARD (default ON) determines whether or not the dBASE status indicators (Ins, Caps, Num, and Del) are displayed on line zero when the status line is off. The parameter is turned off to give full control to the screen design within the program and thus avoid confusion with the customized menus.

SET CONSOLE (default ON) turns output to the screen on (or off). The statement is used in the ADDRECD program immediately before and after a WAIT command to suppress the normal *Press any key to continue* prompt produced by the WAIT statement. This enables the programmer to insert a more specific message, and also to place that message where desired on the screen.

Procedures

The ADDRECD program of Figure 11.4 contains a DO statement for each of the subordinate programs in the hierarchy chart; i.e., there is a DO statement to transfer control to the initialize variable program (DO initvar), a DO statement for the program to obtain user inputs (DO getinput), and so on. There are also three additional DO statements (DO scrnclr, DO printmsg, and DO msgclear), which refer to procedures rather than programs, and these are shown as shaded entries in the revised hierarchy chart of Figure 11.7.

A ***procedure*** is a group of dBASE commands, identified by a procedure name and stored in a procedure file, that is read into memory at the beginning of a program. (Note the **SET PROCEDURE** statement at the start of Figure 11.4.) A procedure is conceptually the same as a program except that it executes more efficiently, because the procedure is already in memory, whereas a program resides on disk and has to be loaded into memory each time it is executed. Note, too, that as with a program, the function of a procedure should be apparent from its name as it appears in the hierarchy chart. Thus the **scrnclr** procedure clears the screen (except for the outside border), the **printmsg** procedure prints a message (in a designated area), while the **msgclear** procedure erases a message.

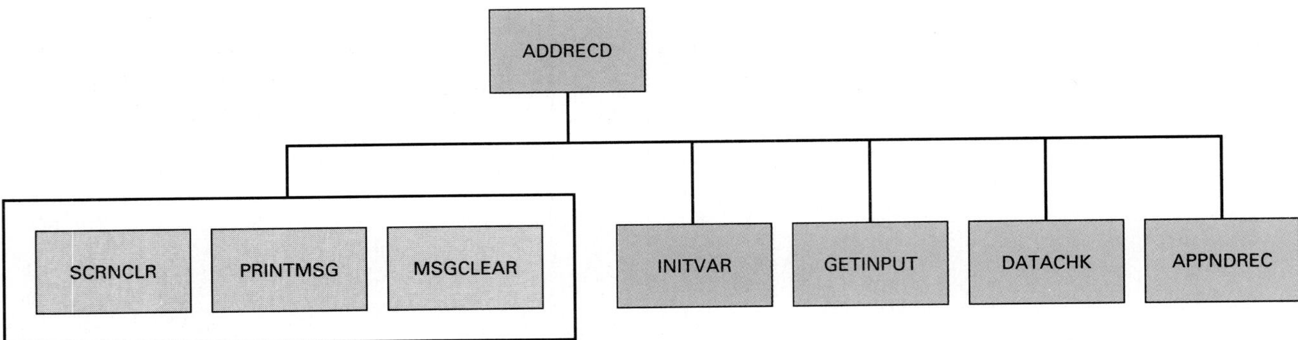

FIGURE 11.7
Revised Hierarchy Chart

Figure 11.8 displays the contents of the procedure file, **PROCLIB.PRG**, which is called by the **ADDRECD** program, and which consists of the three individual procedures (**scrnclr**, **printmsg**, and **msgclear**). Each procedure in Figure 11.8 begins with a **PROCEDURE *name*** and ends with a **RETURN** statement. The **scrnclr** procedure consists of a single **@...CLEAR** statement to clear the entire screen except for the surrounding panel. The **msgclear** procedure performs a similar function except it clears only line 23 near the bottom of the screen.

The **printmsg** procedure designates a **message *parameter*** that contains the contents of the message to be displayed. The parameter is necessary because the **printmsg** procedure is called from several places in the **ADDRECD** program, with the contents of the message determined by a **STORE** statement immediately before the **printmsg** procedure is called. In other words, logic within the **ADDRECD** program determines which message is appropriate (*Enter student's social security number, Record being added,* and so on) and then sends this information to the **printmsg** procedure via the **message** parameter. The message itself is centered on line 23 through use of the **LEN** function (see the Programmer's Notebook for additional information).

The decision as to whether a particular function should be implemented as a program or procedure is somewhat arbitrary. It would have been possible, for example, to change the four subordinate programs in the hierarchy chart to procedures or

FIGURE 11.8
Procedure (PROCLIB.PRG) File

```
***PROCLIB.PRG

*Procedure to clear the inside of the box
PROCEDURE scrnclr
@ 2,1 CLEAR TO 23,78
RETURN

*Procedure to clear message line
PROCEDURE msgclear
@ 23,1 SAY SPACE(78)
RETURN

*Procedure to display a message on the message line
PROCEDURE printmsg
PARAMETERS message
DO MSGCLEAR
@ 23,(80 - LEN(message))/2 SAY message
RETURN
```

to convert the three procedures to programs. We suggest, however, that you use procedures for frequently called routines because of efficiency in execution. Observe, therefore, that each of the procedures in our program (`scrnclr`, `msgclear`, and `printmsg`) is called from several places within the **ADDRECD** program, whereas each program is called only once (for each new record) in the program.

The STORE command

The **STORE** command allocates space for a memory variable, specifies its size and type, and assigns an initial value to that variable. All memory variables *must* be initialized, i.e., defined in a **STORE** statement, prior to being used elsewhere in the program. In the **ADDRECD** program, for example, the variable `duplicate` appears in a **STORE** statement (where it is defined as a logical variable and initialized to `.T.`) immediately prior to its use in a **DO WHILE** statement. In similar fashion, the variable `mssn` is initialized to spaces prior to its appearance in an `@...GET` statement.

The **STORE** command can also assign a new value to a variable that was defined previously in another **STORE** command; e.g., `STORE mline + 1 TO mline`, which increments the value of `mline`. The latter statement assumes that `mline` was previously defined (and initialized) in another **STORE** statement as a numeric variable, e.g., `STORE 0 TO mline`.

The SEEK Command

The **SEEK** command searches the key field of a master index for the first record matching the specified expression. It is similar in concept to the **FIND** command, except that **SEEK** includes the capability to search for an expression that includes a memory variable, and consequently **SEEK** is required in program files. The format of the command is simply, `SEEK expression`, where the expression can be a number, character string (surrounded in single or double quotes), or a memory variable.

Figure 11.9 is extracted from the **ADDRECD** program of Figure 11.4 and illustrates how the **SEEK** command is used to check for the presence of a duplicate social security number. The combination of the `@...GET` and **READ** statements obtains the social security number and stores it in the memory variable, `mssn`. The **SEEK** command then searches the **STUDENTS.DBF** file (which has been opened with an active index on social security number) for the value entered by the user. If the new social security number is found, the duplicate error message is displayed, and the user is asked for another social security number. If, on the other hand, the social security number is not found, the `DO WHILE duplicate` loop ends and the program continues.

Additional Program Listings

The remaining program listings are shown in Figures 11.10, 11.11, 11.12, and 11.13, in the sequence in which they are called from the **ADDRECD** program. We suggest that you concentrate initially on the specific functions of the individual programs, and how control is passed back and forth between the various programs, which in turn requires a discussion of public versus private variables.

Public and Private Variables

Memory variables are, by definition, either ***public*** or ***private,*** with the distinction becoming important when programs are called from one another, as occurs within

```
USE students ORDER ssn ———— Index required for SEEK statement
  .
    .
      .
STORE .T. TO duplicate
DO WHILE duplicate
   DO scrnclr
   STORE "           " TO mssn
   @ 3,20 TO 9,59 PANEL COLOR R
   @ 6,23 SAY "Social Security Number: "
   DO WHILE mssn = "           "          User inputs social security number
      @ 6,47 GET mssn PICTURE "@R 999-99-9999"
      STORE "Enter student's social security number" TO message
      DO printmsg WITH message
      READ
   ENDDO            SEEK statement
   SEEK mssn
   IF FOUND()  ———— FOUND function determines if record is in file
      @ 7,40 TO 13,69 PANEL COLOR GR+
      STORE TRIM(firstname) + " " + lastname TO name
      @ 10,45 SAY name
      STORE "Student in file - Press any key to continue" TO message
      DO printmsg WITH message
      SET CONSOLE OFF
      WAIT
      SET CONSOLE ON
   ELSE
      STORE .F. to duplicate
   ENDIF
ENDDO
```

FIGURE 11.9
Use of the SEEK Statement

FIGURE 11.10
The INITVAR Program

```
***INITVAR.PRG

PUBLIC mlastname,mfirstname,maddress,mcity,mstate,mzipcode
PUBLIC mphone,msex,mbirthdate,mdateadm,mclass,mmajor,mcredits,mqltypts
STORE SPACE(15) TO mlastname
STORE SPACE(12) TO mfirstname
STORE SPACE(25) TO maddress
STORE SPACE(18) TO mcity
STORE "  " TO mstate
STORE "     " TO mzipcode
STORE SPACE(10) TO mphone
STORE " " TO msex
STORE CTOD("  /  /  ") TO mbirthdate
STORE CTOD("  /  /  ") TO mdateadm
STORE "     " TO mclass
STORE "    " TO mmajor
STORE 0 TO mcredits
STORE 0 TO mqltypts
STORE CTOD("  /  /  ") TO mlastcall
RETURN
```

FIGURE 11.11
The GETINPUT Program

```
***GETINPUT.PRG

DO scrnclr
@ 3,4 TO 18,75 DOUBLE
@ 12,5 TO 12,74 DOUBLE
@ 15,5 TO 15,74 DOUBLE
@ 4,21 SAY "Social Security Number:"
@ 4,46 SAY mssn PICTURE "@R 999-99-9999"
@ 6,7 SAY "  First Name: "
@ 6,21 GET mfirstname PICTURE "!XXXXXXXXXX"
@ 6,41 SAY "Last Name: "
@ 6,52 GET mlastname PICTURE "!XXXXXXXXXXXXX"
@ 8,9 SAY "Address: "
@ 8,18 GET maddress PICTURE "XXXXXXXXXXXXXXXXXXXXXXXXX"
@ 8,61 SAY "Sex: "
@ 8,66 GET msex PICTURE "!"
@ 9,12 SAY "City: "
@ 9,18 GET mcity PICTURE "!XXXXXXXXXXXXXXXX"
@ 10,11 SAY "State: "
@ 10,18 GET mstate PICTURE "!!"
@ 10,23 SAY "Zipcode: "
@ 10,32 GET mzipcode PICTURE "99999"
@ 11,11 SAY "Phone: "
@ 11,18 GET mphone PICTURE "@R (999)999-9999"
@ 11,44 SAY "Date of Birth: "
@ 11,59 GET mbirthdate
@ 13,9 SAY "Date Admitted: "
@ 13,24 GET mdateadm
@ 13,47 SAY "Classification:"
@ 13,63 GET mclass PICTURE "!!!9"
@ 14,56 SAY "Major:"
@ 14,64 GET mmajor PICTURE "!!!"
@ 16,13 SAY "Number of Credits:"
@ 16,33 GET mcredits PICTURE "@Z 999"
@ 17,9 SAY "Quality Points Earned:"
@ 17,33 GET mqltypts PICTURE "@Z 999"
READ
@ 16,42 SAY "Grade Point Average: "
@ 16,63 SAY mqltypts/mcredits PICTURE "9.99"
RETURN
```

the **ADDRECD** program. A private variable is available only to the program in which it is created and/or to all programs called by the program in which it was created. A public memory variable, however, is available to any program. All memory variables created in a program are considered private unless they are specifically declared as public.

The **ADDRECD** program is at the top of the hierarchy chart and thus all of its variables are automatically available to every other program; i.e., the **ADDRECD** program contains **DO** statements to call every other program. Variables created in the subordinate programs, however—i.e., the modules on the second level of the hierarchy chart—are not available to other programs on the same or higher level, unless they are declared public.

Consider, for example, the **INITVAR** program shown in Figure 11.10, which defines the memory variables designed to hold the user inputs, e.g., **mlastname** and **mfirstname**. These variables are subsequently accessed by other programs and thus they have to be made available to those other programs; hence the **PUBLIC** declaration at the beginning of Figure 11.10.

FIGURE 11.12
The DATACHK Program

```
***DATACHK.PRG

DO WHILE mfirstname = "              "
   DO msgclear
   STORE "*** Please Enter a First Name ***" TO message
   DO printmsg WITH message
   @ 6,21 GET mfirstname
   READ
ENDDO
DO WHILE mlastname = "                  "
   DO msgclear
   STORE "*** Please Enter a Last Name ***" TO message
   DO printmsg WITH message
   @ 6,52 GET mlastname
   READ
ENDDO
STORE .T. TO notvalid
DO WHILE notvalid
   DO msgclear
   IF msex = "F" .OR. msex = "M"
      STORE .F. TO notvalid
   ELSE
      STORE "Please enter F or M"  TO message
      DO printmsg WITH message
      @ 8,66 GET msex PICTURE "!"
      READ
   ENDIF
ENDDO
RETURN
```

FIGURE 11.13
The APPNDREC Program

```
***APPNDREC.PRG
APPEND BLANK
REPLACE ssn WITH mssn
REPLACE lastname WITH mlastname
REPLACE firstname WITH mfirstname
REPLACE address WITH maddress
REPLACE city WITH mcity
REPLACE state WITH mstate
REPLACE zipcode WITH mzipcode
REPLACE phone WITH mphone
REPLACE sex WITH msex
REPLACE birthdate WITH mbirthdate
REPLACE dateadmtd WITH mdateadm
REPLACE class WITH mclass
REPLACE major WITH mmajor
REPLACE credits WITH mcredits
REPLACE qltypoints WITH mqltypts
RETURN
```

File Maintenance

The addition of records to a system, complex as it may be, is only one component of file maintenance, because as you already know, file maintenance includes a requirement for the modification and/or deletion of existing records. Also, as you might expect, the implementation of the latter two functions requires the development of additional programs to preclude problems of data entry that could otherwise occur at the dot prompt.

It is not our intent, however, to develop these programs in detail, but rather to present you with a completed system for file maintenance. (The programs to which we refer exist on the data disk, and you can explore them at your leisure as the need arises.) We continue, therefore, with a second hands-on exercise to illustrate how the edit and deletion functions are implemented from the view of the end-user. The exercise uses the *erroneous* student file at the end of the first hands-on exercise and directs you to delete the duplicate record for Adams, to delete the blank record, and finally, to edit the incomplete record for the student without a first or last name.

HANDS-ON EXERCISE 2

The File Maintenance Program

Objective
Explore the capabilities of an existing program to perform all operations associated with file maintenance.

STEP 1 **Execute the file maintenance program**
Type **DO FILEMAIN** at the dot prompt to execute the file maintenance program and produce the opening menu of Figure 11.14a. You select options from this menu as you do from any dBASE menu, i.e., by typing the first letter of the desired option or by highlighting the option and pressing the **enter** key.

STEP 2 **Delete the superfluous records**
Select *Delete a record* from the opening menu to produce the delete menu of Figure 11.14. Select *Delete a record* a second time to produce a window listing the last names in alphabetical order as shown in Figure 11.14b. Highlight the second Adams as the

FIGURE 11.14
The File Maintenance Program

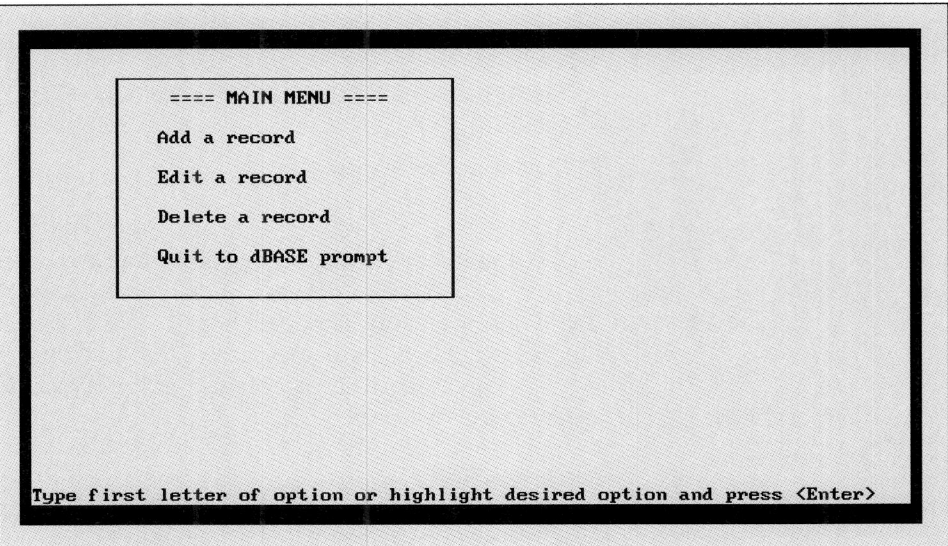

(a) Opening Menu

FIGURE 11.14
The File Maintenance Program (continued)

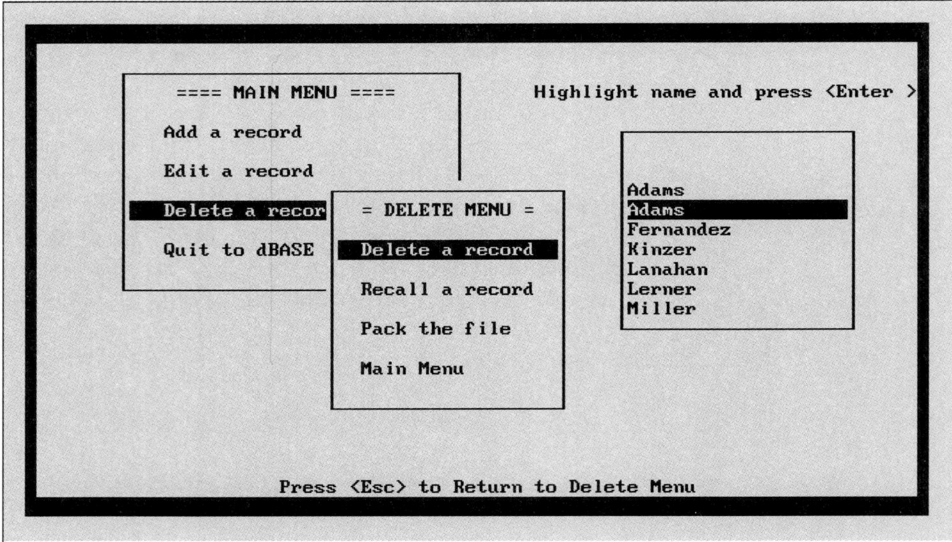

(b) Selecting a Record for Deletion

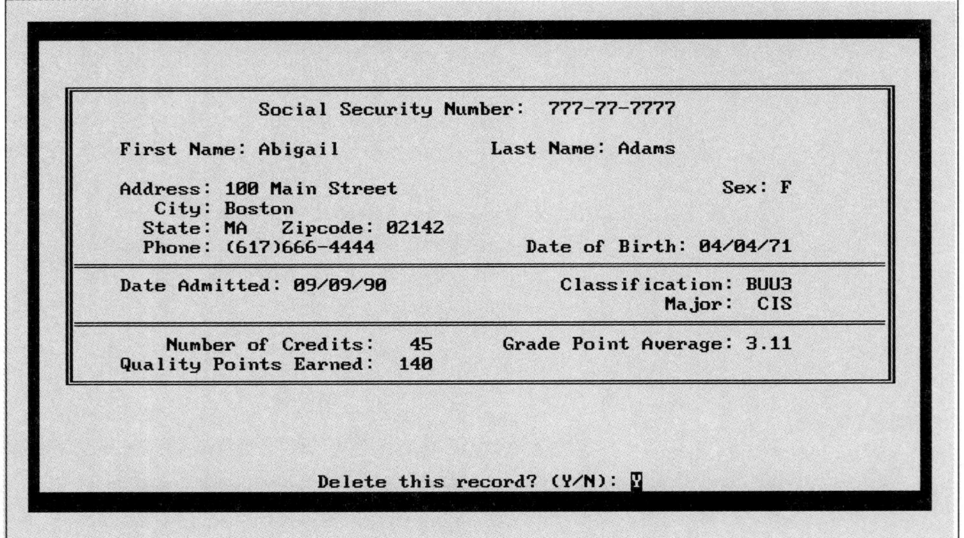

(c) Confirming the Deletion

record slated for deletion, then press **return** to produce the screen of Figure 11.14c. Type **Y** to confirm the deletion of this record, which returns you to the delete menu and window of student names; note, however, that now there is only one Adams in the file, which reflects the deletion of the superfluous record.

Highlight the first blank name and press **return**, then type **Y** to confirm the deletion and return to the delete menu.

STEP 3 **Pack the file**

The two records deleted in step two have been logically, but not physically, deleted from the **STUDENT.DBF** file; i.e., either or both can be recalled if necessary. Eventually, however, you want to permanently (physically) delete the records, which

FIGURE 11.14
The File Maintenance Program (continued)

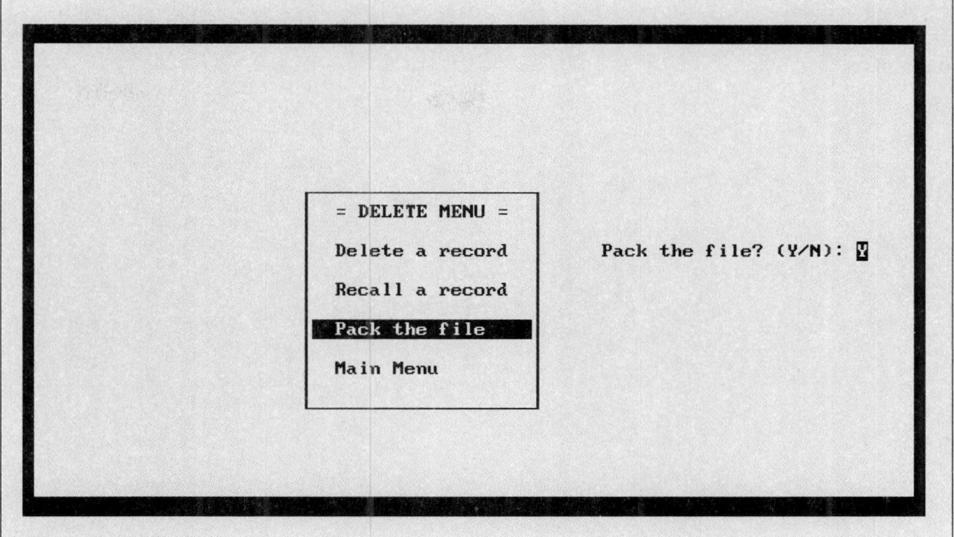

(d) Packing the File

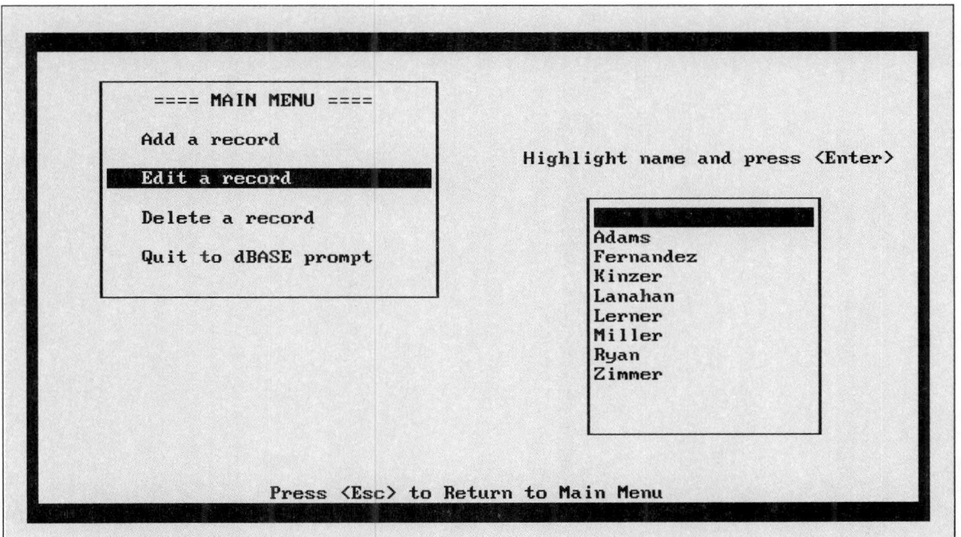

(e) Selecting a Record to Edit

requires that you select *Pack the file* from the delete menu, then type **Y** for confirmation as shown in Figure 11.14d. The records are now permanently deleted from the file with no possibility for recall.

STEP **Edit the incomplete record**

Return to the main menu and select *Edit a record* to produce the window of student names in Figure 11.14e, which no longer contains a duplicate record. Highlight the blank record (i.e., the incomplete record without a first or last name) and press **return** to produce the edit screen of Figure 11.14f. Enter the first and last names as **John** and **Doe**, respectively, then enter **M** as the student's sex. Press the **F2** function key to produce the command summary shown in the middle of the screen, press **Esc**

FIGURE 11.14
The File Maintenance Program (continued)

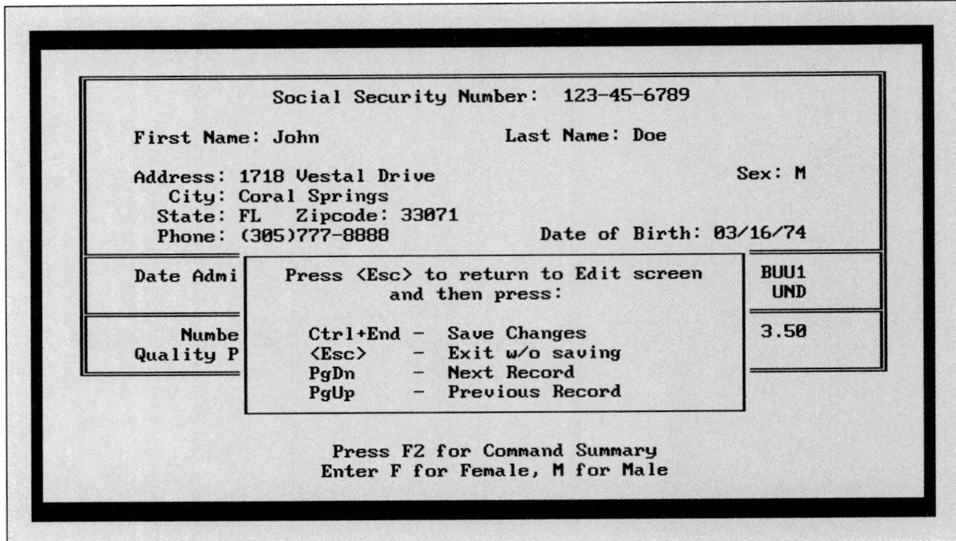

(f) The Edit Screen

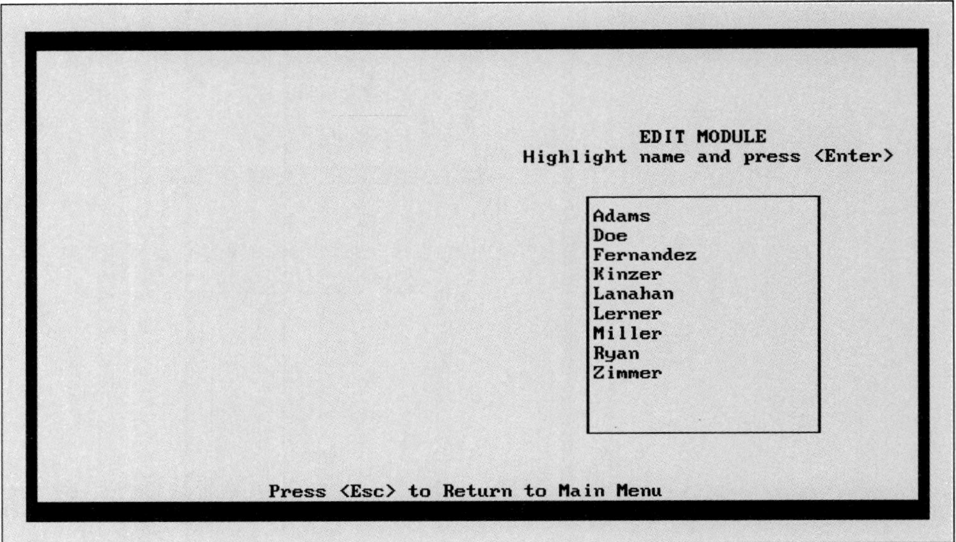

(g) The New File

to return to the edit screen, and finally press **Ctrl+End** to save the changes. You should see the window of names in Figure 11.14g, in which Doe appears in proper sequence.

STEP 5 **Exit dBASE**

Press **Esc** to return to the main menu, then select *Quit to dBASE prompt* to exit the file maintenance program and return to the dot prompt. Type **QUIT** to exit dBASE and return to DOS.

Summary

File maintenance consists of three general operations: the ***addition*** of new records, the ***modification*** of existing records, and the ***deletion*** of existing records. Any of these operations can be accomplished from the dot prompt, the applications generator, or through a custom program.

Adding records from the dot prompt, with or without a format file, cannot prevent the addition of a ***duplicate record*** or one with ***incomplete data;*** this type of data validation can be accomplished only through a custom program.

Pseudocode is a procedurally oriented technique that contains decision-making logic and implies the sequence of operations. A ***hierarchy chart,*** on the other hand, is functionally oriented; it shows what has to be done, but not when or how frequently.

A ***procedure*** is a group of dBASE commands, identified by a procedure name, and stored in a common procedure file. A procedure executes more quickly than a program because procedures reside in memory, whereas program files are read from disk each time they are executed.

The **STORE** command allocates space for a ***memory variable*** and/or assigns a value to a memory variable, erasing what was previously in that variable. All memory variables created in a program are considered ***private*** unless declared ***public.*** A private variable is available only to the program in which it is created and to all lower-level programs called by that program.

Key Words and Concepts

Critical field
Data validation
Duplicate record
File maintenance
Hierarchy chart
Incomplete data
Initialize variables
Key
`LEN()`
Memory variable
`Parameters`
Private variable
Procedure
PROCEDURE header
Pseudocode
Public variable
RETURN
SEEK
SET BELL
SET CONSOLE
SET FORMAT
SET PROCEDURE
SET SAFETY
SET SCOREBOARD
SET STATUS
SET TALK
STORE
Unique key

True/False

1. There are three basic types of file maintenance operations.
2. Certain types of data validation can be accomplished without programming.
3. Use of procedures in lieu of individual program files will speed up program execution.
4. A single procedure file, e.g., **PROCLIB.PRG**, may contain several procedures.
5. A memory variable is defined and initialized in a **STORE** statement.
6. The same procedure can be called from more than one program.
7. A procedure may be written with or without the **PARAMETERS** statement.
8. A **DO** statement may call either a program or a procedure.
9. The **RETURN** statement is normally the last statement in either a called program or a procedure.

10. The **READ** statement may be used in lieu of an **@...GET** statement to obtain the values of input variables.

Exercises

1. Distinguish between:
   (a) A procedure file and a procedure name
   (b) A program and a procedure
   (c) A DO statement and a **RETURN** statement
   (d) A called and a calling program
   (e) Pseudocode and a hierarchy chart

2. Explain the precise function of each group of statements, all of which were extracted from various programs that appeared in the chapter. You can see the effects of some of the statements by executing the commands at the dot prompt; other statements will require you to return to the chapter and/or refer to the Programmer's Notebook.
   (a) `SET CONSOLE OFF`
       `WAIT`
       `SET CONSOLE ON`
   (b) `@ 2,1 CLEAR TO 23,78`
   (c) `@ 0,0 TO 24,79 PANEL COLOR R`
   (d) `@ 23,(80-LEN(message))/2 SAY message`
   (e) `STORE TRIM(lastname) + " " + firstname TO mname`

3. Important as data validation is, it nevertheless extracts a price in terms of increased execution time. The **ADDRECD** program, for example, invokes the lower-level program **DATACHK** to ensure that critical fields have been entered and checks on the validity of the entries. Modify the **ADDRECD** program so that these checks are no longer implemented, then repeat step 8 of the first hands-on exercise.
   (a) Do you notice an appreciable change in the execution time of the program?
   (b) Would this increase significantly as large numbers of records are entered into the file?

4. Answer the following questions with respect to Figure 11.15, which displays the **STUDENTS.DBF** file at the conclusion of the second hands-on exercise.
   (a) Where is the record pointer located?
   (b) Describe two different ways to move to Miller's record.
   (c) Which menu do you pull down to delete Miller once you are there?
   (d) What indicator will appear on the status line to indicate that Miller has been deleted?
   (e) Which menu do you pull down to recall Miller?
   (f) Which menu do you pull down to pack the file and remove all records marked for deletion?

5. Figure 11.16 displays the opening screen of an application that was created through the applications generator. As you can see, the application omits both a report form and a mailing label, but does include all of the maintenance options needed for the **STUDENTS.DBF** file. (The application is on the data disk and can be reached through the control center.)
   (a) Does selection of the Add Information option eliminate the possibility of adding a duplicate and/or incomplete record?

FIGURE 11.15
Screen for Problem 4

Records Organize Fields Go To Exit

SSN	LASTNAME	FIRSTNAME	SEX	ADDRESS	CITY
111111111	Kinzer	Jessica	F	3601 N.W. 75 Terr.	Miami
333333335	Lanahan	Allison	F	5454 S.W. 168 Dr.	Miami
555555555	Zimmer	Kim	F	3456 S.E. 56 St.	Miami
444444444	Miller	Steve	M	444 West Dixie Highway	North M
999999999	Fernandez	Alex	M	8890 Michigan Avenue	New Yor
666666666	Lerner	Allan	M	4321 S.W. 43 Terr.	Denver
888888888	Ryan	Michael	M	4455 S.W. 97 Avenue	Miami
777777777	Adams	Abigail	F	100 Main Street	Boston
123456789	Doe	John		1718 Vestal Drive	Coral S

Browse C:\...student2\STUDENTS Rec 1/9 File

FIGURE 11.16
The Application Generator

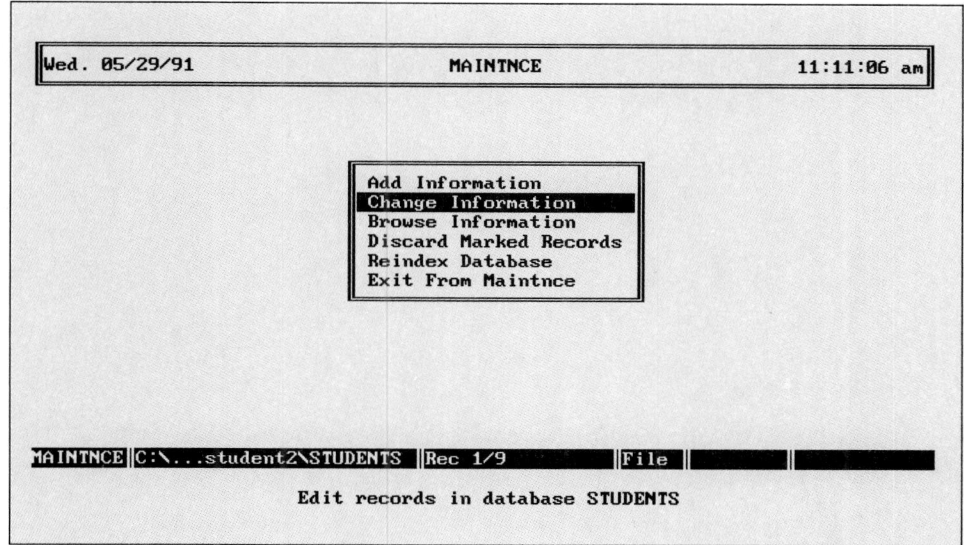

(b) Which menu option enables you to delete and/or recall a record?
(c) Which menu option packs the file?
(d) How do you move to a specific record for subsequent editing?
(e) Other than the opening menu, does the application generator offer you any capabilities beyond those available from the dot prompt?

Relational Databases

CHAPTER

12 Relational Databases

OUTLINE

OBJECTIVES

After reading this chapter you will be able to:

1. Differentiate between a file and a database; describe the advantages of the database approach in file maintenance.
2. List the characteristics of a relational database.
3. Define a one-to-many relationship and describe how it is implemented in a relational database.
4. Define a many-to-many relationship and describe how it is implemented in a relational database.
5. Define referential integrity.

Overview

The concepts of a ***relational database*** are so important that this chapter focuses exclusively on database design. Indeed, it is the only chapter in the entire text *without* any hands-on exercises, because the material is applicable to any data management system, and not just to dBASE. All of the examples in the text thus far were based on a single file and could not be classified as database systems; this chapter, however, moves beyond the earlier single-file examples to true database applications.

Our approach is to present three diverse case studies, each of which embodies a common application with which you are already familiar. The first case study centers on franchises for fast food restaurants and incorporates the concept of a ***one-to-many relationship;*** i.e., one person may own many restaurants, but a given restaurant is owned by only one person. The second case is derived from a system for student transcripts and incorporates a ***many-to-many relationship;*** i.e., one student takes many courses, and one course is taken by many students. The last application is a mail-order business and introduces additional subtleties of database design.

Each case study is introduced by a case preview to familiarize you with the essential elements of the case. The intent in all three examples is to design the file structures necessary to produce the desired information. We begin with the first case study.

CASE PREVIEW: FAST FOOD FRANCHISES

The case you are about to read is set within the context of a national corporation offering franchises for fast food restaurants. The concept of a franchise operation is familiar and exists within many industries. The parent organization develops a model operation, then franchises that concept to qualified individuals (franchisees) seeking to operate their own business. The national company teaches the franchisee to run the business, aids the person in site selection and staffing, coordinates national advertising, and so on. The franchisee pays an initial fee to open the business, followed by subsequent royalties and marketing fees to the parent corporation.

The essence of the case is simply how to relate the data for the various entities or objects, i.e., the *restaurants, franchisees,* and *contracts,* to one another. One approach is to develop a single restaurant file, with each restaurant record containing data about the owner and contract arrangement. As we shall see, that design leads to problems of ***redundancy*** whenever the same person owns more than one restaurant or when several restaurants are governed by the same contract type. A better approach is to develop separate files, one for each of the ***objects*** (restaurants, franchisees, and contracts).

Realize, too, that the objects in the case have a definite relationship to one another, which must be reflected in the file design. The corporation encourages individuals to own multiple restaurants, creating a ***one-to-many relationship*** between franchisees and restaurants. In similar fashion each restaurant is governed by one of three contract types, producing a second one-to-many relationship between contracts and restaurants.

We continue with the case presentation.

CASE STUDY
Fast Food Franchises

The management of a national chain is seeking to automate its restaurant, franchisee, and contract data. The company wants an information system whereby it could obtain, for any given restaurant, the annual sales, type of contract in effect, and/or detailed information about the restaurant owner. The company also needs to know the location of each restaurant, all restaurants in a given state, and all restaurants managed by a particular contract type. The various contract arrangements are described below:

- **Contract 1**—99-year term requiring a one-time fee of $250,000, payable at the time the franchise is awarded. In addition, the franchisee must pay a royalty of two percent of the restaurant's gross sales to the parent corporation, and contribute an additional two percent of sales to the parent corporation for advertising.
- **Contract 2**—5-year term (renewable at franchisee's option), requiring an initial payment of $50,000. In addition, the franchisee must pay a royalty of four percent of the restaurant's gross sales to the parent corporation, and contribute an additional three percent of sales to the parent corporation for advertising.
- **Contract 3**—10-year term (renewable at franchisee's option), requiring an initial payment of $75,000. In addition, the franchisee must pay a royalty of three percent of the restaurant's gross sales to the parent corporation, and contribute an additional three percent of sales to the parent corporation for advertising.

Other contract types may be offered in the future. The company currently has 500 restaurants, of which 200 are company owned. Expansion plans call for opening an additional 200 restaurants each year for the next three years, all of which are to be franchised. There is no limit on the number of restaurants an individual may own, and franchisees are encouraged to apply for multiple restaurants.

Develop a file structure to accommodate all of the above, and in addition enable the company to do all of the following:

1. List all restaurants for a given franchisee.
2. List all restaurants for a given contract type.
3. List all restaurants in the state of Florida with gross sales of over $200,000.
4. List all contract types.
5. List all franchisees in alphabetical order.
6. Display the phone number of a particular franchisee.
7. Display the address of a particular restaurant.
8. Display the initial fee for a particular contract type.

CASE SOLUTION

The initial concern in this, or any other, system is how best to structure the data so that the solution satisfies the information requirements of the client. Since the objective of this case study is to illustrate the advantages of database processing over a single-file representation, we present both ways of structuring the data in order to draw comparisons. Accordingly, the first solution is based on a single restaurant file, and will be shown to have several limitations. The second solution introduces the concept of a relational database and consists of three files (for the restaurants, franchisees, and contracts).

Single-file Solution

The single-file solution is shown in Figure 12.1a. Each record within the file contains data about a particular restaurant, its franchisee (owner), and contract type. There are five restaurants in our example, each with a *unique* restaurant number. At first glance, Figure 12.1a appears to satisfy the case requirements, yet there are three specific types of problems associated with this solution. These are:

1. Difficulties in the modification of data for an existing franchisee or contract type.

Restaurant Number	Restaurant Data (Address, annual sales . . .)	Franchisee Data (Name, telephone, address . . .)	Contract Data (Type, term, initial fee . . .)
R1	Restaurant data for Miami . . .	Franchisee data (Grauer . . .)	Contract data (Type 1 . . .)
R2	Restaurant data for Coral Gables . . .	Franchisee data (Moldof . . .)	Contract data (Type 1 . . .)
R3	Restaurant data for Fort Lauderdale. . .	Franchisee data (Grauer . . .)	Contract data (Type 2 . . .)
R4	Restaurant data for New York . . .	Franchisee data (Glassman . . .)	Contract data (Type 1 . . .)
R5	Restaurant data for Coral Springs . . .	Franchisee data (Coulter . . .)	Contract data (Type 3 . . .)

(a) Single-file Solution

Restaurant Number	Restaurant Data	Franchisee Number	Contract Type
R1	Restaurant data for Miami . . .	F1	C1
R2	Restaurant data for Coral Gables . . .	F2	C1
R3	Restaurant data for Fort Lauderdale. . .	F1	C2
R4	Restaurant data for New York . . .	F3	C1
R5	Restaurant data for Coral Springs . . .	F4	C3

Contract Type	Contract Data
C1	Contract data . . .
C2	Contract data . . .
C3	Contract data . . .

Franchisee Number	Franchisee Data (Name, telephone, address . . .)
F1	Grauer. . .
F2	Moldof. . .
F3	Glassman. . .
F4	Coulter. . .

(b) Multiple-file Solution

FIGURE 12.1
Single- versus Multiple-file Solution

2. Difficulties in the addition of a new franchisee or contract type, in that these entities must first be associated with a particular restaurant.
3. Difficulties in the deletion of a restaurant, in that data for a particular franchisee or contract type may be deleted as well.

The first problem, modification of data about an existing franchisee or contract type, stems from ***redundancy,*** which in turn requires that any change to duplicated data be made in several places throughout the file. In other words, any modification to a duplicated entry, such as a change in data for a franchisee with multiple restaurants (e.g., Grauer, who owns restaurants in Miami and Fort Lauderdale), requires a search through the entire file to find *all* instances of that data so that the *identical modification* can be made to each of the records. A similar procedure would have to be followed should data change about a duplicated contract (e.g., a change in the royalty percentage for contract type 1, which applies to restaurants R1, R2, and R4). This is, to say the least, a time-consuming and error-prone procedure.

The addition of a new franchisee or contract type poses a different type of problem. It is only logical, for example, that potential franchisees must apply to the corporation and qualify for ownership *prior* to having a restaurant assigned to them. It is also logical that the corporation would develop a new contract type *prior* to offering that contract to an existing restaurant. Neither of these events is easily accommodated in the file structure of Figure 12.1a, which requires the *previous existence* of a "dummy" restaurant record to accommodate the new franchisee or contract type.

The deletion of a restaurant creates yet another type of difficulty. What happens, for example, if the company decides to close restaurant R5 because of insufficient sales? The record for this restaurant would disappear as expected, but so too would the data for the franchisee (Coulter), and the contract type (C3), which is not intended. The corporation might want to award Coulter another restaurant in the future and/or offer this contract type to other restaurants. Neither situation would be possible as the relevant data would have been lost with the deletion of the restaurant record.

Multiple-file Solution

A much better solution appears in Figure 12.1b, which uses a *different* file for each of the three ***entities*** (restaurants, franchisees, and contracts) that exist in the system. Every record in the restaurant file is assigned a ***unique*** restaurant number (R1, R2, and so on), just as every record in the franchisee file is given a unique franchisee number (F1, F2, etc.), and every contract record has a unique contract number.

The files are linked to one another through the franchisee and/or contract numbers, which also appear in the restaurant file. Every record in the restaurant file is associated with its appropriate record in the franchisee file through the franchisee number common to both files. In similar fashion, every restaurant is tied to its appropriate contract through the contract number, which appears in the restaurant record. This solution may seem complicated, but it is really quite simple and elegant.

Assume, for example, that we want the name of the franchisee for restaurant R5, and further, that we need the details of the contract type for this restaurant. We retrieve the appropriate restaurant record, which contains franchisee and contract numbers of F4 and C3, respectively. We then search through the franchisee file for franchisee F4 (obtaining all necessary information about Coulter), and search again through the contract file for contract C3 (obtaining the data for this contract type). The process is depicted graphically in Figure 12.1b.

The multiple-file solution may require slightly more effort to retrieve information, but this is more than offset by advantages of file maintenance. Consider, for example, a change in data for contract type 1, which currently governs restaurants R1, R2, and R4. All that is necessary is to go into the contract file, find record C1, and make the changes. The records in the restaurant file are *not* affected because the restaurant records do not contain contract data per se, only the key of the corresponding contract record. In other words, the change in data for contract type 1 is made in one place (the contract file), yet that change is reflected for all affected restaurants. This is in contrast to the single-file solution of Figure 12.1a, which requires the identical modification in three places.

The addition of new records, for franchisees or contracts, is done immediately in the appropriate files of Figure 12.1b. The corporation simply adds a franchisee or contract record as these events occur, without the necessity of a corresponding restaurant record. This is much easier than the approach of Figure 12.1a, which required an existing restaurant in order to add one of the other entities.

The deletion of a restaurant is also easier than with the single-file organization. You could, for example, delete restaurant R5 without losing the associated franchisee and contract data as these records exist in different files.

Queries to the Database

By now you should be convinced of the advantages of the multiple-file approach and how it facilitates all types of file maintenance. However, the ultimate objective of any system is to produce information and it is in this area that the design excels. Consider now Figure 12.2, which expands upon the multiple-file solution to include additional data for the respective files.

To be absolutely sure you understand the multiple-file solution of Figure 12.2, use it to answer the following questions, then check your answers with those provided.

Questions

1. Who owns restaurant R2? What contract type is in effect for this restaurant?
2. What is the address of restaurant R4?
3. Which restaurants are owned by Mr. Grauer?
4. List all restaurants for contract C1.

FIGURE 12.2
Fast Food Franchises

Restaurant Number	Street Address	City	State	Zip Code	Annual Sales	Franchisee Number	Contract Type
R1	11001 Ponce de Leon Blvd	Miami	FL	33361	$600,000	F1	C1
R2	31 West Rivo Alto Road	Coral Gables	FL	33139	$450,000	F2	C1
R3	333 Las Olas Blvd	Fort Lauderdale	FL	33033	$250,000	F1	C2
R4	1700 Broadway	New York	NY	33071	$1,750,000	F3	C1
R5	1300 Sample Road	Coral Springs	FL	10292	$50,000	F4	C3

(a) Restaurant File

Franchisee Number	Franchisee Name	Telephone	Street Address	City	State	Zip Code
F1	Grauer	(305) 755-1000	2133 NW 102 Terrace	Coral Springs	FL	33071
F2	Moldof	(305) 753-4614	1400 Lejeune Blvd	Miami	FL	33365
F3	Glassman	(212) 458-5054	555 Fifth Avenue	New York	NY	10024
F4	Coulter	(305) 755-0910	1000 Federal Highway	Fort Lauderdale	FL	33033

(b) Franchisee File

Contract Type	Term (years)	Initial Fee	Royalty Pct	Advertising Pct
C1	99	$250,000	2%	2%
C2	5	$50,000	4%	3%
C3	10	$75,000	3%	3%

(c) Contract File

5. Which restaurants in Florida have gross sales over $300,000?
6. List all contract types.
7. Which contract type has the lowest initial fee? How much is the initial fee? Which restaurants are governed by this contract?
8. How many franchisees are there? What are their names?
9. What are the royalty and advertising percentages for restaurant R3?

Answers

1. Restaurant R2 is owned by Moldof and governed by contract C1.
2. Restaurant R4 is located at 1700 Broadway, New York, NY.
3. Mr. Grauer owns restaurants R1 and R3.
4. R1, R2, and R4 are governed by contract type C1.
5. The restaurants in Florida with gross sales over $300,000 are R1 ($600,000) and R2 ($450,000).
6. The existing contract types are C1, C2, and C3.
7. Contract type C2 has the lowest initial fee ($50,000); restaurant R3 is governed by this contract type.
8. There are four franchisees: Grauer, Moldof, Glassman, and Coulter.
9. Restaurant R3 is governed by contract C2 with royalty and advertising percentages of four and three percent, respectively.

The Relational Model

The multiple-file structure depicted in Figure 12.2 is an example of a ***relational database,*** a particular type of database organization consisting of a series of two-dimensional tables (also known as files or relations), from where the approach gets its name. Each table in a relational database stores data about a different type of entity in the physical system (e.g., restaurants, franchisees, and contracts). The relational model was first proposed by Dr. ***Edgar F. Codd*** of IBM in 1970.

Table 12.1 displays the terminology used in conjunction with relational databases. The first column displays the formal terms used by Dr. Codd, who spoke in terms of ***relation, tuple,*** and ***attribute.*** Our preference, however, is to use the alternative terms ***table, row,*** and ***column,*** whereas other texts may use traditional data processing terms of ***file, record,*** and ***field.***

The relational model requires that every entity in a system (restaurants, franchisees, or contracts) be given its own table, with every occurrence of that entity (a specific restaurant, franchisee, or contract type) established as a row within the table. The properties of the various entities are entered into the appropriate columns. The order of the various rows and columns within a table is immaterial.

Every row in every table of a relational database is distinct because there must be (at least) one column (or combination of columns) that uniquely identifies that row. The unique column (or combination of columns) is known as the ***primary key.***

TABLE 12.1 **Terminology for the Relational Model**

Formal Term	Alternative Term	Traditional Term
relation	table	file
tuple	row	record
attribute	column	field

The restaurant number, for example, is different for every restaurant in the restaurant table, just as the franchisee number is unique in the franchisee table, and the contract type is distinct in the contract table.

The same column name can, however, appear in multiple tables; e.g., franchisee number appears in both the franchisee table, where its values are unique, and in the restaurant table, where they are not. This is precisely how we implement the one-to-many relationship between franchisees and restaurants; i.e., we enter franchisee number (the primary key in the franchisee table) as a column in the restaurant table where it (the franchisee number) is known as a ***foreign key.*** In similar fashion, contract type (the primary key in the contract table) appears as a foreign key in the restaurant table, to implement the one-to-many relationship between contracts and restaurants.

It is helpful, perhaps, to restate these observations about a relational database in general terms:

1. Every object (entity) requires its own table.
2. Every row is distinct due to the existence of a unique column (or combination of columns) known as the primary key.
3. The order of rows in a table is immaterial.
4. Every column has a distinct name, but the same column name can appear in multiple tables.
5. The order of columns in a table is immaterial although the primary key is generally listed first.
6. The number of columns is the same in every row of the table.

The essence of a relational database can be captured with the phrase, *"The key, the whole key, and nothing but the key . . . so help me Codd,"* adherence to which also ensures the validity of a design. Simply stated, the value of every column other than the primary key depends on the key in that row, on the entire key, and on nothing but that key.

Referential Integrity

One other concept is critical in the study of relational databases, that of ***referential integrity,*** which implies that the tables in a database are consistent with one another. Consider once again the first row in the restaurant table of Figure 12.2a, which indicates that the restaurant is owned by franchisee F1 and governed by contract type C1. Recall, also, how these values are used to obtain additional information about the franchisee or contract type from the appropriate table in Figure 12.2b or 12.2c, respectively.

What if, however, the restaurant table referred to franchisee number F1000 or contract type C9, neither of which exists in the database of Figure 12.2? We would have a problem because the tables are inconsistent with one another; i.e., the restaurant table refers to rows in the franchisee and contract tables that do not exist. Suffice it to say therefore that data validation is critical when establishing or maintaining a database, and that no system, relational or otherwise, can compensate for inaccurate or incomplete data. The responsibility for maintaining the referential integrity of a database is typically left to the user.

CASE PREVIEW: STUDENT TRANSCRIPTS

Our second case is set within the context of student transcripts and expands the concept of a relational database to implement a many-to-many relationship. The system is intended to track *students* and their *courses;* the many-to-many relationship occurs because one student takes many courses, while at the same time one course is taken by many students. The objective of this case is simply how to relate the student and course tables to one another to produce desired information. The resulting file structure must be able to answer queries about a particular student or course, as well as list all courses taken by one student or all students in one course.

CASE STUDY
Student Transcripts

The registrar of a major university is seeking to convert its enrollment and course data to a relational database to facilitate on-line registration. The student table will contain the student's name, address, major, date of entry into the school, cumulative credits, and cumulative quality points. The course table is to contain the unique six-character course identifier, the course title, and the number of credits. Use common sense as to any additional columns for data you deem relevant in either table.

The system should be able to display all facts about a particular student, e.g., John Smith; all facts about a particular course, e.g., CIS120; as well as all facts (grade and semester) about a student/course combination, e.g., John Smith in CIS120.

Develop the file structures to accommodate all of the above, being sure to indicate which columns are unique. Your solution should enable a user to, at a minimum, do all of the following:

1. List all courses currently offered, in sequence by course identifier.
2. List all courses for a particular student.
3. List all students in alphabetical order.
4. List all students who took a specific course in a specific semester.
5. List all students who received an A in a specific course, regardless of when the course was taken.
6. Display the title of a particular course.
7. List all four-credit courses.

CASE SOLUTION

The initial solution of Figure 12.3 consists of two tables, for courses and students, corresponding to the two entities in the physical system. There are no problems of redundancy; i.e., data for a particular course (its description and number of credits) appears only once in the course table, just as data for a particular student appears only once in the student table. New courses will be added directly to the course table, just as new students will be added to the student table.

The design of the student table makes it easy to list all courses for one student; it is more difficult, however, to list all students in one course. Even if this were not the case, the solution is complicated by the irregular shape of the student table; i.e., its rows are of varying length according to the number of courses taken by each student. Not only is this design awkward, but how do we know in advance how much space to allocate for each student?

The problems inherent in Figure 12.3 stem from the many-to-many relationship that exists between students and courses. The solution is to eliminate the ***repeating groups*** (course number, semester, and grade) that occur in each row of the student table in Figure 12.3, in favor of the additional table shown in Figure 12.4. Note, too, that (as required by the relational model) each row in the new table is unique because the combination of student number, course number, and semester is unique.

In other words, a many-to-many relationship requires an additional table, with a ***combined key*** consisting (at a minimum) of the keys of the individual entities. *The many-to-many table may also contain additional columns that exist as a result of the combination* ***(intersection)*** *of the individual keys;* e.g., the combination of student S1, course ACC101, and Spring 1992 is unique and results in a grade of A.

Review once more the properties of a relational database, then verify that the solution in Figure 12.4 adheres to these requirements. Finally, to be absolutely sure that you understand the solution, and to illustrate once again the power of the rela-

Course Number	Course Description	Credits
ACC101	Introduction to Accounting	3
CHM100	Survey of Chemistry	3
CHM101	Chemistry Lab	1
CIS120	Microcomputer Applications	3
ENG100	Freshman English	3
MTH100	Calculus with Analytic Geometry	4
MUS110	Music Appreciation	2
SPN100	Spanish I	3

(a) Course Table

Student Number	Student Data	Courses taken with grade and semester											
S1	Student data (Adams. . .)	ACC101	SP92	A	CIS120	FA91	A	MU100	SP91	B			
S2	Student data (Fox. . .)	ENG100	SP92	B	MTH100	SP92	B	SPN100	SP92	B	CIS120	FA91	A
S3	Student data (Baker. . .)	ACC101	SP92	C	ENG100	SP92	B	MTH100	FA91	C	CIS120	FA91	B
S4	Student data (Jones. . .)	ENG100	SP92	A	MTH100	SP92	A						
S5	Student data (Smith. . .)	CIS120	SP92	C	ENG100	SP92	B	MTH100	SP92	A			

(b) Student Table

FIGURE 12.3
Registration System (repeating groups)

tional model, use Figure 12.4 to answer the following questions about the student database.

Questions

1. How many courses are currently offered?
2. List all three-credit courses.
3. Which courses has Smith taken during his stay at the university?
4. Which students have taken MTH100?
5. Which courses did Adams take during the Fall 1991 semester?
6. Which students took Microcomputer Applications in the Fall 1991 semester?
7. Which students received an A in Freshman English during the Spring 1992 semester?

Answers

1. Eight courses are offered.
2. The three-credit courses are ACC101, CHM100, CIS120, ENG100, and SPN100.
3. Smith has taken CIS120, ENG100, and MTH100.
4. Fox, Baker, Jones, and Smith have taken MTH100.
5. Adams took CIS120 during the Fall 1991 semester.

Course Number	Course Description	Credits
ACC101	Introduction to Accounting	3
CHM100	Survey of Chemistry	3
CHM101	Chemistry Lab	1
CIS120	Microcomputer Applications	3
ENG100	Freshman English	3
MTH100	Calculus with Analytic Geometry	4
MUS110	Music Appreciation	2
SPN100	Spanish I	3

(a) Course Table

Student Number	Student Data
S1	Student data (Adams. . .)
S2	Student data (Fox. . .)
S3	Student data (Baker. . .)
S4	Student data (Jones. . .)
S5	Student data (Smith. . .)

(b) Student Table

Student Number	Course Number	Semester	Grade
S1	ACC101	SP92	A
S1	CIS120	FA91	A
S1	MUS100	SP91	B
S2	ENG100	SP92	B
S2	MTH100	SP92	B
S2	SPN100	SP92	B
S2	CIS120	FA91	A
S3	ACC101	SP92	C
S3	ENG100	SP92	B
S3	MTH100	FA91	C
S3	CIS120	FA91	B
S4	ENG100	SP92	A
S4	MTH100	SP92	A
S5	CIS120	SP92	C
S5	ENG100	SP92	B
S5	MTH100	SP92	A

(c) Student/Course Table

FIGURE 12.4
Registration System (improved design)

6. Adams, Fox, and Baker took Microcomputer Applications in the Fall 1991 semester.
7. Jones was the only student to receive an A in Freshman English during the Spring 1992 semester.

CASE PREVIEW: MAIL-ORDER SYSTEMS

Our final case is set within the context of a mail-order system to monitor *customers, products,* and *orders*. The system contains both a one-to-many and a many-to-many relationship and thus serves as an effective review of all we have covered. In addition, the system has a subtle complexity not found in either the restaurant or transcript example.

CASE STUDY
Mail-order Systems

You have all been on the receiving end of one or more mail-order catalogs, the subject of this discussion. Many of these mail-order companies work the same way; i.e., they publish a catalog describing their product offerings, mail the catalog, and hope for the best.

The mail-order company maintains a list of customers, storing for each customer data associated with that particular customer, e.g., the person's name, address, and credit rating. It also maintains a separate list of products it sells, storing for each product a product number, description, quantity on hand, and cost.

The problem is to design a database capable of tracking orders as they are received. Each incoming order is assigned a unique order number with additional information about the order—e.g., the date the order was received, the customer who placed it, the products that were ordered, and the quantity of each product. One order can contain several products, and one customer can, of course, place multiple orders.

The design must also accommodate a variable-pricing policy, in which the same product is sold at different prices, depending on whether a special is in effect at the time of the order. The system must be able to produce an invoice for the order with the amount due.

Design a relational database to satisfy these requirements, and in addition, to be capable of answering queries such as the following:

1. List all orders.
2. List all customers.
3. List all products.
4. List all orders for a particular customer.
5. Produce an invoice for a particular order, listing the individual products ordered and the total amount of the order.
6. Display the name and address of the customer placing a particular order.
7. List all orders containing a particular product.

CASE SOLUTION

The solution in Figure 12.5 includes tables for two of the three entities, *products* and *customers,* as well as an order/product table to represent the many-to-many relationship between orders and products. It does not, however, contain a separate table for *orders,* which, as we shall see, leads to difficulty later on. Nevertheless, Figure 12.5 appears to satisfy all of the case requirements.

As indicated, the order/product table in Figure 12.5c implements the many-to-many relationship between orders and products (the combination of order number and product number is unique), making it possible to obtain all products in one order or all orders specifying one product. The same table also accommodates the one-to-many relationship between customers and orders, so that we can retrieve the customer associated with a particular order or list all orders for one customer.

What then, if anything, is wrong with Figure 12.5? Look carefully at the first three rows in the order/product table of Figure 12.5c, asking yourself who placed order O1—or, alternatively, on what date was the order placed? The answer is customer C2 on 12/12/91; the problem is that you can obtain the answer from any of the first three rows. In other words, there is a subtle redundancy regarding the placement of order O1 in that the same facts (who and when the order was placed) are stored in more than one row of the table.

A better approach is to include an additional order table, as is done in Figure 12.6c, and a revised order/product table (eliminating the customer number and order date) as shown in Figure 12.6d. The design in Figure 12.6 may appear more complicated in that it contains an additional table, yet it is superior because it eliminates the redundant information about who placed the order and when the order was taken. Note, too, that had we adhered to the original guideline of including a separate table for each physical entity (products, customers, and orders), we would have arrived at Figure 12.6 directly.

Product Number	Product Description	Quantity on Hand	Cost
P1	Widgets	1000	$8.00
P2	Gadgets	750	$1.00
P3	Super Widgets	500	$25.00
P4	Super Gadgets	250	$35.00

(a) Product Table

Customer Number	Customer Name	Credit Rating	Outstanding Balance	Street Address	City	State	Zipcode
C1	Bartolini	A	$0.00	1000 Fifth Avenue	New York	NY	10024
C2	Moldof	A	$500.00	555 Broadway	New York	NY	10036
C3	Simon	B	$350.00	1200 Ninth Avenue	West Orange	NJ	07632
C4	Fegan	C	$125.00	330 Queens Boulevard	Elmhurst	NY	11373
C5	Flynn	B	$0.00	1500 Elm Street	Middle Village	NY	11369

(b) Customer Table

Order Number	Product Number	Quantity Ordered	Price Quoted	Customer Number	Date
O1	P1	50	$10.00	C2	12/12/91
O1	P2	100	$2.00	C2	12/12/91
O1	P3	25	$50.00	C2	12/12/91
O2	P2	500	$1.50	C1	12/12/91
O3	P1	50	$10.00	C5	12/13/91
O3	P3	50	$45.00	C5	12/13/91
O4	P2	500	$1.50	C2	12/14/91
O4	P3	20	$20.00	C2	12/14/91
O5	P1	25	$12.00	C3	12/15/91

(c) Order/Product Table

FIGURE 12.5
Mail-order System (subtle redundancy)

Finally, as we have done throughout the chapter, we conclude the solution by considering the types of queries that can be directed to the database of Figure 12.6. Once again the answers are shown following the questions. Accordingly, review our solution, being sure you can answer the following questions about Figure 12.6:

Questions

1. Which customer placed order O1?
2. How many different products does the company offer?
3. What is the company's cost of product P3?
4. What price was quoted for product P3 in order O1?
5. What was the total cost of order O4?
6. How many units of product P2 were ordered during December 1991?
7. Which orders were placed by Mr. Moldof?

Product Number	Product Description	Quantity on Hand	Cost
P1	Widgets	1000	$8.00
P2	Gadgets	750	$1.00
P3	Super Widgets	500	$25.00
P4	Super Gadgets	250	$35.00

(a) Product Table

Customer Number	Customer Name	Credit Rating	Outstanding Balance	Street Address	City	State	Zipcode
C1	Bartolini	A	$0.00	1000 Fifth Avenue	New York	NY	10024
C2	Moldof	A	$500.00	555 Broadway	New York	NY	10036
C3	Simon	B	$350.00	1200 Ninth Avenue	West Orange	NJ	07632
C4	Fegan	C	$125.00	330 Queens Boulevard	Elmhurst	NY	11373
C5	Flynn	B	$0.00	1500 Elm Street	Middle Village	NY	11369

(b) Customer Table

Order Number	Customer Number	Date
O1	C2	12/12/91
O2	C1	12/12/91
O3	C5	12/13/91
O4	C2	12/14/91
O5	C3	12/15/91

(c) Order Table

Order Number	Product Number	Quantity Ordered	Price Quoted
O1	P1	50	$10.00
O1	P2	100	$2.00
O1	P3	25	$50.00
O2	P2	500	$1.50
O3	P1	50	$10.00
O3	P3	50	$45.00
O4	P2	500	$1.50
O4	P3	20	$20.00
O5	P1	25	$12.00

(d) Order/Product Table

FIGURE 12.6
Mail-order System (improved design)

Answers

1. Moldof placed order O1.
2. The company offers four different products.
3. The company's cost of product P3 is $25.00.
4. The quoted price for product P3 in order O1 was $50.00.
5. The total cost of order O4 was $1150.
6. 1100 units of product P2 were ordered during December 1991.
7. Moldof placed orders O1 and O4.

Summary

A ***relational database*** is a collection of ***tables***, with each table consisting of ***rows*** and ***columns.*** Each ***entity*** in the physical system requires its own table in the database. The order of the rows and columns within a table is immaterial.

A ***one-to-many*** relationship (e.g., one franchisee can own many restaurants) requires that the ***key*** of the *singular* item (franchisee) appear as a ***foreign key*** in the table of the *many* item (restaurant).

A ***many-to-many*** relationship (e.g., one student takes many courses and one course is taken by many students) requires an additional (student/course) table with the combined key consisting of the keys of the individual entities.

Referential integrity ensures that the information in a database is internally consistent. Responsibility for maintaining referential integrity typically rests with the user.

Key Words and Concepts

Attribute
Column
Combined key
Entity
Field
File
Foreign key
Intersection
Many-to-many relationship
Object
One-to-many relationship
Primary key
Queries
Record
Redundancy
Referential integrity
Relation
Relational database
Repeating group
Row
Table
Tuple
Unique

True/False

1. The identical column name can appear in multiple tables within the same database.
2. The individual tables within a database must all contain the same number of rows.
3. Referential integrity refers to the accuracy of the reference manuals.
4. The order of individual rows and/or columns within a table is immaterial.
5. The relational model is incapable of expressing a many-to-many relationship.
6. File, relation, and table are equivalent terms.
7. Relation, attribute, and tuple are equivalent terms.
8. Every one-to-many relationship in a database requires its own table.
9. Repeating groups are necessary to express a many-to-many relationship.
10. The elimination of repeating groups automatically eliminates all redundancy within the database.

Exercises

1. Answer the following with respect to the relational database of Figure 00.2.
   (a) What are the name, address, and telephone number of the owner of restaurant R3?
   (b) Which restaurants have annual sales of $300,000 or less? Who owns the restaurants in question?
   (c) What initial fee was charged for restaurant R5? What are the royalty and advertising percentages in effect for this restaurant?
   (d) How much does restaurant R3 owe to the corporation in royalty and advertising fees for the coming year? (Answer in dollars, as opposed to percentages.)
   (e) Which contract type has the highest initial fee? What is that amount?
   (f) Which restaurant has the highest annual sales? How much?
   (g) Which franchisees do not live in Florida?

(h) What is the total paid to the corporation in initial fees for the five existing restaurants?
(i) Who owns the restaurant with the highest annual sales?

2. Indicate the effect of each of the following transactions on the relational database of Figure 12.2. *Each transaction refers to the original database and thus is to be treated independently of all other transactions.* Note, however, that several of the transactions will introduce integrity problems and/or are invalid as written. All such transactions should be rejected with an appropriate indication of why the transaction is invalid.
(a) A change in the royalty percentage of contract type C2 from four to five percent
(b) The inclusion of a new contract C4 with a term of 15 years, an initial fee of $100,000, and royalty and advertising percentages of three and four percent, respectively
(c) A change in contract for restaurant R3 to contract type C5
(d) The addition of a new franchisee with number F3
(e) The addition of a new restaurant, R6, owned by franchisee F2 and governed by contract C1
(f) The addition of a new restaurant, R7, owned by franchisee F5 and governed by contract C3
(g) A change in address for restaurant R10

3. The university administration is so impressed with the student transcript database of Figure 12.4 that they want it expanded to include faculty data in a fourth table. Each row of the proposed table would include a unique faculty number for each professor, followed by the professor's name, rank, highest degree, salary, address, and other personal data as needed. In addition, the student/course table (Figure 12.4c) would be expanded to include an additional column with the faculty number of the professor who taught the course. Is this design appropriate or are additional modifications necessary?

4. Answer the following with respect to the relational database of Figure 12.6.
(a) What was the total cost of order O1?
(b) How many widgets were ordered during the month?
(c) Which orders were placed by Mr. Fegan?
(d) How many orders were placed by Mr. Flynn?
(e) Who placed order O4?
(f) What is the address of the person placing order O5?
(g) On what day was order O2 taken?

What problems (if any) would result from attempting to process the following transactions?
(h) The addition of a new product, trinkets, with product number P2
(i) The receipt of a new order, O6 (placed by customer C6 on 12/16/91), for 50 units of product P1
(j) The addition of a new customer, Roberts, with customer number C4 and all appropriate customer information
(k) The deletion of product number P3 from the catalog

The next-to-last week of December saw the addition of two new customers (John Smith and Mary Jones with customer numbers C6 and C7) as well as four new products (with product numbers P5 through P8 inclusive). In addition, the following orders were placed:

Order O6 (12/21/91): John Smith ordered 50 units of product P1 and 20 units of product P2.

Order O7 (12/22/91): John Smith placed a second order for 10 additional units of product P1.

Order O8 (12/22/91): Mary Jones placed an order for one unit of each of products P5, P6, and P7.

(l) How many records are added to the customer table?
(m) How many records are added to the product table?
(n) How many records are added to the order table?
(o) How many records are added to the order/product table?

5. Develop the file structures necessary to implement a system for a medical research, intended to track specific people (i.e., subjects) and/or specific studies. A given study will naturally require several subjects, and likewise a specific individual may be a subject in multiple studies.

The system should be able to display all facts about a particular subject, e.g., name, birth date, sex, height, weight, blood pressure, and cholesterol level. It should also be able to display all characteristics associated with a particular study, e.g., the title, beginning date, and ending date. Use your imagination to develop at least five additional fields for each of these records.

Develop the file structure(s) to accommodate all of the above, being sure to indicate which key(s) are unique. In addition, your file structure should enable a user to do all of the following:
(a) List all subjects in a particular study.
(b) List all studies in which a particular subject has participated.
(c) List all subjects who have not yet participated in a study.
(d) List all subjects who are male.
(e) List all males in a designated study.
(f) List all males with high blood pressure in a designated study.
(g) List all studies that were started in 1989.
(h) List all studies that have not yet finished.

6. Develop the file structure to implement a youth sports league intended to track players, coaches, and sponsors. There may be any number of teams in the league, with each team limited to a maximum of 15 players. Each team has one coach, typically the parent of one of the players, and thus the same person can coach several teams. In similar fashion, each team has one sponsor, e.g., a local business, and that sponsor can be associated with multiple teams. A player, however, can be associated with only a single team. Your solution should enable a user to do all of the following:
(a) List all players in the league.
(b) List all teams in the league.
(c) List all coaches.
(d) List all sponsors.
(e) List all players on a given team.
(f) Identify the coach and sponsor for a particular team.
(g) List all teams for one sponsor.
(h) List all teams for one coach.

Your solution should make the system as realistic as possible. The player file, for example, requires not only the identifying information for each player (name, address, phone, and so on) but such additional fields as birth date (to implement age limits on various teams) and ability ratings. The team file could include a team name, team colors, etc. The only limits are your own imagination.

CHAPTER

13 Implementation in dBASE

OUTLINE

OBJECTIVES

After reading this chapter you will be able to:

1. Describe the characteristics of a relational database and how this type of file organization facilitates file maintenance.
2. Design a relational database with several one-to-many relationships.
3. Describe what is meant by the currently selected **DBF** file and how multiple files can be open simultaneously.
4. Explain the **SELECT** and **SET RELATION** commands and how they are used to implement relational concepts in dBASE.
5. Describe the output of the **DISPLAY STATUS** command as it pertains to a relational database.

Overview

The preceding chapter introduced the concept of a ***relational database*** as first postulated by Edgar Codd of IBM. It described the characteristics of a relational database and distinguished between a one-to-many and a many-to-many relationship. That discussion was entirely theoretical and made no mention of implementation.

The present chapter assumes you are familiar with the relational model and focuses entirely on its implementation in dBASE. Note, too, that whereas we previously used the terms ***table, row,*** and ***column*** to describe the relational model, in this chapter we switch to ***file, record,*** and ***field,*** respectively, to be consistent with dBASE terminology.

We begin with presentation of a new case study that provides yet additional practice in database design, then move to a hands-on exercise to illustrate the practical application of these concepts. The essence of this exercise is ***file maintenance*** and how the relational model eliminates problems of redundancy, as well as facilitates the addition or deletion of entities to the system.

The chapter also covers the specific dBASE commands used with a relational database. We include the use of multiple ***work areas,*** the associated **USE** and **SELECT** commands, and the **SET RELATION** command to link the files in various work areas to one another. We present a second hands-on exercise showing how these commands are executed at the dot prompt, then end with a program that ties all of the individual commands together.

CASE PREVIEW

The case you are about to read is set within the context of the Coral Springs Soccer Association (CSSA), a youth-oriented athletic league in South Florida. In essence, the Association is seeking to automate its registration procedure, and to facilitate the monitoring of its *teams, players, coaches,* and *sponsors*. These entities have definite relationships with one another, and the essence of the case becomes how best to structure the data.

Read the case carefully, and as you do, look for the various entities that are present in the system, remembering that each entity requires its own file in the database. Identify the several ***one-to-many relationships*** that are present in the association—e.g., one team has many players—and look for the common fields needed to implement these relationships. Use your imagination as to the type of data the Association requires for each entity—e.g., address, telephone, and birth date for each player.

CASE STUDY
The Coral Springs Soccer Association

Coral Springs, Florida, is a community of 80,000 people located in the northwest corner of Broward County. The city takes great pride in its park and recreational facilities, which have enabled the growth of a number of independently run sports leagues. Foremost among these is the Coral Springs Soccer Association (CSSA), which registered some 3,000 players for the 1991–1992 season. Notification for soccer sign-ups appears several times in local newspapers, at which time parents enroll their youngsters. At registration, the Association gathers data about players, and also about coaches and sponsors. The Board of Directors subsequently meets to decide how many teams it will have in each age group, and manually assigns players, coaches, and sponsors to the individual teams.

The program is open to all children in the city, ages 6 to 16. Age groups are maintained at two-year intervals, beginning with the "Under 8s" and continuing to the "Under 16s." Boys and girls play in separate divisions. Rules of the game are modified to accommodate the younger players and to further the instructional philosophy of the Association. The "Under 8s," for example, play with smaller goals, employ only 7 players to a side, use a size 3 ball, and play 20-minute halves. The "Under 10s" move up to a size 4 ball, a regulation field, and 25-minute halves, and so on.

The Association collects a registration fee of $25 from each participant and raises additional money from the local business community. Sponsors contribute $175 per team, and range from branch offices of national corporations (Wendy's), to local businesses (Poogie's Pools), to individuals (Dr. Getz's Decay Fighters). The money enables the Association to supply every player with a T-shirt and matching soccer socks, as well as provide paid referees for each game. The Association also provides participation trophies to all children in the youngest age group at the end of the season, and provides first- and second-place trophies to players in higher age groups. The money is also used to buy soccer balls, goalie uniforms, and other equipment, and to send selected teams to national tournaments.

Every child who registers is guaranteed a place on a recreational team. The Association maintains a balance among teams by rating players according to their ability prior to devising team assignments. Returning players (those who played last year) are rated by their former coaches at the end of the previous season, whereas new players are evaluated shortly after their initial registration. A player's rating ranges from 1 to 5 (1 being the best). The ratings are kept confidential and used only to balance the teams.

The success of the Coral Springs Soccer Association is due to the phenomenal support of the community. In addition to the nearly 200 sponsors, parents give freely of their time to serve as coaches, to the extent that parents with two children in the program often coach both teams. Most teams practice twice during the week and play on Saturday. The Association expects its coaches to be licensed by the Florida Youth Soccer Association, which requires attendance at one or more coaching clinics.

The growth of the soccer program has prompted the Association to seek its own computer processing. The Board of Directors would like a system to facilitate player registration, and to keep track of coaches, sponsors, and teams.

CASE SOLUTION

Our solution begins with the recognition that each entity—*team, player, coach,* and *sponsor*—requires its own file. In addition, we need to identify the relationships that exist between the entities to determine the common fields that will relate the files to one another. Accordingly, a careful reading of the case presentation reveals the following:

- *A one-to-many relationship between a team and its players;* i.e., a team has many players but a player has only one team. The **TEAM_ID** is the primary key in the team file, where it is *unique* for every record; it is not unique, however, in the player file, where **TEAM_ID** is a foreign key to indicate that several players are on the same team.
- *A one-to-many relationship between a sponsor and its teams;* i.e., a sponsor can have many teams, but a team has only one sponsor. The **SPONSOR_ID** is the primary key in the sponsor file, where it is *unique* for every record; it is not unique, however, in the team file where **SPONSOR_ID** is a foreign key to indicate that several teams can have the same sponsor.
- *A one-to-many relationship between a coach and his (or her) teams;* i.e., a coach can have many teams, but a team has only one coach. (This relationship may sound strange at first, but our case is based on a *youth* league, where the coaches are typically parents, and an enthusiastic parent with two children is apt to coach both teams.) The **COACH_ID** is the primary key in the coach file, where it is *unique* for every record; it is not unique, however, in the team file where **COACH_ID** is a foreign key to indicate that several teams can have the same coach.

These relationships give rise to the database design of Figure 13.1. As indicated, each entity has its own file with its own file structure. The specific fields within each

FIGURE 13.1
dBASE File Structures

```
Field Name    Type          Width
LAST_NAME     Character      12
FIRST_NAME    Character      10
BIRTH_DATE    Date            8
SEX           Character       1
RATING        Character       1
TEAM_ID       Character       6
PHONE         Character       7
STREET        Character      24
CITY          Character      16
STATE         Character       2
ZIP_CODE      Character       5
```

(a) PLAYER.DBF

```
Field Name    Type          Width
TEAM_ID       Character       6
COLORS        Character      16
COACH_ID      Character       2
SPONSOR_ID    Character       2
```

(b) TEAM.DBF

```
Field Name    Type          Width
SPONSOR_ID    Character       2
NAME          Character      20
CONTACT       Character      16
AMOUNT_PD     Numeric         4
PHONE         Character       7
STREET        Character      24
CITY          Character      16
STATE         Character       2
ZIP_CODE      Character       5
```

(c) SPONSOR.DBF

```
Field Name    Type          Width
COACH_ID      Character       2
LAST_NAME     Character      16
FIRST_NAME    Character      12
LICENSE       Character       1
PHONE         Character       7
STREET        Character      24
CITY          Character      16
STATE         Character       2
ZIP_CODE      Character       5
```

(d) COACH.DBF

file were developed from the case description and should be self-explanatory. The player file in Figure 13.1a, for example, contains the player's birth date, sex, and rating, data needed by the Association to assign the player to an appropriate team. A player's record also contains a phone number and address, as well as a **TEAM_ID** to indicate the team to which the player is assigned, thereby linking the player and team files to one another.

The team file in Figure 13.1b contains a *unique* **TEAM_ID** for each team, in addition to both a **COACH_ID** and a **SPONSOR_ID** to provide the links to the coach and sponsor files, respectively. As indicated, multiple teams may have identical values in these fields to indicate that the same individual can coach (or sponsor) more than one team. The team file also contains a field indicating the team colors.

The file structures for the sponsor and coach files are shown in Figures 13.1c and 13.1d, respectively. Each sponsor is assigned a unique **SPONSOR_ID**, just as each coach is given a unique **COACH_ID**, and as indicated, these fields also appear in the team file as foreign keys to link a team to its coach and sponsor. The nature of the remaining fields in each record should be apparent from the field name and case description.

Figure 13.2 contains partial data for each of these files and is a further aid in understanding the solution. Every record in the team file of Figure 13.2b contains a unique **TEAM_ID** (**GU1201**, **GU1202**, and so on). Note, too, that the characters in the **TEAM_ID** field are mnemonic and indicate the nature of the team; e.g., **GU1201** is the the **TEAM_ID** for the first team in the girl's 12 and under division. In similar fashion, every record in the sponsor file of Figure 13.2c contains a unique **SPONSOR_ID** (**S1**,

FIGURE 13.2
Partial File Contents

FIRST_NAME	LAST_NAME	RATING	TEAM_ID
Allison	Aiken	1	GU1201
Meredith	Allen	2	GU1402
Nancy	Anderson	3	GU1201
Maria	Bellizzi	4	GU1401
Aliana	Coulter	3	GU1202
Sara	Coulter	2	GU1201
Tanya	Donati	1	GU1401
Danielle	Ferraro	1	GU1402
Mary Kate	Fetters	3	GU1401
Julianne	Ford	3	GU1202
Laurie	Friedel	1	GU1601
Lori	Fromkin	4	GU1402
Jessica	Granger	1	GU1401
Melissa	Granger	1	GU1601
Heather	Holton	3	GU1402
Jessica	Martineau	1	GU1402
Leah	Martineau	4	GU1201
Cara	O'Brien	2	GU1402
Norma	Pagan	2	GU1401
Laura	Wellbery	1	GU1202
Gina	Wilson	4	GU1202

(a) PLAYER.DBF

TEAM_ID	COLORS	COACH_ID	SPONSOR_ID
GU1201	Red/Black	C3	S1
GU1202	Blue/Yellow		
GU1401	Red/Black	C1	
GU1402	Blue/Yellow	C2	S2
GU1601	Red/Black	C1	S2

(b) TEAM.DBF

SPONSOR_ID	NAME	CONTACT	AMOUNT_PD	PHONE
S1	J.C. Penney	Ralph Cordell	175	7556570
S2	Wendy's	Jill Simmons	350	7551000

(c) SPONSOR.DBF

COACH_ID	FIRST_NAME	LAST_NAME	LICENSE	PHONE
C1	Robert	Granger	F	7530345
C2	Sharon	Zion	E	7522475
C3	John	Osberger	E	7538248

(d) COACH.DBF

S2, and so on), and every record in the coach file of Figure 13.2d contains a unique COACH_ID (C1, C2, etc.).

The relationships between the various keys can be used to derive complete information about any given team. Assume, for example, that we want to know the names of the coach, sponsor, and players assigned to team GU1201. We would retrieve the team record from Figure 13.2b, which contains a COACH_ID and SPONSOR_ID of C3 and S1, respectively. We would then search the coach file for the record whose COACH_ID is C3, and the sponsor file for the record with SPONSOR_ID of S1, obtaining the names of the individuals in the respective files. Finally, we would go through the player file and retrieve every player record whose team is GU1201.

To be absolutely sure you understand the solution, and to appreciate the type of information that can be obtained from the system, consider the following questions (and answers) based on the data in Figure 13.2:

Questions

1. Which players are on team GU1201?
2. Who is the sponsor of team GU1402?
3. Who coaches team GU1601, and what is his phone number?
4. Which coaches have a class F license?
5. What color is Jessica Granger's uniform?
6. What is the phone number of Danielle Ferraro's coach?
7. Is there any team without a coach?
8. Which teams are coached by John Osberger?

Answers

1. Allison Aiken, Nancy Anderson, Sara Coulter, and Leah Martineau are the players on team GU1201.
2. Wendy's is the sponsor of team GU1402.
3. Team GU1601 is coached by Robert Granger, whose phone number is 753-0345.
4. Robert Granger is the only coach with a class F license.
5. Jessica Granger plays for team GU1401, whose colors are red and black.
6. Danielle Ferraro plays for team GU1402, which is coached by Sharon Zion, whose phone number is 752-2475.
7. Team GU1202 is currently without a coach.
8. John Osberger is the coach of team GU1201.

Maintaining the Database

One of the primary attractions of the relational model is the elimination of ***redundancy,*** and the resulting simplification of file maintenance. Consider, for example, a change in phone number for a coach with two teams, e.g., Robert Granger, who coaches teams GU1401 and GU1601. The change will be made only once, i.e., in the coach file of Figure 13.2d, but will be automatically reflected whenever information about the coach for either of these teams is required.

The records for the teams GU1401 and GU1601 in Figure 13.2b contain the same COACH_ID (C1 corresponding to Robert Granger), but do not contain the coach's phone number. The COACH_ID does *not* change because the teams are still coached by the same person, and hence nothing needs to be done to the team records. The coach's phone number does change, however, and we need to modify the appropriate record in the coach file of Figure 13.2d. The change will be made only once, despite the fact that coach C1 has two teams.

The addition of a new record is also facilitated by the relational model because the Association can add a player, coach, or sponsor when these individuals appear at registration, without waiting for an appropriate team assignment. This makes perfect sense within the context of the physical system, because an individual (a player, coach, or sponsor) registers on one date, but the team assignments are not made until several weeks later.

The deletion of a team (or any other record) is also straightforward. You could, for example, delete team **GU1202** from Figure 13.2b without losing data about the players, coach, or sponsor that were assigned to this team. The individuals involved, however, have to be reassigned to other teams because team **GU1202** no longer exists; i.e., the value of the **TEAM_ID** field would change from **GU1202** to **GU1201** for the four players affected in Figure 13.2a.

The ensuing hands-on exercise will demonstrate how relational concepts are implemented in dBASE. The exercise begins with the generation of team rosters based on the four existing **DBF** files (shown in Figure 13.2), which are contained on the data disk. The exercise then directs you to make changes to the individual files, and ends with a revised set of rosters that reflect the changes that have been made. Some things to look for in the exercise:

1. A *change* in a coach's phone number; the coach is Robert Granger, and he currently coaches two teams. The change will be made in only one place (the **COACH.DBF** file), yet the new phone number will be properly reflected in all of the rosters for teams coached by this person.
2. The *deletion* of team **GU1202** from the **TEAM.DBF** file; the individuals associated with this team (the players, coach, and sponsor) remain in their respective files, but must be assigned to new teams.
3. The *addition* of a new sponsor, Poogie's Pools; the sponsor is added in the **SPONSOR.DBF** file and is assigned to a team from the **TEAM.DBF** file.

HANDS-ON EXERCISE 1

Generating Team Rosters

Objective

Demonstrate the basic file maintenance operations within a relational framework.

STEP 1 **Change to the SOCCER subdirectory**

Boot the system, ending at the DOS prompt. Type one of the following two commands, depending on whether you are sharing the hard drive with others:

CD C:\DATADISK\SOCCER — *if you installed the data disk on the hard drive and are not sharing your computer, or*

CD A:\DATADISK\SOCCER — *if you did not install the data disk, i.e., if you are sharing drive C with other students. (Use data disk two if you have 5¼-inch disks.)*

STEP 2 **Load dBASE**

Type **dBASE** to load dBASE, then set the default drive as you have in previous exercises.

STEP 3 **Examine the directory**

Type **DIR** at the dot prompt to obtain information about the DBF files in the current subdirectory. The following should appear on your monitor:

Database Files	# Records	Last Update	Size
COACH.DBF	3	06/22/91	580
PLAYER.DBF	21	06/22/91	2339
SPONSOR.DBF	2	06/11/91	516
TEAM.DBF	5	06/11/91	297

As expected, there are four DBF files—for coaches, players, sponsors, and teams, respectively. Note, too, that the output of the DIR command includes the number of records in each file; i.e., the system currently has three coaches, twenty-one players, two sponsors, and five teams. The SOCCER directory also contains a production index (MDX) file for each DBF, file which can be verified with the command **DIR *.MDX**.

STEP 4 **Print the team rosters**

Type **DO ROSTER** to execute a program that displays the rosters of Figure 13.3, one team at a time. As previously indicated, the objective of this exercise is to consider how changes made to a file within a relational framework affect other files and/or reports based on these files. Accordingly, the next several steps will direct you to make changes in the individual DBF files to see how those changes are reflected in the printed rosters. Step 10, at the conclusion of the editing process, asks you to rerun the roster program to confirm that the various changes were implemented properly.

STEP 5 **Change data for an existing coach (Granger)**

The easiest way to locate a particular record is through the FIND command, which moves the record pointer to the specified record. Recall, however, that the FIND command (discussed previously in Chapter 6 and again in the Programmer's Notebook) requires that the file be open in conjunction with an index whose key is the field on which the search is based. Accordingly, enter these commands:

```
. USE COACH ——————————————————— Opens coach file
. SET ORDER TO TAG LAST_NAME —— Opens the last name index
. FIND Granger ———————————————— The FIND command is case sensitive
. EDIT ———————————————————————— Brings up Granger's record for
                                editing
```

Change the phone number in Granger's record to **753-1752**, then press **Alt+E** to pull down the exit menu, save the change, and return to the dot prompt.

STEP 6 **Delete a team (GU1202)**

The removal of a team requires that we open the team file, move to the appropriate record slated for deletion, and then execute a DELETE and a PACK command. Accordingly, execute the following commands:

```
. USE TEAM ORDER TEAM_ID —— Opens team file and TEAM_ID index
. FIND GU1202 ————————————— GU must be in upper case
. DISPLAY ————————————————— Confirms proper record will be deleted
. DELETE —————————————————— Logically deletes the indicated record
. PACK ———————————————————— Physically deletes the team record
```

The FIND command moves the record pointer to the first record in the team file whose TEAM_ID is GU1202, i.e., the record slated for deletion. The DISPLAY com-

FIGURE 13.3
Team Rosters

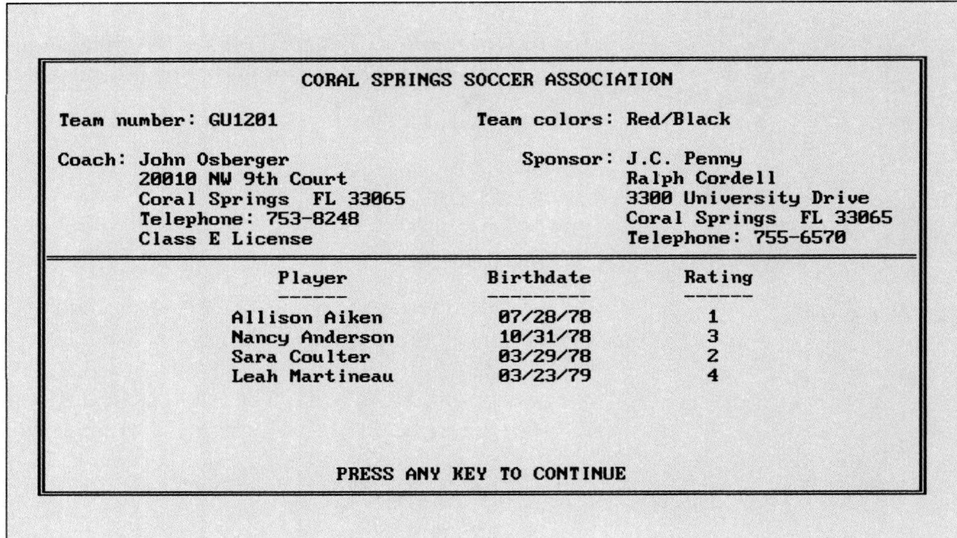

(a) Team GU1201 (girls, 12 and under, team 1)

```
                    CORAL SPRINGS SOCCER ASSOCIATION

Team number: GU1202                         Team colors: Blue/Yellow

Coach:                                          Sponsor:


       Telephone:    -
       Class    License                                 Telephone:     -

                     Player             Birthdate          Rating
                     ------             ---------          ------
                     Aliana Coulter     03/19/79             3
                     Julianne Ford      02/01/78             3
                     Laura Wellbery     10/03/78             1
                     Gina Wilson        03/31/78             4


                       PRESS ANY KEY TO CONTINUE
```

(b) Team GU1202 (girls, 12 and under, team 2)

mand is executed prior to deleting the record to confirm that we have, in fact, found the proper record.

STEP 7 **Reassign players**

The removal of team **GU1202** does *not* delete the associated player, coach, and sponsor records in their respective files, but these individuals must be *reassigned* to different teams. However, since team **GU1202** did not have either a coach or a sponsor, only the players' records need to be changed. Accordingly:

```
. USE PLAYER ORDER TEAM_ID ——— Opens the player file and its index
. FIND GU1202 ——————————————— Finds first player on team GU1202
. EDIT NOFOLLOW —————————————— Brings up the player record for editing
```

You should be positioned at the first player (Aliana Coulter) formerly on team **GU1202**. Change the team assignment for this player to **GU1201**, then press the **PgDn**

FIGURE 13.3
Team Rosters (continued)

```
                    CORAL SPRINGS SOCCER ASSOCIATION

Team number: GU1401                        Team colors: Red/Black

Coach: Robert Granger                            Sponsor:
       2133 NW 102 Terrace
       Coral Springs  FL 33065
       Telephone: 753-0345
       Class E License                                 Telephone:    -

                       Player              Birthdate         Rating
                       ------              ---------         ------
                   Maria Bellizzi           04/15/77            4
                   Tanya Donati             09/20/77            1
                   Mary Kate Fetters        03/16/77            3
                   Jessica Granger          03/16/77            1
                   Norma Pagan              10/10/77            2


                         PRESS ANY KEY TO CONTINUE
```

(c) Team GU1401 (girls, 14 and under, team 1)

```
                    CORAL SPRINGS SOCCER ASSOCIATION

Team number: GU1402                        Team colors: Blue/Yellow

Coach: Sharon Zion                               Sponsor: Wendy's
       10020 NW 6th Court                                 Jill Simmons
       Coral Springs  FL 33065                            1234 Sample Road
       Telephone: 752-2475                                Coral Springs  FL 33065
       Class E License                                    Telephone: 755-1000

                       Player              Birthdate         Rating
                       ------              ---------         ------
                   Meredith Allen           04/16/77            2
                   Danielle Ferraro         03/09/77            1
                   Lori Fromkin             03/06/77            4
                   Heather Holton           05/26/77            3
                   Jessica Martineau        07/28/77            1
                   Cara O'Brien             07/06/77            2


                         PRESS ANY KEY TO CONTINUE
```

(d) Team GU1402 (girls, 14 and under, team 2)

key to move to the next player on this team, make the appropriate change, and so on. (The **NOFOLLOW** parameter is required in the **EDIT** command, or else the record pointer would have been repositioned according to the *new* value of the **TEAM_ID**; i.e., omission of the **NOFOLLOW** parameter would require another **FIND** command to identify the next player from team **GU1202**.) Press **Alt+E** when you have changed the team assignment for the last player on this team (Gina Wilson).

STEP 8 **Add a new sponsor (Poogie's Pools)**

The Association has found a sponsor for the only team (**GU1401**) currently without one. Type **USE SPONSOR** to open the sponsor file, then type **APPEND** to bring up the input template for the new record. Assign the next consecutive number, **S3**, to the new sponsor record. The sponsor's name is **Poogie's Pools**, and the contact person is **Mary Smith**. The new sponsor has not yet paid any money to the Association.

FIGURE 13.3
Team Rosters (continued)

```
                    CORAL SPRINGS SOCCER ASSOCIATION

Team number: GU1601                    Team colors: Red/Black

Coach: Robert Granger                     Sponsor: Wendy's
       2133 NW 102 Terrace                         Jill Simmons
       Coral Springs  FL 33065                     1234 Sample Road
       Telephone: 753-0345                         Coral Springs  FL 33065
       Class E License                             Telephone: 755-1000

                 Player                Birthdate        Rating
                 ------                ---------        ------
             Laurie Friedel            07/04/76           1
             Melissa Granger           01/05/76           1



                        PRESS ANY KEY TO CONTINUE
```

(e) Team GU1601 (girls, 16 and under, team 1)

The phone number is **753-2000**, and the sponsor is located at **10000 Sample Road**, **Coral Springs, FL, 33065**. Press **Alt+E** to return to the dot prompt when you have completed the addition.

STEP 9 **Assign the new sponsor**

The addition of a record to the sponsor file does *not* assign the sponsor to a team; i.e., the latter operation can be done only within the team file. Accordingly, we must once again open the team file, find team **GU1401**, and edit the record to assign a sponsor. Enter these commands:

```
. USE TEAM ORDER TEAM_ID ——— Opens the team file
. FIND GU1401 ———————————— GU must be in upper case
. EDIT ———————————————————— Brings up the record for editing
```

The team file is opened with an index to permit the subsequent **FIND** command to locate the team in question. Enter **S3** as the **SPONSOR_ID**, then press **Alt+E** to save the change and return to the dot prompt.

STEP 10 **Rerun the player rosters**

Type **DO ROSTER** to rerun the roster program, displaying the current rosters on the monitor, one team at a time. Verify that the changes made in the individual **DBF** files are reflected in the new team rosters; i.e., the new rosters should reflect:

(a) Four teams instead of five as team **GU1202** has been deleted.
(b) Eight players on team **GU1201**, including Aliana Coulter, Julianne Ford, Laura Wellbery, and Gina Wilson, who were previously on team **GU1202**. (The players are in alphabetical order because the index for the player file is based on the concatenated key, **TEAM_ID+LAST_NAME**.)
(c) A new phone number for Coach Robert Granger, who appears on two rosters (**GU1401** and **GU1601**).
(d) A new sponsor, Poogie's Pools, for team **GU1401**.

dBASE Commands and Concepts

The exercise just completed demonstrated many of the relational capabilities of dBASE within the context of a completed program. The exercise did not, however, discuss the program per se, and consequently made no mention of the specific commands needed to accomplish these tasks. Accordingly, we present the individual commands in this section, then incorporate the commands into a second hands-on exercise.

The SELECT Command

The relational model requires that all files be open simultaneously, a situation made possible in dBASE through multiple ***work areas.*** dBASE provides ten such work areas (numbered from 1 to 10), each of which can contain one *open* **DBF** file. The **SELECT** command designates the area in which the file will be opened, while a subsequent **USE** command actually opens the file. (The default work area when dBASE is loaded is area one; thus, all of the examples in the previous chapters have taken place in this work area without the requirement of a **SELECT** command.) Consider:

Syntax

```
SELECT <n>
```

Examples

```
SELECT 1
USE TEAM

SELECT 2
USE COACH
```

This particular combination of **SELECT** and **USE** commands opens the **TEAM** and **COACH DBF** files in work areas one and two, respectively. It is important, too, to distinguish between files that are open versus the one that is active; i.e., there can be many ***open files*** but only one ***active file,*** the active file being the file in the currently selected work area (**COACH.DBF** in area two in the example). Most commands (**APPEND**, **EDIT**, **DELETE**, **LIST**, and so on) operate only on the active (currently selected) **DBF** file.

The SET RELATION Command

The **SET RELATION** command relates the currently selected **DBF** file to a **DBF** file in another area, so that when the record pointer in the first file is moved, the record pointer in the related file is moved to the corresponding record. The command requires the presence of a ***common field*** in both files, and further, that the related file be indexed on this field. An abbreviated syntax, together with an example linking the team and coach files, is shown below:

Syntax

```
SET RELATION TO [common-field INTO related file]
```

Examples

```
SELECT 1
USE TEAM

SELECT 2
USE COACH ORDER COACH_ID —— Related file is opened with index

SELECT 1
SET RELATION TO COACH_ID INTO COACH
```

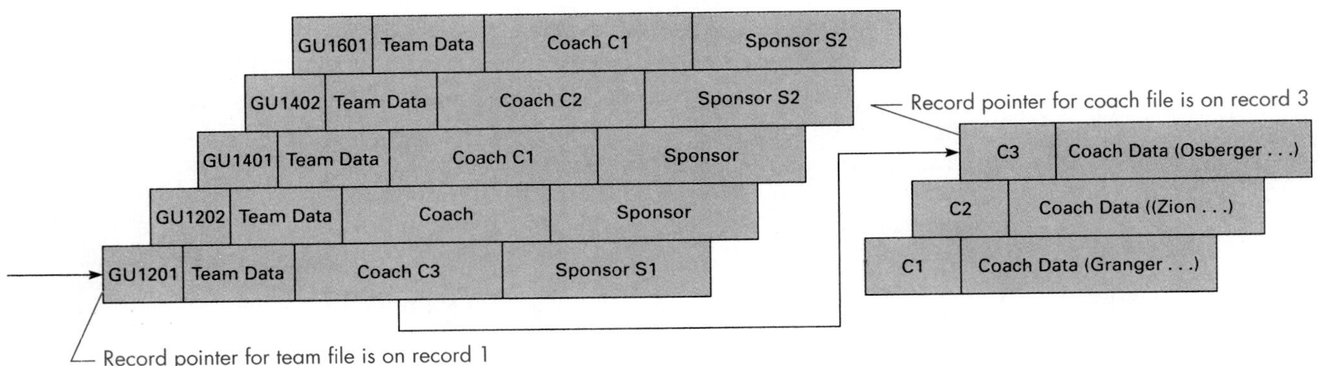

FIGURE 13.4
The SET RELATION Command

The **SET RELATION** command is illustrated in Figure 13.4, which uses **COACH_ID** as the common field to relate the files. The effect of the command is to position the record pointer associated with the coach (i.e., the related) file to the record that matches the value of **COACH_ID** in the team file.

The **SET RELATION** command is further illustrated in Figure 13.5a, in which the team and coach files have been opened in areas one and two, respectively. Note, too, that the coach file has been opened with an active index on **COACH_ID**, the common field present in both files.

The team file is made the active file immediately prior to the **SET RELATION** command. The **DISPLAY** command indicates that record one is the current record in the team file, and that this record has a **TEAM_ID** and **COACH_ID** of **GU1201** and **C3**, respectively.

The fourth (and final) **SELECT** command designates the coach file as the active file, and the **DISPLAY** command that follows indicates that record three is the current record in the coach file. In other words, the **SET RELATION** command moved the record pointer in the coach file to the first record whose **COACH_ID** is **C3** (record three), corresponding to the **COACH_ID** in the current record of the team file.

You can display fields from an open **DBF** file in other than the currently selected work area, by qualifying the field name with the file name; e.g., **COACH->LAST_NAME** refers to the **LAST_NAME** field in the **COACH.DBF** file. The **LIST** command in Figure 13.5b displays the coach's name and phone number for every team, because as the record pointer for work area one moves from team to team, the record pointer in work area two is automatically repositioned at the corresponding coach record.

The syntax of the **SET RELATION** command indicates that the **INTO** clause is optional; i.e., the command can be issued with no additional parameters to cancel the relation in effect.

The DISPLAY STATUS Command

The **DISPLAY STATUS** command shows all currently open files in their associated work areas. It also displays the open indexes and their respective keys, the relationships in effect, the function key settings, and the settings of the **SET** commands.

Figure 13.5c shows partial output produced by the **DISPLAY STATUS** command after the commands in Figures 13.5a and 13.5b were executed. The command confirms the currently selected database (i.e., the active **DBF** file) to be **TEAM.DBF** in area one, and further that this file is related into the **COACH.DBF** file in area two.

```
. SELECT 1
. USE TEAM

. SELECT 2
. USE COACH ORDER COACH_ID

. SELECT 1
. SET RELATION TO COACH_ID INTO COACH
. DISPLAY
Record#  TEAM_ID COLORS               COACH_ID SPONSOR_ID
      1  GU1201  Red/Black            C3       S1
      └──────────────────────── Record pointer is at record 1 in TEAM.DBF

. SELECT 2
. DISPLAY COACH_ID,FIRST_NAME,LAST_NAME,LICENSE,PHONE
Record#  COACH_ID FIRST_NAME    LAST_NAME         LICENSE PHONE
      3  C3       John          Osberger          E       7538248
      └──────────────────────── Record pointer is at record 3 in COACH.DBF
```

(a) The SET RELATION Command

```
                 ┌──── TEAM_ID is displayed from the active (TEAM.DBF) file in area 1
. SELECT 1       │                ┌──── FIRST_NAME is displayed from the COACH.DBF file in area 2
. LIST TEAM_ID,COLORS,COACH->FIRST_NAME,COACH->LAST_NAME,COACH->PHONE
Record#  TEAM_ID COLORS         COACH->FIRST_NAME COACH->LAST_NAME COACH->PHONE
      1  GU1201  Red/Black      John              Osberger         7538248
      2  GU1401  Red/Black      Robert            Granger          7530345
      3  GU1402  Blue/Yellow    Sharon            Zion             7522475
      4  GU1601  Red/Black      Robert            Granger          7530345
```

(b) Displaying Fields from Two Files

```
Currently Selected Database:
Select area:  1, Database in Use: C:\DATADISK\SOCCER\TEAM.DBF
  Alias: TEAM
Production   MDX file:   C:\DATADISK\SOCCER\TEAM.MDX
          Index TAG:       TEAM_ID  Key: TEAM_ID
    Related into: COACH
    Relation: COACH_ID

Select area:  2, Database in Use: C:\DATADISK\SOCCER\COACH.DBF
  Alias: COACH
Production   MDX file:   C:\SOCCER\COACH.MDX
    Master Index TAG:      COACH_ID  Key: COACH_ID
           Index TAG:      LAST_NAME Key:  LAST_NAME
```

(c) The DISPLAY STATUS Command (partial output)

FIGURE 13.5
Implementation in dBASE IV

We continue with a second hands-on exercise to illustrate how the **SELECT** and **SET RELATION** commands are used within the **ROSTER** program to display complete information about each team. The exercise opens each of the four files in a different work area, then uses appropriate **SET RELATION** commands to display information about the coach, sponsor, and players for team **GU1201**. Note, too, that the exercise reflects all changes made in the first hands-on exercise; i.e., there are four teams rather than five, with four additional players assigned to team **GU1201**.

HANDS-ON EXERCISE 2

The SELECT and SET RELATION Commands

Objective

Demonstrate the `SELECT` and `SET RELATION` commands to display all information for team `GU1201`.

STEP 1 **Assign work areas**

Enter the **SELECT** and **USE** commands shown below to open all four files in their designated work areas.

```
. SELECT 1
. USE TEAM ORDER TEAM_ID
. SELECT 2
. USE COACH ORDER COACH_ID
. SELECT 3
. USE SPONSOR ORDER SPONSOR_ID
. SELECT 4
. USE PLAYER ORDER TEAM_ID
```

Type **DISPLAY STATUS** to see the effect of these commands, i.e., to see the open files, their indexes, and associated work areas.

STEP 2 **Relate the team and coach files**

Relate the team file to the coach file by selecting the first work area and entering the `SET RELATION` command shown below. Remember that in order for the **SET RELATION** command to work both files must contain a **COACH_ID** field, and further that the coach file must have been opened with this field as the key of the active index.

```
. SELECT 1
. SET RELATION TO COACH_ID INTO COACH

. DISPLAY TEAM_ID,COLORS,COACH->LAST_NAME,COACH->PHONE

Record# TEAM_ID COLORS     COACH->LAST_NAME COACH->PHONE
      1 GU1201  Red/Black  Osberger              7538248
```

The subsequent `DISPLAY` command shows the **TEAM_ID** and **COLORS** fields from the team file and corresponding coach's **LAST_NAME** and **PHONE** from the related coach file.

STEP 3 **Relate the team and sponsor files**

Relate the team file to the sponsor file as shown below. Note that both files contain a common **SPONSOR_ID** field, and further that the sponsor file was opened (in step 1) with this field as the key of the active index.

```
. SET RELATION TO SPONSOR_ID INTO SPONSOR
. DISPLAY TEAM_ID,SPONSOR->NAME,SPONSOR->CONTACT

Record#  TEAM_ID  SPONSOR->NAME  SPONSOR->CONTACT
      1  GU1201   J.C. Penney    Ralph Cordell
```

The team file is still the active file, but it is now related to the sponsor rather than to the coach file. Accordingly, the DISPLAY command indicates the information associated with the sponsor for team GU1201.

STEP 4 **Relate the team and player files**

Relate the team file to the player file as shown below, then execute the additional commands to list all players on team GU1201. (The one-to-many relationship that exists between a team and its players requires the selection of work area four and the subsequent LIST WHILE command to list all the players on team GU1201.)

```
. SET RELATION TO TEAM_ID INTO PLAYER
. SELECT 4
. LIST FIRST_NAME,LAST_NAME WHILE TEAM_ID = "GU1201"

Record#   FIRST_NAME   LAST_NAME

      1   Allison      Aiken
      3   Nancy        Anderson
      6   Sara         Coulter
      5   Aliana       Coulter
     10   Julianne     Ford
     17   Leah         Martineau
     20   Laura        Wellbery
     21   Gina         Wilson
```

The SELECT command makes the player file active and positions the record pointer at the first player on team GU1201. Note, too, that since the player file was opened with TEAM_ID as the master index, all players on the same team appear together; hence the LIST WHILE command displays all players for team GU1201.

STEP 5 **The DISPLAY STATUS command**

Type **DISPLAY STATUS** to see all files that are currently open, their associated indexes, and the work areas to which they have been assigned. The output of the DISPLAY STATUS command should confirm the results of all commands issued thus far; e.g., it will show the team, coach, sponsor, and player files open in areas one, two, three, and four, respectively.

STEP 6 **Exit dBASE**

Type **QUIT** to exit dBASE and return to DOS.

The Roster Program

Completion of the second hands-on exercise should have familiarized you with two important commands, SELECT and SET RELATION, used in conjunction with the multiple DBF files constituting a relational database. The exercise was restricted, however, in the sense that these commands were entered from the dot prompt, as opposed to being included in a program. Accordingly, we move now to the development of the roster program from the first hands-on exercise, and begin with the pseudocode of Figure 13.6.

FIGURE 13.6
Pseudocode for the Roster Program

```
Open the team, coach, sponsor, and player files
Select the TEAM.DBF file as the active file
DO WHILE team records remain
   Display the appropriate team heading information
   Set relation into the coach file
   Display the associated coach information
   Set relation into the sponsor file
   Display the associated sponsor information
   Set relation into the player file
   Select the PLAYER.DBF file as the active file
   DO WHILE players are on this team
      Display player data
      Get next player record
   ENDDO
   Select the TEAM.DBF file as the active file
   Get next team record
ENDDO
RETURN
```

In essence, the specifications require the preparation of a roster for every record within the team file. Hence, after opening all four files, the team file is selected as the active file, and a **DO WHILE** loop is executed once for every record in the team file. The team information for the current record is displayed, then a relation into the coach file is established, after which the corresponding coach information can be shown. Similar steps are followed for the sponsor file.

The player file requires a different approach in that several players are associated with a given team. Accordingly, an inner loop is entered, which displays data for all players on that team, after which the inner loop ends. (The precise way in which this is accomplished has to do with how the player file is indexed, and is further explained in conjunction with the completed program.) The team file is again made the active file, a new team record is read, and the process begins anew.

The completed program is shown in Figure 13.7 and should present little difficulty. (It may be helpful, however, to review the output produced by this program from the first hands-on exercise.) The program begins with the usual housekeeping commands to disable the **TALK**, **SCOREBOARD**, and **STATUS** features (all of which are discussed further in the Programmer's Notebook). The screen is cleared and a double-line border is drawn.

Four successive pairs of **SELECT** and **USE** commands open the team, coach, sponsor, and player files in areas one, two, three, and four, respectively. A concatenated index, based on **TEAM_ID+LAST_NAME**, is used for the player file, to list the players alphabetically within each team. Area one (containing the team file) is selected as the active area, and the main loop is entered.

Information for the current team record is displayed on the screen through a series of **@...SAY** commands. A relation is set into the coach file, after which the associated coach data is displayed through another series of **@...SAY** commands. A second relation is set into the sponsor file, and the associated sponsor data is also displayed.

A relation is set into the player file, moving the record pointer to the first player for the current team. The player area is made active, and a second loop is entered to display player data, as long as the value in the **TEAM_ID** field in the player record matches the **TEAM_ID** from the team record. (Recall that the player file has **TEAM_ID** as its primary index, so that all players in a given team are retrieved in succession.)

There are two distinct **SKIP** commands within the program. The first occurs within the inner loop that displays all players on one team and moves to the next

```
SET TALK OFF
SET SCOREBOARD OFF
SET STATUS OFF
CLEAR
@ 1,1 TO 23,79  DOUBLE
@ 11,2 TO 11,78 DOUBLE
SELECT 1
USE team ORDER team_id
SELECT 2
USE coach ORDER coach_id
SELECT 3
USE sponsor ORDER sponsor_id
SELECT 4
USE player ORDER team_id
SELECT 1
DO WHILE .NOT. EOF()
   STORE 'CORAL SPRINGS SOCCER ASSOCIATION' TO mtitle
   @ 2,(80 - LEN(mtitle))/2 SAY mtitle
   @ 4,3   SAY "Team number:"
   @ 4,16  SAY team->team_id
   @ 4,39  SAY "Team colors:"
   @ 4,52  SAY team->>colors
   SET RELATION TO coach_id INTO coach
   @ 6,3   SAY "Coach:"
   @ 6,10  SAY TRIM(coach->first_name) + ' ' + TRIM(coach->last_name)
   @ 7,10  SAY coach->street
   @ 8,10  SAY TRIM(coach->city) + '  ' + TRIM(coach->state) + ' ' + ;
     coach-zip_code
   @ 9,10  SAY "Telephone:"
   @ 9,21  SAY coach->phone  FUNCTION "R"  PICTURE "999-9999"
   @ 10,10  SAY "Class"
   @ 10,16  SAY coach->license
   @ 10,18  SAY "License"
   SET RELATION TO sponsor_id INTO sponsor
   @ 6,43  SAY "Sponsor:"
   @ 6,52  SAY sponsor->name
   @ 7,52  SAY sponsor->contact
   @ 8,52  SAY sponsor->street
   @ 9,52  SAY TRIM(sponsor->city) + '  ' + TRIM(sponsor->state) + ' ' + ;
     sponsor->zip_code
   @ 10,52 SAY "Telephone:"
   @ 10,63 SAY sponsor->phone  FUNCTION "R"  PICTURE "999-9999"
   @ 12,16  SAY "      Player                Birthdate         Rating"
   @ 13,16  SAY "      ______                _________         ______"
   SET RELATION TO team_id INTO player
   STORE 14 TO mline
   SELECT 4
   DO WHILE team_id = team->team_id
      @ mline,18 SAY TRIM(player->first_name) + ' ' + player->last_name
      @ mline,41 SAY player->birth_date
      @ mline,59 SAY player->rating
      STORE mline + 1 TO mline
      SKIP
   ENDDO
   STORE 'PRESS ANY KEY TO CONTINUE' TO message
   @ 22,(80 - LEN(message))/2 SAY message
   SET CONSOLE OFF
   WAIT
   SET CONSOLE ON
   SELECT 1
   SKIP
   @ 2,2 CLEAR TO 10,78
   @ 12,2 CLEAR TO 22,78
ENDDO
CLEAR
CLOSE DATABASES
SET STATUS ON
SET SCOREBOARD ON
SET TALK ON
RETURN
```

FIGURE 13.7
The Roster Program

record in the player file; the second occurs within the outer loop to go from one team to the next. The condition in the inner loop determines if the next player is on the same team, and if so, the **SKIP** command in the inner loop is executed. If, however, the player is on a different team, control passes out of the inner loop to the statement that displays the message, *Press any key to continue,* and then to the **SKIP** statement in the outer loop to move to the next team record.

Summary

A ***one-to-many*** relationship (e.g., one team has many players) requires that the primary key of the *singular* item (team) appear as a foreign key in the file of the *many* item (player).

As many as ten **DBF** files can be open at once, provided each file is assigned a different ***work area.*** The **SELECT** command determines the active work area by specifying a number from one to ten.

The **SET RELATION** command establishes a link between records in the active **DBF** file and a **DBF** file in another work area. The relationship is based on a ***common field*** (a field with the same field name, type, width, and contents) in both files, and requires that the related file be indexed on this field.

The **DISPLAY STATUS** command shows all open files and their associated work areas, the key fields for all indexes, and the relations currently in effect. Use of the command is by no means restricted to examples dealing with relational databases.

Key Words and Concepts

Active file
Column
Common field
DISPLAY STATUS
Field
File maintenance
NOFOLLOW
One-to-many relationship
Open file
Record
Redundancy
Relation
Relational database
Row
Table
SELECT
SET RELATION
Work area
->

True/False

1. The identical field name can appear in multiple **DBF** files.
2. A **SET RELATION** command can link more than two **DBF** files at one time.
3. Several **DBF** files can be open simultaneously.
4. Several **DBF** files can be active simultaneously.
5. The individual files in a database must each contain the same number of records.
6. The **SET RELATION** command requires the related file to be open with an index.
7. A single **DISPLAY** command can reference fields from more than one **DBF** file.
8. The **DISPLAY STATUS** command shows all open files and their associated indexes.
9. The **SET RELATION** command with no parameters cancels the existing relation.
10. A database cannot include more than a single one-to-many relationship.

Exercises

1. Distinguish between:
   (a) A file and a database
   (b) An open file and an active file
   (c) A relation and a relational database
   (d) Including (omitting) a **SELECT** command prior to a **USE** command
   (e) **DISPLAY STATUS** versus **DISPLAY STRUCTURE**
   (f) The field names, **COACH_ID** and **COACH->COACH_ID**

2. Use the file contents of Figure 13.2 to answer the following questions:
   (a) How many players are on team **GU1401**?
   (b) Who coaches team **GU1202**?
   (c) What is the sponsor's phone number for team **GU1601**?
   (d) Which coaches have a class E license?
   (e) What color is Norma Pagan's uniform?
   (f) What is the phone number of Gina Wilson's coach?
   (g) Is there any team without a sponsor?
   (h) Which team is coached by John Osberger?

3. Use the existing files in the **SOCCER** subdirectory and the appropriate **LIST** (and other) commands to create the following reports, all of which are to be produced from the dot prompt. Do this problem *after* completing the first hands-on exercise so that every one in the class is working with the identical data and can expect the same answers.
   (a) An alphabetical list of all coaches, listing the coach's first and last name, phone number, and license
   (b) An alphabetical list of all sponsors, listing the sponsor's name, contact person, and phone number
   (c) An alphabetical list of all players with a rating of 1 or 2
   (d) A list of all teams with both a coach and a sponsor

4. Use the existing files in the **SOCCER** subdirectory to make the following roster changes, then rerun the roster program after all changes have been made. As in the previous exercise, be sure you have completed the first hands-on exercise in the chapter, so that everyone in the class is working with the identical data.
   (a) Change the team assignment for Meredith Allen from team **GU1402** to team **GU1401**.
   (b) Drop Coach Granger from team **GU1601**; Coach Osberger will take his place.
   (c) Add the following players:

   ```
   Nicole Johnson, 6/6/77, Rating 2, to team GU1402
   Ivy Cordell, 8/11/76, Rating 1, to team GU1601
   Sara Osberger, 11/24/76, Rating 2, to team GU1601
   Jessica Syltie, 3/23/75, Rating 1, to team GU1601
   ```

   (d) Change the contact person for Wendy's from Jill Simmons to Cory Kruell.
   (e) Change Lori Fromkin's player rating from 4 to 2.
   (f) Delete player Nancy Anderson from the system as her family has moved out of Coral Springs.

5. List the active and open file(s) for each of the command sequences shown below:

   Set 1

   ```
   SELECT 1
   USE PLAYER
   ```

```
Select area:  1, Database in Use: C:\DATADISK\SOCCER\TEAM.DBF
  Alias: TEAM
Production   MDX file:  C:\DATADISK\SOCCER\TEAM.MDX
    Master Index TAG:      TEAM_ID  Key: TEAM_ID
    Related into: PLAYER
    Relation: TEAM_ID

Select area:  2, Database in Use: C:\DATADISK\SOCCER\COACH.DBF
  Alias: COACH
Production   MDX file:  C:\DATADISK\SOCCER\COACH.MDX
    Master Index TAG:      COACH_ID  Key: COACH_ID
           Index TAG:      LAST_NAME Key:  LAST_NAME

Select area:  3, Database in Use: C:\DATADISK\SOCCER\SPONSOR.DBF
  Alias: SPONSOR
Production   MDX file:  C:\DATADISK\SOCCER\SPONSOR.MDX
    Master Index TAG:      SPONSOR_ID  Key: SPONSOR_ID

Currently Selected Database:
Select area:  4, Database in Use: C:\DATADISK\SOCCER\PLAYER.DBF
  Alias: PLAYER
Production   MDX file:  C:\DATADISK\SOCCER\PLAYER.MDX
    Master Index TAG:      TEAM_ID  Key: TEAM_ID+LAST_NAME

Press any key to continue...
```

FIGURE 13.8
DISPLAY STATUS Command for Problem 6

```
SELECT 2
USE COACH
```

Set 2

```
SELECT 1
USE PLAYER
USE COACH
```

Set 3

```
SELECT 1
USE PLAYER
SELECT 2
USE COACH
SELECT 1
```

6. Figure 13.8 contains partial output produced by the **DISPLAY STATUS** command. Answer the following questions, based on information contained in the figure:
   (a) Which **DBF** files are open? To which work areas are they assigned?
   (b) What is the master index tag for each of the files in part a?
   (c) Which **DBF** file is active? To which work area is it assigned?
   (d) What is the master index tag for the file in part c? On what key is the index based?
   (e) What relation is currently in effect?
   (f) What additional information will appear in the next screen(s) after pressing any key to continue?

7. Answer the following with respect to statements within the inner loop of the **ROSTER** program of Figure 13.7:
   (a) On what line (of the monitor) is the information for the first player on a team displayed?

(b) What would be the effect of substituting `mline+2` for `mline+1` in the `STORE` statement within the loop?
(c) What would be the effect of removing the `STORE` statement altogether?
(d) What would be the effect of removing the `SKIP` statement within the loop?
(e) What would be the effect of substituting `SKIP +2` for the original `SKIP` statement?
(f) According to the logic of the program, what is the minimum number of players that will be displayed for each team?

CHAPTER

14 Introduction to SQL

OUTLINE

OBJECTIVES

After reading this chapter you will be able to:

1. Explain the relationship between SQL and dBASE IV and how you go back and forth between the two.
2. Convert a set of existing `DBF` files to a SQL database; describe the purpose of the following SQL commands: `CREATE DATABASE`, `DBDEFINE`, `SHOW DATABASE`, `START DATABASE`, `STOP DATABASE`, and `DROP DATABASE`.
3. Describe the SQL `SELECT` command and the function of the `FROM` and `WHERE` clauses; discuss at least three other clauses in the `SELECT` command.
4. Use the SQL `SELECT` command for multiple-file queries; define the concept of a join operation.
5. Explain the SQL edit window and its use with interactive `SQL` commands.
6. Show how SQL tables can be maintained as `DBF` files through ordinary `dBASE` commands (`APPEND`, `EDIT`, `BROWSE`, `DELETE`, and `PACK`); describe the purpose of the SQL `DBCHECK` and `RUNSTATS` commands.

Overview

Structured Query Language (SQL) was designed originally by IBM in the mid 1970s, and has since become the standard language for accessing a relational database. It is a very eloquent language consisting of approximately 30 commands, which are sufficient to perform all operations associated with a relational database. There are, for example, commands to create tables, and to insert, update, and delete data in those tables. The essence of SQL, however, is the **SELECT** command and its ability to access the data. This single command, and its many parameters, constitute the bulk of our discussion.

SQL (pronounced *sequel*) may be run independently (i.e., as a language unto itself) or its commands may be embedded within other languages such as dBASE or COBOL. You can, for example, maintain files through traditional dBASE commands (APPEND, EDIT, DELETE, etc.), then use the **DBDEFINE** command to convert the DBF files to SQL tables, and finally use the SQL SELECT command to query the database. The dBASE **SET SQL ON/OFF** command alternates between the dBASE/SQL and dBASE-only modes.

Once again, we begin with a new case study, to provide additional practice in database design.

CASE PREVIEW

The case you are about to read is centered on class scheduling within a university, a problem with which you are all familiar. The chairpersons of the individual academic departments are the persons responsible for determining the schedule, as they decide which courses will be given next semester, how many sections of each course to offer, when and where the sections will meet, and finally, the faculty assignments.

Read the case carefully, and as you do, look for the various entities that are present in the system, remembering that each entity requires its own table. Identify the relationships that exist between the different entities (e.g., several sections of the same course can be offered, with each section taught by a different faculty member), then look for the common fields needed to implement these relationships.

CASE STUDY
Class Scheduling

Class scheduling represents a major undertaking at any university and entails the coordination of course offerings as published in a registration schedule with faculty assignments. The essence of the problem can be seen by examining Figure 14.1, which displays different information, depending on the recipient of the report.

Figure 14.1a displays a course schedule as it would appear in a student bulletin, and lists courses in sequence by a course identification number. All courses have a formal title but are more commonly known by a six position course-id; e.g., COBOL Programming is simply CIS223. The first three characters in the course-id denote the department (e.g., CIS stands for Computer Information Systems), whereas the last three indicate the particular course. Figure 14.1a displays the number of credits for each course, the days and hours on which it meets, and finally the location (i.e., the building and room). The complete schedule will contain courses for every department in the university, not just those for the CIS department.

There can, of course, be multiple sections of any given course; e.g., CIS120 is offered four different times—at 9:00, 10:00, 11:00, and 12:00—with all sections meeting three days a week (Mondays, Wednesdays, and Fridays). The information about when a class meets is summarized in the one-letter section designation, e.g., section A meets from 9:00 to 9:50 on Mondays, Wednesdays, and Fridays.

Figure 14.1b displays the course schedule as it might be used by a department chairperson or dean, who needs to know which faculty are teaching which courses, the academic rank of the faculty member, and whether that individual is an adjunct or full-time instructor. The administrator also needs information about a faculty member's salary, highest degree, and sex, although none of that data is displayed in the course schedule.

Design a relational database to satisfy these requirements.

CASE SOLUTION

Our solution recognizes four entities—*offerings, faculty, sections,* and *courses*—each of which requires its own SQL table (dBASE file) as shown in Figure 14.2. The design is easy, almost obvious, once you pick up on a critical sentence in the case preview, i.e., *several sections of the same course can be offered, with each section taught by a different faculty member.* In other words, the combination of a particular course, section, and faculty member is unique, and serves as the primary key for the *offering table* of Figure 14.2a. Let us consider first, however, the other tables in the solution.

The *faculty table* in Figure 14.2b contains data for each faculty member. The individual's last name is assumed to be unique (for the sake of simplicity), and thus **LAST_NAME** becomes the primary key for the faculty table. The other fields—rank, status (full-time or adjunct), degree, and so on—follow directly from the case description and need no further explanation.

The *section table* in Figure 14.2c uses a one-letter **SECTION** designation as its primary key, which in turn will indicate the days and hours a course will meet; e.g., Section A meets from 9:00 to 9:50 on Mondays, Wednesdays, and Fridays. The *course table* in Figure 14.2d uses a unique six-character **COURSE_ID** as its primary key, which determines the course title and number of credits; e.g., CIS223 is a three-credit course in COBOL Programming.

FIGURE 14.1
Course Schedule

COURSE_ID	SECTION	TITLE	CREDITS	DAYS	HOURS	BUILDING	ROOM
CIS120	A	Intro to Computers	3	MWF	9:00 - 9:50	Jenkins	408
CIS120	B	Intro to Computers	3	MWF	10:00 - 10:50	Jenkins	408
CIS120	C	Intro to Computers	3	MWF	11:00 - 11:50	Jenkins	408
CIS120	D	Intro to Computers	3	MWF	12:00 - 12:50	Jenkins	408
CIS223	A	COBOL Programming	3	MWF	9:00 - 10:00	Memorial	210
CIS223	D	COBOL Programming	3	MWF	12:00 - 12:50	Jenkins	401
CIS420	B	Systems Analysis	3	MWF	10:00 - 10:50	Memorial	200
CIS523	D	Intro to Database	3	MWF	12:00 - 12:50	Memorial	305
CIS526	C	Advanced COBOL	3	MWF	11:00 - 11:50	Jenkins	402

(a) Schedule for Student Bulletin

LAST_NAME	COURSE_ID	SECTION	RANK	STATUS
Barber	CIS120	A	Professor	Full time
Barber	CIS120	D	Professor	Full time
Gillenson	CIS523	D	Instructor	Adjunct
Goldsmith	CIS120	C	Assoc Prof	Adjunct
Grauer	CIS223	D	Professor	Full time
Grauer	CIS526	C	Professor	Full time
Stutz	CIS420	B	Instructor	Full time
Vazquez	CIS120	B	Asst Prof	Full time
Vazquez	CIS223	A	Asst Prof	Full time

(b) Schedule for Administration

FIGURE 14.2
dBASE File Structures

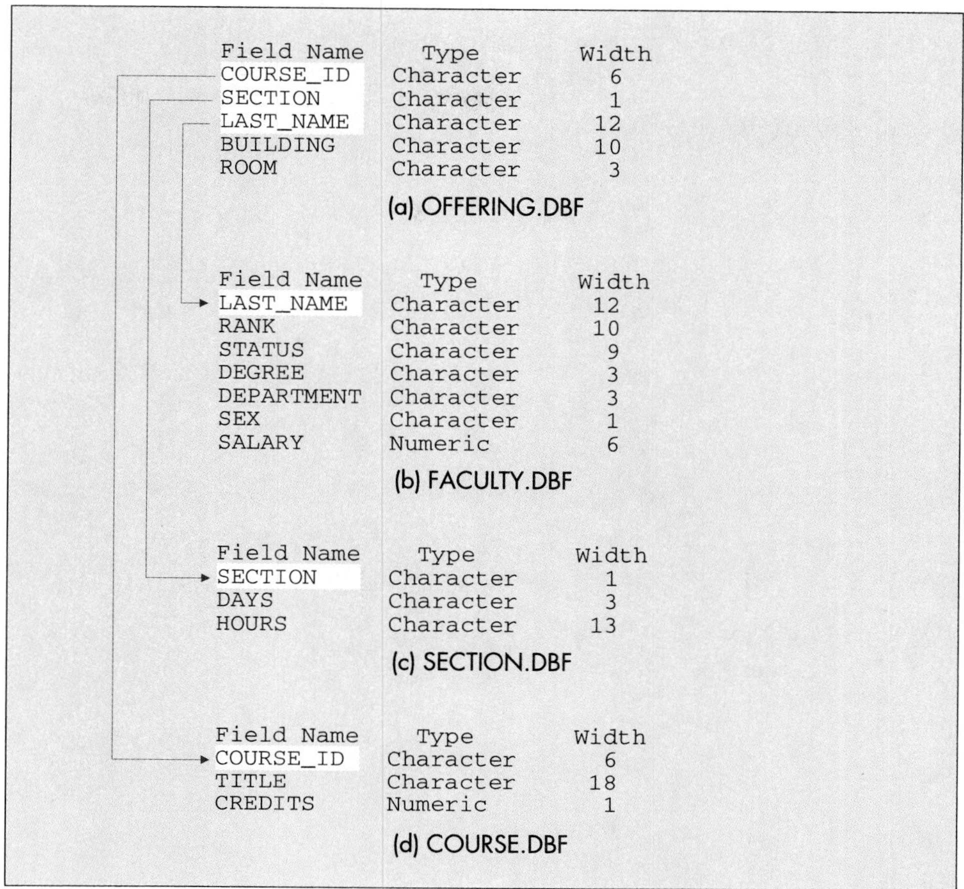

Field Name	Type	Width
COURSE_ID	Character	6
SECTION	Character	1
LAST_NAME	Character	12
BUILDING	Character	10
ROOM	Character	3

(a) OFFERING.DBF

Field Name	Type	Width
LAST_NAME	Character	12
RANK	Character	10
STATUS	Character	9
DEGREE	Character	3
DEPARTMENT	Character	3
SEX	Character	1
SALARY	Numeric	6

(b) FACULTY.DBF

Field Name	Type	Width
SECTION	Character	1
DAYS	Character	3
HOURS	Character	13

(c) SECTION.DBF

Field Name	Type	Width
COURSE_ID	Character	6
TITLE	Character	18
CREDITS	Numeric	1

(d) COURSE.DBF

As indicated, the combination of a course-id, section, and faculty member's last name is unique and becomes the primary key in the offering table. The individual columns—**COURSE_ID**, **SECTION**, and **LAST_NAME** (each of which is a primary key in its respective table)—appear as *foreign keys* in the offering table, which then determines the building and room for that offering.

Remember, too, that all columns other than the primary key must be dependent on *the key, the whole key, and nothing but the key, so help me Codd.*[1] Thus, the building and room in which a class meets (i.e., the other fields in the offering table) are each determined by the *primary key* of the offering table (the combination of **COURSE_ID**, **SECTION**, and **LAST_NAME**), the *whole key* (all three columns are needed), and *nothing but the key* (no other columns are necessary to determine the building or room).

To be absolutely sure that you understand our design, and also to appreciate the types of queries that can be made to the database, use the data in Figure 14.3 to answer the following:

Questions

1. Which courses is Professor Grauer teaching next semester?
2. How many *different* courses are offered next semester?

[1] The relational model was developed by Dr. Edgar F. Codd of IBM in 1970 as mentioned in Chapter 12.

COURSE_ID	SECTION	LAST_NAME	BUILDING	ROOM
CIS120	A	Barber	Jenkins	408
CIS120	D	Barber	Jenkins	408
CIS223	A	Vazquez	Memorial	210
CIS120	B	Vazquez	Jenkins	408
CIS526	C	Grauer	Jenkins	402
CIS420	B	Stutz	Memorial	200
CIS523	D	Gillenson	Memorial	305
CIS120	C	Goldsmith	Jenkins	408
CIS223	D	Grauer	Jenkins	401

(a) OFFERING.DBF

LAST_NAME	RANK	STATUS	DEGREE	DEPARTMENT	SEX	SALARY
Barber	Professor	Full time	PhD	CIS	F	100000
Gillenson	Instructor	Adjunct	MS	CIS	M	22000
Goldsmith	Assoc Prof	Adjunct	PhD	CIS	M	25000
Grauer	Professor	Full time	PhD	CIS	M	75000
Stutz	Instructor	Full time	MS	CIS	M	30000
Vazquez	Asst Prof	Full time	PhD	CIS	F	50000
Hernandez	Instructor	Adjunct	MS	CIS	M	21000

(b) FACULTY.DBF

SECTION	DAYS	HOURS
A	MWF	9:00 - 9:50
B	MWF	10:00 - 10:50
C	MWF	11:00 - 11:50
D	MWF	12:00 - 12:50

(c) SECTION.DBF

COURSE_ID	TITLE	CREDITS
CIS120	Intro to Computers	3
CIS223	COBOL Programming	4
CIS420	Systems Analysis	3
CIS523	Intro to Database	3
CIS526	Advanced COBOL	4
CIS226	Assembler Language	3

(a) COURSE.DBF

FIGURE 14.3
File Contents

3. Where does Professor Goldsmith's CIS120 class meet?
4. When (i.e., at what day and time) is CIS223 offered?
5. Is Assembler Language offered next semester?
6. Which classes meet in the Memorial building?
7. Which professor has the highest salary?
8. Which full-time faculty do not have a PhD?
9. How many women are in the CIS department?

Answers

1. Professor Grauer is teaching CIS526 (Advanced COBOL) and CIS223 (COBOL Programming).
2. Five different courses are offered (CIS120, CIS223, CIS420, CIS523, and CIS526).
3. Professor Goldsmith's CIS120 class meets in Jenkins 408.

4. COBOL Programming, i.e., CIS223, is offered in sections A and D, which meet from 9:00 to 9:50 and from 12:00 to 12:50, respectively, on Mondays, Wednesdays, and Fridays.
5. Assembler Language, i.e., CIS226, is not offered.
6. CIS223 (Section A), CIS420, and CIS523 meet in the Memorial building.
7. Professor Barber has the highest salary (which is wishful thinking on the part of the author).
8. Stutz is the only full-time faculty member without a PhD.
9. There are two women in the CIS department (Barber and Vazquez).

Overview of SQL

The case solution ended with a series of questions about the database, which required you to manually examine one or more of the tables in Figure 14.3. An easier way to obtain the same information would be to develop the equivalent SQL queries, which brings us to a discussion of SQL. It is an eloquent language, consisting of approximately 30 commands, with the exact number dependent on the specific implementation. For ease of presentation, we divide SQL commands into three general categories as follows:

1. Commands that are unique to a specific implementation, e.g., the commands to convert **DBF** files in dBASE IV to the equivalent SQL tables. These commands are discussed in the next section and are the focus of the first hands-on exercise.
2. The **SELECT** command, which is by far the most important SQL command and which is covered in detail in the second half of the chapter. Each of the questions posed in the case solution can be answered with the appropriate **SELECT** command.
3. Additional commands to maintain the SQL tables, which are mentioned briefly toward the end of the chapter. These commands are de-emphasized, however, because the dBASE implementation of SQL makes it possible to maintain SQL tables with traditional dBASE commands (**APPEND**, **EDIT**, **DELETE**, and so on).

As we continue our discussion of SQL and its implementation in dBASE IV, remember that SQL terminology (table, row, and column) differs from that used by dBASE (file, record, and field). The underlying concepts are similar, however, and you generally can understand one by thinking of the other.

Implementation in dBASE IV

The **SET SQL ON/OFF** command alternates between the dBASE/SQL mode and the dBASE-only mode; i.e., you can still execute (some) dBASE commands from within SQL, but you cannot execute any SQL commands from within dBASE. To go from the dBASE-only mode to the dBASE/SQL mode, type **SET SQL ON** at the dot prompt; to leave SQL and go back to dBASE, type **SET SQL OFF** at the **SQL** ***prompt.***

The SQL commands specific to dBASE IV (i.e., that may not exist in other SQL implementations) are listed in Table 14.1. *All SQL commands must end with a semicolon, and failure to do so produces a syntax error.* Upper-case letters indicate a reserved word in SQL, whereas lower-case letters denote a user-supplied entry.

The **CREATE DATABASE** command establishes a set of SQL system tables for the named database, storing those tables in a *separate* DOS directory. (The directory

TABLE 14.1 **SQL Commands Specific to dBASE IV**

Commands to create and/or activate a SQL database:
```
CREATE DATABASE <database name>;
DBDEFINE <filename>;
SHOW DATABASE;
START DATABASE <database name>;
```
Commands to deactivate and/or delete a SQL database:
```
STOP DATABASE;
DROP DATABASE <database name>;
```
Command to update SQL tables:
```
RUNSTATS;
```
Commands to enter or exit SQL:
```
SET SQL ON
SET SQL OFF
```

will be created if it doesn't already exist.) The name of the directory is *always* the same as the database specified in the command; for example, the command `CREATE DATABASE\DATADISK\SCHEDULE;` creates a database that is named `SCHEDULE` in the DOS directory of the same name.

The **DBDEFINE** command converts an existing `DBF` file (together with any associated indexes) to the equivalent SQL table (and indexes).

The **SHOW DATABASE** command lists all SQL databases on the system, displaying the name of the database, its creator, date of creation, and complete DOS path.

The **START DATABASE** command activates an existing database. The `START DATABASE` command is not required after a `CREATE DATABASE` command as the latter automatically starts the newly created database. `START DATABASE` is required, however, at all other times the database is to be accessed.

The **STOP DATABASE** command deactivates the current database. The **DROP DATABASE** command deletes a SQL database, effectively deleting all SQL tables (and corresponding `DBF` files). A `STOP DATABASE` command must be issued prior to deleting an active SQL database.

The **RUNSTATS** command updates the SQL system tables and should be used whenever you modify any SQL tables with traditional dBASE commands.

We are ready now for the first hands-on exercise, in which we create a SQL database from existing `DBF` files. The exercise is straightforward and should be done without difficulty. As you do the exercise, remember that *all SQL commands must end with a semicolon,* and failure to do so will produce a syntax error. All SQL commands in the exercise will be entered interactively at the SQL prompt.

HANDS-ON EXERCISE 1

SQL and dBASE IV

Objective

Create a SQL database from existing `DBF` files; introduce the SQL `SELECT` command to view the contents of a SQL table.

STEP 1 **Change to the SCHEDULE directory**

Boot the system, ending at the DOS prompt. Type one of the following two commands, depending on whether you are sharing the hard drive with others:

CD C:\DATADISK\SCHEDULE — *if you installed the data disk on the hard drive and are not sharing your computer, or*

CD A:\DATADISK\SCHEDULE — *if you did not install the data disk, i.e., if you are sharing drive C with other students. (Use data disk two if you have 5¼-inch disks.)*

STEP 2 **Examine the existing DBF files**

Type **dBASE** to load dBASE, then set the default drive as you have in previous exercises. Type **DIR** at the dot prompt to see the names of the existing DBF files (COURSE, FACULTY, OFFERING, and SECTION) in the SCHEDULE subdirectory.

You are in dBASE and at the dot prompt, and thus you can use any of the normal dBASE commands for file maintenance—e.g. USE, LIST, APPEND, EDIT, BROWSE, DELETE, or PACK. Explore the existing files as you see fit, then enter the SQL mode as described in the next step.

STEP 3 **Enter SQL**

Type **CLOSE ALL** to close all DBF files *prior* to entering SQL. This command is absolutely critical, and you will run into difficulty if you forget it. Type **SET SQL ON** to enter SQL, which in turn produces the SQL prompt.

STEP 4 **Create the SCHEDULE database**

Type **CREATE DATABASE\DATADISK\SCHEDULE;** (*remember the semicolon at the end of the command*) to create the SQL system tables for the database called SCHEDULE in the DOS directory of the same name. You should see the message, *Database SCHEDULE created* after the command has executed successfully. (Note, however, that you cannot create a database more than once; i.e., you cannot create a SQL database if it already exists. Thus, if you see the message that the *SCHEDULE database already exists,* you need to drop the database as described in step 8.)

STEP 5 **The SHOW DATABASE command**

Type **SHOW DATABASE;** to show the SQL databases that exist on your system, whereupon you will see the name of each database, the creator, the date it was created, and the DOS path (i.e., the directory in which it is contained). The output of the command will resemble, but not match exactly, the output below:

```
NAME     CREATOR CREATED   PATH
SAMPLES  SYSTEM  11/17/90  C:\DBASEIV\SAMPLES
SCHEDULE         06/29/91  C:\DATADISK\SCHEDULE
```

At the very least, you should see the SCHEDULE database just created (although your creation date will be different from ours) and most likely the SAMPLES database provided by Ashton-Tate as a SQL demo. You may or may not see other entries, depending on your particular system.

STEP 6 **The HELP command**

The SQL help facility is easily accessed by typing **HELP** (the semicolon is *not* required) at the SQL prompt. Figure 14.4a displays the initial help screen; choosing the *SQL commands* option produces the alphabetical list of commands in Figure 14.4b. Addi-

FIGURE 14.4
SQL Help Facility

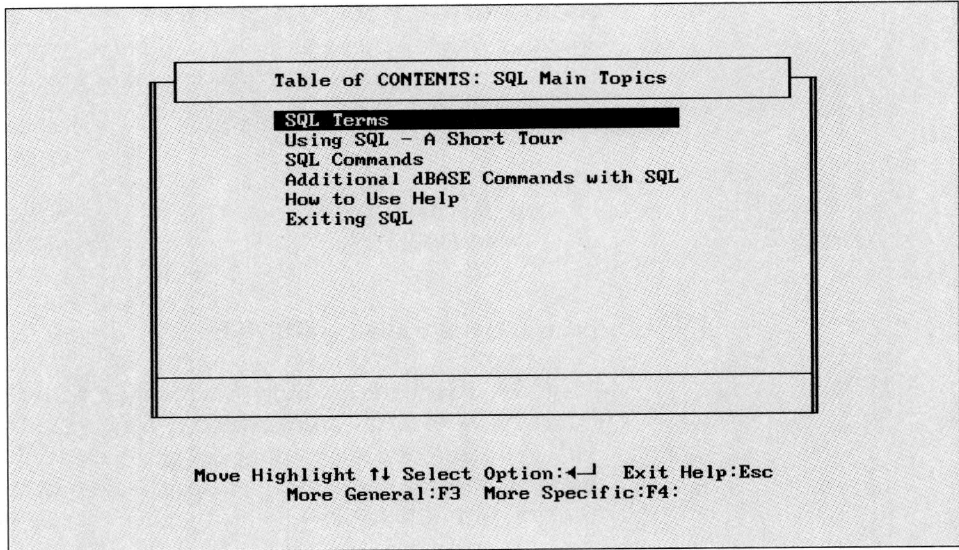

(a) Initial Help Screen

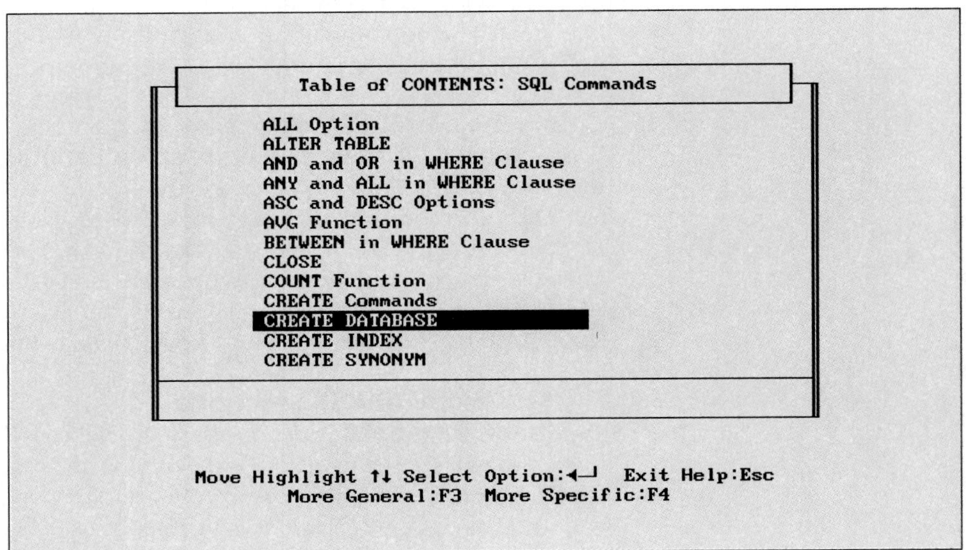

(b) SQL Commands

tional help screens provide the detailed syntax for any highlighted command. Press **Esc** to return to the SQL prompt.

STEP 7 **Define the SQL tables**

The **CREATE DATABASE** command of step 4 established the SQL system tables, but it did not define the tables unique to the scheduling application. Accordingly, we need to issue a series of **DBDEFINE** commands to convert the existing **DBF** files to their SQL equivalents. Type the following commands:

```
SQL. DBDEFINE OFFERING;
SQL. DBDEFINE FACULTY;
```

```
SQL. DBDEFINE SECTION;
SQL. DBDEFINE COURSE;
```

If you followed our instructions exactly, the commands should execute without error and indicate that the referenced tables were successfully defined. If you were successful with all four commands, congratulate yourself on a job well done and move to step 9.

The most common mistake is to omit the semicolon at the end of a command, which produces a message indicating a *syntax error.* Press the **up arrow** key to restore the erroneous command from the command buffer, type a semicolon at the end of the line, then press the **enter** key to re-execute the command. Another common mistake is to misspell one of the table names, which can be corrected in similar fashion.

If you are still having difficulty and are unable to create the database and/or unable to define the tables, it may be necessary for you to drop the database and start over. This is a drastic step and should be done only as a last resort.

STEP 8 **The DROP DATABASE command**

Do this step only if you were unable to create the database in step 4 and/or were unable to successfully define the tables in step 7. Type the following commands:

```
SQL. STOP DATABASE;
SQL. DROP DATABASE SCHEDULE;
```

You will see a warning message indicating that the DROP DATABASE command will drop all SQL tables (i.e., it will erase all DBF files, including OFFERING, STUDENT, COURSE, and FACULTY), making it necessary to recopy these files from the data disk. Select *Proceed,* then locate the data disk that came with the text in order to recopy the original DBF files back to the appropriate subdirectory. Type

RUN COPY C:\DATADISK\BKUP*.DBF C: —— *if you installed the data disk on the hard drive and are not sharing your computer, or*

RUN COPY A:\DATADISK\BKUP*.DBF A: —— *if you did not install the data disk, i.e., if you are sharing drive C with other students. (Use data disk two if you have 5¼-inch disks.)*

Type **DIR** to make sure the DBF files have been restored from the data disk, then return to step 4 and start again.

STEP 9 **The SELECT command**

The syntax of the SELECT command will be covered in detail after the exercise. For the time being, however, enter the following commands to display the contents of the tables in our database:

```
SQL. SELECT * FROM OFFERING;
SQL. SELECT * FROM FACULTY;
SQL. SELECT * FROM SECTION;
SQL. SELECT * FROM COURSE;
```

Should you make a mistake and forget the ending semicolon or misspell a table name, remember to press the **up arrow** key to retrieve the erroneous command, edit the command, then press **enter** to re-execute the corrected command.

```
. DIR
```
DIR command is entered at dot prompt and shows all DBF files

Database Files	# Records	Last Update	Size
OFFERING.DBF	9	06/29/91	491
SECTION.DBF	4	06/29/91	202
COURSE.DBF	6	07/01/91	286
FACULTY.DBF	7	07/01/91	573
SYSIDXS.DBF	0	03/21/88	418
SYSKEYS.DBF	0	03/21/88	226
SYSVIEWS.DBF	0	06/16/88	258
SYSVDEPS.DBF	0	03/21/88	270
SYSSYNS.DBF	0	03/21/88	163
SYSAUTH.DBF	10	06/16/88	1156
SYSCOLAU.DBF	0	03/21/88	226
SYSTIMES.DBF	11	06/16/88	427
SYSTABLS.DBF	14	07/01/91	1391
SYSCOLS.DBF	93	07/01/91	6743

SQL System tables

(a) System Tables

```
. USE SYSTABLS
. LIST OFF TBNAME,CREATOR,COLCOUNT,CLUSTERRID,CREATED
```

TBNAME	CREATOR	COLCOUNT	CLUSTERRID	CREATED
SYSTABLS	SYSTEM	10	10	01/01/88
SYSCOLS	SYSTEM	12	75	01/01/88
SYSIDXS	SYSTEM	12	0	01/01/88
SYSKEYS	SYSTEM	6	0	01/01/88
SYSVIEWS	SYSTEM	7	0	01/01/88
SYSVDEPS	SYSTEM	4	0	01/01/88
SYSSYNS	SYSTEM	4	0	01/01/88
SYSAUTH	SYSTEM	11	10	01/01/88
SYSCOLAU	SYSTEM	6	0	01/01/88
SYSTIMES	SYSTEM	3	11	01/01/88
COURSE		3	6	07/01/91
FACULTY		7	7	07/01/91
OFFERING		5	9	07/01/91
SECTION		3	4	07/01/91

User tables created through DBDEFINE commands

(b) The SYSTABLS.DBF

FIGURE 14.5
SQL Tables

STEP 10 **Exit SQL**

Type **STOP DATABASE;** to close the **SCHEDULE** database, then type **SET SQL OFF** (the semicolon is *not* required) to return to the dot prompt.

STEP 11 **Examine all DBF files**

Type **DIR** at the dot prompt to show the existing **DBF** files; a total of 14 files should appear on your monitor as shown in Figure 14.5a. The first four (**OFFERING**, **SECTION**, **COURSE**, and **FACULTY**) seem familiar, whereas the other 10 files are SQL system tables that were created by the **CREATE DATABASE** command in step 4. You can examine the contents of any **DBF** file exactly as you always have, i.e., by using the file and then listing it; do *not,* however, modify the system tables, or you will destroy the integrity of your database.

The **SYSTABLS.DBF** file is especially interesting as it contains the names and characteristics of the other SQL tables as shown in Figure 14.5b. Observe, for example, the values of the **COLCOUNT** and **CLUSTERID** fields corresponding to the number of columns (fields) and rows (records) in the respective files (tables).

The SELECT Command

The **SELECT** command is the very essence of SQL, as it is the means by which you access data in a relational database. Indeed, you can get along very nicely with just the **SELECT** command, in combination with dBASE specific commands to establish the database, as was done in the hands-on exercise. We begin with the *simplest* form of the **SELECT** command, then expand the discussion to include some of its many optional parameters. Consider:

Syntax

```
SELECT <columns>
   FROM <table>
   [WHERE condition];
```

Example

```
SELECT COURSE_ID, SECTION, BUILDING, ROOM
   FROM OFFERING
   WHERE LAST_NAME = "Vazquez";
```

The **SELECT** command indicates the data (i.e., the columns) to be displayed, the table that contains those columns, and the rows in that table that are to be shown (i.e., only the rows meeting the specified condition will be displayed). Thus, the query in the example will search the offering table for all courses taught by Professor Vazquez, returning the **COURSE_ID**, **SECTION**, **BUILDING**, and **ROOM** for each such offering.

The condition in the **WHERE** clause uses any of the common relational operators as shown below:

Symbol	*Meaning*
<	Less than
<=	Less than or equal to
>	Greater than
>=	Greater than or equal to
=	Equal
<>	Not equal

As indicated, the **SELECT** command can be enhanced through any of several optional clauses, each of which is explained in conjunction with the SQL queries of Figure 14.6. Our intent is not, however, to cover every option of every clause, but to convey an appreciation for the overall power of SQL. Nevertheless, we believe that a willingness to experiment, coupled with an understanding of the SQL command notation, will enable you to become proficient in short order. Consider first the expanded syntax of the **SELECT** statement:

```
SELECT [DISTINCT/ALL] */<expression list>
    FROM <table name> [,<table name>...]
    [WHERE <condition> [AND/OR <condition>...]
          [GROUP BY <column name> [,<column name> ...]
    [HAVING [NOT] <condition> [[AND/OR][NOT]<condition>...]
    [ORDER BY <column name> [DES]...][<column name>[DES]...]
```

It is essential for you to understand the command notation in order to effectively use the **SELECT** command. Accordingly:

- Upper-case letters are used for SQL terms, e.g. **GROUP BY**.
- Lower-case letters enclosed in angled brackets **< >** indicate a user-supplied parameter, e.g., <table name>.
- A slash **/** indicates a choice, e.g., between the terms **DISTINCT** and **ALL**.
- Square brackets [ ] enclose *optional* parameters, and by extension the omis-

```
     Query:  What are the course offerings for next semester?
SQL Command:  SELECT *
                  FROM offering;

   Response:  COURSE_ID SECTION LAST_NAME    BUILDING   ROOM
              CIS120    A       Barber       Jenkins    408
              CIS120    D       Barber       Jenkins    408
              CIS223    A       Vazquez      Memorial   210
              CIS120    B       Vazquez      Jenkins    408
              CIS526    C       Grauer       Jenkins    402
              CIS420    B       Stutz        Memorial   200
              CIS523    D       Gillenson    Memorial   305
              CIS120    C       Goldsmith    Jenkins    408
              CIS223    D       Grauer       Jenkins    401
```

(a) Simplest Form

```
     Query:  Which section of CIS223 is being taught by Professor Grauer?  Where
              does it meet?
SQL Command:  SELECT COURSE_ID, SECTION, BUILDING, ROOM
                  FROM OFFERING
                  WHERE COURSE_ID = "CIS223"
                    AND LAST_NAME = "Grauer";

   Response:  COURSE_ID SECTION BUILDING   ROOM
              CIS223    D       Jenkins    401
```

(b) WHERE Clause

```
     Query:  Which 500 level courses are being offered?
SQL Command:  SELECT COURSE_ID, SECTION, LAST_NAME
                  FROM OFFERING
                  WHERE COURSE_ID LIKE "CIS5%";

   Response:  COURSE_ID SECTION LAST_NAME
              CIS526    C       Grauer
              CIS523    D       Gillenson
```

(c) LIKE Parameter

```
     Query:  Which sections of CIS120 are offered?  List the sections in
              sequence by section number. Who is the instructor for each section?
SQL Command:  SELECT COURSE_ID, SECTION, LAST_NAME
                  FROM OFFERING
                  WHERE COURSE_ID = "CIS120"
                  ORDER BY SECTION;

   Response:  COURSE_ID SECTION LAST_NAME
              CIS120    A       Barber
              CIS120    B       Vazquez
              CIS120    C       Goldsmith
              CIS120    D       Barber
```

(d) ORDER BY Clause

FIGURE 14.6
The SELECT Command

sion of square brackets implies a *required* parameter; e.g., the word **SELECT** is mandatory, as is a choice between an asterisk and an expression list. The *asterisk* has special significance and implies that all columns are to be listed, whereas the expression list may contain specific columns and/or one of five SQL functions (**AVG**, **COUNT**, **MAX**, **MIN**, and **SUM**).

```
         Query:  What are the different courses offered next semester?
   SQL Command:  SELECT DISTINCT COURSE_ID
                     FROM OFFERING;

      Response:  COURSE_ID
                 CIS120
                 CIS223
                 CIS420
                 CIS523
                 CIS526
```

(e) DISTINCT Clause

```
         Query:  How many offerings are scheduled for next semester?
   SQL Command:  SELECT COUNT (COURSE_ID)
                     FROM OFFERING;

      Response:  COUNT1
                 9
```

(f) COUNT Function

```
         Query:  Hom many sections of each course are offered?
   SQL Command:  SELECT COURSE_ID, COUNT (COURSE_ID)
                     FROM OFFERING
                     GROUP BY COURSE_ID;

      Response:  COURSE_ID   COUNT1
                 CIS120           4
                 CIS223           2
                 CIS420           1
                 CIS523           1
                 CIS526           1
```

(g) GROUP BY Clause

```
         Query:  Which courses are offered in more than one section?
   SQL Command:  SELECT COURSE_ID, COUNT (COURSE_ID)
                     FROM OFFERING
                     GROUP BY COURSE_ID
                         HAVING COUNT (COURSE_ID) > 1;

      Response:  COURSE_ID   COUNT1
                 CIS120           4
                 CIS223           2
```

(h) HAVING Clause

FIGURE 14.6
The SELECT Command (continued)

- Three dots **...** indicates the enclosed element can be repeated; e.g., the **ORDER BY** clause can include multiple column names in order to sequence on more than one column.
- A semicolon **;** terminates the command.

The command in Figure 14.6a illustrates the shortest possible form of the **SELECT** command as it omits all optional clauses, specifying only the columns to be displayed (all columns as implied by the asterisk) and the table *from* which they are selected. The query in Figure 14.6b is equally simple and includes specific columns, the associated table, and the condition to be met. All other commands in the figure use one or more of the optional clauses explained below.

LIKE Parameter

The **LIKE** parameter enables the inclusion of a wild card within the condition contained in a WHERE clause. A percent sign stands for any combination of characters (and is analogous to the use of an asterisk in DOS), whereas an underscore denotes a single character (and corresponds to the use of a question mark in DOS). The LIKE parameter is used in the query of Figure 14.6c to select all 500-level courses, i.e., courses whose COURSE_ID begins with CIS5.

ORDER BY Clause

The order of rows in a table within a relational database is immaterial, which means that there is no guarantee as to the sequence in which the results of a particular query are displayed. From a practical standpoint, however, the order is important; thus, the **ORDER BY** clause displays the selected rows in sequence according to values in the specified column(s). The query in Figure 14.6d uses the ORDER BY clause to display the offerings of CIS120 in sequence by section. Note, too, that the sequence in the ORDER BY clause defaults to ascending, unless the DEScending parameter is included.

DISTINCT/ALL Parameter

The **DISTINCT** parameter is included in the query of Figure 14.6e to list the *different* values of COURSE_ID that appear within the offering table. Alternatively, the query could be written with the **ALL** parameter whereby *every* row (including multiple sections for the same course) would be displayed. The DISTINCT/ALL parameter appears in square brackets within the syntax of the SELECT command, meaning that it could be omitted altogether (the default is to ALL). The slash between the two indicates a choice; i.e., one or the other, but not both, is specified.

COUNT Function

The **COUNT** function is one of five aggregate SQL functions (AVG, MIN, MAX, and SUM are the others) that can appear in the expression list of a SELECT command. The function is used in Figure 14.6f to determine the total number of course offerings and in Figure 14.6g (with the GROUP BY clause) to count the sections for each course.

GROUP BY Clause

The **GROUP BY** clause displays the rows with duplicate values for the specified column(s) next to one another. It is similar in concept to an ORDER BY clause, but it is made more powerful through inclusion of the SQL functions (AVG, MAX, MIN, SUM, or COUNT) that operate on each group. The clause is used in the query of Figure 14.6g to count the number of sections for each course.

HAVING Clause

The **HAVING** clause is used in conjunction with the GROUP BY clause to restrict the groups displayed. The clause is used in the query of Figure 14.6h to list all courses with more than one section. The condition specified in the HAVING clause must contain a SQL aggregate function.

Multiple-Table Queries

The syntax of the **SELECT** command indicates that multiple tables can be specified in the **FROM** clause, giving rise to a ***multi-file query*** produced through a ***join*** operation. The process is illustrated in Figure 14.7, and it is this capability that enables SQL to display data from several tables in a single command.

Figure 14.7a depicts an abbreviated version of the offering table with three rows and three columns in each row. Figure 14.7b depicts a similarly abbreviated course table with six rows and two columns in each row. The two tables are joined together in Figure 14.7c such that *every row in the first table is combined with every row in the second table* to produce a joined table with 18 (3 × 6) rows in all.

Only some of the rows in the joined table are of interest, specifically those rows that have *identical* values for the **COURSE_ID** in the original offering and course

FIGURE 14.7
Two-file Query

COURSE_ID	SECTION	LAST_NAME
CIS120	A	Barber
CIS120	D	Barber
CIS223	A	Vazquez

(a) Abbreviated Offering Table

COURSE_ID	TITLE
CIS120	Intro to Computers
CIS223	COBOL Programming
CIS420	Systems Analysis
CIS523	Intro to Database
CIS526	Advanced COBOL
CIS226	Assembler Language

(b) Abbreviated Course Table

COURSE_ID	SECTION	LAST_NAME	COURSE_ID	TITLE
CIS120	A	Barber	CIS120	Intro to Computers
CIS120	A	Barber	CIS223	COBOL Programming
CIS120	A	Barber	CIS420	Systems Analysis
CIS120	A	Barber	CIS523	Intro to Database
CIS120	A	Barber	CIS526	Advanced COBOL
CIS120	A	Barber	CIS226	Assembler Language
CIS120	D	Barber	CIS120	Intro to Computers
CIS120	D	Barber	CIS223	COBOL Programming
CIS120	D	Barber	CIS420	Systems Analysis
CIS120	D	Barber	CIS523	Intro to Database
CIS120	D	Barber	CIS526	Advanced COBOL
CIS120	D	Barber	CIS226	Assembler Language
CIS223	A	Vazquez	CIS120	Intro to Computers
CIS223	A	Vazquez	CIS223	COBOL Programming
CIS223	A	Vazquez	CIS420	Systems Analysis
CIS223	A	Vazquez	CIS523	Intro to Database
CIS223	A	Vazquez	CIS526	Advanced COBOL
CIS223	A	Vazquez	CIS226	Assembler Language

(c) Results of Join Operation

```
SELECT OFFERING.COURSE_ID, SECTION, LAST_NAME, TITLE
    FROM OFFERING, COURSE
    WHERE OFFERING.COURSE_ID = COURSE.COURSE_ID;
```

(d) SQL Query with WHERE Clause

COURSE_ID	SECTION	LAST_NAME	TITLE
CIS120	A	Barber	Intro to Computers
CIS120	D	Barber	Intro to Computers
CIS223	A	Vazquez	COBOL Programming

(e) Final Output

tables. (The interesting rows are shaded for convenience.) The **WHERE** condition in the **SELECT** command of Figure 14.7d is written in such a way as to display the interesting rows, and only those rows, producing the output in Figure 14.7e. Look carefully at that output and see how it contains all of the information in the offering table of Figure 14.7a, together with the appropriate course title as it was taken from the course table of Figure 14.7b. In effect, we have combined data from two tables through a single command, producing output that is far more useful than could have been obtained from either table individually.

Each of the column names in the **SELECT** command belongs to either (or both) of the listed tables. In addition, each column name must be unique, or if not, then the column name must be appropriately qualified to avoid any ***ambiguous reference.*** **SECTION** and **LAST_NAME**, for example, are unique in that they appear in only the offering table. **COURSE_ID**, however, occurs in both tables, and thus is prefixed with the table name, e.g., **OFFERING.COURSE_ID**, to produce an unambiguous (i.e., unique) reference.

Consider, once again, the initial case presentation and the desired course schedules in Figure 14.1a. Can you see that this output was produced by joining columns from three tables (**COURSE_ID**, **SECTION**, **BUILDING**, and **ROOM** from the offering table; **TITLE** and **CREDITS** from the course table; and **DAYS** and **HOURS** from the section table)? In similar fashion, the schedule in Figure 14.1b was produced by joining the **LAST_NAME**, **COURSE_ID**, and **SECTION** columns from the offering table with the **RANK** and **STATUS** columns from the faculty table.

Views

A ***view*** (or virtual table) can be used to simplify queries to a database as will be done in the ensuing hands-on exercise. A view is established through the **CREATE VIEW** command as shown in Figure 14.8a, it is accessed through a **SELECT** command as in Figure 14.8b, and the displayed output is shown in Figure 14.8c. Note, too, the **ORDER BY** clause in the **SELECT** command to display the selected rows in sequence by **LAST_NAME** and **COURSE_ID**. (The output in Figure 14.8c matches the schedule produced for the administration in the original case solution.)

The syntax of the **CREATE VIEW** command requires only the name of the view, e.g., **ADMIN**, the word **AS**, and the **SELECT** command to define the view. After a view has been created, it can be referenced in a **SELECT** statement of its own to retrieve some or all of the data in that view.

The SQL Edit Window

We come shortly to a second hands-on exercise in which you will develop several different SQL commands. The exercise will require you to enter various **SELECT** commands, many of which are more than 80 characters in length and hence will scroll off the screen (a single SQL command can be up to 1,024 characters).

The edit window is intended to simplify the entry (and subsequent editing) of SQL commands as shown in Figure 14.9. You enter the ***edit window*** by pressing **Ctrl+Home** at the SQL prompt, and you execute the command by pressing **Ctrl+End** while still in the edit window. You have only to use the facility once or twice as you do the exercise to appreciate its utility.

FIGURE 14.8
Creating a View

```
CREATE VIEW ADMIN AS
    SELECT LAST_NAME, COURSE_ID, SECTION, RANK, STATUS
    FROM OFFERING,FACULTY
    WHERE OFFERING.LAST_NAME = FACULTY.LAST_NAME;
```

(a) Creating the View

```
SELECT * FROM ADMIN
    ORDER BY LAST_NAME,COURSE_ID;
```

(b) SELECT Command

LAST_NAME	COURSE_ID	SECTION	RANK	STATUS
Barber	CIS120	A	Professor	Full time
Barber	CIS120	D	Professor	Full time
Gillenson	CIS523	D	Instructor	Adjunct
Goldsmith	CIS120	C	Assoc Prof	Adjunct
Grauer	CIS223	D	Professor	Full time
Grauer	CIS526	C	Professor	Full time
Stutz	CIS420	B	Instructor	Full time
Vazquez	CIS120	B	Asst Prof	Full time
Vazquez	CIS223	A	Asst Prof	Full time

(c) Displayed Output

FIGURE 14.9
The Edit Window

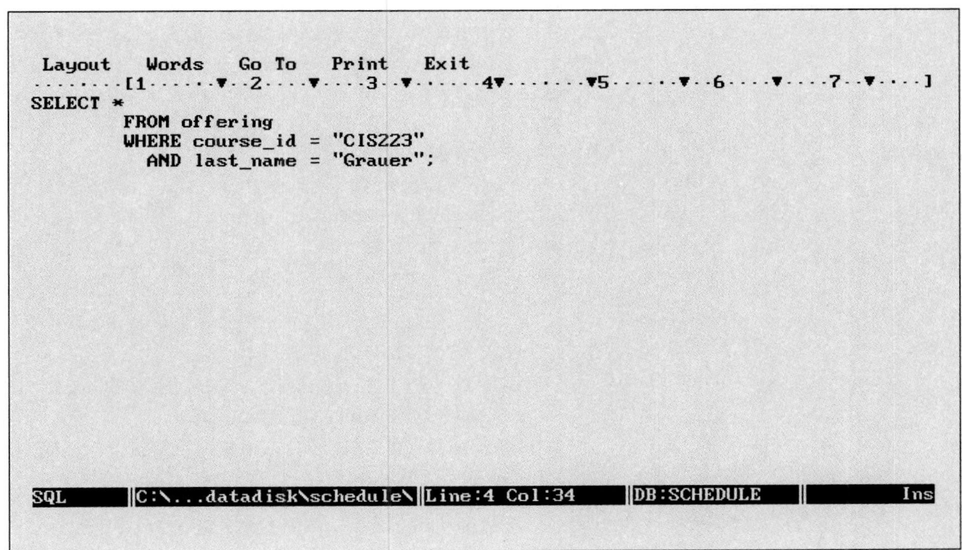

HANDS-ON EXERCISE 2

The SQL SELECT Command

Objective

Develop multiple SQL queries for the `SCHEDULE` database to illustrate the SQL `SELECT` command.

STEP 1 **Start the SCHEDULE database**

Type **SET SQL ON** to enter the SQL mode and produce the SQL prompt, then type

START DATABASE SCHEDULE; to start the existing database. Type the command **SELECT * FROM OFFERING;** to provide the complete list of course offerings.

STEP 2 **The edit window**

Commands may be entered directly at the SQL prompt or more conveniently through the SQL edit window. Press **Ctrl+Home** to bring up the edit window as shown in Figure 14.9, then enter the indicated SELECT command. Within the edit window, press **return** to go from one line to the next, and **Tab** to indent subsequent lines in the command. Type the **semicolon** only at the end of the last line.

Press **Ctrl+End** to execute the command directly from the edit window. Hopefully, you entered the command without error, in which case you should see the expected result. If, however, you made a mistake, SQL will indicate the nature of the error and give you a choice of options; type **E** to edit the command, then press **Ctrl+Home** to return to the edit window. Make corrections as necessary, then press **Ctrl+End** to execute the corrected command from the edit window.

Practice additional SELECT commands from Figure 14.6 as you see fit.

STEP 3 **A two-file query**

Press **Ctrl+Home** to bring up the edit window, then enter the following command:

```
SELECT OFFERING.LAST_NAME,COURSE_ID,SECTION,RANK,STATUS
   FROM OFFERING,FACULTY
   WHERE OFFERING.LAST_NAME = FACULTY.LAST_NAME;
```

Edit the command as necessary until it executes correctly. You will not be pleased with the output, however, because it wraps from one line to the next. Accordingly, we correct the problem by creating a view as described in step 4.

STEP 4 **Create a view**

Press the **up arrow** key to retrieve the command from step 3 (from the command buffer), press **Ctrl+Home** to return to the edit window, then amend the command to create a view as follows:

Add this line to existing command

```
CREATE VIEW ADMIN AS
   SELECT OFFERING.LAST_NAME,COURSE_ID,SECTION,RANK,STATUS
      FROM OFFERING,FACULTY
      WHERE OFFERING.LAST_NAME = FACULTY.LAST_NAME;
```

Press **Ctrl+End** to execute the modified command, which should return you directly to the SQL prompt *without* displaying any output.

STEP 5 **Display the completed view**

Type **SELECT * FROM ADMIN;** to display the identical information as in step 3 but this time *without* wrapping from one line to the next. The problem has been eliminated because all of the displayed columns are from one table (i.e., from the newly created view) and thus there is no need to qualify the column headings.

STEP 6 **The ORDER BY clause**

Press the **up arrow** key to retrieve the command from step 5, press **Ctrl+Home** to return to the edit window, and add the ORDER BY clause as shown below:

```
SELECT * FROM ADMIN
   ORDER BY LAST_NAME,COURSE_ID;
```

Press **Ctrl+End** to execute the amended command, which should produce the output shown in Figure 14.8c. Note, too, that the offerings are displayed in sequence by faculty member, and by course within faculty member.

STEP 7 **Additional practice (optional)**
Develop the SELECT command to produce the class schedule for the student bulletin shown in Figure 14.1a. This command will be slightly more complex than the command just completed, because it retrieves data from three tables (offering, section, and course). Remember, too, the need to create a view so that the displayed information does not wrap from one line to the next.

STEP 8 **Exit SQL**
Type **STOP DATABASE;** to close the SCHEDULE database, type **SET SQL OFF** to return to dBASE, and finally type **QUIT** to exit dBASE and return to DOS.

Maintaining the Database

Data in a DBF file (that has also been defined as a SQL table) can be accessed either through dBASE or SQL. Once you are in the SQL mode, however, you cannot use traditional dBASE commands (APPEND, EDIT, DELETE, and so on) to maintain the file, but must exit SQL and return to the dBASE-only mode, from where these commands can be issued. You can then exit the dBASE-only mode and reenter SQL, from where you use SQL commands to query the database. The process is illustrated in Figure 14.10.

The USE command in Figure 14.10a is executed from the dot prompt (i.e., the dBASE-only mode) and opens the FACULTY.DBF table. The LIST command shows the existing records, after which new records are added through the APPEND command. (The shaded rows in Figure 14.10b contain the new faculty members.) The CLOSE DATABASES command is critical (as omitting the command would produce a *file open error* once in SQL). Finally, the SET SQL ON command exits the dBASE-only mode and enters SQL.

The START DATABASE command is successfully executed from the SQL mode in Figure 14.10b and is followed by the RUNSTATS command to update the SQL system tables. It is the SELECT command, however, that demonstrates the success of the previous APPEND command as the new faculty records are displayed from within the SQL mode although they were added in the dBASE-only mode.

The only limitation to using traditional dBASE commands on SQL tables is a prohibition of the MODIFY STRUCTURE command; i.e., once a DBF file has been defined as a SQL table, you *cannot* modify its structure through dBASE, but must use the SQL ALTER TABLE command as described in the next section.

Additional SQL Commands

Our intent has never been to cover every aspect of every SQL command, but to give you an appreciation for the language and its ability to query a relational database. Our discussion has focused on the SELECT command, which, as we have already stated, is the very essence of SQL. Nevertheless, we provide Table 14.2 to show other basic SQL commands.

```
. USE FACULTY ———— USE command opens the FACULTY.DBF file

. LIST OFF
LAST_NAME     RANK        STATUS    DEGREE DEPARTMENT SEX SALARY
Barber        Professor   Full time PhD    CIS        F   100000
Gillenson     Instructor  Adjunct   MS     CIS        M    22000
Goldsmith     Assoc Prof  Adjunct   PhD    CIS        M    25000
Grauer        Professor   Full time PhD    CIS        M    75000
Stutz         Instructor  Full time MS     CIS        M    30000
Vazquez       Asst Prof   Full time PhD    CIS        F    50000
Hernandez     Instructor  Adjunct   MS     CIS        M    21000

. APPEND ———— APPEND command will add records to the FACULTY.DBF file

   .
     .  ———— Enter data for Friedman, Rushinek, Milgrom, and Rudolph (see Figure 14.10b)
       .

. CLOSE DATABASES ———— Command is critical prior to entering SQL

. SET SQL ON ———— SET command enters dBASEIV/SQL mode
```

(a) dBASE IV Commands

```
SQL. START DATABASE SCHEDULE; ———— SCHEDULE database contains FACULTY table
Database SCHEDULE started

SQL. RUNSTATS; ———— SQL tables are updated to reflect the dBASE APPEND operation
RUNSTATS successful

SQL. SELECT * FROM FACULTY;
 LAST_NAME     RANK        STATUS    DEGREE DEPARTMENT SEX SALARY
 Barber        Professor   Full time PhD    CIS        F   100000
 Gillenson     Instructor  Adjunct   MS     CIS        M    22000
 Goldsmith     Assoc Prof  Adjunct   PhD    CIS        M    25000
 Grauer        Professor   Full time PhD    CIS        M    75000
 Stutz         Instructor  Full time MS     CIS        M    30000
 Vazquez       Asst Prof   Full time PhD    CIS        F    50000
 Hernandez     Instructor  Adjunct   MS     CIS        M    21000
 Friedman      Instructor  Adjunct   MS     ACC        M    29500
 Rushinek      Asst Prof   Full time PhD    ACC        M    49500
 Milgrom       Professor   Full time PhD    ACC        M    82500
 Rudolph       Assoc Prof  Full time PhD    ACC        F    61000

     └———— SELECT command includes the new faculty records
```

(b) SQL Commands

FIGURE 14.10
dBASE IV and SQL

The **SELECT** command is listed first, followed by the available SQL functions. Only the **COUNT** function was illustrated explicitly in the chapter, but the other functions work in a similar way, and their meaning is apparent from the name of the function.

The **DELETE**, **INSERT**, and **UPDATE** commands maintain individual tables in a SQL database. These commands need not be used in a dBASE environment, however, because the identical tasks can be done with traditional dBASE commands as was shown in Figure 14.10. The commands are mentioned for completeness, and to prepare you for a SQL implementation other than dBASE IV.

The **ALTER TABLE** command *must* be used to add a column to an existing table (the dBASE **MODIFY STRUCTURE** command will not work). The **CREATE TABLE** can be circumvented, however, by creating the table in dBASE and executing

TABLE 14.2 **SQL Commands (Abbreviated list and syntax)**

The SELECT command:

```
SELECT [DISTINCT/ALL] */<expression list>
     FROM <table name> [,<table name>...]
     [WHERE <condition> [AND/OR <condition>...]
     [GROUP BY <column name> [,<column name>...]
     [HAVING [NOT] <condition> [AND/OR] [NOT] <condition>...]
     [ORDER BY <column name> [DES]...] [<column name> [DES]...];
```

SQL functions:

```
AVG ([ALL/DISTINCT] <column name>)
COUNT (*/[DISTINCT] <column name>)
MAX ([ALL/DISTINCT] <column name>)
MIN ([ALL/DISTINCT] <column name>)
SUM ([ALL/DISTINCT] <column name>)
```

Commands for table maintenance:

```
DELETE FROM <table name>
     [<WHERE *clause>];

INSERT INTO <table name>
     [<column list>]
     VALUES <value list>;

UPDATE <table name>
     [<column name> = expression...]
     [WHERE <clause>];
```

Commands to modify a database:

```
ALTER TABLE <table name>
     ADD (<column name> <data type>
     [,<column name> <data type>...]);

CREATE TABLE <table name>
     ADD (<column name> <data type>
     [,<column name> <data type>...]);

DROP TABLE <table name>;
```

the appropriate **DBDEFINE** command from within SQL. The **DROP TABLE** command drops a table from an existing database (and is used if a table is no longer necessary).

Summary

The **SET SQL ON** command is issued from the dot prompt and activates the interactive SQL mode. **SET SQL OFF** is issued from within the SQL mode and returns to the dot prompt.

dBASE commands for file maintenance—e.g., **APPEND**, **EDIT**, **BROWSE**, **DELETE**, or **PACK**—*cannot* be executed from within SQL. You can, however, maintain all SQL tables from dBASE, then enter the SQL mode to query the tables. The SQL **RUNSTATS** command updates the SQL tables.

The **CREATE DATABASE** command establishes the SQL system tables for a new database; the name of the database is always the same as the DOS directory in which it is located. The **DBDEFINE** command converts an existing DBF file (together with any associated indexes) to the equivalent SQL tables.

The **SELECT** command is the most important command in SQL. The required **FROM** clause designates the table (or tables) containing the columns to be displayed, and the optional **WHERE** clause restricts the displayed rows to those meeting the specified condition.

A single SELECT command can access data from two (or more) tables by ***joining*** the tables together, and then specifying an appropriate condition in the WHERE clause, to select the rows with identical values in the matching columns.

All SQL commands end with a ***semicolon*** and are entered at the SQL prompt or, more conveniently, through the SQL ***edit window.***

Key Words and Concepts

ALL
Ambiguous reference
ALTER TABLE;
CLOSE ALL
Command buffer
COUNT
CREATE DATABASE;
CREATE VIEW;
Ctrl+End
Ctrl+Home
DBDEFINE;
DISTINCT
DROP DATABASE;
Edit window
FROM clause
GROUP BY clause
HAVING clause
HELP
Join
LIKE parameter
Multi-file query
ORDER BY clause
RUNSTATS;
SELECT;
Semicolon
SET SQL OFF
SET SQL ON
SHOW DATABASE;
SQL
SQL prompt
START DATABASE;
STOP DATABASE;
View
WHERE clause

True/False

1. SQL commands end with a colon or semicolon.
2. SQL commands can be entered at the SQL prompt or through the SQL edit window.
3. There are many other SQL implementations besides dBASE IV.
4. The identical help screen is produced, regardless of whether the HELP command is entered at the dot prompt or the SQL prompt.
5. The CREATE DATABASE command automatically starts the newly created SQL database.
6. The name of a SQL database *cannot* be the same as the DOS directory in which it is located.
7. A single SELECT command cannot join more than two tables.
8. The FROM and WHERE clauses are both required in a SELECT command.
9. The FROM clause in a SELECT command cannot reference more than one table.
10. The DROP DATABASE command will erase only the SQL system tables, but it will leave intact any user tables that existed originally as DBF files.
11. Commands are executed from the SQL edit window by pressing Ctrl+Home.
12. ALL and DISTINCT are mutually exclusive clauses.

Exercises

1. Distinguish between:
   (a) The dot prompt and the SQL prompt
   (b) Typing **HELP** at the dot prompt versus typing it at the SQL prompt
   (c) Pressing the up and down arrow keys at the SQL prompt
   (d) The **FROM** and **WHERE** clauses in a SQL **SELECT** command
   (e) **Ctrl+Home** and **Ctrl+End** with respect to the edit window
   (f) The **DBDEFINE** and **CREATE DATABASE** commands

2. Indicate the specific files in Figure 14.3 where the following changes are to be made, then prepare revised schedules, as shown in Figure 14.1, based on these changes. (You may make the changes with paper and pencil only or implement them in the existing **DBF** files, then rerun the appropriate SQL queries. The choice is yours.)
   (a) Stutz has been promoted to an assistant professor.
   (b) A new three-credit course, CIS422, entitled Systems Design, has been approved, but the course will not be offered next semester.
   (c) Section D of CIS223 has been moved to Memorial 309.
   (d) Goldsmith has replaced Vazquez as the instructor for section B of CIS120.
   (e) A new section of CIS526 has been added; the course will be taught by Vazquez in the section B time slot and meet in Memorial 210.
   (f) Section D of CIS120 will not be offered.
   (g) All class periods will be extended five minutes but will still begin on the hour; e.g., section A will now run from 9:00 to 9:55 and section B from 10:00 to 10:55.

3. Answer the following with respect to the database as it exists in Figure 14.3. (You can answer the queries with paper and pencil or develop the appropriate SQL queries. The choice is yours.)
   (a) Which classes meet in the Memorial building?
   (b) Which faculty have a PhD?
   (c) Which full-time faculty have a PhD?
   (d) Which courses are taught by full-time faculty?
   (e) Which courses are taught by full-time faculty with a PhD?
   (f) Which courses are taught in the section B time slot?
   (g) How many sections of CIS120 are there?
   (h) Which courses is Professor Barber teaching?

4. Figure 14.11 displays five different attempts at a **SELECT** command, four of which are in error. Correct the error in the first four commands, then indicate the expected output (based on the database of Figure 14.2) for the final command.

5. Develop SQL **SELECT** commands to answer the following:
   (a) How many different faculty are teaching next semester?
   (b) Which faculty members are teaching more than one course?
   (c) Which full-time faculty are teaching CIS120?
   (d) Which classes meet on the second floor of the Memorial building?
   (e) Who is teaching CIS223 next semester?
   (f) What is the course title of every course scheduled for the section D time slot?
   (g) How many classes are scheduled in each time slot?

6. Add the additional faculty in Figure 14.10b to the faculty table, then develop SQL **SELECT** commands to answer the following:
   (a) List all faculty by department, and alphabetically within department.

FIGURE 14.11
SQL Error Messages (see Problem 4)

```
SELECT LAST_NAME, COURSE_ID, SECTION, TITLE, STATUS
    FROM FACULTY, OFFER
    WHERE OFFERING.LAST_NAME = FACULTY.LAST_NAME

Error message: SQL syntax error
```

(a) Error 1

```
SELECT LAST_NAME, COURSE_ID, SECTION, TITLE, STATUS
    FROM FACULTY, OFFER
    WHERE OFFERING.LAST_NAME = FACULTY.LAST_NAME;

Error message: Undefined table: OFFER
```

(b) Error 2

```
SELECT LAST_NAME, COURSE_ID, SECTION, TITLE, STATUS
    FROM FACULTY, OFFERING
    WHERE OFFERING.LAST_NAME = FACULTY.LAST_NAME;

Error message: Ambiguous column name: LAST_NAME
```

(c) Error 3

```
SELECT OFFERING.LAST_NAME, COURSE_ID, SECTION, TITLE, STATUS
    FROM FACULTY, OFFERING
    WHERE OFFERING.LAST_NAME = FACULTY.LAST_NAME;

Error message: Memory variable or column name undefined
```

(d) Error 4

```
SELECT OFFERING.LAST_NAME, COURSE_ID, SECTION, STATUS
    FROM FACULTY, OFFERING
    WHERE OFFERING.LAST_NAME = FACULTY.LAST_NAME;
```

(e) Corrected Statement

(b) What is the average salary for the full time faculty in each department?
(c) What is the average salary for each academic rank for full-time faculty? (Answer for the university as a whole, as opposed to individual departments.)
(d) What is the maximum salary for a full-time assistant professor? What is the minimum salary?
(e) How many full-time faculty are there in each department? How many adjunct faculty?
(f) Which full-time faculty do not have a PhD? What is their academic rank?
(g) Which full-time faculty earn less than $50,000? What is their academic rank?

7. The administration is so impressed with the database developed in this chapter that they want to extend its capabilities. In particular, they want to keep track of student grades and be able to retrieve all courses for any given student, the semester the course was taken, and the grade received. They also want to be able to mail this information to the student's home and/or call the student at home.
(a) What additional table(s) need to be added to the existing database to accomplish these goals?
(b) What columns would be present in the new table(s)?

FIGURE 14.12
Output for Problem 8

TBNAME	CREATOR	COLCOUNT	CLUSTERRID	CREATED	UPDATED
SYSTABLS	SYSTEM	10	10	01/01/88	07/03/91
SYSCOLS	SYSTEM	12	75	01/01/88	07/03/91
SYSIDXS	SYSTEM	12	0	01/01/88	01/01/88
SYSKEYS	SYSTEM	6	0	01/01/88	01/01/88
SYSVIEWS	SYSTEM	7	0	01/01/88	01/01/88
SYSVDEPS	SYSTEM	4	0	01/01/88	01/01/88
SYSSYNS	SYSTEM	4	0	01/01/88	01/01/88
SYSAUTH	SYSTEM	11	10	01/01/88	01/01/88
SYSCOLAU	SYSTEM	6	0	01/01/88	01/01/88
SYSTIMES	SYSTEM	3	11	01/01/88	01/01/88
COURSE		3	8	07/01/91	07/02/91
FACULTY		7	7	07/01/91	07/01/91
OFFERING		5	11	07/01/91	07/03/91
SECTION		3	4	07/01/91	07/01/91
STUDENT		7	10	07/03/91	07/03/91
GRADE		4	25	07/03/91	07/03/91

8. Answer the following with respect to the output in Figure 14.12, which was created from the dot prompt within the **SCHEDULE** directory.

(a) What commands were used to create the output?
(b) How many system tables are there in the figure?
(c) Which system table is being displayed?
(d) How many user tables are there?
(e) What is the significance of the different dates in the **CREATED** and **UPDATED** columns for the **OFFERING** table?
(f) What is the significance of the different dates in the **CREATED** column for the **STUDENT** and **FACULTY** table?
(g) How many fields are there in the **GRADE.DBF** file?
(h) How many records are there in the **STUDENT.DBF** file?

The Programmer's Notebook

The ***Programmer's Notebook*** is a convenient reference for the individual learning dBASE, as well as for the experienced programmer. The Notebook lists commands and functions in *alphabetical* order, with the material on each divided into four sections: ***Syntax, Discussion, Tips,*** and ***Related Topics.*** The Notebook is not intended to replace the Ashton-Tate Reference Manual, and hence does not include every command and function available within dBASE IV.

The Notebook does, however, cover the vast majority of commands and functions, and certainly those that are used most frequently. It also presents significant material not found in the Ashton-Tate publication (or elsewhere); hence, we are confident that you will find it to be a useful reference.

Table PN.1 lists the commands and functions appearing in the Programmer's Notebook.

TABLE PN.1 **Commands and Functions in the Programmer's Notebook**

```
?/??
???
*/NOTE
&
&&
@...CLEAR
@...FILL
@...SAY...GET
@...TO
ACTIVATE MENU
ACTIVATE POPUP
ACTIVATE SCREEN
ACTIVATE WINDOW
APPEND
APPEND FROM
ASSIST
AVERAGE
BAR()
BOF()
BROWSE
CALCULATE
CANCEL
CDOW()
CHR()
CLEAR
CLOSE
CMONTH()
COMPILE
CONFIG.DB
CONTINUE
COPY
COPY INDEXES
COUNT
CREATE
CREATE APPLICATION
CREATE LABEL
CREATE QUERY
CREATE REPORT
CREATE SCREEN
CREATE VIEW
CREATE VIEW FROM ENVIRONMENT
CTOD()
DATE()
DAY()
DEACTIVATE MENU
DEACTIVATE POPUP
DEACTIVATE WINDOW
DEBUG
DEFINE BAR
DEFINE MENU
DEFINE PAD
DEFINE POPUP
DEFINE WINDOW
DELETE
DELETE TAG
DELETED()
DIR
DISPLAY
DISPLAY HISTORY
DISPLAY MEMORY
DISPLAY STATUS
DISPLAY STRUCTURE
DO
DO CASE
DO WHILE
DTOC()
DTOS()
EDIT
EJECT
EOF()
FIND
FOUND()
GO
HELP
IF
IIF()
INDEX ON
INSERT
ISCOLOR()
JOIN
LABEL FORM
LEN()
LINENO()
LIST
LIST HISTORY
LIST MEMORY
LIST STATUS
LIST STRUCTURE
LOCATE
LOWER()
LTRIM()
MAX()
MIN()
MODIFY COMMAND
MODIFY LABEL
MODIFY QUERY
MODIFY REPORT
MODIFY SCREEN
MODIFY STRUCTURE
MODIFY VIEW
MONTH()
MOVE WINDOW
ON ERROR/ESCAPE/KEY
ON PAD
ON SELECTION PAD
ON SELECTION POPUP
PACK
PARAMETERS
PRINTSTATUS()
PRIVATE
```

PROCEDURE
PROMPT()
PUBLIC
QUIT
READ
RECALL
RECNO()
REINDEX
RELEASE
REPLACE
REPORT FORM
RESTORE
RESTORE WINDOW
RESUME
RETURN
RTRIM()
RUN
SAVE
SAVE WINDOW
SCAN
SEEK
SELECT
SET
SET ALTERNATE
SET AUTOSAVE
SET BELL
SET BORDER
SET CATALOG
SET CENTURY
SET CLOCK
SET COLOR
SET CONFIRM
SET CONSOLE
SET DATE
SET DEBUG
SET DEFAULT
SET DELETED
SET DELIMITERS
SET DEVELOPMENT
SET DEVICE
SET DISPLAY
SET ECHO
SET ESCAPE
SET EXACT
SET FIELDS
SET FILTER
SET FORMAT
SET FUNCTION
SET HEADING
SET HELP
SET HISTORY
SET INDEX
SET INTENSITY
SET MEMOWIDTH
SET NEAR
SET ORDER
SET PATH
SET PRINTER
SET PROCEDURE
SET RELATION
SET SAFETY
SET SCOREBOARD
SET SKIP
SET SPACE
SET SQL
SET STATUS
SET STEP
SET TALK
SET TRAP
SET TYPEAHEAD
SET UNIQUE
SET VIEW
SET WINDOW
SHOW MENU
SHOW POPUP
SKIP
SORT
SPACE()
STORE
STR()
SUBSTR()
SUM
SUSPEND
TIME()
TRANSFORM()
TRIM()
UPPER()
USE
VAL()
WAIT
YEAR()
ZAP

?

Syntax

```
?/?? [<expression> [PICTURE <expC>]
    [FUNCTION <function list>]
    [AT <expN>] [STYLE <font number>]]...
```

Discussion

The **?/??** command displays the value of an expression list, which may include literals, memory variables, and database fields. The single **?** command produces a carriage return and line feed, causing the expression to be displayed at the beginning of the next line. The double **??**, however, issues neither a carriage return nor a line feed, and displays the expression list at the current cursor position.

The expression list can include an arithmetic, string, date, or logical operation, in which case dBA3E evaluates the operation, then displays the result. For example:

```
? salary * 1.10, salary
? TRIM(lastname)+ ", " + firstname, title
? DATE() + 7
? EOF()
```

Multiple expressions are separated by commas, and each of the expressions may be followed by any of the four optional clauses that control their location, appearance, and format.

The **FUNCTION** and **PICTURE** clauses provide formatting instructions through *function* codes and *template* symbols. A function code affects the display of the entire expression, whereas a template uses a separate symbol for every character and determines the display of the data on a character-by-character basis. Function codes can be used in either the **FUNCTION** clause or the **PICTURE** clause as shown below, and have the same effect regardless of which clause is used.

A **FUNCTION** clause consists of function codes only, whereas a **PICTURE** clause may contain function codes and/or a template. Note, too, that when function codes are used in a **PICTURE** clause, they must appear first and are preceded by an **@** sign; the function codes are also separated from the template symbols by one blank space.

```
FUNCTION "FFFFF"              ———— F represents function codes

PICTURE "@FFFF XXXXXXXXXX"    ———— X represents template symbols
                                   Function codes preceded by @
```

Lists of available function codes and template symbols are shown in Tables PN.2 and PN.3, respectively. Consider the following examples:

```
? lastname FUNCTION "!"
? salary PICTURE "$999,999"
? gpa PICTURE "@Z 9.99"
```

TABLE PN.2 **Function Codes** (?/?? Command)

Function Code	Description
!	Displays letters in upper case
$	Displays numeric data with a leading $
(	Encloses negative numeric data in parentheses
B	Left justifies data within template
C	Displays **CR** after positive numeric data
D	Displays a date in current **SET DATE** format
E	Displays a date in European date format
H	Stretches template horizontally to accommodate data
I	Centers data within template
J	Right justifies data within template
L	Displays leading zeros with numeric data
S<n>	Displays only the first <n> characters of data
T	Trims leading/trailing blanks
V<n>	Stretches template vertically to accommodate data
X	Displays **DB** after negative numeric data
Z	Displays a zero value as a blank space

TABLE PN.3 **Template Symbols** (?/?? Command)

Template Symbol	Description
`!`	Displays letter in upper case (no effect on nonalphabetic characters)
`#`	Displays character unchanged
`$`	Displays a dollar sign instead of leading zero (numeric field only)
`*`	Displays an asterisk instead of leading zero (numeric field only)
`,` (comma)	Inserts comma (numeric field only)
`.` (period)	Specifies the position of the decimal point in displayed number
`9`	Displays character unchanged
`A`	Displays character unchanged
`L`	Displays logical data unchanged
`N`	Displays character unchanged
`X`	Displays character unchanged
`Y`	Displays true entry as Y, false entry as N
`all others`	Displays specified character instead of data

The first example will display the last name in all capital letters, the second will display the salary with leading dollar signs and commas where appropriate, and the third will display the gpa (grade point average) with two decimal places, unless there is no value entered for gpa, in which case the zero will be suppressed and a blank space displayed.

The **`AT`** clause specifies the starting position at which the expression is displayed. The **`STYLE`** clause indicates the *type style* of the data. The codes must be enclosed in quotes and can be combined; e.g., **`? lastname STYLE "BU"`**. Available codes are shown in Table PN.4. The style is dependent on the specific monitor and printer in use. Almost all monitors display boldface, and almost all printers underline; however, the other styles may not be supported.

Tips

1. The **`?`** command with no expression list displays a blank line; i.e., it skips a line.
2. The data types of all fields in a concatenated list must be the same. Accordingly, the display of messages containing numeric or date fields requires the use of string and/or date conversion functions; e.g.,

```
? 'Employee hired on: ' + DTOC(hdate)
? 'Employee's current salary: ' + STR(salary,6)
```

3. The results of the **`?/??`** command are sent to the printer if **`SET PRINTER`** is **`ON`.**
4. The **`?`** can be used to test and debug a complex expression from the dot prompt, before it is incorporated into a report or program.
5. The **`?`** command can be used to evaluate a logical condition. For example, the command **`? lastname = 'Scholl'`** evaluates to true if the value of **`lastname`** is

TABLE PN.4 **Style Codes** (?/?? Command)

Code	Effect
`B`	Boldface
`I`	Italic
`U`	Underline
`R`	Superscript
`L`	Subscript

"Scholl" (i.e., the record pointer is positioned at Mr. Scholl's record), and false if it is not. The command `? 3*3/4 > 2` evaluates to true since 9/4 is indeed greater than 2.

6. The **`AT`** clause can be used to output data in columns; e.g., **`? lastname,salary AT 50`** will display **`lastname`** in column 0 and **`salary`** in column 50.

7. The **`@H`** function code can be used with memo fields to override the default width as established by the **`SET MEMOWIDTH`** command. The **`@H`** function causes the template to expand or contract horizontally, depending on the length of the data to be output. Consider:

```
Without @H function:

SET MEMOWIDTH TO 30
? COMMENT
This is memo field 1 and it is
50 characters long.
```

Memo field wraps to two lines

```
With @H function:

USE ZOO
SET MEMOWIDTH TO 30
? COMMENT FUNCTION "@H"

This is memo field 1 and it is 50 characters long.
```

Memo field doesn't wrap

8. The **`@V <n>`** function is similar to the **`@H`** function, but causes the template to stretch vertically in columnar fashion, the width of the column depending on the value specified by the <n> parameter. It also overrides the default memo field display established by the **`SET MEMOWIDTH`** command. Consider:

```
Without @V function:

SET MEMOWIDTH TO 30
? COMMENT
This is memo field 1 and it is
50 characters long.

With @V function:

SET MEMOWIDTH TO 30
? COMMENT FUNCTION "@V10"
This is
memo field
1 and it
is 50
characters
long.
```

Memo field width determined by @V width

9. The value of the system memory variable **`_wrap`** must be true for the **`@H`** and **`@V`** functions to work as described above. The current value of **`_wrap`** can be determined with the command **`? _wrap`** (or by issuing a **`DISPLAY MEMORY`** command) and can be changed with a **`STORE`** command, e.g., **`STORE .T. TO _wrap.`**

10. When the system memory variable `_wrap` is set to true, the values of `_lmargin` and `_rmargin` determine the left and right margins for the output produced by the `?` command. Current values for `_lmargin` and `_rmargin` can be determined with a `?` command (e.g., `? _lmargin`) and can be changed with a **STORE** command, e.g., `STORE 10 TO _lmargin`.

Related Topics

```
???
@...SAY...GET
DTOC()
SET MEMOWIDTH
SET PRINTER
STR()
```

???

Syntax

```
??? <character expression>
```

Discussion

The `???` command directs output to the printer, bypassing the installed printer driver. It can be used from the dot prompt or from within a program to send control codes to the printer, achieving special effects that the current printer driver does not support. The control codes are hardware dependent; thus, you need to consult a manual for the specific codes required for your printer.

The printer codes must be enclosed in curly braces within quotes and can be any combination of ASCII codes (their decimal equivalent), control character identifiers, and/or ordinary text characters. For example, either of the following two commands will produce italic type on an HP LaserJet III printer:

```
??? "{027}{040}{115}{048}{083}"
??? "{ESC}{040}{115}{048}{083}"
```

Alternatively, the `CHR()` function can be used with the ASCII codes, as follows:

```
??? CHR(27)+CHR(40)+CHR(115)+CHR(48)+CHR(83)
```

Refer to Table PN.5 for a list of ASCII codes and equivalent control character identifiers.

Tips

1. The **STYLE** parameter of the `?/??` command will control the type style of an individual item, whereas the `???` command is best used to control the type style of a group of items.
2. The `???` command directs output to the printer even when **SET PRINTER** is **OFF**.
3. If you specify codes to physically change printer settings (print size, page orientation, and so on), be sure to send codes to return the printer to its default state when you are finished. For example,

```
??? CHR(15)         —— Establishes condensed print on Epson printers
REPORT FORM AREA TO PRINTER
??? CHR(18)         —— Returns to normal print on Epson printers
```

4. Text as well as codes can be output. For example, an overstrike (Ø) can be achieved with the following command:

```
??? "0" + "{BACKSPACE}" + "/"
```

TABLE PN.5 **ASCII Codes and Their Equivalent Control Characters**

ASCII Code	Control Character Identifier
0	{NULL} or {CTRL-@}
1	{CRTL-A}
2	{CTRL-B}
3	{CTRL-C}
4	{CTRL-D}
5	{CTRL-E}
6	{CTRL-F}
7	{BELL} or {CTRL-G}
8	{BACKSPACE} or {CTRL-H}
9	{TAB} or {CTRL-I}
10	{LINEFEED} or {CTRL-J}
11	{CTRL-K}
12	{CTRL-L}
13	{RETURN} or {CTRL-M}
14	{CTRL-N}
15	{CTRL-O}
16	{CTRL-P}
17	{CTRL-Q}
18	{CTRL-R}
19	{CTRL-S}
20	{CTRL-T}
21	{CTRL-U}
22	{CTRL-V}
23	{CTRL-W}
24	{CTRL-X}
25	{CTRL-Y}
26	{CTRL-Z}
27	{ESC} or {ESCAPE} or {CTRL-[}
28	{CTRL-\}
29	{CTRL-]}
30	{CTRL-^}
31	{CTRL-_}
127	{DEL} or {DELETE}

Related Topics

?/??
&&

*

Syntax

```
*/NOTE <comment>
```

Discussion

The word **NOTE** or an * as the first nonblank character of a line indicates a comment; e.g.,

```
***MAINMENU.PRG
***This program maps the main menu screen
```

Comments help to document a program. They are most useful to those involved in program maintenance, as they aid in explaining complex or unusual code.

Tips

1. Don't over comment, as poor comments are sometimes worse than no comments at all. Ill-chosen comments may be redundant with source code, or worse yet, they may be obsolete or inconsistent (which happens when the program is changed but the comments are not). Do comment a program, but choose your comments carefully.
2. The choice between a `&&` or `*` to comment a program is one of personal preference, as one method is not necessarily better than the other. In general, the `*` is used to comment *sections* of code, whereas the && is used to explain an *individual line* of code.
3. The `*` (or the word **NOTE**) need not appear in column one, but can be indented the same number of spaces as the code it explains.
4. Every program should begin with comment lines that give—as a minimum—the name of the program, its function, the name of the author, and the associated called and calling programs.
5. A comment line can be continued to the next line by placing a semicolon at the end of the line, thus eliminating the need to begin the next line with another `*` or **NOTE;** e.g.,

```
* This program maps the screen and displays;
  a choice of report formats for printing or;
  viewing on the screen
```

Related Topics

&&

& - MACRO NOTATION

Syntax

```
& <character variable>
```

Discussion

A single ampersand denotes the dBASE macro function, which causes dBASE to substitute the contents of the memory variable directly into the command in which it appears. The macro function is needed in commands where a literal is expected rather than a character expression; for example,

```
STORE "area" TO mreport
REPORT FORM &mreport
```

The macro function substitutes **area** into the **REPORT FORM** command in place of **&mreport,** effectively creating the command **REPORT FORM area.** The concept may appear confusing at first, but once understood, it provides increased generality within a program.

A more complete example is contained in the code below, which generates one of several different reports, based on a previously entered user response. The case structure stores a tag name and a report form name into two memory variables, depending on the user's input, after which macro substitution is used to produce the desired report.

```
DO CASE
   CASE response = '1'
      STORE "location" TO mtag
      STORE "locrep" TO mreport
   CASE response = '2'
      STORE "salary" TO mtag
      STORE "salrep" TO mreport
   .
    .
     .
ENDCASE
USE EMPLOYEE ORDER &mtag
REPORT FORM &mreport TO PRINTER
```

Tips

1. The data stored in the memory variable associated with the macro function must be a character string.
2. The **FIND** command can search for a character string in a memory variable, but only if the **&** is used with the variable name. For example, the commands

   ```
   STORE 'Borow' TO mname
   FIND &mname
   ```

   will search for the value stored in **mname** rather than the character string "mname". A parallel **SEEK** command (e.g., **SEEK mname**) is easier to use.
3. Macro substitution is useful to obtain user input and then immediately use that input in commands.
4. When a filename has been stored in a memory variable, an alternate to macro substitution is to enclose the variable name within parentheses; e.g.,

   ```
   STORE "usstates" to mname
   STORE "region" TO mrepname
   USE (mname)
   REPORT FORM (mrepname)
   ```

Related Topics

STORE

&&

Syntax

```
[<command>] && <comment>
```

Discussion

The appearance of two ampersands in a dBASE command indicates that the remainder of the line is a comment; i.e., as soon as dBASE encounters the **&&,** it ignores the remainder of the line; e.g.,

```
@ 22,10 SAY SPACE(60) &&Clears the message line
```

Comments help to document a program. They are most useful to those involved in program maintenance, as they aid in explaining complex or unusual code.

Tips

1. Don't over comment, as poor comments are sometimes worse than no comments at all. Ill-chosen comments may be redundant with source code, or worse yet, they may be obsolete or inconsistent (which happens when the program is changed but the comments are not). Do comment a program, but choose your comments carefully.
2. The choice between a **&&** or ***** to comment a program is one of personal preference, as one method is not necessarily better than the other. In general, the ***** is used to comment *sections* of code, whereas the **&&** is used to explain an *individual line* of code.

Related Topics

`*/NOTE`

@...CLEAR

Syntax

```
@ <row,col> CLEAR [TO <row,col>]
```

Discussion

The **@...CLEAR** command clears a portion of the screen, the size of which depends on the row and column coordinates used. The first set of row/column coordinates indicates the upper-left corner of the rectangle to be cleared, while the second set indicates the lower-right corner. Only a single set of coordinates need be specified, in which case the command will clear the designated row, beginning at the indicated column.

Tips

1. The row coordinates can be any integer from 0 to 24 (or 0 to 42 if the **SET DISPLAY** command has been used to change the number of lines displayed), while the column coordinates can be any integer from 0 to 79. If the coordinates specified are not within the allowable limits, a *Coordinates are off the screen* message is displayed.
2. If the same box is used to frame the screen throughout a custom-designed system, the **@...CLEAR TO** command should be used to clear text inside the box, rather than using the **CLEAR** command for the entire screen. This will eliminate the need to constantly redraw the box every time a new screen is mapped.

Related Topics

```
@...FILL
@...SAY
@..TO
CLEAR
SET DISPLAY
```

@...FILL

Syntax

```
@ <row,col> FILL TO <row,col> [COLOR <color>]
```

Discussion

The `@...FILL` command changes the foreground and background colors in the specified rectangular area. The command affects only the text already displayed in that area, and subsequent commands that write to that area use the default colors.

The first set of `<row,col>` coordinates indicates the upper-left corner of the area, while the second set of coordinates designates the lower-right corner. The row coordinates can be any integer from 0 to 24 (or 0 to 42 if the **SET DISPLAY** command has been used to change the number of lines displayed), whereas the column coordinates can be any integer from 0 to 79. If the coordinates specified are not within the allowable limits, a *Coordinates are off the screen* message is displayed.

The **COLOR** clause can specify only the foreground and background colors, separated by a slash, for the standard display area. The available colors and their respective codes are the same as for the **SET COLOR** command. A plus (+) sign may be included with the foreground color to create high-intensity text, and an asterisk (*) may be included to specify blinking text.

Tips

1. The `@...FILL TO` command is used primarily with program and/or format files to create attractive screen displays.
2. The `@...FILL TO` command without a specified color code clears the text by producing a black rectangle. It may be preferable, therefore, to use the **@...CLEAR TO** command to clear areas on the screen.
3. The screen area affected by the **@...FILL TO** command does not distinguish between text and input templates. The command should be used, therefore, only for areas that contain one or the other.

Related Topics

```
@...CLEAR
SET COLOR
```

@...SAY...GET

Syntax

```
@ <row,col> [SAY <expression> [PICTURE <template>]
    [FUNCTION <function list>]]
    [GET <field/memvar>
       [[OPEN]WINDOW <window name>]
       [PICTURE <template>]
       [FUNCTION <function list>]
       [RANGE [<exp>],[<exp>]]
       [VALID <condition>]
       [WHEN <condition>]
       [DEFAULT <expression>]
       [MESSAGE <message>]]
    [COLOR [<standard>][,<enhanced>]]
```

Discussion

The `@...SAY...GET` command allows precise control of screen displays for both input and output, displaying or inputting data at the location specified by the row and column coordinates. These coordinates can be any numeric expression from 0 to 24 (0 to 42 if the **SET DISPLAY** command has been used to change the number of lines displayed) and 0 to 79, respectively. If the coordinates specified are not within the allowable limits, a *Coordinates are off the screen* message is displayed.

The **@...SAY** option displays any valid dBASEIV expression, first evaluating the expression and then displaying the result. For example,

```
@ 10,10 SAY "Soleil America, Inc." —— Character string
@ 12,10 SAY lastname ——————————— Field
@ 14,10 SAY "Social Security Number:" + mssn
             └———————— Complex expression using a memory variable
@ 16,10 SAY 3*2+8 ——————————— Numeric calculation
```

The **@...GET** option defines an input template for an existing field or memory variable, then displays its current value for editing or replacement. Note, however, that the **@...GET** only *defines* the input template, and must be used in conjunction with a **READ** command to activate the full-screen data entry mode.

An **@...SAY...GET** command can consist of a **SAY** clause, a **GET** clause, or both clauses together; e.g.,

```
@ 10,10 SAY 'Enter last name: ' GET lastname
```

Including both clauses in the same command displays the input template for the **GET** clause one space to the right of the text displayed by the **SAY** clause.

The **FUNCTION** and **PICTURE** clauses provide formatting instructions through *function* codes and *template* symbols. A function code affects the display of the entire expression, whereas a template uses a separate symbol for every character and determines the display of the data on a character-by-character basis. Function codes can be used in either the **FUNCTION** clause or the **PICTURE** clause as shown below, and have the same effect, regardless of which clause is used.

A **FUNCTION** clause consists of function codes only, whereas a **PICTURE** clause may contain function codes and/or a template. Note, too, that when function codes are used in a **PICTURE** clause, they must appear first and are preceded by an **@** sign; the function codes are also separated from the template symbols by one blank space.

```
FUNCTION "FFFFF" ——————————— F represents function codes
PICTURE "@FFFF XXXXXXXXXX" —— X represents template symbols
         └——————————————————Function codes preceded by @
```

The standard function codes and template symbols are shown in Tables PN.6 and PN.7, respectively. Consider the following examples:

```
@ 10,10 SAY mgpa PICTURE "9.99"
@ 15,30 GET state FUNCTION "A!"
@ 3,12 GET idcode PICTURE "@! XX999"
```

The first example displays the value of **mgpa** to 2 decimal places. The second example allows only alphabetic input and converts the data to upper case. The third example displays an input template five characters wide, which accepts any character in the two leftmost positions (converting them to upper case if they are alphabetic), but accepts only numeric digits in the remaining three positions.

Any character at all may appear in a template. However, characters other than the standard symbols have no meaning, and will be entered as is into the input template. Consider the following examples,

```
@ 10,5 GET mphone1 PICTURE '(999)999-9999'
@ 10,5 GET mphone2 PICTURE '@R (999)999-9999'
```

TABLE PN.6 **Function Codes** (@...SAY...GET Command)

Function Code	Description (SAY)	Description (GET)
!	Displays alphabetic characters in upper case	Converts alphabetic characters to upper case
$	Displays numeric data with a single leading $	Displays numeric data with a single leading $
(	Encloses negative numeric data in parentheses	No effect
A	No effect	Permits entry of alphabetic characters only
B	Left justifies data within template	Left justifies data within template
C	Displays **CR** after positive numeric data	No effect
D	Displays a date in current **SET DATE** format	Displays a date in current **SET DATE** format
E	Displays a date in European date format	Displays a date in European date format
I	Centers data within template	Centers data within template
J	Right justifies data within template	Right justifies data within template
L	Displays leading zeros with numeric data	Displays leading zeros with numeric data
M <list>	No effect	Multiple choice options presented for selection
R	No effect	Nonstandard template characters used for display but not stored with data
S<n>	Displays only the first **<n>** characters of data	Scrolls data in a template **<n>** characters wide
T	Trims leading/trailing blanks	Trims leading/trailing blanks
X	Displays **DB** after negative numeric data	No effect
Z	Displays a zero value as a blank space	No effect

which differ only in the **@R** function in the second picture clause. In both examples, the nonstandard template characters (the parentheses and the hyphen) are automatically entered into the input template during data entry, and the cursor skips over these positions. Inclusion of the **@R** function in the second example, however, prevents the extra characters from being stored with the field; i.e., **mphone2** requires a field length of 10, whereas **mphone1** requires 13 positions.

The **RANGE** clause is used with character, numeric, and date variables to specify the minimum and maximum values that may be entered. Any entry that falls outside the specified range causes an error message and a prompt for another value. A single boundary (upper or lower) may be specified, provided a comma is placed in the appropriate position to indicate which boundary was supplied; that is, **RANGE 10,** specifies a lower boundary, whereas **RANGE,10000** specifies the upper boundary. Specification of boundary dates requires the dates be enclosed in curly braces; e.g.,

```
@ 10,10 GET mdate RANGE {01/01/91},{12/31/91}
```

to specify January 1, 1991, as the earliest acceptable date and December 31 of the same year as the latest. In all cases, the boundary values must both be the same data type as the field or memory variable to which they apply.

TABLE PN.7 **Template Symbols** (@...SAY...GET Command)

Template Symbol	Description (SAY)	Description (GET)
!	Displays lower-case letters in upper case (has no effect on nonalphabetic characters)	Converts lower-case letters to upper case (has no effect on nonalphabetic characters)
#	Displays character unchanged	Permits entry of only digits and signs (+ or −) and blank spaces
$	Displays dollar sign instead of leading zeros in numeric fields	Displays dollar sign instead of leading zeros in numeric fields
*	Displays asterisks instead of leading zeros in numeric fields	Displays asterisks instead of leading zeros in numeric fields
, (comma)	Inserts commas in numeric fields, as appropriate	Inserts commas in numeric fields, as appropriate
. (period)	Specifies position of decimal in displayed number	Specifies position of decimal in displayed number
9	Displays character unchanged	Permits entry of digits and signs (+ or −) only
A	Displays character unchanged	Permits entry of alphabetic characters only
L	Displays logical data unchanged	Permits entry of **T**, **t**, **Y**, **y**, **F**, **f**, **N**, **n** only
N	Displays character unchanged	Permits entry of alphabetic characters, digits, and underscore only
X	Displays character unchanged	Permits entry of any character
Y	Displays true entry as Y, false entry as N	Permits entry of **Y**, **y**, **N**, **n** only
all others	Displays specified character instead of data	Inserts special characters into data (unless **@R** specified)

The **VALID...ERROR** option establishes a condition that must be met before data will be accepted, and it is used to accomplish complex data validation that cannot be handled by the **RANGE** clause. Any valid logical condition may be specified, and if the condition evaluates to false, dBASE refuses the entry and displays the specified error message (or the message *Editing condition not satisfied* if no message is included).

The **WHEN** option establishes a condition that must be met for the **READ** command to activate the template. As with the **VALID** option, the condition may be any valid logical condition, but this option causes the template to be skipped and the cursor moved to the next template when the condition evaluates to false, effectively making the field read-only.

The **DEFAULT** option displays a default entry in the input template, but may not be used with memory variables, and further, is in effect only when records are being added; i.e., the default value does not appear when records are brought up for editing. The default value may be a character string enclosed in quotes, a number, a date, or a complex expression, but must be of the same data type as the field itself.

The **MESSAGE** option displays a prompting message of up to 79 characters at the bottom of the screen. The message will be displayed only if **SET STATUS** is **ON.**

By default, an **@...GET** command does not display the contents of a memo field, but displays a memo marker in upper case if the memo field contains text, or in lower case if it does not. The **WINDOW** option is used with memo fields to activate a previously defined window when the cursor is moved to the memo field's input template and **Ctrl+Home** is pressed. The contents of the memo field are displayed in the window and can be edited in the normal fashion. The **OPEN WINDOW** option causes the memo field contents to be displayed in the window at all times (rather than having the word "memo" displayed in the input template), even when the cursor is not in the input template. Note, however, that **Ctrl+Home** must still be pressed to access the field contents for data entry/editing.

The **COLOR** option specifies the colors to be used for the **SAY/GET** options. By default, the standard colors (as defined by the **SET COLOR** command) are used for the **SAY** and the enhanced colors for the **GET**. The **COLOR** option follows the same rules and uses the same colors as does the **SET COLOR** command.

Tips

1. Lines 22 through 24 of the screen display are normally used by the status, navigation, and message lines, but can be freed for custom screen displays with the **SET STATUS OFF** command. Note, however, that when **SET STATUS** is **OFF**, dBASE substitutes line 0 for some status messages; hence for complete screen control this line must be freed with **SET SCOREBOARD OFF**.
2. All fields in a concatenated expression must be of the same data type. Thus, if a character string is to be displayed with a date or numeric field, the date or number must be converted to their character equivalents, using a **STR()** or **DTOC()** conversion function; e.g.,

   ```
   @ 10,10 SAY 'Date Hired: ' + DTOC(hdate)
   @ 12,10 SAY 'Salary: ' + STR(salary,6)
   ```

   Alternatively, a pair of statements could be used for each command:

   ```
   @ 10,10 SAY 'Date Hired: '
   @ 10,22 SAY hdate
   @ 12,10 SAY 'Salary: '
   @ 12,18 SAY salary
   ```

3. A memory variable must be explicitly defined in a **STORE** command prior to being used in a **GET** command.
4. The **@R** function is useful in fields such as a telephone or social security number, to display the data in an easily understood format, without storing the insertion characters in the database. For example, the picture clause, **'@R 999-99-9999'**, displays a social security number as 123-45-6789, but requires only nine positions in the database, storing the digits 123456789.
5. Templates may be used to insert commas into numeric fields to produce a more readable number; e.g.,

   ```
   @10,10 SAY salary1 PICTURE '999,999,999'
   ```

   Any comma not preceded by a significant digit will be suppressed; hence, the number 1200 would be displayed as 1,200, while the number 1200000 would appear as 1,200,000.
6. The display of an **@...SAY** command can be rerouted to the printer by issuing a **SET DEVICE TO PRINTER** command. The row and column coordinates can then range from 0 to 32,767 and 0 to 255, respectively, although the printer may have its own, and probably smaller, limitations. When the coordinates specified exceed the allowable limits, dBASE will display an appropriate error message.
7. When the output of an **@...SAY** command is sent to the printer, the page should be mapped from top to bottom and from left to right, to avoid unintentional page breaks. In addition, when a row number lower than the row number in a previous command is encountered, dBASE ejects the page and prints at the proper row and column coordinates on the next page.
8. The **@...SAY** command cannot display the contents of a memo field. Instead, the word "memo" is displayed in the template, in upper case if the field contains text, lower case if it does not.
9. The **CREATE/MODIFY SCREEN** command can be used to lay out the text and fields of a custom form on a blank screen and then automatically generate the format file containing the corresponding **@...SAY...GET** commands. The format file can

then be used with full-screen data entry commands such as **APPEND** and **EDIT** or for incorporation into a more comprehensive **PRG** file.

10. The **S<n>** function can be used only with character data, with the value of **<n>** smaller than the defined field width. The function causes the data to scroll as characters are typed; the **arrow** keys, **Home** key, and **End** key can be used to bring the characters into view.
11. The **M <option list>** function is used only with character data and restricts data entry to the options presented; e.g., **@ 10,10 GET adopt FUNCTION "M B,M,R"** allows a choice of **B**, **M**, or **R** and, further, prevents any other entry. The options are entered as literal strings or numbers and are separated by commas. When the **GET** is activated, you can toggle between the available options with the space bar or type the initial letter of the option. The desired option is selected by pressing the enter key.
12. If no alignment function is used, character data is left justified and numeric data is right justified.
13. The **@R** function applies to character data only. Nonstandard characters are never stored in numeric fields.
14. If a **RANGE** clause is specified for a field or memory variable, but no data is input, the range check is not performed.
15. The **SET CARRY ON** command takes precedence over the **DEFAULT** clause.
16. Whenever a window is active, subsequent **@...SAY...GET** commands refer to addresses within the window. The row and column coordinates are relative to the upper-left corner of the window and not the screen.
17. The **DEFAULT** option does not display the default value for existing records, even when that field is blank. Thus, it is useful only when appending records.
18. The **@...SAY...GET** commands can reference fields from all open **DBF** files, allowing one screen to collect data from multiple files. Field names from **DBF** files in unselected work areas must be preceded by their alias name; for example, **@10,10 GET solemp->lastname.**
19. The appearance of the **@...GET** templates is affected by the status of **SET DELIMITERS** and **SET INTENSITY.** The **SET DELIMITERS** command is used to define characters that mark the boundaries of the input templates. Execution of **SET INTENSITY OFF** causes the standard colors to be used for the **@...GET**s instead of the enhanced colors.

Related Topics

```
?/??
@...CLEAR
@...TO
CLEAR
CREATE SCREEN
DEFINE WINDOW
DTOC()
MODIFY COMMAND
READ
SET CARRY
SET COLOR
SET DELIMITERS
SET DEVICE
SET DISPLAY
SET FORMAT
SET INTENSITY
SET SCOREBOARD
SET STATUS
STR()
```

@...TO

Syntax

```
@ <row,col> TO <row,col>
    [DOUBLE/PANEL/<border definition string>]
    [COLOR <color attribute>]
```

Discussion

The **@...TO** command draws a line or box on the screen, using a single line, double line, solid panel, or the specified characters. The first set of **<row,col>** coordinates indicates the upper-left corner of the box, while the second set of coordinates designates the lower-right corner. Specification of the same row in both parameters produces a horizontal line, whereas specifying the same column coordinates produces a vertical line.

The row coordinate can be any integer from 0 to 24 (or 0 to 42 if the **SET DISPLAY** command has been used to change the number of lines displayed), while the column coordinate can be any integer from 0 to 79. (If the coordinates specified are not within the allowable limits, a *Coordinates are off the screen* message is displayed.) By default the line or box will be drawn with a single line. Consider:

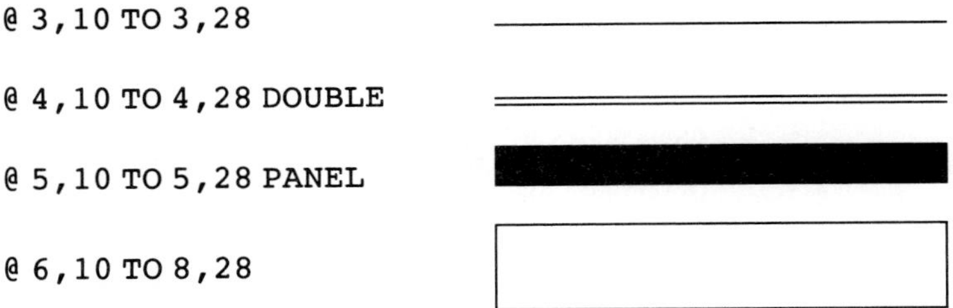

The **COLOR** option will display the line or box in other than the default colors; for example, the command **@ 3,30 TO 3,38 COLOR R/B** draws a single red line on a blue background. A foreground and a background color can be declared for all options except **PANEL**; the first color listed is the foreground (text) color, and the second color is the background color. The **PANEL** option uses a foreground color only. All color codes are the same as in the **SET COLOR** command.

Tips

1. The **@ ... TO** command is used primarily within program and/or format files to create attractive screen displays.
2. A custom border can be created either by specifying the character string itself enclosed in quotes, or by using the character's decimal equivalent (ASCII code value) in the IBM Extended Character Set. For example,

   Note that when the ASCII code value is used, it is not enclosed in quotes.
3. If the same box is used to frame the screen throughout a custom-designed system, the **@...CLEAR TO** command should be used to clear text inside the box, rather than using the **CLEAR** command for the entire screen. This will eliminate the need to constantly redraw the box every time a new screen is mapped.

4. The default setting for the appearance of the line or box can be changed with the **SET BORDER** command. The default for the color can be changed with the **SET COLOR OF NORMAL** command. Both defaults can be changed from the dot prompt, within a program, or within the **CONFIG.DB** file.
5. A custom border definition overrides any default border, as established by the **SET BORDER** command.
6. If different characters are to be used in the custom border definition, they *must* be entered in this order: top line, bottom line, left line, right line, top left corner, top right corner, bottom left corner, bottom right corner.
7. A box and a window function differently. A box is merely a graphic display to accentuate text produced by **@...SAY** commands. A window is more complicated, and must be defined and activated by the appropriate commands, so that output can be rerouted to the active window.

Related Topics

```
@...SAY...GET
ACTIVATE WINDOW
CLEAR
DEFINE WINDOW
SET BORDER
SET COLOR OF NORMAL
SET DISPLAY
```

ACTIVATE MENU

Syntax

```
ACTIVATE MENU <menu name> [PAD <pad name>]
```

Discussion

The **ACTIVATE MENU** command displays a predefined bar menu, overwriting any existing screen display, then activates the menu so that a selection can be made. The most typical menu is a single horizontal bar, but the options can extend over more than one row or even be arranged vertically.

The **ACTIVATE MENU** command requires that you first define the menu with a **DEFINE MENU** command, define the text and placement of the menu options (known as *pads*) with a series of **DEFINE PAD** commands, and specify the action to be taken on selecting each pad with a corresponding series of **ON PAD/ON SELECTION PAD** commands. The menu is displayed with the first pad highlighted unless the **PAD** option indicates a different pad.

Only one bar menu can be active at one time; thus, an **ACTIVATE MENU** command suspends any currently active bar menu before activating the new one. The image of the first menu remains on the screen, unless its display is covered by the new menu.

A **DEACTIVATE MENU** command deactivates the current bar menu, erasing its image from the screen and redisplaying the preexisting screen contents. (If the deactivated bar menu was called from another bar menu, the suspended bar menu is reactivated.) The deactivated menu definition is not erased from memory, and the bar menu can be reactivated with another **ACTIVATE MENU** command; i.e., it is only through a **RELEASE MENUS** or **CLEAR MENUS** command that the menu definitions are erased from memory.

Tips

1. The current bar menu will be deactivated and erased from the screen when the user presses the **Esc** key.

2. Each menu option should begin with a different letter, so that pressing the **Alt** key plus the first letter of the option name selects the desired option.
3. The **SHOW MENU** command displays a bar menu without activating it; use this command to preview the bar menu during menu development.
4. The **ON PAD** command attaches a popup menu to a pad, so that the popup menu is "pulled down" whenever the pad is selected. The **ON SELECTION PAD** command associates any other action with a menu pad.
5. A bar menu and an attached popup menu can both be active at the same time, but the selection procedure is different for each menu. For example, pads are highlighted on a bar menu with the right and left arrow keys, whereas bars are highlighted on a popup menu with the up and down arrow keys. Similarly, options are selected from a bar menu with the **Alt** key plus the first letter of the option name, and from a popup menu by just pressing the first letter of the option name.
6. By default the menu will be placed on row 0, with 3 spaces between each of the defined pads, unless this default is overridden by using the **AT** option in the **DEFINE PAD** command, to place the pads explicitly on the screen.

Related Topics

```
CLEAR MENUS
DEACTIVATE MENU
DEFINE MENU
DEFINE PAD
ON PAD
ON SELECTION PAD
RELEASE MENUS
SHOW MENU
```

ACTIVATE POPUP

Syntax

```
ACTIVATE POPUP <popup name>
```

Discussion

The **ACTIVATE POPUP** command displays a predefined vertical menu (called a popup menu), overwriting any existing screen display, then activates the menu so that a selection can be made.

The **ACTIVATE POPUP** command requires that you first define the menu with a **DEFINE POPUP** command, define the text and placement of the menu options (known as *bars*) with a series of **DEFINE BAR** commands, and specify the action to be taken upon selecting a bar with an **ON SELECTION POPUP** command.

The menu is displayed with the first selectable bar highlighted; selections are made by using the up and down arrow keys to highlight a bar, and then pressing the enter key; or, alternatively, by pressing the first letter of the option name.

Only one popup menu can be active at one time; thus, an **ACTIVATE POPUP** command suspends any currently active popup menu before activating the new one. The image of the first menu remains on the screen, unless it is covered by the new menu.

A **DEACTIVATE POPUP** command deactivates the current popup menu, erasing its image from the screen and redisplaying the underlying screen contents. (If the deactivated popup menu was called from another popup menu, the suspended popup is reactivated.) The deactivated menu definition is not erased from memory, and the popup menu can be reactivated with another **ACTIVATE POPUP** command; it is only through a **RELEASE POPUPS** or **CLEAR POPUPS** command that the menu definitions are erased from memory.

Tips

1. The current menu will be deactivated and erased from the screen when the user presses the **`Esc`** key.
2. Each menu option should begin with a different letter, so that pressing the first letter of the option name selects the desired option.
3. The **`SHOW POPUP`** command displays a popup menu on the screen without activating it; use this command to preview the menu during menu development.
4. The **`SET BORDER`** command determines the border that surrounds the popup menu. The default border of a single line can be changed by executing a **`SET BORDER`** command prior to the **`DEFINE POPUP`** command.
5. A bar menu and an attached popup menu can both be active at the same time, but the selection procedure is different for each menu. For example, pads are highlighted on a bar menu with the right and left arrow keys, whereas bars are highlighted on a popup menu with the up and down arrow keys. Similarly, options are selected from a bar menu by pressing the **`Alt`** key plus the first letter of the option name, and from a popup menu by just pressing the first letter of the option name.

Related Topics

```
BAR()
CLEAR POPUPS
DEACTIVATE POPUP
DEFINE BAR
DEFINE POPUP
ON SELECTION POPUP
RELEASE POPUPS
SET BORDER
SHOW POPUP
```

ACTIVATE SCREEN

Syntax

```
ACTIVATE SCREEN
```

Discussion

The **`ACTIVATE SCREEN`** command redirects output to the area of the screen outside the boundaries of the active window, without clearing the window from the screen. Screen output is otherwise displayed within the active window. The combination of **`ACTIVATE SCREEN`** and **`ACTIVATE WINDOW`** alternates between displaying output on the screens and in a window. For example,

```
DEFINE WINDOW win1 FROM 3,15 TO 7,65
DO WHILE .NOT. EOF()
     ACTIVATE WINDOW win1
     DISPLAY lastname, firstname, salary
     ACTIVATE SCREEN
     @ 11,20 SAY "Press any key to see the next record"
     SET CONSOLE OFF
     WAIT
     SET CONSOLE ON
     SKIP
ENDDO
```

Tips

1. The active window remains on the screen after the **ACTIVATE SCREEN** command has been issued, but subsequent screen output may overwrite the window. Thus, care must be taken to see that the position of the window is not affected by the screen output.
2. A window will remain on the screen until it is deactivated, overwritten, or scrolled off the screen by subsequent screen output. Even after it is cleared from the screen, however, the window definition remains in memory and can be reactivated with an **ACTIVATE WINDOW** command; i.e., it is only through a **RELEASE WINDOWS** or **CLEAR WINDOWS** command that the window definition is released from memory.
3. A **CLEAR** command issued after an **ACTIVATE SCREEN** command will clear the entire screen, including the window, but it does not release the window definition from memory.

Related Topics

```
ACTIVATE WINDOW
CLEAR
DEACTIVATE WINDOW
DEFINE WINDOW
```

ACTIVATE WINDOW

Syntax

```
ACTIVATE WINDOW <window name list>/ALL
```

Discussion

The **ACTIVATE WINDOW** command displays one or more predefined windows on the screen, overwriting any existing screen display, then activates one window, so that all subsequent screen output is sent to that window. The active window is determined as follows:

1. If only one window is specified, it becomes the active window.
2. If multiple windows are specified, the active window is the last one listed.
3. If **ALL** is specified, the active window is the one most recently defined.

The **ACTIVATE WINDOW** command requires the previous execution of a **DEFINE WINDOW** command to define the name, size, location, and border appearance of the window. Once activated, all screen output is sent to the window, including output from the following commands: **?/??**, **@...SAY...GET**, **LIST**, **DISPLAY**, **REPORT FORM**, **LABEL FORM**, etc. All output scrolls within the window and is automatically wrapped to fit within its borders.

Only one window can be active at one time; thus, an **ACTIVATE WINDOW** command suspends any currently active window before activating the new one. The image of the first window remains on the screen, unless it is covered by the new window.

A **DEACTIVATE WINDOW** command deactivates one or more windows, erasing their images from the screen and redisplaying the underlying screen contents. If another window was suspended when the window was activated, it is reactivated; otherwise dBASE returns to the full screen. The deactivated window definition is not erased from memory, and the window can be reactivated with another **ACTIVATE WINDOW** command; i.e, it is only through a **RELEASE WINDOWS** or a **CLEAR WINDOWS** command that the window definitions are erased from memory.

Tips

1. Up to twenty window definitions can be in memory at one time.
2. A window can be activated and deactivated as many times as needed during a session.

3. The **MOVE WINDOW** command can be used to assign new row and column coordinates to a window definition, changing its location on the screen.
4. A **SAVE WINDOW** command is used to save one or more window definitions currently in memory to a disk file, from which the definitions can subsequently be restored to memory with the **RESTORE WINDOW** command.
5. The **ACTIVATE SCREEN** command can be used to display text outside a window without deactivating the window. Output will continue to be displayed outside the window borders until an **ACTIVATE WINDOW** command is issued.
6. A defined window can be used as an editing window for a memo field by issuing a **SET WINDOW OF MEMO** command.

Related Topics

```
ACTIVATE SCREEN
CLEAR WINDOWS
DEACTIVATE WINDOW
DEFINE WINDOW
MOVE WINDOW
RELEASE WINDOW
RESTORE WINDOW
SAVE WINDOW
SET WINDOW OF MEMO
```

APPEND

Syntax

```
APPEND [BLANK]
```

Discussion

The **APPEND** command places you in a full-screen data entry mode, from which new records can be added to the end of the currently selected database file. The command produces an *input template* on the screen for the next successive record in the file; e.g., if there are currently 120 records in the active file, an input template is produced for record 121. The default template shows every field in the file structure, providing an amount of space for each field equal to its respective width. The cursor is positioned initially in field 1, column 1, from where data can be entered into the desired fields. A custom screen that replaces the default can be designated with the **SET FORMAT TO** command.

If the number of characters entered into a given field does not fill the space allocated for that field, the return key must be pressed to move to the next successive field. If, however, the allocated space is filled completely, the cursor moves automatically to the next field (or to the first field of the next record, if you are in the last field of the current record).

Any attempt to enter an illegal character (e.g., a letter in a numeric or date field, or any character other than a **T, F, N, Y, t, f, n,** or **y** in a logical field) will produce a beep, and the entry will be ignored. The cursor will remain in position, waiting for a valid entry. If no data is to be entered for a particular field, press the return key to move the cursor to the next field.

You can move between fields within a given record by using the **F3** (Previous) and **F4** (Next) keys. The contents of any existing entry can be edited by merely typing over what was previously entered, or by inserting or deleting characters. Table PN.8 summarizes the keystroke combinations used in the **APPEND** mode.

As alluded to earlier, entering data in the last field of a record automatically brings up the input template for the next record. You may continue adding records in this fashion, or you may terminate the append process, and return to the dot prompt—saving all of the records previ-

TABLE PN.8 **Keystroke Combinations for APPEND Command**

Keystroke	Function
→ or ←	Moves cursor one character to the right orleft
↓ or ↑	Moves cursor down/up one row (**BROWSE**) or field (**EDIT**)
F3/F4 or **Shift+Tab/Tab**	Moves cursor to the previous/next field within the current record
Home/End	Moves cursor to beginning/end of the current record (**BROWSE**) or current field (**EDIT**)
PgUp/PgDn	Moves cursor to the previous/next screen (**BROWSE**) or previous/next record (**EDIT**) in the database file (accessing records in physical order of entry when no index is active, or in order according to the master index)
Ins	Toggles between the insert and replacement modes
Del	Deletes character the cursor is on
Ctrl+Home	Opens a memo field for editing
Ctrl+Y	Deletes all characters in the entry template of the present field, beginning at the cursor position
Ctrl+U	Marks/unmarks the current record for deletion (toggle switch)
Ctrl+W, Ctrl+End	Saves all appended records, including the current record, and returns to the dot prompt; saves changes to a memo field
Ctrl+Q, Esc	Saves all appended records, except for the current record, and returns to the dot prompt
F2	Toggles between the **EDIT** and **BROWSE** screens
Shift+F8	Copies data in same field of previous record to the current record
F9	Toggles memo field open and closed, saving the edits
F10	Accesses the **APPEND** menu bar

ously appended—by pressing the return key *immediately* when the input template for the new record appears.

Ctrl+End and **Ctrl+W** also terminate the append process, saving all of the records added. However, these commands should not be used when a blank record is displayed in the input template, as pressing either **Ctrl+End** or **Ctrl+W** at this point will cause a blank (superfluous) record to be added to the file. **Ctrl+Q** and/or the **Esc** key also return to the dot prompt, saving all appended records except the one whose input template is currently displayed on the screen.

All indexes that are a part of the production index file will be automatically updated as new records are appended. However, all indexes that are not a part of the production index file must be explicitly opened with a **SET INDEX TO** command in order to be updated as new records are appended. Conversely, indexes not open are not updated, and so no longer match the database. If these indexes are subsequently opened, they must be reindexed before they can be used reliably.

The APPEND BLANK option adds one blank record to the end of the currently selected database, moves the record pointer to that blank record, and returns to the dot prompt. It does not invoke the full-screen input mode, and is primarily used with command programs.

Tips

1. You may design a custom screen for data entry by creating either a format file or a program file with the appropriate **@...SAY and @...GET** commands. This

enables you to supply more meaningful prompts for each field's entry template, include necessary messages to guide data entry, include data validation procedures, and even restrict access to certain fields for security reasons. This is especially useful if the data entry operator has little or no dBASE experience.

2. Use the `F2` key to toggle between the **`BROWSE`** and **`EDIT`** screens.
3. To enter data into a memo field, position the cursor in the input template of the memo field and press **`Ctrl+Home`** or **`F9`** to activate the memo text editor. Text can then be entered and/or edited as with a word processor. (See **`MODIFY COMMAND`** for specifics regarding working with the dBASE text editor.) To exit the text editor, press **`Ctrl+End`** to save the memo text, or the **`Esc`** key to exit without saving, at which point you will be returned to the full-screen append mode to continue data entry.
4. Use of the **`PgUp`** and **`PgDn`** keys in the append mode moves between screens/records in the database according to the physical order of the database if no index is active, or according to the logical order of any active index.
5. Existing records can be edited in the append mode by paging to the appropriate record and editing the field contents.
6. If a field entry is longer than the field width, and you continue to type past the last position in the field, the extra characters will appear in the next field. **`SET CONFIRM ON`** will prevent this from happening as it requires that the return key be pressed at the end of every field (regardless of whether or not the field is filled) to move to the next field. However, given that **`SET CONFIRM ON`** requires an extra keystroke, many users prefer **`CONFIRM`** set to **`OFF`** (the default setting). If **`CONFIRM`** is off, it is wise to **`SET BELL ON`** (also the default setting) so that a warning beep is produced at the end of a field.
7. Records can be appended only to the currently selected database file.
8. The appearance of the template within the append mode can be changed with the **`SET DELIMITERS`**, **`SET INTENSITY`**, and **`SET COLOR`** commands.
9. The **`SET CARRY ON`** command copies all of the data from the previous record to the newly appended record. It can be used when most of the fields in the subsequent record will contain the same data values as the current record, to save retyping those entries. Any fields that should contain different data values can then be edited.
10. If **`SET AUTOSAVE`** is **`OFF`**, some of the newly appended records are stored in buffers and are not written to disk until the data file is closed. In this case the appended records may not be reflected in the directory until after the database file is closed. If **`SET AUTOSAVE`** is **`ON`**, however, each newly appended record is written to disk as it is added to the file, and the directory is updated after each addition.
11. Many users choose to **`SET CONFIRM ON`** when **`SET BELL`** is **`OFF`**, so that pressing the return key is necessary at the end of every input template. This prevents a user from overtyping one field into the next without any warning.
12. To access the menu bar within the **`APPEND`** mode, press the **`F10`** key.

Related Topics

```
APPEND FROM
BROWSE
EDIT
SET AUTOSAVE
SET BELL
SET CARRY
SET CONFIRM
SET FORMAT
SET INDEX
USE
```

APPEND FROM

Syntax

```
APPEND FROM <filename> [FOR <condition>]
    [[TYPE] <file type>]
```

Discussion

The **APPEND FROM** command copies records from an existing file to the end of the currently selected database. The file from which the records are copied is assumed to be a database (**DBF**) file unless otherwise specified. The other file types include **dBASEII**, **DELIMITED**, **DELIMITED WITH BLANK**, **DELIMITED WITH <delimiter>**, **FW2**, **SDF**, **DIF**, **SYLK**, **RPD**, and **WKS**, and are discussed in more detail with the **COPY** command.

Specification of a **DBF** file as the source file will copy data only for fields common to both files; i.e., fields in the target file that have no matching field name in the source file are left blank. Fields in the source file that are larger than their counterparts in the target file are truncated if they contain character data, or replaced by asterisks if they are numeric.

Specification of a **DELIMITED** file as the source file assumes that the fields are separated by commas, that character fields are surrounded by double quotes (unless the **DELIMITED WITH** clause has been used to specify a different delimiter), and that each record ends with a carriage return and a line feed. The data is copied field by field, beginning with the leftmost character in each field. If the source file has more fields than the target database, the data in the extra fields is lost; if, however, the source file has fewer fields, the remaining fields in the target database are left blank.

Specification of an **SDF** file as the source file assumes that the records are fixed length, that a carriage return and line feed are at the end of each record, and that the fields are exactly the same length as those in the target database. Data is appended character by character, starting with the leftmost character, and no delimiters are used. As in a **DELIMITED** file, extra fields in the source file are lost, whereas missing fields result in blank fields in the target database.

Specification of a **SYLK**, **WKS**, or **DIF** file as the source file causes each row in the spreadsheet to be treated as a record, and each column as a field. The layout of the spreadsheet columns should match the structure of the target database for the data to be appended properly. In addition, column headings in the spreadsheet should be deleted before the **APPEND** is executed (i.e., row 1 should contain the first record).

Specification of a **dBASEII** file assumes that the source file is a dBASE II database file, whereas specification of an **RPD** or an **FW2** file assumes a RapidFile data file or a Framework II file, respectively.

Tips

1. If the source file is a **DBF** file, records marked for deletion in the source file will be appended to the target database, but will not be similarly marked after the append operation is completed. Specification of **SET DELETED ON**, however, prevents the marked records from being appended in the first place.
2. When appending from another database file, fields common to both files do not have to be in the same order in the file structure, nor do they have to be of the same type (although the data does have to be consistent with the new type). The fields do, however, have to be identically named.
3. A **DELIMITED WITH BLANK** clause assumes that the character fields in the source file are separated by one blank space. A **DELIMITED WITH <delimiter>** clause assumes fields are separated by commas, and that character data is surrounded by the specified delimiter.
4. Any open indexes in the currently selected work area are automatically updated when the data is appended.
5. If a **FOR** clause is used, the field on which the condition is based must be present in both the source and target files.

6. If no extension is specified with the source filename and no **TYPE** clause is used, dBASE will assume that the source file has a **DBF** extension. If, however, the extension is omitted and a **TYPE** clause is used, dBASE will assume that the source file has the default extension supplied by the respective software package.
7. If the source file is a spreadsheet file, rows that are blank in the source file become blank records in the **DBF** file.

Related Topics

```
APPEND
COPY
MODIFY STRUCTURE
SET DELETED
```

ASSIST

Syntax

```
ASSIST
```

Discussion

The **ASSIST** command invokes the dBASE IV control center, through which you can access the menu system. Through the control center, data files can be viewed, appended, browsed, and edited; reports and labels can be generated; queries can be created or modified; and programs can be executed. The control center is intended to simplify the execution of commands that would otherwise be issued at the dot prompt, and is covered in detail in Chapter 8.

Tips

1. The control center presents six panels, each of which provides access to a different design screen and through which the following file types can be created, modified, and activated: database file, query file, screen form, report form, label form, and application program.
2. Whenever the control center is activated, it opens a catalog—either the most recently opened catalog or, if no catalog exists, it opens **UNTITLED.CAT**. Files in the open catalog are placed in their appropriate panels and are available for use. New files that are created through the control center will be added to the open catalog as they are created and placed in their appropriate panel, available for immediate use.
3. The menu bar at the top of the screen can be accessed with either the **F10** key or by pressing the **Alt** key and the first letter of the option name (e.g., **Alt+C** for the Catalog option). To exit the menu bar, press the **Esc** key.
4. The navigation line and the message line at the bottom of the screen provide context-specific instructions and descriptive information, respectively.
5. To exit the control center, press **Esc** or **Alt+E** to access the exit menu. Pressing **Esc** takes you to the dot prompt, whereas accessing the exit menu allows a choice of exiting to the dot prompt or to DOS.
6. The control center provides only limited access to commands executed at the dot prompt; e.g., running a report from the report panel does not allow access to many options in the **REPORT FORM** command as executed from the dot prompt.

Related Topics

```
CONFIG.DB
HELP
```

AVERAGE

Syntax

```
AVERAGE [<expression list>][<scope>][WHILE <condition>]
    [FOR <condition>][TO <memvar list>]
```

Discussion

The **AVERAGE** command computes the arithmetic mean of numeric fields and/or arithmetic expressions involving numeric fields. The command computes an average for every numeric field in the currently selected database, unless an expression list is included in the command; i.e., inclusion of the expression list will restrict the computation to only those numeric fields specified in the list.

Every record in the database will be included in the computation unless the command contains a scope, **FOR**, or **WHILE** parameter. Thus, the command,

```
AVERAGE salary
```

includes every record in the **DBF** file in computing the average salary, whereas the command,

```
AVERAGE salary NEXT 10
```

includes only the next 10 records, beginning with the current record. In similar fashion, the command

```
AVERAGE salary FOR location = 'FL'
```

computes the average salary for only those employees located in Florida.

The results of the **AVERAGE** command (the field names and their respective averages) are displayed on the screen immediately after the command is issued (as long as **SET TALK** is **ON**), but are not otherwise saved. To preserve the results for future use, the **TO** clause must be specified with a valid memory variable included for each field expression averaged.

Tips

1. In the absence of an expression list, an average is computed for every numeric field in the current database, whether it makes sense to do so or not. Thus, if zip code were defined as a numeric field, an average of the zip codes would be computed, even though it would be a meaningless number.
2. When using a **TO** clause to save multiple averages to memory variables, the averages are computed in the order that the fields are listed in the expression list, and then assigned to the memory variables in the order of the memvar list. Thus, in the command

   ```
   AVERAGE field1,field2 TO memvar1,memvar2
   ```

   the average of **field1** is assigned to **memvar1** and the average of **field2** to **memvar2.**
3. If a filter condition has been established with a **SET FILTER** command, only those records that meet the filter condition will be included when calculating the average. In similar fashion, if **SET DELETED** is **ON**, only records not marked for deletion will be included in the calculation.

Related Topics

```
CALCULATE
COUNT
SET DELETED
SET FILTER
SUM
```

BAR FUNCTION

Syntax

```
BAR()
```

Discussion

The **BAR()** function returns an integer representing the most recently selected bar from the active popup menu. The function is used to evaluate the user's menu choice and transfer control accordingly. Consider:

```
DEFINE POPUP mainmenu FROM 6,25 TO 17,54
DEFINE BAR 1 OF mainmenu PROMPT "Add a record"
DEFINE BAR 2 OF mainmenu PROMPT "Edit a record"
DEFINE BAR 3 OF mainmenu PROMPT "Return to Main Menu"
ON SELECTION POPUP mainmenu DO mainprg
ACTIVATE POPUP mainmenu

PROCEDURE mainprg
DO CASE
   CASE BAR() = 1
      DO addrec
   CASE BAR() = 2
      DO editrec
   CASE BAR() = 3
      DEACTIVATE POPUP
ENDCASE
```

Selection of the first bar, *Add a record*, transfers control to **ADDREC.PRG**; selection of the second bar, to **EDITREC.PRG**; and so on. The bar numbers reflect the actual line number within the popup borders, and *not* the position of the menu choice; e.g., the menu options could be displayed on bars 2, 4, and 6. The bar number in each **CASE** condition reflects the bar number in the corresponding **DEFINE BAR** command, and not the position of the choice. The commands:

```
DEFINE BAR 2 OF mainmenu PROMPT "Add a record"
DEFINE BAR 4 OF mainmenu PROMPT "Edit a record"
DEFINE BAR 6 OF mainmenu PROMPT "Return to Main Menu"
```

offer *Add a record* as the first menu choice, but the corresponding **CASE** condition must reference bar 2 to transfer control to **ADDREC.PRG**.

Tips

1. The **BAR()** function returns a value of zero if there is no active popup menu or if the **Esc** key was used to deactivate the menu.
2. **DEFINE BAR** commands are not used when the **PROMPT** option is specified in the **DEFINE POPUP** command, eliminating the need for the **BAR()** function.

Related Topics

```
ACTIVATE POPUP
CLEAR POPUPS
DEACTIVATE POPUP
DEFINE BAR
```

```
DEFINE POPUP
ON SELECTION POPUP
RELEASE POPUPS
```

BOF FUNCTION

Syntax

```
BOF([<alias>])
```

Discussion

The `BOF()`, **B**eginning **O**f **F**ile, function indicates whether or not an attempt has been made to move the record pointer above the first record in the file, returning a logical value of true or false, respectively. The function is typically used in programs that process a file in reverse order, i.e., from the last record to the first. A simple example of such a program, to print the name and salary for every record, is shown here:

```
USE solemp ORDER salary
GO BOTTOM
DO WHILE .NOT. BOF()
 ? name,salary
 SKIP -1
ENDDO
```

The `BOF()` condition is considered true only when an attempt has actually been made to move above the first record; i.e., it is not true when the record pointer is on the first record. Consider:

```
USE solemp
GO TOP
? BOF()
.F. ———————————————— dBASE response
SKIP -1
? BOF()
.T. ———————————————— dBASE response
```

The `BOF()` function will not be reset to false until the record pointer is repositioned to the first record or beyond.

Tips

1. The first logical record (according to the master index) will be considered the beginning of file, unless no index is open, in which case it is the first physical record.
2. Any attempt to move the record pointer above the beginning of the file causes the record pointer to remain positioned on record 1. This differs from the `EOF()` condition, where an attempt to move beyond the last record actually does so, moving it to an end-of-file marker with a record number one greater than that of the last physical record in the file.
3. A separate value of the `BOF()` function is maintained for each of the 10 available work areas. When testing for the condition in an unselected work area, the number of the work area or the name of the **DBF** file, enclosed in quotation marks, must be indicated within the parentheses. For example, `? BOF(3)` is used to indicate whether or not an attempt has been made to move above the first record in the file open in work area three, whereas `? BOF("zoo")` tests the condition in the **ZOO.DBF** file in whichever work area the file is open. `BOF()`, with no work area specified, tests the condition in the currently selected work area.

Related Topics

```
EOF()
RECNO()
SKIP
```

BROWSE

Syntax

```
BROWSE [NOINIT] [NOAPPEND] [NOEDIT] [NODELETE]
    [COMPRESS] [FORMAT] [WINDOW <window name>]
    [FREEZE <field>][LOCK <n>]
    [NOFOLLOW] [NOMENU] [WIDTH <n>]
    [FIELDS <field name>[/R][/<column width>] ...
```

Discussion

BROWSE is a full-screen command that permits file maintenance operations to the currently selected database, including the appending, editing, and deleting of records. Up to 17 records may be displayed on the screen at one time, with each record displayed on a single line. The fields are presented in columnar fashion, in the order that they appear in the database file or the current view.

The current position of the record pointer determines the first record shown in the screen display (i.e., the record that is highlighted). The keystrokes in Table PN.9 may then be used to edit fields in the highlighted record, and/or to move to another record. All fields can be edited except calculated or read-only fields. Changes made to the data file that affect calculated fields will cause the calculated fields to be recalculated and the new results displayed. If an index is open, editing a key value will immediately reposition the record in the data file.

To append new records, move the highlight beyond the last record in the database, at which point you will be asked if new records are to be added. A response of **Y** brings up an input template for the new record, whereas a response of **N** returns to the **BROWSE** mode.

The **NOINIT** clause causes dBASE to use the same command options as were used with the previous **BROWSE** command.

The **NOAPPEND** clause prevents the appending of records while in the **BROWSE** mode.

The **NOEDIT** clause prevents the editing of any of the displayed fields. However, records may still be appended and/or deleted.

The **NODELETE** clause prevents the deleting/recalling of records with **Ctrl+U**. Records may still be appended and/or edited.

The **COMPRESS** clause changes the screen display so that 19 records, rather than the default of 17, will fit on the screen at one time.

The **FORMAT** clause causes the **BROWSE** command to use the picture clauses, messages, and data validation restrictions as defined in the active format file. In fact, all of the **@...GET** instructions specified in the format file are honored, other than the row and column coordinates that affect the positioning of the fields on the screen. Note that the format file must be opened with a **SET FORMAT TO** command prior to issuing the **BROWSE** command with this option.

The **WINDOW** clause causes the **BROWSE** command to display the data in a previously defined window. The window will be automatically deactivated when the **BROWSE** mode is exited.

The **FREEZE** clause restricts editing to the specified field, while still displaying the other fields. For example, the command

```
BROWSE FIELDS lastname,location,salary FREEZE salary
```

displays the three fields listed for each record, but highlights only the salary field; i.e., salary is the only field on which editing is possible. Only one field can be frozen at a time.

TABLE PN.9 **Keystroke Combinations for BROWSE Command**

Keystroke	Function
→ or ←	Moves cursor one character to the right or left
↓ or ↑	Moves cursor down/up one row
`F3/F4` or `Shift+Tab/Tab`	Moves cursor to the previous/next field within the current record
`Home/End`	Moves cursor to beginning/end of the current record
`PgUp/PgDn`	Moves cursor to the previous/next screen in the database file (accessing records in physical order of entry when no index is active, or in order according to the master index)
`Ins`	Toggles between the insert and replacement modes
`Del`	Deletes character the cursor is on
`Ctrl+Home`	Opens a memo field for editing
`Ctrl+Y`	Deletes all characters in the entry template of the present field, beginning at the cursor position
`Ctrl+U`	Marks/unmarks the current record for deletion (toggle switch)
`Ctrl+W, Ctrl+End`	Saves all appended records, including the current record, and returns to the dot prompt; saves changes to a memo field
`Ctrl+Q, Esc`	Saves all appended records, except for the current record and returns to the dot prompt
`F2`	Toggles between the **EDIT** and **BROWSE** screens
`Shift+F8`	Copies data in same field of previous record to the current record
`F9`	Toggles memo field open and closed, saving the edits
`F10`	Accesses the **BROWSE** menu bar

The **LOCK** clause specifies the number of contiguous fields that will remain fixed on the left side of the screen during a horizontal scrolling operation, and is quite helpful when certain fields are needed on the screen at all times (e.g., last name or account number).

The **NOFOLLOW** clause is significant only when an index is in use, and further when the key field (according to the active index) is being edited. Assume, for example, that account number is the active index, and that an account number is changed from 111 to 666. Normally, i.e., without the **NOFOLLOW** clause, the screen display would shift immediately to the next several records, beginning with account number 666. Specification of **NOFOLLOW**, however, will keep the display where it is (i.e., to records following 111), even though the edited record has been logically moved. This is a very important clause when you are performing a great many edits on a very large database, and you want to perform the edits in the order of the original logical sequence.

The **NOMENU** clause prevents access to the **BROWSE** menu bar.

The **WIDTH** clause specifies the maximum width that any field can have in the screen display. The entire contents of a field can still be accessed, even if not displayed, by using the right and left arrow keys to scroll through the field contents. If both a **WIDTH** clause and a **<column width>** option for a specific field are used, the smaller of the two is honored.

The **FIELDS** clause will include just the listed fields in the screen display, thereby making these fields the only ones available for modification. (The order in which the fields are listed is also the order in which they are displayed.) The **/R** switch makes the designated field read-only. The column-width switch specifies the width of the column display for the designated field, and can be a numeric value between 4 and 100 for a character field or a value between 8 and 100 for a numeric or date field. Values smaller than 8 for date fields or smaller than the defined width of a numeric field are ignored. A column width should not be specified for memo and logical fields, and will be ignored if specified. If the entire contents of the field do not fit within the width specified, the right and left arrow keys can be used to scroll through the field contents.

Tips

1. The easiest way to view a large data file whose fields will not all fit on the screen at one time is to limit the display width of the visible fields with the **WIDTH** clause and/or limit the number of fields displayed with a **FIELD** list (using the column-width switch in the field list). Either of these techniques is generally preferable to scrolling.
2. Do not append records when the **FIELDS** clause has been specified, as data input will be restricted to these fields.
3. **NOMENU**, **NOAPPEND**, **NODELETE**, and **NOEDIT** are useful when the **BROWSE** mode is initiated from a program, as they limit the operations a data entry operator can perform. The **FIELDS** clause and the **/R** switch can also be helpful in this situation, in that they prevent access to designated fields for security purposes.
4. The **LOCK** clause should not include so many fields as to prevent scrolling. The number of fields that can be locked will vary from file to file and will depend on the widths of the specific fields involved.
5. The **PgUp** and **PgDn** keys move between screens according to the physical order of the database if no index is open, or according to the logical order of the open master index.
6. In the event that data is entered beyond the last position in an input template, the extra characters are made part of the next field. This can be prevented if **SET CONFIRM** is **ON**, which requires that the enter key be pressed at the end of every field (regardless of whether or not the field is filled) to move to the next field.
7. Deleted records are not displayed by the **BROWSE** command if **SET DELETED** is **ON**. The same holds true for records not meeting an active filter condition.
8. The contents of a memo field can be edited by positioning the cursor in the input template of the memo field and pressing **Ctrl+Home** or **F9** to activate the memo text editor. Text can then be entered and/or edited as with a word processor. (See **MODIFY COMMAND** for specifics regarding working with the dBASE text editor.) To exit the text editor, press **Ctrl+End** to save the memo text or **Esc** to exit without saving the text, at which point you will be returned to the full-screen **BROWSE** mode to continue data entry.
9. The **F2** key can be used to toggle between the **BROWSE** and **EDIT** modes. When called from the **BROWSE** mode with the **F2** key, the **EDIT** command respects all of the **BROWSE** options that were specified, except for **COMPRESS**, **FREEZE**, **LOCK**, and **WIDTH**.
10. If **SET AUTOSAVE** is **OFF**, some of the newly appended records are stored in buffers and are not written to disk until the data file is closed; i.e., the appended records may not be reflected in the directory until after the database file is closed. If **SET AUTOSAVE** is **ON**, however, each newly appended record is written to disk as it is added to the file, and the directory is updated after each addition.
11. The **FIELDS** clause can include a calculated field, in which case both a field name and the expression used to calculate the desired result must be specified. For example,

    ```
    BROWSE FIELDS
        name,credits,qltypoints,gpa=credits/qltypoints
    ```

    Note that the calculated field is read-only and as such cannot be edited.
12. The **F10** key can be used to access the **BROWSE** menu bar.

Related Topics

```
APPEND
EDIT
SET AUTOSAVE
SET FORMAT
```

CALCULATE

Syntax

```
CALCULATE [scope]<option list>[FOR <condition>]
    [WHILE <condition>][TO <memvar list>]
```

Discussion

The **CALCULATE** command computes one or more financial and/or statistical functions for designated fields in the currently selected **DBF** file. The available functions are shown in the table below:

Function	Calculation Performed
AVG(<expN>)	The average of the specified numeric field or expression
CNT()	The number of records in the **DBF** file
MAX(<exp>)	The largest value for the specified numeric, date, or character field or expression
MIN(<exp>)	The smallest value for the specified numeric, date, or character field or expression
NPV(<rate>,<flows>,<initial>)	The net present value of the designated cash flow field
STD(<expN>)	The standard deviation of the specified numeric field or expression
SUM(<expN>)	The sum of the specified numeric field or expression
VAR(<expN>)	The variance of the specified numeric field or expression

The option list indicates the desired function(s) and associated argument, which can be a field name or an expression including a field name. Every record is included in the computation unless the command contains a scope, **FOR**, or **WHILE** parameter. Thus, the command,

```
CALCULATE MAX(popltn)
```

includes all of the records in the **DBF** file in determining the maximum population, whereas the command,

```
CALCULATE MAX(popltn) NEXT 10
```

includes only the next ten records in the calculation, beginning with the current record.

The results of the command (the field names and their respective results) are displayed on the screen (as long as **SET TALK** is **ON**), but are not otherwise saved. To preserve the results for future use, the **TO** clause must be specified with a valid memory variable included for each field expression calculated. The functions are calculated in the order listed and assigned to the memory variables in the order of the memory variable list. Thus, in the command,

```
CALCULATE MAX(popltn),MAX(area) TO maxpop,maxarea
```

the maximum population will be assigned to **maxpop**, and the maximum area will be assigned to **maxarea**.

Tips

1. A function argument can contain a single field or a single expression involving multiple fields; it cannot, however, contain two distinct fields. Thus, **CALCULATE MIN(population,area)** is invalid, but **CALCULATE MIN(population/area)** is a valid command.
2. The **MAX()** and **MIN()** functions can process date and/or character data; e.g., **CALCULATE MIN(state)** will return the first state in alphabetic order (i.e., Alabama), while **CALCULATE MAX(yradmtd)** returns the latest chronological date.
3. The **CNT()** function has no argument.
4. The parameters in the **NPV()** function are the discount rate (expressed as a decimal number), the field containing the periodic cash flows (expressed as positive or negative numbers, depending on whether there was a cash inflow or outflow), and the initial investment (expressed as a negative value since it is a cash outflow).
5. If a filter condition has been established with a **SET FILTER** command, only those records meeting the filter condition are included in the calculation. In similar fashion, only records not marked for deletion will be included in the calculation if **SET DELETED** is **ON**.
6. Averages, sums, and counts can also be obtained with the **AVERAGE**, **SUM**, and **COUNT** commands, respectively. There are no equivalent commands for the maximum and minimum functions, or for the financial functions.

Related Topics

```
AVERAGE
COUNT
SET DELETED
SET FILTER
SUM
```

CANCEL

Syntax

```
CANCEL
```

Discussion

The **CANCEL** command terminates execution of the current program, closes all open program files, and returns control to the dot prompt. It is used primarily in debugging as part of an error routine or as a response to a dBASE error message (e.g., the *Cancel Ignore Suspend* message, which is displayed by dBASE as errors are detected).

Tips

1. The **CANCEL** command does not close an open procedure file.
2. The **CANCEL** command does not close an open **DBF** file; thus, the position of the record pointer remains unchanged from where it was when the error occurred. Accordingly, you can execute commands such as **DISPLAY STATUS**, **DISPLAY**, and **? RECNO()** to track down the problem.
3. The **CANCEL** command releases all private memory variables; hence it may be preferable to **SUSPEND**, rather than **CANCEL**, execution, in order to display the contents of the memory variables. Additional commands can also be entered from the dot prompt during the suspension, after which execution can be resumed or canceled.
4. The **RESUME** command resumes execution at the point where it was suspended.

5. If a program has been suspended, and a serious error detected and resolved, you should **CANCEL** rather than **SUSPEND** execution. Close all databases; release all memory variables, window definitions, and menu definitions; edit the file, and reexecute the program.

Related Topics

RESUME
SUSPEND

CDOW FUNCTION

Syntax

```
CDOW(<date expression>)
```

Discussion

The **CDOW()** function returns the day of the week in character format (Sunday, Monday, etc.) corresponding to the specified date expression. The argument in the **CDOW()** function must be a date-type argument and may assume several different forms as shown in the following table:

Function	Name of the Argument
CDOW(hiredate)	Date field
CDOW(memdate)	Date memory variable
CDOW(DATE())	**DATE()** function itself
CDOW{12/25/92}	Literal date
CDOW(CTOD(hiredate))	**CTOD()** conversion function
CDOW(DATE() + 10)	Expression with date arithmetic

Tips

1. If the argument of a **CDOW()** function is a character string enclosed in quotes or a character field or memory variable, it must first be converted to a date-type variable with the **CTOD()** conversion function. The shorthand format, using curly braces, is often easier and more convenient, but may be used only with a literal date; i.e., it cannot be used with a character string enclosed in quotes or with a character field or memory variable. (Note that a literal date is *not* enclosed in quotes as is a date expressed as a character string.)
2. The **CDOW()** function is often used in program files and/or report forms to display a date in a more attractive format. For example, given a system date of 08/03/92, the command,

```
@ 20,20 SAY + CDOW(DATE()) + ", " + DTOC(DATE())
```

returns the string "Thursday, 08/03/92".

Related Topics

CMONTH()
CTOD()
DATE()
DTOC()

CHR FUNCTION

Syntax

```
CHR(<ASCII number>)
```

Discussion

The **CHR()** function returns the ASCII character corresponding to the number specified in the function. (The number itself must be a positive integer between 0 and 255.) The function provides access to the complete ASCII character set, most importantly those characters with no direct keyboard equivalent (e.g., printer control codes, foreign language characters, and graphics characters).

Tips

1. The ASCII character 7 rings the bell in a program, perhaps to signal that an invalid response has been entered. (The bell will be sounded regardless of whether **SET BELL** is **ON** or **OFF**.) Consider:

```
DO CASE
   CASE opt = '1'
      .
         .
            .
   OTHERWISE
      ? CHR(7)
      @ 22,25 SAY "Please enter 1 - 5"
ENDDO
```

2. ASCII characters can be sent to the printer to produce special effects, such as condensed or boldfaced print. The particular ASCII characters are hardware specific; e.g., the ASCII character 15 indicates compressed print on many Epson and Okidata printers. Consider:

```
??? CHR(15)          ??? sends ASCII control code to printer
REPORT FORM employee
??? CHR(18)
```

The ASCII character 18 is used on these same printers to return to normal print, which should be done as a matter of course at the end of printing.

3. Not all printers support the extended ASCII character set (128–255), which are the graphic, scientific, and foreign language characters. Thus, it is possible that a character from the extended set will appear on the screen, but not on the printer.

Related Topics

```
???
SET BELL
SET PRINTER
```

CLEAR

Syntax

```
CLEAR
CLEAR ALL
```

```
CLEAR FIELDS
CLEAR GETS
CLEAR MEMORY
CLEAR MENUS
CLEAR POPUPS
CLEAR TYPEAHEAD
CLEAR WINDOWS
```

Discussion

The **CLEAR** command functions differently, depending upon the option specified. Consider:

1. **CLEAR**, issued with no option, erases the entire screen and repositions the cursor to the lower-left corner of the screen. Note that if a window is active when the **CLEAR** command is issued, only the window is cleared and not the entire screen.
2. **CLEAR ALL** closes all open database (**DBF**) and related (**MDX**, **NDX**, **FMT**, **FRM**, **DBT**, and **CAT**) files; releases all memory variables; releases all popup and menu definitions; releases all window definitions; releases all field lists; and selects work area 1. It does not affect the system memory variables nor does it close any open **ALTERNATE** or **PROCEDURE** files.
3. **CLEAR FIELDS** releases the current field list in all work areas, regardless of whether the field list was established through a **SET FIELDS TO** command, or by opening a view file. The command also executes the equivalent of a **SET FIELDS OFF** command.
4. **CLEAR GETS** releases all **@...GET**s issued since the last **CLEAR ALL**, **CLEAR GETS**, or **READ** command. Note that unless otherwise increased or decreased in the **CONFIG.DB** file, a total of 128 **@...GET** statements are permitted before a **CLEAR GETS** must be issued.
5. From the dot prompt, **CLEAR MEMORY** is the same as a **RELEASE ALL** command, releasing all public and private memory variables. In a program, however, **CLEAR MEMORY** releases all public and private memory variables, whereas **RELEASE ALL** releases only the private memory variables created in the current or lower-level programs. In either case **CLEAR MEMORY** does not affect system memory variables.
6. **CLEAR MENUS** clears all user-defined horizontal bar menus from the screen and releases their definitions from memory.
7. **CLEAR POPUPS** clears all user-defined popup menus from the screen and releases their definitions from memory. The popups are deactivated, as are their respective **ON SELECTION** commands.
8. **CLEAR TYPEAHEAD** clears all characters from the keyboard buffer and is intended to prevent fast typists from outrunning the keyboard. The existence of a buffer allows data entry in anticipation of future prompts, a dangerous practice that can result in unintended or erroneous characters remaining in the buffer. Accordingly, **CLEAR TYPEAHEAD** is most useful immediately prior to a **READ** or **WAIT** command, to ensure that the buffer is empty, and that dBASE acts upon intentionally typed characters, rather than incorrectly typed ones remaining in the buffer.
9. **CLEAR WINDOWS** clears all user-defined windows from the screen and erases them from memory. Any definitions not saved are lost. Any text covered by a window is restored.

Tips

1. **CLEAR** can be used in conjunction with the **@...TO** function to erase a rectangular portion of the screen, as specified by the two sets of row and column coordinates; e.g., the statement,

   ```
   @ 2,10 CLEAR TO 14,20
   ```

   will clear the screen from row 2, column 10 to row 14, column 20. Given that dBASE recognizes a screen of 25 rows and 80 columns, the row value(s) may be any integer from 0 through 24, whereas the column value(s) may be any integers from 0 through 79.

2. **CLEAR GETS** cancels any **@...GET** commands that have not been collected by a **READ** command. Accordingly, any pending **GET** statements must be read prior to a **CLEAR GETS** command.
3. All memory variables needed for future processing must be saved prior to executing a **CLEAR MEMORY** command.
4. A window definition can be saved to a disk file prior to being cleared with a **SAVE WINDOW** command and then can be recreated with a **RESTORE WINDOW** command.

Related Topics

```
@...CLEAR
@...GET
CLOSE
READ
RELEASE
RESTORE WINDOW
SAVE
SAVE WINDOW
SET FIELDS
SET TYPEAHEAD
```

CLOSE

Syntax

```
CLOSE <filetype>/ALL
```

Discussion

The **CLOSE** command closes all open files, or only open files of a specific file type, depending on the option specified. The command cannot be issued without an option; i.e., **CLOSE** by itself is not a valid command and will result in an error message. The effect of the command depends on the indicated file type as follows:

1. CLOSE ALL	Closes all open files of all types and selects work area 1.
2. CLOSE ALTERNATE	Closes the current alternate file, as previously opened with the **SET ALTERNATE** command.
3. CLOSE DATABASES	Closes all database files and their associated indexes (**MDX** and **NDX**), format files, and memo files in all ten work areas.
4. CLOSE FORMAT	Closes an open format file in the currently selected work area, as previously opened with a **SET FORMAT** command.
5. CLOSE INDEX	Closes all open indexes in the currently selected work area except for the production **MDX** file.
6. CLOSE PROCEDURE	Closes the current procedure file, as previously opened with a **SET PROCEDURE** command.

Tips

1. The **USE** command with no parameters will close the **DBF** file and its associated index in the currently selected work area only. This is often preferable to issuing a **CLOSE**

DATABASES command, which closes the **DBF** files in all ten areas, as opposed to just the current area.

Related Topics

```
QUIT
SET ALTERNATE
SET FORMAT
SET INDEX
SET PROCEDURE
USE
```

CMONTH FUNCTION

Syntax

```
CMONTH(<date expression>)
```

Discussion

The **CMONTH()** function returns the character name (January, February, etc.) corresponding to the month in the specified date expression. The argument in the **CMONTH()** function must be a date-type argument and may assume several different forms as shown in the following table:

Function	Nature of the Argument
`CMONTH(hiredate)`	Date field
`CMONTH(memdate)`	Date memory variable
`CMONTH(DATE())`	**DATE()** function itself
`CMONTH{12/25/92}`	Literal date
`CMONTH(CTOD(hiredate))`	**CTOD()** conversion function
`CMONTH(DATE()+10)`	Expression with date arithmetic

Tips

1. If the argument of a **CMONTH()** function is a character string enclosed in quotes or a character field or memory variable, it must first be converted to a date-type variable with the **CTOD()** conversion function. The shorthand format using curly braces, is often easier and more convenient, but may be used only with a literal date; i.e., it cannot be used with a character string enclosed in quotes or with a character field or memory variable. (Note that a literal date is *not* enclosed in quotes as is a date expressed as a character string.)
2. The **CMONTH()** function is often used in program files and/or report forms to display a date in a more attractive format. For example, given a system date of 01/08/93, the command,

Command entered on one line

```
@ 20,20 SAY "Today is " + CMONTH(DATE()) + " " +
   STR(DAY(DATE()),2) + ", " + STR(YEAR(DATE()),4)
```

returns the string "Today is January 08, 1993". (Note that the day and year must be converted to strings to be concatenated with the other character-type data.)

Related Topics

CDOW()
CTOD()
DATE()
DAY()
STR()
YEAR()

COMPILE

Syntax

```
COMPILE <filename> [RUNTIME]
```

Discussion

The **COMPILE** command translates the specified source program to an execute-only form called an object program, without executing the resultant file. The object code is in a form closer to the native language of the microprocessor, and thus executes much faster than if dBASE had to continually read, interpret, and then execute commands in the source program one-by-one (as it did in all previous versions).

Normally, dBASE compiles a source program when it is first executed. Regular program files (**PRG**), SQL program files (**PRS**), and update query files (**UPD**) are compiled by the **DO** command, producing an object program with an extension of **DBO**. Format files (**FMT**) are compiled by the **SET FORMAT TO** command to produce object programs with an **FMO** extension. Report form files (**FRG**) and label form files (**LBG**) are compiled by the **REPORT FORM** and **LABEL FORM** commands and produce files with an extension of **FRO** and **LBO**, respectively. Query files (**QBE**) are compiled with the **SET VIEW TO** command and produce object code files with an extension of **QBO**.

During compilation, dBASE checks for syntactical and structural accuracy (e.g., every **DO WHILE** must have a corresponding **ENDDO**, and all terms must be spelled correctly), and it displays error messages when violations are found.

Realize, too, that once the program has cleanly compiled, it is the object code that is executed, not the source code. However, when you edit a program, it is the source code that is edited and not the object code, and the program must, therefore, be recompiled for the changes to take effect. If editing is done through a dBASE facility (e.g., **MODIFY COMMAND**, **MODIFY REPORT**), the object program is erased from disk when the edits are saved, thus automatically recompiling the source code the next time the program is run. If, however, you use an external word processor to edit the file, the program is recompiled only if **SET DEVELOPMENT** is **ON**. When **SET DEVELOPMENT** is **OFF**, either the obsolete object program must be explicitly deleted or the program must be recompiled with the **COMPILE** command.

The **RUNTIME** option causes dBASE to identify the commands that will cause errors in a runtime version of the program.

Tips

1. The **COMPILE** command searches for a default extension of **PRG**; any other extension must be explicitly specified in the filename.
2. The **COMPILE** command assigns the resultant object program an extension of **DBO**, regardless of the file type of the source code; i.e., compilation of **FMT**, **FRG**, **LBG**, and **QBE** files produces files with a **DBO** extension. It is recommended, therefore, that these

files not be edited with an external word processor and, further, that they not be compiled through the **COMPILE** command.

3. The **COMPILE** command can be used to compile a program without executing it.

Related Topics

CREATE/MODIFY LABEL
CREATE/MODIFY QUERY
CREATE/MODIFY REPORT
CREATE/MODIFY SCREEN
DEBUG
DO
MODIFY COMMAND
SET DEVELOPMENT

CONFIG.DB

Discussion

The **CONFIG.DB** file enables you to customize dBASE IV to your personal needs. The file can be created with the nondocument mode of a word processor, or with dBASE's **DBSETUP** program, or with the **MODIFY COMMAND** text editor. The commands in the **CONFIG.DB** file are entered one command per line, in no particular order, and in any combination of upper and lower case. Their purpose can be to:

1. Reconfigure the dBASE operating environment.
2. Redefine memory allocation.
3. Redefine the function keys.
4. Change the default status of various **SET** commands (including the **SET** commands that control the color of the screen display).

The syntax of commands used in the **CONFIG.DB** file is simply **<keyword> = <value>** and as such, is often different from that of the equivalent command when issued at the dot prompt. Consider:

Dot Prompt Command	CONFIG.DB Command
SET BELL OFF	BELL=OFF
SET AUTOSAVE ON	AUTOSAVE=ON
SET DEFAULT TO A	DEFAULT=A
SET COLOR OF FIELDS TO B/W	COLOR OF FIELDS=B/W
SET FUNCTION 6 TO "USE FILE1"	F6="USE FILE1;"

The **CONFIG.DB** file is read from the logged subdirectory when **dBASE** is loaded; or if no **CONFIG.DB** file exists in that subdirectory, the directories in the **DOS PATH** command will be searched. Accordingly, if the same **CONFIG.DB** is to be read every time dBASE is loaded, it should be stored in the same subdirectory as the **DBASE** program. If, however, a different **CONFIG.DB** is to be read, depending on the application being run, the various **CONFIG.DB** files should be stored in the same subdirectory as their respective applications, and that subdirectory should be made the default prior to loading dBASE. Note, too, that the dBASE program subdirectory should be included in the **DOS PATH** command. A **CONFIG.DB** file is not required as dBASE will establish default settings in its absence.

Any changes to the configuration and/or memory allocation must be done from a **CONFIG.DB** file; i.e., the changes cannot be done at the dot prompt. Consider:

Command	Effect
COMMAND=<command>	Executes indicated command when dBASE is loaded
PROMPT=<expression>	Changes the appearance of the dBASE prompt
TEDIT=<filename>	Specifies an external word processor for use with **MODIFY COMMAND**
WP=<filename>	Specifies an external word processor for use with memo fields
FILES=<number>	Specifies the maximum number of files that can be open at one time (15–99)

For a full list of the commands that can be used in the **CONFIG.DB** file, consult the dBASE manual.

Tips

1. Modification of the **CONFIG.DB** file requires you to reload dBASE for the changes to take effect.
2. The **CONFIG.DB** file can be made to execute a particular dBASE program file automatically whenever dBASE is loaded by including a **COMMAND = statement**; for example,

   ```
   COMMAND = DO MAINMENU
   ```

   This is especially useful when setting up a custom system for users who never work from the dot prompt, and who are interested only in a specific application program.
3. Specifying a program filename in the command line when you load dBASE (e.g., **DBASE MAINMENU**) will execute the named program as soon as dBASE is loaded, overriding any **COMMAND** = in the **CONFIG.DB** file.
4. Examination of the **CONFIG.DB** file that is provided with dBASE reveals a **COMMAND=ASSIST** statement to bring up the control center automatically. You can eliminate the automatic appearance of the control center simply by deleting this command from the **CONFIG.DB** file.
5. The **PROMPT** = command will change the dBASE dot prompt to a new prompting character; e.g.,

   ```
   PROMPT = COMMAND>
   ```

   will replace the dot prompt with **COMMAND>**
6. The **CONFIG.DB** file is not to be confused with **CONFIG.SYS**, which is used by DOS to establish various system parameters, e.g., the maximum number of files and buffers that can be open at one time. The **CONFIG.SYS** file must be located in the root directory of the drive from where the system is booted. Note that the **FILES** = command in the **CONFIG.DB** file cannot be greater than the **FILES** = command in the **CONFIG.SYS** file.
7. In theory, an external word processor may be used instead of the dBASE text editor by including a **TEDIT=** command in the **CONFIG.DB** file. In practice, however, sophisticated word processors are too large to load in this manner. Another option to consider is the use of a RAM resident utility, such as Sidekick, but again memory problems may interfere with complex operations.
8. If the **TEDIT** command is used to substitute an external word processor for dBASE's text editor, be sure to include a **DEVELOPMENT=ON** command in the **CONFIG.DB** file to delete the matching **DBO** files when a **PRG** file is modified.

9. The `F1` and `Shift+F10` function keys cannot be redefined.
10. When redefining the function keys, include a semicolon at the end of the command to cause the command to execute when the function key is pressed. (The semicolon represents the enter key.)

Related Topics

SET
SET DEVELOPMENT

CONTINUE

Syntax

```
CONTINUE
```

Discussion

The **CONTINUE** command searches the currently selected database, beginning with the current record, for the next record meeting the search condition in the most recently issued **LOCATE** command. The command operates within the scope of the **LOCATE** command if one was specified; if not, it searches until the end of file is reached or a record is found.

The record number of the found record is displayed on the screen (as long as **SET TALK** is **ON**), and the record pointer is moved to that record. If, however, a record meeting the designated condition is not found, an *End of LOCATE scope* message is displayed instead, and the record pointer is moved to the end of file, or to the last record included in the scope of the associated **LOCATE** command.

As many **CONTINUE** commands as necessary can be issued until the end of file (or scope) is reached, in order to find all of the records meeting the search condition.

Tips

1. The **CONTINUE** command repositions the record pointer, but does not display the found record. Accordingly, a subsequent **DISPLAY** command is necessary to view the found record.
2. The **CONTINUE** command begins its search at the current position of the record pointer, as determined by the previously executed **LOCATE** (or **CONTINUE**) command. Hence, commands that move the record pointer should not be issued between a **LOCATE** and subsequent **CONTINUE** command, or the search will be compromised. This same principle holds true between successive **CONTINUE** commands.
3. If a filter condition is active, records not meeting the filter condition are ignored by the **CONTINUE** command. In similar fashion, records marked for deletion are also ignored when **SET DELETED** is **ON**.

Related Topics

LOCATE
SET DELETED
SET FILTER

COPY

Syntax

```
COPY TO <new filename> [<scope>][FIELDS <field list>]
    [WHILE <condition>][FOR <condition>][TYPE<filetype>]
```

Discussion

The **COPY** command creates a new database file with an identical file structure to that of the currently selected database. All of the records in the currently selected database are copied to the new file, including those marked for deletion, unless a scope parameter, or a **FOR** or **WHILE** clause, is included. Specification of these clauses copies only a subset of the records to the new file, as specified by the scope or as determined by the condition. For example, the command,

```
COPY TO newfile NEXT 20
```

will copy the next 20 records in the database (beginning with the current record) to the file named **NEWFILE.DBF**, whereas the command,

```
COPY TO newfile2 FOR location = 'FL'
```

will copy only those records having a location code of Florida.

All of the fields in the original file structure will be copied to the new file unless a **FIELDS** clause is included to limit the fields that are copied. The command,

```
COPY TO newfile3 FIELDS lastname,initials
```

creates a new database file named **NEWFILE3.DBF**, consisting of only two fields (with identical types and widths to those in the source file) in its file structure.

Omission of the **TYPE** clause produces a dBASE IV file (with the default extension of **DBF**), whereas its inclusion produces a file in different formats for use in other application programs, e.g., Lotus.

Other **TYPE** specifications are discussed below:

1. DELIMITED [WITH <delimiter>/BLANK], for example:

   ```
   COPY TO newfile TYPE DELIMITED
   COPY TO newfile TYPE DELIMITED WITH *
   COPY TO newfile TYPE DELIMITED WITH BLANK
   ```

   The **DELIMITED** option creates an ASCII text file with variable-length records. Each record in the target file ends with a carriage return and line feed. Commas separate the fields within a record, double quotes surround character data (although a different delimiter can be specified by using **DELIMITED WITH <delimiter>**), and trailing blanks are not included. Dates are converted to eight-digit numbers in which the first four digits indicate the year, and the second four, the month and day. The copied file is assigned a default extension of **TXT**. The **DELIMITED WITH BLANK** option uses a single blank space to separate the fields, and no delimiters surround the character data.

2. **SDF** (System Data Format), for example:

   ```
   COPY TO newfile TYPE SDF
   ```

   The **SDF** option creates an ASCII text file, which consists of fixed-length records. The field widths of the original database file are maintained in that blanks are used to pad the field when necessary (character fields are copied left justified, and numeric fields are copied right justified). Each record ends with a carriage return and a line feed. No delimiters are used between fields, as individual fields can be identified by their starting position in the file. The copied file is assigned a default extension of **TXT**.

3. **WKS**, for example:

```
COPY TO newfile TYPE WKS
```

The **WKS** option creates a file suitable for input to Lotus 1–2-3, release 1A or higher. Fields are converted to columns, and records are converted to rows. The copied file is assigned a default extension of **WKS**.

4. **RPD**, for example:

```
COPY TO newfile TYPE RPD
```

The **RPD** option creates a RapidFile data file with an extension of **RPD**.

5. **FW2**, for example:

```
COPY TO newfile TYPE FW2
```

The **FW2** option creates a Framework II database file with an extension of **FW2**.

Tips

1. Records marked for deletion will be copied to the new file unless **SET DELETED** is **ON**.
2. The existence of a filter condition causes only those records meeting the filter condition to be included in the copied file. Note, too, that if a filter has been set, and a **FOR** or **WHILE** clause is included, only those records meeting the filter condition will be tested in the **FOR** or **WHILE** condition.
3. The existence of a field list causes only those fields to be copied to the new file. If a field list is active and a **FIELDS** clause is included in the **COPY** command, the clause may include only the active fields.
4. The **COPY** command copies record by record, and consequently is time consuming in a large file. Thus, when copying from one **DBF** file to another, the **DOS COPY** command is faster and more efficient.
5. The **COPY** command can be used to make a temporary backup copy of a database file, a wise decision prior to making major changes in the data.
6. The directory date for the new database file will be the date the file was copied.
7. The order in which the records are copied to the new file is determined by whether or not an index is active. If no index is active, the records are copied in physical order; if an index is active, the records are copied to the new file in the logical order of the active index.
8. Inclusion of a period (.) as the last character of the filename will override the default extension, resulting in no extension at all.
9. The **COPY** command overwrites an existing file of the same name with no warning, unless **SET SAFETY** is **ON**.
10. Memo fields are copied only if the target file is another dBASE IV data file.
11. When the target file is a spreadsheet file, field names are converted to column headers.
12. If a relationship has been established to a file in another work area, and fields from the related file have been included in the active field list, the target file will contain data from the related records.

Related Topics

```
APPEND FROM
SET DELETED
SET DELIMITED
SET FIELDS
SET SAFETY
```

COPY INDEXES

Syntax

```
COPY INDEXES <file list> [TO <mdx filename>]
```

Discussion

The **COPY INDEXES** command converts one or more *open* single index files (**NDX**) to tags in a multiple index file (**MDX**). The **NDX** files will be copied to the production **MDX** file, unless the **TO** clause is used to specify an independent **MDX** file.

A maximum of 47 **NDX** files can be copied in a single command, which is also the maximum number of tags allowed in a multiple index file.

Tips

1. If the target **MDX** file does not exist, dBASE will create either a production **MDX** file with the same name as the **DBF** file, or an independent **MDX** file with the specified name, depending on whether or not the **TO** clause was used.
2. A **SET INDEX TO** command (or a **USE** command with the **INDEX** option) must be issued to open the **NDX** files prior to executing a **COPY INDEXES** command.
3. Although up to 47 **NDX** files can be included in the file list, there can be only one target **MDX** file specified.
4. This command is used primarily to convert dBASE III Plus applications to dBASE IV.

Related Topics

SET INDEX TO
USE

COUNT

Syntax

```
COUNT [<scope>][WHILE <condition>][FOR <condition>]
    [TO <memvar>]
```

Discussion

The **COUNT** command counts (tallies) the number of records in the currently selected database. Every record will be counted unless the command contains a scope parameter, or a **FOR** or **WHILE** clause. In other words, **COUNT** with no parameters returns a count of all of the records in the current **DBF** file.

Inclusion of either a **FOR** or **WHILE** parameter causes only those records that match the specified condition to be counted; e.g., the command,

```
COUNT FOR location = 'TX',
```

returns the number of records with a location of Texas. Specification of **REST** as the scope parameter, e.g.,

```
COUNT REST FOR location = 'TX',
```

causes counting to begin at the current record (as opposed to the beginning of the file as is done with the default scope of **ALL**).

The tally determined by the **COUNT** command is displayed on the screen immediately after the command is issued (as long as **SET TALK** is **ON**), but is not otherwise saved. Specification of the **TO** clause, e.g.,

```
COUNT FOR location = 'TX' TO locnumbr
```

will, however, save the tally to a valid numeric memory variable. The print (**?**) command, i.e., **? locnumbr**, may then be used to view the results of the **COUNT** command.

Tips

1. If **SET DELETED** is **ON**, records marked for deletion will not be counted. In similar fashion, if a filter condition has been established, records not meeting the filter condition will be ignored, and thus, not counted.

Related Topics

```
AVERAGE
CALCULATE
RECCOUNT()
SET DELETED
SET FILTER
SUM
```

CREATE

Syntax

```
CREATE <filename>
```

Discussion

The **CREATE** command defines the structure of a new database (**DBF**) file, adds the new file to the disk directory, and, if requested, opens the newly created file for data entry. The command may be specified with or without a filename; e.g., **CREATE SOLEMP**, or simply **CREATE**, in which case dBASE prompts for a filename.

Execution of the command displays a design screen through which the fields in the file structure are defined one at a time, to a maximum of 255 fields. The following information is required for each field: field name, field type, field width, number of decimals (numeric fields only), and an index flag.

The ***field name*** must be one to ten characters in length, must begin with a letter, and can consist of letters, numbers, and an embedded underscore character. Blanks are *not* permitted.

The ***field type*** is specified as character, numeric, floating point numeric, logical, date, or memo. A character field can contain any ASCII character, but may *not* be used in mathematical operations. A numeric field can contain only the digits 0 through 9, a decimal point, and a minus sign; commas or dollar signs are *not* permitted. A floating point numeric field is used only with applications that process extremely large or small numbers, and is not discussed further. A logical field can contain only a value of true (**T**, **t**, **Y**, **y**) or false (**F**, **f**, **N**, **n**).

A date field is displayed in one of several formats, as determined by the **SET DATE** and/or **SET CENTURY** commands. The default format is **mm/dd/yy**, and the slashes are displayed automatically in the input templates. Arithmetic calculations can be performed on date fields, e.g., subtracting one date from another to determine the number of days between the two dates.

A memo field contains a block of text, which is physically stored in a separate file; the ancillary file is created automatically when the memo field is defined, and is given the same name as the **DBF** file, but with a **DBT** extension. The memo field in the **DBF** file contains a pointer to the beginning position of the text in the **DBT** file.

The maximum ***field width*** depends on the field type, as shown in the following table. Note, however, that the width of a numeric field includes a position for both the decimal point and an (optional) minus sign, that a maximum of 18 decimal places is permitted, and finally that the number of decimals must be two less than the total field width (to allow for the decimal point and a possible minus sign).

Field Type	Width
Character	User-defined width up to 254 characters
Numeric	User-defined width up to 20 characters
Date	Predefined width of 8 characters
Logical	Predefined width of 1 character
Memo	Predefined width of 10 characters

The ***index flag***, entered as a **Y** or **N**, determines whether a tag will be created in the associated production index, which is given the same name as the **DBF** file, but an extension of **MDX**. The **MDX** file is opened in conjunction with the **DBF** file, and updated automatically as changes are made to the **DBF** file.

The definition of each field begins with the field name, which as indicated earlier, must be 10 characters or less. Pressing the enter key (if the name is less than 10 characters) moves the cursor to the input template for the field type, which is chosen in one of three ways:

1. By pressing the enter key if the default type of character is desired.
2. By pressing the first letter of the desired type, i.e., **N**, **C**, **D**, **L**, or **M** for numeric, character, date, logical, or memo, respectively.
3. By pressing the space bar to toggle through the different field types, and pressing the enter key after the desired type appears.

The specification of the field width depends on the field type. Default widths are entered automatically for date, logical, and memo fields, whereas explicit specification is required for character and numeric fields; the latter also requires additional input for the number of decimal places.

The index flag is entered in one of two ways, by:

1. Pressing the space bar to toggle between **N** and **Y**, then pressing the enter key after the desired response appears.
2. Typing either **Y** or **N** immediately.

Informational messages are displayed at the bottom of the screen to remind you of dBASE rules and limitations. Any mistake in data entry produces a beep and an associated error message; this error must be corrected before proceeding further. The status line at the bottom of the screen also shows the name and location of the current file, and the position of the current field within the file structure. The number of bytes remaining (from the maximum record size of 4000) is indicated in the upper right-hand corner of the screen.

The newly defined file structure is saved by pressing **Ctrl+End** or **Ctrl+W**, or by pressing the enter key when the cursor is positioned in a blank field name template; the latter action produces the message *Press ENTER key to confirm - Press any other key to resume.* Table PN.10 contains the keystroke combinations associated with the **CREATE** mode.

Once the file structure has been saved, dBASE displays the message *Input data records now? (Y/N).* A response of **Y** takes you to the full-screen **APPEND** mode, whereas an **N** returns to the dot prompt.

TABLE PN.10 **Keystroke Combinations for CREATE Command**

Keystroke	Function
→ or ←	Moves cursor one character to the right or left
↑ or ↓	Moves cursor to the previous or next field
`PgUp, PgDn`	Scrolls through field definitions when more than one screen is required
`Ins`	Toggles between the insert and replacement modes
`Del`	Deletes character cursor is on
`Enter key`	Moves cursor one column to the right
`Ctrl+Y`	Deletes all characters in entry template, beginning at the current cursor position
`Ctrl+U`	Deletes entire field definition at current cursor position
`Ctrl+N`	Inserts a field definition template at current cursor position
`Ctrl+W, Ctrl+End`	Saves definition and exits to dot prompt
`Ctrl+Q, Esc`	Aborts operation and exits to dot prompt

Tips

1. Field names should be as descriptive as possible so they are easy to remember.
2. dBASE reserved words (i.e., command or function names) are not allowed as field names.
3. "Numeric" fields such as zip code or social security number, that are not used in calculations, should be defined as character rather than numeric fields. This is done for two reasons: to increase processing efficiency, and to display leading zeros (which do not appear for numeric fields).
4. Logical fields should be named to reflect the true condition to make programming statements easier to follow; for example:

```
IF ltr_sent
   statements if letter sent
ELSE
   statements if letter not sent
ENDIF
```

5. Logical fields are automatically initialized to false; i.e., you need only press the enter key (during data entry) to accept the default value.
6. All date fields have a width of eight, even if **SET CENTURY** is **ON**; i.e., **SET CENTURY** affects the input template but not how dates are stored internally.
7. Any **MDX** file created during the design of the **DBF** file must be available with the **DBF** file; i.e., if an attempt is made to open the **DBF** file and the **MDX** file cannot be found, dBASE will display an error message that the *Production MDX file cannot be found.*
8. Any **DBT** file created during the design of the **DBF** file must be available with the **DBF** file; i.e., if an attempt is made to open the **DBF** file and the **DBT** file cannot be found, dBASE prompts to create an empty memo file.
9. The **MODIFY STRUCTURE** command is used to change to the structure of an existing **DBF** file.
10. The database design screen can be accessed through the data panel from the control center.

Related Topics

```
ASSIST
MODIFY STRUCTURE
SET CENTURY
SET DATE
```

CREATE APPLICATION

Syntax

```
CREATE APPLICATION <filename>
```

Discussion

The **CREATE APPLICATION** command invokes the application generator, a full-screen, menu-driven procedure that steps you through the design of a menu-driven application. The result is a set of programs that contain the design specifications of the application objects. The application allows data management tasks to be performed through a system of menus that require no real knowledge of dBASE, other than how to pick menu options and how to enter and/or edit data.

An application is a set of related programs that perform a particular task, the development of which can be a long and detailed process. The application generator creates the programs for you, so that both simple and complex applications can be built without having to write a single line of program code.

The application generator differs from the other design screens in that it works with multiple *objects* at one time; both nonapplication objects (**DBF** files and their indexes, query files, screen form files, report form files, and label form files) and application objects (the application object, bar menus, popup menus, file lists, structure lists, value lists, and batch processes). The nonapplication objects can be created from the dot prompt or the control center. The application objects are created on the application generator work surface and are each given a name and stored in a separate file, as described more fully in the following table:

Object	Extension	Description
Application object	**APP**	Stores environment settings and essential characteristics of the application (e.g., application name, main menu name, sign-on text, **DBF** file or view)
Bar Menu	**BAR**	Stores menu options that appear on a horizontal bar
Popup Menu	**POP**	Stores menu options that appear in a vertical frame
Files List	**FIL**	Stores list of file names that match a specific pattern
Structure List	**STR**	Stores list of field names in the active **DBF** file or view
Values List	**VAL**	Stores list of values in one field of the **DBF** file or view
Batch Process	**BCH**	Stores series of actions associated with a menu item or list

The files in the table are not required to run the application as dBASE incorporates the associated code in the program it creates; they are required, however, to edit the objects on the application generator work surface.

A simple application containing a **DBF** file (with a single master index), screen form, report form, and label form may be generated in a manner of minutes by selecting the *generate quick application* option from the application menu. The resultant application allows the user to perform file maintenance operations and print a report and/or mailing labels, but it is by definition simple, and therefore limited in what it can do. The development of this type of simple application requires knowledge of the various design screens for the nonapplication objects, but no knowledge of how to develop the system of menus that tie the operations together.

A more complex application can also be built, but often proves to be more trouble than it is worth. Despite the fact that programming per se is not required, much time must still be spent designing, testing, and debugging the system. The application generator does not have the flexibility inherent in building programs from scratch, and hence, you often must embed your own dBASE code to achieve the desired result. You are well advised, therefore, to develop your own application programs through accepted structured programming techniques rather than through the application generator.

Tips

1. **CREATE** and **MODIFY** can be used interchangeably to create and/or modify applications. The determining factor in whether a new application is created or an existing application is modified is whether or not the **APP** file already exists.
2. The application generator can be accessed through the applications panel from the control center.
3. The application object and the main menu cannot be given the same name.
4. There is no limit to the number of times an application may be generated, a process that is repeated many times during development.
5. An application can be run from the dot prompt with a DO command that references the file that was given the same name as the application object.

Related Topics

```
CREATE
CREATE/MODIFY LABEL
CREATE/MODIFY QUERY
CREATE/MODIFY REPORT
CREATE/MODIFY QUERY
DO
```

CREATE LABEL

Syntax

```
CREATE LABEL <filename>
```

Discussion

The **CREATE LABEL** command invokes a full-screen, menu-driven procedure that steps you through the design of a mailing label, envelope, or Rolodex card. The result is a label format file (with an extension of **LBL**) containing the design specifications needed by the layout editor, and a file (with an extension of **LBG**) containing the source code to produce the eventual labels.

The label form is created on a work surface equal to the size of the selected label. You may choose a predefined label size (described in terms of the height and width of one label as well as the number of labels across the page) or define one of your own by specifying the height (in rows), width (in characters), number of lines between labels, number of spaces between labels, etc. (The maximum label size is 255 lines by 255 characters.)

The label form may include fields from the currently selected **DBF** file (or view), calculated fields (which you create), predefined fields (date, time, record number, page number), and/or descriptive character text. The **TRIM()** function is automatically assigned to each field, provided a blank is entered via the space bar (as opposed to leaving empty work surface) between the trimmed field and the data to its right. Other picture functions and templates are available through the *modify field* option of the fields menu. (See the **@...SAY...GET** command for a description of the various function codes and template symbols.)

The label form menu bar has seven pull-down menus (*Layout, Dimensions, Fields, Words, Go To, Print,* and *Exit*), which are accessed by pressing the `F10` key or the `Alt` key and the first letter of the menu name. The availability of individual menu items is context sensitive, with items that make no sense in the current operation unavailable. Additionally, some options are bulleted (i.e., marked with a > to the left of the option name), indicating that there is a submenu attached to that menu item.

Tips

1. A database (`DBF`) file must be open for a label form to be created.
2. `CREATE` and `MODIFY` can be used interchangeably to create and/or modify label forms. The determining factor in whether a new form is created or an existing form modified is whether or not the label form already exists.
3. A new `LBL` file is created whenever `MODIFY LABEL` is used to edit existing labels. In addition, any existing `LBO` file is deleted from disk, ensuring that the modified label form will be recompiled when the labels are subsequently generated.
4. Labels are generated with the `LABEL FORM` command, which merges data from the currently selected `DBF` file with the label form. Execution of the `LABEL FORM` command checks for the existence of an object code (`LBO`) file, and if none exists, the label form is compiled, after which the resultant `LBO` file is executed.
5. The design of a label should take into consideration the default spacing of 10 characters per inch horizontally and six lines per inch vertically. The label height is specified as the number of lines between the top of one label and the top of the next.
6. dBASE automatically suppresses blank lines that result from empty fields; however, lines that are deliberately left blank on the work surface are left blank when the labels are printed.
7. An `IIF()` function can be used to conditionally print a field; e.g.,

```
IIF(initial = " ",TRIM(firstname),TRIM(firstname)
    + " " + initial) + " " + lastname
```

   Use of the `IIF()` function prevents an extra blank from appearing between the first and last names if there is no middle initial. This function can be entered onto the work surface as a calculated field, with the `IIF()` function entered as the field expression. The `IIF()` function can also be used to print out code values; e.g.,

```
IIF(adopt="B","Bird",IIF(adopt="M","Mammal","Reptile"))
```

   The function prints out Bird if the content of `adopt` is a `B`, Mammal if the content is `M`, and Reptile if the content is `R`.
8. To add a field to an existing label form, place the cursor at the position of the new field and pull down the fields menu. To move or copy a field, press the `F6` key to select the item, highlight the desired text or fields with the cursor keys, then press the enter key to complete the selection process; move the cursor to the new position, press `F7` (Move) or `F8` (Copy), and finally, press the enter key to complete the operation. To delete a field, highlight the field and press the `Del` key.
9. If a label form includes fields from a `DBF` file other than the currently selected file, those files must be open and any necessary relationships explicitly established prior to generating the labels. The commands for establishing the relationship can be entered from the dot prompt, or the appropriate view query file can be opened.
10. The label form design screen can be accessed through the labels panel in the control center.

Related Topics

```
@...SAY...GET
CREATE/MODIFY REPORT
IIF()
LABEL FORM
TRIM()
```

CREATE QUERY

Syntax

```
CREATE QUERY <filename>
```

Discussion

The **CREATE QUERY** command invokes a full-screen, menu-driven facility to assist in building conditions for extracting specific records, linking multiple **DBF** files into a view, and updating data for specific records. The result is either a *view query* file (**QBE**) or an *update query* file (**UPD**), depending on the activities performed. Both are ASCII text files containing dBASE IV commands, but differ as follows.

A view query contains the source code to open one or more **DBF** files and their indexes in selected work areas, establish the relationship between the open files, establish an active filter condition for each file, and establish an active field list for the system of related files. The file is executed with a **SET VIEW TO** command, which activates the stored view, thereby establishing the working environment for all subsequent commands. An update query, on the other hand, includes source code to modify data through the equivalent of the **APPEND**, **DELETE**, **RECALL**, and **PACK** commands. An update query is fast and powerful, and is executed with a **DO** command; the complete filename, including the extension, must be specified, or the **DO** command will not find the file.

The query design screen uses a *query by example* (QBE) interface to create the view and update queries. The work surface consists of a *file skeleton* at the top of the screen, an optional *calculated field skeleton* in the middle, and a *view skeleton* at the bottom. Up to eight file skeletons can appear on the work surface at one time, but there can be only one view skeleton for a view query. (An update query does not produce a view, and therefore has no view skeleton.)

The **F3** and **F4** keys move between the skeletons, while the **Tab** and **Shift+Tab** keys move from field to field within a skeleton. Fields are added to (and removed from) the view skeleton with the **F5** key or through the fields menu. All fields are affected when the cursor is beneath the file name, whereas only a single field is added (removed) if the cursor is below the field name.

Filter conditions are entered by placing the condition beneath the field name in the file skeleton or by building a condition in a condition box (accessed through the condition menu); e.g., you can either enter **"FL"** under **state** in the file skeleton or enter **state = "FL"** in a condition box. The filter condition may be any valid dBASE IV expression, and in addition, may include the relational operators **LIKE** and **SOUNDS LIKE**. **LIKE** is used with the wildcard characters (***** and **?**) to match character patterns; e.g., **LIKE "331*"** entered under **zipcode** in the file skeleton will select all records whose **zipcode** begins with 331. The **SOUNDS LIKE** operator matches close spellings; e.g., **SOUNDS LIKE "Lea"** entered under **firstname** in the file skeleton will select a first name of Leah, Lee, or Lea.

Conditions placed on the same row of the file skeleton are combined with an **.AND.** operation; i.e., all individual conditions must be met for a record to be selected. Conditions placed on different rows are combined with an **.OR.** operation; i.e., only one of the conditions must be met for the record to be selected.

A logical order for the file can be established by using one of four sorting operators: ascending, descending, ascending dictionary, and descending dictionary. Ascending differs from ascending dictionary in that the first differentiates between upper- and lower-case letters (with all upper-case letters coming before lower-case letters), whereas the latter does not. The same is true for descending and descending dictionary. The sort order is selected by entering Asc, Des, AscDict, or DesDict below the field name in the file skeleton, or by selecting the desired sort order from the fields menu. If a sort is performed on more than one key, a number reflecting the key's position within the sort order must be included; e.g., Asc1 indicates the primary key and Asc2 indicates the secondary key.

Relationships between files are established by placing the name of the same *example variable* beneath the corresponding field names in the file skeletons of the files to be linked. An example variable is a nonspecific identifier that is used as a place holder, and as long as the name is the same for both fields, it does not matter what name is used. The resultant view matches each record with its corresponding record in the linked file.

An update query is created when an update operator is entered beneath a file name, either by typing in the operator (Replace, Append, Mark, or Unmark) or by accessing the update menu. While there may be more than one file skeleton on the screen, only one can contain an update operator, and that is the only file updated. Any view skeleton on the screen when the update operator is entered is removed. The replace operator requires a replacement instruction in the file skeleton, beginning with the word `WITH`, followed by the appropriate dBASE expression; e.g., `WITH salary * 1.1`. Other fields may contain conditions, but those conditions are used to select the records to be updated. Append is used to append records from one `DBF` file to another. The target `DBF` file is the one with the append operator specified. Filters can be specified in the source `DBF` file so that only selected records are appended to the target file. Mark and Unmark are used to delete and recall records from the specified `DBF` file. Filter conditions can also be specified so that only selected records are processed.

The query design menu bar has five pull-down menus (*Layout, Fields, Condition, Update,* and *Exit*), which are accessed by pressing the `F10` key or the `Alt` key and the first letter of the menu name. The availability of the individual menu items is context sensitive, with items that make no sense in the current operation unavailable. Additionally, some options are bulleted (i.e., marked with a > to the left of the option name), indicating that there is a submenu attached to that menu item.

Tips

1. The keywords `VIEW` and `QUERY` can be used interchangeably in this command, as can `CREATE` and `MODIFY`. The determining factor in whether a new file is created or an existing file modified is whether or not the file already exists. dBASE looks first for a file with a `QBE` or `UPD` extension; if none exists, it then looks for a file with a `VUE` extension, and if none is found, dBASE creates the file with a `QBE` or `UPD` extension.
2. View queries are activated with the `SET VIEW TO` command, which opens the stored view. When the `SET VIEW TO` command is executed, dBASE checks to see if a compiled object code file (`QBO`) exists, and if not, the query file is compiled and the resultant `QBO` file is executed.
3. Update queries are activated with the `DO` command, which actually performs the update. When the `DO` command is executed, dBASE checks to see if a compiled object code file (`DBO`) exists, and if not, the update query file is compiled and the resultant `DBO` file is executed.
4. A new `QBE` file is created whenever `MODIFY QUERY` is used to edit existing queries. In addition, any existing `QBO` file is deleted, ensuring that the modified query will be recompiled when the queries are activated. However, changes made to a `UPD` file do not delete the old `DBO` file, and `SET DEVELOPMENT` must be `ON` to ensure that the file will be recompiled when it is next activated.
5. The `DBO` file generated from the `UPD` file may be renamed with a `UPO` extension to keep the update queries distinguishable from program files. Indeed, this must be done if you want the update queries to appear in the queries panel of the control center.
6. The `CREATE VIEW FROM ENVIRONMENT` command creates a `VUE` file, storing information about the currently established environment (e.g., information about the open `DBF` files and respective work areas, the active relationships, and any active filter conditions or format files). These `VUE` files, as well as ones created in dBASE III Plus, can be read by the `CREATE/MODIFY QUERY` command, but a `QBE` file will be created when the file is saved.
7. The `TYPE <filename.ext>` command can be used to see the source code in either the `QBE` or `UPD` files.
8. `MODIFY COMMAND`, or the nondocument mode of a word processor, can be used to edit a `QBE` or `UPD` file, but the changes will not be made to the corresponding `QBO` or `DBO` files. Thus, you must delete the obsolete files from the disk so that the source code will be recompiled when they are next activated.

9. The query design screen can be reached from the **BROWSE** and **EDIT** modes by selecting *transfer to query design* from the exit menu or by pressing **Shift+F2**. It can also be reached from the database design screen, and the label form, report form, and form design screens, with **Shift+F2**.
10. A field used in a filter condition does not have to be included in the view skeleton.
11. When building a condition, you may select field names, operators, and functions from a list presented by pressing the **Shift+F1** key.
12. Up to 20 calculated fields can be created for a query.
13. The query form design screen can be accessed through the queries panel in the control center. Update queries are listed in the panel with an * to the left of their file name.

Related Topics

```
APPEND
CREATE/MODIFY VIEW
DELETE
DO
MODIFY COMMAND
PACK
RECALL
SELECT
SET DEVELOPMENT
SET FIELDS
SET FILTER
SET RELATION
USE
```

CREATE REPORT

Syntax

```
CREATE REPORT <filename>
```

Discussion

The **CREATE REPORT** command invokes a full-screen, menu-driven procedure that steps you through the design of a report. The result is a report form file (with an extension of **FRM**) that contains the design specifications needed by the layout editor, and an associated program file (with extension of **FRG**) that contains the source code to produce the eventual report.

Three types of report layouts are possible: columnar, form, and mail merge. The columnar layout displays fields horizontally across a page (much like the output of a **LIST** command) and prints one line for each record in the **DBF** file. The form layout arranges fields vertically and thus prints several lines for each record. The mail-merge layout is for form letters, with text and fields intermingled on the page.

The design surface is divided into report bands that extend horizontally across the page. Each report band consists of one or more lines and prints at designated places within a report. There are seven different types of report bands, five of which appear by default as described in the following table.

Band	Purpose
Page Header	Prints at the top of every page; used primarily for information such as the date, time, page number, page title (if different from the report title), and column headings
Report Intro Band	Prints once, at the beginning of the report; used for report title, cover page, introductory narratives
Detail Band	Prints once for each record; used for fields and explanatory text
Report Summary Band	Prints once, at the end of the report; used for totals, summary statistics, or concluding narratives
Page Footer	Prints at the bottom of every page; used primarily for date and page number (if not printed in the page header)

Two additional bands, the Group Intro Band and the Group Summary Band, can be added through the bands menu when summary information is required for groups (subsets) of records with a **DBF** file. The groups can be determined by record count (e.g., every 10 records) or by the contents of a field or expression (records with the same value in the field or expression are grouped together). The group intro band appears at the beginning of each group and typically contains an explanation of the criteria that define the group. The group summary band appears at the end of each group and contains subtotals, counts, and other summary statistics.

Text and/or data is entered into a band by moving the cursor to that band and typing the text or adding a field through the fields menu. Permissible fields include the fields in the current **DBF** file or view, calculated fields (which you create), predefined fields (date, time, record number, and page number), and summary fields (average, count, maximum, minimum, sum, standard deviation, and variance). Function codes and picture templates can be assigned as a field is entered, or added later through the *modify field* option of the fields menu. (See the **@...SAY...GET** command for a description of the various function codes and template symbols.)

The report form menu bar has seven pull-down menus (*Layout, Fields, Bands, Words, Go To, Print,* and *Exit*), which are accessed by pressing the **F10** key or the **Alt** key and the first letter of the menu name. The availability of the menu items is context sensitive, with items that make no sense in the current operation unavailable. Additionally, some options are bulleted (i.e., marked with a > to the left of the option name), indicating that there is a submenu attached to that menu item.

Tips

1. A database (**DBF**) file must be open for a report form to be created.
2. **CREATE** and **MODIFY** can be used interchangeably to create and/or modify report forms. The determining factor in whether a new form is created or an existing form modified is whether or not the report form already exists.
3. A new **FRG** file is created whenever **MODIFY REPORT** is used to edit an existing report form. In addition, any existing **FRO** file is deleted, ensuring that the modified report form will be recompiled when the labels are generated.
4. Execution of the **REPORT FORM** command checks for the existence of an object (**FRO**) file, and if none exists, the report form is compiled, after which the resultant **FRO** file is executed.
5. Text can be entered with or without word wrap; word wrap is turned on and off through the bands menu.
6. All report bands default to one blank line.
7. A band may be closed to hide data within that band or to compress the design screen and bring distant bands closer together. For example, you may want to hide the detail band and print just summary data (which is analogous to using the **SUMMARY** option

in the **REPORT FORM** command), or you may want to close the report header band, bringing the detail band closer to the page header band for aligning fields and column headers. The contents of a closed band do not appear when the report is printed. A band is toggled open and closed by placing the cursor on the border of the band and pressing the enter key.

8. Any report using a group band requires the DBF file to be open, with a master index whose key expression matches the groups in the report form. A new group is created every time the value within a field changes, and therefore records with like values must be together in the data file.
9. Group bands can be added only when the cursor is above the detail band, i.e., in the page header band, report intro band, or an existing group intro band.
10. Group bands can be nested to allow groups within groups, e.g., grouping cities within states.
11. The quick report option can be used to create columnar, form, or mail-merge reports. Column layout presents templates for all of the fields in the detail band, with the field name used as the column header in the page header band. Form layout presents the field templates in a vertical list in the detail band, with one field per line and the field name to the left of the template. The mail-merge layout leaves only the detail band open, with the word wrap on.
12. The form layout can be used to design reports that require more than one line per record. Distinct columns do not appear, and fields and text can be spread across the page.
13. An IIF() function can be used to conditionally print a field; e.g.,

    ```
    IIF(initial = " ",TRIM(firstname),TRIM(firstname)
        + " " + initial) + " " + lastname
    ```

    Use of the IIF() function prevents an extra blank from appearing between the first and last names if there is no middle initial. This function can be entered onto the work surface as a calculated field, with the IIF() function entered as the field expression. The IIF() function can also be used to print out code values; e.g.,

    ```
    IIF(adopt="B","Bird",IIF(adopt="M","Mammal","Reptile"))
    ```

    The function prints out Bird if the content of adopt is a B, Mammal if the content is M, and Reptile if the content is neither B nor M.
14. To add a field to an existing report form, place the cursor at the position of the new field and pull down the fields menu. To move or copy a field, press the F6 key to select the item, highlight the desired text or fields with the cursor keys, then press the enter key to complete the selection process; move the cursor to the new position, press F7 (Move) or F8 (Copy), and finally, press the enter key to complete the operation. To delete a field, highlight the field and press the Del key.
15. If a report form includes fields from a DBF file other than the currently selected file, those files must be open and any necessary relationships explicitly established prior to generating the report. The commands for establishing the relationship can be entered from the dot prompt or by opening the appropriate view or query file.
16. The report form design screen can be accessed through the reports panel in the control center.

Related Topics

```
@...SAY...GET
CREATE/MODIFY LABEL
IIF()
REPORT FORM
```

CREATE SCREEN

Syntax

```
CREATE SCREEN <filename>
```

Discussion

The **CREATE SCREEN** command invokes a full-screen, menu-driven procedure to design a custom data entry screen for use with the currently selected database. The result is a screen file (with an extension of **SCR**) containing the design specifications needed by the layout editor, and an associated format file (with an extension of **FMT**) containing the source code for drawing the screen. The format file is automatically activated as soon as it is saved.

A custom screen is preferable to the normal data entry screen because:

1. The custom screen is more attractive, apt to contain more explicit prompting messages, and is certainly more user friendly.
2. Additional formatting and data validation procedures, as well as security precautions, are possible.
3. Fields from related databases can be included in the same input screen.

Five design elements can be placed on the work surface: fields from the currently selected **DBF** file (or view), calculated fields (which you create), text, boxes, and lines. Text is typed onto the work surface exactly where it is to be displayed. Fields are added by positioning the cursor where the field is to be located and selecting the *add field* option from the fields menu. Function codes and picture templates can be assigned as the field is entered or added later through the *modify field* option of the fields menu. (See the **@...SAY...GET** command for a description of the various function codes and template symbols.)

Edit options can be assigned to each field to validate data as it is being entered: *editing allowed* (determines if a field will be read-only), *permit edit* (assigns read-only status to a field if the specified condition is not met), *message* (displays a message at the bottom of the screen when the cursor is in the input template), *carry forward* (displays data from the corresponding field in the previous record as the default value when a new record is added), *default value* (specifies the default value when a new record is added), *smallest/largest value allowed* (defines the range within which the data must fall), *accept new value* (specifies the condition that must be met before new data can be accepted), and *unaccepted message* (displays an error message at bottom of screen when the *accept new value* condition is not met). Lines and boxes are placed on the work surface through the layout menu.

The screen form design menu bar has five pull-down menus (*Layout, Fields, Words, Go To,* and *Exit*), which are accessed by pressing the **F10** key or the **Alt** key and the first letter of the menu name. The availability of the individual menu items is context sensitive, with items that make no sense in the current operation unavailable. Additionally, some options are bulleted (i.e., marked with a > to the left of the option name), indicating that there is a submenu attached to that menu item.

Tips

1. **CREATE** and **MODIFY** can be used interchangeably to create and/or modify screen forms. The determining factor in whether a new screen form is created or an existing screen form modified is whether or not the report form already exists.
2. Changes are made to the **SCR** file when the **MODIFY SCREEN** command is used to edit an existing screen. When the edits are saved, a new **FMT** file is generated and the **FMO** file is recompiled.
3. An existing format file is opened with the **SET FORMAT TO** command, and is subsequently activated by any full-screen editing command, such as **APPEND** or **EDIT**. The custom data entry screen appears in lieu of the input templates normally associated with these commands.

4. The format file produced by the **CREATE SCREEN** command can be used as the basis for a program (**PRG**) file that appends or edits data; i.e., the program would be developed around the **@... SAY** commands in the format file.
5. The screen design form respects the number of lines per screen as determined by the **SET DISPLAY TO** command.
6. The appearance of the data entry form can be improved through color or monochrome screen attributes (e.g., blinking, bold) selected from the words menu.
7. When the format file is activated, dBASE reads the fields horizontally across one line before moving down to the next line. This order cannot be changed, regardless of the order in which the fields were entered onto the design surface.
8. Memory variables can be placed on the design surface through the fields menu. The variables do not need to be active during the design process, although they do need to be activated prior to the data entry process.
9. The contents of a calculated field cannot be edited, as its value depends on the values in existing fields.
10. Boxes visually connect related information and may be drawn with a single line, double line, or a user specified character selected from a list of ASCII characters. To draw a box, choose the box option from the layout menu. Select the border type, then use the arrow keys to position the cursor at the upper-left corner of where the box is to be placed, and press the enter key; use the arrow keys to position the cursor at the lower-right corner of the box and press the enter key a second time. The box can be seen as it is being drawn. The box can be deleted by placing the cursor anywhere on the box border and pressing the **Del** key.
11. Drawing a line is done in similar fashion to drawing a box, but you will need to press the enter key to begin the line and to signal its end. The cursor can be moved in any direction so that a variety of shapes can be created. Text can be entered as the line is being drawn, and is displayed in the current direction of the cursor. Use the **Backspace** key to erase segments of the line as it is being drawn. Once a line has been completed, it can be edited with the same keystrokes as ordinary text.
12. To add a field to an existing screen form, place the cursor at the position of the new field and pull down the fields menu. To move or copy a field, press the **F6** key to select the item, highlight the desired text or fields with the cursor keys, then press the enter key to complete the selection process; move the cursor to the new position, press **F7** (Move) or **F8** (Copy), and finally, press the enter key to complete the operation. To delete a field, highlight the field and press the **Del** key.
13. Memo fields can be displayed as a memo marker (the default) or within a window by accessing the *Display as* option of the modify field menu. The size of the window is changed by placing the cursor in the window, pressing **Shift+F7**, and using the arrow keys to increase or decrease the size of the window; press the enter key to complete the operation. The window can be deleted or moved in the same way as any other field.
14. Clear, well-laid-out screens are critical to the ease with which an application can be used. Consistency from screen to screen within a system is also very important.
15. If a screen form includes fields from a **DBF** file other than the currently selected file, those files must be open and any necessary relationships explicitly established prior to generating the report. The commands for establishing the relationship can be entered from the dot prompt or by opening the appropriate view query file.
16. The screen form work surface can be accessed through the forms panel in the control center.

Related Topics

```
@...SAY...GET
APPEND
EDIT
MODIFY COMMAND
READ
```

```
SET DISPLAY
SET FORMAT
```

CREATE VIEW

Syntax

```
CREATE VIEW <filename>
```

Discussion

The discussion of the **CREATE VIEW** command is identical to that which was presented for the **CREATE QUERY** command. (See the **CREATE QUERY** command for additional information.)

CREATE VIEW FROM ENVIRONMENT

Syntax

```
CREATE VIEW <filename> FROM ENVIRONMENT
```

Discussion

The **CREATE VIEW FROM ENVIRONMENT** command creates a view file (with an extension of **VUE**), saving the following information from the currently active dBASE IV environment:

1. The names of all open **DBF** files (including the associated indexes and memo files) and their assigned work areas.
2. The number of the currently selected work area.
3. The currently established relationships between the files.
4. The active field list.
5. The names of open format files.
6. Any filter conditions currently in effect.

When the view file is subsequently activated with the **SET VIEW TO** command, the stored environment is reactivated; i.e., the files are opened in the appropriate work areas, the relationships are established, the field list and the filter conditions are activated, and the specified work area is made current.

Tips

1. The view file created by the **CREATE VIEW FROM ENVIRONMENT** command is essentially a dBASE III Plus file. Although it has been maintained in dBASE IV, it has been effectively replaced by the more powerful **CREATE/MODIFY QUERY** command. It is still used, however, by advanced users who find it faster and more convenient to work from the dot prompt rather than from within the menu-driven query design screen.
2. The **SET VIEW TO** command is used to activate the stored view. The command searches first for a **QBO** or **QBE** file, and if none can be found, for a **VUE** file. Therefore, a **VUE** file cannot have the same name as a **QBO** or **QBE** file, or else the extension must be specified when the file is referenced.
3. A **VUE** file can be converted to a **QBE** file by opening the **VUE** file with a **MODIFY QUERY** command and selecting the save and exit option from the exit menu.
4. A view file is unlike a normal file in that once it establishes the environment, it is no longer considered an open file and thus, never needs to be closed. The files it opens, however, are closed with appropriate **CLOSE** or **CLEAR** commands.
5. The **DISPLAY STATUS** command will show all environmental information.

Related Topics

CLEAR
CLOSE
CREATE/MODIFY QUERY
CREATE/MODIFY VIEW
DISPLAY STATUS
SELECT
SET FIELDS
SET FILTER
SET RELATION
USE

CTOD FUNCTION

Syntax

```
CTOD(<character expression>)
```

Discussion

The **CTOD()**, **C**haracter **TO D**ate function, converts a date entered as a character string to its equivalent date value. The default format is "mm/dd/yy", but can be changed with the **SET DATE** and/or **SET CENTURY** commands. When the argument of the **CTOD()** function is a literal date, a shorthand notation using curly braces may be used in lieu of the function; for example, **{01/05/92}** is equivalent to **CTOD("01/05/92")** and may be used in its place in any command using a literal date. Note that with the curly brace notation, the date is *not* enclosed within quotes.

The curly braces are easier and more convenient to use with literal dates than the equivalent **CTOD()** function. However, they cannot be used with field names and/or memory variables, and in those situations the **CTOD()** function must be used. For example, the command **STORE "07/01/92" TO mdate**, followed by the command **? CDOW{mdate}**, produces a *Syntax error*, whereas the same command, followed by **? CDOW(CTOD(mdate))**, returns a response of *Wednesday.*

The curly braces or the **CTOD()** function is required to create a date-type memory variable, to replace a date field with a character date, or to create conditions that compare date fields to character dates; e.g.,

```
STORE {01/02/92} TO mhiredate
LIST FOR hiredate > {01/01/90}
REPLACE birthdate WITH CTOD(mbirthdate)
```

Using neither the **CTOD()** function nor the curly braces would, in the first case, result in a numeric variable being created, and in the other two instances, a *Data type mismatch* error. Note, also, that whereas either the curly braces or the **CTOD()** function can be used with the first two examples, only the **CTOD()** format can be used with the third example.

Tips

1. The **CTOD()** function enables date arithmetic to be performed with character dates. For example, the command,

   ```
   ? DATE() - CTOD("05/31/92")
   ```

   will return the number of days between today's date and May 31, 1992. (Note that if today's date is the earlier date, a negative number will be returned.)

2. An error message will not be produced if an invalid date is entered within the curly braces or as the argument of the **CTOD()** function, but rather the invalid date will be converted to its equivalent calendar date. For example, the command,

```
STORE {10/45/92} TO mdate
```

results in 11/14/92 being stored in the memory variable **mdate**.

3. If the **SET DATE** command is in effect to establish a different format, be sure to use the new format, or erroneous dates will be generated. For example, if the date has been set to **ANSI** (yy.mm.dd), in lieu of the default **AMERICAN** format (mm/dd/yy), the command,

```
STORE {05/31/92} TO mdate
```

will place 07.10.05 (that is not a typographical error) into **mdate**, without any indication of an error.

4. Regardless of whether **CENTURY** is **ON** or **OFF**, any date entered with a two-digit year is assumed to be a twentieth century date; i.e., to enter a date from another century, you must specify a four-digit year; e.g.,

```
STORE CTOD("04/18/1775") TO olddate
```

Related Topics

```
DATE()
DTOC()
SET CENTURY
SET DATE
```

DATE FUNCTION

Syntax

```
DATE()
```

Discussion

The **DATE()** function returns the system date as obtained from DOS, in the default format of mm/dd/yy. (A different format, e.g., dd/mm/yy, can be established with the **SET DATE** command.) The value returned by the **DATE()** function is a date (as opposed to a character) field, and can be used in date arithmetic with no conversion required (e.g., **DATE() + 7**). However, displaying the function in a character string requires that it first be converted to character data with the **DTOC()** conversion function; e.g.,

```
? "Today is " + DTOC(DATE())
```

Tips

1. Be sure to enter the system date correctly upon booting the system, as that is the date returned by the **DATE()** function (as well as the date stamped on all files created).
2. The dBASE **DATE()** function cannot be used to set the system date. The DOS **DATE** command can, however, be accessed from within dBASE to set the system date by using a **RUN** command, e.g., **RUN DATE**.
3. The **DATE()** function may itself be the argument of other dBASE date functions, e.g., **CMONTH(DATE())** or **CDOW(DATE())**.

4. The **DATE()** function can be used to store the system date to a date-type memory variable; e.g.,

```
STORE DATE() TO mtoday
```

Related Topics

CDOW()
CMONTH()
DAY()
DTOC()
MONTH()
RUN
SET DATE
YEAR()

DAY FUNCTION

Syntax

```
DAY(<date expression>)
```

Discussion

The **DAY()** function returns a numeric value corresponding to the day of the month in the specified date expression. The argument in the **DAY()** function must be a date-type value and may assume several different forms as shown in the following table:

Function	Nature of the Argument
DAY(hiredate)	Date field
DAY(memdate)	Date memory variable
DAY(DATE())	**DATE()** function
DAY{12/25/92}	Literal date
DAY(CTOD(hiredate))	**CTOD()** conversion function
DAY(DATE() + 10)	Expression with date arithmetic

Tips

1. If the argument of a **DAY()** function is a character string enclosed in quotes or a character field or memory variable, it must first be converted to a date-type variable with the **CTOD()** conversion function. The shorthand format using curly braces, which is often easier and more convenient to use, may be used only with a literal date, and cannot be used with a character string enclosed in quotes or with a character field or memory variable. (Note that a literal date is *not* enclosed in quotes as is a date expressed as a character string.)
2. The **DAY** function is often used in program files and/or report forms to display a date in a more attractive format. For example, given a system date of 01/08/92, the command,

Command is entered on one line

```
@ 20,20 SAY "Today is " + CMONTH(DATE()) + " "
+ STR(DAY(DATE()),2) + ", " + STR(YEAR(DATE()),4)
```

returns the string "Today is January 08, 1992". (Note that the day and year must be converted to strings in order to be concatenated with the other character-type data.)

Related Topics

CDOW()
CMONTH()
CTOD()
DATE()
MONTH()
STR()
YEAR()

DEACTIVATE MENU

Syntax

```
DEACTIVATE MENU
```

Discussion

The **DEACTIVATE MENU** command deactivates the current bar menu, erasing it from the screen and redisplaying the preexisting screen contents. It is typically issued in an **ON SELECTION PAD** command or in conjunction with a choice to exit from the current menu. For example,

```
DEFINE MENU bar1
DEFINE PAD add OF bar1 AT 3,2 PROMPT "Add a record"
DEFINE PAD edit OF bar1 AT 3,10 PROMPT "Edit a record"
DEFINE PAD quit OF bar1 AT 3,18 PROMPT "Return to Main Menu"
ON SELECTION PAD add OF bar1 DO addprg
ON SELECTION PAD edit OF bar1 DO editprg
ON SELECTION PAD quit OF bar1 DEACTIVATE MENU
ACTIVATE MENU bar1
```

The menu definition is not released from memory when it is deactivated, and thus can be reactivated at any time with an **ACTIVATE MENU** command. It is only through a **RELEASE MENUS** or **CLEAR MENUS** command that the bar menu definitions are released from memory. Note, too, that a bar menu must be deactivated before its definition can be released from memory.

Tips

1. The current bar menu will be deactivated and erased from the screen when the user presses the **Esc** key.
2. Only one bar menu can be active at one time. Therefore, an **ACTIVATE MENU** command suspends (but does not deactivate) any currently active bar menu, and when the new menu is subsequently deactivated, the suspended bar menu is automatically reactivated.
3. A **DEACTIVATE MENU** command returns control to the line beneath the **ACTIVATE MENU** command. Therefore, if the **DEACTIVATE MENU** command is part of a procedure, any statements following it are not executed.
4. The **DEACTIVATE MENU** command has no effect from the dot prompt.

Related Topics

```
ACTIVATE MENU
CLEAR MENUS
DEFINE MENU
DEFINE PAD
ON PAD
ON SELECTION PAD
RELEASE MENUS
SHOW MENU
```

DEACTIVATE POPUP

Syntax

```
DEACTIVATE POPUP
```

Discussion

The **DEACTIVATE POPUP** command deactivates the current popup menu, erasing it from the screen and redisplaying the preexisting screen contents. It is typically issued in a program or procedure called by an **ON SELECTION POPUP** command or in conjunction with a choice to exit from the current menu. For example,

```
DEFINE POPUP mainmenu FROM 6,25 TO 17,54
DEFINE BAR 1 OF mainmenu PROMPT "ADD"
DEFINE BAR 2 OF mainmenu PROMPT "EDIT"
DEFINE BAR 3 OF mainmenu PROMPT "QUIT"
ON SELECTION POPUP mainmenu DO mainprg
ACTIVATE POPUP mainmenu

PROCEDURE mainprg
DO CASE
 CASE BAR() = 1
  DO addrec
 CASE BAR() = 2
  DO editrec
 CASE BAR() = 3
  DEACTIVATE POPUP
ENDCASE
```

The menu definition is not released from memory when it is deactivated, and it can be reactivated at any time with an **ACTIVATE POPUP** command. It is only through a **RELEASE POPUPS** or **CLEAR POPUPS** command that the popup menu definitions are released from memory. Note, too, that a popup menu must be deactivated before its definition can be released from memory.

Tips

1. The current popup menu will be deactivated and erased from the screen when the user presses the **Esc** key.
2. Only one popup menu can be active at one time. Therefore, an **ACTIVATE POPUP** command suspends (but does not deactivate) any currently active popup menu, and when the new menu is subsequently deactivated, the suspended popup menu is automatically reactivated.

3. A **DEACTIVATE POPUP** command returns control to the line beneath the **ACTIVATE POPUP** command. Therefore, any statements following the **DEACTIVATE POPUP** command are not executed.
4. The **DEACTIVATE POPUP** command has no effect from the dot prompt.

Related Topics

```
ACTIVATE POPUP
BAR()
CLEAR POPUPS
DEFINE POPUP
ON SELECTION POPUP
RELEASE POPUPS
SHOW POPUP
```

DEACTIVATE WINDOW

Syntax

```
DEACTIVATE WINDOW <window name list>/ALL
```

Discussion

The **DEACTIVATE WINDOW** command deactivates one or more current windows, erasing them from the screen and redisplaying the preexisting screen contents. Specifying a window list deactivates the listed windows; **ALL** deactivates all current windows and restores the full-screen mode.

Only one window can be active at one time. Therefore, an **ACTIVATE WINDOW** command suspends (but does not deactivate) any currently active window before activating the new one. The image of the first window remains on the screen unless its display is covered by the new window, and when the new window is subsequently deactivated, the suspended window is reactivated. dBASE returns to using the full-screen mode when the last window is deactivated.

The window definition is not erased from memory when it is deactivated, and thus can be reactivated at any time with an **ACTIVATE WINDOW** command. It is only through a **RELEASE WINDOWS** or **CLEAR WINDOWS** command that the window definitions are released from memory. Note, too, that a window must be deactivated before its definition can be released from memory.

Tips

1. A window can be activated and deactivated as many times as necessary during a session.
2. The **ACTIVATE SCREEN** command can be used to display text outside a window without deactivating the window. Output will continue to be displayed outside the window borders until an **ACTIVATE WINDOW** command is issued.

Related Topics

```
ACTIVATE SCREEN
ACTIVATE WINDOW
CLEAR WINDOWS
DEFINE WINDOW
RELEASE WINDOWS
RESTORE WINDOW
SAVE WINDOW
```

DEBUG

Syntax

```
DEBUG <filename>/<procedure name>
    [WITH <parameter list>]
```

Discussion

The **DEBUG** command loads the specified program or procedure into the full-screen debugger to monitor its execution and let you see the commands as they execute. It is of tremendous assistance in identifying and correcting errors in program logic. The screen display is divided into four windows as follows:

Window	Location	Purpose
Edit	Upper-left corner of the screen	Displays up to eleven lines of a program, highlighting the next command to be executed.
Debugger	Bottom of the screen	Displays status information (the currently selected work area, **DBF** file, master index, current record number, program name, procedure name, and current line number); contains the **ACTION** prompt, where commands are entered.
Display	Below the edit window	Displays the contents of up to 10 fields, memory variables, and/or expressions.
Breakpoint	To the right of the display window	Displays up to ten logical conditions that, when true, cause the program to pause execution and the cursor to be positioned at the **ACTION** prompt.

The cursor is positioned initially at the **ACTION** prompt in the debugger window, awaiting a command. A help screen (which can be toggled on and off with the **F1** key) is displayed in the upper-right corner, and lists the available debugger commands, as shown in Table PN.11.

In essence, the debugger lets you run a program until an error occurs or a breakpoint is reached (the **R** command), or you may choose the single-step mode (with an **S** or **N** command), in which one line (or a specified number of lines) is executed. When execution is suspended, you may view the program in the edit window, display the contents of designated variables, set new breakpoints, or enter any commands.

The **E** command places the cursor in the edit window where the program can be modified. Changes are saved and the window exited with **Ctrl+End**, but unless you exit the debugger and recompile the program, the previously compiled version continues to run; i.e., the changes are not in effect.

The display and breakpoint windows are entered with the **D** and **B** commands, respectively. Only four entries can be seen in each of these windows at one time, but the up and down arrow keys will scroll to as many as ten entries. The windows are exited with **Ctrl+End**, and the cursor is repositioned at the **ACTION** prompt for the next command.

The **F9** key functions as a toggle switch between the debugger window and the output screen produced by the program. The **F9** key can also be used in the edit window, to expand the window for easier editing.

TABLE PN.11 **Debugger Commands**

Command	Result
`B`	Accesses breakpoint window where breakpoint conditions are entered
`D`	Accesses the display window to enter variable names and/or examine the contents of the indicated variables or expressions
`E`	Accesses the edit window where changes to the program are made
`L`	Runs the program, beginning at the line number specified
`[<n>]N`	Executes the next line or next `n` lines in current program/procedure; called programs/procedures are executed normally, without displaying their commands in the edit window
`P`	Displays the program traceback information (chain of programs that called the current program)
`Q`	Quits the debugger and cancels the current program
`R`	Runs the program until an error is encountered, the **`Esc`** key is pressed, or a breakpoint condition is reached
`[<n>]S`	Executes the next line or the next `n` lines in current program/procedure, including lines from any called programs and procedures
`X`	Suspends execution and returns control to the dot prompt, from where other commands can be executed; **`RESUME`** returns control to the debugger; **`CANCEL`** terminates execution and returns control to the dot prompt
↵	Executes either an `S` or `N` command, depending on which was last executed

The **`WITH`** clause allows parameters to be passed to a program that contains a **`PARAMETERS`** statement.

Tips

1. Multiple lines can be scrolled in the edit window by entering a number and then pressing the up/down arrow key.
2. Breakpoints are best used with the `R` command to run the program continuously until the breakpoints are reached. Typical breakpoints include the **`PROGRAM()`** and the **`LINENO()`** functions, to pause when a particular program is called or a specified line number is reached, e.g., **`PROGRAM() = "INITVAR.PRG"`** or **`LINENO() = 15`**.
3. The **`X`** command suspends execution so that additional commands can be entered from the dot prompt, e.g., **`DISPLAY MEMORY`** or **`DISPLAY STATUS`**. You can return to the debugger with the **`RESUME`** command or cancel it altogether with the **`CANCEL`** command.
4. The **`SET TRAP ON`** command can be issued from the dot prompt (prior to the **`DO`** command, which executes the program) to automatically invoke the debugger if an error is encountered during program execution or if the **`Esc`** key is pressed. This is helpful when most of a program is working correctly, and the problem can be traced to a small section of code.
5. Use the `N` command when called programs and/or procedures have been tested and proven correct; this will run the called program/procedure in its entirety, and return to the single-step mode when control returns to the calling program.

Related Topics

```
CANCEL
COMPILE
```

```
LINENO()
RESUME
SUSPEND
```

DEFINE BAR

Syntax

```
DEFINE BAR <line number> OF <popup name>
    PROMPT <expression> [MESSAGE <expression>]
    [SKIP [FOR <condition>]
```

Discussion

The **DEFINE BAR** command defines the location and the text of an option or prompt in a previously defined popup menu; one bar must be defined for each option and/or prompt that is to appear. The **DEFINE BAR** command is the second step in the design of a popup menu and requires the previous execution of a **DEFINE POPUP** command.

The lines in a popup menu are known as *bars* and are assigned numbers beginning with 1, starting with the first line in the window. The location of each bar is determined solely by its line number, and not by the sequence of the **DEFINE BAR** commands in the program. A bar is not needed for every line in the window, and any bar numbers that are omitted are left blank.

By default, the menu is displayed with the first selectable bar highlighted. Selections are made by using the up and down arrow keys to highlight a bar and pressing the enter key, or alternatively by pressing the first letter of the option name. When the actions associated with the selected bar are exhausted, the menu reappears on the screen and another bar can be selected.

The **OF** clause specifies the name of the associated popup menu. The **PROMPT** clause provides the text that will be displayed for that bar, which must be a character expression enclosed in quotation marks. The **SKIP** option renders a bar unavailable for selection; the **SKIP FOR** or **SKIP WHEN** clause makes it unavailable only when the specified condition is true, e.g., **SKIP WHEN mcode = "1"**. Consider:

```
DEFINE POPUP mainmenu FROM 6,25 TO 13,54
DEFINE BAR 1 OF mainmenu PROMPT "MAIN MENU" SKIP
DEFINE BAR 3 OF mainmenu PROMPT "ADD"
DEFINE BAR 4 OF mainmenu PROMPT "EDIT"
DEFINE BAR 5 OF mainmenu PROMPT "RETURN"
```

The six-line popup menu has four defined bars (lines 2 and 6 are blank). The menu title appears on the first line of the window, but cannot be selected because of the **SKIP** clause.

The **MESSAGE** clause displays a message centered on the bottom of the screen when the bar is highlighted. The message can contain up to 79 characters and must be enclosed in quotation marks; it will overwrite any currently displayed message, including one displayed as a result of the **DEFINE POPUP** command.

Tips

1. The **DEFINE BAR** command cannot be used if a **PROMPT** clause was specified in the **DEFINE POPUP** command.
2. Specification of a bar number greater than the total number of lines in the window produces vertical scrolling within the window. However, if the length of the prompt is greater than the width of the window, the prompt is truncated as no horizontal scrolling is permitted.
3. If the same bar number is specified in two different **DEFINE BAR** commands, the text displayed by the second **DEFINE BAR** command overwrites the first.

4. The highlighted bar is displayed in the colors of the enhanced display area, or in the colors established by a **SET COLOR OF HIGHLIGHT** command, if one was issued. The color of the other bars is the same as the standard display area, or those established by a **SET COLOR OF NORMAL** command. The text for available bars is always brighter than that for unavailable ones.
5. Each **DEFINE BAR** command requires an equivalent **CASE BAR()** statement in the program or procedure called by the **ON SELECTION POPUP** command.
6. By default, the first character of the bar text will appear immediately to the right of the menu border. The text can be positioned elsewhere by adding spaces to the **PROMPT** expression, e.g., **PROMPT "   ADD"**.
7. Each menu option should begin with a different letter, so that pressing the first letter of the option name selects the desired option.
8. The **SHOW POPUP** command displays a popup menu without activating it, and is used to preview the menu during development.

Related Topics

```
BAR()
CLEAR POPUPS
DEACTIVATE POPUP
DEFINE BAR
DEFINE POPUP
ON SELECTION POPUP
RELEASE POPUPS
SET COLOR
SHOW POPUP
```

DEFINE MENU

Syntax

```
DEFINE MENU <menu name> [MESSAGE <expression>]
```

Discussion

The **DEFINE MENU** command is the first step in the design of a horizontal bar menu. The command assigns a name to the menu and optionally displays a message at the bottom of the screen when the menu is activated. The other steps in the design process include:

1. Defining the individual menu options (called *pads*) through a series of **DEFINE PAD** commands.
2. Specifying the action to be taken as a result of selecting each pad with a series of **ON SELECTION PAD** and **ON PAD** commands.
3. Writing the programs and/or procedures referenced by the **ON SELECTION PAD** and **ON PAD** commands.
4. Activating the menu with an **ACTIVATE MENU** command.

By default, the menu is displayed with the first pad highlighted. The **PAD** option of the **ACTIVATE MENU** can be used to override this default, specifying a different pad as the default. Selections are made by using the right and left arrow keys to highlight a pad and pressing the enter key, or alternatively, by pressing **Alt** and the first letter of the pad name and then pressing the enter key. When the actions associated with the selected pad are exhausted, the menu reappears on the screen and another pad can be selected.

The horizontal bar is placed on row 0, with three spaces between each of the defined pads, unless the **AT** option is included in the **DEFINE PAD** command to place the pads elsewhere on the screen. No frame is drawn around the menu, although one can be created with the **@...TO** command.

The commands to create and activate a bar menu are shown below:

```
DEFINE MENU bar1 MESSAGE "Select ADD, EDIT, or QUIT"
DEFINE PAD add OF bar1 AT 3,2 PROMPT "ADD"
DEFINE PAD edit OF bar1 AT 3,10 PROMPT "EDIT"
DEFINE PAD quit OF bar1 AT 3,18 PROMPT "QUIT"
ON SELECTION PAD add OF bar1 DO addprg
ON SELECTION PAD edit OF bar1 DO editprg
ON SELECTION PAD quit OF bar1 DEACTIVATE MENU
ACTIVATE MENU bar1
```

The programs associated with the **ON SELECTION PAD** commands (e.g., **ADDPRG.PRG** and **EDITPRG.PRG**) must be available prior to activating the menu.

The **MESSAGE** clause displays a message centered at the bottom of the screen when the menu is activated. It can contain up to 79 characters and must be enclosed in quotation marks.

Tips

1. Each **DEFINE PAD** command can have its own message, which overrides the **DEFINE MENU** message; thus, if every pad had an associated message, the **DEFINE MENU** message would never be displayed.
2. Each menu option should begin with a different letter, so that pressing the **Alt** key and the first letter of the option name selects the desired option.
3. The **SHOW MENU** command displays a bar menu without activating it and is used to preview the bar menu during development.
4. The **ON PAD** command attaches a popup menu to a pad, so that the popup menu is "pulled down" whenever the pad is highlighted. To associate a popup menu with a pad in a bar menu without the popup menu automatically appearing whenever the pad is highlighted, issue an **ON SELECTION PAD** command that specifies an **ACTIVATE POPUP** command as the command to be executed. For example,

   ```
   ON SELECTION PAD add OF bar1 ACTIVATE POPUP addpop
   ```

   The user will have to press the enter key when the pad name is highlighted to cause the popup menu to appear.
5. Only one bar menu can be active at one time, although a bar menu and an attached popup menu can both be active simultaneously. The commands to select from each of the menus differ, so that dBASE can differentiate between the two. For example, pads are highlighted on a bar menu with the right and left arrow keys, whereas bars are highlighted on a popup menu with the up and down arrow keys. Similarly, options are selected from a bar menu by pressing the **Alt** key and the first letter of the option name, and from a popup menu by pressing just the first letter of the option name.
6. The **DEACTIVATE MENU** command deactivates the current bar menu and erases it from the screen. A **RELEASE MENUS** or **CLEAR MENUS** command releases the menu definition from memory. A menu must be deactivated before it can be released.
7. The current bar menu will be deactivated and erased from the screen when the user presses the **Esc** key.

Related Topics

```
CLEAR MENUS
DEACTIVATE MENU
DEFINE MENU
DEFINE PAD
ON PAD
ON SELECTION PAD
RELEASE MENUS
SHOW MENU
```

DEFINE PAD

Syntax

```
DEFINE PAD <pad name> OF <menu name> PROMPT <expression>
    [AT <row,col>] [MESSAGE <expression>]
```

Discussion

The **DEFINE PAD** command defines the text of an option (pad) in a previously defined bar menu; one pad must be defined for each option that will appear. The **DEFINE PAD** command is the second step in the design of a bar menu and requires the previous execution of a **DEFINE MENU** command.

The pad name may be up to 10 characters long and may consist of letters, numbers, and an optional underscore. The **OF** clause specifies the name of the associated bar menu. The **PROMPT** clause provides the text that will be displayed for that pad, which must be a character expression enclosed in quotation marks.

By default, the menu is displayed with the first pad highlighted. The **PAD** option in the **ACTIVATE MENU** command can be used to override this default, specifying a different pad as the default. Selections are made by using the right and left arrow keys to highlight a pad and pressing the enter key, or alternatively, by pressing **Alt** and the first letter of the pad name and pressing the enter key. When the actions associated with the selected pad are exhausted, the menu reappears on the screen and another pad can be selected.

The menu is placed on row 0, with three spaces between each pad, unless the **AT** clause is used to explicitly position the pads, in which case, care must be taken to space the pads attractively. **SET SCOREBOARD** should be **OFF** so that the menu cannot be overwritten by the status indicators.

An **ON PAD** or **ON SELECTION PAD** command is needed for each pad defined, to specify the action taken whenever the pad is selected. The **ON PAD** command attaches a popup menu to a pad, so that the popup menu is "pulled down" whenever the pad is selected. The **ON SELECTION PAD** command associates any other action with a menu pad. For example,

```
DEFINE MENU bar1 MESSAGE "Select ADD, EDIT, or QUIT"
DEFINE PAD add OF bar1 AT 3,2 PROMPT "ADD"
DEFINE PAD edit OF bar1 AT 3,10 PROMPT "EDIT"
DEFINE PAD quit OF bar1 AT 3,18 PROMPT "QUIT"
ON SELECTION PAD add OF bar1 DO addprg
ON SELECTION PAD edit OF bar1 DO editprg
ON SELECTION PAD quit OF bar1 DEACTIVATE MENU
ACTIVATE MENU bar1
```

The programs associated with the **ON SELECTION PAD** commands (e.g., **ADDPRG.PRG** and **EDITPRG.PRG**) must be available prior to activating the menu.

The **MESSAGE** clause displays a message centered at the bottom of the screen when the pad is highlighted. The message can contain up to 79 characters and must be enclosed in quotation marks; it will overwrite any currently displayed message, including one displayed as a result of the **DEFINE MENU** command.

Tips

1. If the same pad name is specified in two different **DEFINE PAD** commands, the text displayed by the second **DEFINE PAD** command overwrites the first.
2. The highlighted pad is displayed in the colors of the enhanced display area, or in the colors established by a **SET COLOR OF HIGHLIGHT** command, if one was issued. The color of the other pads is the same as the standard display area, or those established by a **SET COLOR OF MESSAGES** command.
3. Each pad should begin with a different letter, so that pressing the **Alt** key and the first letter of the option name selects the desired option.

4. The **SHOW MENU** command displays a bar menu without activating it and is used to preview the menu during development.

Related Topics

```
@...TO
CLEAR MENUS
DEACTIVATE MENU
DEFINE MENU
DEFINE PAD
ON PAD
ON SELECTION PAD
RELEASE MENUS
SET SCOREBOARD
SHOW MENU
```

DEFINE POPUP

Syntax

```
DEFINE POPUP <popup name> FROM <row,col> [TO <row,col>]
    [PROMPT FIELD <field>/PROMPT FILES
    [LIKE <skeleton>]/PROMPT STRUCTURE]
    [MESSAGE <expression>]
```

Discussion

The **DEFINE POPUP** command is the first step in the design of a popup menu, which consists of a vertical list of menu options displayed in a window frame. The command assigns a name to the menu, positions it on the screen, and optionally displays a message at the bottom of the screen when the menu is activated. The other steps in the design process include:

1. Defining the individual menu options (called *bars*) through a series of **DEFINE BAR** commands.
2. Specifying the action to be taken as a result of making a selection from the menu with an **ON SELECTION POPUP** command.
3. Writing the program and/or procedure referenced by the **ON SELECTION POPUP** command.
4. Activating the menu with an **ACTIVATE POPUP** command.

The first set of **<row,col>** coordinates defines the upper-left corner of the menu window, and the optional **TO** clause designates the lower-right corner. Vertical scrolling within the window will occur if a bar number is greater than the total number of lines in the window. However, if the length of the prompt is greater than the width of the window, the prompt is truncated, as no horizontal scrolling is permitted.

Omission of the **TO** clause causes the window to default to a width corresponding to the longest bar and a height corresponding to the highest bar number defined. The window frame defaults to a single line, but can be changed by issuing a **SET BORDER TO** command prior to the **DEFINE POPUP** command. The color of the frame corresponds to the colors of the enhanced display area, or to the colors established by the **SET COLOR OF BOX** command, if one has been previously issued.

The optional **PROMPT** clauses result in specialized menus called *pick lists.* The **PROMPT FIELD** option causes the data values in the specified field to become the bars of the popup menu. There will be one bar for each record, and if there are more records then lines in the window, vertical scrolling is permitted. The field whose values are displayed must be from the currently selected **DBF** file, or else a file alias must be specified with the field name.

The **PROMPT FILES** option causes file names to become the bars of the popup menu. The files from the current catalog will be listed, or if no catalog is active, files from the current subdirectory. If the **LIKE** option is included, only files that match the specified skeleton will be listed. If there are more files than fit within the window, vertical scrolling is permitted.

The **PROMPT STRUCTURE** option causes the field names in the currently selected **DBF** file or view to become the bars of the popup menu. The field names are listed in alphabetical order, and vertical scrolling is permitted if they cannot all be listed within the defined window. Note that after an item is picked, dBASE does not automatically process the selection in any way. Choosing a field value does not move the record pointer to that field, nor does selecting a file name open that file. The code to process the item selected must be included in the program/procedure named in the **ON SELECTION POPUP** command or in a program that it calls.

By default, the menu is displayed with the first selectable bar highlighted. Selections are made by using the up and down arrow keys to highlight a bar and pressing the enter key, or alternatively, by pressing the first letter of the option name. When the actions associated with the selected bar are exhausted, the menu reappears on the screen and another bar can be selected.

The commands to create and activate a popup menu are shown below:

```
DEFINE POPUP mainmenu FROM 6,25 TO 17,54
DEFINE BAR 1 OF mainmenu PROMPT "ADD"
DEFINE BAR 2 OF mainmenu PROMPT "EDIT"
DEFINE BAR 3 OF mainmenu PROMPT "QUIT"
ON SELECTION POPUP mainmenu DO mainprg
ACTIVATE POPUP mainmenu

PROCEDURE mainprg
DO CASE
 CASE BAR() = 1
  DO addrec
 CASE BAR() = 2
  DO editrec
 CASE BAR() = 3
  DEACTIVATE POPUP
ENDCASE
```

Note, too, that each **DEFINE BAR** command has an equivalent **CASE BAR()** statement in the procedure called by the **ON SELECTION POPUP** command.

The **MESSAGE** clause displays a message centered at the bottom of the screen when the menu is activated; it can contain up to 79 characters and must be enclosed in quotation marks.

Tips

1. Each **DEFINE BAR** command can have its own message, which overrides the **DEFINE POPUP** message; thus, if every bar had an associated message, the **DEFINE POPUP** message would never be displayed.
2. Each menu option should begin with a different letter, so that pressing the first letter of the option name selects the desired option.
3. The **SHOW POPUP** command displays a popup menu without activating it and is used to preview the menu during development.
4. The **DEACTIVATE POPUP** command deactivates the current popup menu and erases it from the screen. A **RELEASE POPUPS** or **CLEAR POPUPS** command releases the menu definition from memory. A menu must be deactivated before it can be released.
5. **DEFINE BAR** commands are not used when the **PROMPT** clause is specified in the **DEFINE POPUP** command, nor is there a need for the **BAR()** function to evaluate the

user's choice and transfer control. The **PROMPT()** function returns the character string equivalent of the prompt text from the bar selected, and so can be used in a program to carry out actions based on the user's choice; e.g.,

```
SEEK PROMPT()                     ─┐  Positions record pointer
LOCATE FOR city = PROMPT()        ─┘  to selected record
REPORT FORM PROMPT() TO PRINT     ──  Prints selected file
```

The first two examples are appropriate after a selection is made from a menu defined with the **PROMPT FIELD** option; the third example implies a selection was made from a menu defined with the **PROMPT FILES** option.

6. The **PROMPT FIELD** option can specify only a single field; field expressions are not permitted.

Related Topics

```
ACTIVATE POPUP
BAR()
CLEAR POPUPS
DEFINE BAR
DEFINE POPUP
ON SELECTION POPUP
PROMPT()
RELEASE POPUPS
SET BORDER
SET COLOR
SHOW POPUP
```

DEFINE WINDOW

Syntax

```
DEFINE WINDOW <window name> FROM <row,col> TO <row,col>
    [DOUBLE/PANEL/NONE/<border definition string>]
    [COLOR [<standard>] [,<enhanced>] [,<frame>]]
```

Discussion

The **DEFINE WINDOW** command defines the name, location, and border appearance of the specified window. Once activated, the window will be displayed on the screen, overwriting any existing screen display, with all subsequent screen input and output being sent to the window rather than the screen. The output scrolls within the window and is automatically wrapped to fit within its borders.

The first set of **<row,col>** coordinates specifies the upper-left corner of the window, whereas the second set designates the lower-right corner. When the command is executed, the coordinates are checked, and if they are not within the allowable screen limits (i.e., 80 columns and 25 or 43 rows, depending on the status of the **SET DISPLAY** command), an *Illegal value* message is displayed. If, on the other hand, the values are within the screen limitations, but the size of the window conflicts with the presence of the status line, a *Window coordinates outside of allowable screen space* message is displayed.

By default, the window border is a single line, but the appearance can be changed by issuing a **SET BORDER TO** command prior to the **DEFINE WINDOW** command or by specifying **DOUBLE**, **PANEL**, **NONE**, or a border definition string within the **DEFINE WINDOW** command. (See the **SET BORDER** command for details.) Note that the window always reflects the border in effect when it was defined, rather than the border settings when it is activated.

The **COLOR** clause of the **DEFINE WINDOW** command overrides the default screen colors for the standard and enhanced display areas, and the border (frame). Commas are required to indicate omitted parameters if only the border colors are changed; e.g., the command,

```
DEFINE WINDOW WIN1 FROM 5,10 TO 15,70 COLOR ,,GR+/R
```

changes just the color of the border. (See the **SET COLOR** command for the list of allowable color codes.) As with the border definition, the window reflects the colors in effect when the window was defined, rather than when it is activated.

Only one window can be active at one time. Therefore, an **ACTIVATE WINDOW** command temporarily suspends (not deactivates) any currently active window before activating the new one. The image of the first window remains on the screen unless its display is covered by the new window, and when the new window is subsequently deactivated, the suspended window is reactivated. If only one window had been activated, dBASE returns to using the full screen when that window is deactivated.

The window definition is not erased from memory when it is deactivated, and thus can be reactivated at any time with an **ACTIVATE WINDOW** command. It is only through a **RELEASE WINDOWS** or **CLEAR WINDOWS** command that the window definitions are released from memory. Note, too, that a window must be deactivated before its definition can be released from memory.

Tips

1. Up to twenty window definitions can be in memory at one time.
2. The character for a custom border is specified by enclosing the character in quotes, or by using the character's decimal equivalent (ASCII code value) in the IBM Extended Character Set. For example,

   ```
   DEFINE WINDOW FROM 5,10 TO 15,50 "*"
   DEFINE WINDOW FROM 5,10 TO 15,50 3
   ```

   The first command draws a frame or border of asterisks, whereas the second draws a frame made of hearts (ASCII character 3 is ♥). The ASCII code value is not enclosed in quotes.
3. The **MOVE WINDOW** command assigns new row and column coordinates to a window definition, changing its location on the screen.
4. A **SAVE WINDOW** command saves one or more window definitions currently in memory to disk, from where they can be subsequently restored to memory with the **RESTORE WINDOW** command.
5. The **ACTIVATE SCREEN** command displays text outside a window without deactivating the window. Output will be displayed outside the window borders until an **ACTIVATE WINDOW** command is issued.
6. A defined window can be used as an editing window for a memo field by issuing a **SET WINDOW OF MEMO** command.

Related Topics

```
ACTIVATE WINDOW
CLEAR WINDOWS
DEACTIVATE WINDOW
MOVE WINDOW
RELEASE WINDOWS
RESTORE WINDOW
SAVE WINDOW
SET BORDER
SET COLOR
SET DISPLAY
SET WINDOW OF MEMO
```

DELETE

Syntax

```
DELETE [<scope>][WHILE <condition>][FOR <condition>]
```

Discussion

The **DELETE** command marks a record(s) in the currently selected database for deletion. Only the current record will be deleted unless a scope parameter, or a **FOR** or **WHILE** condition, is specified to mark more than one record at a time, for example, **DELETE NEXT 10** or **DELETE FOR location = 'FL'**.

The position of the record pointer is unaffected if **DELETE** is specified with no additional parameters. **DELETE ALL** or **DELETE REST**, however, moves the record pointer to the end of the file, whereas any other scope parameter will reposition the record pointer at the last record marked for deletion. Inclusion of a **WHILE** condition moves the record pointer to the record after the last record meeting the condition, while specification of a **FOR** condition moves the record pointer to the end of the file.

Records marked for deletion are still accessible, and are processed by subsequent dBASE commands. However, when these records are displayed or listed, they are identified by an asterisk in the first byte of the record. In similar fashion, **Del** appears on the status line when deleted records are browsed or edited.

Tips

1. **SET DELETED ON** causes subsequent dBASE commands to ignore records marked for deletion, treating them as if they were not physically present; i.e., the logically deleted records are "hidden" from dBASE commands. **SET DELETED OFF** returns to the default processing mode in which all records are processed, regardless of their deleted status.
2. Commands that access records by record number (e.g., **GOTO 3** or **EDIT RECORD 3**) will operate even if **SET DELETED** is **ON**. The **INDEX** and **SORT** commands will also process deleted records, regardless of whether **SET DELETED** is **ON** or **OFF**.
3. The **DELETED()** function returns a value of true if a record has been marked for deletion and a value of false if it has not. This function can be used to display or count the records marked for deletion, as shown:

   ```
   LIST FOR DELETED()
   COUNT FOR DELETED()
   ```

   or to archive deleted records, as in

   ```
   COPY TO archive FOR DELETED()
   ```

   Remember, however, that the status of **SET DELETED** must be **OFF** for these commands to execute properly.
4. A record other than the current record can be deleted with the command, **DELETE RECORD <n>**, where n is a valid record number.
5. The **RECALL** command is used to unmark a previously deleted record. The **PACK** command is used to physically remove the deleted records from the file.
6. **Ctrl+U** can be used to delete/recall the current record from within the **EDIT** or **BROWSE** mode.

Related Topics

```
DELETED()
PACK
RECALL
SET DELETED
ZAP
```

DELETE TAG

Syntax

```
DELETE TAG <tag name> [OF <mdx filename>]
    /<ndx filename> [...]
```

Discussion

The **DELETE TAG** command deletes one or more tags from an open **MDX** file. The tag will be deleted from the production **MDX** file unless an **OF** clause is used to specify an independent **MDX** file. For example,

```
DELETE TAG donation ———— Deletes a single tag from production MDX file
DELETE TAG city,zipcode —— Deletes two tags from production MDX file
DELETE TAG last OF second —— Deletes a single tag from independent MDX file
```

If all tags in an **MDX** file are deleted, the **MDX** file is deleted from the disk as well. If it is the production **MDX** file, the **DBF** file header is updated to indicate that no production **MDX** file exists.

Tips

1. Tags should be deleted when they are no longer required, in order to speed up data entry. Additionally, when a tag is deleted, the disk space is freed and the **MDX** file has one less tag toward its limit of 47 tags.
2. The **DISPLAY STATUS** command indicates the tags that exist in the production **MDX** file (and any other open **MDX** file). This helps to determine which tags, if any, are no longer needed.

Related Topics

```
CREATE
DISPLAY STATUS
INDEX ON
SET ORDER TO
USE
```

DELETED FUNCTION

Syntax

```
DELETED([<alias>])
```

Discussion

The **DELETED()** function returns a logical value of true if the current record is marked for deletion, or false, if it is not. The status of the current record (i.e., whether or not it is marked for deletion) can be viewed with the command, **? DELETED()**, which will display **.T.** or **.F.**, for marked and unmarked records, respectively.

```
USE solemp
GO 3
? DELETED()
.F.  ———————————— dBASE response
DELETE
? DELETED()
.T.  ———————————— dBASE response
```

The **DELETED()** function operates on the currently selected **DBF** file unless an alias is specified within the parentheses, in which case it is used to determine whether or not the current record in an unselected work area is deleted, for example, **? DELETED(2)** or **? DELETED("SOLEMP")**. The alias can be specified as the number of the work area or the name of the **DBF** file enclosed in quotes.

Tips

1. Whenever **SET DELETED** is **ON**, records marked for deletion are hidden, so that the **DELETED()** condition will not find any records. In other words, **SET DELETED** must be **OFF** for commands using the **DELETED()** function to work properly.
2. The function is often used to process all of the deleted records in the currently selected data file with a single command; e.g.,

```
SET DELETED OFF
LIST FOR DELETED()
COPY TO archive FOR DELETED()
COUNT FOR DELETED()
```

Related Topics

```
DELETE
SET DELETED
```

DIR

Syntax

```
DIRECTORY/DIR [<drive:>][<path>]<skeleton>]
```

Discussion

The dBASE **DIR** command displays information about the files stored on the designated disk. It is parallel in function to the DOS command except that it is executed from within dBASE, and is therefore more convenient.

If the command is issued with no parameters (e.g., **DIR**), it displays the names of all **DBF** files on the default drive together with the number of records, the date of the last update, and the file size in bytes. It also indicates the total number of bytes used by the **DBF** files, the total number of **DBF** files, and the number of bytes remaining on the disk. If a drive or path is included in the command (e.g., **DIR A:** or **DIR C:\DBASE\SOLEIL**), it will display the aforementioned information for all **DBF** files on the designated drive or subdirectory.

The skeleton parameter enables the use of the DOS wild card characters, the ? and the *, within the **DIR** command. The question mark represents any single character in its position in the filename, whereas the asterisk denotes any number of characters in the filename. For example:

1. **DIR ?.DBF** lists all files with one character filenames that have a **DBF** extension.
2. **DIR *.PRG** lists all filenames that have a **PRG** extension, regardless of the length of the filename.
3. **DIR S?.FRM** lists all two-character filenames that have an **FRM** extension and begin with the letter S.
4. **DIR S*.FRM** lists all filenames that have an **FRM** extension and begin with the letter S, regardless of the length of the filename.

Whenever the skeleton parameter is used, the filenames are listed in columns across the screen (for a maximum of four columns), and the only information given is the filename, the total number of bytes used by the files listed, the total number of files listed, and the number of bytes remaining on the disk.

Tips

1. If **SET AUTOSAVE** is **OFF**, the directory listing may not reflect all changes made to a database file until after the file is closed with a **CLOSE DATABASES** or **USE** command.
2. A **SET PATH TO** command does not affect the results of a **DIR** command, in that only files from the current (logged) subdirectory are listed. A path must be included in the **DIR** command, e.g., **DIR C:\DATADISK**, to list files in subdirectories other than the logged directory.
3. The DOS **DIR** command can be accessed from within dBASE through a **RUN** command, i.e., **RUN DIR**.

Related Topics

DISPLAY FILES
RUN
SET PATH TO

DISPLAY

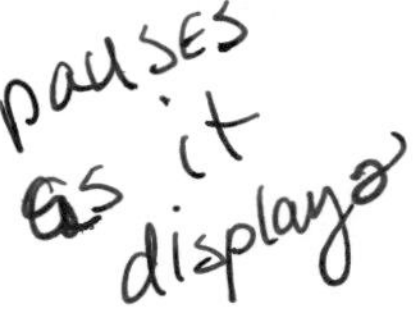

Syntax

```
DISPLAY [[FIELDS]<expN list>][<scope>]
[WHILE <condition>] [FOR <condition>][OFF]
[TO PRINTER/TO FILE <filename>]
```

Discussion

The **DISPLAY** command shows all fields for the current record in the currently selected database. The default scope is one, so that issuing the command with no parameters causes only the current record to be displayed. A scope, **FOR**, or **WHILE** parameter may be used to output multiple records; e.g.,

```
DISPLAY ALL
DISPLAY NEXT 10
DISPLAY FOR location = 'NY'
```

If the output produced by the command requires more than 20 lines, the data is exhibited one screen at a time with a pause between screens; i.e., a key has to be pressed for the display to continue.

The **DISPLAY** command with no parameters does not reposition the record pointer, whereas including a scope parameter, or a **FOR** or **WHILE** clause, alters its position. Specification of a scope of **ALL** or **REST** moves the record pointer to the end of file, as does inclusion of a **FOR** condition. Specification of **NEXT** as the scope parameter repositions the pointer to the last record in the scope, while inclusion of a **WHILE** condition moves it to the record beyond the last record meeting the condition.

An expression list can be included to show only selected fields and/or to display complex expressions; e.g.,

```
DISPLAY ssn,initials,lname
DISPLAY ALL ssn,TRIM(initials) + ' ' + lname
DISPLAY ssn,(salary2-salary1)/salary1*100
```

The screen display is always preceded by a heading line, which includes the field names (or expressions) of the individual fields. The width of each expression is determined by either the field width (as established by the file structure) or the width of the heading, whichever is greater.

The contents of a memo field are not displayed, unless the field name is specified in an expression list. Omission of the memo field name displays the word "memo" in lower case if the field does not contain any text, and in upper case if text is present. The default display width for a memo field is 50 columns, but that can be modified with the **SET MEMOWIDTH** command.

The **OFF** parameter suppresses the record number. The **TO PRINTER** parameter echoes the results of the command to the printer. The **TO FILE** option prints the output to a disk file.

Tips

1. If the data to be displayed is too long to fit on one line, both the heading and the data wrap to successive lines, making the output difficult to read. The **SET FIELDS** command or an expression list can be used to limit the display to essential fields, and avoid the wrap to the next line.
2. The heading line shows the field names and expressions exactly as they were entered in the command line; i.e., if the command was typed in upper case, the heading line will also be in upper case.
3. The heading line is suppressed with the **SET HEADING OFF** command, a useful procedure when using a long or complex expression.
4. No record is displayed if the record pointer is at the end of file.
5. Deleted records will not be displayed if **SET DELETED** is **ON**, unless the record pointer is explicitly moved to the specific record; e.g.,

   ```
   DISPLAY RECORD 5
   ```

   or

   ```
   GOTO 5
   DISPLAY
   ```

   The same principle holds for records not matching the condition set by a **SET FILTER** command; i.e., records not matching the filter condition are ignored, unless the record pointer is specifically moved to the record.
6. Fields from database files in other than the currently selected work area can be displayed by including the file alias with the field name in the command; e.g.,

   ```
   DISPLAY ssn,lname,location->locname
   ```

   This is usually done only when a **SET RELATION** command is in effect.

7. The **LIST** command operates in similar fashion, except that its default scope is **ALL**. In addition, **LIST** does not pause between screens of data.
8. To halt execution of the **DISPLAY** command, press the **Esc** key.

Related Topics

```
?/??
@...SAY...GET
LIST
SET DELETED
SET FIELDS
SET FILTER
SET MEMOWIDTH
SET RELATION
```

DISPLAY HISTORY

Syntax

```
DISPLAY HISTORY [LAST <n>]
    [TO PRINTER/TO FILE <filename>]
```

Discussion

The **DISPLAY HISTORY** command displays the list of the commands currently stored in history memory, which is, by default, the 20 most recently executed commands. (The number can be increased or decreased with the **SET HISTORY** command.)

Specification of the **LAST <n>** clause, where **<n>** is a number less than the history's capacity, will list only the most recently executed n commands.

Inclusion of the **TO PRINTER** clause echoes the results to the printer. The **TO FILE** clause outputs the result to a disk file.

Tips

1. The screen display pauses between screens until a key is pressed to continue the listing.
2. Any of the commands stored in the history memory can be recalled to the dot prompt, where they may be edited and/or reissued. Repeatedly pressing the up arrow key redisplays the previous commands, beginning with the one most recently executed. Once the desired command is at the dot prompt, the right and left arrow keys are used to edit the command (in either the insert or replacement modes), whereas the return key will reexecute the command. Note, too, that while the up arrow key progressively lists earlier commands, the down arrow key moves towards the most recently issued commands.
3. Newly executed commands will not be stored in the history memory when the status of **SET HISTORY** is **OFF**, although previous commands can still be recalled, edited, and reissued. **SET HISTORY** must be turned back **ON** to resume storing commands.
4. **LIST HISTORY** displays the same information as **DISPLAY HISTORY**, except that it does not pause between screens of information.

Related Topics

```
LIST HISTORY
SET HISTORY
```

DISPLAY MEMORY

Syntax

```
DISPLAY MEMORY [TO PRINTER/TO FILE <filename>]
```

Discussion

The **DISPLAY MEMORY** command provides information about the current memory variables, including:

1. The name, status (public or private), type, stored value, and size of every active user memory variable.
2. The number of active user memory variables.
3. The amount of memory used by existing user memory variables.
4. The names and amount of memory used by all active windows, popup menus, bar menus, and pads.
5. The settings and amount of memory used by all system memory variables.
6. The amount of available memory remaining.

The maximum number of memory variables that can exist at one time is determined by the **MVBLKSIZE** and **MVMAXBLKS** settings, which specify the number of memory variable slots per block (default is 50) and the number of blocks allocated for memory variables (default of 10), respectively. This default of 500 can be increased by changing the appropriate setting in **CONFIG.DB**.

If the display of the memory variables exceeds what will fit on one screen, the display pauses after each screen, waiting for the user to press a key to continue. The **TO PRINTER** clause echoes the screen display to the printer. If the printer is not ready, an error message will be displayed. The **TO FILE** clause writes the output to a disk file.

Tips

1. The **DISPLAY MEMORY** command is a very useful debugging tool when programming problems occur.
2. The display of a numeric memory variable shows the variable both as it appears in displays, and as it is stored in memory (the two can be very different, especially in regard to the number of decimal places).
3. Private memory variables (those created in programs or procedures and not explicitly declared as public) are released from memory as soon as the program or procedure that created them is terminated. These variables will not, therefore, be included in a **DISPLAY MEMORY** output obtained from the dot prompt at the program's conclusion. Hence to view the contents of private memory variables, you must either include **DISPLAY MEMORY** (and **WAIT**) commands at strategic points in the program, or temporarily declare the memory variables **PUBLIC** (either in the program itself or from the dot prompt before running the program).
4. Memory variables saved to **MEM** files for use in future dBASE sessions with the **SAVE** command can be viewed only after they have been loaded into memory with the **RESTORE** command.
5. **LIST MEMORY** displays the same information as **DISPLAY MEMORY**, except that it does not pause between screens of information.
6. System memory variables control the appearance of printed and screen output. Their names begin with an underscore, and they are automatically created and maintained by dBASE. These variables may be changed through report and label design screens and from the dot prompt with a **STORE** command. They cannot be **RELEASE**d.

Related Topics

CONFIG.DB
DISPLAY MEMORY
PRIVATE
PUBLIC
RELEASE
RESTORE
SAVE
STORE

DISPLAY STATUS

Syntax

```
DISPLAY STATUS [TO PRINTER/TO FILE <filename>]
```

Discussion

The **DISPLAY STATUS** command provides information about the current dBASE IV session, including:

1. The current search path.
2. The default drive/directory.
3. The destination printer port.
4. The left margin setting for reports and labels.
5. The currently selected work area.
6. The status of most of the **ON/OFF SET** commands.
7. The function key settings.

In addition, the command will display the names of all open database files, and for each file the number of its work area and its alias. As applicable, it will also supply for each work area the name of an active format file, information regarding an active relationship or any active filter condition, the names of all of the open indexes and their respective keys, and the name of an open memo (**DBT**) file.

Specification of **TO PRINTER** will direct the output to the printer, as well as the screen. The **TO FILE** clause will write the output to a disk file.

Tips

1. **DISPLAY STATUS** is a helpful debugging tool.
2. **LIST STATUS** provides the same information, and differs only in that it does not pause between screens as does the **DISPLAY STATUS** command.
3. **DISPLAY STATUS** also provides information on the status of file and record locks in a networked system.

Related Topic

DISPLAY MEMORY

DISPLAY STRUCTURE

Syntax

```
DISPLAY STRUCTURE [IN <alias>]
    [TO PRINTER/TO FILE <filename>]
```

Discussion

The **DISPLAY STRUCTURE** command displays the following information about the currently selected database file:

1. The filename (including the drive and path name).
2. The number of records in the file.
3. The date of the last update to the file.
4. The name, type, width (including decimals for numeric fields), and whether or not there is an **MDX** tag for that field, for every field in the file structure.
5. The total number of bytes per record.

If the structure is large enough to require more than one screen (i.e., it contains more than 16 fields), the display pauses after each screen, prompting you to press any key to continue.

The **DISPLAY STRUCTURE** command operates on the currently selected **DBF** file unless an **IN <alias>** clause is specified, in which case it is used to display the file structure of a file open in an unselected work area, e.g, **DISPLAY STRUCTURE IN 2** or **DISPLAY STRUCTURE IN ZOO**. The alias can be specified as the number of the work area or the name of the **DBF** file.

Specification of **TO PRINTER** will direct the output display to the printer, as well as the screen. The **TO FILE** clause will write the output to a disk file.

Tips

1. The total number of bytes per record is one more than the sum of all of the field widths. The extra byte is for the deleted record marker (*).
2. This command can be used to verify the spelling of a field name, the width of a field, and/or the field type.
3. If there is an active field list, the active fields are marked with >.
4. The **IN <alias>** clause allows the structure of a file in an unselected work area to be displayed.

Related Topics

```
LIST STRUCTURE
```

DO

Syntax

```
DO <filename> [WITH <parameter list>]
```

Discussion

The **DO** command executes either a command file, an individual procedure stored within a command file, or a procedure file. If the command file or procedure file has not yet been compiled, or if it has been revised since its last compilation, dBASE compiles the source code and saves it to disk as an object file with a **DBO** extension; it is the **DBO** file that is executed, and it executes much faster than the equivalent **PRG** file.

When a **DO** command is issued, dBASE searches for the program/procedure as follows:

1. dBASE will search for a like-named procedure in the current **DBO** file.
2. dBASE will search for a like-named procedure in the open procedure file (if there is one).
3. dBASE will search for a like-named procedure in another open **DBO** file.
4. dBASE will search for a like-named **DBO** file.
5. dBASE will search for a like-named **PRG** file, which it will then compile to execute the generated **DBO** file.
6. dBASE will search for a like-named **PRS** file (SQL command file), which it will then compile to execute the generated **DBO** file.

The program containing the **DO** command is known as the *calling program*; the program named in the **DO** command is termed the *called program*. When the called program terminates, control is passed back to the calling program, to the statement immediately following the **DO** command.

The **WITH** clause is used to pass parameters to the called program, which stores the values in private memory variables initialized through a **PARAMETERS** command. (This command must be the first executable command in the called program.) The values of the parameters in the **WITH** clause are assigned sequentially to the memory variables in the **PARAMETERS** command, requiring that the number of parameters in the **WITH** clause equal the number of memory variables in the **PARAMETERS** command. The names of the parameters, however, do not have to be the same as the memory variables in the **PARAMETERS** command.

Tips

1. If a procedure in an open procedure or **DBO** file has the same name as an unopened **PRG** or **DBO** file, the procedure will always be executed.
2. Each **DO** that specifies a program file counts as an open file toward the total number of files allowed open at one time. Individual procedures are considered part of a procedure file and do not count toward the limit; i.e., only the procedure file itself is counted.
3. Memory variables created within the calling program are available to the called program and to any program that it calls. Changes made in the value of any of these variables are passed back to the calling program. On the other hand, memory variables created within a called program are not available to the calling program, unless they are first declared **PUBLIC**.
4. A program ends when the last command in the file has been executed and control is returned to the calling program (or the dot prompt). A **RETURN** command should be entered as the last line of every program, although this is not required.
5. Do not include a drive and path with the name of a procedure.
6. A procedure may be stored within a program file or in a separate procedure file. Each procedure must begin with a **PROCEDURE** statement, and each file may contain as many procedures as the available memory will permit, up to 1,170 procedures per file. dBASE maintains a list of all of the available procedures at the beginning of every **DBO** file, whether the procedures are a part of the file itself or called from a separate procedure file.
7. As many as 32 **DBO** files may be active at one time. A **DO** command can call a procedure found in any one of the active **DBO** files.
8. **MODIFY COMMAND** deletes the old **DBO** file when a command file is modified, ensuring that a new **DBO** file will be created when the program is run. Since external text editors do not automatically delete the old **DBO** file, **SET DEVELOPMENT** must be **ON** when an external text editor is used to modify a program file, to ensure that the outdated object file is replaced.
9. Any frequently used routine should be coded as a procedure. If the routine is used by only one program, it should be stored within that program, whereas if it is used by many different programs, it should be coded as part of a separate procedure file.

10. The use of parameters permits generalized coding in a called program to perform a specific task, as designated by the different programs that call it. For example, the procedure **PRINTMSG.PRG** (shown below),

```
PROCEDURE PRINTMSG
PARAMETERS message,mrow,mcol
@ mrow,mcol SAY message
RETURN
```

will display a message at a given screen location, depending on the values passed to it by the calling program. Thus, in the following program,

```
STORE 20 TO mrow
STORE 10 TO mcol
STORE 'Please enter a Y or N' TO msg
DO printmsg WITH msg,mrow,mcol
```

the message will be displayed at line 20, column 10, whereas another program whose coding is

```
STORE 12 TO mrow
STORE 15 TO mcol
STORE 'Please enter option' TO msg
DO printmsg WITH msg,mrow,mcol
```

will display a different message at line 12, column 15.

11. The **WITH** option can pass up to 64 parameters to a single procedure.
12. Update queries are activated with the **DO** command, which performs the update. When the **DO** command is executed, dBASE checks to see if a compiled object code file (**DBO**) exists, and if not, the update query file is compiled and the resultant **DBO** file is executed.
13. The **MODIFY QUERY** command edits the **UPD** file but does *not* delete the old **DBO** file. **SET DEVELOPMENT** must be **ON**, therefore, to ensure that the modified query file will be recompiled when it is next activated. The update query file will not be recompiled (and the old **DBO** file will be executed) if **SET DEVELOPMENT** is **OFF**.

Related Topics

```
CREATE/MODIFY QUERY
CREATE/MODIFY VIEW
MODIFY COMMAND
PARAMETERS
PROCEDURE
RETURN
SET DEVELOPMENT
SET PROCEDURE
```

DO CASE

Syntax

```
DO CASE
   CASE <condition>
      <commands>
   [CASE <condition>
      <commands>]
   .
    .
     .
   [OTHERWISE
      <commands>]
ENDCASE
```

Discussion

DO CASE is a structured programming command that selects one of several alternative courses of action. Execution begins with evaluation of the first condition and, if necessary, continues with each subsequent condition until a true condition is found. Upon reaching a true condition, every subsequent command is executed until another **CASE**, **OTHERWISE**, or **ENDCASE** is reached. Any remaining lines are then skipped, and control passes to the first command after the **ENDCASE** statement.

The **CASE** structure begins and ends with **DO CASE** and **ENDCASE**, respectively, each of which must be coded on its own line. Every **CASE** statement is also coded on its own line, as is the optional **OTHERWISE** statement, which follows the last **CASE**, and which specifies commands to be executed if none of the preceding conditions is true. If **OTHERWISE** is omitted and none of the preceding conditions is true, control passes directly to the first command after the **ENDCASE** statement. The command following either a **CASE** or **OTHERWISE** statement may be any valid dBASE command.

Indentation within a **CASE** statement is used only to improve readability, and is not required by the rules of dBASE. However, as with the **IF** and **DO WHILE** structures, indentation is highly recommended as it helps tremendously in making program logic more understandable.

Tips

1. A **DO CASE** statement is preferable to a series of nested **IF**'s, especially when there are more than three levels. **DO CASE** runs slightly faster and is also easier to follow.
2. **DO CASE** is ideal when one course of action must be chosen from several alternatives, and consequently is recommended for the creation of menu-driven programs. Consider:

```
DO CASE
   CASE input = 1
      DO program_1
   CASE input = 2
      DO program_2
   CASE input = 3
      DO program_3
   OTHERWISE
      DISPLAY 'error message'
ENDCASE
```

3. Nested **CASE** structures are permitted. In addition, **IF** and **DO WHILE** structures may be used within the **CASE** structure as one of the commands to be executed. Be careful, however, to ensure that the nested structures are complete (i.e., every **IF** has an **ENDIF**, every **DO WHILE** an **ENDDO**, and every **DO CASE** an **ENDCASE**).
4. Consistent indentation (typically 3 spaces) within the structure is strongly recommended.
5. Any number of **CASE** statements may be placed between the **DO CASE** and the **ENDCASE**.

Related Topics

DO WHILE
IF...ELSE...ENDIF
IIF()

DO WHILE

Syntax

```
DO WHILE <condition>
    <commands>
ENDDO
```

Discussion

DO WHILE is a structured programming command that executes the included commands repeatedly as long as the specified condition is true. The condition is tested *prior* to execution of any of the included commands. Hence, if the initial test of the condition is false, control passes immediately to the first command after the **DO WHILE** statement.

If, however, the condition is true, the included commands are executed until the **ENDDO** is reached, whereupon control returns to the **DO WHILE** statement and the condition is retested. The process is repeated until the condition becomes false, whereupon control passes to the statement after **ENDDO**, terminating the loop.

As indicated, the condition is tested at the beginning of the loop, meaning that if the condition becomes false midway through the list of commands, the rest of the commands are still executed. Only when the **ENDDO** is reached, and control is transferred back to the **DO WHILE**, will the condition be evaluated as false and the loop terminated.

Provision must be made to ensure that the condition in the **DO WHILE** statement eventually becomes false, or else the loop will be repeated indefinitely. Should this occur, the only way to terminate processing is to press the **Esc** key.

Nested **DO WHILE** loops (one **DO WHILE** performed within another **DO WHILE**) are permitted, provided that each **DO WHILE** is terminated by an **ENDDO**. Since dBASE ignores any additional text appearing on the same line as an **ENDDO** statement, it is helpful to label the **ENDDO** portion of the command as shown:

```
DO WHILE city = 'Miami'
  .
    .
      .
   DO WHILE zipcode = '33176'
     .
       .
         .
   ENDDO  &&zipcode
ENDDO  &&city
```

Indentation within a `DO WHILE` statement is used only to improve readability, and is not required by the rules of dBASE syntax. However, as with the `IF` and `DO CASE` structures, indentation is highly recommended as it makes program logic easier to follow.

Tips

1. `DO WHILE .NOT. EOF()` is used to perform the same set of steps for all records in a file; e.g.,

```
USE solemp
DO WHILE .NOT. EOF()
   ? lastname,firstname
   SKIP
ENDDO
```

   The `SKIP` command is necessary within the loop to move the record pointer to the next record in the file; indeed, if `SKIP` were erroneously omitted, the condition controlling the loop would never be false, and the program would loop indefinitely.
2. Consistent indentation (typically 3 spaces) within the structure is strongly recommended.
3. Compound conditions may be included through use of the logical operators `.AND.` and `.OR.` You must, however, repeat the field name or memory variable in each part of a complex clause, even if the field name or variable name is the same, for example, `DO WHILE city = 'Miami' .OR. city = 'New York'`.
4. The `SCAN...ENDSCAN` command is a simplified version of the `DO WHILE` command, and is primarily used for processing a subset of the records in a data file. For example,

```
SCAN FOR location = 'FL'
   ? lastname,firstname
ENDSCAN
```

5. A `LOOP` command may be included within the `DO WHILE` structure to bypass remaining commands and go directly to the `ENDDO` statement, in effect returning to the top of the `DO WHILE` structure to reevaluate the condition. Consider:

```
DO WHILE condition 1
   Statement 1
   IF condition 2
      LOOP
   ENDIF
   Statement 2
ENDDO
```

   We recommend, however, that `LOOP` statements be avoided (by reworking logic) as they violate the basic precepts of structured programming.
6. An `EXIT` command may be included within the `DO WHILE` structure to make an abnormal (premature) exit from the loop, by passing control directly to the first command after the `ENDDO`. We recommend, however, *against* the use of `EXIT`, as it, too, violates the precepts of structured programming.

Related Topics

88
DO CASE
IF...ELSE...ENDIF
SCAN

DTOC FUNCTION

Syntax

```
DTOC(<date expression>)
```

Discussion

The **DTOC()**, **D**ate **TO** **C**haracter function, converts a date expression to an equivalent character string. The argument of the function can be a date field, a date memory variable, the result of the **DATE()** function, the result of a **CTOD()** conversion function, or the result of an expression involving date arithmetic. The default format of the argument is mm/dd/yy, but that can be changed with the **SET DATE** and **SET CENTURY** commands.

The **DTOC()** function is required when storing a date (e.g., the system date or a date field) to a character-type memory variable, when replacing character-type fields with date-type data, or more importantly, when concatenating a date with a character string; for example,

```
STORE DTOC(DATE()) TO mdate
REPLACE cdate WITH DTOC(DATE())
? "Today is " + DTOC(DATE())
```

Not using the **DTOC()** function would, in the first example, result in a date variable being created rather than a character variable and would, in the next two examples, result in a *Data type mismatch* error.

Tips

1. If the display format of the date has been changed with the **SET DATE** command, the format of the character date returned by the **DTOC()** will reflect the change.
2. **SET CENTURY** must be **ON** for the **DTOC()** function to display a four-digit year. This is especially important if the century is other than the twentieth century.
3. In an index whose key expression consists of both a character and a date field, the date cannot simply be converted to character data with a **DTOC()** function. This is because character data is sequenced by comparing the characters one by one, beginning with the leftmost character, implying that all dates beginning with 01 come before dates beginning with 02, regardless of the year; for example, 01/01/88 would come before 02/15/87. Correction of this problem requires a **SET DATE ANSI** command to rearrange the date into yy/mm/dd format; e.g.,

   ```
   SET DATE ANSI
   INDEX ON location + DTOC(hiredate) TAG locdate
   ```

   or more simply a single **INDEX ON** command, using a **DTOS()** function:

   ```
   INDEX ON location + DTOS(hiredate) TAG locdate
   ```

Related Topics

```
CTOD()
DATE()
DTOS()
INDEX
SET CENTURY
SET DATE
```

DTOS FUNCTION

Syntax

```
DTOS(<date expression>)
```

Discussion

The **DTOS()**, **D**ate **TO** **S**tring function, converts a date expression to a character string, returning an eight-character string in the form **YYYYMMDD**. The argument of the function can be a date field, a date memory variable, the result of the **DATE()** function, the result of a **DTOC()** conversion function, a literal date enclosed in curly braces, or the result of an expression involving date arithmetic. For example,

```
STORE {12/25/92} TO mdate
? mdate
12/25/92 ——————————— dBASE response
? DTOS(mdate)
19921225 ——————————— dBASE response
```

The **DTOS()** function is used primarily when combining a date with a character string in the key expression of an index, as it preserves the correct chronological order for the date, e.g., **INDEX ON department + DTOS(app_date) TAG appdate**.

Tips

1. The format of the character string returned by the **DTOS()** function is **YYYYMMDD**, regardless of the settings of the **SET CENTURY** and **SET DATE** commands.
2. A date cannot be concatenated with a character field unless it is first converted to a character string, or a *Data type mismatch* error message will occur.
3. In an index whose key expression consists of both a character and a date field, the date cannot simply be converted to character data with a **DTOC()** function. This is because character data is sequenced by comparing the characters one by one, beginning with the leftmost character, implying that all dates beginning with 01 come before dates beginning with 02, regardless of the year; for example, 01/01/88 would come before 02/15/87. Correction of this problem requires either a **SET DATE ANSI** command to rearrange the date into yy/mm/dd format; e.g.,

   ```
   SET DATE ANSI
   INDEX ON location + DTOC(hiredate) TAG locdate
   ```

   or more simply a single **INDEX ON** command, using the **DTOS()** function:

   ```
   INDEX ON location + DTOS(hiredate) TAG locdate
   ```

Related Topics

```
DTOC()
SET CENTURY
SET DATE
```

EDIT

Syntax

```
EDIT [NOINIT] [NOAPPEND] [NOEDIT] [NODELETE] [NOFOLLOW]
    [NOMENU] [<scope>] [<record number>]
    [FIELDS <field list>] [WHILE <condition>]
    [FOR <condition>]
```

Discussion

EDIT is a full-screen command used to modify the contents of a record or group of records in the currently selected database. Issuing the command with no parameters, i.e., **EDIT**, displays the contents of every field for the current record, with the cursor positioned at the first character of the first field. The contents of any field can be modified by moving the cursor to the desired field with the up or down arrow keys and entering the necessary changes (using either the insertion or replacement modes, and/or by deleting characters). After editing the current record, the next (or previous) record may be edited by using the **PgUp** or **PgDn** key. The keystroke combinations used with the **APPEND** command pertain to **EDIT** as well (see Table PN.12), as do many of the principles for data entry.

Records may be appended to a file while in the **EDIT** mode by moving the cursor beyond the last record, producing the prompt, *Add new records? (Y/N)*. Answer Yes, and dBASE brings up a blank input template for data entry, exactly as it does in the **APPEND** mode.

The edit mode can be exited at any time by pressing **Ctrl+W or Ctrl+End** to save the changes made to all records, or by pressing the **Esc** key or **Ctrl+Q** to save all changes except those made to the current record.

The **NOINIT** clause causes dBASE to use the same command options as were used with the previous **EDIT** command.

The **NOAPPEND** clause prevents the appending of records while in the **EDIT** mode.

The **NOEDIT** clause prevents the editing of any of the displayed fields. However, records may still be appended and/or deleted.

The **NODELETE** clause prevents the deleting/recalling of records with **Ctrl+U**. Records may still be appended and/or edited.

The **NOFOLLOW** clause has an affect only when an index is in use, and further when the key field (according to the active index) is the field being edited. For example, if an index whose key is zip code is the master index, and a zip code is changed from 33124 to 10020, the screen display would normally shift immediately to the group of records beginning with zip code 10020. Specification of **NOFOLLOW**, however, will keep the display where it is (i.e., the records following 33124), even though the edited record has been logically moved. This is a very important clause when you are performing multiple edits, and you want to perform the edits in the order of the original logical sequence.

The **NOMENU** clause prevents access to the **EDIT** menu bar.

The **FIELDS** clause limits editing to those fields specified in the field list, as they are the only ones for which input templates are displayed on the screen. The fields will be listed in the order in which they appear in the field list, rather than their position in the file structure.

Inclusion of a **FOR** or **WHILE** condition will limit access to those records meeting the specified condition; e.g., **EDIT FOR location = 'FL'** allows editing of only those records with a location code of Florida. Note, too, that regardless of where the record pointer is positioned (e.g., on record 10), the first record meeting the condition is the record that is displayed, even if that record is above the current record. Pressing the **PgDn** key will then display the next record meeting the condition, rather than the next physical record (or next logical record in the case of an open index).

Tips

1. The contents of a memo field can be edited by positioning the cursor in the input template of the memo field and pressing **Ctrl+Home** or **F9** to activate the memo text editor. Text can then be entered and/or edited as with a word processor. (See

TABLE PN.12 **Keystroke Combinations for EDIT Command**

Keystroke	Function
→ or ←	Moves cursor one character to the right or left
↑ or ↓	Moves cursor up/down one field
`F3/F4` or `Shift+Tab/Tab`	Moves cursor to the previous/next field within the current record
`Home/End`	Moves cursor to beginning/end of the current field
`PgUp/PgDn`	Moves cursor to the previous/next record in the database file (accessing records in physical order of entry when no index is active, or in order according to the master index)
`Ins`	Toggles between the insert and replacement modes
`Del`	Deletes character the cursor is on
`Ctrl+Home`	Opens a memo field for editing
`Ctrl+Y`	Deletes all characters in the entry template of the present field, beginning at the cursor position
`Ctrl+U`	Marks/unmarks the current record for deletion (toggle switch)
`Ctrl+W, Ctrl+End`	Saves all appended records, including the current record, and returns to the dot prompt; saves changes to a memo field
`Ctrl+Q, Esc`	Saves all appended records except for the current record, and returns to the dot prompt
`F2`	Toggles between the `EDIT` and `BROWSE` screens
`Shift+F8`	Copies data in same field of previous record to the current record
`F9`	Toggles memo field open and closed, saving the edits
`F10`	Accesses the `EDIT` menu bar

MODIFY COMMAND for specifics regarding working with the dBASE text editor.) To exit the text editor, press **Ctrl+End** to save the memo text or the **Esc** key to exit without saving the text, at which point you will be returned to the full-screen **EDIT** mode to continue data entry.

2. The record number of the record to be edited can be specified in the **EDIT** command, e.g., **EDIT 5**, in which case the specified record is displayed rather than the current record. The **PgUp** and **PgDn** keys can then be used to access other records in the file for editing. If, however, the command **EDIT RECORD 5** is issued, only record 5 can be edited, and the **PgUp** and **PgDn** keys cannot be used to access other records.
3. A custom screen for data editing may be created with either a format or program file, which contains the appropriate **@...SAY...GET** commands. Custom screens enable you to supply more meaningful prompts for input templates, include necessary messages to guide data entry, and even restrict access to certain fields for security.
4. The **PgUp** and **PgDn** keys move between records according to the physical order of the database if no index is open, or according to the logical order of the open master index.
5. In the event that data is entered beyond the last position in an input template, the extra characters are made part of the next field. This can be prevented if **SET CONFIRM** is **ON**, which requires that the enter key be pressed at the end of every field (regardless of whether or not the field is filled) in order to move to the next field.
6. The appearance of the template within the **EDIT** mode can be changed with the **SET DELIMITERS**, **SET INTENSITY**, and **SET COLOR OF FIELDS** commands.
7. Editing is limited to the field list established by a **SET FIELDS** command. A **FIELDS** clause may also be included in the **EDIT** command to further limit the subset of

available fields; however, the **FIELDS** clause can specify only active fields, or else a *Variable not found* error message will result.

8. Deleted records are not accessed by the **EDIT** command if **SET DELETED** is **ON**, unless the record pointer is specifically moved to the deleted record with a **GOTO** command. Alternatively, an **EDIT RECORD** command may be used to explicitly specify the record number of a deleted record. The same holds true for records not meeting an active filter condition.
9. If **SET AUTOSAVE** is **OFF**, some of the newly appended records are stored in buffers and are not written to disk until the data file is closed; thus, the appended records may not be reflected in the directory until after the database file is closed. If **SET AUTOSAVE** is **ON**, however, each newly appended record is written to disk immediately, and the directory is updated after each addition.
10. The **F2** key can be used to toggle between the **EDIT** and **BROWSE** modes. The **EDIT** options specified are honored in the **BROWSE** mode, although if a scope, **FOR**, or **WHILE** clause is specified with the **EDIT** command, the **F2** key is disabled and the **BROWSE** mode cannot be accessed.
11. When called from the **BROWSE** mode with the **F2** key, the **EDIT** command respects all of the **BROWSE** options that were specified, except for **COMPRESS**, **FREEZE**, **LOCK**, and **WIDTH**.
12. The **F10** key can be used to display the **EDIT** menu bar.

Related Topics

```
APPEND
BROWSE
SET COLOR
SET CONFIRM
SET DELETED
SET DELIMITERS
SET FIELDS
SET FILTER
SET FORMAT
SET INTENSITY
SET MENU
```

EJECT

Syntax

```
EJECT
```

Discussion

The **EJECT** command issues a form feed to the printer, causing the paper to advance to the top of the next page. With a tractor feed printer, the paper has to be manually aligned initially and the printer set to top of form for the command to work properly. In addition, the form length setting in the printer should be consistent with the length of paper being used. Refer to the printer's manual for specific instructions.

Tips

1. The status of **SET PRINTER** does not affect the **EJECT** command; i.e., the command can be issued whether **PRINTER** is **ON** or **OFF**.
2. If the printer is not on-line when the command is issued, an error message will appear on the screen. In some cases the computer may even lock and require rebooting, a

situation that can result in data loss. To prevent this from happening from within a program, include a **PRINTSTATUS()** function prior to the **EJECT** command, to verify that the printer is on-line and ready for output.

3. An **EJECT** command is not needed if the row number in the current **@...SAY** command is less than the row number in the previous **@...SAY** command, as the form feed will be done automatically.
4. In some instances the last line to be printed is held in the print buffer and will not appear until the next printing operation begins. Issuing an **EJECT** command will force the line from the buffer as it advances the page, completing the report or listing.
5. The **REPORT FORM** command automatically issues a form feed before printing, unless a **NOEJECT** clause is specified.
6. The value of the **_padvance** system memory variable can be changed with a **STORE** command to **"LINEFEEDS"** to cause the **EJECT** command to issue a line feed rather than form feed. (The default value is **"FORMFEEDS"**.)

Related Topics

```
PRINTSTATUS()
REPORT FORM
SET DEVICE
SET PRINTER
```

EOF FUNCTION

Syntax

```
EOF([<alias>])
```

Discussion

The **EOF()**, **E**nd **O**f **F**ile function, indicates whether or not the record pointer has moved beyond the last record in the file, returning a logical value of true or false, respectively. The function is typically used in programs that process a file sequentially, from the first record to the last. A simple example of such a program, to print the name and salary for every record, is shown below:

```
USE solemp
DO WHILE .NOT. EOF()
   ? name,salary
   SKIP
ENDDO
```

The **EOF()** condition is considered true only when the record pointer has moved beyond the last record; i.e., it is not true when the record pointer is on the last record. Consider:

```
USE solemp
GO BOTTOM
? EOF()
.F.  ------------------------  dBASE response
SKIP 1
? EOF()
.T.  ------------------------  dBASE response
```

The **EOF()** function will not be reset to false until the record pointer is moved back into the file, e.g., by a **GO TOP** command.

Tips

1. The last logical record (according to the master index) will be considered the end of file, unless no index is open, in which case it is the last physical record.
2. Any attempt to move the record pointer beyond the last record in the file actually moves it to an end-of-file marker, with a record number one greater than that of the last record. This differs from the **`BOF()`** situation, where an attempt to move the record pointer above the first record leaves it set at record 1.
3. A separate value of the **`EOF()`** function is maintained for each of the ten available work areas. When testing for the condition in an unselected work area, the number of the work area or the name of the **`DBF`** file, enclosed in quotation marks, must be indicated within the parentheses. For example, **`? EOF(3)`** is used to indicate whether or not the record pointer has been moved beyond the last record in the file open in work area three, whereas **`? EOF("ZOO")`** tests the condition in the **`ZOO.DBF`** file in whichever area the file is open. **`EOF()`** with no work area specified tests the condition in the currently selected work area.
4. In general, commands that process all of the records in a database file (e.g., **`LIST`**, **`REPORT FORM`**, **`COPY FOR`**, **`DISPLAY FOR`**) set the **`EOF()`** function to true. In addition, unsuccessful **`LOCATE`**, **`FIND`**, and **`SEEK`** commands also set the function to true.

Related Topics

```
BOF()
RECNO()
SKIP
```

FIND

Syntax

```
FIND <character string/numeric value>
```

Discussion

The **`FIND`** command searches the key field of the master index for the first record matching the specified string or numeric value and, if a record is found, moves the record pointer to that record. The **`FIND`** command merely repositions the record pointer and does not display the found record; a subsequent **`DISPLAY`** command is needed to view the record. If the search is unsuccessful, a *Find not successful* message is displayed (as long as **`SET TALK`** is **`ON`**), and the record pointer is repositioned to the end of file.

The character string in a **`FIND`** command need not be enclosed in quotes unless leading blanks are an essential portion of the string. Note, however, that the command **`FIND Jones`** is different from the command **`FIND "    Jones"`**. Nor is it necessary to specify the complete character string being sought so long as **`SET EXACT`** is **`OFF`**. In other words, the command, **`FIND B`**, will position the record pointer at the first record whose key value begins with a "B", whereas the command, **`FIND Bor`**, will position the record pointer at the first record beginning with "Bor".

The requirement of the **`FIND`** command to use an active index implies that records with like values of the search key will be grouped together; i.e., if there is another record with the same key value, it will be sequenced immediately beneath the found record. Hence that record can be accessed with a **`SKIP`** command (to move the record pointer), and viewed with a **`DISPLAY`** command (to verify that the key does, in fact, match). Indeed, all records with the same key value can be retrieved by repeated **`SKIP`** and **`DISPLAY`** commands, until the value of the key field no longer matches the character string or numeric value specified in the original **`FIND`** command.

Tips

1. A numeric value used in a **FIND** command must be specified as a numeric constant, e.g., **FIND 11122**. Moreover, the **FIND** command will *not* search for a partial numeric value as it will for a partial character string; i.e., **FIND 111** will not retrieve a record whose key is 11122.
2. Upper- and lower-case letters are treated as different characters, regardless of whether **EXACT** is **SET ON** or **OFF**. For example, the command **FIND MILLER** will not find a key value of "Miller" or "miller".
3. **FIND** conducts a much more rapid search than does the corresponding **LOCATE** command. **FIND**, however, requires an index and limits the search to a value equal to the character string or numeric value. **LOCATE**, on the other hand, can search for values greater than, less than, or not equal to.
4. The **FIND** command can search for a character string stored in a memory variable, but only if the macro symbol (**&**) is used with the memory variable name. For example, the commands,

   ```
   STORE 'Borow' TO mname
   FIND &mname
   ```

   instruct dBASE to search for the value stored in **mname** rather than the character string "mname". However, the **FIND** command is so clumsy with memory variables that a parallel **SEEK** command is more likely to appear in program files. The **FIND** command is better used only at the dot prompt.
5. The **FIND** command cannot search for a numeric value stored in a memory variable, even if the macro symbol (&) is used with the memory variable name. Nor can numeric expressions such as **(newsalary - oldsalary)/oldsalary * 100** be used in the **FIND** command. (A **SEEK** command is required in both instances.)
6. Records not meeting an active filter condition are ignored by the **FIND** command. In similar fashion, records marked for deletion are also ignored when **SET DELETED** is **ON**.
7. When **SET NEAR** is **ON** and a matching record is not found, the record pointer is positioned at the record immediately below where the matching record should have been found, rather than at the end of file.

Related Topics

```
LOCATE
SEEK
SET DELETED
SET FILTER
SET NEAR
SKIP
```

FOUND FUNCTION

Syntax

```
FOUND([<alias>])
```

Discussion

The **FOUND()** function returns a logical value of true if the previous **FIND**, **SEEK**, **LOCATE**, or **CONTINUE** command was successful, false if it was not. The function is used to control program flow, based on the outcome of a search operation. For example,

```
SEEK mlast
IF FOUND()
   ? lastname, firstname, donation
ELSE
   ? "Record not in file"
ENDIF
```

The data from the designated fields will be printed if the indicated record is in the **DBF** file; the message *Record not found* will be printed if the record is not in the file.

Tips

1. A separate value of the **FOUND()** function is maintained for each of the ten available work areas. When testing for the condition in an unselected work area, the number of the work area or the name of the **DBF** file, enclosed in quotation marks, must be indicated within the parentheses. For example, **? FOUND(3)** tests the results of the last search operation in work area three, whereas ? **FOUND("zoo")** tests the condition for the **ZOO.DBF** file in whichever work area the file is open. **FOUND()** with no work area specified tests the condition in the currently selected work area.
2. The **IF FOUND()** syntax is equivalent to **IF .NOT. EOF()**, but is easier to read and recommended for that reason.

Related Topics

```
BOF()
CONTINUE
EOF()
FIND
IF
LOCATE
SEEK
```

GO/GOTO

Syntax

```
GO/GOTO [RECORD] <expN> [IN <alias>]
GO/GOTO TOP/BOTTOM [IN <alias>]
<record number>
```

Discussion

The **GO/GOTO** command positions the record pointer at a specified record, by providing either the record number or an expression from which the record number may be calculated.

Specification of **GO/GOTO TOP** will position the record pointer at record 1 if no index is active, or if an index is active, at the first record according to the logical order of the index. **GO/GOTO BOTTOM** functions in similar fashion, positioning the record pointer at the last physical record in the database if no index is active, or if an index is active, at the last record in the logical sequence of the index.

The record pointer may also be repositioned by entering just the record number at the dot prompt; e.g., entering the number 4 at the dot prompt will position the record pointer at record 4 and is equivalent to the command **GOTO 4**.

The use of a record number in the command always refers to the physical record number and not a record's relative position in the file. For example, **GO 4** (or simply **4**) moves the record pointer to record number 4 and not the fourth record in the file. This concept is important when an index is active, as record 4 and the fourth record will most likely not be the same record.

The **GO/GOTO** command will place the record pointer on records marked for deletion, even if **SET DELETED** is **ON**. In similar fashion, the command will also position the record pointer on records currently hidden from view by a **SET FILTER** command.

Tips

1. A numeric expression may be used in place of a record number; e.g., **GO 6/2** will position the record pointer to record 3.
2. After a **GO/GOTO** command has been executed, dBASE merely responds with another dot prompt. To verify that the record pointer has been positioned correctly, issue a **DISPLAY** command or a **? RECNO()** command.
3. For clarity in a program file, use the **GO/GOTO** form of the command, rather than just record number.
4. The **SKIP**, **FIND**, and **LOCATE** commands also reposition the record pointer.
5. The record pointer may be moved in an unselected work area by using the **IN<alias>** option; e.g., the commands **GO 3 IN 2** or **GO 4 IN SOLEMP** move the record pointer to record 3 in whichever file is open in work area 2, or to record 4 in the **SOLEMP.DBF** file regardless of the work area in which it is open.
6. If a relationship has been established between two files, moving the record pointer in the controlling file with a **GO/GOTO** command moves the record pointer to the related record in the dependent file.

Related Topics

```
FIND
LOCATE
SET DELETED
SET FILTER
SKIP
```

HELP

Syntax

```
HELP [keyword]
```

Discussion

The **HELP** command brings up the dBASE on-line help facility. If the command is entered with a keyword, e.g., **HELP DISPLAY**, the help screen specific to the keyword is brought up immediately. If, however, the command is entered without a keyword, i.e., **HELP**, the Dot Prompt Commands and Functions Menu is displayed instead.

Selections are made from the menu by highlighting the desired option and pressing the enter key or the **F4** key. The first three options on the menu present an alphabetical list of their respective commands, from which a command can be selected to obtain specific information on the command and its syntax. The System Memvars option presents a list of the system memory variables, their type, and their range of values. The Error Messages option presents a menu of potential error messages, from which a message can be selected and the possible reasons for its occurrence displayed.

The help facility is in actuality a nested series of menus, with the initial menu dependent on the context from which help was requested. The Dot Prompt Command and Functions menu, for example, is a submenu of the main Help System, and is displayed whenever help is requested from the dot prompt. Other menus include the Control Center, SQL Main Topics, Help on help, and Reference, any of which can be the initial menu, depending on the context from which help is requested. The **F3** key is used to access a higher-level menu, while the **F4** key will access a lower-level menu.

Information on the various commands/topics is organized like pages in a book. After a selection of a particular command or topic has been made, the **F3** and **F4** keys move to the previous and next help page (screen), respectively. Additionally, *buttons* are presented at the bottom of the screen that allow a choice of Contents (return to the current menu), Related Topics (display help on a related topic), Backup (return to previously displayed help screens), or Print (print the current help page). A button can be selected by highlighting it with the right or left arrow key and pressing the enter key.

The **Esc** key terminates the help facility and returns to the dBASE screen from which help was called.

Tips

1. The **F1** function key always brings up the **HELP** program; i.e., the **F1** key cannot be reprogrammed with the **SET FUNCTION** command, or with the **F1 = command** in the **CONFIG.DB** file.
2. If the **dBASE1.HLP** and **dBASE2.HLP** files are erased from the dBASE disk or subdirectory, the help facility will not be available.
3. **HELP** and **ASSIST** are not equivalent commands; i.e., **ASSIST** brings up the Control Center, whereas **HELP** provides descriptive information on dBASE commands and topics.
4. If an invalid command is entered (i.e., the syntax is improper), dBASE will automatically offer help unless **SET HELP** is **OFF**.
5. Even if **SET HELP** is **OFF**, the help facility can still be accessed by typing in **HELP** at the dot prompt, or pressing **F1**. In other words, the **SET HELP OFF** command controls the offer of help (when command syntax is incorrect), but does not affect its availability.
6. When returning from a help screen to the dot prompt, the help screen is not cleared until the enter key is pressed; the command is typed in while the correct syntax is still displayed on the screen.

Related Topics

ASSIST
SET HELP

IF

Syntax

```
IF <condition>
    <command>
[ELSE
    <command>]
ENDIF
```

Discussion

IF...ELSE...ENDIF is a structured programming command that evaluates a condition, then selects a course of action, depending on whether the condition is true or false. Indentation of commands under both **IF** and **ELSE** is not required by dBASE, but is highly recommended to make the program easier to read. The **ELSE** clause is optional, but when present, must be coded on a line by itself. **ENDIF**, however, is required to mark the end of the decision structure. In its simplest form:

```
IF <condition>
    <command>
ENDIF
```

every command between **IF** and **ENDIF** is executed if the condition is true. If, however, the condition is false, control passes immediately to the command after **ENDIF**. In its more complex form:

```
IF <condition>
    <command>
ELSE
    <command>
ENDIF
```

the command tests the condition and executes the commands between **IF** and **ELSE** if the condition is true. If, however, the condition is false, it executes the commands between **ELSE** and **ENDIF**. In either case (i.e., after the appropriate set of commands has been executed) control passes to the first command after **ENDIF**.

The condition in an **IF** statement may be any dBASE IV expression that can assume a value of either true or false, e.g., a comparison using relational operators, as in **IF age < 40**; a more complex comparison using **.AND.**, **.OR.**, or **.NOT.**, as in **IF age < 40 .AND. city = 'Chicago'**; a logical variable, such as **IF bill_pd**; or a function that is either true or false, such as **IF DELETED()** or **IF EOF()**.

The commands within the **IF...ELSE...ENDIF** structure may be any valid dBASE IV command, including another **IF** structure. Inclusion of one **IF** command within another is called nesting, an example of which is shown here:

```
IF condition1
    <commands if condition1 is true>
ELSE
    IF condition2
        <commands if condition2 is true>
    ELSE
        <commands if condition2 is false>
    ENDIF  (condition2)
ENDIF  (condition1)
```

In this example, $condition_2$ is evaluated only if $condition_1$ is false. Each **IF** has its own **ENDIF**, and the entire second **IF** command (the **IF** and its associated **ELSE** and **ENDIF**) is located completely within the first **IF** statement.

Tips

1. There may be only one **ELSE** statement for each **IF...ENDIF**.
2. **ELSE** and/or **ENDIF** refer to the closest previously unpaired **IF**. Be sure that all **ELSE** clauses are properly paired with the appropriate **IF**, and that there is an **ENDIF** for every **IF**.

3. Any text coded on the same line as **ENDIF** is ignored (i.e., treated as a comment). Accordingly, parenthetical information can be included to indicate a reference to the associated **IF**, and is especially helpful with multiple and/or nested ifs. For example:

```
IF EOF()
   RETURN
ELSE
   IF bill-pd
      ? 'The bill is paid'
   ELSE
      ? 'The bill is not paid'
   ENDIF (bill-pd)
ENDIF (eof)
```

4. Compound conditions may be evaluated with the use of the logical operators **.AND.** and **.OR.** However, the field name or memory variable must be repeated in each portion of a complex clause, even if the field or variable name is the same; e.g.,

```
IF choice = 0 .OR. choice = 9
```

5. The proper syntax for a logical field or variable is **IF <logical name>** or **IF.NOT. <logical name>**. In other words, you may *not* use **IF <logical name> = .T.** or, alternately, **IF <logical name> = .F.**
6. Consistent indentation (typically 3 spaces) within the structure is strongly recommended.
7. Nested **IF**s should not go beyond three levels or else they become too difficult to follow. A **DO CASE** command should be used instead.
8. **IF** cannot be used from the dot prompt.

Related Topics

DO CASE
DO WHILE
IIF()

IIF FUNCTION

Syntax

```
IIF(<logical expression>,<expression1>,<expression2>)
```

Discussion

The **IIF()** function (immediate **IF**) provides conditional processing in situations where an **IF...ELSE...ENDIF** cannot be used, e.g., at the dot prompt, in report forms, or in mailing labels. The function evaluates the logical expression and returns either expression$_1$ or expression$_2$, depending on whether the condition is true (expression$_1$) or false (expression$_2$).

The logical expression can be anything that evaluates to true or false. Expression$_1$ and Expression$_2$ can be expressions, constants, fields, or memory variables of any type.

Tips

1. The **IF..ELSE..ENDIF** command is more powerful and more conducive to structured programming; it should be used exclusively in program files in lieu of a comparable **IIF()** function. **IIF()** should be used only in instances where the other is not possible.

2. The `IIF()` function is useful as a content entry in report forms and/or mailing labels. Consider, for example, the situation in which a middle initial is not always present, and where it is desirable to eliminate the extra space that would appear if no initial were supplied. An `IIF()` function could be used as a content entry as follows:

Command is entered on one line

```
IIF(initial = " ",TRIM(firstname) + " " + lastname,
   TRIM(firstname) + " " + initial + " " + lastname)
```

3. The `IIF()` function can prevent calculations that do not make sense, as well as calculations whose execution would produce erroneous results. The following `LIST` command lists the last name, salary, and percent salary increase (where appropriate) for all employees in the currently selected database file.

Command is entered on one line

```
LIST lastname,salary,IIF(oldsalary =
   0,0,(salary-oldsalary)/oldsalary * 100)
```

The percent salary increase is computed only for employees who have a nonzero value for old salary (i.e., new employees would not have an old salary and hence no increase could be determined). Note, too, that in the absence of the `IIF()` function, any attempt to compute a percent salary increase where the old salary did not exist would result in division by zero.

4. The `IIF()` function can be used to enhance the unappealing `.T.` or `.F.` normally displayed for logical variables. Consider:

Command is entered on one line

```
LIST lastname,IIF(fee-paid,"Fee has been
   paid","Fee has not been paid")
```

The `LIST` command would display the last name of every person in the file, together with an indication of whether or not the fee has been paid. The results of such a command are clearer and more attractive than a display showing just a `.T.` or an `.F.`

5. Nested (embedded) `IIF()` functions are also possible, though in general are not recommended. Consider:

Command is entered on one line

```
? IIF(size = "S", "Small",IIF(size =
   "M","Medium","Large"))
```

The function will display "Small" if the size equals `"S"`, "Medium" if the size = `"M"`, and "Large" otherwise.

6. Expression$_1$ and expression$_2$ do not have to be of the same data type.

Related Topics

```
CREATE LABEL
CREATE REPORT
IF...ELSE...ENDIF
```

INDEX ON

Syntax

```
INDEX ON <key expression> TO <.ndx filename>/TAG <tag name>
   [OF <.mdx filename>] [UNIQUE] [DESCENDING]
```

Discussion

The **INDEX ON** command creates either a *tag* in a *multiple index file* (**MDX**) or an entirely new *single index file* (**NDX**) associated with the currently selected database file. An index allows a **DBF** file to be processed in a logical sequence different from the physical order in which the records were appended. The index itself contains only the key expression and corresponding record number of every record in the database file.

A multiple index file can contain up to 47 indexes, each identified by a tag name. The same naming conventions are used for index tags as for field names. They may be ten characters long, must begin with a letter, and can consist of letters, numbers, and the underscore. Each database file may have one production **MDX** file, which is created when the database file is created. It is assigned the same filename as the database file, but given an **MDX** extension, and is automatically opened/closed whenever the database file is opened/closed. New tags are added to the production **MDX** file with the **TAG** clause, e.g., **INDEX ON lastname + firstname TAG alpha**. Tags can be created in a multiple index file other than the production **MDX** by using the **OF** clause, e.g., **INDEX ON zipcode TAG zipcode OF newindex**.

Single index files (**NDX**) are created with the **TO** clause, and have been included in dBASE IV primarily to maintain compatibility with dBASE III Plus. They need rarely, if ever, be used, and then only when the files will be used with dBASE III Plus also. Most of the information that applies to **MDX** files also applies to **NDX** files, unless otherwise noted.

Indexes are, by default, created in ascending order. The key expression can be a single character, numeric, or date field, or it can be an expression involving several fields; note, however, that while the key expression can be up to 220 characters in length, the evaluated result of that expression cannot exceed 100 characters. The data type of the expression determines whether the records are ordered alphabetically (character expression), numerically (numeric expression), or chronologically (date expression). When the key expression consists of multiple fields, they must all be of the same data type or be converted to the same data type by using the appropriate dBASE functions. Multiple keys are listed in the expression according to their importance, with the most important (primary) key listed first, the next most important (secondary) key listed next, and so on, down to the least important key.

The **UNIQUE** option results in an index file that has only one entry for each value of the key field, so that if two or more records have the same key value, only the first record encountered will be included in the index. Specification of the **UNIQUE** clause produces the same results as indexing the file when **SET UNIQUE** is **ON**.

Tips

1. Indexes based on a single field are more easily created through the **CREATE** or **MODIFY STRUCTURE** command. The **INDEX ON** command is typically used to create indexes whose keys are complex expressions or are in descending order.
2. A memo field cannot be used in the key expression of an **INDEX** command, either as a single field or as part of a complex expression. A logical field can be used only if it is first converted to a character field with an **IIF()** function; e.g.,

```
INDEX ON IIF(paid,"T","F")+lastname TAG paidname
```

3. When an index is created, it becomes the controlling (master) index, and the data file will be processed in the logical order of that index. There may be multiple indexes open at one time, but there can be only one master index.
4. The **SET INDEX** and **SET ORDER** commands change the master index. The **SET INDEX** command opens **NDX** files and independent **MDX** files, whereas the **SET ORDER** command changes the master index to a tag or index file that is already open. Note, also, that the **SET INDEX** command first closes any open **NDX** or **MDX** files (other than the production **MDX** file) and then opens only the listed files, whereas the **SET ORDER TO** command establishes a new master index without closing any other open index **NDX** or **MDX** files.
5. Whenever possible, a tag name should reflect the expression used to create the index, as doing so causes the name to indicate the sequence of the index.

6. When converting data types for use in key expressions, the **STR()** function is used to convert a numeric field to character data, and the **DTOS()** function is used to convert a date field to character data; e.g.,

```
INDEX ON STR(donation,3)+lastname TAG donlast
INDEX ON DTOS(donor_date)+lastname TAG datename
```

7. An index can be created according to the results of a calculation; e.g.,

```
INDEX ON (new-old)/old*100 TAG increase
```

   Although the index is based on the result of the calculation, the database file has not been modified to include the result. Hence, to display the result with the file, the calculation itself would have to be included in a **DISPLAY** or **LIST** command.
8. Updating a database file will automatically update all open indexes (those in the production **MDX** file as well as those explicitly opened with a **SET INDEX TO** command). If any indexes (e.g., independent **MDX** files or **NDX** files) were not open when the database file was updated, the nonopen indexes must be subsequently opened and reindexed. This is extremely important as opening an out-of-date index does not produce an error message, just unreliable results.
9. The **INDEX ON** command operates on the entire database. Records marked for deletion are included in the index even if **SET DELETED** is **ON**, as are records not matching the active filter condition.
10. An index can be created on any (character, numeric, or date) field in the file structure, even if that field is not included in an active field list.
11. The **SORT** command should not be used to physically sequence a file, as sorting a large file is quite time consuming. Index the file instead, then copy the file to a new file with the index open. The original database file can then be deleted, and the new file renamed with the name of the original file. The same procedure should be used periodically on heavily updated index files, as processing slows remarkably when the logical and the physical order grow more disparate.
12. If the target of an **INDEX ON** command has the same name as an existing file, and the status of **SET SAFETY** is **ON**, dBASE will ask before overwriting the index. If, however, **SET SAFETY** is **OFF**, the index will be overwritten with no warning.
13. If the **TAG** clause is used when creating an index, without specifying an **OF** clause, the tag is placed in the production **MDX** file.
14. The **DESCENDING** clause, used to create indexes in descending order, can be used only when creating tags in an **MDX** file. Additionally, it applies to the entire key expression, and cannot be applied to only one field of a key expression using several fields.
15. Single **NDX** files are not automatically opened when the **DBF** file is opened, but must be explicitly opened with a **USE...INDEX** command or with a **SET INDEX TO** command; e.g.,

```
USE student INDEX major
```

   or

```
USE student
SET INDEX TO major
```

   where **student** is the **DBF** file and **major** is the single index file.

Related Topics

```
CREATE STRUCTURE
DTOS()
MODIFY STRUCTURE
REINDEX
SET DELETED
SET FILTER
SET INDEX
SET ORDER
SET SAFETY
SET UNIQUE
SORT
STR()
USE
```

INSERT

Syntax

```
INSERT [BLANK] [BEFORE]
```

Discussion

The **INSERT** command displays an input template, enabling a single record to be added to the active database, immediately *below* the current record. Hence, if the command is issued when the record pointer is on record six, an input template for record seven will be displayed (and all of the remaining records will be renumbered after the insertion). Only one record at a time may be inserted, so that after data for the new record has been entered, control is returned to the dot prompt.

Data entry is accomplished in the same way as in the **APPEND** mode, except that paging to previous or subsequent records is not allowed. (See Table NB.8 in the discussion of the **APPEND** command.) Pressing **Ctrl+W** or **Ctrl+End** will save the inserted record, whereas the **Esc** key cancels the insertion.

Inclusion of the **BLANK** clause causes a blank (empty) record to be inserted immediately below the current record, without displaying the input template. The record pointer is repositioned at the blank record, from where an **EDIT**, **BROWSE**, or **REPLACE** command can be used to enter data.

Specification of the **BEFORE** clause inserts the new record immediately above the current record rather than below. **BEFORE** and **BLANK** may appear together in the same command; e.g., **INSERT BLANK BEFORE** inserts a blank record above the current record.

Tips

1. Multiple records can be appended if the **INSERT** command is issued when the record pointer is on the last record; i.e., **INSERT** will function identically to **APPEND** when the record pointer is so located.
2. If an index is active when the **INSERT** command is issued, the new record will be appended to the end of the database, regardless of where the record pointer is positioned. The record pointer is then on the last record, and multiple records can be appended if desired.
3. If a field list has been established with the **SET FIELDS** command, the input template will contain only the active fields.

Related Topics

APPEND
SET FIELDS

ISCOLOR FUNCTION

Syntax

```
ISCOLOR()
```

Discussion

The **ISCOLOR()** function returns a logical value of true if the current display is a color monitor, false if it is not. The function is used to set the display colors or monochrome attributes accordingly. For example,

```
IF ISCOLOR()
   SET COLOR TO W/R
ELSE
   SET COLOR TO W+
ENDIF
```

The program segment specifies white text on a red background for the standard display area for a color monitor and high-intensity text in a monochrome environment.

Tips

1. The **ISCOLOR()** function can be used at the beginning of a program to establish different settings for use at different points in the program. For example,

```
IF ISCOLOR()
   STORE "W+/B,R/W" TO color1
   STORE "W/B,R/W" TO color2
   STORE "R/B,R/W" TO color3
ELSE
   STORE "W+/N,N/W" TO color1
   STORE "W/N,N/W" TO color2
   STORE "W+/N,N/W" TO color3
ENDIF
```

   Commands to change the screen colors could then be issued at various points in the program as follows:

```
SET COLOR TO &mcolor1
```

Related Topics

&
SET COLOR

JOIN

Syntax

```
JOIN WITH <alias> TO <filename> FOR <condition>
    [FIELDS <field list>]
```

Discussion

The JOIN command creates a new database by merging records from the currently selected database with records from a second open database, as identified in the WITH clause of the command. The file structure of the new file contains all of the fields in the current database together with all of the fields in the second database, unless a field list is included, in which case the new file contains only the listed fields. Duplicate field names are not permitted, so that if the same field name is present in both files, only the field from the currently selected file is copied. (To include the field name from the unselected file instead, precede the field name with the file alias.)

The joining process begins by setting the record pointer to the first record in the currently selected database. Every record in the second file is checked against the FOR condition, and whenever a match is found, data from the two records is combined to form a single record in the new (joined) file. After all of the records in the second file have been evaluated, the record pointer is positioned to the next record in the current database. The second file is again searched record by record for a matching condition, and again whenever a match is found, data in the two records is combined to form a new record in the joined file. This process is repeated for every record in the currently selected database.

Consider, for example, a banking application that maintains two distinct files, for accounts and customers, respectively. (One customer can have several accounts, but each account can be associated with only one customer.) The commands,

```
SELECT 2
USE customer
SELECT 1
USE account
JOIN WITH customer TO custacct FOR c_id = customer->c_id
```

will combine data from the existing customer and account files into a new file, CUSTACCT.DBF, which has as many records as the original account file. However, each record in the new file will have the corresponding customer data appended to the account data.

Tips

1. The joining process is expensive in terms of time and space requirements, especially when large databases are involved. The SET RELATION command provides a faster and more efficient way to relate two databases.
2. The maximum number of fields in the joined file cannot exceed 255, and any fields beyond this number are lost from the second file. For example, if the currently selected file contains 200 fields and the second file contains 100, only the first 55 fields from the WITH file are included, with the remainder being discarded.

Related Topics

SET RELATION
SET SQL

LABEL FORM

Syntax

```
LABEL FORM <label filename> [<scope>] [SAMPLE]
    [WHILE <condition>] [FOR <condition>]
    [TO PRINTER/TO FILE <filename>]
```

Discussion

The **LABEL FORM** command merges data from the currently selected **DBF** file with the specified label form, printing the generated labels to the screen. The default scope is **ALL**, so one label will be created for every record in the **DBF** file, unless a scope, **FOR**, or **WHILE** clause is included in the command. The labels are printed according to the logical sequence of the master index, or if no index is open, according to the physical order of the file.

After the labels are generated, the record pointer is repositioned at the end of the file, unless **NEXT** is indicated as the scope or a **WHILE** condition is included. Specification of the **NEXT** parameter repositions the record pointer at the last record listed (unless **NEXT** goes beyond the end of file, in which case the record pointer is set to the end of file), whereas a **WHILE** condition moves the record pointer one record beyond the last record meeting the specified condition.

The **TO PRINTER** clause produces the labels on the printer as well as the screen. The **SAMPLE** clause provides the opportunity to align labels in the printer before the labels are generated by printing a row of dummy labels with X's to indicate positioning. After the dummy labels are printed, dBASE displays the message *Do you want more samples?*, so that rows of dummy labels can continue to be printed until the alignment is satisfactory. The **TO FILE** clause directs the output to a file, which can be subsequently modified with a word processor.

Tips

1. The labels panel in the control center provides simplified but limited access to capabilities available through the **LABEL FORM** command.
2. When a **LABEL FORM** command is executed, dBASE checks to see if an **LBO** file exists. If not, the label form is compiled and the resultant **LBO** file is executed. When a label form file is edited, dBASE deletes the old **LBO** file from the disk so that the modified label form will be recompiled when the labels are subsequently generated.
3. The printed output of the **LABEL FORM** command is not restricted to mailing labels per se, but can also be used for other forms where a "mailing label" format is appropriate, e.g., envelopes and Rolodex cards.
4. All necessary **DBF** files and their associated indexes must be opened prior to the **LABEL FORM** command being issued. Additionally, if the label form references fields from unselected work areas, the proper relationships must have been previously set.
5. A label form can be used with any **DBF** file that has a structure compatible with the one that was open when the form was designed.
6. Mailing labels are generated only for those records meeting an existing filter condition. In similar fashion, labels are not generated for any records marked for deletion when **SET DELETED** is **ON**.
7. An error message will be displayed if the label form includes fields not specified in the active field list; i.e., all fields in the label form must appear in any current **SET FIELDS** command.
8. The **SET CONSOLE OFF** command, when used in a program file, will suppress the screen display during printing. Remember to set the console back on when the printing is complete, so that processing can proceed normally; e.g.,

   ```
   SET CONSOLE OFF
   LABEL FORM employee TO PRINTER
   SET CONSOLE ON
   ```

   The **SET CONSOLE OFF** command has no effect from the dot prompt.
9. ASCII characters may be sent to printer prior to actual printing, perhaps to specify compressed print or some other option; e.g.,

   ```
   ??? CHR(15)
   LABEL FORM employee
   ??? CHR(18)
   ```

   Although the ASCII character 15 is shown in the example, it is by no means universally used by all printers. (Consult your own printer manual for specifics.) Remember, too, to restore the printer to normal printing as soon as the labels are completed.

10. An error will occur if the printer is not on-line when a **LABEL FORM** command is issued. In some cases the computer may lock and require rebooting, possibly resulting in data loss. It is advisable, therefore, to test the value of the **PRINTSTATUS()** function prior to printing.

Related Topics

```
CHR()
CREATE/MODIFY LABEL
PRINTSTATUS()
REPORT FORM
SET CONSOLE
SET DELETED
SET FIELDS
SET FILTER
SET PRINTER
SET RELATION
```

LEN FUNCTION

Syntax

```
LEN(<character expression>)
```

Discussion

The **LEN()** function returns the number of characters in the specified character expression, which can be a character field, memory variable, memo field, character expression enclosed in quotes, concatenated character expression, or the result of a function that returns a string. The **LEN()** function is illustrated in the following table, in which "Chris" and "Anderson" have been stored to the memory variables, **mfirst** and **mlast**, respectively.

Function	Value
LEN(mfirst)	5
LEN(mlast)	8
LEN(mfirst + mlast)	13
LEN("Chris Anderson")	14

Tips

1. Specification of a character field as the argument of a **LEN()** function returns the field length as defined in the file structure, not the length of the data entered into the field. Specification of a memory variable as the argument returns the actual length of the data entered into the variable.
2. The **TRIM()** function physically deletes trailing blanks so that they are no longer counted by the **LEN()** function. For example, if Milgrom is stored in the character field **lastname** (defined as a 12-position field in the file structure), the functions **LEN(lastname)** and **LEN(TRIM(lastname))** return lengths of 12 and 7, respectively.
3. The **LEN()** function can be used to center the screen display of messages produced by a program; e.g.,

```
STORE "Please enter another option" TO message
@ 20,(80 - LEN(message))/2 SAY message
```

The length of the message is first subtracted from 80 (the number of characters that can fit across the screen) to determine the number of blank spaces remaining on the line. This value is then divided by two to obtain the starting column of the message (effectively centering the message).

Related Topics

```
@...SAY
TRIM()
```

LINENO FUNCTION

Syntax

```
LINENO()
```

Discussion

The **`LINENO()`** function returns the line number of the next command to be executed and is used primarily with the debugger to create breakpoints. It can also be used with any custom routine to track down errors in program execution.

The **`LINENO()`** function is entered in the breakpoint window of the debugger as follows:

```
LINENO() = 56
```

The debugger will pause when line 56 is reached, with the cursor positioned at the **`ACTION`** prompt. You can then elect to view the expressions in the display window, edit the program, or exit to the dot prompt, from where more debugging alternatives can be explored.

1. The **`PROGRAM()`** function returns the name of the current program or procedure, and is used in similar fashion to the **`LINENO()`** command.
2. The current value of **`LINENO()`** can be displayed with the **`?`** command, e.g., **`? LINENO()`**.

Related Topics

```
?
DEBUG
PROGRAM()
```

LIST

Syntax

```
LIST [OFF][<scope>][<expression list>]
     [WHILE <condition>]
     [FOR <condition>][TO PRINTER]
```

Discussion

The **`LIST`** command displays information about records in the currently selected **`DBF`** file. The default scope is **`ALL`**, and the default expression list contains every field; thus, a **`LIST`** command with no additional parameters displays every field for every record. A **`FOR`** and/or **`WHILE`** condition can be included to limit the records that are displayed, just as specification of an expression list will restrict the fields that are shown. Records are listed in the physical order of the database file unless there is an active index, in which case they are listed according to the logical sequence of the index.

After listing the records, the record pointer is positioned at the end of the file, unless **NEXT** is indicated as the scope or a **WHILE** condition is included. Specification of the **NEXT** parameter repositions the record pointer to the last record listed (unless **NEXT** goes beyond the end of file, in which case the record pointer is set to the end of file), whereas including a **WHILE** condition moves the record pointer one record beyond the last record meeting the specified condition.

An expression list can be included to show only selected fields and/or to display complex expressions; e.g.,

```
LIST ssn,initials,lname
LIST ssn,TRIM(initials) + ' ' + lname
LIST ssn,(salary2-salary1)/salary1*100
```

The screen display is always preceded by a heading line, which includes the field names (or expressions) of the individual fields. The width of each expression is determined by either the field width (as established by the file structure) or the width of the heading, whichever is greater.

The contents of a memo field are not displayed unless the field name is specified in an expression list. Omission of the memo field name displays the word "memo" in lower case if the field does not contain any text, and in upper case if text is present. The default display width for a memo field is 50 columns, but that can be modified with the **SET MEMOWIDTH** command.

The **OFF** parameter suppresses the display of the record number. The **TO PRINTER** clause echoes the results of the command to the printer. The **TO FILE** option directs the output to a disk file.

Tips

1. The **LIST** command begins with the first record in the file (or the first record according to the active index) unless **NEXT** or **REST** is specified as the scope parameter. Inclusion of **NEXT** (or **REST**) causes the command to begin with the current record.
2. When a record is too long to be displayed on one line, the output is wrapped to the next line(s), making it difficult to determine which data belongs to which field, especially when multiple records are displayed. The **SET FIELDS** command or an expression list can be used to limit the display to the essential fields and avoid the wrap to the next line(s).
3. The heading line shows the field names and expressions exactly as they were entered in the command line; i.e., if the command was typed in upper case, the heading line will also be in upper case.
4. The heading line can be suppressed with the **SET HEADING OFF** command, a useful procedure when using a long or complex expression.
5. Deleted records will not be listed if **SET DELETED** is **ON**. The same principle holds for records not matching the condition established by a **SET FILTER** command; i.e., records not matching the filter condition are treated as if they were not in the file.
6. Fields from database files in other than the currently selected work area can be displayed by including the file alias with the field name in the command; e.g.,

   ```
   LIST ssn,lname,location->loccode
   ```

   This is usually done only when a **SET RELATION** command is in effect.
7. The **LIST** command does not pause between screens when the display requires more than a single screen; i.e., the display continues to scroll until the last record is listed. (This is the major difference between **LIST** and **DISPLAY ALL**, which pauses every 20 lines). You can, however, press **Ctrl+S** to interrupt the listing, then press any key to continue. You can also press the **Esc** key to cancel the command entirely.

Related Topics

```
?/???
DISPLAY
SET DELETED
SET FIELDS
SET FILTER
SET HEADING
SET MEMOWIDTH
SET RELATION
```

LIST HISTORY

Syntax

```
LIST HISTORY [TO PRINTER]
```

Discussion

The **LIST HISTORY** command displays the same information as the **DISPLAY HISTORY** command, but without pausing between screens. (See the **DISPLAY HISTORY** command for additional information.)

LIST MEMORY

Syntax

```
LIST MEMORY [TO PRINTER]
```

Discussion

The **LIST MEMORY** command displays the same information as the **DISPLAY MEMORY** command, but without pausing between screens. (See the **DISPLAY MEMORY** command for additional information.)

LIST STATUS

Syntax

```
LIST STATUS [TO PRINTER]
```

Discussion

The **LIST STATUS** command displays the same information as the **DISPLAY STATUS** command, but without pausing between screens. (See the **DISPLAY STATUS** command for additional information.)

LIST STRUCTURE

Syntax

```
LIST STRUCTURE [TO PRINTER]
```

Discussion

The **LIST STRUCTURE** command displays the same information as the **DISPLAY STRUCTURE** command, but without pausing between screens. (See the **DISPLAY STRUCTURE** command for additional information.)

LOCATE

Syntax

```
LOCATE [<scope>][WHILE <condition>][FOR <condition>]
```

Discussion

The **LOCATE** command searches the currently selected database for the first record meeting the specified **FOR** condition. A successful search displays the record number (as long as **SET TALK** is **ON**) and repositions the record pointer to that record. If, however, the search is unsuccessful (i.e., no record is found), the message *End of LOCATE scope* is displayed, and the record pointer is repositioned at the end of file (or end of scope, if one was specified).

The **LOCATE** command begins its search with the first record in the file, and continues until a record is found or the end of file is reached, whichever occurs first. Inclusion of a scope parameter and/or a **WHILE** condition will, however, alter the way in which the search is performed. A scope of **NEXT** begins at the current (rather than first) record, and continues only through the specified number of records. A scope of **REST** also begins at the current record, but continues through the remainder of the file or until a record is found. A **WHILE** condition also begins at the current record, but continues only until the condition is no longer true.

Additional records meeting the search condition are found with the **CONTINUE** command; i.e., **CONTINUE** causes dBASE to search for the next record meeting the condition in the most recently executed **LOCATE** command. A successful search moves the record pointer to that record, from where another **CONTINUE** command may be issued, and so on, until all of the records meeting the condition have been located. Eventually an *End of LOCATE scope* message will appear, at which point the record pointer will have been moved to the end of file.

Tips

1. **LOCATE** can be used to search for values equal to, greater than, or less than the specified condition, and does not require a master index. **FIND** and **SEEK**, on the other hand, can search only the key field of the master index for equal values.
2. The **LOCATE** command does not display the found record, but merely repositions the record pointer to that record. A subsequent **DISPLAY** command is necessary to view the record.
3. Only one search condition can be in effect at any one time in any one work area, although a different condition can be in effect for each of the ten available work areas. If a particular work area is left and later reactivated, the last search condition is retained. Be sure, however, that the record pointer has not been repositioned since the last record was found, or the results of the search may be unreliable when subsequent **CONTINUE** commands are issued.

4. When **SET EXACT** is **OFF**, a match is found if the characters in the search string match the characters in the same positions in the field value, even if the strings are of different lengths; e.g.,

```
LOCATE FOR lastname = 'B'
```

will find the first record in which the last name begins with the letter B. Note, however, that case is always considered, and that B does not match b, even when **SET EXACT** is **OFF**.
5. Records not meeting the filter condition are ignored by the **LOCATE** operation. In similar fashion, records marked for deletion are also ignored when **SET DELETED** is **ON**.
6. The search condition can include a field that was not specified in the field list established by a **SET FIELDS** command.

Related Topics

CONTINUE
FIND
SEEK
SET DELETED
SET EXACT
SET FIELDS
SET FILTER

LOWER FUNCTION

Syntax

```
LOWER(<character string>)
```

Discussion

The **LOWER()** function converts all of the upper-case letters in the specified character string to their lower-case equivalents. The argument may be a character string, character field, memory variable, or a concatenated string expression, as shown in the following table:

Function Code	Nature of the Argument
LOWER("THIS IS A STRING")	Character string
LOWER(lastname)	Character field
LOWER(memname)	Memory variable
LOWER("TODAY IS " + DTOC(DATE()))	Concatenated string

Tips

1. The **LOWER()**, **UPPER()**, and **SUBSTR()** functions can be combined to convert the initial character in a field to upper case, and the remaining characters to lower case; i.e.,

Command is entered on one line

```
REPLACE lname WITH UPPER(LEFT(lname,1)) +
    LOWER(SUBSTR(lname,2))
```

A single **REPLACE** command can be used to make this same substitution for every record in the currently selected **DBF** file by specifying a scope of **ALL**.

2. Most systems allow the user to respond in upper or lower case, complicating the process of data validation. The problem is solved by converting the response to a uniform standard (either upper or lower), and then testing for only one set of permitted responses. For example, in a system in which **A**, **B**, **C**, or **D** or (**a**, **b**, **c**, or **d**) are valid, the following code would suffice:

```
@ 10,20 GET response PICTURE A
STORE LOWER(response) to response
IF response < 'a' .OR. response > 'd'
   @ 12,2 SAY 'Please respond with a, b, c, or d'
ENDIF
```

Related Topics

```
LEFT()
SUBSTR()
UPPER()
```

LTRIM FUNCTION

Syntax

```
LTRIM(<character expression>)
```

Discussion

The **LTRIM()** function strips leading blanks from a character expression. The expression may be a character field, memory variable, character string enclosed in quotes, or a concatenated string. The **LTRIM()** function is especially useful when working with a string produced as a result of the **STR()** conversion function, in that the latter often contains leading blanks. Consider, for example, the difference in two concatenated strings, with and without the **LTRIM()** function:

Without the **LTRIM()** function:

```
? "Your raise is " + STR(raise,7) + " dollars"
Your raise is     750 dollars
```

With the **LTRIM()** function:

```
? "Your raise is " + LTRIM(STR(raise,7)) + " dollars"
Your raise is 750 dollars
```

Tips

1. The **LTRIM()** function can improve the appearance of lists, report forms, and/or mailing labels by using it in a field entry to concatenate character data.

Related Topics

```
CREATE LABEL
CREATE REPORT
RTRIM()
STR()
TRIM()
```

MAX FUNCTION

Syntax

MAX(<expression$_1$>,<expression$_2$>)

Discussion

The **MAX()** function returns the larger of two expressions of the same data type; i.e., it compares two numeric, two date, or two character expressions and selects the larger of the two. The function, **MAX(1000,salary * .05)**, for example, multiplies the salary value in the current record by 0.05, compares it to 1000, and returns the larger of the two values. The function, **MAX({12/25/92},{01/31/93})**, returns the date 01/31/93, as it is the later of the two dates; while the function, **MAX("Black","Rice")**, returns the character string "Rice".

The **MAX()** function can be used for conditional processing or display purposes at the dot prompt, within a report or label form, or in any other situation where an **IF...ELSE...ENDIF** structure cannot be used. You could, for example, update records from the dot prompt to reflect a 5% across the board salary increase, with a minimum raise of $1,000, using the command:

```
REPLACE ALL salary WITH MAX(salary + 1000,salary * 1.05)
```

In similar fashion, a report form can be constructed to reflect the new salary level by entering the same **MAX()** function with the appropriate field entry.

Tips

1. The **MAX()** function cannot be used to search all records in a **DBF** file to find the maximum value in a particular field. The **MAX()** option of the **CALCULATE** command is used instead; e.g. **? CALCULATE MAX(salary)** would return the largest salary in the **DBF** file.

Related Topics

```
CALCULATE
IIF()
MIN()
```

MIN FUNCTION

Syntax

```
MIN(<expression1>,<expression2>)
```

Discussion

The `MIN()` function returns the smaller of two expressions of the same data type; i.e., it compares two numeric, two date, or two character expressions and selects the smaller of the two. The function, `MIN(1000,salary * .05)`, for example, multiplies the salary value in the current record by 0.05, compares it to 1000, and returns the smaller of the two values. The function, `MIN({12/25/92},{01/31/93})`, returns the date 12/25/92, as it is the earlier of the two dates; while the function `MIN("Black","Rice")`, returns the character string "Black".

The `MIN()` function can be used for conditional processing or display purposes at the dot prompt, within a report or label form, or in any other situation where an `IF...ELSE...ENDIF` structure cannot be used. You could, for example, update records from the dot prompt to reflect a 5% across the board salary increase, with a maximum raise of $1,000, using the command:

```
REPLACE ALL salary WITH MIN(salary + 1000,salary * 1.05)
```

In similar fashion, a report form can be constructed to reflect the new salary level by entering the same `MIN()` function with the appropriate field entry.

Tips

1. The `MIN()` function cannot be used to search all records in a **DBF** file to find the minimum value in a particular field. The `MIN()` option of the `CALCULATE` command is used instead; e.g. `? CALCULATE MIN(salary)` would return the smallest salary in the **DBF** file.

Related Topics

```
CALCULATE
IIF()
MAX()
```

MODIFY COMMAND

Syntax

```
MODIFY COMMAND/FILE <filename>
     [WINDOW <window name>]
```

Discussion

`MODIFY COMMAND` activates the dBASE IV text editor and is used primarily to create and/or edit program (**PRG**) and format (**FMT**) files, although it can also be used to create or edit any standard ASCII text file.

The text editor may be invoked with or without specification of the desired filename; i.e., if no filename is specified, dBASE will prompt for one. dBASE will then search for the named file and, if it exists, load it into memory for editing. If, however, no file with that name exists, a new file is opened and a clear screen presented for text entry. The `MODIFY COMMAND` text

TABLE PN.13 **Keystroke Combinations for MODIFY COMMAND**

Keystroke	Task
→ or ←	Moves cursor one character to the right or left
↑ or ↓	Moves cursor to the previous line or to the next line
`Home/End`	Moves cursor to the beginning/end of current line
`PgUp/PgDn`	Moves cursor to previous/next screen
`Ctrl+PgUp/Ctrl+PgDn`	Moves cursor to beginning/end of file
`Tab` or `Shift+Tab`	Moves cursor to next/previous tab stop
`Ctrl+Enter`	Saves and continues editing
`Ctrl+End, Ctrl+W`	Saves and exits
`Esc`	Exits without saving
`F6`	Begins select block operation
`F7`	Moves block
`F8`	Copies block
`Ctrl+N, Enter` key	Adds a blank line at cursor
`Ctrl+Y`	Deletes current line
`Del` key	Deletes character at cursor or selected block
`Shift+F5`	Specifies search string; searches forward from current cursor position
`Shift+F3`	Searches for *previous* occurrence of search string
`Shift+F4`	Searches for *next* occurrence of search string
`Shift+F6`	Searches and replaces
`Ctrl+KR`	Reads a disk file into current file
`Ctrl+KW`	Writes selected block to separate disk file

editor displays a *ruler line* immediately beneath the menu bar, with square brackets to indicate the margins, and triangles to indicate tab stops. The default margins are 1 and 1024, and cannot be changed in the **MODIFY COMMAND** mode.

Table PN.13 summarizes the keystroke combinations to be used with the text editor. As indicated in the table, advanced word processing features such as a search-and-replace are available, meaning that an external word processor is no longer required to create more complex programs as it was with dBASE III Plus. Note, too, that most of the operations described in Table NB.13 can also be performed by making selections from the menu bar.

The **WINDOW** option displays the text editor in a previously defined window. Prior to executing **MODIFY COMMAND**, the window must have been defined with a **DEFINE WINDOW** command or restored to memory with a **RESTORE WINDOW** command. If no window definition exists, dBASE displays a *Window name not found* error message.

Tips

1. Every line in a program file must end with a hard carriage return.
2. The drive and directory designators may be specified with the filename, to create and/or edit files in other than the default directory.
3. Any time an existing file is edited, and the edited version is saved, the previous version is saved as a backup file with an extension of **BAK**.
4. **MODIFY COMMAND** supplies the default extension of **PRG** when a file is created; thus, if a different extension (e.g., **FMT**) is desired, it must be specified explicitly when assigning the filename. In similar fashion, when searching for the file named in the **MODIFY COMMAND** instruction, dBASE will look only for files with a **PRG** extension unless a different extension is specified; e.g., **MODIFY COMMAND STOCK.FMT**.
5. **MODIFY FILE** is an alternative syntax for this command. In this form of the command, no default extension is assigned to the filename, and any extension desired must be explicitly specified.

6. The maximum file size is limited more by the available disk space than by the dBASE file size limitation. The text editor can handle 32,000 lines of 1,024 characters each, resulting in a maximum file size of 32,768,000 bytes. Program files should not even begin to approach this limit.
7. As indicated, the maximum line length is 1,024 characters. However, a command line that extends beyond 80 characters is difficult to read (and print), so it may be preferable to manually divide the line at a logical breakpoint by typing a semicolon (;), pressing the enter key, and continuing the command on the next line. The semicolon prevents dBASE from interpreting the hard carriage return at the end of the line. Continued lines can be indented for clarity, but remember that the command continues with the first character of the next line, and hence you must be careful not to omit any necessary spaces.
8. In theory, an external word processor may be used instead of the dBASE text editor by including a `TEDIT =` command in the `CONFIG.DB` file. In practice, however, sophisticated word processors are too large to load in this manner. Another option to consider is the use of a RAM resident utility, such as Sidekick, but again memory problems may interfere with complex operations.
9. Block operations can be performed by first selecting the text to be processed and then executing the desired operation. To select text, move to the beginning of the block and press `F6` (Extend Select). Highlight the desired block by using the cursor keys and then press the enter key to complete the selection. The block may then be moved, copied, deleted, or written to a separate file by using the keystrokes as indicated in Table PN.13.
10. To move the cursor to a specific line number, select the Go To Menu from the menu bar.
11. A hard copy of a `PRG` file or `FMT` file may be obtained with the command, `TYPE <filename.ext> TO PRINTER`, or by selecting the Print menu from the menu bar. The latter method is preferable when debugging, as programs may be printed with line numbers, a helpful tool since error messages always indicate a line number.
12. Memo fields cannot be edited with `MODIFY COMMAND`.

Related Topics

```
CONFIG.DB
DEBUG
DEFINE WINDOW
RESTORE WINDOW
RUN
SAVE WINDOW
TYPE
```

MODIFY LABEL

Syntax

```
MODIFY LABEL <filename>
```

Discussion

The discussion on the `MODIFY LABEL` command is essentially identical to that which was presented for the `CREATE LABEL` command. (See the `CREATE LABEL` command for additional information.)

MODIFY QUERY

Syntax

```
MODIFY QUERY <filename>
```

Discussion

The discussion on the **MODIFY QUERY** command is essentially identical to that which was presented for the **CREATE QUERY** command. (See the **CREATE QUERY** command for additional information.)

MODIFY REPORT

Syntax

```
MODIFY REPORT <filename>
```

Discussion

The discussion on the **MODIFY REPORT** command is essentially identical to that which was presented for the **CREATE REPORT** command. (See the **CREATE REPORT** command for additional information.)

MODIFY SCREEN

Syntax

```
MODIFY SCREEN <filename>
```

Discussion

The discussion on the **MODIFY SCREEN** command is essentially identical to that which was presented for the **CREATE SCREEN** command. (See the **CREATE SCREEN** command for additional information.)

MODIFY STRUCTURE

Syntax

```
MODIFY STRUCTURE
```

Discussion

The **MODIFY STRUCTURE** command displays the file structure of the currently selected database file, allowing new fields to be added and/or existing fields to be edited or deleted. The screen display is the same as for the **CREATE** command, except that the **MODIFY STRUCTURE** command displays existing information in the templates. The keystroke combinations for the **CREATE** command are applicable as well (see Table NB.10), as is the general discussion and tips.

The **MODIFY STRUCTURE** command automatically creates a temporary copy of the structure of the original **DBF** file, with no data in it, and makes the changes to this temporary copy. After the changes have been made and saved, records from the original **DBF** file are appended to the file with the changed structure. Then the original file is renamed with a **DBK** extension, and the modified file is made the **DBF** file. If there is an associated memo field file (**DBT**), a backup is also made and given an extension of **TBK**. The rules for copying the data to the new file are quite precise and depend on whether fields were added or deleted, field names were changed, field widths increased or decreased, and field types altered.

As might be expected, a newly created field will be blank in the modified file, whereas data for a field that was deleted will be irretrievably lost. Changing the name of an existing field produces a prompt, asking if the original data should be copied from all fields; an affirmative response will copy the data into the renamed field, whereas a negative response results in its loss.

Increasing the field width of an existing field does not pose any problems; decreasing the width, however, will truncate character data if it is too long to fit in the modified field, and will convert numeric data to asterisks.

Changing the field type does not result in data loss, provided the original data is consistent with the new type. A date field, numeric field, or logical field can be changed to a character field without data loss. A character field in a date format can be converted to a date field without difficulty, but converting a character field to a numeric field will result in data loss if nonnumeric data is encountered. (Numeric characters will be converted to digits until a nonnumeric character is encountered. If the first character in the field is nonnumeric, the data will be converted as a zero.) A logical field cannot be converted to a numeric field.

Tips

1. Field names and widths should not be changed in the same session of **MODIFY STRUCTURE**, even if they are being changed for different fields, as data will be lost for the field whose name is changed. If it is necessary to modify both names and widths, change the name in one session and the width in another.
2. A field's name and its type should not be changed in the same session of **MODIFY STRUCTURE**. Change each separately, issuing two **MODIFY STRUCTURE** commands.
3. Do not insert/delete fields and change the name of a field in the same session of **MODIFY STRUCTURE**.
4. If you modify the name, type, or width of a field for which an index tag exists in the production **MDX** file, the index will be rebuilt.
5. Backup files will not be created if there is insufficient room on the disk. However, since data is easily lost during a **MODIFY STRUCTURE** session, you should make sure that there is enough room on the disk to accommodate the backup files.

Related Topics

CREATE

MODIFY VIEW

Syntax

```
MODIFY VIEW <filename>
```

Discussion

The discussion on the **MODIFY VIEW** command is essentially identical to that which was presented for the **CREATE QUERY** command. (See the **CREATE QUERY** command for additional information.)

MONTH FUNCTION

Syntax

```
MONTH(<date expression>)
```

Discussion

The **MONTH()** function returns a numeric value from 1 to 12, corresponding to the month in the specified date expression. The argument in the **MONTH()** function may assume several different forms as shown in the following table:

Function	Nature of the Argument
MONTH(hiredate)	Date field
MONTH(memdate)	Date memory variable
MONTH(DATE())	**DATE()** function itself
MONTH{12/25/92}	Literal date
MONTH(CTOD(hiredate))	**CTOD()** conversion function
MONTH(DATE() + 10)	Expression with date arithmetic

Tips

1. If the argument of a **MONTH()** function is a character string enclosed in quotes or a character field or memory variable, it must first be converted to a date-type variable with the **CTOD()** conversion function. The shorthand format using curly braces is often easier and more convenient, but may be used only with a literal date; i.e., it cannot be used with a character string enclosed in quotes or with a character field or memory variable. (Note that a literal date is *not* enclosed in quotes as is a date expressed as a character string.)

Related Topics

CMONTH()
CTOD()
DATE()
DAY()
STR()
YEAR()

MOVE WINDOW

Syntax

```
MOVE WINDOW <window name> TO <row,col>/BY
    <delta row,delta col>
```

Discussion

The **MOVE WINDOW** command repositions the named window to a new location on the screen. If the window is active when the command is issued, the relocation is effective immediately, moving both the window and its contents; if, however, the window is not active, it will be positioned at the new location when it is next activated. In either case the new coordinates become a permanent part of the window definition, and a new **MOVE WINDOW** command is necessary to return the window to its original location.

The **TO** clause specifies *absolute* row and column coordinates for the upper-left corner of the window; e.g., the command **MOVE WINDOW win1 TO 5,10** moves the window named **win1** so that its upper-left corner is in row 5, column 10. The **BY** clause, on the other hand, executes a *relative* move, specifying the number of rows and/or columns that the window should be moved from its current position. The window is moved down if the delta row integer is positive, up if it is negative. Similarly, the window is moved to the right if the delta column integer is positive, to the left if it is negative. Thus, the command **MOVE WINDOW win2 BY 6,12** moves the upper-left corner of the window down six rows and right twelve columns, whereas the command **MOVE WINDOW win2 BY -3,-10** moves the window up three rows and left ten columns.

A *Coordinates are off the screen* message is displayed if the window will not fit on the screen at its new location, and the window is not moved.

Tips

1. The window definition must be in memory prior to executing a **MOVE WINDOW** command; i.e., once the window definition has been released or cleared, the window can no longer be assigned a new screen location.

Related Topics

```
ACTIVATE WINDOW
CLEAR WINDOWS
DEACTIVATE WINDOW
DEFINE WINDOW
RELEASE WINDOWS
RESTORE WINDOW
SAVE WINDOW
```

ON ERROR/ESCAPE/KEY

Syntax

```
ON ERROR <command>
ON ESCAPE <command>
ON KEY [LABEL <keyname>][<command>]
```

Discussion

The **ON ERROR/ESCAPE/KEY** command executes the indicated program when an error occurs, the **Esc** key is pressed, or a specified key is pressed. The commands are used for *event trapping* in application programs by interrupting the normal program flow and transferring control to an error or help routine. Control returns to the original program (at the point where it left off) when the called routine terminates.

The **ON ERROR** trap is triggered when a dBASE IV error, such as a syntax or evaluation error, occurs. The **ON ERROR** command prevents the normal interruption of the program and the associated error message, and sends control to a programmer-supplied error routine. The latter may use the **ERROR()** function to evaluate the generated error number and/or the **MESSAGE()** function to output the associated error message. A list of error messages and their associated error numbers can be found in the *dBASE IV Language Reference.*

The **ON ESCAPE** trap is triggered when the user presses the **Esc** key. The **ON ESCAPE** command is similar to the **ON ERROR** command in that it prevents program interruption and, instead, sends control to an error or help routine. The **ON ESCAPE** command will work only if **SET ESCAPE** is **ON**.

The **ON KEY** command transfers control to the specified routine when any key is pressed. Inclusion of the **LABEL** clause, however, transfers control only for a specific keystroke or keystroke combination. The key name is entered without quotation marks and can be any keyboard character, typically a function key or function key combination. (See the **SET FUNCTION** command.)

Event trapping is disabled by issuing the command without any parameters; for example, **ON ERROR** disables error trapping.

Tips

1. The **ON ERROR** trap is disabled until the called routine has terminated. Thus, if **ON ERROR** is needed within the called routine, a second **ON ERROR** command is required within the called routine.
2. The order of precedence in event trapping is **ON ERROR**, **ON ESCAPE**, and then **ON KEY**. Thus, if both the **ON KEY** and **ON ESCAPE** commands have been issued, the **ON ESCAPE** routine will be executed when the **Esc** key is pressed, as it takes precedence.
3. The **ON KEY** trap takes effect immediately in the **APPEND**, **EDIT**, **BROWSE**, and **INSERT** modes or when a **READ** command, bar menu, or popup menu is active. Other commands—such as **SORT**, **INDEX**, and **LIST**—will complete execution prior to responding to the trapped keystroke.
4. The **ON ESCAPE** trap takes effect immediately, regardless of the command being executed. Therefore, you can include an **ON ESCAPE** trap in a program to press the **Esc** key to interrupt a list or print command.
5. The **ON KEY** command can be used to trap the **Esc** key when **SET ESCAPE** is **OFF**.
6. The **ON KEY** command takes precedence over the **SET FUNCTION TO** command if both reference the same function key.
7. All three commands can be used in the same program.

Related Topics

SET ESCAPE
SET FUNCTION

ON PAD

Syntax

```
ON PAD <pad name> OF <menu name>
    [ACTIVATE POPUP <popup>]
```

Discussion

The **ON PAD** command activates the specified popup menu when the indicated pad is highlighted on the named bar menu. The pad and menu names in the **ON PAD** command must match the corresponding entries in the **DEFINE PAD** and **DEFINE MENU** commands, respectively. Additionally, the referenced popup menu must have been previously built by:

1. Defining the name and location of the popup menu with a **DEFINE POPUP** command.
2. Defining the individual menu options (called *bars*) through a series of **DEFINE BAR** commands.
3. Specifying the action to be taken as a result of making a selection from the menu with an **ON SELECTION POPUP** command.

4. Writing the program and/or procedure referenced by the **ON SELECTION POPUP** command.

For example,

```
***Commands to define the bar menu
DEFINE MENU bar1
DEFINE PAD add OF bar1 AT 3,2 PROMPT "ADD"
DEFINE PAD edit OF bar1 AT 3,10 PROMPT "EDIT"
DEFINE PAD quit OF bar1 AT 3,18 PROMPT "QUIT"
ON PAD add OF bar1 ACTIVATE POPUP popmenu
ON SELECTION PAD edit OF bar1 DO editprg
ON SELECTION PAD quit OF bar1 DEACTIVATE MENU

***Commands to define the popup menu
DEFINE POPUP popmenu FROM 4,2
DEFINE BAR 1 OF popmenu PROMPT "ACCOUNT FILE"
DEFINE BAR 2 OF popmenu PROMPT "CUSTOMER FILE"
ON SELECTION POPUP popmenu DO addprg

***Activate the bar menu
ACTIVATE MENU bar1


***Procedure called when a selection is made from popup
    menu
PROCEDURE addprg
DO CASE
   CASE BAR() = 1
        DO acctadd
   CASE BAR() = 2
        DO custadd
ENDCASE
```

If the **ACTIVATE POPUP** clause is omitted, the pad is disabled and has no effect when highlighted or selected.

Tips

1. The **ON PAD** command is used to attach a popup menu to a pad, so that the popup menu is "pulled down" whenever the pad is highlighted. To associate a popup menu with a pad in a bar menu, *without* the popup menu appearing when the pad is highlighted, the user must specify an **ACTIVATE POPUP <popup name>** command in an **ON SELECTION PAD** command. For example,

   ```
   ON SELECTION PAD add OF bar1 ACTIVATE POPUP addpop
   ```

   The user will have to press the enter key when the pad name is highlighted to cause the popup menu to appear.
2. Only one bar menu can be active at one time, although a bar menu and an attached popup menu can both be active simultaneously. The commands to select from each of the menus differ, so that dBASE can differentiate between the two. For example, pads are highlighted on a bar menu with the right and left arrow keys, whereas bars are highlighted on a popup menu with the up and down arrow keys. Similarly, options are selected from a bar menu with **Alt** and the first letter of the option name, and from a popup menu by just pressing the first letter of the option name.
3. When the actions associated with the selected bar of the popup menu are exhausted, the popup menu reappears on the screen and another bar can be selected.
4. The popup menu is deactivated when another pad is highlighted on the bar menu.

Related Topics

ACTIVATE MENU
ACTIVATE POPUP
BAR()
DEACTIVATE MENU
DEACTIVATE POPUP
DEFINE BAR
DEFINE MENU
DEFINE PAD
DEFINE POPUP
ON SELECTION PAD
ON SELECTION POPUP
PROMPT()

ON SELECTION PAD

Syntax

```
ON SELECTION PAD <pad name> OF <menu name> [<command>]
```

Discussion

The **ON SELECTION PAD** command specifies the action taken when the specified pad is selected from the named bar menu. The pad and menu names in the **ON SELECTION PAD** command must match the corresponding entries in the **DEFINE PAD** and **DEFINE MENU** commands, respectively. Consider:

```
DEFINE MENU bar1
DEFINE PAD add OF bar1 AT 3,2 PROMPT "ADD"
DEFINE PAD edit OF bar1 AT 3,10 PROMPT "EDIT"
DEFINE PAD quit OF bar1 AT 3,18 PROMPT "QUIT"
ON SELECTION PAD add OF bar1 DO addprg
ON SELECTION PAD edit OF bar1 DO editprg
ON SELECTION PAD quit OF bar1 DEACTIVATE MENU
ACTIVATE MENU bar1
```

The command to be executed can be any valid dBASE IV command, including a **DO** command to call another program or procedure. When the actions associated with the selected pad are exhausted, the menu reappears on the screen and another pad can be selected.

Tips

1. The programs associated with the **ON SELECTION PAD** commands (e.g., **ADDPRG.PRG** and **EDITPRG.PRG**) must be available prior to activating the menu.
2. The **ON PAD** command is used to attach a popup menu to a pad, so that the popup menu is "pulled down" whenever the pad is highlighted. To associate a popup menu with a pad in a bar menu *without* the popup menu appearing when the pad is highlighted, specify an **ACTIVATE POPUP <popup name>** in an **ON SELECTION PAD** command. For example,

   ```
   ON SELECTION PAD add OF bar1 ACTIVATE POPUP addpop
   ```

   The user will have to press the enter key when the pad name is highlighted to cause the popup menu to appear.
3. If the **ON SELECTION PAD** command does not specify a command to be executed, the pad is disabled and has no effect when selected.

Related Topics

```
ACTIVATE MENU
DEACTIVATE MENU
DEFINE BAR
DEFINE MENU
DEFINE PAD
ON PAD
```

ON SELECTION POPUP

Syntax

```
ON SELECTION POPUP <popup name>/ALL [<command>]
```

Discussion

The **ON SELECTION POPUP** command specifies the command to be executed when a selection is made from the named popup menu. The command can be any valid dBASE IV command, but is typically a **DO** command to transfer control to a program or procedure. In addition, if the associated **DEFINE POPUP** command did not use the **PROMPT** clause, the program will most likely contain a **DO CASE** structure to evaluate the user's selection and transfer control accordingly. For example,

```
DEFINE POPUP mainmenu FROM 6,25 TO 17,54
DEFINE BAR 1 OF mainmenu PROMPT "ADD"
DEFINE BAR 2 OF mainmenu PROMPT "EDIT"
DEFINE BAR 3 OF mainmenu PROMPT "QUIT"
ON SELECTION POPUP mainmenu DO mainprg
ACTIVATE POPUP mainmenu

PROCEDURE mainprg
DO CASE
   CASE BAR() = 1
    DO addrec
   CASE BAR() = 2
    DO editrec
   CASE BAR() = 3
    DEACTIVATE POPUP
ENDCASE
```

Execution of **ON SELECTION POPUP** without a specified command disables the active popup menu; i.e., its options can be highlighted, but not selected.

Tips

1. When the actions associated with the selected bar are exhausted, the menu reappears on the screen and another bar can be selected.
2. The **ALL** clause causes the same command to be executed when a selection is made from a popup menu, regardless of which previously defined popup menu is activated.

Related Topics

```
ACTIVATE POPUP
BAR()
CLEAR POPUPS
DEFINE BAR
DEFINE POPUP
PROMPT()
RELEASE POPUPS
```

PACK

Syntax

```
PACK
```

Discussion

The **PACK** command physically removes all records marked for deletion from the active **DBF** file. The records are permanently removed and can no longer be recalled (recovered). Note, too, that since there are no scope, **FOR**, or **WHILE** clauses associated with the command, every marked record is affected. After the **PACK** operation has been completed, the records are renumbered and all open indexes rebuilt.

Tips

1. Records marked for deletion should be checked prior to issuing a **PACK** command so that erroneously marked records can be recalled. A listing of the records slated for deletion can be obtained with either of the following commands:

   ```
   DISPLAY ALL FOR DELETED()
   LIST TO PRINTER FOR DELETED()
   ```

2. The **PACK** command does not save a backup copy of the **DBF** file prior to deleting the records. Should there be any doubt about the records being deleted, execute a **COPY** command prior to the **PACK**.
3. After a **PACK** command has been issued, the space previously used by the deleted records is free for use by the system. The space is not, however, made available until after the file has been closed. In similar fashion, if **SET AUTOSAVE** is **OFF**, the **DIR** command does not reflect the decrease in file size until the file has been closed.
4. **ZAP** is equivalent to the combination of a **DELETE ALL** and **PACK** command. The **ZAP** command will irretrievably remove every record in the database, leaving only an empty file structure.

Related Topics

```
DELETE
RECALL
SET AUTOSAVE
ZAP
```

PARAMETERS

Syntax

```
PARAMETERS <parameter list>
```

Discussion

The **PARAMETERS** command is the means by which data is passed to a called program or procedure and then returned to the calling program. It must be the first executable statement in a program, or the first executable line after the **PROCEDURE** header.

When a program is called, data is sent via the **WITH** clause of the **DO** command in the calling program, e.g., **DO prog1 WITH msalary,mincrease,mnewsalary**. Each parameter in the **WITH** clause can be any legitimate dBASE IV expression. Values are passed *sequentially* to the memory variables in the **PARAMETERS** command, requiring that the number of parameters in the **WITH** clause equal the number of memory variables in the **PARAMETERS** command. The names of the parameters in the **WITH** clause do *not* have to be the same as those in the **PARAMETERS** command.

The values of the parameters are passed back to the calling program when control is returned, including values that were changed by the called program. Consider:

```
STORE 10000 TO msalary
STORE .10 TO mincrease
STORE 0 TO mnewsalary
DO raise WITH msalary,mincrease,mnewsalary
? mnewsalary

PROCEDURE raise
PARAMETERS msal,minc,mnew
STORE msal*(1+minc) TO mnew
RETURN
```

The value of **mnewsalary** is calculated by the procedure, and the result is passed back to the calling program, which displays 11000 as a result of the **? mnewsalary** command.

Tips

1. A *Wrong number of parameters* error message is displayed if the number of parameters in the **DO** command does not equal the number in the **PARAMETERS** command.
2. The use of parameters permits a generalized procedure to perform specific tasks, according to the needs of the calling program. For example, the procedure, PRINTMSG,

```
PROCEDURE PRINTMSG
PARAMETERS message,mrow,mcol
@ mrow,mcol SAY message
RETURN
```

displays a message at a given location, depending on the values passed to it by the calling program. Thus, given the following program,

```
STORE 20 TO mrow
STORE 10 TO mcol
STORE 'Please enter a Y or N' TO msg
DO printmsg WITH msg,mrow,mcol
```

the message will be displayed at row 20, column 10, whereas the program below,

```
STORE 12 TO mrow
STORE 15 TO mcol
STORE 'Please enter option' TO msg
DO printmsg WITH msg,mrow,mcol
```

will display a different message at row 12, column 15.

3. The **WITH** option can pass up to 64 parameters to a single procedure.
4. The memory variables defined in the **PARAMETERS** command are released when control is returned to the calling program.

Related Topics

DO
PROCEDURE
RELEASE
STORE

PRINTSTATUS FUNCTION

Syntax

```
PRINTSTATUS()
```

Discussion

The **PRINTSTATUS()** function returns a logical value of true if the printer is ready, false if it is not. It is used to determine if a print operation can be executed, or whether a message should be displayed to the user to bring the printer on-line. For example,

```
DO WHILE .NOT. PRINTSTATUS()
   @ 20,10 SAY "Turn printer on—press any key to continue"
   SET CONSOLE OFF
   WAIT
   SET CONSOLE ON
ENDDO
REPORT FORM salaries TO PRINT
```

Tips

1. It is entirely possible that the computer will lock and require rebooting if the printer is not on-line when a print command is issued. (This is true regardless of whether the printing results from a **SET PRINTER** command, **SET DEVICE** command, **Ctrl+P** command, or a **TO PRINTER** clause.) It is always advisable, therefore, to test the value of **PRINTSTATUS()** before printing.

Related Topics

SET CONSOLE
SET DEVICE
SET PRINTER
WAIT

PRIVATE

Syntax

```
PRIVATE <memvar list>
PRIVATE ALL [LIKE/EXCEPT <skeleton>]
```

Discussion

Memory variables created within a program are, by default, private, making them available to only that program or those programs that it calls. Thus, the **PRIVATE** command is needed only when a local memory variable has the same name as a variable in a higher-level program, to prevent interference between the two. The higher-level variable will be "hidden" until control is returned to the calling program, at which time it is reinstated with its original value intact.

The **ALL** parameter declares all memory variables in the program private, whereas the **LIKE/EXCEPT** option declares only a subset of the memory variables private, depending on whether they match (**ALL LIKE**) or do not match (**ALL EXCEPT**) the specified skeleton. The skeleton can use either or both of the wild card characters, i.e., the * and the **?**. The * matches one or more characters from its position in the variable name, whereas the **?** matches any single character in the exact position.

Private memory variables are released from memory when control returns to the calling program or the dot prompt.

Tips

1. The **SAVE** command saves all or some of the currently active memory variables to a file, from where they can be restored to memory. The restored variables are public if the **RESTORE** command is executed from the dot prompt; the variables are private (local to the program) if the **RESTORE** command is executed from within a program. To restore variables as public from within a program, declare them public and issue a **RESTORE** command with the **ADDITIVE** option.
2. Private memory variables that will be needed in future sessions must be saved prior to termination of the program in which they are contained, or they will be released when the program ends.
3. A common prefix should be chosen for a subset of memory variables that will be declared private so that the **LIKE/EXCEPT** clause can be used.
4. **ALL LIKE** and **ALL EXCEPT** are mutually exclusive; i.e., they *cannot* appear in the same command.
5. A **DISPLAY MEMORY** command can be used to view the contents of memory variables in a suspended program, as well as the names of the programs in which they were created. Memory variables that are hidden from view are marked as such.

Related Topics

PUBLIC
RELEASE
RESTORE
SAVE

PROCEDURE

Syntax

```
PROCEDURE <procedure name>
```

Discussion

The **PROCEDURE** command is the first line in a (subroutine or) procedure. The procedure may be located in the program file in which it is called, in another program file, or in a separate file that contains only procedures. Regardless of its location, a procedure is executed with a **DO** command that searches first for a like-named procedure, and if none is found, for a like-named program. (See the **DO** command for specifics.)

All procedures begin with the **PROCEDURE** header and end with a **RETURN** command to transfer control back to the calling program. In between is an optional **PARAMETERS** command to pass data to and from the calling program, and (of course) the commands to carry out the designated task of the procedure.

The use of parameters permits a generalized procedure to perform a specific task according to the values of the passed parameters. For example, the procedure, **PRINTMSG,** shown below, accepts two parameters, a message and the row in which the message is to appear. The procedure centers the message in the indicated row (after first clearing the row of any previous text).

```
PROCEDURE printmsg
PARAMETERS message,mrow
@ mrow,1 CLEAR TO mrow,80
@ mrow,(80 - LEN(message))/2 SAY message
RETURN
```

Once established, the procedure can be called from one or several programs, each time with different parameters. For example:

```
STORE 12 TO mrow
STORE 'Please enter a Y or N' TO message
DO printmsg WITH message,mrow
.
  .
    .

STORE 20 TO mrow
STORE 'Please enter option' TO message
DO printmsg WITH message,mrow
```

The messages will be centered in rows 12 and 20, respectively.

Tips

1. A procedure name can be up to eight characters long, can consist of letters, numbers, and an underscore, and must begin with a letter.
2. The individual procedures in a procedure file should be separated from one another with a blank line to make each procedure easily identifiable.
3. A procedure located in a procedure file cannot be accessed until the procedure file is opened with a **SET PROCEDURE TO** command.
4. Any frequently used routine should be coded as a procedure. If the routine is used by only one program, it should be stored within that program, whereas if it is used by many different programs, it should be coded as part of a separate procedure file.

5. The same procedure file can be used by many different applications.
6. A procedure file may contain as many procedures as the available memory will permit, up to 1,170 procedures per file. dBASE maintains a list of all of the available procedures at the beginning of every **DBO** file, whether the procedures are a part of the file itself or called from a separate procedure file.

Related Topics

```
DO
PARAMETERS
RETURN
SET PROCEDURE TO
```

PROMPT FUNCTION

Syntax

```
PROMPT()
```

Discussion

The **PROMPT()** function returns the **PROMPT** expression corresponding to the bar or pad most recently selected from a popup or bar menu. Its most important use is in conjunction with the *pick lists* created when a popup menu has been defined with a **PROMPT** clause. The **PROMPT FIELD** option of the **DEFINE POPUP** command causes the data values in the specified field to become the bars of the popup menu, the **PROMPT FILES** option causes file names to become the bars of the popup menu, and the **PROMPT STRUCTURE** option causes the field names in the currently selected **DBF** file or view to become the bars of the popup menu.

Once an item is selected from the pick list, dBASE does not automatically process the selection; i.e., choosing a field value does not move the record pointer to that field, nor does selecting a file name open that file. Instead, the instructions to process the selected item must be included in the program or procedure named in the **ON SELECTION POPUP** command.

The **PROMPT()** function returns the character string equivalent of the text from the selected bar and can be used to carry out actions based on the user's choice. Consider:

```
LOCATE FOR lastname = PROMPT()
REPORT FORM PROMPT() TO PRINT
```

The **LOCATE** command is appropriate for a menu defined with the **PROMPT FIELD** option and moves the record pointer to the selected record. The **REPORT FORM** command could be used with a menu defined through the **PROMPT FILES** option as it produces a report according to the selected report form.

Tips

1. The **PROMPT FIELD** option of the **DEFINE POPUP** command can specify only a field name; a field expression may *not* be used.
2. Pressing the **Esc** key in response to the active menu causes the **PROMPT()** function to return a null value.

Related Topics

```
BAR()
DEFINE POPUP
ON SELECTION POPUP
```

PUBLIC

Syntax

```
PUBLIC <memvar list>
```

Discussion

The **PUBLIC** command declares one or more memory variables global, making them accessible to all programs, including higher-level programs, and causing them to be retained in memory even after the program in which they were created is terminated. By contrast, a memory variable that is not made public is released from memory as soon as the program in which it was created returns control to its calling program or to the dot prompt.

Tips

1. Changes made to any variable in a called program are passed back to the calling program.
2. A memory variable must be declared public before it is initialized.
3. A memory variable declared as private in one program may have the same name as a memory variable declared as public in a higher-level program; i.e., changes made to the private variable during execution of the lower-level program will not interfere with the original value of the like-named public variable. The latter is, in fact, hidden until the private memory variable is released from memory, at which time it is reinstated with its original values intact.
4. The **SAVE** command saves all or some of the currently active memory variables to a file, from where they can be restored to memory. The restored variables are public if the **RESTORE** command is executed from the dot prompt; the variables are private (local to the program) if the **RESTORE** command is executed from within a program. To restore variables as public from within a program, declare them public and issue a **RESTORE** command with the **ADDITIVE** option.
5. Private memory variables that will be needed in future sessions must be saved prior to termination of the program in which they are contained, or they will be released when the program ends.
6. A **DISPLAY MEMORY** command can be executed at the dot prompt to view the contents of the public memory variables.
7. System memory variables are, by default, public; their values may be changed in a program, but their original values will be reinstated when the program terminates.

Related Topics

PUBLIC
RELEASE
RESTORE
SAVE

QUIT

Syntax

```
QUIT
```

Discussion

The **QUIT** command closes all open files, releases all memory variables, and returns control to the operating system. The command may be safely issued at any time, and need not be preceded by a **CLOSE DATABASES** (or similar) command. In other words, the **QUIT** command automatically saves all changes made since the last save operation.

The **QUIT** command is the only safe way to exit dBASE; i.e., rebooting the system, or removing a floppy disk without quitting, can result in damage to open files, with a resultant loss of data that renders the database unusable.

Tips

1. Use a **QUIT** command rather than **RETURN** to exit from a custom system; this takes the user to DOS rather than leaving him or her stranded at the dot prompt.

Related Topics

```
CLOSE DATABASES
RETURN
```

READ

Syntax

```
READ [SAVE]
```

Discussion

The **READ** command is used in program files in conjunction with **@...SAY...GET** commands to create custom screens for full-screen data entry and editing. A series of **@...SAY...GET** commands are issued to map the screen, after which a **READ** command initiates the actual data entry process by placing the cursor in the first input template. The cursor can then be moved forward or backward into any of the templates for the fields and/or memory variables displayed by the **@...SAY...GET** commands.

No data value is stored into its corresponding field or memory variable until the user exits from the full-screen mode by pressing the **Esc** key or by completing the entry for the last input template. Until that time, the user may go back and forth between fields, editing data as desired. The segment below illustrates this concept, first mapping the screen, then allowing the user to move between all six templates until the data in **mcity** is completed or the **Esc** key is pressed. At that time, all of the **GET**s are cleared, and the cursor can no longer be moved back to those fields for further editing. Consider:

```
CLEAR
@ 2,5 SAY 'Enter last name:' GET mlname
@ 3,5 SAY 'Enter first name:' GET mfname
@ 4,5 SAY 'Enter age:' GET mage
@ 5,5 SAY 'Enter sex:' GET msex
@ 6,5 SAY 'Enter street address:' GET maddress
@ 7,5 SAY 'Enter city:' GET mcity
READ
.
  .
    .
```

The **READ** command activates only the templates defined since the last **READ**, **CLEAR**, **CLEAR ALL**, or **CLEAR GETS** command. What if, however, the program specifications required the value of **msex** to be validated immediately after input, requiring the insertion of an additional **READ** command (as well as a validation routine) after the **GET msex** command line? Execution of the first **READ** would result in the data being stored in the memory variables for **mlname**, **mfname**, **mage**, and **msex** and those **GET**s being cleared. The second **READ** command would then position the cursor in the input template for **maddress**, with the first four input templates now inaccessible for further editing. Data could be entered in the templates for **maddress** and **mcity** only.

Specification of the **SAVE** clause, however, does not clear the **GET**s, so a subsequent **READ** activates not only the **GET**s immediately preceding it, but also those preceding the **READ SAVE**. Hence, in the preceding example, insertion of a **READ SAVE** command after the **GET msex** command line (in lieu of a simple **READ**) permits the value of **msex** to be validated without rendering the first four input templates inaccessible. The drawback to this approach is that after the **READ SAVE**, the cursor is repositioned in the input template for **mlname**, requiring the user to move through all of the data already entered to return to the template where data entry left off (in this case, **maddress**).

A **READ** command has a much different use when it appears in a format file, where it creates multiple screen formats, marking the point where each new screen is to begin. The **PgUp** and **PgDn** keys can be used when the format file is active, to page back and forth between screens. This use of the **READ** command is permitted in format files only, and not in program files with **@..SAY...GET** commands.

Tips

1. Memory variables must be initialized with a **STORE** command prior to the **@...SAY..GET** and **READ** commands being executed.
2. Excessive use of the **READ SAVE** command will eventually exceed the number of **GET**s permitted in a program. Issuing a **CLEAR GETS** command periodically will eliminate the problem. Alternatively, you can increase the maximum number of **GET**s permitted from 128 to as many as 1,023, by placing a **GETS=** command in the **CONFIG.DB** file.
3. Any dBASE commands physically above a **READ SAVE** command are not re-executed; i.e., a **READ SAVE** command makes the previous **GET**s accessible for data entry, but does not send control backward in the program.
4. A single data validation procedure which is executed after the data has been entered for an entire record, is often preferable to validating each field immediately as it is entered.

Related Topics

```
@...SAY...GET
CLEAR GETS
CREATE SCREEN
SET FORMAT TO
```

RECALL

Syntax

```
RECALL [<scope>][WHILE <condition>][FOR <condition>]
```

Discussion

The **RECALL** command removes the deletion marker from a record marked for deletion, reinstating it as an active record. Only the current record will be recalled unless a scope parameter, or a **FOR** or **WHILE** condition, is specified to unmark more than one record at a time, e.g., **RECALL NEXT** 10 or **RECALL FOR** location = '**FL**'. The command will have no effect, however, if the current record is not marked for deletion.

The position of the record pointer is unaffected if **RECALL** is specified with no additional parameters. **RECALL ALL** or **RECALL REST**, however, moves the record pointer to the end of the file, whereas any other scope parameter will reposition the record pointer at the last record recalled. Inclusion of a **WHILE** condition moves the record pointer to the record after the last record meeting the condition, while specification of a **FOR** condition moves the record pointer to the end of the file.

Tips

1. A record other than the current record can be recalled with the command, **RECALL RECORD** <n>, where n is a valid record number.
2. The **RECALL** command has no effect once deleted records have been physically removed from the database with the **PACK** or **ZAP** command.
3. When **SET DELETED** is **ON**, records marked for deletion are hidden from processing; i.e., the logically deleted records will not be found in a **FIND** or **LOCATE** command, nor will they appear when the file is edited or browsed. To access a deleted record, you must explicitly specify the record number in the command and thus can recall a record in one of only two ways:

   ```
   RECALL RECORD 4
   ```

   or

   ```
   GO 4
   RECALL
   ```

4. Ctrl+U can be used to recall/delete the current record from within the **EDIT** or **BROWSE** modes.

Related Topics

```
DELETE
PACK
SET DELETED
ZAP
```

RECNO FUNCTION

Syntax

```
RECNO([<alias>])
```

Discussion

The **RECNO()** function returns the record number of the current record (the record that the record pointer is on) in the currently selected **DBF** file. The command **? RECNO()** displays the record number on the screen.

The **RECNO()** function can be used to determine the record number in an unselected area by specifying the number of the work area or the name of the file enclosed in quotation marks; e.g., **? RECNO(3)** displays the record number of the current record in the file open in work area 3, whereas **? RECNO("zoo")** displays the record number of the current record in the **ZOO.DBF** file in whichever work area the file is open.

Tips

1. Any attempt to move the record pointer beyond the last record in the file repositions it to the end-of-file marker, with a record number one greater than that of the last record. By contrast, any attempt to move the record pointer above the first record, leaves it positioned on the first record.
2. The **RECNO()** function returns a value of one when there are no records in the currently selected **DBF** file, or a value of zero when no **DBF** file is open.

Related Topics

BOF()
EOF()

REINDEX

Syntax

```
REINDEX
```

Discussion

The **REINDEX** command rebuilds all of the open index files in the currently selected work area, using the original key expressions stored with the index. Indexes that are open when a database file is updated are themselves automatically updated and, in theory, never need to be reindexed. Unopened indexes, however, become immediately obsolete when the database file is updated, and must be rebuilt to reflect the changes. The production **MDX** file is automatically opened when the **DBF** file is opened; hence the **REINDEX** command is used primarily to update single index files and/or independent multiple index files.

Tips

1. A production **MDX** file can be damaged and require reindexing if there is a hardware failure, the power goes out, or the machine is rebooted when the **DBF** file is open.
2. If an index file is damaged to the extent that dBASE cannot read the key expression, a **REINDEX** command will not work. In this situation, the indexes will need to be rebuilt

the same way they were first created, through a **CREATE/MODIFY STRUCTURE** command or through an **INDEX ON** command.

3. Opening an obsolete index will not always produce an error message, but will most likely result in inconsistent and/or incorrect information. This is the best argument for placing all indexes as tags in the production **MDX** file.
4. The **PACK** command automatically reindexes all open index files.
5. An index file that was created with a **UNIQUE** clause or when the status of **SET UNIQUE** was **ON** will retain its **UNIQUE** status when reindexed, regardless of whether **SET UNIQUE** is **ON** or **OFF**.

Related Topics

```
INDEX
PACK
SET INDEX
SET UNIQUE
```

RELEASE

Syntax

```
RELEASE <memvar list>
RELEASE ALL [LIKE/EXCEPT <skeleton>]
RELEASE MENUS [<menu name list>]
RELEASE POPUPS [<popup name list>]
RELEASE WINDOWS [<window name list>]
```

Discussion

The **RELEASE** command removes active memory variables, bar menus, popup menus, and windows from memory, thereby freeing the associated space for use.

Specification of a memory variable list releases one or more memory variables, e.g., **RELEASE mnumber** or **RELEASE mlname,mfname,mssn**. A group of memory variables can be released with a single command as follows:

1. RELEASE ALL	From the dot prompt, releases all currently active user memory variables; from within a program, releases all **PRIVATE** memory variables created in that program.
2. RELEASE ALL LIKE	Uses wild card characters (* and ?) to release groups of similarly named memory variables; e.g., **RELEASE ALL LIKE z*** releases all memory variables that begin with the letter z.
3. RELEASE ALL EXCEPT	Uses wild card characters (* and ?) to release all memory variables except those that match the skeleton; e.g., **RELEASE ALL EXCEPT z*** releases all memory variables *except* those that begin with the letter z.

Once a memory variable is released from memory, it is permanently deleted and cannot be retrieved. However, a **SAVE** command can be issued prior to the **RELEASE** to save the memory variables to a **MEM** file, from which they can later be restored.

RELEASE MENUS, without a menu list, clears from the screen any currently displayed horizontal bar menus. It also releases from memory all horizontal bar menu definitions, including their associated pad definitions, **ON SELECTION PAD** commands, and **ON PAD** commands. The menus must be deactivated before they can be released. Inclusion of a menu name list affects only the named menus.

RELEASE POPUPS, without a menu list, clears from the screen any currently displayed popup menus. It also releases from memory all popup menu definitions, including their associated bar definitions and **ON SELECTION POPUP** commands. The popup menus must be deactivated before they can be released. Inclusion of a menu list affects only the named popups.

RELEASE WINDOWS, without a list of window names, clears from the screen any currently displayed windows. It also releases from memory all window definitions. Text covered by the released window(s) is restored. Inclusion of a window list affects only the named windows.

Tips

1. The wild card characters — the asterisk and the question mark — are used in the skeleton. The ***** matches one or more characters from its position to the end of the variable name; the **?** matches any single character in its exact position.
2. **CLEAR MEMORY** and **RELEASE ALL** are equivalent when issued from the dot prompt, in that both release all current memory variables. When issued from a program, however, **RELEASE ALL** will release only the memory variables created within that specific program (private), whereas **CLEAR MEMORY** releases all memory variables (public and private).
3. When a program terminates and passes control back to its calling program, all private memory variables are automatically released, and no explicit **RELEASE ALL** command is required. Hence, to preserve any of the program's private variables, a **SAVE** command should be issued, or the variables should be declared public.
4. Memory variables saved to **MEM** files for use in future dBASE sessions with the **SAVE** command can be accessed only after they have been loaded into memory with the **RESTORE** command.
5. By default, up to 500 memory variables can be active at one time, but this number can be increased or decreased by changing the **MVBLKSIZE** and/or **MVMAXBLKS** settings in the **CONFIG.DB** file. A maximum of 25,000 memory variables is possible, if your system has enough memory.
6. System memory variables, which control the appearance of printed and screen output, are not affected by the **RELEASE** command.

Related Topics

ACTIVATE MENU
ACTIVATE POPUP
CLEAR MEMORY
DEACTIVATE MENU
DEACTIVATE POPUP
DEFINE BAR
DEFINE MENU
DEFINE PAD
DEFINE POPUP
ON PAD
ON SELECTION PAD
ON SELECTION POPUP
RESTORE
SAVE

REPLACE

Syntax

```
REPLACE <field> WITH <exp> [ADDITIVE]
    [,<field> WITH <exp> [ADDITIVE],...] [<scope>]
    [WHILE <condition>] [FOR <condition>]
```

Discussion

The **REPLACE** command stores new data in specified fields of one or more records in the currently selected database, in effect overwriting the existing data. The default scope is one, so that issuing the command with no scope or **FOR** parameter affects only the current record. Careful attention should be paid to the sequence in which multiple **REPLACE** commands are issued for the same record; e.g., the commands

```
REPLACE salary2 WITH salary1
```

and

```
REPLACE salary1 WITH msalary
```

will store the value previously in **salary1** in **salary2**, and then store the value in the memory variable **msalary** in **salary1**. (Issuing the commands in reverse order would have an entirely different result.) Alternatively, the two commands could have been combined into a single command as shown:

```
REPLACE salary2 WITH salary1,salary1 WITH msalary
```

The field and its corresponding **WITH** expression must be of the same data type, otherwise a *Data type mismatch* error results. A numeric field, for example, cannot be replaced with character data, nor can a character field be replaced with numeric data. In addition, the width of the **WITH** expression should not be larger than the width of the replaced field. Should this occur, character data will be truncated, and numeric data will be lost and asterisks displayed in the field. The **ADDITIVE** clause allows the **WITH** expression to be added to the end of the existing contents in a memo field, rather than replacing it.

A scope clause can be included to replace the field contents of a group of records uniformly with the same expression; e.g.,

```
REPLACE ALL salary WITH salary * 1.10
```

will reflect an across the board 10% increase in every record, whereas the command

```
REPLACE NEXT 5 salary WITH salary * 1.10
```

gives a 10% increase to the next 5 employees (beginning with the employee whose record is the current record).

Inclusion of a **FOR** or **WHILE** condition will replace the field contents for only those records that meet the specified condition; e.g.,

```
REPLACE salary WITH salary * 1.10 FOR location = 'NY'
```

gives a 10% raise to only those employees in New York.

Issuing the **REPLACE** command with no parameters does not reposition the record pointer, whereas including a scope parameter, or a **FOR** or **WHILE** clause, alters its position. Specification of a scope of **ALL** or **REST** moves the record pointer to the end of file, as does inclusion of a **FOR** condition. Specification of **NEXT** as the scope parameter repositions the pointer to the last record in the scope, while inclusion of a **WHILE** condition moves it to the record beyond the last record meeting the condition.

Tips

1. The **REPLACE** command is often the last command in programs that append new records to a database. Commands are issued to **GET** memory variables, validation tests are performed, a blank record is appended to the **DBF** file, and finally the contents of the memory variables replace the blank fields in the newly appended record.
2. Any attempt to replace an inactive field (i.e., a field not contained in the field list of the current **SET FIELDS** command) produces a *Variable not found* error message.
3. Only those records meeting an active filter condition are affected by the **REPLACE** command; e.g., **REPLACE ALL** does not alter values in records outside the filter. The same principle holds true if **SET DELETED** is **ON**; i.e., records marked for deletion are not affected by the **REPLACE** command.
4. The **ADDITIVE** clause affects only memo fields. It is ignored when used with other field types.

Related Topics

APPEND
REINDEX
SET DELETED
SET FIELDS
SET FILTER
STORE

REPORT FORM

Syntax

```
REPORT FORM <filename> [<scope>] [WHILE <condition>]
    [FOR <condition>] [PLAIN] [HEADING <expression>]
    [NOEJECT] [TO PRINTER/TO FILE <filename>][SUMMARY]
```

Discussion

The **REPORT FORM** command merges data from the currently selected **DBF** file with the specified report format, printing the generated report to the screen. The default scope is **ALL**, so a report created with no additional parameters will include every record in the **DBF** file. The records will be listed according to the logical sequence of the master index, or if no index is open, according to the physical order of the currently selected database.

After the report is generated, the record pointer is repositioned to the end of file, unless **NEXT** is indicated as the scope parameter or a **WHILE** condition is included. Specification of the **NEXT** parameter repositions the record pointer to the last record listed (unless **NEXT** goes beyond the end of file, in which case the record pointer is set to the end of file), whereas inclusion of a **WHILE** condition moves the record pointer one record beyond the last record meeting the specified condition.

The **HEADING** option prints a page heading (in addition to the report header defined when the report was created) on every page of the report, automatically centering the heading on the line immediately beneath the report header. The heading line can be used to indicate the criteria on which records were selected for the report, and the text of the heading must be enclosed in quotes; e.g.,

```
REPORT FORM usstates HEADING "Pacific Coast States"
```

The **PLAIN** option suppresses the printing of the date and page number, if they were included in the report heading, and prints the report header on only the first page of the report.

The **SUMMARY** option suppresses the display of detail lines, producing a report that shows group subtotals and totals only. To use this option effectively, summary fields should have been placed in a group summary band or a report summary band when the report form was created.

The **TO PRINTER** clause produces a copy of the report on the printer as well as the screen. An initial form feed is executed before the printing begins, although this can be suppressed with a **NOEJECT** clause. The **TO FILE** clause directs the output to an ASCII text file, which can be subsequently modified with a word processor.

Tips

1. The reports panel in the control center provides simplified but limited access to capabilities available through the **REPORT FORM** command.
2. When a **REPORT FORM** command is executed, dBASE checks to see if an **FRO** or **FRG** file exists. If not, the report form is compiled and the resultant **FRO** file is executed. If the report form file is modified, dBASE deletes the old **FRO** file from the disk so that the modified report form will be recompiled when the report is subsequently generated.
3. All necessary database files and their associated indexes must be opened prior to the **REPORT FORM** command being issued. Additionally, if the report form references fields from unselected work areas, the proper relationships must have been previously established.
4. A report form can be used with any **DBF** file that has a structure compatible with the one that was open when the form was designed.
5. Detail lines are generated only for those records meeting an active filter condition. In similar fashion, detail lines are not generated for any records marked for deletion when **SET DELETED** is **ON**.
6. A syntax error results if the report form includes fields not specified in the active field list; i.e., all fields in the report form must appear in any current **SET FIELDS** command.
7. The **PLAIN** option is mutually exclusive with the **HEADING** option, suppressing a page heading on all pages of the report, including the first page.
8. The **PLAIN** option can be used to suppress page numbers when printing the report to a disk file for later use with a word processor. This is recommended since modifications made with the word processor will change the original pagination.
9. The **SET CONSOLE OFF** command, when used in a program, will suppress the screen display during printing. The console should be set back on when the printing is complete, so that processing can proceed normally; e.g.,

   ```
   SET CONSOLE OFF
   REPORT FORM employee TO PRINTER
   SET CONSOLE ON
   ```

   The **SET CONSOLE** command has no effect from the dot prompt.
10. ASCII characters may be sent to printer prior to actual printing, perhaps to specify compressed print or some other option; e.g.,

    ```
    ??? CHR(15)
    REPORT FORM employee
    ??? CHR(18)
    ```

    The ASCII character 15 shown in the example is by no means universally used by all printers. (Consult your own printer manual for specifics.) Remember, too, to restore the printer to normal printing as soon as the report is finished.
11. An error will occur if the printer is not on-line when a **REPORT FORM** command is issued. In some cases, the computer may lock and require rebooting, possibly resulting in data loss. It is advisable, therefore, to test the value of the **PRINTSTATUS()** function prior to printing.

Related Topics

```
CHR()
CREATE/MODIFY REPORT
LABEL FORM
PRINTSTATUS()
SET CONSOLE
SET DELETED
SET FIELDS
SET FILTER
SET PRINTER
SET RELATION
```

RESTORE

Syntax

```
RESTORE FROM <filename> [ADDITIVE]
```

Discussion

The **RESTORE** command brings the values of memory variables stored in the specified file into memory, simultaneously releasing any variables already in memory when the command was executed. Specification of the **ADDITIVE** clause, however, will add the memory variables in the file to those already in memory; existing memory variables with the same name as a restored variable will be overwritten and the original value lost.

Tips

1. If the **RESTORE** command is executed from the dot prompt, the restored variables are **PUBLIC**; if, on the other hand, the command is executed from within a program, the restored variables are **PRIVATE** (local to the program). To restore variables as public from within a program, declare them public with a **PUBLIC** statement and then issue a **RESTORE** command with the **ADDITIVE** option.
2. Up to 500 memory variables can be active at one time, but this number can be increased or decreased by changing the **MVBLKSIZE** and/or **MVMAXBLKS** settings in the **CONFIG.DB** file. A maximum of 25,000 memory variables is possible, if your system has sufficient memory.
3. The value of a restored memory variable can be changed with a subsequent **STORE** command.

Related Topics

```
CLEAR
CONFIG.DB
DISPLAY MEMORY
PRIVATE
PUBLIC
RELEASE
SAVE
STORE
```

RESTORE WINDOW

Syntax

```
RESTORE WINDOW <window list>/ALL FROM <filename>
```

Discussion

The **RESTORE WINDOW** command loads one or more window definitions into memory from the specified file, adding to the definitions already in memory. The **ALL** clause restores all of the stored window definitions, whereas a window list restores only the named windows. The window list may be in any order, and does not have to be the same as was used in the **SAVE WINDOW** command.

Once in memory, the **ACTIVATE WINDOW** command activates the windows in any desired order.

Tips

1. The **RESTORE WINDOW** command assumes an extension of **WIN**; any other extension must be explicitly specified with the file name.
2. The **SAVE WINDOW** command saves one or more window definitions in memory to disk. If one of the windows is active when the **SAVE WINDOW** command is executed, that window will be automatically activated when it is restored.
3. If there are window definitions already in memory, and the **RESTORE WINDOW** command will cause the total number to exceed the upper limit of twenty, dBASE will load as many definitions as it can and then display a *No more windows available* message.
4. If a window definition being restored to memory has the same name as a definition already in memory, the latter will be overwritten.

Related Topics

ACTIVATE WINDOW
CLEAR WINDOWS
DEACTIVATE WINDOW
DEFINE WINDOW
RELEASE WINDOWS
SAVE WINDOW

RESUME

Syntax

```
RESUME
```

Discussion

The **RESUME** command continues execution of a suspended program at the point where it was originally interrupted. The command makes sense only within the context of a debugging session, initiated by the user's decision to temporarily halt execution of a program, to execute additional debugging statements (**DISPLAY MEMORY**, **DISPLAY STATUS**, and so on).

Tips

1. A program may have been suspended as a result of pressing the **Esc** key or as a result of a **SUSPEND** command issued from within the program.
2. A **RESUME** command issued from the dot prompt restarts a suspended **DEBUG** command, returning to the debugger at the command line following the one on which execution was suspended.

Related Topics

```
CANCEL
DEBUG
DISPLAY MEMORY
DISPLAY STATUS
SUSPEND
```

RETURN

Syntax

```
RETURN [TO MASTER/TO <procedure name>]
```

Discussion

The **RETURN** command terminates the current program or procedure, transferring control to either the calling program or the dot prompt, depending on where the program or procedure was called. Control is returned in a calling program to the command line immediately following the one that originally transferred control (typically a **DO** command).

The **TO MASTER** clause returns control directly to the highest-level calling program, typically the user's entry into the system. The **TO <procedure name>** clause returns control to the named procedure.

Tips

1. In the absence of a **RETURN** statement, a program terminates with the last physical command, whereupon control is transferred to the calling program (or dot prompt). Good coding standards suggest, however, that a **RETURN** command be included in every program and procedure.
2. The **TO MASTER/TO <procedure name>** options should rarely if ever be used, as they violate the one entry point/one exit point philosophy of structured programming.
3. Execution of a **RETURN** command also releases all private memory variables (those created within the program). However, database files, index files, format files, alternate files, and procedure files opened in the program are not affected by the **RETURN** command, and thus remain open after the transfer of control has taken place. If necessary, the aforementioned files can be closed with the appropriate **CLOSE** command.

Related Topics

```
CLOSE
DO
QUIT
```

RTRIM FUNCTION

Syntax

```
RTRIM(<character expression>)
```

Discussion

The **RTRIM()** function strips trailing blanks from the specified character string and is identical in all respects to the **TRIM** function. (See the **TRIM()** function for additional information.)

Related Topics

```
LTRIM()
TRIM()
```

RUN

Syntax

```
RUN <command>
! <command>
```

Discussion

The **RUN** command executes a DOS command or an external program from within dBASE. Execution of the command temporarily suspends dBASE processing, executes the specified DOS command or program, and then returns to dBASE at the point where it was interrupted. Use of the **RUN** command requires sufficient memory so that **COMMAND.COM** (and the external program) can be loaded into memory along with dBASE; if not enough memory is available, dBASE will display an *Insufficient memory* error message. **COMMAND.COM** must also be available to dBASE when the **RUN** command is issued, and thus must be in the root directory of the disk used to boot the system or in the directory specified in the DOS **SET COMSPEC** command.

Tips

1. It is easier to **RUN** the DOS **COPY**, **ERASE**, and **RENAME** commands to process groups of files than it is to use the equivalent dBASE commands. This is because dBASE does not recognize wild card characters in these commands; for example, the command **ERASE *.BAK** results in a syntax error, whereas **RUN ERASE *.BAK** executes successfully.
2. Execution of an external program can be a complicated undertaking and often requires more memory than is available. Hence it is often best to exit dBASE and then run the external program.
3. The **RUN** command makes it easy to change subdirectories while in dBASE, for example, **RUN CD C:\DATADISK\USSTATES**. Be sure to specify the full path, starting from the root and including the drive letter.

Related Topics

```
CONFIG.DB
```

SAVE

Syntax

```
SAVE TO <filename> [ALL LIKE/EXCEPT <skeleton>]
```

Discussion

The **SAVE** command stores all currently active memory variables in the specified file; the latter is assigned a default extension of **MEM** unless another extension is explicitly specified. The saved memory variables can be subsequently restored to memory with the **RESTORE** command.

The **ALL LIKE** and **ALL EXCEPT** clauses may be used to save only a subset of the current memory variables, depending on whether they match (**ALL LIKE**) or do not match (**ALL EXCEPT**) the specified skeleton. The skeleton can use either or both of two wild card characters, the * and the ?. The * matches one or more characters from its position to the end of the filename, whereas the ? matches any *single* character in its exact position. For example,

```
SAVE TO constant ALL LIKE mr*
```

will save all current memory variables beginning with "mr" to a file named **CONSTANT.MEM**, regardless of the length of the memory variable name. By contrast, the command,

```
SAVE TO constant ALL EXCEPT ???3
```

will save all current memory variables *except* those having a "3" as the last character of a four-character name.

Tips

1. Program constants that need to be preserved from one dBASE session to the next can be saved in one session and restored in the next.
2. Private memory variables that will be needed in future dBASE sessions must be saved prior to the termination of the program in which they are contained, otherwise they will be automatically released when the program returns control to its calling program.
3. The skeleton need not use a wild card character, and thus can be used to save a single memory variable. For example,

   ```
   SAVE TO memfile ALL LIKE mcount
   ```

   will save only the memory variable **mcount** to the **MEM** file.
4. **ALL LIKE** and **ALL EXCEPT** are mutually exclusive; i.e., they *cannot* be used in the same command.
5. To view the contents of a **MEM** file, it must first be restored to memory with a **RESTORE** command. The contents of memory can then be viewed with a **DISPLAY MEMORY** command. The **RESTORE** command will delete all current memory variables unless the **ADDITIVE** option is used.
6. A **SAVE** command that specifies an existing filename overwrites the entire file, and does *not* add the newly saved variables to those already in the file. dBASE will ask if the file should be overwritten, provided **SET SAFETY** is **ON**. If **SAFETY** is **OFF**, however, the existing file is overwritten with no warning, and the values of the formerly saved variables are irretrievably lost.

Related Topics

```
CLEAR
DISPLAY MEMORY
RELEASE
RESTORE
SET SAFETY
```

SAVE WINDOW

Syntax

```
SAVE WINDOW <window list>/ALL TO <filename>
```

Discussion

The **SAVE WINDOW** command saves one or more current window definitions to a disk file. The **ALL** clause saves all current definitions, whereas a window list saves only the named windows.

Tips

1. The disk file is automatically assigned a **WIN** extension, unless another extension is specified.
2. **SET SAFETY ON** will prevent dBASE from overwriting an existing file with the same name. If **SET SAFETY** is **OFF**, however, the file is overwritten without warning.
3. Up to 20 window definitions can be in memory at one time; therefore, a maximum of 20 definitions can be saved in one file.
4. The **RESTORE WINDOW** command restores one or more window definitions to memory.

Related Topics

ACTIVATE WINDOW
CLEAR WINDOWS
DEACTIVATE WINDOW
DEFINE WINDOW
RELEASE WINDOWS
RESTORE WINDOW
SET SAFETY

SCAN

Syntax

```
SCAN [<scope>] [FOR <condition>] [WHILE condition>]
    [<commands>]
ENDSCAN
```

Discussion

The **SCAN** command is a simplified alternative to the **DO WHILE** command. The default scope is **ALL**, and processing begins with the first record in the currently selected **DBF** file (or the first record according to the active index). A scope of **NEXT** or **REST**, however, begins at the current record, and includes only the records within the specified scope. A **FOR** or **WHILE** condition can also be specified to further limit the affected records.

The commands between the **SCAN** and **ENDSCAN** are executed for every included record, with the record pointer *automatically* advancing to the next record each time the **ENDSCAN** statement is encountered. When all records have been processed, the record pointer is positioned at the end of the file, unless a scope of **NEXT** or a **WHILE** condition was specified, in which case the record pointer is positioned at the last record processed, or one record beyond the last record meeting the specified condition.

The **SCAN** command does not offer any additional capability over an ordinary **DO WHILE** command; it does, however, accomplish the same task with fewer commands. Thus:

```
SCAN FOR city = 'Miami'
   ? lastname,firstname,donation
ENDSCAN
```

is equivalent to, but simpler than:

```
DO WHILE .NOT. EOF()
   IF city = 'Miami'
      ? lastname,firstname,donation
   ENDIF
   SKIP
ENDDO
```

Tips

1. The **SCAN** command, with no additional parameters, executes the identical instructions for every record in the file; e.g., to print the last name and salary of every record, use the commands:

   ```
   SCAN
      ? lastname,salary
   ENDSCAN
   ```

2. Inclusion of a **WHILE** condition requires the record pointer to be explicitly positioned on the first record meeting the specified condition prior to entering the **SCAN** structure.
3. An **EXIT** command may be included within the **SCAN** structure to make an abnormal (premature) exit from the loop, by passing control directly to the first command after the **ENDSCAN**. We recommend, however, *against* the use of **EXIT**, as it violates the one entry point/one exit point philosophy of structured programming.

Related Topics

DO WHILE
FIND
LOCATE
SKIP

SEEK

Syntax

```
SEEK <expression>
```

Discussion

The **SEEK** command searches the key field of the master index for the first record matching the specified string or numeric value and, if a record is found, moves the record pointer to that record. The **SEEK** command merely repositions the record pointer and does not display the found record; a subsequent **DISPLAY** command is needed to view the record. If the search is unsuccessful, a *Find not successful* message is displayed (as long as **SET TALK** is **ON**), and the record pointer is repositioned to the end of file.

The **SEEK** command contains all of the capabilities inherent in the **FIND** command and, in addition, enables a search on an expression involving one or more memory variables. Because the **FIND** command cannot search for an expression, and because it is cumbersome to use the macro notation in finding values stored in memory variables, **SEEK** is more likely to be used in program files. **FIND**, on the other hand, is more convenient to use from the dot prompt.

As with the **FIND** command, the requirement to use an active index implies that records with like values of the search key will be grouped together; i.e., if there is another record with the same key value, it will be sequenced immediately beneath the found record. Hence that record can be accessed with a **SKIP** command (to move the record pointer), and viewed with a **DISPLAY** command (to verify that the key does, in fact, match). Indeed, all records with the same key value can be retrieved by repeatedly issuing **SKIP** and **DISPLAY** commands until the value of the key field no longer matches the character string or numeric value specified in the original **SEEK** command.

Tips

1. The **SEEK** command requires that a character string used as the search expression be enclosed in quotes to differentiate it from a memory variable. This differs from the **FIND** command, where quotation marks are optional; i.e.,

   `FIND Jones` ——— *Valid for* ***FIND****; invalid with* ***SEEK***

   `FIND "Jones"` ——— *Valid for both* ***FIND*** *and* ***SEEK***

2. A partial character string may be stored in the memory variable used in the search expression, as long as **SET EXACT** is **OFF** and the specified string consists of the initial characters in the key value. For example,

   ```
   STORE "Sm" to mname
   SEEK mname
   ```

   will position the record pointer at the first record having a key value that begins with "Sm".
3. The **SEEK** command will not search for a partial numeric value as it will for a partial character string; i.e., **SEEK 111** will not retrieve a record whose key is **111222**.
4. Upper- and lower-case letters are treated as different characters, regardless of whether **SET EXACT** is **ON** or **OFF**. The commands,

   ```
   STORE 'MILLER' to mname
   SEEK mname
   ```

   will not find a key value of "Miller" or "miller".
5. **SEEK** conducts a much more rapid search than does the corresponding **LOCATE** command. **SEEK**, however, requires an index and limits the search to a value equal to the character string or numeric value. **LOCATE**, on the other hand, can search for values greater than, less than, or not equal to.
6. Records not meeting an active filter condition are ignored by the **SEEK** command. In similar fashion, records marked for deletion are also ignored when **SET DELETED** is **ON**.
7. When **SET NEAR** is **ON** and a matching record is not found, the record pointer is positioned at the record immediately below where the matching record should have been found, rather than at the end of file.

Related Topics

FIND
LOCATE
SET DELETED
SET FILTER
SET NEAR

SELECT

Syntax

```
SELECT <work area/alias>
```

Discussion

The **SELECT** command designates one of ten available work areas as the currently selected work area. Subsequent dBASE commands will apply to the **DBF** file in that work area, unless an unselected work area is explicitly specified in the command. For example, **? EOF()** returns the end of file condition in the current work area, whereas **? EOF(5)** returns the end of file condition in work area five. Only one work area can be currently selected at any one time.

Work area one is the default work area when dBASE is loaded initially. A different work area may be selected in one of three ways:

1. By indicating the number of the work area (a value from 1 to 10), e.g., **SELECT 3**.
2. By indicating the work area letter (a letter from A through J), e.g., **SELECT C**.
3. By giving the name or alias of the open **DBF** file in the work area, e.g., **SELECT employee**.

Only one **DBF** file may be open at a time in any one work area. Thus, the simultaneous use of more than one **DBF** file requires that each file be placed in its own work area, by first selecting the area and then opening the file. For example, the commands:

```
SELECT 2
USE location
SELECT 3
USE title
```

open the files **LOCATION.DBF** and **TITLE.DBF** in work areas 2 and 3, respectively.

Each work area also contains the data file's affiliated files (memo files, index files, a query file and/or a format file) as well as any active filter condition and/or established relationship. Note that as with the **DBF** file, these affiliated files can be open in only one work area at any given time.

dBASE maintains an independent record pointer in each of the work areas; i.e., selecting a particular area and repositioning the record pointer in that area does not affect the record pointers for files in other work areas. In other words, if the record pointer in area one is on record 15 and area three is selected, the record pointer in area one remains on record 15, despite movements of the record pointer in area three. In addition, when area one is reselected, its record pointer is still on record 15 (and will not be moved to record 1, as happens when the file is opened).

Relationships can be established between open files, enabling more sophisticated systems to be developed than if just one **DBF** file were available. This is accomplished by the **SET RELATION** command, which links files together in such a way that the record pointers move in conjunction with one another. In other words, commands that move the record pointer in one file will automatically reposition the record pointer in a second file to the corresponding record.

Tips

1. The first file opened does not have to be placed in work area one; i.e., any of the other areas may be used.
2. If an alias is not specified when a **DBF** file is first opened, the filename, without the extension, is assigned as the default alias.
3. Fields from a **DBF** file in an unselected work area can be accessed by using the file alias with the field name; e.g.,

   ```
   SELECT employee
   DISPLAY lastname,location->locname
   ```

The **lastname** field belongs to the **EMPLOYEE.DBF** file in the current work area and is included in the **DISPLAY** command in the usual fashion; **locname**, however, belongs to **LOCATION.DBF** and is preceded by the appropriate file alias. (A relationship between these two files should have been established to make the display meaningful.)

4. A **SET FIELDS** command may include fields from database files in unselected work areas by preceding the field name with the file alias; e.g.,

```
SET FIELDS TO lname,loc,location->locname
```

5. The **USE** command with no filename specified closes the database file in the currently selected work area, whereas **CLOSE DATABASES** closes the database files in *all* of the work areas.
6. The maximum number of files that may be open at one time is determined by the **FILES=** command in the **CONFIG.DB** file (or the **FILES=** command in the **CONFIG.SYS** file), and in any case cannot be more than 99. Any attempt to open more than the maximum will result in a *Too many files open* error message.
7. Work area ten is reserved for an open catalog. A **DBF** file may not be opened in this work area if a catalog is already open. If, on the other hand, a **DBF** file is open in work area ten when a catalog is opened, the **DBF** file will automatically be closed and the catalog opened.
8. The **CLEAR ALL** command automatically selects work area one.

Related Topics

CLEAR
CLOSE
CONFIG.DB
SET FIELDS
SET RELATION
USE

SET

Syntax

```
SET
```

Discussion

The **SET** command invokes a full-screen menu for viewing and/or changing the status of other **SET** commands. The command produces a menu bar across the top of the screen, offering a choice of five menus, each representing a subset of available **SET** commands. A menu is accessed by pressing the **Alt** key and the first letter of the menu name. The menus are:

1. **OPTIONS** — **SET** commands for approximately 40 of the most common options.
2. **DISPLAY** — **SET** commands for screen colors and display attributes.
3. **KEYS** — **SET** commands to reset the function keys.
4. **DISK** — **SET** commands for the default drive and search path.
5. **FILES** — **SET** commands to open alternate, format, device, and index files.

The status of a particular **SET** command is changed by selecting the appropriate menu, highlighting the menu choice by using the up/down arrow keys, and then—depending on the item chosen—pressing the return key or entering the appropriate information.

The **SET** command is exited by pressing the **Esc** key. All changes remain in effect until they are modified or the dBASE session is terminated.

Tips

1. On a color monitor a selection from the display menu presents a popup menu from which foreground and background colors can be selected. Use the up/down arrow keys to highlight the desired foreground color; use the right/left arrow keys to move to the column of background colors; use the up/down arrow keys to highlight the desired background color; and press **Ctrl+End** to accept the changes made. The effect of all color changes is seen immediately as the change is made. Note that pressing **B** while in this menu toggles the blinking option on and off.
2. The individual **SET** commands are discussed in the next several pages of the Programmer's Notebook. The syntax of those **SET** commands with an **ON/OFF** option shows the default value in **boldface** type.
3. The default setting of many **SET** commands can be permanently changed through the **CONFIG.DB** file.
4. The status of individual **SET** commands can also be changed by issuing the appropriate **SET** command from the dot prompt or from within program files.
5. **SET** commands altered in a program file should be returned to the default setting before exiting the program.
6. **F1** and **Shift+F10** are reserved for Help and Macro recording, respectively, and are not available for reprogramming.

Related Topics

CONFIG.DB

SET ALTERNATE

Syntax

```
SET ALTERNATE TO [<filename> [ADDITIVE]]
SET ALTERNATE ON/OFF
```

Discussion

The **SET ALTERNATE** commands work in conjunction with one another to echo all screen output (commands as well as the output of those commands) to a file, with the exception of the output of full-screen commands such as **@...SAY** or **APPEND**. The **SET ALTERNATE TO** command creates and opens an ASCII text file (with a default extension of **TXT**) to hold the output, and the **SET ALTERNATE ON** initiates the echoing process. All subsequent screen output is sent to the file until a **SET ALTERNATE OFF** command is issued. **SET ALTERNATE** can be reset to **ON** to append additional output to the open alternate file.

The alternate file is closed with either a **CLOSE ALTERNATE** or **SET ALTERNATE TO** command with no filename specified. Once the alternate file has been closed, a subsequent **SET ALTERNATE TO** command specifying the same filename causes the existing file to be overwritten, unless the **ADDITIVE** option is specified, in which case the new output is appended to the end of the file.

Tips

1. Alternate files are widely used to record a sequence of commands from the dot prompt, together with dBASE's responses, for documentation or problem solving.
2. Commands issued after a **SET ALTERNATE TO <filename>** command, but before the **SET ALTERNATE ON** command, are not recorded.
3. **SET ALTERNATE OFF** and **CLOSE ALTERNATE** should both be issued before attempting to edit an alternate file. This ensures that the buffers are emptied and that the file was properly saved.

4. The alternate file may be subsequently edited with a word processor, to facilitate the development of system documentation and/or dBASE tutorials.
5. The **TYPE** command (**TYPE <filename>.TXT**) can be used to view the contents of an alternate file from the dot prompt. Inclusion of the **TO PRINTER** parameter produces hard copy as well.
6. If a file already exists with the same name as the one specified in the **SET ALTERNATE TO** command, and the **ADDITIVE** option is not specified, the file will be overwritten with no warning unless **SET SAFETY** is **ON**.
7. Output from **@...SAY** commands can be sent to a file with the **SET DEVICE TO FILE** command.

Related Topics

```
CLOSE
SET DEBUG
SET DEVICE
SET ECHO
SET SAFETY
```

SET AUTOSAVE

Syntax

```
SET AUTOSAVE ON/OFF
```

Discussion

SET AUTOSAVE ON saves each record to disk immediately after it is appended or modified. In the default mode (**SET AUTOSAVE OFF**), changes made to the **DBF** file are stored in buffers and saved to disk only when the buffers become full or the **DBF** file is closed.

Tips

1. The status of **SET AUTOSAVE** is especially important during full-screen data entry operations, e.g., **APPEND**, **BROWSE**, **EDIT**, and **INSERT**.
2. **SET AUTOSAVE ON** reduces the chance of data loss in the event of a system failure (e.g., a power failure), but also slows performance as it writes to disk after every change is made.
3. The disk directory is updated after each addition or change to the file.

Related Topics

```
APPEND
BROWSE
EDIT
INSERT
```

SET BELL

Syntax

```
SET BELL ON/OFF
SET BELL TO [<frequency>, <duration>]
```

Discussion

The **SET BELL** command determines whether or not a bell will ring when a user attempts to enter invalid data (e.g., character data in a numeric field) or when data completely fills an input template. The command can also be used to control the frequency and duration of the signal.

The choice between **SET BELL ON** (bell rings) and **SET BELL OFF** (bell doesn't ring) is one of personal preference, with valid arguments both pro and con. Leaving it on during data entry serves as a warning when an error occurs, but can become annoying as the bell also sounds whenever the data fills the template. For example, the bell will sound when data is entered into a logical field, as the input template consists of only one character and is always filled.

The frequency of the signal determines its pitch and can be any value between 10 and 10,000 (the default is 512). A lower pitch is achieved by setting the frequency to a value between 20 and 550, and a higher pitch by using values between 550 and 5,500. The duration of the signal determines its length and can be any value between 2 and 19 (the default is 2). A value of 19 ticks is approximately equal to one second.

Tips

1. The ASCII character 7 rings the bell within a program, regardless of the status of **SET BELL**. Consider:

```
DO CASE
   CASE opt = '1'
     .
       .
         .
   OTHERWISE
      ? CHR(7)
      @ 21,15 SAY "Please re-enter"
ENDDO
```

2. Many users choose to **SET CONFIRM ON** when **BELL** is **OFF**, so that pressing the return key is necessary at the end of every input template. This prevents a user from overtyping one field into the next without any warning.
3. Consistency throughout a system regarding the status of **BELL** and **CONFIRM** is important, so that the user always knows what is expected, and does not have to guess at data entry.
4. When changing the frequency and/or duration of the bell, both parameters must be specified.

Related Topics

```
?/??
CHR()
SET CONFIRM
```

SET BORDER

Syntax

```
SET BORDER TO
    [SINGLE/DOUBLE/PANEL/NONE/<border defn string>]
```

Discussion

The **SET BORDER** command defines the border style for all subsequently defined menus, windows, and boxes created with the **@...TO** command. The default border is a single line, but it can be changed to a double line or solid panel. Consider:

```
SET BORDER TO SINGLE
@ 2,4 TO 4,20
```

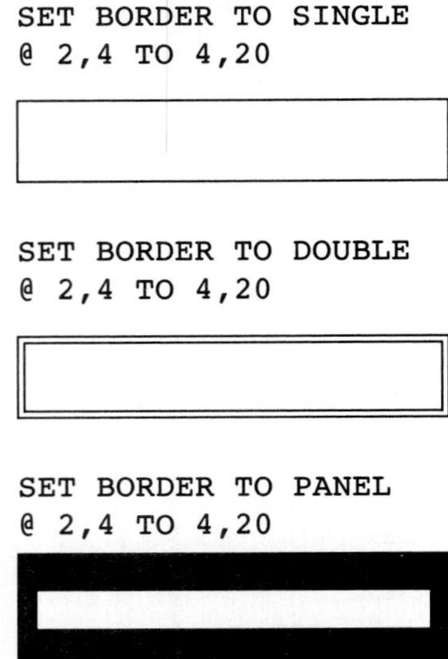

```
SET BORDER TO DOUBLE
@ 2,4 TO 4,20
```

```
SET BORDER TO PANEL
@ 2,4 TO 4,20
```

A custom frame can be created by specifying either the desired character string itself, enclosed in quotes, or by using the character's decimal equivalent (ASCII code value) in the IBM Extended Character Set, not enclosed in quotes. Consider,

```
SET BORDER TO PANEL "*"
@ 2,4 TO 4,20
*****************
*               *
*****************
```

```
SET BORDER TO PANEL "3"
@ 2,4 TO 4,20
♥♥♥♥♥♥♥♥♥♥♥♥♥♥♥♥♥♥
♥                ♥
♥♥♥♥♥♥♥♥♥♥♥♥♥♥♥♥♥♥
```

Tips

1. The **SET BORDER** command does not affect any menu or border definition that is already in memory.
2. The default border established by the **SET BORDER** command is overridden when the border is defined in the **@...TO** or **DEFINE WINDOW** command itself; for example,

```
@ 2,10 TO 6,30 DOUBLE
DEFINE WINDOW win1 FROM 5,10 TO 15,70 PANEL
```

3. The **NONE** keyword is a valid option when establishing the border style for a window or menu, but makes little sense for a box.
4. The **SET BORDER TO** command with no parameter resets the border style to a single=line box.
5. The custom border definition does not have to use the same character for the entire box, but can specify a different character for the top, bottom, left side, right side,

upper-left corner, upper-right corner, lower-left corner, and lower-right corner, in exactly that order. For example,

```
SET BORDER TO 205,205,179,179,213,184,212,190
@ 2,4 TO 4,20
```

Related Topics

```
@...TO
DEFINE MENU
DEFINE POPUP
DEFINE WINDOW
```

SET CATALOG

Syntax

```
SET CATALOG TO <filename>
SET CATALOG ON/OFF
```

Discussion

The **SET CATALOG TO** command opens an existing catalog file, or if there is no such file, creates and opens a new file. The specified catalog is activated (set on), and then, as long as the catalog remains open, information about each file created and/or opened during a session is stored in that catalog. The file information includes the file name and path, alias, type, and an 80-character description of the file (which is requested by dBASE when the file is created or opened). In addition, each nondatabase file (an index file, format file, and so on) is linked in the catalog to its particular database file.

A catalog groups all files used in a particular application, and its utility revolves around a query feature that provides assistance in selecting the correct file. Any command that uses a filename as part of its syntax can include a query (**?**) in place of the filename. The command, **USE ?**, for example, displays all of the database files in the open catalog. The up and down arrow keys will highlight the various files, simultaneously displaying the description entered at the time the file was created. Pressing the return key opens the highlighted file.

In similar fashion, a query can be used in other commands that access files contained in the catalog, as shown in the examples below:

```
SET FORMAT TO ?
SET INDEX TO ?
MODIFY REPORT ?
MODIFY SCREEN ?
SET VIEW TO ?
SET FILTER TO ?
REPORT FORM ?
```

However, rather than listing all files of the particular file type, only those associated with the currently selected database are shown, making it easier to select the proper ancillary files.

To ensure that the catalog is kept current, it should be opened with a **SET CATALOG TO** command at the beginning of every session. If it is necessary, however, to create or open a file that is not to be stored in the catalog, the cataloging should be turned off with a **SET CATALOG OFF** command. A subsequent **SET CATALOG ON** will resume catalog maintenance.

A catalog is not closed until a **SET CATALOG TO** command is issued without a file name. In other words, **SET CATALOG OFF** does not close a catalog, but merely suspends the cataloging process. The query feature can still be used when **SET CATALOG** is **OFF** as long as the catalog is still open.

Tips

1. A separate catalog should be maintained for each application, and should be opened before any of the files belonging to the application are created.
2. An open catalog file is automatically placed in work area ten, thereby reducing the number of available work areas to nine.
3. A catalog file is, in reality, a database file, except that it is given an extension of **CAT**. One record is appended to the catalog for every file created while the catalog is open. The file structure contains seven fields: **PATH**, **FILE_NAME**, **ALIAS**, **TYPE**, **TITLE**, **CODE**, and **TAG**.

   The contents of the first four fields are entered automatically when the file is created or opened. A **CODE** is assigned by dBASE to associate files with their particular **DBF** file. The **TITLE** stores the description entered when the file was created/opened, and **TAG** is an optional field that is generally not used.
4. The contents of a **CAT** file can be displayed and edited from the dot prompt, as can any database file. The **CAT** extension must be specified when opening the catalog file; e.g., **USE ZOO.CAT** so that dBASE will not assume a **DBF** extension. You should not edit dBASE-supplied information or modify the structure, as it can render the catalog file unusable; i.e., editing should be limited to the title field.
5. Many of the functions implicit in the concept of a dBASE catalog can be achieved by placing each application in its own subdirectory, with a lot less effort.
6. When a catalog is active, the **SET TITLES OFF** command will suppress the prompt for file descriptions when creating/opening files.
7. The first time you create a catalog, dBASE creates a master catalog that is named **CATALOG.CAT** in the default directory and uses this catalog to keep track of other catalogs created while logged into that directory. The structure of the master catalog is the same as for any other catalog, the only difference being that it records information about catalog files.
8. The **SET CATALOG TO ?** command can be used to select a catalog from among the **CAT** files in the master catalog.
9. Each time you activate the control center, dBASE loads the catalog previously in use in the current subdirectory, and displays only those filenames in its panels. If you have not created any catalogs in the current subdirectory, dBASE automatically opens **UNTITLED.CAT** to catalog all files created/opened during that session at the control center.
10. The catalog menu can be used at the control center to add/remove files from the current catalog, change the current catalog, and edit the file descriptions.
11. When a catalog is opened, dBASE checks the contents of the catalog against the current disk directory. Files erased from the disk since the catalog was last opened are automatically deleted from the catalog. However, files that were copied to the subdirectory or created while the catalog was closed are *not* added to the catalog.
12. When **SET CATALOG** is **ON**, an entry to the catalog will be made when any of the following commands are executed: **CREATE**, **CREATE/MODIFY LABEL**, **CREATE/MODIFY QUERY**, **CREATE/MODIFY REPORT**, **CREATE/MODIFY SCREEN**, **CREATE/MODIFY VIEW**, **INDEX**, **JOIN**, **SET FORMAT**, **SET VIEW**, **SORT**, and **USE**.

SET CENTURY

Syntax

```
SET CENTURY ON/OFF
```

Discussion

The **SET CENTURY** command determines how the year portion of a date is input and displayed. The default format is two digits, with the twentieth century assumed. **SET CENTURY ON** changes the display to four digits, making it possible to work with dates from other centuries.

Tips

1. **SET CENTURY** does not affect how dates are stored internally, only how they are input or displayed. For example, if a date of 12/25/2010 is entered when **CENTURY** is **ON**, it will be displayed as 12/25/10 when **SET CENTURY** is **OFF**, but as 12/25/2010 when **SET CENTURY** is reset to **ON**.
2. The width of a date field in the structure of a **DBF** file is 8, regardless of whether **SET CENTURY** is **ON** or **OFF**.
2. Non–twentieth-century dates cannot be entered when **CENTURY** is **OFF**, as the input template provides only two digits for year. Non–twentieth-century memory variables can, however, be created by entering a four-digit year; e.g.,

   ```
   STORE {07/04/1776} TO memdate
   ```

   Note, however, that the date will be displayed as 07/04/76 until **SET CENTURY** is set **ON**, at which time it will be shown as 07/04/1776.
3. The **YEAR()** function returns a four-digit year, regardless of the status of **SET CENTURY**. All other commands displaying a date will show either a two- or four-digit year, corresponding to the status of **SET CENTURY**.
4. If a date calculation results in a nontwentieth century date, the correct century will be retained even if **SET CENTURY** is **OFF**.

Related Topics

CTOD()
DATE()
DTOC()
SET DATE
YEAR()

SET CLOCK

Syntax

```
SET CLOCK ON/OFF
SET CLOCK TO [<row,col>]
```

Discussion

The **SET CLOCK** command controls the display of the system clock. The **SET CLOCK ON** command displays the current time in the format *hh:mm:ss am/pm* in column 69 of row 0. The **SET CLOCK TO** command displays the clock at the specified row and column.

The command, **SET CLOCK TO**, issued with no parameters, redisplays the clock at its default location.

Tips

1. The clock is displayed during full-screen menu commands, regardless of the status of `SET CLOCK`.
2. Be sure to enter the system time correctly when booting the system.
3. Execution of an `@...SAY TIME()` command in a program displays the time when the screen was mapped and will not be updated until another `@...SAY TIME()` command is executed. For this reason the `SET CLOCK` command is preferred.

Related Topics

```
CLEAR
TIME()
```

SET COLOR

Syntax

```
SET COLOR ON/OFF
SET COLOR TO [[<standard>][,[<enhanced>]
    [,[<perimeter>][,[<background>]]]]]
SET COLORS OF NORMAL TO [<color>]
SET COLORS OF MESSAGES TO [<color>]
SET COLORS OF TITLES TO [<color>]
SET COLORS OF BOX TO [<color>]
SET COLORS OF HIGHLIGHT TO [<color>]
SET COLORS OF INFORMATION TO [<color>]
SET COLORS OF FIELDS TO [<color>]
```

Discussion

The `SET COLOR ON/OFF` command enables the user to switch back and forth between a color and a monochrome monitor in systems with both. The default value is determined by the monitor in use when dBASE is loaded.

The effects of the `SET COLOR TO` command differ, depending on what type of monitor is in use. In any event, the command provides for three distinct areas known as the standard display area, enhanced display area, and perimeter. Both a foreground and background color can be specified for the standard and enhanced display areas, whereas only one color is specified for the perimeter. The `<background>` parameter is used only with monitors that require the same background color for both the standard and enhanced areas (see Tip 6 below). Available colors, and their respective codes, are shown in the following table:

Color	Code
Black	N
Blank	X
Blue	B
Brown	GR
Cyan	BG
Gray	N+
Green	G
Magenta	RB
Red	R
White	W
Yellow	GR+

The **SET COLOR TO** command separates the foreground and background colors for a given area by a slash, and separates the different areas by a comma. Thus, the command,

```
SET COLOR TO W/B,R/W,N
```

displays white text on a blue background in the standard display area, displays red text on a white background in the enhanced area, and provides a black perimeter.

A plus (+) sign may be included with either foreground color to create high-intensity text, whereas an asterisk specifies blinking text; e.g.,

```
SET COLOR TO W+/B,R/W,N
SET COLOR TO W/B,R*/W,N
```

The background color may not be set to high intensity on EGA monitors.

You need not change the colors in all three areas every time, although you must use comma(s) to indicate the omission of positional fields. For example, to change the display in the enhanced area to red on white, leaving the standard area and perimeter as is, use the command:

```
SET COLOR TO ,R/W
```

The **SET COLOR OF** command controls the appearance of predefined screen areas, as follows:

Command	Area Affected
SET COLOR OF NORMAL	Most standard listings; output of **@...SAY** commands; layout design surfaces
SET COLOR OF MESSAGES	Special text displays; navigation line messages; available menu items; control center panels
SET COLOR OF TITLES	Field headings in **LIST** and **DISPLAY** commands; ruler line; column labels
SET COLOR OF BOX	Menu and list borders; prompt box borders
SET COLOR OF HIGHLIGHT	Highlighted menu options; selected fields; information box borders
SET COLOR OF INFORMATION	Clock and status line; error box borders
SET COLOR OF FIELDS	Selected fields in **BROWSE** mode

The **SET COLOR TO** command can be used with a *monochrome monitor* to create inverse video or high-intensity, underlined, or blinking text. Consider:

Code	Effect
+	High-intensity text
U	Underlined text
U+	High-intensity text that is underlined
I	Inverse video
*	Blinking text

For example, the commands,

```
SET COLOR TO W+/N
SET COLOR TO U
```

provide high-intensity white text on a black background, which is underlined as well.

The **SET COLOR TO** command, with no additional parameters, resets the screen to the dBASE IV program defaults (white text on a black background in the standard area, black text on a white background in the enhanced area, and a black perimeter), not the default colors established in the **CONFIG.DB** file.

Tips

1. The standard and enhanced display areas may each be assigned any pair of colors. Choose carefully, however, as an attractive screen is very important.
2. Specification of **X** as the background color within the **SET COLOR TO** command displays blank text (effectively hiding it from view), a feature that can be used to suppress user-supplied passwords, security codes, and so on.
3. Blinking and high-intensity attributes can be specified for color or monochrome monitors. Underlining and inverse video, however, can be used only on monochrome monitors, and then not with all monochrome monitors. You must try the special effects to see if they work with your monitor.
4. The default colors can be changed with a **COLOR** command or a **COLOR OF** command in the **CONFIG.DB** file. In addition, inclusion of a **COLOR = ON** command will designate the color monitor as the active monitor (in systems with two monitors), regardless of which was in use when dBASE was loaded.
5. Cyan, magenta, brown, and yellow are created from combinations of other colors. In similar fashion, additional colors can be created with different code combinations.
6. Some display adapters require that the background color be the same for standard and enhanced display areas. For these monitors, specify the foreground colors for each area and then the background color; e.g., **SET COLOR TO B,G,R** establishes blue text on a red background in the standard display area and green text on a red background in the enhanced display area.
7. If either the foreground or background color is omitted from a color pair, black is selected.
8. The **ISCOLOR()** function returns a logical true if the current monitor is a color monitor, and a logical false if it is a monochrome monitor. A program can test the value of this condition, then set color codes accordingly.

Related Topics

```
CONFIG.DB
ISCOLOR()
SET DELIMITERS
SET INTENSITY
```

SET CONFIRM

Syntax

```
SET CONFIRM ON/OFF
```

Discussion

The **SET CONFIRM** command determines whether or not the cursor moves automatically to the next input template when data completely fills the current template. The choice between **ON** (having to confirm each entry with the return key even when the template is filled) and **OFF** (automatic advancement to the next field) is one of personal preference, with valid arguments both pro and con. Setting **CONFIRM ON** lends consistency to data entry, but also slows it to some degree.

Tips

1. Many users choose to **SET CONFIRM ON** when **SET BELL** is **OFF**, so that pressing the return key is necessary at the end of every input template. This prevents a user from overtyping one field into the next without any warning.
2. Consistency throughout a system regarding the status of **BELL** and **CONFIRM** is important, so that the user always knows what is expected, and does not have to guess at data entry.

Related Topics

SET BELL

SET CONSOLE

Syntax

```
SET CONSOLE ON/OFF
```

Discussion

The **SET CONSOLE** command turns the screen display on and off and affects such output as listings, report and label forms, as well as output produced by the **?**, **LIST**, and **DISPLAY** commands. It does not, however, affect screen displays resulting from full-screen commands such as **@...SAY**, **APPEND**, or **EDIT**, nor does it inhibit dBASE error or safety messages.

Tips

1. **SET CONSOLE OFF** has no effect when issued from the dot prompt; that is, **SET CONSOLE** is always **ON** in the interactive mode.
2. dBASE error messages and command responses (for example, *Find not successful* and *100% indexed*) are suppressed with **SET TALK OFF**, and are not affected by the **SET CONSOLE** command.
3. The screen display is often suppressed during the printing of report forms or mailing labels; e.g.,

```
SET CONSOLE OFF
REPORT FORM ... TO PRINTER
LABEL FORM ... TO PRINTER
SET CONSOLE ON
```

   It is important, however, to turn the console back on when printing is finished.
4. The **WAIT** command is often preceded with **@ ... SAY** commands to print custom messages, then bracketed with **SET CONSOLE ON** and **OFF**, to suppress the standard message produced by the **WAIT** command; e.g.,

```
@ ... SAY commands for custom messages
SET CONSOLE OFF
WAIT
SET CONSOLE ON
```

Related Topics

```
?
DISPLAY
LABEL FORM
LIST
REPORT FORM
SET DEVICE
SET TALK
WAIT
```

SET DATE

Syntax

```
SET DATE AMERICAN
SET DATE ANSI
SET DATE BRITISH
SET DATE FRENCH
SET DATE GERMAN
SET DATE ITALIAN
SET DATE JAPAN
SET DATE USA
SET DATE MDY
SET DATE DMY
SET DATE YMD
```

Discussion

The **SET DATE** command determines which of eleven date formats will be used with the display and input of all date fields. The choices are shown in the table:

Format	Appearance
AMERICAN	mm/dd/yy
ANSI	yy.mm.dd
BRITISH	dd/mm/yy
FRENCH	dd/mm/yy
GERMAN	dd.mm.yy
ITALIAN	dd-mm-yy
JAPAN	yy/mm/dd
USA	mm-dd-yy
MDY	mm/dd/yy
DMY	dd/mm/yy
YMD	yy/mm/dd

The default format is **AMERICAN**. Date arithmetic, indexing on a single date field, and date comparisons are done, regardless of the format in effect.

Tips

1. Character or literal dates that are input into date fields or stored in memory variables must be in a format consistent with the current setting of the **`SET DATE`** format; e.g.,

```
SET DATE FRENCH
STORE {25/12/92} TO memdate
```

2. The input templates for date fields reflect the format as established with the **`SET DATE`** command.
3. The **`DTOS()`** function must be used to convert a date field to character data to produce a concatenated character expression, regardless of the date format; e.g.,

```
SET DATE ITALIAN
INDEX ON DTOS(donor_date)+lastname TAG datename
```

4. **`SET CENTURY`** must be **`ON`** to display and input a four-digit year, and is essential when working with nontwentieth century dates.

Related Topics

```
CTOD()
DTOS()
INDEX
SET CENTURY
```

SET DEBUG

Syntax

SET DEBUG ON/**OFF**

Discussion

The **`SET DEBUG`** command determines whether output from the **`SET ECHO`** command is sent to the screen (**`DEBUG OFF`**) or to the printer (**`DEBUG ON`**). The **`SET DEBUG`** command is used as a debugging tool in conjunction with the **`SET ECHO`** command, and has no effect unless **`SET ECHO`** is **`ON`**. When **`SET ECHO`** is **`ON`**, each program command is displayed on the screen as it is executed. Thus, **`SET DEBUG ON`**, in conjunction with **`SET ECHO ON`**, directs the display of the command to the printer rather than the screen, preventing interference with the program's formatted screen displays.

Tips

1. The **`SET DEBUG`** command, in conjunction with the **`SET ECHO`** command, is an excellent debugging tool, especially when trying to determine whether conditional processing and/or looping structures are executing properly. It is helpful to **`SET TALK ON`** as well, to provide yet additional information.
2. The **`SET DEBUG`** command causes line numbers to be included in the printout, a further aid in debugging conditional processing and looping structures.
3. The **`SET ECHO`** and **`SET DEBUG`** commands can both be issued from within a program as well as from the dot prompt. Rather than issuing the commands prior to running a program, it is often more efficient to isolate the problem to a particular section of code, set the parameters **`ON`** from within the program immediately prior to that section, and then **`OFF`** again immediately below it. When the errors have been corrected, remember to delete the commands from the program altogether.

4. When **SET DEBUG** and **SET ECHO** are both **ON**, output from **SET TALK**, **LIST**, and **DISPLAY** commands is not sent to the printer unless **SET PRINTER** is **ON**.

Related Topics

```
DEBUG
SET ECHO
SET PRINTER
SET STEP
SET TALK
```

SET DEFAULT TO

Syntax

```
SET DEFAULT TO <drive>[:]
```

Discussion

The **SET DEFAULT** command changes the default drive; i.e., the drive to which dBASE refers when it is reading or writing files. The command does not refer to the drive containing the dBASE program files; i.e., if dBASE itself is executing from drive C, and the data files are on drive A, **SET DEFAULT TO A** is required immediately after loading dBASE.

The **SET DEFAULT** command cannot be used to change subdirectories; i.e., the default directory on any given drive is the directory logged prior to loading dBASE.

Tips

1. The **SET DEFAULT TO** command does not check that the specified drive actually exists, and no error message is given if it does not. If an invalid drive is designated, the logged drive remains the default.
2. The **DISPLAY STATUS** command verifies the default drive.
3. Each dBASE application should be kept in its own subdirectory, with the dBASE program files stored in yet another subdirectory. In no event should the program files and data files be stored in the same subdirectory.
4. The following procedure may be used to log into the appropriate subdirectory prior to loading dBASE:
   i. From DOS, change to the directory containing the particular dBASE application; e.g,

      ```
      C:\>CD C:\DATADISK\ZOO
      ```

   ii. Set a path to the dBASE program files (if it hasn't already been done through the **AUTOEXEC.BAT** file) with the DOS **PATH** command; e.g.,

      ```
      C:\DATADISK\ZOO>PATH C:\DBASEIV
      ```

   iii. Load dBASE from the logged subdirectory; e.g.,

      ```
      C:\DATADISK\ZOO>DBASE
      ```

   iv. Type **DISPLAY STATUS** to confirm that dBASE is defaulting to the data drive; if not, issue the appropriate **SET DEFAULT** command.
5. The **RUN** command can be used to change subdirectories after dBASE has been loaded; e.g.,

   ```
   RUN CD C:\DATADISK\USSTATES
   ```

The path must begin with the drive letter and include the complete path (starting with the root directory) to the desired subdirectory.

Related Topics

```
DISPLAY STATUS
SET PATH
```

SET DELETED

Syntax

```
SET DELETED ON/OFF
```

Discussion

The **SET DELETED** command determines whether records marked for deletion are processed by other dBASE commands; i.e., **SET DELETED ON** causes dBASE to ignore records marked for deletion, treating them as though they were not physically in the database.

A deleted record can still be accessed when **SET DELETED** is **ON** if the record pointer is explicitly moved to the deleted record with a **GO** command or if the record number of the deleted record is explicitly specified. For example, if record 3 is marked for deletion and the command **GO 3** is executed immediately before a **DISPLAY** command, dBASE will display the record even though it is marked for deletion. In similar fashion, **EDIT RECORD 3** will bring up record 3 for editing, whereas it would not be accessible through the **PgUp** and **PgDn** keys during an **EDIT** session.

Tips

1. The **INDEX ON** and **REINDEX** commands process all of the records in a database, including those marked for deletion, regardless of whether **SET DELETED** is **ON** or **OFF**.
2. The **RECALL ALL** command has no effect (i.e., no records are recalled) when **SET DELETED** is **ON**. A specific record can still be recalled by including the record number in the command; e.g., **RECALL RECORD 3**.
3. **SET DELETED ON** does not affect the position of the record pointer; i.e., if a deleted record is the current record when a **SET DELETED ON** command is issued, it remains the current record.

Related Topics

```
DELETE
DELETED()
INDEX
PACK
RECALL
```

SET DELIMITERS

Syntax

```
SET DELIMITERS TO <character expression/DEFAULT>
SET DELIMITERS ON/OFF
```

Discussion

The **SET DELIMITERS** command determines whether the input templates displayed through an **APPEND**, **EDIT**, or **@...GET** command are offset by a beginning and ending character (i.e., delimiters). The use of delimiters is in addition to (or, if **SET INTENSITY** is **OFF**, instead of) the reverse video effect, which appears by default.

The choice of delimiter is determined by the **SET DELIMITERS TO** command; the delimiters appear, however, only if **SET DELIMITERS** is **ON**. Thus, the combination of

```
SET DELIMITERS TO "<>"
SET DELIMITERS ON
```

will create input templates delimited by the less than/greater than signs (e.g., < ░ >). The delimiters can be reset to their default value (:) with a **SET DELIMITERS TO DEFAULT** command.

Tips

1. If only one delimiter is specified in the **SET DELIMITERS TO** command, it will appear before and after the input template. If two different delimiters are specified, the first appears before the input template, and the second one appears after.
2. Common delimiters used are [ ], { }, | |, ( ), and < >.
3. The reverse video display of the input templates is suppressed with **SET INTENSITY OFF**, causing the templates to be differentiated only by delimiters. Accordingly, the **INTENSITY** and **DELIMITERS** parameters should not both be off at the same time.
4. A **SET COLOR OF FIELDS** command has no effect on input templates if **SET INTENSITY** is **OFF**; i.e., the input templates will have the same appearance as the standard display area.
5. New default delimiters can be established with a **DELIMITERS =** command in the **CONFIG.DB** file.
6. **SET DELIMITERS ON**, with no subsequent **SET DELIMITERS TO** command, displays the default delimiters (colon) for all input templates. A **SET DELIMITERS TO** command has no effect unless accompanied by a **SET DELIMITERS ON** command, however.

Related Topics

CONFIG.DB
SET COLOR
SET INTENSITY

SET DEVELOPMENT

Syntax

SET DEVELOPMENT **ON**/OFF

Discussion

The **SET DEVELOPMENT** command determines whether dBASE will compare the date and time stamps of a **PRG** file and its associated **DBO** file prior to executing the **DBO** file. By default, **SET DEVELOPMENT** is **ON**, causing the program to be recompiled whenever the **DBO** file has an earlier date and time than the **PRG** file. There is no comparison when **SET DEVELOPMENT** is **OFF**, so that any existing **DBO** file is immediately executed regardless of whether it is current.

Tips

1. **MODIFY COMMAND** automatically deletes the **DBO** file when the **PRG** file is edited, forcing dBASE to recompile the program.
2. When an external word processor is used to edit a **PRG** file, the program is not recompiled unless **SET DEVELOPMENT** is **ON**. If **SET DEVELOPMENT** is **OFF**, the **DBO** file must be erased, or a **COMPILE** command must be issued to explicitly recompile the program.

Related Topics

```
COMPILE
MODIFY COMMAND
```

SET DEVICE

Syntax

```
SET DEVICE TO PRINTER/SCREEN/FILE <filename>
```

Discussion

The **SET DEVICE** command determines whether output produced by an **@...SAY** command is sent to the printer, screen, or a text file. It is important to reset the **DEVICE** to the **SCREEN** after output is rerouted, so that processing will resume normal operations; e.g.,

```
SET DEVICE TO PRINTER
@ 5,10 SAY "Employee Last Name: " + lastname
@ 7,10 SAY "Employee Initials: " + initials
.
. ——————————— Additional @...SAY commands
.
SET DEVICE TO SCREEN
```

Tips

1. **SET DEVICE TO PRINTER** affects only the output produced by **@...SAY** commands; i.e., output from other commands (e.g., **LIST**, **DISPLAY**, **REPORT FORM**, and **LABEL FORM**), as well as dBASE error and informational messages, continue to go to the screen. Note, too, output produced by the **@...TO** command cannot be rerouted to the printer with a **SET DEVICE TO PRINTER** command.
2. Printing may not begin immediately as data is held in the printer's buffer area. It is good practice, therefore, to follow the final **@...SAY** command with an **EJECT** command, to force the last of the data from the buffer area.
3. Output of **@...SAY** commands can be sent to only one device at a time. Therefore, parallel sets of **@...SAY** commands (with **DEVICE** alternately set to **SCREEN**, **PRINTER**, and **FILE**) are necessary if output is to be sent to more than one device.
4. Any **GET** commands, included within an **@...SAY...GET** command, are ignored when **DEVICE** is set to the **PRINTER**.
5. A file created with a **SET DEVICE TO FILE** command has a default extension of **TXT** and remains open until the device is set back to **SCREEN**. The text file can be subsequently modified with a word processor.
6. When the output of an **@...SAY** command is rerouted to the printer, the row and column coordinates can range from 0 to 32,767 and 0 to 255, respectively, although the printer may have its own, and probably smaller, limitations.

7. When the output of an **@...SAY** command is sent to the printer, the page should be mapped from top to bottom and from left to right, to avoid unintentional page breaks. In addition, when a row number lower than the row number in a previous command is encountered, dBASE ejects the page and prints at the proper row and column coordinates on the next page.
8. Output from **@...SAY** commands cannot be written to a file using the **SET ALTERNATE** command.
9. Output from dBASE commands such as **?**, **LIST**, **DISPLAY**, **REPORT FORM**, and **LABEL FORM** is sent to the printer by including a **TO PRINTER** clause with the command or by first issuing a **SET PRINTER ON** command.

Related Topics

```
@...SAY
EJECT
SET ALTERNATE
SET PRINTER
```

SET DISPLAY

Syntax

```
SET DISPLAY TO MONO/COLOR/EGA25/EGA43/MONO43
```

Discussion

The **SET DISPLAY** command is used to switch between a color and a monochrome monitor in systems that have both and/or to switch between the 25- and 43-line display modes on monitors supporting both. A *Display mode not available* message is displayed if the selected mode is not supported.

Tips

1. The **SET COLOR** command can also be used to switch between a color and monochrome monitor.
2. The display mode determines the maximum row value for an **@...FILL**, **@...CLEAR**, **@...SAY**, **@...TO**, **DEFINE POPUP**, or **DEFINE WINDOW** command.
3. The monitor remains in the 43-line mode even after exiting dBASE.

Related Topics

```
@...CLEAR
@...FILL
@...SAY
@...TO
DEFINE POPUP
DEFINE WINDOW
SET COLOR
```

SET ECHO

Syntax

```
SET ECHO ON/OFF
```

Discussion

The **SET ECHO** command is a debugging tool that displays commands from a program as they are executed. Output from the command is intermingled with the normal screen display unless **SET DEBUG** is **ON**, in which case it is directed to the printer.

Tips

1. The **SET ECHO** command is an excellent debugging tool, especially when trying to determine whether conditional processing and/or looping structures are executing properly. It is helpful to **SET TALK ON** as well, to provide yet additional information.
2. The line numbers are included in the display as a further aid in debugging.
3. The display of executed commands will generally scroll by too quickly to permit detailed study, making it necessary to press the **Pause** key or **Ctrl+S** to pause the display (pressing any key to continue). Alternatively, you can **SET DEBUG ON** to direct output of the **ECHO** command to the printer.
4. The **SET STEP ON** command executes one command at a time, pausing until the space bar is pressed, before continuing to the next command. This prevents rapid scrolling when **SET ECHO** is **ON**, but the screen becomes very hard to read because dBASE displays the message *Press SPACE to skip, S to suspend, or Esc to cancel . . .* after each command.
5. The **SET ECHO** and **SET DEBUG** commands can both be issued from within a program as well as from the dot prompt. Rather than issuing the commands prior to running a program, it is often more efficient to isolate the problem to a particular section of code, set the parameters **ON** from within the program immediately prior to that section, and then **OFF** again immediately below it. When the errors have been corrected, remember to delete the commands from the program altogether.
6. When **SET DEBUG** and **SET ECHO** are both **ON**, output from **SET TALK**, **LIST**, and **DISPLAY** commands is not sent to the printer unless **SET PRINTER** is **ON**.

Related Topics

DEBUG
SET DEBUG
SET PRINTER
SET STEP
SET TALK

SET ESCAPE

Syntax

```
SET ESCAPE ON/OFF
```

Discussion

The **SET ESCAPE** command determines whether pressing the **Esc** key will interrupt the command or program being executed. When **SET ESCAPE** is **ON**, pressing the **Esc** key during execution of a command from the dot prompt terminates the command, displays the message

****Interrupted****, and returns control to the dot prompt. Pressing the key during execution of a program halts processing, displays the current command, and prompts with a choice of *Cancel Ignore Suspend.* A choice of cancel will terminate the program and return to the dot prompt, whereas ignore simply resumes execution. Suspend halts execution, but allows additional commands (**DISPLAY HISTORY**, **DISPLAY MEMORY**, and so on) to be entered from the dot prompt to aid in debugging. The **RESUME** command can be entered to continue execution at the point in the program where it was suspended.

SET ESCAPE OFF from the dot prompt disables the key so that it has no effect, except for full-screen commands (**BROWSE**, **APPEND**, and so on); i.e., they will still be terminated when the **Esc** key is pressed, even if **SET ESCAPE** is **OFF**. **SET ESCAPE OFF** from a program, however, disables the key completely.

Tips

1. **SET ESCAPE** should be **OFF** at the beginning of a program, so that a user is not returned to the dot prompt if the **Esc** key is inadvertently pressed (or if the user purposefully tries to interrupt a lengthy, but crucial, process). Remember, however, to **SET ESCAPE ON** at the end of the program.
2. **SET ESCAPE** should be **ON** during program development and debugging.
3. When **SET ESCAPE** is **OFF**, a program can be interrupted only by turning the computer off or rebooting the system.
4. Pressing **Ctrl+S** to pause the display has no effect when **SET ESCAPE** is **OFF**.

Related Topics

CANCEL
RESUME
SUSPEND

SET EXACT

Syntax

```
SET EXACT ON/OFF
```

Discussion

The **SET EXACT** command determines whether two character strings must be the same length to be considered equal. When **SET EXACT** is **OFF** (the default), the two strings are considered equal as long as all the characters in the string on the right of the relational operator are identical to the characters in the same position in the string on the left, regardless of the length of the respective strings. For example, the commands,

```
SET EXACT OFF
LIST FOR lname = "Sm"
```

will return records for Smith, Smitty, Smithson; i.e, any name beginning with "Sm" will be included, regardless of its length.

SET EXACT ON, however, imposes the additional requirement that the strings be the same length; i.e., no records will be returned in the above example unless someone has the unusual last name of "Sm".

Tips

1. The status of **SET EXACT** pertains to any command involving the comparison of two character strings; e.g., implicit comparisons in commands such as **SEEK** and **FIND**, as well as the explicit comparisons in a **FOR** or **WHILE** clause.
2. Upper- and lower-case letters are treated as different characters, regardless of whether **SET EXACT** is **ON** or **OFF**. For example, the command

   ```
   FIND MILLER
   ```

   will not find either "Miller" or "miller".

Related Topics

```
FIND
LOCATE
SEEK
```

SET FIELDS

Syntax

```
SET FIELDS TO
    [<field> [/R]/<calculated field id=expression,...]
SET FIELDS TO ALL [LIKE/EXCEPT <skeleton>]
SET FIELDS ON/OFF
```

Discussion

The **SET FIELDS TO** command establishes an active field list for a **DBF** file, effectively hiding the other fields from view; i.e., only those fields included in the field list are accessible by dBASE commands.

Any subsequently issued **SET FIELDS** command adds to, rather than replaces, the existing field list; for example, in the commands,

```
SET FIELDS TO ssn,lastname
SET FIELDS TO initials
```

the first command establishes a field list consisting of **ssn** and **lastname**; the second command adds **initials**, so that the active list contains all three fields.

Fields may be designated as read-only by specifying the **/R** parameter with the field name, e.g., **SET FIELDS TO lastname,salary/R**. The read-only fields will be displayed as usual, but will not be available for editing.

Calculated fields that are not a part of the **DBF** file can be included by specifying a field identifier and necessary expression, e.g., **SET FIELDS TO state,density=popltn/area**. The calculated field does not become part of the **DBF** file, but is displayed as though it were. The field identifier is used as the column heading.

The active field list applies to all open **DBF** files, regardless of which work area they are in; i.e., there is a single field list applicable to all ten work areas, as opposed to ten individual field lists. The active list must therefore contain every field from every **DBF** file that needs to be accessed. Fields from different databases can be added to the active list in one of two ways, by

1. Including fields from nonselected **DBF** files with the file alias preceding the field name.
2. Selecting a work area and issuing a **SET FIELDS** command for the fields in that work area, then selecting a second work area and issuing another **SET FIELDS** command. The latter group will be added to the existing field list.

Activating fields from multiple work areas does not establish any relationship between files, nor does it require one; in general, however, a relationship is established with the **SET RELATION** command prior to establishing the field list.

The **SET FIELDS TO ALL** command adds all fields in the currently selected **DBF** file to the active field list. **ALL LIKE/EXCEPT** option allows wild card characters (* and **?**) to be used to activate or exclude groups of similarly named fields; e.g., **SET FIELDS TO ALL LIKE tr*** adds all fields that begin with "tr", whereas **SET FIELDS TO ALL EXCEPT tr*** adds all fields *except* those that begin with "tr".

A **CLEAR FIELDS** command eliminates the effect of all previous **SET FIELDS** commands, returning to the default status where all fields are accessible.

Tips

1. The error message *No fields to process* will be displayed if a **SET FIELDS ON** command is issued before a field list has been established.
2. The **SET FIELDS TO** command eliminates the need to continually specify the same field list.
3. A **SET FIELDS OFF** command should be issued prior to working with an unrelated **DBF** file open in another work area. Otherwise, if a field list is active when a new **DBF** file is opened, no fields in that file will be active.
4. With commands that honor the field list, attempts to access inactive fields will result in a *Variable not found* error message.
5. If several **DBF** files have fields with identical names included in the active field list, distinguish between the fields with the file alias. Otherwise, dBASE will use the first field name that it finds in the active field list.
6. The **DISPLAY STRUCTURE** command indicates all active fields by placing a greater than sign (>) to the left of the field name.
7. Indexes whose key expressions include fields not in the active field list may still be used.
8. The **LOCATE**, **SET FILTER**, and **SET RELATION** commands ignore the active field list and can access all fields.
9. A field list should not be active when records are appended to a file; i.e., it is best to append records to one **DBF** file at a time, with all fields accessible.
10. A **SET FIELDS TO** command cancels the active field list. **SET FIELDS OFF** temporarily disables the active field list, and a subsequent **SET FIELDS ON** will restore it.
11. Do not include a field in a **SET FIELDS TO** command that was specified in a previous **SET FIELDS TO** command, or the field will be displayed twice. In similar fashion, do not issue a **SET FIELDS TO ALL** command if any of the fields is already in the active field list.
12. The wild card characters—the asterisk and the question mark—are used in the skeleton. The * matches one or more characters from its position to the end of the variable name; the **?** matches any single character in its exact position.

Related Topics

CLEAR
DISPLAY STRUCTURE
SET RELATION

SET FILTER

Syntax

```
SET FILTER TO [FILE <filename>]/[condition]
```

Discussion

The **SET FILTER** command hides from view all records in the currently selected **DBF** file that do not meet the specified filter condition. It is analogous to the **SET DELETED** command in that once a filter has been set, records not meeting the condition are treated as though they were not physically present in the database. However, as with the **SET DELETED** command, a record not meeting the filter condition will still be processed if it is the current record, or if it is explicitly referenced in a command; e.g., **EDIT RECORD 3**.

A filter condition can be based on any valid expression and is established in one of two ways, either by specifying the condition in a **SET FILTER** command; e.g.,

```
SET FILTER TO hiredate > {03/16/87}
```

or by opening a query file in which the filter condition was previously saved; e.g.,

```
SET FILTER TO FILE hirespec
```

The **SET FILTER** command is most useful when the same subset of records is to be processed by many different commands; e.g.,

Without filter condition:

```
LIST FOR salary > 20000
REPORT FORM employee FOR salary > 20000
LABEL FORM employee FOR salary > 20000
COPY TO mail.txt FOR salary > 20000 DELIMITED
```

With filter condition:

```
SET FILTER TO salary > 20000
LIST
REPORT FORM employee
LABEL FORM employee
COPY TO mail.txt DELIMITED
```

The two sets of commands produce equivalent results. The second set, however, is easier to use, and less susceptible to error as the condition is entered only once.

An existing filter condition is deactivated, with all records once again accessible, by issuing a **SET FILTER TO** command with neither a condition nor a file name.

Tips

1. Most dBASE commands respect the filter condition and process only those records meeting the specified condition. **INDEX ON**, **REINDEX**, and **ZAP** are exceptions, as they ignore the filter condition and process all records. Similarly, **RECCOUNT()** also ignores the filter condition, returning the total number of records in the file.
2. A filter condition can be built with any of the relational operators (=, <>, >, >=, <, <=) and/or any of the logical operators (**.AND.**, **.OR.**, **.NOT.**).
3. There can be only one **FILTER** condition in effect in a work area at one time; i.e., issuing a second **SET FILTER** command deactivates the first filter condition. A different filter condition can, however, be in effect in each of the ten work areas.

4. A filter condition can be stored in a memory variable and subsequently activated with macro notation; e.g.,

```
STORE "salary > 20000" TO mcond
SET FILTER TO &mcond
```

5. A filter condition is not activated until the record pointer is moved, even if the current record does not meet the filter condition; hence commands that begin processing with the current record may produce invalid results. It is recommended, therefore, that the record pointer be repositioned to a record meeting the condition (or to the top of the file) before issuing any additional commands.

Related Topics

```
CREATE/MODIFY QUERY
SET DELETED
```

SET FORMAT

Syntax

```
SET FORMAT TO [<filename>]
```

Discussion

The **SET FORMAT TO** command opens an existing format file containing a previously designed data entry screen. The effect is visible, however, only in conjunction with a subsequent full-screen editing command, such as **APPEND**, **EDIT**, or **INSERT**. The custom screen in the format file is displayed instead of the input templates associated with the full-screen commands and is preferable because:

1. It is more attractive, apt to contain more explicit prompting messages, and certainly more user friendly.
2. Additional formatting and data validation procedures, as well as security precautions, are possible.
3. Fields from related databases can be included in the same input screen.

Only one format file can be open in one work area at one time; i.e., issuing a second **SET FORMAT** command closes the open format file and opens the new file. A different format file can, however, be open in each of the ten work areas.

A format file remains open until a **CLOSE FORMAT** or a **SET FORMAT TO** command (with no filename) is specified, or until its associated **DBF** file is closed.

Tips

1. When a **SET FORMAT TO** command is executed, dBASE looks for an **FMO** file. If one does not exist, dBASE then looks for an **FMT** file, compiles it, and executes the resultant **FMO** file. When a **MODIFY SCREEN** command is used to edit a format file, dBASE automatically generates a new **FMT** file and recompiles it.
2. A format file is best created through the **CREATE/MODIFY SCREEN** command.
3. If a format file includes fields from other than the currently selected **DBF** file, those files must be open and any necessary relationships established.
4. A **READ** command activates an open format file, producing a problem in programs attempting to read memory variables while the format file is open. Close the format file prior to getting the memory variables.
5. A **BROWSE** command that specifies the **FORMAT** option uses the picture clauses, messages, and data validation restrictions as defined in the active format file. The format

file must be opened with a **SET FORMAT TO** command prior to issuing the **BROWSE** command.

Related Topics

```
APPEND
BROWSE
CLOSE
CREATE SCREEN
EDIT
INSERT
MODIFY COMMAND
READ
SET VIEW
```

SET FUNCTION

Syntax

```
SET FUNCTION <expression> TO <character expression>[;]
```

Discussion

The **SET FUNCTION** command is used to reprogram a function key or a combination of the function key with the **Shift** or **Ctrl** key. The key to be reprogrammed may be identified by name (**F2** through **F10**, **Ctrl-F1** through **Ctrl-F10**, and **Shift-F1** through **Shift-F9**), by number (2 to 29, respectively), or by a using a memory variable storing a string value equivalent to its name (e.g., **STORE "Shift-F2 TO mname**, followed by **SET FUNCTION mname TO "USE ZOO"**). The expression assigned to the key must be a character expression of 238 characters or fewer, and must be enclosed in quotation marks.

The function key may be set in such a way as to execute the command immediately, or merely display the command at the dot prompt. A semicolon represents the enter key, and including the semicolon in the expression will execute the command. Omitting the semicolon, on the other hand, requires the user to press the return key to execute the command. Consider:

```
SET FUNCTION 5 TO "USE solemp;"
SET FUNCTION 6 TO "MODIFY COMMAND"
```

Pressing the **F5** key will open the file **SOLEMP.DBF**. Pressing the **F6** key, however, will display **MODIFY COMMAND** at the dot prompt with the cursor positioned to the right of the command. The desired filename can then be entered, and the return key pressed to execute the command.

Tips

1. The **F1** and the **Shift-F10** keys cannot be reprogrammed as they are reserved for **HELP** and macro recording, respectively. Nor can the **Alt** key be programmed in conjunction with the function keys, as those key combinations are reserved for macro operations.
2. On enhanced keyboards the **F11** and **F12** keys cannot be programmed, either alone or in combination with the **Shift** or **Ctrl** keys.
3. The **DISPLAY STATUS** command will list the current settings of the programmable function keys. The default settings are shown in the following table:

Key	Setting
F2	ASSIST;
F3	LIST;
F4	DIR;
F5	DISPLAY STRUCTURE;
F6	DISPLAY STATUS;
F7	DISPLAY MEMORY;
F8	DISPLAY;
F9	APPEND;
F10	EDIT;

4. Multiple commands can be stored to the same function key by separating them with semicolons; e.g.,

```
SET FUNCTION 3 TO "USE solemp; SET ORDER TO"
```

   Pressing the **F3** key will open **SOLEMP.DBF**, then display **SET ORDER TO** at the dot prompt, allowing the user to enter the name of the index tag. Pressing the return key executes the latter command.
5. The expression assigned to a function key through a **SET FUNCTION** command is overridden by an **ON KEY** assignment for the same key, issued from within a program.

Related Topics

DISPLAY STATUS
ON KEY

SET HEADING

Syntax

```
SET HEADING ON/OFF
```

Discussion

The **SET HEADING** command determines whether a heading line is displayed in conjunction with the **DISPLAY**, **LIST**, **AVERAGE**, **CALCULATE**, and **SUM** commands. If present, the heading will show the field names and/or expressions exactly as they were entered in the command; i.e., if the command was typed in lower case, the heading line will also be in lower case. The width of each column is determined by the field width, as established by the file structure, or by the width of the field expression, whichever is greater. If, however, headings are not displayed (**SET HEADING** is **OFF**), the column width is determined by the field width.

Tips

1. Complex field expressions are difficult to read when they appear in a heading line; **SET HEADING OFF** may be worthwhile in such instances.
2. It may also be advantageous to **SET HEADING OFF** in a program that prints a listing with **DISPLAY ALL** or **LIST**, as more descriptive headings can be created by the **@...SAY** or **?** commands.

Related Topics

```
@...SAY
AVERAGE
CALCULATE
DISPLAY
LIST
SUM
```

SET HELP

Syntax

```
SET HELP ON/OFF
```

Discussion

The **SET HELP** command determines whether dBASE offers help in the event of a syntax error at the dot prompt. The default status is **ON**, so that when an error is made, dBASE displays an error box that allows a choice of *Cancel Edit Help*. Cancel returns you to the dot prompt, Edit allows the command line to be edited and reexecuted, and Help brings up the help menu. Setting **HELP** to **OFF** precludes the offer of help, presenting a choice of only Cancel or Edit.

Tips

1. The F1 function key will bring up the **HELP** menu, regardless of the status of **SET HELP**.
2. A choice is made from the error box by highlighting the desired item and pressing the enter key or by pressing the initial letter of the item name.

Related Topics

```
HELP
```

SET HISTORY

Syntax

```
SET HISTORY ON/OFF
SET HISTORY TO <numeric expression>
```

Discussion

The **SET HISTORY** commands determine whether commands entered at the dot prompt are stored in history memory, and if so, the number of commands that can be held at one time. The default status is **ON**, which enables commands to be recalled by using the up and down arrow keys, edited if necessary, and reissued. Commands are displayed from the most recent to the least recent, and when the maximum number of commands is reached, the least recent are cleared one by one as new commands are executed.

SET HISTORY OFF prevents newly issued commands from being stored until **HISTORY** is turned back **ON**. Commands already in the history buffer can still be listed, but cannot be accessed and reissued.

The **SET HISTORY TO** command changes the number of commands that can be held in history memory from its default value of 20 to any integer between 0 and 16,000.

Tips

1. Commands executed from within a program file are not stored in history memory.
2. **SET HISTORY TO 0** clears all commands from history memory.
3. The commands stored in history memory can be viewed with a **DISPLAY/LIST HISTORY** command.
4. A further restriction on the size of history memory is established by the amount of available memory in the system.

Related Topics

DISPLAY/LIST HISTORY

SET INDEX

Syntax

```
SET INDEX TO [<filename list> [ORDER [TAG] <filename>/
    <mdx tagname> [OF <mdx filename>]]]
```

Discussion

The **SET INDEX TO** command opens one or more existing single index files (**NDX**) and/or independent multiple index files (**MDX**) that are associated with the currently selected **DBF** file. The command is *not* used with the production **MDX** file as it is automatically opened in conjunction with the **DBF** file. A maximum of ten **NDX** and **MDX** files can be opened, with the master index being determined as follows:

1. If an **NDX** file is the first (or only) file listed, it becomes the master index.
2. If an independent **MDX** file is the first (or only) file listed, the **DBF** file will be processed in physical order if no **ORDER** clause is specified, or in the logical order of the indicated tag if an **ORDER** clause is specified.

The master index determines the logical sequence in which records are accessed, and the one used by the **SEEK** and **FIND** commands. When multiple indexes are opened in the same command, the indexes listed in addition to the master index have no effect on how the records are processed, but are open only so that they will be updated as changes are made to the **DBF** file.

A **CLOSE INDEXES** or a **SET INDEX TO** command, with no filenames listed, will close all open indexes (**NDX** and **MDX**), except for the production **MDX** file. Closing the **DBF** file with a **USE** or **CLOSE DATABASES** command closes all open index files, including the production **MDX** file.

Tips

1. Existing single index files can also be opened with the **INDEX** clause in the **USE** command; e.g., the single command,

   ```
   USE file1 INDEX lastname,location,title
   ```

   is equivalent to the two commands:

   ```
   USE file1
   SET INDEX TO lastname,location,title
   ```

2. A **SET INDEX TO** command closes any open single index files and independent **MDX** files, then opens the indexes specified in the file list.
3. A **SET INDEX TO** command repositions the record pointer to the first record of the master index.
4. Updating a **DBF** file will automatically update all open indexes (those in the production **MDX** file as well as those explicitly opened with a **SET INDEX TO** command). If any indexes (e.g., independent **MDX** files or **NDX** files) were not open when the database file was updated, the nonopen indexes must be subsequently opened and reindexed. This is extremely important, as opening an out-of-date index does not produce an error message, just unreliable results.
5. The **OF** clause should be used when the tag specified as the master index is contained in an **MDX** file other than the production **MDX** file and/or when two or more open **MDX** files all contain that tag name.
6. Inadvertently opening an **NDX** or **MDX** file not matching the currently selected database produces an error message. However, opening an **NDX** file normally associated with another **DBF** file, but which has a key expression appropriate for the current **DBF** file, will not produce an error message, just bizarre results.
7. The **SET ORDER TO** command changes the master index without closing any of the open indexes.

Related Topics

```
CLOSE
INDEX ON
REINDEX
SET ORDER
USE
```

SET INTENSITY

Syntax

```
SET INTENSITY ON/OFF
```

Discussion

The **SET INTENSITY** command determines whether input templates for full-screen data entry operations are displayed in reverse video. The default status is **ON**, and reverse video is initially in effect. A **SET INTENSITY OFF** command removes the highlighting, so that the input templates are no longer differentiated from the standard display area.

Tips

1. The input templates displayed by the **APPEND**, **EDIT**, **INSERT**, and **@...GET** commands are affected by the **SET INTENSITY** command.
2. **SET INTENSITY** and **SET DELIMITERS** should not be **OFF** at the same time, as the input templates would no longer be differentiated from the standard display area.
3. The codes specified for the enhanced display area in the **SET COLOR** command determine the colors of the input templates. These colors can be overridden in a **SET COLOR OF FIELDS** command, which affects only the input templates and not the enhanced display areas.

Related Topics

```
SET COLOR
SET DELIMITERS
```

SET MEMOWIDTH

Syntax

```
SET MEMOWIDTH TO <numeric expression>
```

Discussion

The **SET MEMOWIDTH** command determines the width of the column used to display the contents of a memo field in the field list of a **LIST**, **DISPLAY**, or **?** command. The default width of 50 can be changed to any value between 8 and 255. Note, however, that setting a width larger than the display area (whether for the screen or a printed page) causes the individual lines to wrap around, making the display difficult to read. (On some printers the contents will be truncated rather than wrapped.)

Tips

1. The **@H** function code can be used with memo fields to override the default width as established by the **SET MEMOWIDTH** command. The **@H** function causes the template to expand or contract horizontally, depending on the length of the data to be output. Consider:

   Without @H function:

   ```
   SET MEMOWIDTH TO 30
   ? COMMENT
   This is memo field 1 and it is
       50 characters long
   ```

   Memo field wraps to two lines

   With @H function:

   ```
   USE ZOO
   SET MEMOWIDTH TO 30
   ? COMMENT FUNCTION "@H"
   This is memo field 1 and it is 50 characters long.
   ```

   Memo field doesn't wrap

2. The **@V<n>** function is similar to the **@H** function, but causes the template to stretch vertically in columnar fashion, the width of the column depending on the value specified by the **<n>** parameter. It also overrides the default memo field display established by the **SET MEMOWIDTH** command. Consider:

   Without @V function:

   ```
   . SET MEMOWIDTH TO 30
   . ? COMMENT
   This is memo field 1 and it is
   50 characters long.
   ```

   With @V function:

   ```
   . SET MEMOWIDTH TO 30
   . ? COMMENT FUNCTION "@V10"
   This is
   memo field
   1 and it
   is 50
   characters
   long.
   ```

   Memo field width determined by @V width

3. The value of the system memory variable `_wrap` must be true for the `@H` and `@V` functions to work as described above. The current value of `_wrap` can be determined with the command `? _wrap` (or by issuing a `DISPLAY MEMORY` command) and can be changed with a `STORE` command, e.g., `STORE .T. TO _wrap`.
4. When the system memory variable `_wrap` is set to true, the values of `_lmargin` and `_rmargin` determine the left and right margins for the output produced by the `?` command. Current values for `_lmargin`, `_rmargin` can be determined with a `?` command (e.g., `? _lmargin`) and can be changed with a `STORE` command, e.g., `STORE 10 TO _lmargin`.

Related Topics

```
?
DISPLAY
LIST
```

SET NEAR

Syntax

```
SET NEAR ON/OFF
```

Discussion

The `SET NEAR` command determines the position of the record pointer after an unsuccessful `FIND` or `SEEK` command. The record pointer is placed immediately below where the matching record should have been when `SET NEAR` is `ON`, and at the end of file when `SET NEAR` is `OFF`.

Tips

1. The `SET NEAR` respects both the `SET DELETED` and the `SET FILTER` commands, ignoring deleted records when `SET DELETED` is `ON`, and ignoring all records that do not meet an active filter condition.

Related Topics

```
FIND
SEEK
SET DELETED
SET FILTER
```

SET ORDER

Syntax

```
SET ORDER TO [TAG] <filename>/<mdx tagname>
    [OF <mdx filename>]
SET ORDER TO <numeric expression>
```

Discussion

The **SET ORDER** command selects a currently active index or tag as the master index without closing any other active index or moving the record pointer. The master index determines the logical sequence in which the records are processed, and the one used by the **FIND** and **SEEK** commands.

A **SET ORDER TO** command, with no parameters specified, deactivates all open indexes/tags without closing them. The file is processed in physical order, but all the indexes remain open for updating.

Tips

1. Updating a **DBF** file automatically updates all open indexes (those in the production **MDX** file as well as those opened with a **SET INDEX TO** command). Any indexes (e.g., independent **MDX** files or **NDX** files) that were not open when the database file was updated, must be subsequently opened and reindexed. This is extremely important, as opening an out-of-date index does not produce an error message, just unreliable results.
2. The **SET ORDER** command does *not* reposition the record pointer to the top of the file (as does a **SET INDEX** command); i.e., the current record remains the current record. A **GO TOP** command can be issued to position the record pointer at the first logical record.
3. The **OF** clause should be used when the tag specified as the master index is contained in an **MDX** file other than the production **MDX** file and/or when two or more open **MDX** files all contain that tag name.
4. The use of the keyword **TAG** is recommended whenever **NDX** and **MDX** files are both open, to differentiate between **NDX** filenames and tag names.
5. The **SET ORDER TO <numeric expression>** is retained in dBASE IV for compatibility with dBASE III Plus and can be used only in the absence of an **MDX** file. The numeric expression must be a number between 0 and 10, and establishes as the master index the **NDX** file whose position in the field list of the **SET INDEX TO** or **USE** command corresponds to the number specified. **SET ORDER TO 0** causes the database to be processed in physical order, as no master index is established, but leaves all of the **NDX** files open for updating.

Related Topics

```
INDEX ON
SET INDEX
USE
```

SET PATH

Syntax

```
SET PATH TO <path list>
```

Discussion

The dBASE **SET PATH** command specifies alternate subdirectories that are to be searched when the specified file cannot be found in the default directory. The command does *not*, however, store newly created files in the alternate directory. In other words, **SET PATH** does not change directories, but only provides an alternate place for dBASE to look for files not found in the present subdirectory.

Multiple paths may be specified, and are separated by commas or semicolons; e.g.,

```
SET PATH TO b:\soleil,b:\solstub
```

or

```
SET PATH TO b:\soleil;b:\solstub
```

The path list may not exceed 60 characters, and the paths are searched in the order that they are listed. Each path should begin with the drive letter and specify the full path, starting with the root directory.

The **SET PATH TO** command (with no path list) deactivates any existing path, restricting future searches to the current subdirectory.

Tips

1. The dBASE **SET PATH** command is different from the DOS **PATH** command in that the latter searches only for files with extensions of **BAT**, **COM**, or **EXE**, whereas the dBASE command searches for files of all types.
2. The following procedure may be used to log into the appropriate subdirectory prior to loading dBASE:
   i. From DOS, change to the directory containing the particular dBASE application; e.g,

      ```
      C:\>CD C:\DATADISK\ZOO
      ```

   ii. Set a path to the dBASE program files (if it hasn't already been done through the **AUTOEXEC.BAT** file) with the DOS **PATH** command; e.g.,

      ```
      C:\DATADISK\ZOO>PATH C:\DBASEIV
      ```

   iii. Load dBASE from the logged subdirectory; e.g.,

      ```
      C:\DATADISK\ZOO>DBASE
      ```

   iv. Type **DISPLAY STATUS** to confirm that dBASE is defaulting to the data drive; if not, issue the appropriate **SET DEFAULT** command.
3. The **RUN** command is used to change subdirectories after dBASE has been loaded; e.g.,

   ```
   RUN CD C:\DATADISK\USSTATES
   ```

   The path must begin with the drive letter and include the complete path (starting with the root directory) to the desired subdirectory.
4. The **DISPLAY STATUS** command displays the current search paths.
5. A path must be specified in the dBASE **DIR** command to obtain a listing of files in other than the default subdirectory; e.g.,

   ```
   DIR C:\DATADISK\SOLEIL\*.PRG
   ```

6. dBASE does not recognize paths established with the DOS **PATH** command (except through use of the **RUN** command, where the operating system actually takes control, searching the DOS path for the appropriate **COM**, **EXE**, or **BAT** file).
7. The control center does not recognize the paths established with a **SET PATH** command.

Related Topics

DIR
DISPLAY STATUS

SET PRINTER

Syntax

```
SET PRINTER ON/OFF
SET PRINTER TO <DOS device>
SET PRINTER TO FILE <filename>
```

Discussion

SET PRINTER ON directs all screen output (except for that of full-screen commands and text formatted with **@...SAY** commands) to the printer as well as to the screen. Included in the output sent to the printer are commands entered at the dot prompt, as well as the responses that dBASE displays on the screen. Accordingly, specification of **SET PRINTER ON** creates a printed record of all commands issued and their results.

The **SET PRINTER TO <DOS device>** command changes the default printer from **PRN** or **LPT1** to **LPT2**, **LPT3**, **COM1**, or **COM2**, depending on the destination printer.

The **SET PRINTER TO FILE** command sends output to the named disk file, following the specifications of the installed printer driver. The file can thereafter be printed from the DOS prompt with the command,

```
COPY filename.ext PRN
```

where *filename.ext* is the name of the file to be printed and **PRN** is the destination printer.

SET PRINTER OFF returns to the default mode, where output is displayed on the screen only.

Tips

1. **SET DEVICE TO PRINTER** must be issued to direct text formatted with **@...SAY** commands to the printer.
2. A **SET CONSOLE OFF** command, issued prior to **SET PRINTER ON**, suppresses the screen display while directing output to the printer.
3. The printer must be on-line before issuing a **SET PRINTER ON** command. If not, an error message will result.
4. **Ctrl+P** acts as a toggle switch to set the printer on and off, and can be used from the dot prompt instead of **SET PRINTER ON/OFF**.
5. The system memory variable **_pdriver** stores the name of the installed printer driver. Its value can be displayed with the command **? _pdriver**, and can be changed with a **STORE** command; e.g., **STORE "HPLAS100.PR2" TO _pdriver**. The installed printer driver determines the formatting codes used when creating a print file with a **SET PRINTER TO FILE** command.
6. The value of **_pdriver** can be set to **"ASCII.PR2"** to create an ASCII text file, or for that matter, to any other available printer driver name to create a file formatted for that specific printer. This is useful when printing current output at another location or on another printer.
7. Files created with the **SET PRINTER TO FILE** command, when the printer driver is **ASCII.PR2**, can be sent to any line printer or over any telecommunications link.
8. Do *not* print the file created with the **SET PRINTER TO FILE** command with the DOS **PRINT** command.
9. **SET PRINTER TO FILE** command stays in effect until another **SET PRINTER TO** command is issued.

Related Topics

```
SET CONSOLE
SET DEVICE
```

SET PROCEDURE

Syntax

```
SET PROCEDURE TO [<filename>]
```

Discussion

The **SET PROCEDURE** command loads the designated procedure file into memory, from where its individual procedures are available to other programs and/or procedures.

The advantage of a procedure over a program is speed; i.e., access to a procedure is nearly instantaneous as the procedure is already in memory, whereas a program has to be read from disk into memory before it can be executed.

Procedures that are called from only one program should be stored within that program, whereas procedures called by several different programs should be coded as part of a separate procedure file, and loaded into memory when the application is first started. This is done with the **SET PROCEDURE TO** command, which names the procedure file.

A procedure file may contain as many procedures as available memory will permit, up to a maximum of 1,170 procedures per file. Each procedure within the procedure file begins with a **PROCEDURE** statement and ends with a **RETURN** command. An individual procedure is executed by a **DO** command, which searches first for a like-named procedure, and if none is found, for a like-named program. (See the **DO** command for specifics.)

Only one procedure file can be open at one time; thus, opening a second procedure file implicitly closes the first one. A procedure file can also be explicitly closed with a **CLOSE PROCEDURE** command or a **SET PROCEDURE TO** command with no filename specified.

Tips

1. A procedure file is created in the same way as a program file; in other words, with **MODIFY COMMAND**, or with the nondocument mode of a word processor. The procedure file should be given a **PRG** extension.
2. If a **DBO** file does not exist when a **SET PROCEDURE** command is executed, dBASE compiles the corresponding **PRG** file, then executes the resulting **DBO** file.
3. The individual procedures in a procedure file should be separated from one another with a blank line to make each procedure easily identifiable.
4. A **DO...WITH** command passes data from the calling program to a procedure through a **PARAMETERS** statement, which must be the first executable statement in the procedure. This allows a generalized procedure to perform specific tasks, according to the needs of the calling program. For example, the procedure **PRINTMSG**,

```
PROCEDURE PRINTMSG
PARAMETERS message,mrow,mcol
@ mrow,mcol SAY message
RETURN
```

displays a message at a given location, depending on the values passed to it by the calling program. Thus, given the following program,

```
STORE 20 TO mrow
STORE 10 TO mcol
STORE 'Please enter a Y or N' TO msg
DO printmsg WITH msg,mrow,mcol
```

the message will be displayed at row 20, column 10, whereas the program below,

```
STORE 12 TO mrow
STORE 15 TO mcol
```

```
STORE 'Please enter option' TO msg
DO printmsg WITH msg,mrow,mcol
```

will display a different message at row 12, column 15.

5. The same procedure file can be used by many different applications.

Related Topics

```
DO
MODIFY COMMAND
PARAMETERS
PROCEDURE
```

SET RELATION

Syntax

```
SET RELATION TO
    [<key expression>/<expN> INTO <alias>],...]
```

Discussion

The **SET RELATION** command establishes a link between records in the currently selected **DBF** file and those in a second **DBF** file open in another work area, so that moving the record pointer in the currently selected file also moves the record pointer in the related file. The relationship can be based on a common field (the usual approach), or on record numbers, but either way the command enables data from two **DBF** files to be processed as though it were coming from a single file.

Consider, for example, a banking application with two files, for customers and loans, with a *one-to-many* relationship between customers and loans; i.e., one customer can have many loans. The following commands,

```
SELECT 1
USE customer ORDER cust_num
SELECT 2
USE loan
SET RELATION TO cust_num INTO customer
```

establish a relationship between the records in the currently selected (controlling) **DBF** file and those in the related file (i.e., the file specified in the **INTO** clause). The relationship is built on a common field (**cust_num**), and the related file must be open with a master index based on that common field. As the record pointer is moved in the controlling file, the record pointer is also moved in the related file so that data can be displayed from the two files as if it were contained in one. Thus, the commands,

```
SELECT 2
SET ORDER TO loan_num
LIST loan_num,loan_type,customer->last_name
```

will produce a list of loans in sequence by loan number, together with the corresponding customer names. Note that fields from the related file (**CUSTOMER.DBF**) must be preceded by the file alias in the **LIST** command.

Multiple relationships for the same file can be established with a single **SET RELATION** command. For example, to list all loans, together with the corresponding customer names *and* the primary loan officer, use the commands:

```
SELECT 3
USE officer ORDER off_id
SELECT 2
SET RELATION TO cust_num INTO customer,off_id INTO officer
LIST loan_amt,customer->last_name, officer->off_name
```

A relationship can also be established based on record numbers (rather than a key expression), in which case the related database is opened *without* an index, and a common field need not exist. If the relationship is established in this way, then whenever the record pointer moves to a new record in the controlling file, the record pointer in the related file is moved to the record with the corresponding record number. A numeric expression can be used in place of **RECNO( )**, where the result of the numeric expression determines the record number in the related file.

Issuing the command with no parameters (**SET RELATION TO**) deactivates the relationship; i.e., the record pointers will once again move independently in the two files.

Tips

1. The **SET RELATION** command moves the record pointer to the first matching record in the related file, but gives no indication whether other matching records exist, and further, makes no provision to find those other records. A **SET SKIP** command is needed to cause dBASE to find all of the matching records in the related file before it moves the record pointer to the next record in the controlling file. In our above example, the **SET SKIP** command can be used to list all loans for each customer, in sequence by customer number, as shown here:

   ```
   SELECT 1
   SET SKIP TO loan
   LIST last_name,loan->loan_num,loan->loan_type
   ```

   This time the customer file is the active file as it (**CUSTOMER.DBF**) is in the most recently selected work area; the **LIST** command includes the file alias for the unselected (loan) file.
2. A different relationship can be in effect for each of the ten work areas, making possible an intricate network of related files. The **DISPLAY STATUS** command shows the relationships in the various work areas, e.g., the name of the related file and the field upon which the relationship is based.
3. The **CREATE VIEW FROM ENVIRONMENT** command will save current relationships in a view (**VUE**) file, from where they can be reestablished in future sessions with a **SET VIEW** command. Relationships can also be created through the command **CREATE/MODIFY VIEW**.
4. If no matching record is found in the related file, the record pointer in that file is positioned at the end-of-file marker, and fields displayed for that record are blank.
5. The controlling file may or may not be indexed, depending on whether it is to be processed in logical or physical order.
6. The active field list (established with a **SET FIELDS TO** command) may contain fields from all open files; however, the relationship between the files must be established before attempting to output any data.

Related Topics

```
CREATE/MODIFY QUERY
CREATE/MODIFY VIEW
CREATE VIEW FROM ENVIRONMENT
DISPLAY STATUS
JOIN
SELECT
SET FIELDS
SET SKIP
SET VIEW
```

SET SAFETY

Syntax

```
SET SAFETY ON/OFF
```

Discussion

The **SET SAFETY** command determines whether dBASE will display a warning before overwriting an existing file. The default status is **ON**, and produces the message *File already exists* if an attempt is made to create a file with the same name as an existing file. A decision to *Overwrite* replaces the existing file, whereas *Cancel* returns to the dot prompt.

The file is overwritten with no warning if **SET SAFETY** is **OFF**.

Tips

1. **SET SAFETY** is normally **OFF** within a program where the intention is to overwrite existing files. Moreover, the message produced by **SET SAFETY ON** would only clutter the custom screen and confuse the user.
2. **SET SAFETY** should always be **ON** at the dot prompt, where inadvertently specifying the name of an existing file can lead to very unfortunate results.
3. The **SET SAFETY** message is unaffected by the status of **SET TALK**; i.e., when **SET SAFETY** is **ON**, the message appears regardless of whether **SET TALK** is **ON** or **OFF**.
4. The **ZAP** command will ask you to verify that you want to delete and pack all of the records if **SET SAFETY** is **ON**.

Related Topics

```
SET TALK
ZAP
```

SET SCOREBOARD

Syntax

```
SET SCOREBOARD ON/OFF
```

Discussion

SET SCOREBOARD, in conjunction with **SET STATUS**, determines whether or not the status of the toggle switches (**Ins**, **Caps**, **Num**, and **Del**) will be displayed, and if so, where. The effects of various combinations of **ON** and **OFF** settings for the two commands are explained in the following table:

Status	Scoreboard	Result
ON	Immaterial	Status indicators appear in the status line (line 22)
OFF	ON	Status indicators appear on line 0
OFF	OFF	Status indicators do not appear at all

Tips

1. Either (or both) **SET STATUS** or **SET SCOREBOARD** should be **ON** at the dot prompt. In a program file, however, they should both be **OFF** so that the program has complete control over every line of the screen display.
2. The error message displayed by inputting a value outside the specified range in an **@...GET** command is also affected by the **SET SCOREBOARD** and **SET STATUS** combination.

Related Topics

SET STATUS

SET SKIP

Syntax

```
SET SKIP TO [<alias> [,...]]
```

Discussion

The **SET SKIP** command provides access to *all* matching records in the related file and is used when a one-to-many relationship exists between the controlling and related files. Without the command, dBASE will process only the first matching record in the related file, whereas with the **SET SKIP** command, it processes all matching records in the related file *before* moving the record pointer in the controlling file. Note, however, that a relationship *must* be established in order for the **SET SKIP** command to work. Consider, for example, a banking application with two files, customers and loans, where one customer can have many loans. Establishing a relationship without the **SET SKIP** command lists only the first loan for each customer as shown here:

```
. SELECT 2
. USE loan ORDER cust_id
```

```
. SELECT 1
. USE customer ORDER lastname
. SET RELATION TO cust_id INTO loan
. LIST lastname,loan->loan_id,loan->loan_amt
lastname     loan->loan_id    loan->loan_amt
Butler       L08              20000
Morris       L04              10000
Rice         L01              10000
```

The **SET SKIP** command, however, lists all loans for each customer. Consider:

```
. SELECT 2
. USE loan ORDER cust_id
. SELECT 1
. USE customer ORDER lastname
. SET RELATION TO cust_id INTO loan
. SET SKIP TO loan
. LIST lastname,loan->loan_id,loan->loan_amt
lastname    loan->loan_id    loan->loan_amt
Butler        L08             20000
Butler        L10             35000
Morris        L04             10000
Morris        L07             10000
Morris        L11             12500
Rice          L01             10000
Rice          L09             15000
```

Tips

1. The **SET RELATION** command must be issued prior to the **SET SKIP** command.
2. When more than one file is listed in the **SET SKIP TO** command, the record pointer is moved through all of the matching records in the first related file, then it is moved through all of the matching records in the second file, and so on. After all of the matching records have been found in all of the related files, the record pointer is moved to the next matching record in the controlling file.
3. The **SET SKIP TO** command with no filename deactivates skipping in the related files.

Related Topics

SELECT
SET RELATION

SET SPACE

Syntax

```
SET SPACE ON/OFF
```

Discussion

The **SET SPACE** command determines whether a space is printed between expressions separated with a comma in the **?** and **??** commands. The expressions are separated by a space when **SET SPACE** is **ON**, but not when **SET SPACE** is **OFF**. Consider:

```
.SET SPACE ON
.? "First Name:",firstname
First Name: Jessica
```
Space between colon and Jessica

```
.SET SPACE OFF
.? "First Name:",firstname
First Name:Jessica
```
No space between colon and Jessica

Tips

1. The **SET SPACE** command has no effect on listings produced with the **LIST**, **DISPLAY**, or **@...SAY** commands.

Related Topics

?/??

SET SQL

Syntax

```
SET SQL ON/OFF
```

Discussion

The **SET SQL** command alternates between the dBASE only and the dBASE SQL mode. When **SET SQL** is **ON**, SQL commands, as well as a subset of dBASE commands, can be executed; whereas when it is **OFF**, you are in the default dBASE mode, where only dBASE commands can be executed.

SQL is an advanced relational database language consisting of fewer than 30 commands that define, update, and access data in relational tables. SQL provides a fast and efficient way of querying the tables, reducing the amount of programming necessary to access data. SQL commands can be entered interactively at the SQL prompt or embedded in dBASE programs; the latter must have a **PRS** extension (rather than **PRG**) to alert dBASE to the fact that there will be embedded SQL code.

Tips

1. The **SET SQL** command must be issued from the dot prompt, and not from within a program; dBASE will automatically switch to the SQL mode when a program file with a **PRS** extension is executed.
2. The combination of SQL and dBASE provides the best of both worlds; SQL offers a more efficient way to retrieve data from a relational database, whereas dBASE presents the data in a more attractive format.
3. The subset of dBASE commands that are allowed in the SQL mode is found in the *Advanced Topics Handbook* provided by Ashton-Tate.
4. Chapter 14 in the main portion of the text provides a thorough introduction to SQL.

SET STATUS

Syntax

```
SET STATUS ON/OFF
```

Discussion

The **SET STATUS** command determines whether the status bar is displayed at the bottom of the screen. The status bar indicates:

1. The current screen or program being executed.
2. The path to the currently selected **DBF** file.
3. The cursor location on a work surface or the current record number in a **DBF** file.
4. The name of the file supplying the data for the current operation.
5. The status of the toggle switches.

In addition, a *navigation line* (which provides context-sensitive help information about the current operation) and a *message line* (which provides context-sensitive descriptive information) are displayed immediately below the status line when **SET STATUS** is **ON**.

Tips

1. The status bar appears during a **CREATE** operation, regardless of whether **STATUS** is **ON** or **OFF**.
2. Either (or both) **SET STATUS** or **SET SCOREBOARD** should be **ON** at the dot prompt. In a program file, however, they should both be **OFF** so that the program has complete control over every line of the screen display.
3. When **SET STATUS** is **OFF**, the status indicators appear on line 0, as long as **SET SCOREBOARD** is **ON**.
4. In full-screen commands, such as **BROWSE** and **APPEND**, the navigation and message lines appear when the **F10** key is used to access the menus, regardless of whether **SET STATUS** is **OFF**.
5. The **SET MESSAGE TO** command displays a user-defined message on the message line if **SET STATUS** is **ON**.

Related Topics

SET MESSAGE
SET SCOREBOARD

SET STEP

Syntax

```
SET STEP ON/OFF
```

Discussion

SET STEP ON is a debugging tool that pauses program execution after each command, displaying the result of the command together with a prompting message. The user is given the choice of continuing with the next command (by pressing the spacebar), suspending program execution (by pressing **S**), or terminating the program (by pressing the **Esc** key). Suspending execution returns control to the dot prompt, from where other debugging commands may be executed (e.g., **DISPLAY STATUS** or **DISPLAY MEMORY**). Control returns to the program with execution of a **RESUME** command.

Tips

1. **SET STEP** is best used with **SET ECHO ON** and **SET TALK ON**, to see the command as it is executed (**SET ECHO**) and then to see the dBASE response (**SET TALK**).
2. The interactive debugger is easier and more powerful and is recommended for that reason.

Related Topics

DEBUG
SET DEBUG
SET ECHO
SET TALK

SET TALK

Syntax

```
SET TALK ON/OFF
```

Discussion

The **SET TALK** command determines whether dBASE displays a response detailing the action taken as a result of the command just executed. When **SET TALK** is **ON**, for example, dBASE responds to a **STORE** command by showing the data stored, to a **COUNT** command by indicating the number of the records counted, to a successful **LOCATE** command by indicating the new position of the record pointer, and to a **COPY** command by indicating the number of records copied. **SET TALK OFF** prevents these messages from appearing.

Tips

1. **SET TALK ON** is informative at the dot prompt but disruptive in a program, where it only confuses the user.
2. **SET TALK** should always be **ON** during debugging a program to obtain all possible information.
3. The **SET SAFETY** message (*File already exists*) is unaffected by the status of **SET TALK**.
4. dBASE error messages regarding problems in data entry and/or command syntax appear, regardless of the status of **SET TALK**.

Related Topic

SET SAFETY

SET TRAP

Syntax

```
SET TRAP ON/OFF
```

Discussion

The **SET TRAP** command determines whether the dBASE debugger is invoked when an error is encountered during program execution or when the **Esc** key is pressed. When **SET TRAP** is **ON**, the debugger is activated, with the line where the error occurred highlighted in the edit window. When **SET TRAP** is **OFF**, dBASE merely offers a choice of *Cancel, Ignore, Suspend.*

Tips

1. The **ON ERROR** trap takes precedence over the **SET TRAP** command.
2. **SET TRAP ON** is especially helpful when most of a program is working and the problem can be traced to a specific block of code.

Related Topics

DEBUG
ON ERROR/ESCAPE/KEY

SET TYPEAHEAD

Syntax

```
SET TYPEAHEAD TO <numeric expression>
```

Discussion

The **SET TYPEAHEAD** command determines the size of the typeahead buffer, which in turn controls the number of keystrokes that can be entered ahead of actual processing. The default value of 20 may be changed to any number between 0 and 32,000. The typeahead buffer increases the speed of input from the dot prompt because a new command can be entered while the previous command is processing. In other words, commands in the buffer are executed as soon as the previous commands are completed, so that no time is lost waiting for a new command to be entered.

Tips

1. Any characters entered when the typeahead buffer is full are ignored (i.e., lost). The bell will ring, however (if **SET BELL** is **ON**), to warn that the buffer is full.
2. **SET TYPEAHEAD TO 0** disables the buffer; i.e., the buffer is immediately "full" and will not accept any characters.
3. The typeahead buffer becomes a liability within a program file as incorrect anticipation (by the user) of the next response will produce erroneous results. Accordingly, disable the buffer entirely, or use a **CLEAR TYPEAHEAD** command before each input is read.
4. The **SET TYPEAHEAD** command has no effect if **SET ESCAPE** is **OFF**.

Related Topics

```
SET BELL
SET ESCAPE
```

SET UNIQUE

Syntax

```
SET UNIQUE ON/OFF
```

Discussion

The **SET UNIQUE** command determines whether an index entry is generated for every record in a **DBF** file, or only for those records with unique values of the key expression. The default is **SET UNIQUE OFF**, so that an index normally contains an entry for every record in its associated **DBF** file. When **SET UNIQUE** is **ON**, however, the resulting index includes only those records having a unique value of the key expression. In other words, if multiple records contain the same value in the key field, only the first record is included in the index.

An index created with **SET UNIQUE ON** provides a list of the *different* key values that exist in a database. It can be used to increase processing efficiency in extremely large databases by finding the starting location of each of the different key values.

Tips

1. Indexing with **SET UNIQUE ON** is equivalent to specifying the **UNIQUE** clause in an **INDEX** command.
2. A unique index retains its status when it is reindexed, or when changes are made to the database, regardless of whether **SET UNIQUE** is **ON** or **OFF**. Newly appended or edited records are added to a unique index only if their key values do not already exist.
3. A unique index will not permit access to all of the records in the database whenever there are duplicate values of the key expression. Therefore, a unique index should not be opened as the master index unless it is specifically needed for its unique status.

Related Topics

```
INDEX
REINDEX
```

SET VIEW

Syntax

```
SET VIEW TO <filename>
```

Discussion

The **SET VIEW** command opens an existing view (query) file and establishes the relational environment specified in the view file. All **DBF** files, memo files, and associated indexes are placed in their assigned work areas; relationships between the files are established; the field list (if present) is activated; the filter conditions (if present) are established; and the format files (if present) are opened.

Tips

1. If a **QBO** file does not exist when a **SET VIEW** command is executed, dBASE compiles the associated **QBE** file and then executes the resultant **QBO** file. If **MODIFY QUERY** is used to edit the query file, dBASE deletes the old **QBO** file, causing the modified query file to be recompiled when the query is subsequently opened. If dBASE cannot find either a **QBO** or **QBE** file, it will open the corresponding **VUE** file.
2. A **VUE** file, created with the **CREATE VIEW FROM ENVIRONMENT** command, is considered a holdover from dBASE III Plus, and should be converted to a **QBE** file. To do so, open the **VUE** file with a **MODIFY QUERY** command, and when you exit, a **QBE** file will be generated.
3. A view file is unlike a normal file in that once it establishes the environment, it is no longer considered an open file and hence, never needs to be closed. The files it opens, however, are closed with appropriate **CLOSE** or **CLEAR** commands.
4. The **DISPLAY STATUS** command shows all environmental information.

Related Topics

```
CREATE/MODIFY QUERY
CREATE/MODIFY VIEW
CREATE VIEW FROM ENVIRONMENT
DISPLAY STATUS
```

SET WINDOW

Syntax

```
SET WINDOW OF MEMO TO <window name>
```

Discussion

The **SET WINDOW** command specifies a previously defined window as the editing window that will be activated for a memo field accessed by a full-screen data entry command (e.g., **APPEND**, **BROWSE**, **EDIT**, or **@...GET**). The memo field appears as a memo marker until the cursor is moved to the input template and **Ctrl+Home** pressed, which causes the contents of the memo field to be displayed in the window.

Tips

1. The **WINDOW** clause in the **@...GET** command takes precedence over the window specified in a **SET WINDOW** command.
2. If a **SET WINDOW** command specifies a window that has not yet been defined, a *Window has not yet been defined message* appears.

Related Topics

```
@...GET
DEFINE WINDOW
MOVE WINDOW
RESTORE WINDOW
SAVE WINDOW
```

SHOW MENU

Syntax

```
SHOW MENU <menu name> [PAD <pad name>]
```

Discussion

The **SHOW MENU** command displays a bar menu on the screen without activating it, allowing you to preview a menu as it is being built. The **SHOW MENU** command can be issued periodically as the individual pads are defined, without having to wait until the associated programs and procedures have been written.

The **PAD** clause highlights the specified pad when the menu is displayed. If no **PAD** clause is specified, none of the pads is highlighted.

Tips

1. The **SHOW MENU** command does *not* activate the menu; thus, the cursor cannot be moved, and no selections can be made.
2. A **DEFINE MENU** command and at least one **DEFINE PAD** command must be issued prior to executing a **SHOW MENU** command, otherwise a *Menu has not been defined* message or a *Pad has not been defined for this menu* message will appear.
3. The menu is displayed on the screen, overwriting any existing screen display; the cursor returns to the dot prompt to await the next command.

Related Topics

```
ACTIVATE MENU
DEACTIVATE MENU
DEFINE MENU
DEFINE PAD
```

SHOW POPUP

Syntax

```
SHOW POPUP <popup name>
```

Discussion

The **SHOW POPUP** command displays a popup menu on the screen without activating it, allowing you to preview a menu as it is being built. The **SHOW POPUP** command can be issued periodically as the individual bars are defined, without having to wait until the associated programs and procedures have been written.

Tips

1. The **SHOW POPUP** command does *not* activate the menu; thus, the cursor cannot be moved, and no selections can be made.
2. A **DEFINE POPUP** command and at least one **DEFINE BAR** command must be issued prior to executing a **SHOW POPUP** command, otherwise a *Popup not defined* message or a *No bars have been defined for this popup* message will appear.
3. The menu is displayed on the screen, overwriting any existing screen display; the cursor returns to the dot prompt to await the next command.

Related Topics

```
ACTIVATE POPUP
DEACTIVATE POPUP
DEFINE BAR
DEFINE POPUP
```

SKIP

Syntax

```
SKIP [<numeric expression>] [IN <alias>]
```

Discussion

The **SKIP** command moves the record pointer forward or backward in the currently selected database, moving forward when the numeric expression is positive and backward when it is negative. The default is to move forward one record, otherwise to move the specified number of records in the indicated direction. **SKIP 10** and **SKIP -5** move the record pointer forward ten positions and backward five positions, respectively. The new position of the record pointer is displayed on the screen, provided **SET TALK** is **ON**.

The **SKIP** command operates within the physical sequence of the records in the database when no index is active. If an index is active, however, the command operates within the logical sequence according to that index.

Deleted records are treated as if they weren't there when **SET DELETED** is **ON**; i.e., if the record pointer is at record 3, and record 4 has been marked for deletion, **SKIP** will reposition the record pointer to record 5. The same principle holds true when a filter condition has been established; i.e., records that do not meet the filter condition are treated as if they are not physically present.

Tips

1. If the record pointer is on record 3 and a **SKIP -7** command is issued, and no index is active, the record pointer will be repositioned to record 1 and the **BOF()** function will be set to true. If, however, record 1 is the current record and a **SKIP -1** command is executed, a *Beginning of file encountered* error message is displayed.
2. If the record pointer is on record 20, and a **SKIP 10** is issued, assuming a 25-record file, the record pointer will be repositioned to record 26 (the end-of-file marker) and the **EOF()** function set to true. If, however, the record pointer is at record 26 (the end-of-file marker), and a **SKIP** command is executed, an *End of file encountered* error message is displayed.
3. A **SKIP** command, which moves the record pointer in the currently selected database, will also move the record pointer in a related database, given that a relationship has been set between the files.
4. The numeric expression can be a formula, constant, or numeric memory variable; e.g., **SKIP 5*2**, **SKIP 10**, and **SKIP mnum**, are all equivalent (assuming **mnum** contains the numeric constant 10).
5. The record pointer may be moved in an unselected work area by using the **IN <alias>** option; e.g., the command **SKIP IN 2** moves the record pointer to the next record in the file open in work area two, whereas **SKIP IN SOLEMP** moves the record pointer to the next record in the **SOLEMP.DBF** file in whichever work area the file is open.

Related Topics

```
BOF()
EOF()
GOTO
SET DELETED
SET FILTER
SET INDEX
SET RELATION
```

SORT

Syntax

```
SORT <scope> ON <field1>[/A][/C][/D]
    [,<field>[/A][/C][/D]...]
    [WHILE <condition>][FOR <condition>]
    [ASCENDING] [DESCENDING] TO <filename>
```

Discussion

The **SORT** command creates a copy of the currently selected **DBF** file, in which the records are physically reordered according to the specified key field(s). The newly sorted file, specified in the **TO** clause, is a database file in its own right, and is assigned a default extension of **DBF** (unless another extension is explicitly specified). The new file is completely independent of the file from which it was created.

Character, numeric, and date fields may be designated as keys (memo and logical fields may not be used) to reorder the file in alphabetical, numerical, or chronological sequence, respectively. For example, the command,

```
SORT ON lastname TO alpha
```

creates a new database file named **ALPHA.DBF**, in which the records are sequenced alphabetically (A–Z) by last name; whereas the command,

```
SORT ON salary TO salary
```

puts records in ascending sequence of salary.

A maximum of ten keys is permitted in the same **SORT** command, and the individual keys need not be of the same data type. The first field listed is the primary key, within which records are sorted according to a secondary key, and so on. For example, the command,

```
SORT ON location,salary TO locsal
```

creates a new file in which the records are sequenced by location, and then by salary within each location.

Unless otherwise indicated, all sorts are performed in ascending (ASCII) sequence. This can be changed, however, as follows:

/A	Ascending order
/D	Descending order
/C	Ignore the difference between upper- and lower-case letters (upper-case letters normally precede lower case)

The **/A** and **/D** parameters apply only to the field with which they are used and are mutually exclusive for the same key. Either one can, however, be combined with the **/C** parameter for use with character fields; e.g.,

```
SORT ON loc/AC,salary/D TO locatsal
```

Note that when the **/C** is combined with another parameter, only one **/** is used. The **ASCENDING** and **DESCENDING** options affect all key fields that do not have an individual **/A** or **/D** option, and are mutually exclusive; i.e., they cannot be used in the same **SORT** command.

A scope, **FOR**, or **WHILE** clause can be included to copy only a subset of records in the currently selected database to the new file; e.g.,

```
SORT NEXT 20 ON lastname TO newfile
SORT ON lastname FOR state = 'NY' TO nylist
```

Tips

1. A file cannot be sorted to itself or to any other open file.
2. If a filter condition is active, only those records meeting the specified filter condition will be sorted and copied to the new file. The same is true if **SET DELETED** is **ON**; i.e., records marked for deletion will not be included in the sorting process.
3. The **SORT** command will not accept an expression as a key. If it is necessary to sort on an expression, you can issue an **INDEX** command, using the expression as the key of the index, then copy the indexed file to a new **DBF** file, which will be sequenced according to the desired expression.
4. If a field list has been established with the **SET FIELDS** command, all fields will still be copied to the sorted file, whether or not they are in the field list. However, the key field(s) must be included in the field list, or a *Field not found* error message is displayed.
5. The **SORT** command positions the record pointer at the end of file unless a **NEXT**, scope, or **WHILE** condition is used, in which case the record pointer is positioned one record below the last record processed.
6. If the source database file contains a memo field, a copy of the **DBT** file will be automatically created for the sorted file, having the same name as the sorted file but with a **DBT** extension.
7. If the target file of the **SORT** command has the same name as an existing file and the status of **SAFETY** is **ON**, dBASE will ask before overwriting the existing file. If, however, **SAFETY** is **OFF**, no warning will be given before the file is overwritten.

Related Topics

```
INDEX
SET DELETED
SET FIELDS
SET FILTER
USE
```

SPACE FUNCTION

Syntax

```
SPACE(<numeric expression>)
```

Discussion

The **SPACE()** function generates a character string consisting of the indicated number of spaces. The function may specify any valid numeric expression (i.e., a numeric field, memory variable, constant, or arithmetic expression). The value of the expression, however, must result in a positive number between 0 and 254 or else an error message will be displayed.

Tips

1. The `SPACE()` function can initialize a character-type memory variable with blanks; e.g., `STORE SPACE(13) TO mlname` is easier and more efficient than the equivalent `STORE '             ' TO mlname`.
2. The `SPACE()` function is often used in a program to clear an individual line prior to mapping new text; e.g.,

```
@ 20,20 SAY SPACE(68)
```

This is especially important if the new text is a shorter string than what it replaces. A single `@...CLEAR TO` command will clear a rectangular area of more than one line, and is the equivalent of several individual `@...SAY SPACE()` commands.

Related Topics

@...CLEAR
STORE

STORE

Syntax

```
STORE <expression> TO <memvar list>
<memvar> = <expression>
```

Discussion

The **STORE** command initializes one or more memory variables, simultaneously creating the variables if they do not already exist. The expression is evaluated first, then the result is stored in the named memory variable. If it is an existing memory variable, any previous value is overwritten and therefore lost.

The expression may be comprised of constants, fields, functions, and/or other memory variables. The nature of the expression determines the data type of the memory variable (character, numeric, date, or logical), as follows:

```
STORE 'hello' TO mgreeting
STORE 10 TO mnumber
STORE {06/12/92} TO mdate
STORE .T. TO mloop
```

A numeric memory variable is created by supplying a value consisting of only digits and an optional decimal point. Numeric memory variables default to a length of 10, with no decimal places. This default may be overridden by the assigned value if it is longer than 10 digits and/or explicitly includes decimal places.

A character memory variable is created by enclosing the value in quotes, with the length of the character string determining the length of the memory variable; the maximum length is 254 characters.

A date memory variable is created by enclosing a literal date in curly braces or by converting a character string date with a `CTOD()` function. The default length is eight.

A logical memory variable is created with a true or false value set off by periods (e.g., **.T.**, **.Y.**, **.F.**, or **.N.**); the default length is one position.

Tips

1. In the = form of the command, the name of the memory variable must be to the left of the equal sign and the expression to be stored to the right.

2. The **STORE** form of the command is superior to the = form of the command as it can initialize several memory variables (to the same value) at one time; e.g.,

```
STORE 0 TO mnum,mrow,mcol
```

3. A memory variable cannot be assigned a memo data type.
4. The name of a memory variable can consist of up to ten characters and be comprised of letters, numbers, and underscores; it must, however, begin with a letter. Although single-character names are permitted, the letters A–J should not be used as they might conflict with references to the various work areas.
5. If a field in the currently selected **DBF** file has the same name as a memory variable, the field name takes precedence in all operations except macro (**&**) substitution. This can produce unpredictable results; hence it is best not to give fields and memory variables common names. One solution is to begin all memory variable names with a common letter (e.g., m) and simultaneously avoid this letter when selecting field names. Another solution is to precede memory variable names with **m–>**, e.g., m–>mainopt.
6. A common prefix can be used for memory variables that are somehow related, to enable subsequent statements such as **RELEASE ALL LIKE/EXCEPT** or **SAVE ALL LIKE/EXCEPT**.
7. It is often necessary to create memory variables, with no particular initial values, so that other values may be input through subsequent **GET** statements. Assign a zero to numeric variables, a blank character string of the desired length to character variables, and a blank date to date variables. For example:

```
STORE 0 TO mnumber
STORE SPACE(50) TO mcompany
STORE {} TO mdate
```

Logical variables, however, cannot be assigned a blank value, and must be initialized to either true or false.

8. The value stored in a memory variable can be either a simple value or a complex expression, such as:

```
STORE TRIM(first) + " " + TRIM(last) TO mname
STORE UPPER(mchoice) TO mchoice
STORE mprice * 1.15 TO mincrease
STORE mcounter + 1 TO mcounter
STORE {12/25/92} - DATE() TO moredays
```

9. Memory variables created at the dot prompt are, by default, public (global), and can be accessed by any program or procedure. Memory variables created in a program are private (local) to that program and can be accessed only by that program or a program that it calls, unless they are declared public prior to being created.
10. Up to 500 memory variables can be active at one time, but this default can be increased or decreased by changing the **MVBLKSIZE** and/or **MVMAXBLKS** settings in the **CONFIG.DB** file. A maximum of 25,000 memory variables is possible.

Related Topics

```
@...SAY...GET
DISPLAY MEMORY
PRIVATE
PUBLIC
RELEASE
RESTORE
SAVE
WAIT
```

STR FUNCTION

Syntax

```
STR(<numeric expression>, [<length>], [<decimals>])
```

Discussion

The **STR()** function returns the character string equivalent of the numeric expression specified in the function argument. The length parameter specifies the length of the character string (the default is 10), whereas the decimal parameter indicates the number of decimal places (the default is 0). These parameters may be any valid numeric expression (i.e., a numeric field, memory variable, constant, or arithmetic expression).

The length parameter must account for the total number of characters to be output, including a minus sign, decimal point, and the appropriate number of decimal places. If the length is smaller than the number of digits to the left of the decimal, dBASE returns asterisks rather than a character string; if the length can accommodate the digits to the left of the decimal, but not the decimal point or the decimal places, the appropriately rounded integer will be returned. Similarly, if the decimals parameter is less than the number of decimals in the numeric expression, the result will be rounded to the specified number of decimals. In any event the number of decimal places must be less than the total length, or an execution error message results and no string is returned.

Consider, for example, the following table, which assumes the value 1234.5678 has been stored in **mnum**:

Function	Displayed Value
`STR(mnum)`	1235
`STR(mnum,3)`	***
`STR(mnum,5,2)`	1235
`STR(mnum,7,2)`	1234.57
`STR(mnum,2,6)`	*Execution error*

Tips

1. The **STR()** function enables the concatenation of numeric values and character strings in the same print statement (i.e., **?** or **@...SAY**). In addition, the appearance of the conatenated string can be improved with the **LTRIM()** function; e.g.,

```
? "Your raise is " + STR(raise,7) + " dollars"
Your raise is     750 dollars
? "Your raise is " + LTRIM(STR(raise,7)) + " dollars"
Your raise is 750 dollars
```

2. The **STR()** function is necessary to build an index based on a combination of character and numeric fields; e.g.,

```
INDEX ON location + STR(salary,6) TAG locsal
```

Related Topics

```
CREATE REPORT
INDEX ON
LTRIM()
VAL()
```

SUBSTR FUNCTION

Syntax

```
SUBSTR(<expC>, <starting position>, [<length>])
```

Discussion

The **SUBSTR** function returns a portion (substring) of the specified character string, beginning with the character in the indicated starting position, and ending with either the last character in the string, if no length is provided, or with the appropriate character as determined by the optional length parameter. Consider:

Function	Value
`SUBSTR("United States of America",1,6)`	`United`
`SUBSTR("United States of America",8,6)`	`States`
`SUBSTR("United States of America",18)`	`America`

The character expression can be a character field, memo field, memory variable, character string enclosed in quotes, concatenated character expression, or the result of a function that returns a string.

The starting position and length parameters can be any valid numeric expression (i.e., a numeric field, memory variable, numeric constant, or arithmetic expression). The starting position must, however, be a positive integer and cannot be greater than the total length of the original string, otherwise an error results. The length parameter can be greater than the number of characters between the starting position and the end of the character string, in which case the substring ends with the last character in the string.

Tips

1. The **SUBSTR** function can be used to embed literal constants in a field for display purposes; e.g., hyphens in a social security number (assuming that the social security number is defined as a nine-position character field); e.g.,

```
LIST SUBSTR(ssn,1,3) + "-" + SUBSTR(ssn,4,2)
    + "-" + SUBSTR(ssn,6)
```

2. The **@R** insertion function provides an alternative to the **SUBSTR()** function and is applicable to **@...SAY...GET** commands, report forms, and label forms; e.g.,

```
@ 2,15 SAY ssn PICTURE "@R 999—99—9999"
```

Related Topics

```
@...SAY...GET
STR()
```

SUM

Syntax

```
SUM [<expression list>][<scope>][WHILE <condition>]
    [FOR <condition>][TO <memvar list>]
```

Discussion

The **SUM** command computes the sum of numeric fields and/or arithmetic expressions involving numeric fields. The command computes the total of every numeric field in the currently selected **DBF** file, unless an expression list is included in the command; i.e., inclusion of the expression list restricts the computation to only those numeric fields specified in the list.

Every record in the database will be included in the computation unless the command contains a scope, **FOR**, or **WHILE** parameter. Thus, the command,

```
SUM salary
```

includes every record in the database in computing the total salary amount, whereas the command,

```
SUM salary NEXT 10
```

includes only the next ten records, begining with the current record. In similar fashion, the command,

```
SUM salary FOR location = 'NY'
```

computes the total salary amount for only those employees located in New York.

The results of the **SUM** command (the field names and their respective totals) are displayed on the screen immediately after the command is issued (as long as **SET TALK** is **ON**), but are not otherwise saved. To preserve the totals for future use, the **TO** clause must be specified, with a valid memory variable included for each field expression summed.

Tips

1. In the absence of an expression list, a sum is computed for every numeric field in the current database, whether it makes sense to do so or not. Thus, if a social security number is defined as a numeric field, a sum of the social security numbers will be computed, even though it will be a meaningless number.
2. When using a **TO** clause to save multiple sums to memory variables, the sums are computed in the order that the fields are listed in the expression list and then assigned to the memory variables in the order of the memvar list. Thus, in the command,

   ```
   SUM field1,field2 TO memvar1,memvar2
   ```

   the sum of **field1** is assigned to **memvar1** and the sum of **field2** to **memvar2**.
3. If a filter condition is active, records not meeting the filter condition are ignored by the **SUM** command. In similar fashion, records marked for deletion are also ignored when **SET DELETED** is **ON**.

Related Topics

AVERAGE
CALCULATE
COUNT
SET DELETED
SET FILTER

SUSPEND

Syntax

```
SUSPEND
```

Discussion

The **SUSPEND** command temporarily interrupts execution of a program and returns control to the dot prompt. It is used primarily in debugging as part of an error routine or as a response to a dBASE error message (e.g., the *Cancel, Ignore, Suspend* message, which is displayed by dBASE as errors are detected). The command does not release memory variables, all **DBF** files are kept open, and the position of the record pointers remains unchanged. Accordingly, commands such as **DISPLAY MEMORY**, **DISPLAY STATUS**, **DISPLAY**, and **? RECNO()** are typically issued immediately after a **SUSPEND** command as an aid in debugging.

Program execution can be continued from where it was suspended with a **RESUME** command or terminated with a **CANCEL** command.

Tips

1. Do not issue a **DO** command to reexecute a suspended program as the suspended program remains in memory until it is explicitly cancelled or resumed.
2. The **CANCEL** command releases all private memory variables, and thus a program must be suspended rather than cancelled to display memory variables. Additional commands can be entered from the dot prompt during suspension, after which execution can be resumed or cancelled.
3. Once a serious error has been detected and corrected, you should **CANCEL** rather than **RESUME** execution. Close all databases; release all memory variables, window definitions, and menu definitions; edit the file; and reexecute the program.

Related Topics

CANCEL
DEBUG
RESUME

TIME FUNCTION

Syntax

```
TIME()
```

Discussion

The **TIME()** function returns the system time as obtained from DOS, in the default format of hh:mm:ss. The system time is based on a 24-hour clock, so that times from 1:00 PM to one second before midnight are displayed as 13:00:00 to 23:59:59. The value returned by the **TIME()** function is a character string, and can be displayed in concatenated strings without conversion; e.g.,

```
? "Time printed: " + TIME()
```

To use the time in arithmetic operations, it must first be converted to a numeric value with the **VAL()** function. Note, too, that dBASE does not provide time arithmetic as it does date arithmetic; hence a program must be written to compute time intervals if desired.

Tips

1. Be sure to enter the system time correctly when booting the system, as that is the time returned by the **TIME** function. It is also the time stamped on all files that are created or modified.
2. The dBASE **TIME** function cannot be used to set the system time. The DOS **TIME** command can, however, be accessed from within dBASE to set the system time by using a **RUN** command, e.g., **RUN TIME**.
3. Execution of an **@...SAY TIME()** command in a program displays the time when the screen was mapped and will not be updated until another **@...SAY TIME()** command is executed. The **SET CLOCK** command, however, continually displays the current time.

Related Topics

DATE()
SET CLOCK

TRANSFORM FUNCTION

Syntax

```
TRANSFORM(<expression>,<character expression>)
```

Discussion

The **TRANSFORM()** function formats a character, numeric, date, or logical expression, producing a character-type data value. The first argument is the expression to be formatted; the second is a formatting template that uses the same function codes and template symbols as the **@...SAY...GET** command. Function codes affect the display of the entire expression, whereas a template uses a separate symbol for every character and determines the display of the data on a character-by-character basis. When function codes are used, they must appear first and are preceded by an **@** sign; the function codes are also separated from the template symbols by one blank space. Consider:

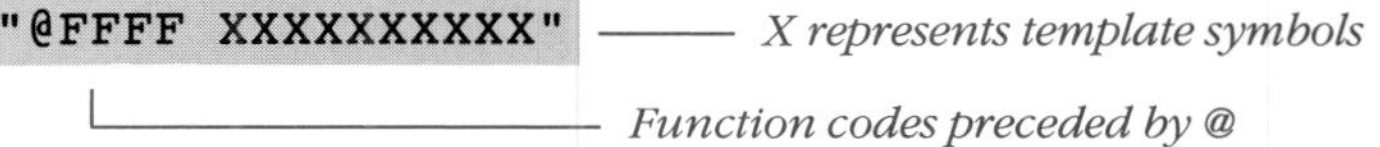

A list of available function codes and template symbols is shown in Tables NB.2 and NB.3, respectively. Consider:

```
DISPLAY TRANSFORM(lastname,"@!")
DISPLAY TRANSFORM(salary,"$999,999")
DISPLAY TRANSFORM(gpa,"@Z 9.99")
```

The first example displays the last name in capital letters, the second displays the salary with leading dollar signs and commas where appropriate, and the third displays the gpa with two decimal places. (Note, however, that if no value is entered for the grade point average, the zero will be suppressed and a blank space displayed.)

Tips

1. The **TRANSFORM()** function is most useful with commands that do not allow a **PICTURE** clause, such as **LIST** and **DISPLAY**, e.g.,
   DISPLAY "Population: " + TRANSFORM(popltn,"999,999,999").
2. The command **DISPLAY "Population: " + popltn** causes a *Data type mismatch* message as a character string cannot be concatenated with a numeric field.

3. The expression to be formatted can be any valid dBASE IV expression, including a literal, memory variable, field, or complex expression.

Related Topics

```
?/??
@...SAY
DISPLAY
LIST
```

TRIM FUNCTION

Syntax

```
TRIM(<character expression>)
```

Discussion

The **TRIM()** function strips trailing blanks from the specified character expression. (The expression may be a character field, memory variable, character string enclosed in quotation marks, or a concatenated string expression). The function is especially useful when concatenating character fields to one another; e.g.,

Without TRIM() function:

```
LIST lastname,initials TO PRINTER
Arnold       JS
Baker        MJ
.
  .
    .
Sugrue       PK
```

With TRIM() function:

```
LIST TRIM(lastname),initials TO PRINTER
Arnold JS
Baker MJ
.
  .
    .
Sugrue PK
```

Tips

1. The **TRIM()** function followed by a comma inserts one space before the next field, whereas **TRIM()** followed by a plus sign (+) does not insert any space; the latter requires that a blank be explicitly concatenated as follows:

```
LIST TRIM(lastname) + ",  " + initials
```

2. The **TRIM()** function is identical to the **RTRIM()** function.

3. The length of the trimmed character string is less than that of the untrimmed version; e.g.,

```
STORE "Jessica       "  TO mname
? LEN(mname)
1  ——————————— dBASE response
? LEN(TRIM(mname))
72 ——————————— dBASE response
```

4. The `TRIM()` function can improve the appearance of a simple listing by using it to concatenate character data. For example, to insert a comma immediately after the city name, use the expression:

```
LIST TRIM(city) + ", " + state + " " + zipcode
```

5. The `TRIM()` function is automatically added to character fields as report forms are designed and to character, numeric, and memo fields as label forms are designed. Note, however, that for the `TRIM()` function to work in the report and label forms, a space must be explicitly typed between the trimmed field and the field to its right to keep them together, rather than leaving empty work surface space. (The `TRIM()` function can also be turned on and off when designing forms by selecting the appropriate picture function in the modify field menu.)

Related Topics

```
CREATE LABEL
CREATE REPORT
LTRIM()
RTRIM()
```

UPPER FUNCTION

Syntax

```
UPPER(<character string>)
```

Discussion

The `UPPER()` function converts all of the lower-case letters in the specified character string to their upper-case equivalents. The argument may be a character string, character field, or memory variable, or a concatenated string expression, as shown in the following table:

Function	Nature of the Argument
`UPPER("this is a string")`	Character string
`UPPER(lastname)`	Character field
`UPPER(memname)`	Memory variable
`UPPER("Today is" + DTOC(DATE()))`	Concatenated string

Tips

1. The **UPPER()**, **LOWER()**, and **LEFT()** functions can be combined to convert the initial character in a field to upper case, and the remaining characters to lower case; i.e.,

   Command entered on one line

   ```
   REPLACE lname WITH UPPER(LEFT(lname,1)) +
       LOWER(SUBSTR(lname,2))
   ```

   A single **REPLACE** command will make the substitution for every record in the currently selected database, by specifying a scope of **ALL**.
2. Most systems allow the user to respond in upper or lower case, complicating the process of data validation. The problem is solved by converting the response to a uniform standard (either upper or lower), and then testing for only one set of permitted responses. For example, in a system in which A, B, C, or D or (a, b, c, or d) are valid, the following code would suffice:

   ```
   @10,20 GET response PICTURE A
   STORE UPPER(response) to response
   IF response < 'A' .OR. response > 'D'
       @12,2 SAY 'Please respond with A, B, C, or D'
   ENDIF
   ```

Related Topics

```
LEFT()
LOWER()
SUBSTR()
```

USE

Syntax

```
USE [<filename>] [IN <work area number>]
    [INDEX <index list>]
    [ORDER [TAG] <.ndx filename/.mdx tag name>
    [OF <.mdx filename>]]
    [ALIAS <alias name>] [NOUPDATE]
```

Discussion

The **USE <filename>** command opens an existing **DBF** file, its production **MDX** file, and any associated memo (**DBT**) files in the currently selected work area. The full drive specification and/or pathname is required if the file exists on a drive other than the default drive, or in a subdirectory other than the logged directory.

As indicated, the production **MDX** file is automatically opened and closed whenever the **DBF** file is opened and closed. However, single index files (**NDX**) and independent multiple index files must be explicitly opened by using either the **INDEX** clause or a **SET INDEX TO** command. Up to ten **NDX** and **MDX** files, in addition to the production **MDX** file, can be opened for a single **DBF** file at one time. Only open indexes are updated when changes are made to the **DBF** file.

The record pointer is positioned at record one and the file is processed in physical order when the production **MDX** file is the only open index and no **ORDER** clause is specified. If, however, an **ORDER** clause is specified, the record pointer is positioned at the first logical record according to the index tag, and the file is processed in the logical order of the index.

When the **INDEX** clause is used to open indexes in addition to the production **MDX** file, and the first file listed is an **NDX** file, it becomes the master (controlling) index. If the first file listed is an independent multiple index file, the **DBF** file will be processed in physical order if no **ORDER** clause is specified or else in the logical order of the indicated tag if an **ORDER** clause is specified.

An alias of up to ten characters can be assigned by using the **ALIAS** option. The alias is a temporarily assigned name, and is lost when the file is closed. The rules for assigning an alias name are the same as those for field names (use only letters, numbers, and an underscore and begin them with a letter), and if no **ALIAS** is explicitly assigned, the alias defaults to the filename. A short, meaningful alias is particularly useful when the filename itself is difficult to remember.

The **NOUPDATE** clause makes the file read-only, preventing records from being appended, modified, and/or deleted.

Up to ten database (**DBF**) files can be open at any one time, with each file placed in its own work area. There can, however, be only one open database file per work area, and a given database file can be open in only one work area; i.e., **SOLEMP.DBF** cannot be open in work areas 1 and 4 simultaneously. Database files are assigned to a work area by selecting a work area and then issuing the appropriate form of the **USE** command. Thus, the command sequence:

```
SELECT 1
USE solemp ORDER lname
SELECT 2
USE location ORDER locname
```

places the **SOLEMP.DBF** in work area 1 with **lname** as the controlling index, while **LOCATION.DBF** is placed in work area 2 with **locname** as the controlling index. If no files have been opened and no work area is specified (selected), the **USE** command opens the specified file in work area 1, and it becomes the currently selected work area.

The **USE** command, issued by itself with no parameters, closes the database file and its associated indexes in the currently selected work area.

The **IN** clause opens/closes the database file (and its indexes) in the specified work area rather than the currently selected work area. The work area may be a number from 1–10 or a letter A–J.

Tips

1. The **DISPLAY STATUS** command displays the following information for each open database file:

    Filename
    Work area number
    Alias
    Active filter condition
    Any database relations
    Open index files and their respective keys
    Open memo files (DBT)
    Open format file

2. Only one **DBF** file can be open in a work area at one time. Hence, if a file is open in the currently selected work area and a **USE <filename>** command is executed to open another **DBF** file, without first selecting another work area, the first file (and any open indexes) is closed.
3. Updating a **DBF** file will automatically update all open indexes (those in the production **MDX** file as well as those explicitly opened with a **SET INDEX TO** command). If any indexes (e.g., independent **MDX** files or **NDX** files) were not open when the database file was updated, the nonopen indexes must be subsequently opened and rein-

dexed. This is extremely important as opening an out-of-date index does not produce an error message, just unreliable results.

4. The **OF** clause should be used when the tag name specified as the master index is contained in an **MDX** file other than the production **MDX** file and/or when two or more open **MDX** files all contain that tag name.
5. Inadvertently opening an **NDX** or **MDX** file not matching the currently selected database produces an error message. However, opening an **NDX** file normally associated with another **DBF** file, but which has a key expression appropriate for the current **DBF** file, will not produce an error message, just bizarre results.
6. The **SET ORDER** command is used to change the controlling index of an open **DBF** file without closing any of the open indexes.
7. If the production **MDX** file is accidently erased from disk, you will not be able to open the **DBF** file. Therefore, be sure to keep backup copies of both the **DBF** and the **MDX** files.

Related Topics

```
DISPLAY STATUS
SELECT
SET INDEX
SET ORDER
```

VAL FUNCTION

Syntax

```
VAL(<character expression>)
```

Discussion

The **VAL()** function returns a numeric value, equivalent to the character-type number specified in the argument. The function is used when arithmetic operations are performed on data that has been stored (for whatever reason) in character format.

Tips

1. The **VAL()** function will display a rounded numeric value according to the number of places established with the **SET DECIMALS** command. (The full decimal value is used in arithmetic operations.)

```
SET DECIMALS TO 5
? VAL('3.555678')
3.55568 ———————— dBASE response
SET DECIMALS TO 2
? VAL('3.555678')
3.56 ———————— dBASE response
```

2. A numerical value of zero is returned for any character string beginning with a non-numeric character other than a blank. If, however, the character string begins with a digit or a blank followed by a digit, but contains a subsequent letter or special char-

acter, the digits are converted and the remaining characters are ignored. Consider the following examples:

Function	Numeric Equivalent
`VAL("ABC")`	0
`VAL("ABC123")`	0
`VAL("123")`	123
`VAL("123ABC")`	123

3. The **`TIME()`** function returns a character string (hh:mm:ss) rather than a numeric value, and cannot be used in a calculation unless it is first converted to a numeric equivalent. Remember, too, that dBASE does not provide time arithmetic as it does date arithmetic; thus, considerable programming may be required.

Related Topics

```
SET DECIMALS
STR()
TIME()
```

WAIT

Syntax

```
WAIT [<prompt>][TO <memvar>]
```

Discussion

The **`WAIT`** command suspends processing while simultaneously displaying the default message, *Press any key to continue ...* in column 0 of the next available line. Compliance with the message (i.e., pressing any key) causes dBASE to resume processing at the point where it was interrupted.

The prompt clause substitutes a custom message for the default message. The prompt must be enclosed in quotes. In addition, the proper number of spaces must appear at the beginning of the prompt string, if the message is to begin in any column other than 0.

Inclusion of the **`TO`** parameter stores the next keystroke entered into the specified memory variable (which is automatically initialized as a one-byte character variable). This can be useful in a custom program, as demonstrated by the following code:

```
WAIT "Please enter choice: " TO manswer
DO CASE
   CASE manswer = '1'
      DO addrec
   CASE manswer = '2'
      DO editrec
   .
     .
       .
ENDCASE
```

If, however, the return key is pressed in response to a **WAIT TO** command, the length of the newly created memory variable is 0 rather than 1. This enables the following test for the return key:

```
WAIT "Press return key to continue" TO manswer
IF LEN(manswer) = 0
   DO prog1
ELSE
   DO error
ENDIF
```

Tips

1. User input associated with the **WAIT** command is limited to a single character, meaning that processing continues as soon as any key is hit. Any extra keystrokes are stored in the typeahead buffer, which can cause problems later in the program. It is good practice, therefore, always to issue a **CLEAR TYPEAHEAD** command after a **WAIT** command.
2. Sophisticated menus that go beyond a one-character user response, or which contain enhanced data validation capabilities, and/or which use more attractive prompting messages are better produced with combinations of the **@...SAY...GET** and **READ** commands.
3. The **WAIT** command can be used after error messages or important informational screens, to give the user sufficient time to read the screen before processing continues.
4. The default *Press any key to continue ...* message can be suppressed by setting the console off immediately prior to the **WAIT** statement. The user's response is still collected, after which the console should be set back on. Consider:

```
SET CONSOLE OFF
WAIT
SET CONSOLE ON
```

Related Topics

```
@...SAY...GET
READ
SET CONSOLE
```

YEAR FUNCTION

Syntax

```
YEAR(<date expression>)
```

Discussion

The **YEAR()** function returns a four-digit number corresponding to the year in the specified date expression. The argument in the **YEAR()** function must be a date-type value and may assume several different forms as shown in the following table:

Function	Nature of the Argument
`YEAR(hiredate)`	Date field
`YEAR(memdate)`	Date memory variable
`YEAR(DATE())`	`DATE()` function itself
`YEAR{12/25/92}`	Literal date
`YEAR(CTOD(hiredate))`	`CTOD()` conversion function
`YEAR(DATE()+10)`	Expression with date arithmetic

Tips

1. If the argument of a **YEAR()** function is a character string enclosed in quotes, or a character field or memory variable, it must first be converted to a date-type variable with the **CTOD()** conversion function. The shorthand format using curly braces, which is often easier and more convenient to use, may be used only with a literal date, and cannot be used with a character string enclosed in quotes or with a character field or memory variable. (Note that a literal date is *not* enclosed in quotes as is a date expressed as a character string.)
2. The **YEAR()** function is often used in program files and/or report forms to display a date in a more attractive format. For example, given a date of 01/08/92, the command,

   Command is entered on one line

   ```
   @ 20,20 SAY "Today is " + CMONTH(DATE()) + " "
      + STR(DAY(DATE()),2) + ", " + STR(YEAR(DATE()),4)
   ```

   returns the string "Today is January 08, 1992". (Note that the day and year must be converted to strings to be concatenated with the other character-type data.)
3. The **YEAR** function supplies a four-digit value, regardless of the status of **SET CENTURY**.

Related Topics

CMONTH()
CTOD()
DATE()
DAY()
MONTH()
SET CENTURY
STR()

ZAP

Syntax

ZAP

Discussion

The **ZAP** command physically deletes every record from the currently selected database, leaving the file open and the file structure intact. It is equivalent to combining the **DELETE ALL** and **PACK** commands, except that it executes more quickly. Note, too, that it is not possible to recall records after a **ZAP** command has been executed.

Tips

1. If **SET SAFETY** is **ON**, confirmation of the procedure is requested prior to deleting the records. If **SET SAFETY** is **OFF**, however, the file will be zapped with no warning.
2. Be sure you have a current backup copy of the file in question before issuing the **ZAP** command. If you are unsure of the backup, copy the file before you zap it.
3. The **ZAP** command is often used to clear a temporary work file.
4. Any open index files in the currently selected work area are automatically updated to reflect the fact that the associated database file has been cleared of all its records.

Related Topics

DELETE
PACK
RECALL

Index